JUSTICE STATISTICS

AN EXTENDED LOOK AT CRIME IN THE UNITED STATES

Seventh Edition
2022

Edited by
Shana Hertz Hattis

Lanham • Boulder • New York • London

Published by Bernan Press

An imprint of The Rowman & Littlefield Publishing Group, Inc.

4501 Forbes Boulevard, Suite 200, Lanham, Maryland 20706

www.rowman.com

86-90 Paul Street, London, EC2A 4NE

ISBN 9781636710761 (paperback) | ISBN 9781636710778 (ebook)

Contents

Expanded Offense Tables

Federal Crime Data

Human Trafficking

Cargo Theft

PART 4: FEDERAL JUSTICE STATISTICS, 2020 271

PART 5: HATE CRIME STATISTICS, 2020 285

PART 8: LAW ENFORCEMENT OFFICERS KILLED AND ASSAULTED, 2020....................................391

INTRODUCTION

Bernan Press is pleased to present the seventh edition of its comprehensive collection of justice statistics in the United States. This volume provides a fresh look at the valuable information compiled by the Department of Justice, including its subsidiaries, the Bureau of Justice Statistics (BJS) and the Federal Bureau of Investigation (FBI).

The book brings together 12 key reports that fall under the general topic of "justice," including criminal victimization, identity theft, crime in the United States, hate crimes, probation, parole, school violence, and law enforcement officers killed and assaulted. Tables in this volume provide a comprehensive account of each of these subjects; for more information, including full-scope methodologies and information about standard errors for each table, please see the full reports at the URLs listed below.

Each section contains statistical tables and figures highlighting the data, as well as a brief summary of the report's methodology and at-a-glance highlights of the most compelling information. Data from 2020 and 2021 (where applicable) should be interpreted with caution, especially in comparison to previous years, due to the circumstances imposed by the COVID-19 pandemic.

The reports include:

- *Capital Punishment, 2020*, discusses both prisoners on death row in the United States and prisoners executed in the applicable year. It can be found at https://bjs.ojp.gov/content/pub/pdf/cp20st.pdf.
- *Crime in the United States, 2020*, provides an introduction to overall crime trends. This report is more fully presented in Bernan Press's companion volume *Crime in the United States*. However, given the importance of this data in the understanding of justice and crime trends in the United States, its most relevant tables have been included in this volume. Once again appearing in this book, and not contained in the complementary *Crime* volume, is the full range of the UCR's expanded offense tables. Also included are three supplementary reports: *Federal Crime Data*, *Human Trafficking*, and *Cargo Theft*. Full data can be accessed at https://crime-data-explorer.fr.cloud.gov/pages/home.
- *Criminal Victimization, 2020*, takes a close look at the victims of violent and property crime in the United States. The full report is accessible at https://bjs.ojp.gov/library/publications/criminal-victimization-2020.
- *Federal Justice Statistics, 2020*, returns with an updated report to this volume. It describes the activities, workloads, and outcomes of the federal judicial system from arrest to conviction and imprisonment. It can be found at https://bjs.ojp.gov/library/publications/federal-justice-statistics-2020.

- *Hate Crime Statistics, 2020*, details the hate crimes committed in the United States throughout 2020. Full data can be accessed at https://crime-data-explorer.fr.cloud.gov/pages/home.
- *Indicators of School Crime and Safety, 2020*, is an annual report that presents data on crime and safety at school from the perspectives of students, teachers, and principals. Conducted jointly by the Bureau of Justice Statistics and the National Center for Education Statistics, the report's data sources include the National Crime Victimization Survey (NCVS), the School Crime Supplement to the NCVS, the Youth Risk Behavior Survey, and the School Survey on Crime and Safety. The full report can be accessed at https://nces.ed.gov/pubsearch/pubsinfo.asp?pubid=2022092.
- *Jail Inmates in 2020* presents estimates of the inmate populations of jails based on various demographic characteristics. The full report can be accessed at https://bjs.ojp.gov/library/publications/jail-inmates-2020-statistical-tables.
- *Law Enforcement Officers Killed and Assaulted, 2020 (LEOKA)*, is the primary resource for data about harm done to law enforcement officers. This volume provides a comprehensive sample of the report; full data can be accessed at https://crime-data-explorer.fr.cloud.gov/pages/home.
- *Probation and Parole in the United States, 2020*, details data about post-release inmates still in the legal system. The report can be accessed at https://bjs.ojp.gov/library/publications/probation-and-parole-united-states-2020.
- *Recidivism of Prisoners Released in 24 States in 2008: A 10-Year Follow-Up Period (2008–2018)* is expanded in this edition. It examines the rate, number, and percentage of prisoners who were arrested at least once during the nine years following their release. It can be found at https://bjs.ojp.gov/library/publications/recidivism-prisoners-released-24-states-2008-10-year-follow-period-2008-2018.
- *The Impact of COVID-19 on the Local Jail Population, January–June 2020*, appears in more complete form in this edition. The full report can be found at https://bjs.ojp.gov/library/publications/impact-covid-19-local-jail-population-january-june-2020.

ABOUT THE EDITOR

Shana Hertz Hattis is an editor with over a decade of experience in statistical and government research publications. Past titles include *State Profiles: The Population and Economy of Each U.S. State*, *Crime in the United States*, and *The Almanac of American Education*. She earned her bachelor of science in journalism and master of science in education degrees from Northwestern University.

PART 1

Capital Punishment, 2020

HIGHLIGHTS

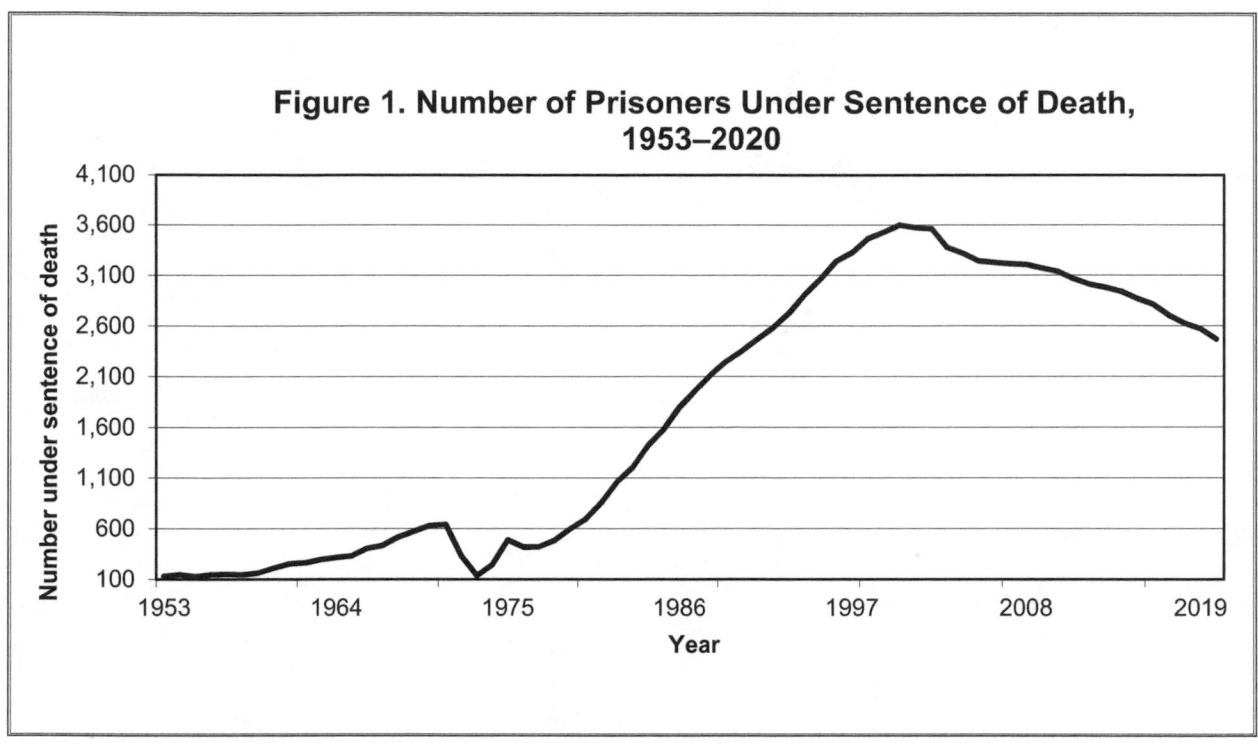

Figure 1. Number of Prisoners Under Sentence of Death, 1953–2020

- At yearend 2020, 28 states and the Federal Bureau of Prisons (BOP) held 2,570 prisoners under sentence of death, 94 persons (4 percent) fewer than at yearend 2019. This was the 20th consecutive year in which this number has decreased. California (28 percent), Florida (14 percent), and Texas (8 percent) held half of the prisoners under sentence of death in the country, while BOP held 51 prisoners under sentence of death.

- Colorado repealed the death-penalty provision in July 2020; the three inmates under sentence of death received commuted sentences of life imprisonment without the possibility of parole.

- Seventeen prisoners were executed in the United States in 2020 by five states and the BOP; 10 were White, 5 were Black, and 1 was American Indian/Alaska Native. One prisoner was of Hispanic/Latino origin. These prisoners had been on death row for an average of nearly 19 years.

- The number of prisoners executed in 2020 represented the smallest number of executions since 1991, when 14 prisoners were executed.

- During 2020, 17 states and the BOP reported a decrease in the number of prisoners held under sentence of death, 16 states reported no change, and no states reported an increase in the number of prisoners held under sentence of death.

- Approximately 56 percent of prisoners under sentence of death at yearend 2020 were White, while approximately 41 percent were Black; approximately 15 percent were of Hispanic or Latino origin (in cases in which origin was known).

- Approximately 98 percent of prisoners under sentence of death were male.

- Seven states and the BOP received a total of 14 prisoners under sentence of death in 2020, the smallest intake since the U.S. Supreme Court invalidated capital punishment statutes in several states in 1972 (see *Furman v. Georgia*, 408 U.S. 238 [1972]).

Table 1. Status of the Death Penalty, December 31, 2020

(Number.)

State	Executions in 2020	Number of prisoners under sentence of death
Total[2]	22	2,469
Alabama..	1	170
Arizona...	0	116
Arkansas...	0	29
California..	0	703
Delaware	0	0
Federal Bureau of Prisons...	10	51
Florida	0	337
Georgia	1	40
Idaho...	0	8
Indiana	0	8
Kansas	0	10
Kentucky	0	26
Louisiana..	0	66
Mississippi..	0	40
Missouri	1	20
Montana...	0	2
Nebraska..	0	12
Nevada	0	67
New Hampshire[1]..	0	1
New York..	0	0
North Carolina	0	137
Ohio...	0	137
Oklahoma...	0	45
Oregon...	0	24
Pennsylvania	0	118
South Carolina..	0	36
South Dakota..	0	1
Tennessee...	1	50
Texas..	3	206
Utah	0	7
Virginia...	0	2
Washington	0	0
Wyoming..	0	0

NOTE: Jurisdictions without the death penalty in 2020 include Alaska, Colorado, Connecticut, District of Columbia, Hawaii, Illinois, Iowa, Maine, Maryland, Massachusetts, Michigan, Minnesota, New Hampshire, New Jersey, New Mexico, North Dakota, Rhode Island, Vermont, West Virginia, and Wisconsin.While the Washington Supreme Court has declared the state's death penalty statute unconstitutional as applied (State v. Gregory, 192 Wash. 2d 1, 427 P.3d 621 (2018)), no legislative action has been taken to revise or repeal the statute. The state continues to report that the death penalty is authorized.
[1]New Hampshire repealed its death penalty statute, effective May 30, 2019. As of December 31, 2020, one male prisoner remained under a previously imposed sentence of death.
[2]New York, Delaware, Washington, and Wyoming held no inmates under sentence of death on December 31, 2020.

Table 2. Prisoners Under Sentence of Death, by Region, Jurisdiction, and Race, 2019 and 2020

(Number.)

Region and jurisdiction	Prisoners under sentence of death, 12/31/19			Received under sentence of death, 2020			Removed from death row (excluding executions), 2020[1]			Executed, 2020			Prisoners under sentence of death, 12/31/20		
	Total[2]	White[3]	Black[3]	Total[2]	White[3]	Black[3]	Total[2]	White[3]	Black[3]	Total[2]	White[3]	Black[3]	Total[2]	White[3]	Black[3]
U.S. Total................................	2,563	1,443	1,057	14	8	6	91	46	43	17	11	5	2,469	1,394	1,015
Federal[4]	61	35	25	0	0	0	0	0	0	10	5	4	51	30	21
State....................................	2,502	1,408	1,032	14	8	6	91	46	43	7	6	1	2,418	1,364	994
Northeast............................	133	64	67	1	0	1	15	5	10	0	0	0	119	59	58
New Hampshire	1	0	1	0	0	0	0	0	0	0	0	0	1	0	1
New York	0	0	0	0	0	0	0	0	0	0	0	0	0	0	0
Pennsylvania	132	64	66	1	0	1	15	5	10	0	0	0	118	59	57
Midwest............................	194	99	94	0	0	0	5	1	4	1	1	0	188	97	90
Indiana	8	6	2	0	0	0	0	0	0	0	0	0	8	6	2
Kansas...............................	10	7	3	0	0	0	0	0	0	0	0	0	10	7	3
Missouri.............................	22	15	7	0	0	0	1	1	0	1	1	0	20	13	7
Nebraska............................	12	9	3	0	0	0	0	0	0	0	0	0	12	9	3
Ohio.................................	141	61	79	0	0	0	4	0	4	0	0	0	137	61	75
South Dakota.......................	1	1	0	0	0	0	0	0	0	0	0	0	1	1	0
South.................................	1,217	642	558	11	6	5	38	18	18	6	5	1	1,184	625	544
Alabama.............................	175	88	87	0	0	0	4	1	3	1	0	1	170	87	83
Arkansas.............................	30	15	15	0	0	0	1	1	0	0	0	0	29	14	15
Delaware	0	0	0	0	0	0	0	0	0	0	0	0	0	0	0
Florida	338	212	126	7	4	3	8	5	3	0	0	0	337	211	126
Georgia	44	23	21	0	0	0	3	2	1	1	1	0	40	20	20
Kentucky	27	24	3	0	0	0	1	1	0	0	0	0	26	23	3
Louisiana	68	23	45	0	0	0	2	1	1	0	0	0	66	22	44
Mississippi..........................	40	17	22	1	0	1	1	0	1	0	0	0	40	17	22
North Carolina	143	58	78	0	0	0	6	0	5	0	0	0	137	58	73
Oklahoma...........................	46	22	20	1	1	0	2	0	1	0	0	0	45	23	19
South Carolina......................	36	17	19	0	0	0	0	0	0	0	0	0	36	17	19
Tennessee	52	25	26	0	0	0	1	1	0	1	1	0	50	23	26
Texas................................	216	118	94	2	1	1	9	6	3	3	3	0	206	110	92
Virginia..............................	2	0	2	0	0	0	0	0	0	0	0	0	2	0	2
West.................................	958	603	313	2	2	0	33	22	11	0	0	0	927	583	302
Arizona..............................	116	89	20	1	1	0	1	1	0	0	0	0	116	89	20
California............................	727	432	264	1	1	0	25	17	8	0	0	0	703	416	256
Colorado............................	3	0	3	0	0	0	3	0	3	0	0	0	0	0	0
Idaho................................	8	8	0	0	0	0	0	0	0	0	0	0	8	8	0
Montana.............................	2	2	0	0	0	0	0	0	0	0	0	0	2	2	0
Nevada	69	44	23	0	0	0	2	2	0	0	0	0	67	42	23
Oregon	26	23	2	0	0	0	2	2	0	0	0	0	24	21	2
Utah.................................	7	5	1	0	0	0	0	0	0	0	0	0	7	5	1
Washington	0	0	0	0	0	0	0	0	0	0	0	0	0	0	0
Wyoming............................	0	0	0	0	0	0	0	0	0	0	0	0	0	0	0

NOTE: Some counts for yearend 2019 are revised from those reported in Capital Punishment, 2019 - Statistical Tables (NCJ 300381, BJS, June 2021). The revised counts include 5 prisoners who were either reported late to the National Prisoner Statistics program or were not in the custody of state correctional authorities on December 31, 2019 (4 in California and 1 in Ohio). The revised counts exclude 13 prisoners who were relieved of a death sentence before December 31, 2019 (3 in Oregon; 2 each in Pennsylvania, Florida, Georgia, and Nevada; and 1 each in California and Idaho). Data for December 31, 2019 also include 1 prisoner in Ohio who was erroneously reported as being removed from under sentence of death in a previous year.
[1]Includes 38 deaths from natural causes (17 in California; 4 in Florida; 3 in Ohio; 2 each Alabama, Louisiana, and Texas; and 1 each in Pennsylvania, Missouri, Georgia, Kentucky, Tennessee, Arizona, Nevada, and Oregon), 3 deaths by suicide (1 each in Alabama, Florida, and California), and 1 death from an undetermined cause (California).
[2]Includes American Indians or Alaska Natives and Asians, Native Hawaiians, or Other Pacific Islanders.
[3]Includes persons of Hispanic origin.
[4]Excludes persons held under the jurisdiction of the U.S. Armed Forces with a military death sentence for murder.

Table 3. Prisoners Removed from Under Sentence of Death, by Region, Jurisdiction, and Method of Removal, 2020

(Number.)

Region and jurisdiction	Total	Execution	Other death[1]	Sentence commuted	Appeals court or higher court overturned	
					Capital conviction	Death sentence
U.S. Total..	108	17	42	4	11	34
Federal	10	10	0	0	0	0
State..	98	7	42	4	11	34
Northeast..	15	0	1	0	2	12
Pennsylvania	15	0	1	0	2	12
Midwest..	6	1	4	0	0	1
Missouri..	2	1	1	0	0	0
Ohio	4	0	3	0	0	1
South..	44	6	15	1	6	16
Alabama....................................	5	1	3	0	1	0
Arkansas....................................	1	0	0	0	0	1
Florida	8	0	5	0	1	2
Georgia	4	1	1	1	1	0
Kentucky	1	0	1	0	0	0
Louisiana	2	0	2	0	0	0
Mississippi..................................	1	0	0	0	1	0
North Carolina............................	6	0	0	0	1	5
Oklahoma..................................	2	0	0	0	1	1
Tennessee	2	1	1	0	0	0
Texas..	12	3	2	0	0	7
West..	33	0	22	3	3	5
Arizona......................................	1	0	1	0	0	0
California....................................	25	0	19	0	3	3
Colorado....................................	3	0	0	3	0	0
Nevada..	2	0	1	0	0	1
Oregon..	2	0	1	0	0	1

[1]In 2020, other deaths were due to natural causes, suicide, and unspecified causes.

Table 4. Demographic Characteristics for Prisoners Under Sentence of Death, 2020

(Number; percent; years; grade level.)

Characteristic	Total yearend	Admissions	Removals
Total (number)..	2,469	14	108
Sex (percent)			
Male...	97.9	100.0	98.1
Female...	2.1	0.0	1.9
Race (percent)			
White[1]	56.5	57.1	52.8
Black[1]	41.1	42.9	44.4
American Indian/Alaska Native[1]	0.7	0.0	2.8
Asian/Native Hawaiian/Other Pacific Islander[1,2]	1.7	0.0	0.0
Ethnicity (percent)[3]			
Hispanic/Latino..................................	15.3	0.0	15.2
Non-Hispanic/Latino.............................	84.7	100.0	84.8
Age (percent)			
18 to 19 years..................................	0.0	0.0	0.0
20 to 24 years..................................	0.0	0.0	0.9
25 to 29 years..................................	1.2	14.3	0.9
30 to 34 years..................................	4.4	7.1	0.9
35 to 39 years..................................	7.5	21.4	4.6
40 to 44 years..................................	12.8	14.3	13.9
45 to 49 years..................................	16.3	14.3	15.7
50 to 54 years..................................	17.7	14.3	9.3
55 to 59 years..................................	15.9	7.1	15.7
60 to 64 years..................................	11.9	7.1	13.9
65 years and older	12.2	0.0	24.1
Average Age (years)			
Mean..	52	43	55
Median..	52	41	56
Education (percent)[4]			
8th grade or less..................................	11.6	0.0	14.8
9th to 11th grade	34.9	66.7	35.2
High school graduate/GED	44.4	33.3	40.9
Any college..	9.2	0.0	9.1
Median Education Level			
Grade	12th	NC	12th
Marital Status (percent)[5]			
Married...	21.1	18.2	27.2
Divorced/separated	20.0	18.2	14.1
Widowed..	3.5	9.1	6.5
Never married	55.4	54.5	52.2

NOTE: Percentages are based on prisoners for whom data were reported. Details may not sum to totals due to rounding.
NC = Not calculated.
[1]Includes persons of Hispanic origin.
[2]Includes 36 Asians and 6 Native Hawaiians or Other Pacific Islanders at yearend 2020.
[3]Excludes 221 prisoners from total yearend and 9 removals because ethnicity was unknown.
[4]Excludes 535 prisoners from total yearend, 11 admissions, and 20 removals because education level was unknown.
[5]Excludes 365 prisoners from total yearend, 3 admissions, and 16 removals because marital status was unknown.

Table 5. Advance Count of Executions, January 1, 2021–December 31, 2021

(Number.)

Year	Number of executions
Total	11
Federal...	3
Texas..	3
Oklahoma..	2
Missouri...	1
Alabama...	1
Mississippi	1

Table 6. Authorized Method of Execution, by State, 2019

(Percent; number.)

State	Lethal injection[1]	Electrocution	Lethal gas	Hanging[1]	Firing squad	Nitrogen hypoxia
Total	31	9	3	2	3	3
Alabama.............................	√	√				√
Arizona[2]...........................	√		√			
Arkansas[3].........................	√	√				
California[4]........................	√					
Delaware[5]........................	√			√		
Florida	√	√				
Georgia	√					
Idaho..................................	√					
Indiana	√					
Kansas	√					
Kentucky[6]........................	√	√				
Louisiana	√					
Mississippi[7]......................	√	√			√	√
Missouri	√		√			
Montana	√					
Nebraska	√					
Nevada	√					
New York............................	√					
North Carolina	√					
Ohio	√					
Oklahoma[7].......................	√	√			√	√
Oregon	√					
Pennsylvania	√					
South Carolina	√	√				
South Dakota[8]	√					
Tennessee[9]	√	√				
Texas..................................	√					
Utah[10].............................	√				√	
Virginia	√	√				
Washington	√			√		
Wyoming[11]	√		√			

NOTE: The method of execution of federal prisoners is lethal injection, pursuant to 28 C.F.R. Part 26. For offenses prosecuted under the Violent Crime Control and Law Enforcement Act of 1994, the execution method is that of the state in which the conviction took place (18 U.S.C. ß 3596).
[1]Counts exclude New Hampshire, which repealed the death penalty effective May 30, 2019. The one male prisoner remaining under sentence of death is subject to execution by lethal injection or by hanging if lethal injection cannot be given.
[2]Authorizes lethal injection for persons sentenced after November 23, 1992. Prisoners sentenced before that date may select lethal injection or gas.
[3]Authorizes lethal injection for persons whose offense occurred on or after July 4, 1983 (Act 774 of 1983). Prisoners whose offense occurred before that date may select lethal injection or electrocution. Electrocution is the authorized method if lethal injection is invalidated by an unappealable court order (Ark. Code Ann. ß 5-4-617).
[4]Both lethal injection and lethal gas are authorized by statute (Cal. Pen. Code 3604). However, use of lethal gas was invalided by a federal court (Fierro v. Terhune, 147 F.3d 1158, 1160 (9th Cir. 1998)).
[5]Authorizes hanging if lethal injection is held to be unconstitutional by a court of competent jurisdiction.
[6]Authorizes lethal injection for persons sentenced on or after March 31, 1998. Prisoners sentenced before that date may select lethal injection or electrocution.
[7]Authorizes nitrogen hypoxia if lethal injection is held to be unconstitutional, electrocution if both lethal injection and nitrogen hypoxia are held to be unconstitutional, and firing squad if all other methods are held to be unconstitutional.
[8]Any person convicted of a capital offense or sentenced to death prior to July 1, 2017 may choose to be executed by lethal injection or in the manner provided by South Dakota law at the time of the personís conviction or sentence.
[9]Authorizes lethal injection for persons whose capital offense occurred after December 31, 1998. Prisoners whose offense occurred before that date may select electrocution by written waiver. Electrocution is the authorized method if a court or the commissioner of corrections determines that lethal injection cannot be given. If both methods are ruled unconstitutional, state law allows for the use of any method that is constitutional.
[10]Authorizes firing squad if lethal injection is held unconstitutional. Prisoners who selected execution by firing squad prior to May 3, 2004 may still be entitled to execution by that method.
[11]Authorizes lethal gas if lethal injection is held to be unconstitutional.

Table 7. Number of Persons Executed Under Civil Authority in the United States, 1930–2020

(Number.)

Year	Executions
1930	155
1931	153
1932	140
1933	160
1934	168
1935	199
1936	195
1937	147
1938	190
1939	160
1940	124
1941	123
1942	147
1943	131
1944	120
1945	117
1946	131
1947	153
1948	119
1949	119
1950	82
1951	105
1952	83
1953	62
1954	81
1955	76
1956	65
1957	65
1958	49
1959	49
1960	56
1961	42
1962	47
1963	21
1964	15
1965	7
1966	1
1967	2
1968	0
1969	0
1970	0
1971	0
1972	0
1973	0
1974	0

(Number.)

Year	Executions
1975	0
1976	0
1977	1
1978	0
1979	2
1980	0
1981	1
1982	2
1983	5
1984	21
1985	18
1986	18
1987	25
1988	11
1989	16
1990	23
1991	14
1992	31
1993	38
1994	31
1995	56
1996	45
1997	74
1998	68
1999	98
2000	85
2001	66
2002	71
2003	65
2004	59
2005	60
2006	53
2007	42
2008	37
2009	52
2010	46
2011	43
2012	43
2013	39
2014	35
2015	28
2016	20
2017	23
2018	25
2019	22
2020	17

NOTE: Excludes 160 executions carried out by military authorities from 1930 to 1961.

Table 8. Number of Persons Under Sentence of Death, 1953–2020

(Number.)

Year	Number of prisoners under sentence of death	Year	Number of prisoners under sentence of death
1953	131	1988	2,117
1954	147	1989	2,243
1955	125	1990	2,346
1956	146	1991	2,465
1957	151	1992	2,580
1958	147	1993	2,727
1959	164	1994	2,905
1960	212	1995	3,064
1961	257	1996	3,242
1962	267	1997	3,328
1963	297	1998	3,465
1964	315	1999	3,527
1965	331	2000	3,601
1966	406	2001	3,577
1967	435	2002	3,562
1968	517	2003	3,377
1969	575	2004	3,320
1970	631	2005	3,245
1971	642	2006	3,228
1972	334	2007	3,215
1973	134	2008	3,210
1974	244	2009	3,173
1975	488	2010	3,139
1976	420	2011	3,065
1977	423	2012	3,011
1978	482	2013	2,983
1979	593	2014	2,942
1980	692	2015	2,872
1981	860	2016	2,797
1982	1,066	2017	2,703
1983	1,209	2018	2,626
1984	1,420	2019	2,570
1985	1,575	2020	2,469
1986	1,800		
1987	1,907		

Table 9. Admissions to and Removal from Under Sentence of Death, 1973–2020

(Number.)

Year	Admissions	Removals
1973	44	240
1974	161	55
1975	318	67
1976	249	317
1977	159	156
1978	211	150
1979	172	61
1980	202	101
1981	249	84
1982	287	79
1983	266	123
1984	305	90
1985	291	130
1986	320	109
1987	311	142
1988	317	165
1989	275	149
1990	270	152
1991	285	159
1992	300	173
1993	299	162
1994	330	153
1995	325	171
1996	323	155
1997	283	187
1998	310	174
1999	287	221
2000	235	173
2001	164	194
2002	172	191
2003	156	346
2004	140	198
2005	143	216
2006	125	145
2007	129	140
2008	122	136
2009	118	166
2010	116	143
2011	84	155
2012	85	124
2013	85	118
2014	70	116
2015	54	122
2016	33	99
2017	37	133
2018	41	117
2019	31	87
2020	14	108

Table 10. Number of Prisoners Under Sentence of Death, by Race, 1968–2020

(Number.)

Year	White[1]	Black[1]	All other races[1,2]
1968	243	271	3
1969	263	310	2
1970	293	335	3
1971	306	332	4
1972	167	166	1
1973	64	68	2
1974	110	128	6
1975	218	262	8
1976	225	195	0
1977	229	192	2
1978	281	197	4
1979	354	236	3
1980	424	264	4
1981	499	353	8
1982	613	441	12
1983	692	505	12
1984	806	598	16
1985	896	664	15
1986	1,013	762	25
1987	1,128	813	26
1988	1,235	848	34
1989	1,308	898	37
1990	1,368	940	38
1991	1,449	979	37
1992	1,511	1,031	38
1993	1,575	1,111	41
1994	1,653	1,203	49
1995	1,732	1,284	48
1996	1,833	1,358	51
1997	1,864	1,408	56
1998	1,917	1,489	59
1999	1,960	1,515	65
2000	1,989	1,541	71
2001	1,968	1,538	71
2002	1,939	1,551	72
2003	1,882	1,417	78
2004	1,856	1,390	74
2005	1,802	1,366	77
2006	1,806	1,353	74
2007	1,806	1,338	71
2008	1,795	1,343	72
2009	1,779	1,318	76
2010	1,743	1,309	87
2011	1,721	1,274	70
2012	1,684	1,258	69
2013	1,670	1,251	62
2014	1,647	1,233	62
2015	1,606	1,202	64
2016	1,553	1,179	65
2017	1,508	1,129	66
2018	1,470	1,091	65
2019	1,443	1,064	63
2020	1,394	1,015	60

NOTE: Data on Hispanic origin was not collected prior to 1977.
[1]Includes persons of Hispanic origin.
[2]Includes American Indians or Alaska Natives; Asians, Native Hawaiians, or Other Pacific Islanders; and persons for whom only ethnicity was identified.

Table 11. Female Prisoners Under Sentence of Death, by Region, Jurisdiction, and Race, 2019 and 2020

(Number.)

Region and jurisdiction	Female prisoners under sentence of death, 12/31/19[1]			Received under sentence of death, 2020			Removed from death row, 2020			Female prisoners under sentence of death, 12/31/20		
	Total[2]	White[3]	Black[3]	Total[2]	White[3]	Black[3]	Total[2]	White[3]	Black[3]	Total[2]	White[3]	Black[3]
U.S. Total	53	39	11	0	0	0	2	1	0	51	38	11
Federal	1	1	0	0	0	0	0	0	0	1	1	0
State	52	38	11	0	0	0	2	1	0	50	37	11
Midwest	1	1	0	0	0	0	0	0	0	1	1	0
Ohio	1	1	0	0	0	0	0	0	0	1	1	0
South	23	14	8	0	0	0	1	0	0	22	14	8
Alabama	5	4	1	0	0	0	0	0	0	5	4	1
Florida	3	1	2	0	0	0	0	0	0	3	1	2
Georgia	1	0	1	0	0	0	0	0	0	1	0	1
Kentucky	1	1	0	0	0	0	0	0	0	1	1	0
Louisiana	1	0	1	0	0	0	0	0	0	1	0	1
Mississippi	1	1	0	0	0	0	0	0	0	1	1	0
North Carolina	3	1	1	0	0	0	1	0	0	2	1	1
Oklahoma	1	1	0	0	0	0	0	0	0	1	1	0
Tennessee	1	1	0	0	0	0	0	0	0	1	1	0
Texas	6	4	2	0	0	0	0	0	0	6	4	2
West	28	23	3	0	0	0	1	1	0	27	22	3
Arizona	3	3	0	0	0	0	0	0	0	3	3	0
California	23	18	3	0	0	0	0	0	0	23	18	3
Idaho	1	1	0	0	0	0	0	0	0	1	1	0
Oregon	1	1	0	0	0	0	1	1	0	0	0	0

[1]Counts of female prisoners under sentence of death at yearend 2019 have been revised from those reported in Capital Punishment, 2019 - Statistical Tables (NCJ 300381, BJS, June 2021). The revised counts include one prisoner in California who was originally reported as a male prisoner. Following sex reassignment surgery, she is now housed in a female facility and included in the count of female prisoners.
[2]Includes American Indians or Alaska Natives and Asians, Native Hawaiians, or Other Pacific Islanders.
[3]Includes persons of Hispanic origin.

Table 12. Hispanic Prisoners Under Sentence of Death, by Region and Jurisdiction, 2019 and 2020

(Number.)

Region and jurisdiction	Hispanic prisoners under sentence of death, 12/31/19	Received under sentence of death, 2020	Removed from death row (excluding executions), 2020	Executed, 2020	Hispanic prisoners under sentence of death, 12/31/20
U.S. Total	358	0	14	1	343
Federal	7	0	0	0	7
State	351	0	14	1	336
Northeast	14	0	0	0	14
Pennsylvania	14	0	0	0	14
Midwest	10	0	0	0	10
Nebraska	6	0	0	0	6
Ohio	4	0	0	0	4
South	95	0	6	1	88
Alabama	1	0	0	0	1
Florida	22	0	0	0	22
Georgia	2	0	0	0	2
Louisiana	2	0	0	0	2
Mississippi	1	0	0	0	1
North Carolina	3	0	0	0	3
Oklahoma	1	0	0	0	1
South Carolina	1	0	0	0	1
Tennessee	1	0	0	0	1
Texas	61	0	6	1	54
West	232	0	8	0	224
Arizona	24	0	1	0	23
California	196	0	7	0	189
Idaho	1	0	0	0	1
Nevada	6	0	0	0	6
Oregon	3	0	0	0	3
Utah	2	0	0	0	2

NOTE: Counts of Hispanic prisoners under sentence of death at yearend 2019 have been revised from those reported in Capital Punishment, 2019 - Statistical Tables (NCJ 300381, BJS, June 2021). The revised counts include four prisoners in California who were not included in the counts for December 31, 2019.

Table 13. Criminal History of Prisoners Under Sentence of Death, by Race or Ethnicity, 2020

(Percent; number.)

Characteristic	All prisoners	White[1]	Black[1]	Hispanic	American Indian/ Alaska Native[1]	Asian/ Native Hawaiian/ Other Pacific Islander[1]
U.S. Total	100.0	100.0	100.0	100.0	100.0	100.0
Number of prisoners	2,469	1,062	1,006	343	18	40
Prior Felony Convictions[2]						
Yes	67.6	63.8	72.8	65.4	68.8	56.8
No	32.4	36.2	27.2	34.6	31.3	43.2
Prior Homicide Convictions[3]						
Yes	9.5	9.8	9.6	9.1	5.6	5.0
No	90.5	90.2	90.4	90.9	94.4	95.0
Legal Status at Time of Capital Offense[4]						
Charges pending	7.9	9.6	7.0	5.8	6.3	5.6
On probation	11.4	9.9	11.5	14.8	18.8	13.9
On parole	16.0	13.7	17.9	17.4	25.0	13.9
On escape	1.2	1.7	0.8	1.0	0.0	0.0
Incarcerated	4.6	5.9	3.7	3.5	12.5	0.0
Other status	0.1	0.0	0.1	0.3	0.0	0.0
None	58.8	59.2	58.9	57.2	37.5	66.7

NOTE: Percentages are based on prisoners for whom data were reported. Details may not sum to totals due to rounding.
[1]Excludes persons of Hispanic origin (e.g., "White" refers to non-Hispanic Whites and "Black" refers to non-Hispanic Blacks).
[2]Excludes 191 prisoners because data were not reported.
[3]Excludes 31 prisoners because data were not reported.
[4]Excludes 285 prisoners because data were not reported.

Table 14. Prisoners Under Sentence of Death on December 31, 2020, by Year of Sentencing

(Number; years.)

Region and jurisdiction	Year of sentence for prisoners under sentence of death, 12/31/20													Under sentence of death, 12/31/20	Average years under sentence of death, 12/31/20
	1976 to 1980	1981 to 1985	1986 to 1990	1991 to 1995	1996 to 2000	2001 to 2005	2006 to 2010	2011 to 2015	2016	2017	2018	2019	2020		
U.S. Total	20	106	208	398	513	360	421	293	30	34	39	33	14	2,469	19.4
Federal	0	0	0	2	3	16	19	6	0	2	2	1	0	51	13.5
Alabama	0	1	9	22	37	30	36	24	4	1	3	3	0	170	17.2
Arizona	1	4	8	18	10	16	34	16	1	4	2	1	1	116	17.2
Arkansas	1	0	0	7	5	5	4	5	0	0	2	0	0	29	18
California	5	46	88	125	156	76	106	72	10	9	4	5	1	703	21.2
Florida	8	18	35	66	58	30	50	47	3	3	7	5	7	337	20.2
Georgia	0	0	2	4	12	7	10	4	0	0	0	1	0	40	18.2
Idaho	0	0	1	3	1	2	1	0	0	0	0	0	0	8	NC
Indiana	0	0	0	1	2	1	1	3	0	0	0	0	0	8	NC
Kansas	0	0	0	0	0	3	4	2	1	0	0	0	0	10	12.4
Kentucky	1	3	4	4	7	2	4	1	0	0	0	0	0	26	24.9
Louisiana	0	2	3	10	25	11	7	7	0	0	1	0	0	66	20.1
Mississippi	0	1	3	6	5	8	7	6	0	1	2	0	1	40	17.4
Missouri	0	2	1	0	0	4	8	4	0	0	1	0	0	20	15.6
Montana	0	1	0	1	0	0	0	0	0	0	0	0	0	2	NC
Nebraska	0	0	0	0	1	5	3	0	0	1	2	0	0	12	12.5
Nevada	1	11	5	10	16	5	8	5	1	4	1	0	0	67	21.9
New Hampshire	0	0	0	0	0	0	1	0	0	0	0	0	0	1	NC
North Carolina	0	1	1	44	47	23	13	4	1	0	0	3	0	137	21.3
Ohio	0	6	15	21	26	23	16	15	4	1	4	6	0	137	19.1
Oklahoma	0	1	0	1	6	13	13	6	0	2	1	1	1	45	14.2
Oregon	0	0	0	4	8	3	7	2	0	0	0	0	0	24	19
Pennsylvania	0	2	15	18	24	16	18	21	1	2	0	0	1	118	19.3
South Carolina	0	2	1	1	7	11	11	1	0	0	0	2	0	36	17.6
South Dakota	0	0	0	0	0	0	0	1	0	0	0	0	0	1	NC
Tennessee	0	3	8	8	13	6	6	5	0	0	1	0	0	50	22.2
Texas	3	1	7	21	42	43	33	35	4	4	6	5	2	206	16.6
Utah	0	1	2	1	2	0	0	1	0	0	0	0	0	7	NC
Virginia	0	0	0	0	0	1	1	0	0	0	0	0	0	2	NC

NOTE: For persons sentenced to death more than once, counts are based on the year of the most recent death sentence.
NC = Not calculated. A reliable average cannot be calculated from fewer than 10 cases.

Table 15. Average Time Elapsed Between Sentencing and Execution, Selected Years, 1977–2020

(Number; months.)

Year[1]	Executions	Average elapsed time (months) from sentence to execution[2]
Total	1,529	147
1977...	1	NC
1979...	2	NC
1981...	1	NC
1982...	2	NC
1983...	5	NC
1984...	21	74
1985...	18	71
1986...	18	87
1987...	25	86
1988...	11	80
1989...	16	95
1990...	23	95
1991...	14	116
1992...	31	114
1993...	38	113
1994...	31	122
1995...	56	134
1996...	45	125
1997...	74	133
1998...	68	130
1999...	98	143
2000...	85	137
2001...	66	142
2002...	71	127
2003...	65	131
2004...	59	132
2005...	60	147
2006...	53	145
2007...	42	153
2008...	37	139
2009...	52	169
2010...	46	178
2011...	43	198
2012...	43	190
2013...	39	186
2014...	35	218
2015...	28	195
2016...	20	204
2017...	23	243
2018...	25	238
2019...	22	264
2020...	17	227

NOTE: In 1972, the U.S. Supreme Court invalidated capital punishment statutes in several states (*Furman v. Georgia*, 408 U.S. 238 (1972)), effecting a moratorium on executions. Executions resumed in 1977 when the court found that revisions to statutes in several states had effectively addressed the issues previously held unconstitutional (*Gregg v. Georgia*, 428 U.S. 153 (1976)) and its companion cases).
[1]No executions were carried out in 1978 or 1980.
[2]Average time was calculated from the most recent sentencing date.

METHODOLOGY

Capital punishment information is collected annually as part of the Bureau of Justice Statistics' (BJS) National Prisoner Statistics program (NPS-8). This data series is collected in two parts:

- Data on persons under sentence of death are obtained from the department of corrections in each jurisdiction currently authorizing capital punishment.

- The status of death penalty statutes is obtained from the Office of the Attorney General in each of the 50 states, the U.S. Attorney's Office in the District of Columbia, and Federal Bureau of Prisons for the federal government.

Data collection forms are available on the BJS website at https://bjs.ojp.gov.

The NPS-8 covers all persons under a state or federal civil sentence of death at any time during the year. This includes capital offenders transferred from prison to mental hospitals and those who may have escaped from custody. It excludes persons sentenced to death under the Uniform Code of Military Justice and those whose death sentences have been overturned by a court or executive action, regardless of their current incarceration status.

Statistics in this report may differ from data collected by other organizations for various reasons:

- The NPS-8 adds prisoners to the population under sentence of death not at sentencing but at the time they are admitted to a state or federal correctional facility.

- If prisoners entered prison under a death sentence or were reported as being relieved of a death sentence in one year but the admission or removal had occurred in a previous year, counts are adjusted to reflect the actual dates of sentence or removal.

- NPS-8 counts are for the last day of the calendar year and will differ from counts for more recent periods.

Readers should use caution in interpreting data, especially as compared to previous years, due to the conditions imposed by the COVID-19 pandemic.

DEFINITIONS

Aggravating factor: Specific elements of a crime defined by statute. When present, these factors may allow a jury to impose a death sentence for a person convicted of a capital offense. Sometimes these are also called aggravating circumstances.

Capital conviction: A formal declaration that a defendant is guilty of a capital offense, made by the verdict of a jury, the decision of a judge, or a guilty plea by the defendant in a court of law.

Capital offense: A criminal offense punishable by death. Offenses that are eligible for a death sentence are defined by statute in each jurisdiction that authorizes capital punishment. The most common is first-degree murder accompanied by at least one aggravating factor.

Lists of capital offenses by state and by federal can be found at the end of this section.

Capital punishment: The process of sentencing convicted offenders to death for the most serious crimes and carrying out that sentence. The specific offenses and circumstances which determine if a crime is eligible for a death sentence are defined by statute and are prescribed by Congress or a state legislature.

Capital statute: State or federal laws dictating specific crimes that are eligible for a death sentence and specific procedures to be followed in carrying out such sentences.

Civil authority: For the purposes of this report, the state or federal entities responsible for implementation and enforcement of capital punishment laws, excluding military authorities.

Commutation: Reduction of a death sentence by a governor or a board of advisors empaneled to review sentences. Criteria for granting a commutation vary by state. The new sentence can be to life or a term of years.

Death row: A slang term referring to the area of a prison in which prisoners under sentence of death are housed. Usage of the term "death row" continues despite the fact that many states do not maintain a separate unit or facility for prisoners under sentence of death.

Received under sentence of death: Persons admitted to prison after being sentenced to death by a court.

Removal from under sentence of death: A prisoner who was previously under sentence of death and is no longer included in the count of persons under sentence of death. An inmate can be relieved of a death sentence by several methods: execution, death by causes other than execution, commutation, or an overturned capital conviction or sentence.

Sentence of death: A sentence imposed by a court for a capital offense which authorizes the state to execute a convicted offender.

Yearend: As of December 31 of the calendar year.

State	Offenses
Alabama	Intentional murder (Ala. Stat. Ann. § 13A-5-40(a)(1)–(21)) with 14 aggravating factors (Ala. Stat. Ann. § 13A-5-49).
Arizona	First-degree murder, including premeditated murder and felony murder, accompanied by at least 1 of 10 aggravating factors (A.R.S. § 13-703(F)).
Arkansas	Capital murder (Ark. Code Ann. § 5-10-101) with a finding of at least 1 of 10 aggravating circumstances; and treason (Ark. Code Ann. § 5-51-201).
California	First-degree murder with special circumstances; military sabotage; train wreck causing death; treason; perjury resulting in the execution of an innocent person; and fatal assault by a prisoner serving a life sentence.
Delaware	First-degree murder (11 Del. C. § 636) with at least 1 statutory aggravating circumstance (11 Del. C. § 4209). The Delaware Supreme Court held that a portion of Delaware's death penalty sentencing statute (11 Del. C. § 4209) was unconstitutional (*Rauf v. State*, 145 A.3d 430 (Del. 2016)). No legislative action has been taken to amend the statute. As a result, capital cases are no longer pursued in Delaware.
Florida	First-degree murder with aggravating factors; felony murder; and capital drug-trafficking felonies.
Georgia	Murder with aggravating circumstances; rape, armed robbery, or kidnapping with bodily injury or ransom when the victim dies; aircraft hijacking; and treason (O.C.G.A. § 17-10-30).
Idaho	First-degree murder with aggravating factors; first-degree kidnapping; and perjury resulting in the execution of an innocent person.
Indiana	Murder with 1 or more of 18 aggravating circumstances (I.C. 35-50-2-9).
Kansas	Intentional and premeditated killing of a person in 1 or more of 7 different circumstances (K.S.A. 21-5401).
Kentucky	Capital murder with the presence of at least 1 statutory aggravating circumstance; and capital kidnapping (K.R.S. 532.025).
Louisiana	First-degree murder (La. R.S. 14:30) with aggravating circumstances (La. C.Cr.P. 905.4); and treason (La. R.S. 14:113).
Mississippi	Capital murder with aggravating circumstances (Miss. Code Ann. § 97-3-19(2)); and aircraft piracy (Miss. Code Ann. § 97-25-55(1)).
Missouri	First-degree murder with at least 1 statutory aggravating circumstance (565.020 R.S.M.O. 2000).
Montana	Deliberate homicide, including felony murder, with 1 of 9 aggravating circumstances (Mont. Code Ann. § 46-18-303); aggravated kidnapping resulting in death of victim or rescuer; attempted deliberate homicide; aggravated assault or kidnapping while in detention; and capital sexual intercourse without consent (Mont. Code Ann. § 45-5-503).
Nebraska	First-degree murder with a finding of 1 or more statutory aggravating circumstances.
Nevada	First-degree murder with at least 1 of 15 aggravating circumstances (N.R.S. 200.030, 200.033, 200.035).
New York	First-degree murder with 1 of 13 aggravating factors (NY Penal Law § 125.27). The New York Court of Appeals held that a portion of New York's death penalty sentencing statute (C.P.L. 400.27) was unconstitutional (*People v. Taylor*, 9 N.Y.3d 129 (2007)). No legislative action has been taken to amend the statute. As a result, capital cases are no longer pursued in New York.
North Carolina	First-degree murder (N.C. Gen. Stat. § 14-17) with the finding of at least 1 of 11 statutory aggravating circumstances (N.C. Gen. Stat. § 15A-2000).
Ohio	Aggravated murder with at least 1 of 10 aggravating circumstances (O.R.C. 2903.01, 2929.02, 2929.04).

State	Offenses
Oklahoma	First-degree murder (21 O.S. § 701.7) in conjunction with a finding of at least 1 of 8 statutorily defined aggravating circumstances (21 O.S. § 701.12).
Oregon	Aggravated murder (O.R.S. 163.095).
Pennsylvania	First-degree murder (18 Pa.C.S.A. § 2502(a)) with 18 aggravating circumstances (42 Pa.C.S.A. § 9711).
South Carolina	Murder with at least 1 of 12 aggravating circumstances (S.C. Code § 16-3-20(C)(a)).
South Dakota	First-degree murder (S.D.C.L. 22-16-4) with 1 of 10 aggravating circumstances (S.D.C.L. 23A-27A-1).
Tennessee	First-degree murder (Tenn. Code Ann. § 39-13-202) with 1 of 18 aggravating circumstances (Tenn. Code Ann. § 39-13-204).
Texas	Capital murder, defined as criminal homicide with 1 of 9 statutory aggravators (Tex. Penal Code § 19.03).
Utah	Aggravated murder (Utah Code Ann. § 76-5-202).
Virginia	Capital murder, defined as the willful, deliberate, and premeditated murder accompanied by 1 of 15 aggravating circumstances (VA Code § 18.2-31(A)(1-15)).
Washington	Aggravated first-degree murder. The Washington Supreme Court has declared the state's death penalty statute unconstitutional as applied (*State v. Gregory*, 192 Wash. 2d 1, 427 P.3d 621 (2018)). No legislative action has been taken to revise or repeal the statute.
Wyoming	First-degree murder, including premeditated murder and murder during the commission of sexual assault, sexual abuse of a minor, arson, robbery, burglary, escape, resisting arrest, kidnapping, or abuse of a minor younger than age 16 (W.S.A. § 6-2-101(a)).

NOTE: New Hampshire repealed its death penalty effective May 30, 2019. One male prisoner remains under a previously imposed sentence of death.

Federal Capital Offenses, 2020

Statute	Description
8 U.S.C. 1342	Murder related to the smuggling of aliens.
18 U.S.C. 32-34	Destruction of aircraft, motor vehicles, or related facilities resulting in death.
18 U.S.C. 36	Murder committed during a drug-related drive-by shooting.
18 U.S.C. 37	Murder committed at an airport serving international civil aviation.
18 U.S.C. 115(b)(3) [by cross-reference to 18 U.S.C. 1111]	Retaliatory murder of a member of the immediate family of law enforcement officials.
18 U.S.C. 241, 242, 245, 247	Civil rights offenses resulting in death.
18 U.S.C. 351 [by cross-reference to 18 U.S.C. 1111]	Murder of a member of Congress, an important executive official, or a Supreme Court Justice.
18 U.S.C. 794	Espionage.
18 U.S.C. 844(d), (f), (i)	Death resulting from offenses involving transportation of explosives, destruction of government property, or destruction of property related to foreign or interstate commerce.
18 U.S.C. 924(i)	Murder committed by the use of a firearm during a crime of violence or a drug-trafficking crime.
18 U.S.C. 930	Murder committed in a federal government facility.
18 U.S.C. 1091	Genocide.
18 U.S.C. 1111	First-degree murder.

Statute	Description
18 U.S.C. 1114	Murder of a federal judge or law enforcement official.
18 U.S.C. 1116	Murder of a foreign official.
18 U.S.C. 1118	Murder by a federal prisoner.
18 U.S.C. 1119	Murder of a U.S. national in a foreign country.
18 U.S.C. 1120	Murder by an escaped federal prisoner already sentenced to life imprisonment.
18 U.S.C. 1121	Murder of a state or local law enforcement official or other person aiding in a federal investigation; murder of a state correctional officer.
18 U.S.C. 1201	Murder during a kidnapping.
18 U.S.C. 1203	Murder during a hostage taking.
18 U.S.C. 1503	Murder of a court officer or juror.
18 U.S.C. 1512	Murder with the intent of preventing testimony by a witness, victim, or informant.
18 U.S.C. 1513	Retaliatory murder of a witness, victim, or informant.
18 U.S.C. 1716	Mailing of injurious articles with intent to kill or resulting in death.
18 U.S.C. 1751 [by cross-reference to 18 U.S.C. 1111]	Assassination or kidnapping resulting in the death of the President or Vice President.
18 U.S.C. 1958	Murder for hire.
18 U.S.C. 1959	Murder involved in a racketeering offense.
18 U.S.C. 1992	Willful wrecking of a train resulting in death.
18 U.S.C. 2113	Bank robbery-related murder or kidnapping.
18 U.S.C. 2119	Murder related to a carjacking.
18 U.S.C. 2245	Murder related to rape or child molestation.
18 U.S.C. 2251	Murder related to sexual exploitation of children.
18 U.S.C. 2280	Murder committed during an offense against maritime navigation.
18 U.S.C. 2281	Murder committed during an offense against a maritime fixed platform.
18 U.S.C. 2332	Terrorist murder of a U.S. national in another country.
18 U.S.C. 2332a	Murder by the use of a weapon of mass destruction.
18 U.S.C. 2340	Murder involving torture.
18 U.S.C. 2381	Treason.
21 U.S.C. 848(e)	Murder related to a continuing criminal enterprise or related murder of a federal, state, or local law enforcement officer.
49 U.S.C. 1472–1473	Death resulting from aircraft hijacking.

Crime in the United States, 2020

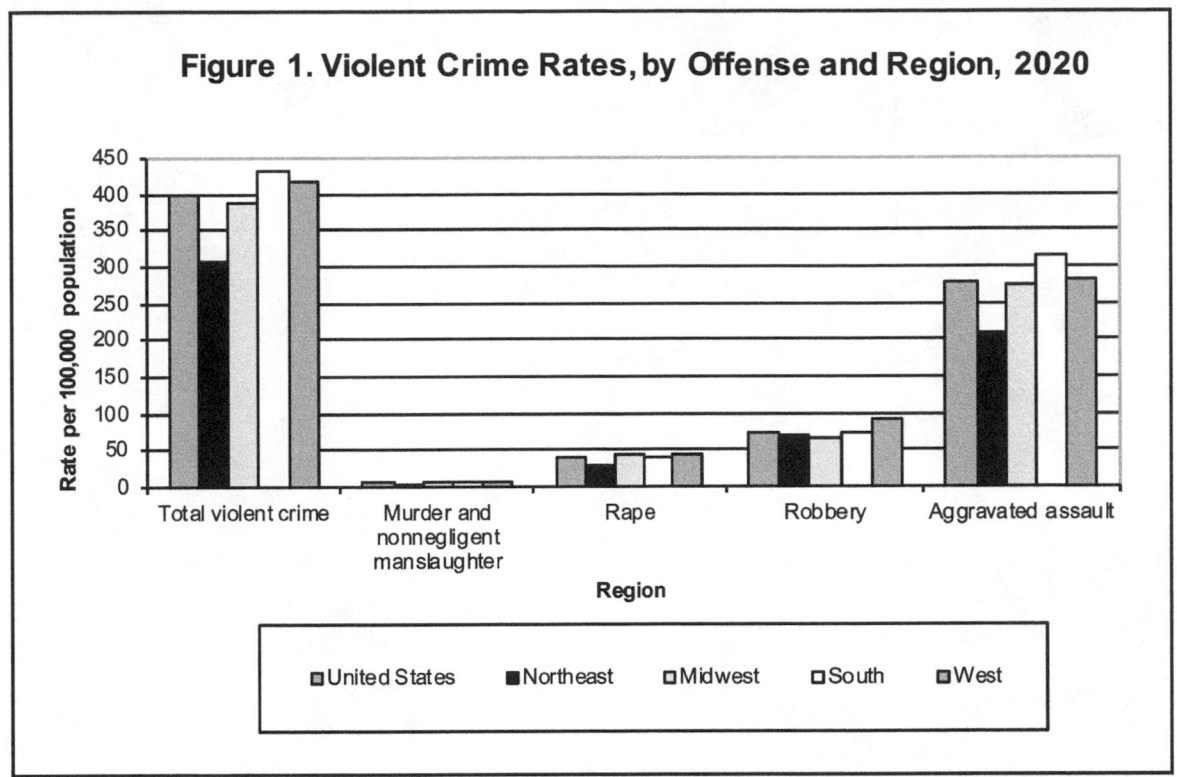

Figure 1. Violent Crime Rates, by Offense and Region, 2020

- An estimated 1,277,696 violent crimes occurred nationwide, an increase of 5.6 percent from the 2019 estimate. Aggravated assaults accounted for 64.3 percent of violent crimes reported to law enforcement in 2020.
- The 2-year trend showed that property crime offenses (an estimated total of 6,452,038) declined 7.8 percent in 2020 when compared with the 2019 estimate. Larceny-theft accounted for 71.4 percent of all property crimes in 2020.
- In 2020, 41.7 percent of violent crimes and 14.6 percent of property crimes were cleared by arrest or exceptional means.
- Law enforcement made an estimated 7,632,473 arrests nationwide in 2020. Of these arrests, 482,408 were for

violent crimes and 871,370 were for property crimes. The highest number of arrests were for drug abuse violations (estimated at 1,155,610 arrests).
- Nationwide, the rate of sworn officers in cities was 2.2 per 1,000 inhabitants. The percentage of full-time civilian law enforcement employees was 30.7 percent.
- There were 571 crimes known to law enforcement at federal agencies in 2020.
- Of participating states, Texas had the most human trafficking violations in 2020, with 484.
- In 2020, 1,118 cargo theft incidents were reported among participating states and 25.4 percent of these thefts were recovered.

Table 1. Crime in the United States, by Volume and Rate Per 100,000 Inhabitants, 2001–2020

(Number, rate per 100,000 population.)

Year	Population[1]	Violent crime[2] Number	Rate	Murder and nonnegligent manslaughter Number	Rate	Rape (revised definition)[3] Number	Rate	Rape (legacy definition)[4] Number	Rate	Robbery Number	Rate	Aggravated assault Number	Rate
2001[5]	285,317,559	1,439,480	504.5	16,037	5.6	X	X	90,863	31.8	423,557	148.5	909,023	318.6
2002	287,973,924	1,423,677	494.4	16,229	5.6	X	X	95,235	33.1	420,806	146.1	891,407	309.5
2003	290,788,976	1,383,676	475.8	16,528	5.7	X	X	93,883	32.3	414,235	142.5	859,030	295.4
2004	293,656,842	1,360,088	463.2	16,148	5.5	X	X	95,089	32.4	401,470	136.7	847,381	288.6
2005	296,507,061	1,390,745	469.0	16,740	5.6	X	X	94,347	31.8	417,438	140.8	862,220	290.8
2006	299,398,484	1,435,123	479.3	17,309	5.8	X	X	94,472	31.6	449,246	150.0	874,096	292.0
2007	301,621,157	1,422,970	471.8	17,128	5.7	X	X	92,160	30.6	447,324	148.3	866,358	287.2
2008	304,059,724	1,394,461	458.6	16,465	5.4	X	X	90,750	29.8	443,563	145.9	843,683	277.5
2009	307,006,550	1,325,896	431.9	15,399	5.0	X	X	89,241	29.1	408,742	133.1	812,514	264.7
2010	309,330,219	1,251,248	404.5	14,722	4.8	X	X	85,593	27.7	369,089	119.3	781,844	252.8
2011	311,587,816	1,206,005	387.1	14,661	4.7	X	X	84,175	27.0	354,746	113.9	752,423	241.5
2012	313,873,685	1,217,057	387.8	14,856	4.7	X	X	85,141	27.1	355,051	113.1	762,009	242.8
2013	316,497,531	1,168,298	369.1	14,319	4.5	113,695	36	82,109	25.9	345,093	109.0	726,777	229.6
2014	318,907,401	1,153,022	361.6	14,164	4.4	118,027	37.0	84,864	26.6	322,905	101.3	731,089	229.2
2015	320,896,618	1,199,310	373.7	15,883	4.9	126,134	39.3	91,261	28.4	328,109	102.2	764,057	238.1
2016	323,405,935	1,250,162	386.6	17,413	5.4	132,414	40.9	96,970	30.0	332,797	102.9	802,982	248.3
2017	325,147,121	1,247,917	383.8	17,294	5.3	135,666	41.7	99,708	30.7	320,596	98.6	810,319	249.2
2018	326,687,501	1,209,997	370.4	16,374	5.0	143,765	44.0	101,363	31.0	281,278	86.1	810,982	248.2
2019[6]	328,329,953	1,210,229	368.6	16,669	5.1	143,224	43.6	103,060	31.4	268,483	81.8	822,017	250.4
2020	329,484,123	1,277,696	387.8	21,570	6.5	126,430	38.4	91,021	27.6	243,600	73.9	921,505	279.7

Year	Property crime Number	Rate	Burglary Number	Rate	Larceny-theft Number	Rate	Motor vehicle theft Number	Rate
2001[5]	10,437,189	3,658.1	2,116,531	741.8	7,092,267	2,485.7	1,228,391	430.5
2002	10,455,277	3,630.6	2,151,252	747.0	7,057,379	2,450.7	1,246,646	432.9
2003	10,442,862	3,591.2	2,154,834	741.0	7,026,802	2,416.5	1,261,226	433.7
2004	10,319,386	3,514.1	2,144,446	730.3	6,937,089	2,362.3	1,237,851	421.5
2005	10,174,754	3,431.5	2,155,448	726.9	6,783,447	2,287.8	1,235,859	416.8
2006	10,019,601	3,346.6	2,194,993	733.1	6,626,363	2,213.2	1,198,245	400.2
2007	9,882,212	3,276.4	2,190,198	726.1	6,591,542	2,185.4	1,100,472	364.9
2008	9,774,152	3,214.6	2,228,887	733.0	6,586,206	2,166.1	959,059	315.4
2009	9,337,060	3,041.3	2,203,313	717.7	6,338,095	2,064.5	795,652	259.2
2010	9,112,625	2,945.9	2,168,459	701.0	6,204,601	2,005.8	739,565	239.1
2011	9,052,743	2,905.4	2,185,140	701.3	6,151,095	1,974.1	716,508	230.0
2012	9,001,992	2,868.0	2,109,932	672.2	6,168,874	1,965.4	723,186	230.4
2013	8,651,892	2,733.6	1,932,139	610.5	6,019,465	1,901.9	700,288	221.3
2014	8,209,010	2,574.1	1,713,153	537.2	5,809,054	1,821.5	686,803	215.4
2015	8,024,115	2,500.5	1,587,564	494.7	5,723,488	1,783.6	713,063	222.2
2016	7,928,530	2,451.6	1,516,405	468.9	5,644,835	1,745.4	767,290	237.3
2017	7,682,988	2,362.9	1,397,045	429.7	5,513,000	1,695.5	772,943	237.7
2018	7,219,084	2,209.8	1,235,013	378.0	5,232,167	1,601.6	751,904	230.2
2019[6]	6,995,235	2,130.6	1,118,096	340.5	5,152,267	1,569.2	724,872	220.8
2020	6,452,038	1,958.2	1,035,314	314.2	4,606,324	1,398.0	810,400	246.0

NOTE: Although arson data are included in the trend and clearance tables, sufficient data are not available to estimate totals for this offense. Therefore, no arson data are published in this table.
X = Not applicable.
[1] Populations are U.S. Census Bureau provisional estimates as of July 1 for each year except 2000 and 2010, which are decennial census counts.
[2] The violent crime figures include the offenses of murder, rape (legacy definition), robbery, and aggravated assault.
[3] The figures shown in this column for the offense of rape were estimated using the revised UCR definition of rape.
[4] The figures shown in this column for the offense of rape were estimated using the legacy UCR definition of rape.
[5] The murder and nonnegligent homicides that occurred as a result of the events of September 11, 2001, are not included in this table.
[6] The crime figures have been adjusted.

Table 1A. Crime in the United States, Percent Change in Volume and Rate Per 100,000 Inhabitants for 2 Years, 5 Years, and 10 Years, 2011–2020

(Percent change.)

Year	Violent crime[1]		Murder and nonnegligent manslaughter		Rape (revised definition)[2]		Rape (legacy definition)[3]		Robbery	
	Number	Rate	Number	Rate	Number	Rate	Number	Rate	Number	Rate
2011–2020...........................	+5.9	+0.2	+47.1	+39.1	X	X	+8.1	+2.3	-31.3	-35.1
2016–2020...........................	+2.2	+0.3	+23.9	+21.6	-4.5	-6.3	-6.1	-7.9	-26.8	-28.2
2019–2020...........................	+5.6	+5.2	+29.4	+28.9	-11.7	-12.0	-11.7	-12.0	-9.3	-9.6

X = Not applicable.
[1] The violent crime figures include the offenses of murder, rape (legacy definition), robbery, and aggravated assault.
[2] The figures shown in this column for the offense of rape were estimated using the revised UCR definition of rape.
[3] The figures shown in this column for the offense of rape were estimated using the legacy UCR definition of rape.

Table 2. Crime in the United States,[1] by Region, Geographic Division, and State, 2019–2020

(Number, rate per 100,000 population, percent.)

Area	Population[2]	Violent crime[3]		Murder and nonnegligent manslaughter		Rape (revised definition)[4]		Robbery	
		Number	Rate	Number	Rate	Number	Rate	Number	Rate
UNITED STATES[5,6,7,8,9]									
2019.................	328,329,953	1,250,393	380.8	16,669	5.1	143,224	43.6	268,483	81.8
2020.................	329,484,123	1,313,105	398.5	21,570	6.5	126,430	38.4	243,600	73.9
Percent change		+5.0	+4.6	+29.4	+28.9	-11.7	-12.0	-9.3	-9.6
NORTHEAST[5]									
2019.................	56,002,934	164,411	293.6	1,856	3.3	17,487	31.2	40,222	71.8
2020.................	55,849,869	172,219	308.4	2,526	4.5	15,066	27.0	38,535	69.0
Percent change		+4.7	+5.0	+36.1	+36.5	-13.8	-13.6	-4.2	-3.9
New England									
2019.................	14,849,662	36,609	246.5	352	2.4	4,963	33.4	6,578	44.3
2020.................	14,847,468	34,734	233.9	380	2.6	4,093	27.6	5,898	39.7
Percent change		-5.1	-5.1	+8.0	+8.0	-17.5	-17.5	-10.3	-10.3
Connecticut									
2019	3,566,022	6,583	184.6	107	3.0	797	22.3	1,942	54.5
2020	3,557,006	6,459	181.6	140	3.9	594	16.7	2,033	57.2
Percent change		-1.9	-1.6	+30.8	+31.2	-25.5	-25.3	+4.7	+5.0
Maine									
2019	1,345,770	1,562	116.1	22	1.6	520	38.6	192	14.3
2020	1,350,141	1,466	108.6	22	1.6	486	36.0	170	12.6
Percent change		-6.1	-6.4	+0.0	-0.3	-6.5	-6.8	-11.5	-11.7
Massachusetts									
2019	6,894,883	22,662	328.7	153	2.2	2,244	32.5	3,625	52.6
2020	6,893,574	21,288	308.8	160	2.3	1,851	26.9	3,015	43.7
Percent change		-6.1	-6.0	+4.6	+4.6	-17.5	-17.5	-16.8	-16.8
New Hampshire									
2019	1,360,783	2,152	158.1	33	2.4	606	44.5	327	24.0
2020	1,366,275	2,000	146.4	12	0.9	542	39.7	280	20.5
Percent change		-7.1	-7.4	-63.6	-63.8	-10.6	-10.9	-14.4	-14.7
Rhode Island									
2019	1,058,158	2,357	222.7	26	2.5	498	47.1	421	39.8
2020	1,057,125	2,440	230.8	32	3.0	407	38.5	336	31.8
Percent change		+3.5	+3.6	+23.1	+23.2	-18.3	-18.2	-20.2	-20.1
Vermont									
2019	624,046	1,293	207.2	11	1.8	298	47.8	71	11.4
2020	623,347	1,081	173.4	14	2.2	213	34.2	64	10.3
Percent change		-16.4	-16.3	27.3	+27.4	-28.5	-28.4	-9.9	-9.8
Middle Atlantic[5]									
2019.................	41,153,272	127,802	310.6	1,504	3.7	12,524	30.4	33,644	81.8
2020.................	41,002,401	137,485	335.3	2,146	5.2	10,973	26.8	32,637	79.6
Percent change		+7.6	+8.0	+42.7	+43.2	-12.4	-12.1	-3.0	-2.6
New Jersey									
2019	8,891,258	18,382	206.7	263	3.0	1,537	17.3	5,730	64.4
2020	8,882,371	17,353	195.4	329	3.7	1,277	14.4	4,384	49.4
Percent change		-5.6	-5.5	+25.1	+25.2	-16.9	-16.8	-23.5	-23.4

Table 1A. Crime in the United States, Percent Change in Volume and Rate Per 100,000 Inhabitants for 2 Years, 5 Years, and 10 Years, 2011–2020—*Continued*

(Percent change.)

Year	Aggravated assault		Property crime		Burglary		Larceny-theft		Motor vehicle theft	
	Number	Rate	Number	Rate	Number	Rate	Number	Rate	Number	Rate
2011–2020	+22.5	+15.8	-28.7	-32.6	-52.6	-55.2	-25.1	-29.2	+13.1	+7.0
2016–2020	+14.8	+12.6	-18.6	-20.1	-31.7	-33.0	-18.4	-19.9	+5.6	+3.7
2019–2020	+12.1	+11.7	-7.8	-8.1	-7.4	-7.7	-10.6	-10.9	+11.8	+11.4

Table 2. Crime in the United States,[1] by Region, Geographic Division, and State, 2019–2020—*Continued*

(Number, rate per 100,000 population, percent.)

Area	Aggravated assault		Property crime		Burglary		Larceny-theft		Motor vehicle theft	
	Number	Rate	Number	Rate	Number	Rate	Number	Rate	Number	Rate
UNITED STATES[5,6,7,8,9]										
2019	822,017	250.4	6,995,235	2,130.6	1,118,096	340.5	5,152,267	1,569.2	724,872	220.8
2020	921,505	279.7	6,452,038	1,958.2	1,035,314	314.2	4,606,324	1,398.0	810,400	246.0
Percent change	+12.1	+11.7	-7.8	-8.1	-7.4	-7.7	-10.6	-10.9	+11.8	+11.4
NORTHEAST[5]										
2019	104,846	187.2	759,192	1,355.6	94,329	168.4	613,608	1,095.7	51,255	91.5
2020	116,092	207.9	765,478	1,370.6	99,884	178.8	601,250	1,076.5	64,344	115.2
Percent change	+10.7	+11.0	+0.8	+1.1	+5.9	+6.2	-2.0	-1.7	+25.5	+25.9
New England										
2019	24,716	166.4	191,098	1,286.9	26,541	178.7	149,097	1,004.0	15,460	104.1
2020	24,363	164.1	179,648	1,210.0	23,124	155.7	137,588	926.7	18,936	127.5
Percent change	-1.4	-1.4	-6.0	-6.0	-12.9	-12.9	-7.7	-7.7	+22.5	+22.5
Connecticut										
2019	3,737	104.8	51,076	1,432.3	6,468	181.4	38,616	1,082.9	5,992	168.0
2020	3,692	103.8	55,670	1,565.1	6,656	187.1	40,592	1,141.2	8,422	236.8
Percent change	-1.2	-1.0	+9.0	+9.3	+2.9	+3.2	+5.1	+5.4	+40.6	+40.9
Maine										
2019	828	61.5	16,791	1,247.7	2,360	175.4	13,705	1,018.4	726	53.9
2020	788	58.4	15,610	1,156.2	2,009	148.8	12,739	943.5	862	63.8
Percent change	-4.8	-5.1	-7.0	-7.3	-14.9	-15.1	-7.0	-7.3	+18.7	+18.3
Massachusetts										
2019	16,640	241.3	81,399	1,180.6	12,323	178.7	62,944	912.9	6,132	88.9
2020	16,262	235.9	72,602	1,053.2	10,323	149.7	55,444	804.3	6,835	99.2
Percent change	-2.3	-2.3	-10.8	-10.8	-16.2	-16.2	-11.9	-11.9	+11.5	+11.5
New Hampshire										
2019	1,186	87.2	16,552	1,216.4	1,783	131.0	13,826	1,016.0	943	69.3
2020	1,166	85.3	15,014	1,098.9	1,412	103.3	12,558	919.1	1,044	76.4
Percent change	-1.7	-2.1	-9.3	-9.7	-20.8	-21.1	-9.2	-9.5	+10.7	+10.3
Rhode Island										
2019	1,412	133.4	16,312	1,541.5	2,321	219.3	12,628	1,193.4	1,363	128.8
2020	1,665	157.5	13,166	1,245.5	1,763	166.8	9,894	935.9	1,509	142.7
Percent change	+17.9	+18.0	-19.3	-19.2	-24.0	-24.0	-21.7	-21.6	+10.7	+10.8
Vermont										
2019	913	146.3	8,968	1,437.1	1,286	206.1	7,378	1,182.3	304	48.7
2020	790	126.7	7,586	1,217.0	961	154.2	6,361	1,020.5	264	42.4
Percent change	-13.5	-13.4	-15.4	-15.3	-25.3	-25.2	-13.8	-13.7	-13.2	-13.1
Middle Atlantic[5]										
2019	80,130	194.7	568,094	1,380.4	67,788	164.7	464,511	1,128.7	35,795	87.0
2020	91,729	223.7	585,830	1,428.8	76,760	187.2	463,662	1,130.8	45,408	110.7
Percent change	+14.5	+14.9	+3.1	+3.5	+13.2	+13.7	-0.2	+0.2	+26.9	+27.3
New Jersey										
2019	10,852	122.1	118,637	1,334.3	16,399	184.4	91,902	1,033.6	10,336	116.2
2020	11,363	127.9	102,875	1,158.2	12,983	146.2	79,614	896.3	10,278	115.7
Percent change	+4.7	+4.8	-13.3	-13.2	-20.8	-20.8	-13.4	-13.3	-0.6	-0.5

Table 2. Crime in the United States,[1] by Region, Geographic Division, and State, 2019–2020—*Continued*

(Number, rate per 100,000 population, percent.)

Area	Population[2]	Violent crime[3]		Murder and nonnegligent manslaughter		Rape (revised definition)[4]		Robbery	
		Number	Rate	Number	Rate	Number	Rate	Number	Rate
New York									
2019..................	19,463,131	70,260	361.0	565	2.9	6,642	34.1	18,165	93.3
2020..................	19,336,776	70,339	363.8	808	4.2	5,468	28.3	17,525	90.6
Percent change............		+0.1	+0.8	+43.0	+43.9	-17.7	-17.1	-3.5	-2.9
Pennsylvania[5]									
2019..................	12,798,883	39,160	306.0	676	5.3	4,345	33.9	9,749	76.2
2020..................	12,783,254	49,793	389.5	1,009	7.9	4,228	33.1	10,728	83.9
Percent change............		+27.2	+27.3	+49.3	+49.4	-2.7	-2.6	+10.0	+10.2
MIDWEST[6,7]									
2019..................	68,340,091	250,007	365.8	3,527	5.2	35,056	51.3	46,597	68.2
2020..................	68,316,744	264,915	387.8	4,803	7.0	30,157	44.1	43,368	63.5
Percent change		+6.0	+6.0	+36.2	+36.2	-14.0	-13.9	-6.9	-6.9
East North Central[6,7]									
2019..................	46,903,910	173,323	369.5	2,573	5.5	24,278	51.8	35,202	75.1
2020..................	46,834,910	180,379	385.1	3,538	7.6	20,575	43.9	31,821	67.9
Percent change		+4.1	+4.2	+37.5	+37.7	-15.3	-15.1	-9.6	-9.5
Illinois[6]									
2019..................	12,667,017	52,601	415.3	851	6.7	6,161	48.6	12,660	99.9
2020..................	12,587,530	53,612	425.9	1,151	9.1	5,090	40.4	12,261	97.4
Percent change............		+1.9	+2.6	+35.3	+36.1	-17.4	-16.9	-3.2	-2.5
Indiana									
2019..................	6,731,010	25,006	371.5	373	5.5	2,553	37.9	5,335	79.3
2020..................	6,754,953	24,161	357.7	505	7.5	2,348	34.8	4,215	62.4
Percent change............		-3.4	-3.7	+35.4	+34.9	-8.0	-8.4	-21.0	-21.3
Michigan									
2019..................	9,984,795	43,793	438.6	576	5.8	7,356	73.7	5,352	53.6
2020..................	9,966,555	47,641	478.0	754	7.6	6,065	60.9	4,438	44.5
Percent change............		+8.8	+9.0	+30.9	+31.1	-17.6	-17.4	-17.1	-16.9
Ohio[7]									
2019..................	11,696,507	34,618	296.0	584	5.0	5,850	50.0	8,861	75.8
2020..................	11,693,217	36,104	308.8	820	7.0	5,052	43.2	7,826	66.9
Percent change............		+4.3	+4.3	+40.4	+40.5	-13.6	-13.6	-11.7	-11.7
Wisconsin									
2019..................	5,824,581	17,305	297.1	189	3.2	2,358	40.5	2,994	51.4
2020..................	5,832,655	18,861	323.4	308	5.3	2,020	34.6	3,081	52.8
Percent change............		+9.0	+8.8	63.0	+62.7	-14.3	-14.5	+2.9	+2.8
West North Central									
2019..................	21,436,181	76,684	357.7	954	4.5	10,778	50.3	11,395	53.2
2020..................	21,481,834	84,536	393.5	1,265	5.9	9,582	44.6	11,547	53.8
Percent change		+10.2	+10.0	+32.6	+32.3	-11.1	-11.3	+1.3	+1.1
Iowa[5]									
2019..................	3,159,596	9,086	287.6	70	2.2	1,365	43.2	919	29.1
2020..................	3,163,561	9,601	303.5	111	3.5	1,289	40.7	943	29.8
Percent change............		+5.7	+5.5	+58.6	+58.4	-5.6	-5.7	+2.6	+2.5
Kansas									
2019..................	2,912,635	11,811	405.5	95	3.3	1,500	51.5	1,157	39.7
2020..................	2,913,805	12,385	425.0	100	3.4	1,263	43.3	928	31.8
Percent change............		+4.9	+4.8	+5.3	+5.2	-15.8	-15.8	-19.8	-19.8
Minnesota									
2019..................	5,640,053	13,395	237.5	127	2.3	2,499	44.3	3,155	55.9
2020..................	5,657,342	15,698	277.5	190	3.4	2,211	39.1	3,877	68.5
Percent change............		+17.2	+16.8	+49.6	+49.1	-11.5	-11.8	+22.9	+22.5
Missouri									
2019..................	6,140,475	30,680	499.6	576	9.4	3,019	49.2	4,995	81.3
2020..................	6,151,548	33,385	542.7	723	11.8	2,661	43.3	4,575	74.4
Percent change............		+8.8	+8.6	+25.5	+25.3	-11.9	-12.0	-8.4	-8.6
Nebraska									
2019..................	1,932,571	5,887	304.6	45	2.3	1,284	66.4	795	41.1
2020..................	1,937,552	6,473	334.1	69	3.6	1,163	60.0	799	41.2
Percent change............		+10.0	+9.7	+53.3	+52.9	-9.4	-9.7	+0.5	+0.2
North Dakota									
2019..................	763,724	2,302	301.4	25	3.3	464	60.8	184	24.1
2020..................	765,309	2,518	329.0	32	4.2	396	51.7	151	19.7
Percent change............		+9.4	+9.2	+28.0	+27.7	-14.7	-14.8	-17.9	-18.1
South Dakota									
2019..................	887,127	3,523	397.1	16	1.8	647	72.9	190	21.4
2020..................	892,717	4,476	501.4	40	4.5	599	67.1	274	30.7
Percent change............		+27.1	+26.3	+150.0	+148.4	-7.4	-8.0	+44.2	+43.3

Table 2. Crime in the United States,[1] by Region, Geographic Division, and State, 2019–2020—*Continued*

(Number, rate per 100,000 population, percent.)

Area	Aggravated assault Number	Rate	Property crime Number	Rate	Burglary Number	Rate	Larceny-theft Number	Rate	Motor vehicle theft Number	Rate
New York										
2019	44,888	230.6	269,787	1,386.1	28,065	144.2	228,672	1,174.9	13,050	67.0
2020	46,538	240.7	272,788	1,410.7	32,003	165.5	221,129	1,143.6	19,656	101.7
Percent change	+3.7	+4.4	+1.1	+1.8	+14.0	+14.8	-3.3	-2.7	+50.6	+51.6
Pennsylvania[5]										
2019	24,390	190.6	179,670	1,403.8	23,324	182.2	143,937	1,124.6	12,409	97.0
2020	33,828	264.6	210,167	1,644.1	31,774	248.6	162,919	1,274.5	15,474	121.0
Percent change	+38.7	+38.9	+17.0	+17.1	+36.2	+36.4	+13.2	+13.3	+24.7	+24.9
MIDWEST[6,7]										
2019	164,827	241.2	1,327,238	1,942.1	216,869	317.3	979,942	1,433.9	130,427	190.8
2020	186,587	273.1	1,219,817	1,785.5	195,963	286.8	877,996	1,285.2	145,858	213.5
Percent change	+13.2	+13.2	-8.1	-8.1	-9.6	-9.6	-10.4	-10.4	+11.8	+11.9
East North Central[6,7]										
2019	111,270	237.2	850,783	1,813.9	141,753	302.2	632,167	1,347.8	76,863	163.9
2020	124,445	265.7	755,390	1,612.9	123,212	263.1	547,556	1,169.1	84,622	180.7
Percent change	+11.8	+12.0	-11.2	-11.1	-13.1	-13.0	-13.4	-13.3	+10.1	+10.3
Illinois[6]										
2019	32,929	260.0	235,033	1,855.5	34,789	274.6	181,225	1,430.7	19,019	150.1
2020	35,110	278.9	196,287	1,559.4	31,020	246.4	143,935	1,143.5	21,332	169.5
Percent change	+6.6	+7.3	-16.5	-16.0	-10.8	-10.3	-20.6	-20.1	+12.2	+12.9
Indiana										
2019	16,745	248.8	131,097	1,947.7	21,586	320.7	95,745	1,422.4	13,766	204.5
2020	17,093	253.0	120,453	1,783.2	18,938	280.4	86,080	1,274.3	15,435	228.5
Percent change	+2.1	+1.7	-8.1	-8.4	-12.3	-12.6	-10.1	-10.4	+12.1	+11.7
Michigan										
2019	30,509	305.6	158,317	1,585.6	28,574	286.2	111,900	1,120.7	17,843	178.7
2020	36,384	365.1	135,633	1,360.9	23,231	233.1	94,017	943.3	18,385	184.5
Percent change	+19.3	+19.5	-14.3	-14.2	-18.7	-18.6	-16.0	-15.8	+3.0	+3.2
Ohio[7]										
2019	19,323	165.2	240,540	2,056.5	44,232	378.2	177,610	1,518.5	18,698	159.9
2020	22,406	191.6	216,363	1,850.3	37,279	318.8	159,007	1,359.8	20,077	171.7
Percent change	+16.0	+16.0	-10.1	-10.0	-15.7	-15.7	-10.5	-10.4	+7.4	+7.4
Wisconsin										
2019	11,764	202.0	85,796	1,473.0	12,572	215.8	65,687	1,127.8	7,537	129.4
2020	13,452	230.6	86,654	1,485.7	12,744	218.5	64,517	1,106.1	9,393	161.0
Percent change	+14.3	+14.2	+1.0	+0.9	+1.4	+1.2	-1.8	-1.9	+24.6	+24.5
West North Central										
2019	53,557	249.8	476,455	2,222.7	75,116	350.4	347,775	1,622.4	53,564	249.9
2020	62,142	289.3	464,427	2,162.0	72,751	338.7	330,440	1,538.2	61,236	285.1
Percent change	+16.0	+15.8	-2.5	-2.7	-3.1	-3.4	-5.0	-5.2	+14.3	+14.1
Iowa[5]										
2019	6,732	213.1	58,446	1,849.8	12,406	392.6	40,479	1,281.1	5,561	176.0
2020	7,258	229.4	53,725	1,698.2	11,739	371.1	35,751	1,130.1	6,235	197.1
Percent change	+7.8	+7.7	-8.1	-8.2	-5.4	-5.5	-11.7	-11.8	+12.1	+12.0
Kansas										
2019	9,059	311.0	66,306	2,276.5	9,996	343.2	49,420	1,696.7	6,890	236.6
2020	10,094	346.4	64,077	2,199.1	9,655	331.4	47,193	1,619.6	7,229	248.1
Percent change	+11.4	+11.4	-3.4	-3.4	-3.4	-3.5	-4.5	-4.5	+4.9	+4.9
Minnesota										
2019	7,614	135.0	117,971	2,091.7	16,026	284.1	90,685	1,607.9	11,260	199.6
2020	9,420	166.5	120,212	2,124.9	17,370	307.0	88,696	1,567.8	14,146	250.0
Percent change	+23.7	+23.3	+1.9	+1.6	+8.4	+8.1	-2.2	-2.5	+25.6	+25.2
Missouri										
2019	22,090	359.7	163,223	2,658.1	26,617	433.5	115,324	1,878.1	21,282	346.6
2020	25,426	413.3	155,698	2,531.0	23,300	378.8	108,209	1,759.1	24,189	393.2
Percent change	+15.1	+14.9	-4.6	-4.8	-12.5	-12.6	-6.2	-6.3	+13.7	+13.5
Nebraska										
2019	3,763	194.7	39,553	2,046.7	4,763	246.5	29,817	1,542.9	4,973	257.3
2020	4,442	229.3	36,991	1,909.2	4,455	229.9	27,488	1,418.7	5,048	260.5
Percent change	+18.0	+17.7	-6.5	-6.7	-6.5	-6.7	-7.8	-8.0	+1.5	+1.2
North Dakota										
2019	1,629	213.3	15,270	1,999.4	2,646	346.5	10,785	1,412.2	1,839	240.8
2020	1,939	253.4	16,256	2,124.1	3,196	417.6	10,986	1,435.5	2,074	271.0
Percent change	+19.0	+18.8	+6.5	+6.2	+20.8	+20.5	+1.9	+1.7	+12.8	+12.5
South Dakota										
2019	2,670	301.0	15,686	1,768.2	2,662	300.1	11,265	1,269.8	1,759	198.3
2020	3,563	399.1	17,468	1,956.7	3,036	340.1	12,117	1,357.3	2,315	259.3
Percent change	+33.4	+32.6	+11.4	+10.7	+14.0	+13.3	+7.6	+6.9	+31.6	+30.8

(Number, rate per 100,000 population, percent.)

Area	Population[2]	Violent crime[3]		Murder and nonnegligent manslaughter		Rape (revised definition)[4]		Robbery	
		Number	Rate	Number	Rate	Number	Rate	Number	Rate
SOUTH[5,7,8,9]									
2019....................	125,686,544	511,209	406.7	8,063	6.4	53,738	42.8	102,414	81.5
2020....................	126,662,754	546,535	431.5	10,156	8.0	48,307	38.1	91,100	71.9
Percent change		+6.9	+6.1	+26.0	+25.0	-10.1	-10.8	-11.0	-11.7
South Atlantic[5,8,9]									
2019....................	65,870,942	244,720	371.5	4,140	6.3	23,711	36.0	51,332	77.9
2020....................	66,392,969	258,241	389.0	5,102	7.7	21,529	32.4	44,562	67.1
Percent change............		+5.5	+4.7	+23.2	+22.3	-9.2	-9.9	-13.2	-13.9
Delaware									
2019	976,668	4,128	422.7	47	4.8	329	33.7	789	80.8
2020	986,809	4,262	431.9	73	7.4	261	26.4	700	70.9
Percent change		+3.2	+2.2	+55.3	+53.7	-20.7	-21.5	-11.3	-12.2
District of Columbia[8]									
2019	708,253	7,403	1,045.2	166	23.4	345	48.7	2,714	383.2
2020	712,816	7,127	999.8	201	28.2	311	43.6	2,373	332.9
Percent change		-3.7	-4.3	+21.1	+20.3	-9.9	-10.4	-12.6	-13.1
Florida									
2019	21,492,056	81,291	378.2	1,122	5.2	8,463	39.4	16,234	75.5
2020	21,733,312	83,368	383.6	1,290	5.9	7,686	35.4	13,521	62.2
Percent change		+2.6	+1.4	+15.0	+13.7	-9.2	-10.2	-16.7	-17.6
Georgia[9]									
2019	10,628,020	34,666	326.2	605	5.7	3,005	28.3	7,488	70.5
2020	10,710,017	42,850	400.1	943	8.8	3,420	31.9	7,016	65.5
Percent change		+23.6	+22.7	+55.9	+54.7	+13.8	+12.9	-6.3	-7.0
Maryland[5]									
2019	6,054,954	27,511	454.4	545	9.0	1,944	32.1	9,215	152.2
2020	6,055,802	24,215	399.9	553	9.1	1,732	28.6	7,174	118.5
Percent change		-12.0	-12.0	+1.5	+1.5	-10.9	-10.9	-22.1	-22.2
North Carolina									
2019	10,501,384	39,773	378.7	653	6.2	3,364	32.0	7,700	73.3
2020	10,600,823	44,451	419.3	852	8.0	2,922	27.6	7,340	69.2
Percent change		+11.8	+10.7	+30.5	+29.3	-13.1	-14.0	-4.7	-5.6
South Carolina									
2019	5,157,702	26,307	510.1	455	8.8	2,528	49.0	3,325	64.5
2020	5,218,040	27,691	530.7	549	10.5	2,086	40.0	3,122	59.8
Percent change		+5.3	+4.0	+20.7	+19.3	-17.5	-18.4	-6.1	-7.2
Virginia									
2019	8,556,642	17,916	209.4	447	5.2	2,915	34.1	3,520	41.1
2020	8,590,563	17,925	208.7	524	6.1	2,279	26.5	2,947	34.3
Percent change		+0.1	-0.3	+17.2	+16.8	-21.8	-22.1	-16.3	-16.6
West Virginia									
2019	1,795,263	5,725	318.9	100	5.6	818	45.6	347	19.3
2020	1,784,787	6,352	355.9	117	6.6	832	46.6	369	20.7
Percent change		+11.0	+11.6	+17.0	+17.7	+1.7	+2.3	+6.3	+7.0
East South Central[5,7]									
2019....................	19,188,862	83,328	434.3	1,432	7.5	7,659	39.9	13,868	72.3
2020....................	19,252,403	88,888	461.7	1,772	9.2	6,805	35.3	12,029	62.5
Percent change		+6.7	+6.3	+23.7	+23.3	-11.2	-11.4	-13.3	-13.5
Alabama[5]									
2019	4,907,965	24,769	504.7	390	7.9	2,119	43.2	3,922	79.9
2020	4,921,532	22,322	453.6	471	9.6	1,608	32.7	2,666	54.2
Percent change............		-9.9	-10.1	+20.8	+20.4	-24.1	-24.3	-32.0	-32.2
Kentucky									
2019	4,472,345	9,872	220.7	229	5.1	1,673	37.4	2,162	48.3
2020	4,477,251	11,600	259.1	323	7.2	1,371	30.6	2,369	52.9
Percent change............		+17.5	+17.4	+41.0	+40.9	-18.1	-18.1	+9.6	+9.5
Mississippi[7]									
2019	2,978,227	7,779	261.2	298	10.0	924	31.0	1,620	54.4
2020	2,966,786	8,638	291.2	315	10.6	1,148	38.7	1,419	47.8
Percent change............		+11.0	+11.5	+5.7	+6.1	+24.2	+24.7	-12.4	-12.1
Tennessee									
2019	6,830,325	40,908	598.9	515	7.5	2,943	43.1	6,164	90.2
2020	6,886,834	46,328	672.7	663	9.6	2,678	38.9	5,575	81.0
Percent change............		+13.2	+12.3	+28.7	+27.7	-9.0	-9.8	-9.6	-10.3
West South Central									
2019....................	40,626,740	183,161	450.8	2,491	6.1	22,368	55.1	37,214	91.6
2020....................	41,017,382	199,406	486.1	3,282	8.0	19,973	48.7	34,509	84.1
Percent change		+8.9	+7.8	+31.8	+30.5	-10.7	-11.6	-7.3	-8.2

(Number, rate per 100,000 population, percent.)

Area	Aggravated assault		Property crime		Burglary		Larceny-theft		Motor vehicle theft	
	Number	Rate	Number	Rate	Number	Rate	Number	Rate	Number	Rate
SOUTH[5,7,8,9]										
2019.................	346,994	276.1	3,008,909	2,394.0	498,381	396.5	2,229,081	1,773.5	281,447	223.9
2020.................	396,972	313.4	2,668,302	2,106.6	441,688	348.7	1,929,682	1,523.5	296,932	234.4
Percent change	+14.4	+13.5	-11.3	-12.0	-11.4	-12.1	-13.4	-14.1	+5.5	+4.7
South Atlantic[5,8,9]										
2019............................	165,537	251.3	1,498,001	2,274.1	223,239	338.9	1,151,490	1,748.1	123,272	187.1
2020............................	187,048	281.7	1,269,388	1,911.9	192,836	290.4	948,880	1,429.2	127,672	192.3
Percent change............	+13.0	+12.1	-15.3	-15.9	-13.6	-14.3	-17.6	-18.2	+3.6	+2.8
Delaware										
2019	2,963	303.4	21,932	2,245.6	2,984	305.5	17,343	1,775.7	1,605	164.3
2020	3,228	327.1	19,355	1,961.4	2,508	254.2	15,182	1,538.5	1,665	168.7
Percent change	+8.9	+7.8	-11.7	-12.7	-16.0	-16.8	-12.5	-13.4	+3.7	+2.7
District of Columbia[8]										
2019	4,178	589.9	30,819	4,351.4	1,843	260.2	26,643	3,761.8	2,333	329.4
2020	4,242	595.1	24,899	3,493.0	1,964	275.5	19,536	2,740.7	3,399	476.8
Percent change	+1.5	+0.9	-19.2	-19.7	+6.6	+5.9	-26.7	-27.1	+45.7	+44.8
Florida										
2019	55,472	258.1	460,966	2,144.8	63,338	294.7	358,537	1,668.2	39,091	181.9
2020	60,871	280.1	384,556	1,769.4	52,293	240.6	293,992	1,352.7	38,271	176.1
Percent change	+9.7	+8.5	-16.6	-17.5	-17.4	-18.4	-18.0	-18.9	-2.1	-3.2
Georgia[9]										
2019	23,568	221.8	294,817	2,774.0	37,476	352.6	234,850	2,209.7	22,491	211.6
2020	31,471	293.8	214,988	2,007.4	31,139	290.7	158,343	1,478.5	25,506	238.2
Percent change	+33.5	+32.5	-27.1	-27.6	-16.9	-17.5	-32.6	-33.1	+13.4	+12.5
Maryland[5]										
2019	15,807	261.1	118,091	1,950.3	16,872	278.6	89,938	1,485.4	11,281	186.3
2020	14,756	243.7	97,487	1,609.8	15,261	252.0	71,757	1,184.9	10,469	172.9
Percent change	-6.6	-6.7	-17.4	-17.5	-9.5	-9.6	-20.2	-20.2	-7.2	-7.2
North Carolina										
2019	28,056	267.2	251,135	2,391.4	54,033	514.5	178,332	1,698.2	18,770	178.7
2020	33,337	314.5	236,026	2,226.5	49,952	471.2	165,554	1,561.7	20,520	193.6
Percent change	+18.8	+17.7	-6.0	-6.9	-7.6	-8.4	-7.2	-8.0	+9.3	+8.3
South Carolina										
2019	19,999	387.8	151,970	2,946.5	27,439	532.0	109,366	2,120.4	15,165	294.0
2020	21,934	420.3	141,987	2,721.1	23,377	448.0	103,892	1,991.0	14,718	282.1
Percent change	+9.7	+8.4	-6.6	-7.6	-14.8	-15.8	-5.0	-6.1	-2.9	-4.1
Virginia										
2019	11,034	129.0	140,944	1,647.2	13,972	163.3	116,656	1,363.3	10,316	120.6
2020	12,175	141.7	125,114	1,456.4	11,465	133.5	102,796	1,196.6	10,853	126.3
Percent change	+10.3	+9.9	-11.2	-11.6	-17.9	-18.3	-11.9	-12.2	+5.2	+4.8
West Virginia										
2019	4,460	248.4	27,327	1,522.2	5,282	294.2	19,825	1,104.3	2,220	123.7
2020	5,034	282.1	24,976	1,399.4	4,877	273.3	17,828	998.9	2,271	127.2
Percent change	+12.9	+13.5	-8.6	-8.1	-7.7	-7.1	-10.1	-9.5	+2.3	+2.9
East South Central[5,7]										
2019.................................	60,369	314.6	465,641	2,426.6	88,682	462.2	328,965	1,714.4	47,994	250.1
2020.................................	68,282	354.7	418,860	2,175.6	76,034	394.9	293,222	1,523.0	49,604	257.7
Percent change	+13.1	+12.7	-10.0	-10.3	-14.3	-14.5	-10.9	-11.2	+3.4	+3.0
Alabama[5]										
2019.................................	18,338	373.6	128,726	2,622.8	24,805	505.4	91,225	1,858.7	12,696	258.7
2020.................................	17,577	357.1	105,161	2,136.8	19,660	399.5	74,575	1,515.3	10,926	222.0
Percent change............	-4.1	-4.4	-18.3	-18.5	-20.7	-21.0	-18.3	-18.5	-13.9	-14.2
Kentucky										
2019	5,808	129.9	85,387	1,909.2	15,567	348.1	59,535	1,331.2	10,285	230.0
2020	7,537	168.3	79,673	1,779.5	15,407	344.1	52,769	1,178.6	11,497	256.8
Percent change............	+29.8	+29.6	-6.7	-6.8	-1.0	-1.1	-11.4	-11.5	+11.8	+11.7
Mississippi[7]										
2019	4,937	165.8	69,727	2,341.2	18,341	615.8	45,665	1,533.3	5,721	192.1
2020	5,756	194.0	62,351	2,101.6	14,488	488.3	41,780	1,408.3	6,083	205.0
Percent change............	+16.6	+17.0	-10.6	-10.2	-21.0	-20.7	-8.5	-8.2	+6.3	+6.7
Tennessee										
2019	31,286	458.0	181,801	2,661.7	29,969	438.8	132,540	1,940.5	19,292	282.4
2020	37,412	543.2	171,675	2,492.8	26,479	384.5	124,098	1,802.0	21,098	306.4
Percent change	+19.6	+18.6	-5.6	-6.3	-11.6	-12.4	-6.4	-7.1	+9.4	+8.5
West South Central										
2019.................................	121,088	298.1	1,045,267	2,572.9	186,460	459.0	748,626	1,842.7	110,181	271.2
2020.................................	141,642	345.3	980,054	2,389.4	172,818	421.3	687,580	1,676.3	119,656	291.7
Percent change	+17.0	+15.9	-6.2	-7.1	-7.3	-8.2	-8.2	-9.0	+8.6	+7.6

Table 2. Crime in the United States,[1] by Region, Geographic Division, and State, 2019–2020—*Continued*

(Number, rate per 100,000 population, percent.)

Area	Population[2]	Violent crime[3]		Murder and nonnegligent manslaughter		Rape (revised definition)[4]		Robbery	
		Number	Rate	Number	Rate	Number	Rate	Number	Rate
Arkansas									
2019.........................	3,020,985	17,547	580.8	237	7.8	2,420	80.1	1,576	52.2
2020.........................	3,030,522	20,363	671.9	321	10.6	2,226	73.5	1,577	52.0
Percent change............		+16.0	+15.7	+35.4	+35.0	-8.0	-8.3	+0.1	-0.3
Louisiana									
2019.........................	4,658,285	26,072	559.7	547	11.7	2,282	49.0	4,129	88.6
2020.........................	4,645,318	29,704	639.4	734	15.8	2,136	46.0	3,747	80.7
Percent change............		+13.9	+14.2	+34.2	+34.6	-6.4	-6.1	-9.3	-9.0
Oklahoma									
2019.........................	3,960,676	17,279	436.3	275	6.9	2,363	59.7	2,383	60.2
2020.........................	3,980,783	18,255	458.6	296	7.4	2,102	52.8	2,351	59.1
Percent change............		+5.6	+5.1	+7.6	+7.1	-11.0	-11.5	-1.3	-1.8
Texas									
2019.........................	28,986,794	122,263	421.8	1,432	4.9	15,303	52.8	29,126	100.5
2020.........................	29,360,759	131,084	446.5	1,931	6.6	13,509	46.0	26,834	91.4
Percent change............		+7.2	+5.8	+34.8	+33.1	-11.7	-12.8	-7.9	-9.0
WEST[7]									
2019[7].......................	78,300,384	324,766	414.8	3,223	4.1	36,943	47.2	79,250	101.2
2020.........................	78,654,756	329,436	418.8	4,085	5.2	32,900	41.8	70,597	89.8
Percent change..............		+1.4	+1.0	+26.7	+26.2	-10.9	-11.3	-10.9	-11.3
Mountain									
2019.........................	24,883,416	104,857	421.4	1,105	4.4	15,032	60.4	17,354	69.7
2020.........................	25,213,395	110,732	439.2	1,366	5.4	13,508	53.6	16,927	67.1
Percent change..............		+5.6	+4.2	+23.6	+22.0	-10.1	-11.3	-2.5	-3.7
Arizona									
2019.........................	7,291,843	32,603	447.1	397	5.4	3,650	50.1	6,305	86.5
2020[7].......................	7,421,401	35,980	484.8	513	6.9	3,263	44.0	6,211	83.7
Percent change............		+10.4	+8.4	+29.2	+27.0	-10.6	-12.2	-1.5	-3.2
Colorado									
2019.........................	5,758,486	22,149	384.6	229	4.0	4,087	71.0	3,716	64.5
2020.........................	5,807,719	24,570	423.1	294	5.1	3,652	62.9	3,964	68.3
Percent change............		+10.9	+10.0	+28.4	+27.3	-10.6	-11.4	+6.7	+5.8
Idaho									
2019.........................	1,789,060	4,162	232.6	28	1.6	918	51.3	161	9.0
2020.........................	1,826,913	4,432	242.6	41	2.2	832	45.5	174	9.5
Percent change............		+6.5	+4.3	+46.4	+43.4	-9.4	-11.2	+8.1	+5.8
Montana									
2019.........................	1,070,123	4,472	417.9	32	3.0	679	63.5	209	19.5
2020.........................	1,080,577	5,077	469.8	54	5.0	598	55.3	279	25.8
Percent change............		+13.5	+12.4	+68.8	+67.1	-11.9	-12.8	+33.5	+32.2
Nevada									
2019.........................	3,090,771	15,334	496.1	144	4.7	2,155	69.7	3,289	106.4
2020.........................	3,138,259	14,445	460.3	180	5.7	1,851	59.0	2,785	88.7
Percent change............		-5.8	-7.2	+25.0	+23.1	-14.1	-15.4	-15.3	-16.6
New Mexico									
2019.........................	2,099,634	17,302	824.0	185	8.8	1,355	64.5	2,477	118.0
2020.........................	2,106,319	16,393	778.3	164	7.8	1,170	55.5	2,086	99.0
Percent change............		-5.3	-5.6	-11.4	-11.6	-13.7	-13.9	-15.8	-16.1
Utah									
2019.........................	3,203,383	7,588	236.9	77	2.4	1,865	58.2	1,130	35.3
2020.........................	3,249,879	8,471	260.7	102	3.1	1,809	55.7	1,362	41.9
Percent change............		+11.6	+10.0	+32.5	+30.6	-3.0	-4.4	+20.5	+18.8
Wyoming									
2019.........................	580,116	1,247	215.0	13	2.2	323	55.7	67	11.5
2020.........................	582,328	1,364	234.2	18	3.1	333	57.2	66	11.3
Percent change............		+9.4	+9.0	+38.5	+37.9	+3.1	+2.7	-1.5	-1.9
Pacific[7]									
2019.........................	53,416,968	219,909	411.7	2,118	4.0	21,911	41.0	61,896	115.9
2020.........................	53,441,361	218,704	409.2	2,719	5.1	19,392	36.3	53,670	100.4
Percent change..............		-0.5	-0.6	+28.4	+28.3	-11.5	-11.5	-13.3	-13.3
Alaska									
2019.........................	733,603	6,346	865.0	69	9.4	1,102	150.2	826	112.6
2020.........................	731,158	6,126	837.8	49	6.7	1,132	154.8	712	97.4
Percent change............		-3.5	-3.1	-29.0	-28.7	+2.7	+3.1	-13.8	-13.5
California									
2019.........................	39,437,610	174,341	442.1	1,690	4.3	14,801	37.5	52,306	132.6
2020.........................	39,368,078	174,026	442.0	2,203	5.6	13,449	34.2	44,728	113.6
Percent change............		-0.2	*	+30.4	+30.6	-9.1	-9.0	-14.5	-14.3

(Number, rate per 100,000 population, percent.)

Area	Aggravated assault		Property crime		Burglary		Larceny-theft		Motor vehicle theft	
	Number	Rate	Number	Rate	Number	Rate	Number	Rate	Number	Rate
Arkansas										
2019............................	13,314	440.7	86,029	2,847.7	17,706	586.1	60,843	2,014.0	7,480	247.6
2020............................	16,239	535.8	79,200	2,613.4	15,854	523.1	55,413	1,828.5	7,933	261.8
Percent change............	+22.0	+21.6	-7.9	-8.2	-10.5	-10.7	-8.9	-9.2	+6.1	+5.7
Louisiana										
2019............................	19,114	410.3	148,429	3,186.3	27,440	589.1	110,123	2,364.0	10,866	233.3
2020............................	23,087	497.0	133,989	2,884.4	23,698	510.1	97,891	2,107.3	12,400	266.9
Percent change............	+20.8	+21.1	-9.7	-9.5	-13.6	-13.4	-11.1	-10.9	+14.1	+14.4
Oklahoma										
2019............................	12,258	309.5	113,504	2,865.8	26,820	677.2	73,199	1,848.1	13,485	340.5
2020............................	13,506	339.3	107,705	2,705.6	24,415	613.3	68,243	1,714.3	15,047	378.0
Percent change............	+10.2	+9.6	-5.1	-5.6	-9.0	-9.4	-6.8	-7.2	+11.6	+11.0
Texas										
2019............................	76,402	263.6	697,305	2,405.6	114,494	395.0	504,461	1,740.3	78,350	270.3
2020............................	88,810	302.5	659,160	2,245.0	108,851	370.7	466,033	1,587.3	84,276	287.0
Percent change............	+16.2	+14.8	-5.5	-6.7	-4.9	-6.1	-7.6	-8.8	+7.6	+6.2
WEST[7]										
2019............................	205,350	262.3	1,899,896	2,426.4	308,517	394.0	1,329,636	1,698.1	261,743	334.3
2020............................	221,854	282.1	1,798,441	2,286.5	297,779	378.6	1,197,396	1,522.3	303,266	385.6
Percent change..............	+8.0	+7.6	-5.3	-5.8	-3.5	-3.9	-9.9	-10.4	+15.9	+15.3
Mountain										
2019............................	71,366	286.8	591,703	2,377.9	96,771	388.9	423,075	1,700.2	71,857	288.8
2020............................	78,931	313.1	582,926	2,312.0	90,292	358.1	408,988	1,622.1	83,646	331.8
Percent change	+10.6	+9.2	-1.5	-2.8	-6.7	-7.9	-3.3	-4.6	+16.4	+14.9
Arizona										
2019............................	22,251	305.1	177,628	2,436.0	29,170	400.0	130,427	1,788.7	18,031	247.3
2020............................	25,993	350.2	165,323	2,227.7	24,488	330.0	122,898	1,656.0	17,937	241.7
Percent change............	+16.8	+14.8	-6.9	-8.6	-16.1	-17.5	-5.8	-7.4	-0.5	-2.3
Colorado										
2019............................	14,117	245.2	150,564	2,614.6	20,266	351.9	108,575	1,885.5	21,723	377.2
2020............................	16,660	286.9	164,582	2,833.8	23,246	400.3	110,884	1,909.3	30,452	524.3
Percent change............	+18.0	+17.0	+9.3	+8.4	+14.7	+13.7	+2.1	+1.3	+40.2	+39.0
Idaho										
2019............................	3,055	170.8	22,244	1,243.3	4,045	226.1	16,591	927.4	1,608	89.9
2020............................	3,385	185.3	20,313	1,111.9	3,731	204.2	14,815	810.9	1,767	96.7
Percent change............	+10.8	+8.5	-8.7	-10.6	-7.8	-9.7	-10.7	-12.6	+9.9	+7.6
Montana										
2019............................	3,552	331.9	23,929	2,236.1	2,968	277.4	18,547	1,733.2	2,414	225.6
2020............................	4,146	383.7	22,917	2,120.8	2,919	270.1	17,322	1,603.0	2,676	247.6
Percent change............	+16.7	+15.6	-4.2	-5.2	-1.7	-2.6	-6.6	-7.5	+10.9	+9.8
Nevada										
2019............................	9,746	315.3	72,028	2,330.4	15,630	505.7	45,127	1,460.1	11,271	364.7
2020............................	9,629	306.8	60,462	1,926.6	11,574	368.8	38,332	1,221.4	10,556	336.4
Percent change............	-1.2	-2.7	-16.1	-17.3	-26.0	-27.1	-15.1	-16.3	-6.3	-7.8
New Mexico										
2019............................	13,285	632.7	66,744	3,178.8	14,640	697.3	42,749	2,036.0	9,355	445.6
2020............................	12,973	615.9	59,859	2,841.9	13,665	648.8	37,188	1,765.5	9,006	427.6
Percent change............	-2.3	-2.7	-10.3	-10.6	-6.7	-7.0	-13.0	-13.3	-3.7	-4.0
Utah										
2019............................	4,516	141.0	69,469	2,168.6	8,658	270.3	54,078	1,688.2	6,733	210.2
2020............................	5,198	159.9	80,091	2,464.4	9,444	290.6	60,359	1,857.3	10,288	316.6
Percent change............	+15.1	+13.5	+15.3	+13.6	+9.1	+7.5	+11.6	+10.0	+52.8	+50.6
Wyoming										
2019............................	844	145.5	9,097	1,568.1	1,394	240.3	6,981	1,203.4	722	124.5
2020............................	947	162.6	9,379	1,610.6	1,225	210.4	7,190	1,234.7	964	165.5
Percent change............	+12.2	+11.8	+3.1	+2.7	-12.1	-12.5	+3.0	+2.6	+33.5	+33.0
Pacific[7]										
2019............................	133,984	250.8	1,308,193	2,449.0	211,746	396.4	906,561	1,697.1	189,886	355.5
2020............................	142,923	267.4	1,215,515	2,274.5	207,487	388.3	788,408	1,475.3	219,620	411.0
Percent change	+6.7	+6.6	-7.1	-7.1	-2.0	-2.1	-13.0	-13.1	+15.7	+15.6
Alaska										
2019............................	4,349	592.8	21,293	2,902.5	3,558	485.0	15,118	2,060.8	2,617	356.7
2020............................	4,233	578.9	16,528	2,260.5	2,775	379.5	11,784	1,611.7	1,969	269.3
Percent change............	-2.7	-2.3	-22.4	-22.1	-22.0	-21.7	-22.1	-21.8	-24.8	-24.5
California										
2019............................	105,544	267.6	921,177	2,335.8	152,551	386.8	626,865	1,589.5	141,761	359.5
2020............................	113,646	288.7	842,054	2,138.9	145,529	369.7	528,202	1,341.7	168,323	427.6
Percent change............	+7.7	+7.9	-8.6	-8.4	-4.6	-4.4	-15.7	-15.6	+18.7	+18.9

Table 2. Crime in the United States,[1] by Region, Geographic Division, and State, 2019–2020—*Continued*

(Number, rate per 100,000 population, percent.)

Area	Population[2]	Violent crime[3]		Murder and nonnegligent manslaughter		Rape (revised definition)[4]		Robbery	
		Number	Rate	Number	Rate	Number	Rate	Number	Rate
Hawaii									
2019.................	1,415,615	3,745	264.5	37	2.6	625	44.2	1,079	76.2
2020.................	1,407,006	3,576	254.2	41	2.9	569	40.4	867	61.6
Percent change............		-4.5	-3.9	+10.8	+11.5	-9.0	-8.4	-19.6	-19.2
Oregon[7]									
2019.................	4,216,116	12,382	293.7	117	2.8	1,886	44.7	2,329	55.2
2020.................	4,241,507	12,380	291.9	125	2.9	1,565	36.9	2,180	51.4
Percent change............		*	-0.6	+6.8	+6.2	-17.0	-17.5	-6.4	-7.0
Washington									
2019.................	7,614,024	23,095	303.3	205	2.7	3,497	45.9	5,356	70.3
2020.................	7,693,612	22,596	293.7	301	3.9	2,677	34.8	5,183	67.4
Percent change............		-2.2	-3.2	+46.8	+45.3	-23.4	-24.2	-3.2	-4.2
Puerto Rico									
2019.................	3,193,553	6,479	202.9	606	19.0	215	6.7	2,121	66.4
2020.................	3,159,343	5,196	164.5	529	16.7	148	4.7	1,177	37.3
Percent change		-19.8	-18.9	-12.7	-11.8	-31.2	-30.4	-44.5	-43.9

NOTE: Although arson data are included in the trend and clearance tables, sufficient data are not available to estimate totals for this offense. Therefore, no arson data are published in this table.
* = Less than one-tenth of 1 percent.
[1]The previous year's crime figures have been adjusted.
[2]Population figures are U.S. Census Bureau provisional estimates as of July 1, 2020.
[3]The violent crime figures include the offenses of murder, rape (revised definition), robbery, and aggravated assault.
[4]The figures shown in this column for the offense of rape were estimated using the revised Uniform Crime Reporting (UCR) definition of rape. See chapter notes for more detail.
[5]Limited data for 2018 were available for Alabama, Maryland, and Pennsylvania.
[6]The FBI determined that the state did not follow national UCR Program guidelines for reporting an offense. Consequently, those figures are not included in this table. The agency of Rockford submits independently and therefore includes all offenses.
[7]This state's agencies submitted rape data according to the legacy UCR definition of rape.
[8]Includes offenses reported by the Metro Transit Police and the District of Columbia Fire and Emergency Medical Services: Arson Investigation Unit.
[9]Because of changes in the state/local agency's reporting practices, figures are not comparable to previous years' data.

(Number, rate per 100,000 population, percent.)

Area	Aggravated assault		Property crime		Burglary		Larceny-theft		Motor vehicle theft	
	Number	Rate	Number	Rate	Number	Rate	Number	Rate	Number	Rate
Hawaii										
2019.................	2,004	141.6	40,617	2,869.2	5,534	390.9	29,878	2,110.6	5,205	367.7
2020.................	2,099	149.2	33,928	2,411.4	4,630	329.1	23,954	1,702.5	5,344	379.8
Percent change............	+4.7	+5.4	-16.5	-16.0	-16.3	-15.8	-19.8	-19.3	+2.7	+3.3
Oregon[7]										
2019.................	8,050	190.9	117,567	2,788.5	15,127	358.8	86,922	2,061.7	15,518	368.1
2020.................	8,510	200.6	112,782	2,659.0	14,386	339.2	81,811	1,928.8	16,585	391.0
Percent change............	+5.7	+5.1	-4.1	-4.6	-4.9	-5.5	-5.9	-6.4	+6.9	+6.2
Washington										
2019.................	14,037	184.4	207,539	2,725.7	34,976	459.4	147,778	1,940.9	24,785	325.5
2020.................	14,435	187.6	210,223	2,732.4	40,167	522.1	142,657	1,854.2	27,399	356.1
Percent change............	+2.8	+1.8	+1.3	+0.2	+14.8	+13.7	-3.5	-4.5	+10.5	+9.4
Puerto Rico										
2019.................	3,537	110.8	22,441	702.7	4,291	134.4	14,483	453.5	3,667	114.8
2020.................	3,342	105.8	13,241	419.1	2,952	93.4	8,311	263.1	1,978	62.6
Percent change................	-5.5	-4.5	-41.0	-40.4	-31.2	-30.5	-42.6	-42.0	-46.1	-45.5

NOTE: Although arson data are included in the trend and clearance tables, sufficient data are not available to estimate totals for this offense. Therefore, no arson data are published in this table.

* = Less than one-tenth of 1 percent.

[1]The previous year's crime figures have been adjusted.

[2]Population figures are U.S. Census Bureau provisional estimates as of July 1, 2020.

[3]The violent crime figures include the offenses of murder, rape (revised definition), robbery, and aggravated assault.

[4]The figures shown in this column for the offense of rape were estimated using the revised Uniform Crime Reporting (UCR) definition of rape. See chapter notes for more detail.

[5]Limited data for 2018 were available for Alabama, Maryland, and Pennsylvania.

[6]The FBI determined that the state did not follow national UCR Program guidelines for reporting an offense. Consequently, those figures are not included in this table. The agency of Rockford submits independently and therefore includes all offenses.

[7]This state's agencies submitted rape data according to the legacy UCR definition of rape.

[8]Includes offenses reported by the Metro Transit Police and the District of Columbia Fire and Emergency Medical Services: Arson Investigation Unit.

[9]Because of changes in the state/local agency's reporting practices, figures are not comparable to previous years' data.

Table 3. Crime in the United States, by State and Area, 2020

(Number, percent, rate per 100,000 population.)

Area	Population[1]	Violent crime[2]	Murder and nonnegligent manslaughter	Rape (revised definition)[3]	Robbery	Aggravated assault	Property crime	Burglary	Larceny-theft	Motor vehicle theft
Alabama[4]										
Metropolitan statistical area	3,750,044									
Area actually reporting	86.6%	16,638	319	1,147	2,260	12,912	75,971	13,921	53,997	8,053
Estimated total	100.0%	17,789	336	1,243	2,374	13,836	84,113	15,452	59,871	8,790
Cities outside metropolitan areas	527,001									
Area actually reporting	87.4%	2,834	73	188	204	2,369	13,407	2,276	10,061	1,070
Estimated total	100.0%	3,174	81	210	242	2,641	15,217	2,673	11,313	1,231
Nonmetropolitan counties	644,487									
Area actually reporting	71.5%	798	18	89	29	662	3,863	953	2,358	552
Estimated total	100.0%	1,359	54	155	50	1,100	5,831	1,535	3,391	905
State total	4,921,532	22,322	471	1,608	2,666	17,577	105,161	19,660	74,575	10,926
Rate per 100,000 inhabitants		453.6	9.6	32.7	54.2	357.1	2,136.8	399.5	1,515.3	222.0
Alaska										
Metropolitan statistical area	338,179									
Area actually reporting	100.0%	3,853	21	596	608	2,628	11,760	1,668	8,678	1,414
Cities outside metropolitan areas	127,563									
Area actually reporting	90.6%	900	8	266	55	571	2,147	315	1,685	147
Estimated total	100.0%	946	9	269	64	604	2,391	355	1,860	176
Nonmetropolitan counties	265,416									
Area actually reporting	100.0%	1,327	19	267	40	1,001	2,377	752	1,246	379
State total	731,158	6,126	49	1,132	712	4,233	16,528	2,775	11,784	1,969
Rate per 100,000 inhabitants		837.8	6.7	154.8	97.4	578.9	2,260.5	379.5	1,611.7	269.3
Arizona										
Metropolitan statistical area	7,066,114									
Area actually reporting	93.0%	30,068	431	2,971	6,094	20,572	152,680	21,627	114,824	16,229
Estimated total	100.0%	31,245	457	3,083	6,134	21,571	158,648	22,997	118,727	16,924
Cities outside metropolitan areas	126,679									
Area actually reporting	85.2%	4,000	37	158	57	3,748	4,253	1,012	2,625	616
Estimated total	100.0%	4,207	39	168	67	3,933	4,929	1,092	3,170	667
Nonmetropolitan counties	228,608									
Area actually reporting	73.0%	314	10	9	8	287	1,204	321	655	228
Estimated total	100.0%	528	17	12	10	489	1,746	399	1,001	346
State total	7,421,401	35,980	513	3,263	6,211	25,993	165,323	24,488	122,898	17,937
Rate per 100,000 inhabitants		484.8	6.9	44.0	83.7	350.2	2,227.7	330.0	1,656.0	241.7
Arkansas										
Metropolitan statistical area	1,927,318									
Area actually reporting	95.0%	13,909	184	1,353	1,153	11,219	53,598	10,190	37,829	5,579
Estimated total	100.0%	14,275	189	1,390	1,216	11,480	55,526	10,497	39,220	5,809
Cities outside metropolitan areas	494,464									
Area actually reporting	97.9%	3,637	91	449	228	2,869	15,072	3,329	10,673	1,070
Estimated total	100.0%	3,674	91	451	237	2,895	15,277	3,362	10,820	1,095
Nonmetropolitan counties	608,740									
Area actually reporting	79.8%	1,957	33	338	48	1,538	5,998	1,608	3,648	742
Estimated total	100.0%	2,414	41	385	124	1,864	8,397	1,995	5,373	1,029
State total	3,030,522	20,363	321	2,226	1,577	16,239	79,200	15,854	55,413	7,933
Rate per 100,000 inhabitants		671.9	10.6	73.5	52.0	535.8	2,613.4	523.1	1,828.5	261.8
California										
Metropolitan statistical area	38,539,958									
Area actually reporting	99.9%	170,104	2,158	12,997	44,286	110,663	827,403	141,667	519,418	166,318
Estimated total	100.0%	170,131	2,158	13,000	44,291	110,682	827,545	141,689	519,521	166,335
Cities outside metropolitan areas	268,242									
Area actually reporting	100.0%	1,583	9	149	281	1,144	6,887	1,501	4,407	979
Nonmetropolitan counties	559,878									
Area actually reporting	100.0%	2,312	36	300	156	1,820	7,622	2,339	4,274	1,009
State total	39,368,078	174,026	2,203	13,449	44,728	113,646	842,054	145,529	528,202	168,323
Rate per 100,000 inhabitants		442.0	5.6	34.2	113.6	288.7	2,138.9	369.7	1,341.7	427.6
Colorado										
Metropolitan statistical area	5,093,407									
Area actually reporting	99.5%	22,960	277	3,289	3,862	15,532	151,647	21,038	101,466	29,143
Estimated total	100.0%	23,015	277	3,297	3,872	15,569	152,467	21,104	102,105	29,258
Cities outside metropolitan areas	345,449									
Area actually reporting	96.4%	963	10	223	74	656	8,425	1,151	6,610	664
Estimated total	100.0%	989	10	228	75	676	8,696	1,184	6,819	693
Nonmetropolitan counties	368,863									
Area actually reporting	91.5%	523	7	118	16	382	3,103	872	1,775	456
Estimated total	100.0%	566	7	127	17	415	3,419	958	1,960	501

(Number, percent, rate per 100,000 population.)

Area	Population[1]	Violent crime[2]	Murder and nonnegligent manslaughter	Rape (revised definition)[3]	Robbery	Aggravated assault	Property crime	Burglary	Larceny-theft	Motor vehicle theft
State total................................	5,807,719	24,570	294	3,652	3,964	16,660	164,582	23,246	110,884	30,452
Rate per 100,000 inhabitants		423.1	5.1	62.9	68.3	286.9	2,833.8	400.3	1,909.3	524.3
Connecticut										
Metropolitan statistical area..........................	2,958,732									
Area actually reporting	100.0%	6,159	130	530	1,982	3,517	52,571	6,158	38,631	7,782
Cities outside metropolitan areas........................	111,501									
Area actually reporting	100.0%	87	1	13	24	49	1,225	124	952	149
Nonmetropolitan counties	486,773									
Area actually reporting	100.0%	213	9	51	27	126	1,874	374	1,009	491
State total................................	3,557,006	6,459	140	594	2,033	3,692	55,670	6,656	40,592	8,422
Rate per 100,000 inhabitants		181.6	3.9	16.7	57.2	103.8	1,565.1	187.1	1,141.2	236.8
Delaware										
Metropolitan statistical area..........................	986,809									
Area actually reporting	100.0%	4,262	73	261	700	3,228	19,355	2,508	15,182	1,665
Cities outside metropolitan areas........................	None									
Nonmetropolitan counties	None									
State total................................	986,809	4,262	73	261	700	3,228	19,355	2,508	15,182	1,665
Rate per 100,000 inhabitants		431.9	7.4	26.4	70.9	327.1	1,961.4	254.2	1,538.5	168.7
District of Columbia[5]										
Metropolitan statistical area..........................	712,816									
Area actually reporting	100.0%	7,127	201	311	2,373	4,242	24,899	1,964	19,536	3,399
Cities outside metropolitan areas........................	None									
Nonmetropolitan counties	None									
District total................................	712,816	7,127	201	311	2,373	4,242	24,899	1,964	19,536	3,399
Rate per 100,000 inhabitants		999.8	28.2	43.6	332.9	595.1	3,493.0	275.5	2,740.7	476.8
Florida										
Metropolitan statistical area..........................	21,043,573									
Area actually reporting	99.8%	80,320	1,238	7,441	13,205	58,436	371,991	49,202	285,586	37,203
Estimated total	100.0%	80,538	1,240	7,456	13,241	58,601	373,436	49,404	286,718	37,314
Cities outside metropolitan areas........................	140,051									
Area actually reporting	92.0%	843	18	50	102	673	3,756	839	2,607	310
Estimated total	100.0%	885	18	54	111	702	3,983	876	2,769	338
Nonmetropolitan counties	549,688									
Area actually reporting	93.5%	1,810	30	163	145	1,472	6,423	1,900	3,989	534
Estimated total	100.0%	1,945	32	176	169	1,568	7,137	2,013	4,505	619
State total................................	21,733,312	83,368	1,290	7,686	13,521	60,871	384,556	52,293	293,992	38,271
Rate per 100,000 inhabitants		383.6	5.9	35.4	62.2	280.1	1,769.4	240.6	1,352.7	176.1
Georgia[6]										
Metropolitan statistical area..........................	8,903,595									
Area actually reporting	70.7%	27,159	615	2,092	4,533	19,919	129,465	16,813	95,500	17,152
Estimated total	100.0%	37,571	855	2,843	6,496	27,377	182,131	24,901	134,357	22,873
Cities outside metropolitan areas........................	641,416									
Area actually reporting	61.6%	1,842	38	180	234	1,390	12,023	1,767	9,555	701
Estimated total	100.0%	2,700	47	274	353	2,026	18,207	2,740	14,355	1,112
Nonmetropolitan counties	1,165,006									
Area actually reporting	75.9%	1,905	28	244	105	1,528	10,588	2,403	7,078	1,107
Estimated total	100.0%	2,579	41	303	167	2,068	14,650	3,498	9,631	1,521
State total................................	10,710,017	42,850	943	3,420	7,016	31,471	214,988	31,139	158,343	25,506
Rate per 100,000 inhabitants		400.1	8.8	31.9	65.5	293.8	2,007.4	290.7	1,478.5	238.2
Hawaii										
Metropolitan statistical area..........................	1,133,616									
Area actually reporting	14.7%	379	5	71	59	244	3,537	496	2,612	429
Estimated total	100.0%	2,769	27	401	798	1,543	28,815	3,791	20,438	4,586
Cities outside metropolitan areas........................	None									
Nonmetropolitan counties	273,390									
Area actually reporting	100.0%	807	14	168	69	556	5,113	839	3,516	758
State total................................	1,407,006	3,576	41	569	867	2,099	33,928	4,630	23,954	5,344
Rate per 100,000 inhabitants		254.2	2.9	40.4	61.6	149.2	2,411.4	329.1	1,702.5	379.8
Idaho										
Metropolitan statistical area..........................	1,361,287									
Estimated total	99.9%	3,582	26	693	159	2,704	16,647	2,974	12,205	1,468
Area actually reporting	100.0%	3,583	26	693	159	2,705	16,653	2,975	12,210	1,468
Cities outside metropolitan areas........................	186,575									
Area actually reporting	96.3%	366	3	49	10	304	2,052	362	1,543	147
Estimated total	100.0%	380	3	51	10	316	2,135	380	1,603	152

Table 3. Crime in the United States, by State and Area, 2020—*Continued*

(Number, percent, rate per 100,000 population.)

Area	Population[1]	Violent crime[2]	Murder and nonnegligent manslaughter	Rape (revised definition)[3]	Robbery	Aggravated assault	Property crime	Burglary	Larceny-theft	Motor vehicle theft
Nonmetropolitan counties	279,051									
Area actually reporting	100.0%	469	12	88	5	364	1,525	376	1,002	147
State total..	1,826,913	4,432	41	832	174	3,385	20,313	3,731	14,815	1,767
Rate per 100,000 inhabitants		242.6	2.2	45.5	9.5	185.3	1,111.9	204.2	810.9	96.7
Illinois[7]										
Metropolitan statistical area......................	11,178,842									
Area actually reporting	94.3%	48,707	1,086	4,258	11,829	31,534	170,797	25,705	125,469	19,623
Estimated total	100.0%	49,959	1,105	4,438	12,019	32,397	178,768	27,076	131,388	20,304
Cities outside metropolitan areas.............	800,198									
Area actually reporting	81.3%	2,047	13	380	157	1,497	11,607	2,131	8,870	606
Estimated total	100.0%	2,324	13	402	168	1,741	13,375	2,564	10,139	672
Nonmetropolitan counties	608,490									
Area actually reporting	88.9%	1,268	33	239	74	922	3,639	1,208	2,115	316
Estimated total	100.0%	1,329	33	250	74	972	4,144	1,380	2,408	356
State total..	12,587,530	53,612	1,151	5,090	12,261	35,110	196,287	31,020	143,935	21,332
Rate per 100,000 inhabitants		425.9	9.1	40.4	97.4	278.9	1,559.4	246.4	1,143.5	169.5
Indiana										
Metropolitan statistical area......................	5,294,758									
Area actually reporting	88.2%	20,174	458	1,692	3,998	14,026	95,762	14,562	68,534	12,666
Estimated total	100.0%	21,151	464	1,812	4,104	14,771	102,523	16,051	73,029	13,443
Cities outside metropolitan areas.............	560,706									
Area actually reporting	55.8%	726	8	88	33	597	5,881	705	4,756	420
Estimated total	100.0%	1,345	11	176	60	1,098	11,226	1,398	9,016	812
Nonmetropolitan counties	899,489									
Area actually reporting	52.0%	1,133	27	211	35	860	3,491	723	2,154	614
Estimated total	100.0%	1,665	30	360	51	1,224	6,704	1,489	4,035	1,180
State total..	6,754,953	24,161	505	2,348	4,215	17,093	120,453	18,938	86,080	15,435
Rate per 100,000 inhabitants		357.7	7.5	34.8	62.4	253.0	1,783.2	280.4	1,274.3	228.5
Iowa										
Metropolitan statistical area......................	1,947,544									
Area actually reporting	97.4%	6,581	90	774	813	4,904	39,132	8,154	26,184	4,794
Estimated total	100.0%	6,721	90	801	825	5,005	39,935	8,334	26,736	4,865
Cities outside metropolitan areas.............	568,224									
Area actually reporting	96.3%	1,922	14	308	100	1,500	10,086	2,145	7,080	861
Estimated total	100.0%	1,992	14	317	102	1,559	10,450	2,222	7,337	891
Nonmetropolitan counties	647,793									
Area actually reporting	98.0%	859	7	169	8	675	3,151	1,118	1,591	442
Estimated total	100.0%	888	7	171	16	694	3,340	1,183	1,678	479
State total..	3,163,561	9,601	111	1,289	943	7,258	53,725	11,739	35,751	6,235
Rate per 100,000 inhabitants		303.5	3.5	40.7	29.8	229.4	1,698.2	371.1	1,130.1	197.1
Kansas										
Metropolitan statistical area......................	2,032,826									
Area actually reporting	79.5%	8,485	76	773	697	6,939	40,181	5,580	29,847	4,754
Estimated total	100.0%	9,430	83	881	774	7,692	47,379	6,354	35,268	5,757
Cities outside metropolitan areas.............	561,423									
Area actually reporting	92.4%	2,017	8	291	125	1,593	12,770	2,028	9,782	960
Estimated total	100.0%	2,205	9	310	131	1,755	13,453	2,226	10,180	1,047
Nonmetropolitan counties	319,556									
Area actually reporting	96.1%	722	8	68	23	623	3,089	1,003	1,679	407
Estimated total	100.0%	750	8	72	23	647	3,245	1,075	1,745	425
State total..	2,913,805	12,385	100	1,263	928	10,094	64,077	9,655	47,193	7,229
Rate per 100,000 inhabitants		425.0	3.4	43.3	31.8	346.4	2,199.1	331.4	1,619.6	248.1
Kentucky										
Metropolitan statistical area......................	2,672,178									
Area actually reporting	99.9%	9,441	241	809	2,117	6,274	60,950	10,833	41,376	8,741
Estimated total	100.0%	9,446	241	809	2,119	6,277	61,003	10,841	41,415	8,747
Cities outside metropolitan areas.............	528,590									
Area actually reporting	99.5%	846	15	180	157	494	10,407	1,957	7,336	1,114
Estimated total	100.0%	849	15	180	157	497	10,475	1,970	7,384	1,121
Nonmetropolitan counties	1,276,483									
Area actually reporting	100.0%	1,305	67	382	93	763	8,195	2,596	3,970	1,629
State total..	4,477,251	11,600	323	1,371	2,369	7,537	79,673	15,407	52,769	11,497
Rate per 100,000 inhabitants		259.1	7.2	30.6	52.9	168.3	1,779.5	344.1	1,178.6	256.8

Table 3. Crime in the United States, by State and Area, 2020—*Continued*

(Number, percent, rate per 100,000 population.)

Area	Population[1]	Violent crime[2]	Murder and nonnegligent manslaughter	Rape (revised definition)[3]	Robbery	Aggravated assault	Property crime	Burglary	Larceny-theft	Motor vehicle theft
Louisiana										
Metropolitan statistical area	3,917,340									
Area actually reporting	94.3%	24,966	626	1,774	3,312	19,254	114,133	19,428	84,040	10,665
Estimated total	100.0%	25,881	638	1,857	3,459	19,927	119,029	20,211	87,609	11,209
Cities outside metropolitan areas	264,144									
Area actually reporting	76.6%	1,757	51	68	164	1,474	7,688	1,793	5,494	401
Estimated total	100.0%	1,985	51	92	202	1,640	8,934	1,991	6,394	549
Nonmetropolitan counties	463,834									
Area actually reporting	91.1%	1,677	42	172	56	1,407	5,184	1,361	3,292	531
Estimated total	100.0%	1,838	45	187	86	1,520	6,026	1,496	3,888	642
State total	4,645,318	29,704	734	2,136	3,747	23,087	133,989	23,698	97,891	12,400
Rate per 100,000 inhabitants		639.4	15.8	46.0	80.7	497.0	2,884.4	510.1	2,107.3	266.9
Maine										
Metropolitan statistical area	803,976									
Area actually reporting	100.0%	797	11	236	119	431	9,312	1,011	7,795	506
Cities outside metropolitan areas	254,490									
Area actually reporting	100.0%	353	4	111	42	196	3,917	501	3,242	174
Nonmetropolitan counties	291,675									
Area actually reporting	100.0%	316	7	139	9	161	2,381	497	1,702	182
State total	1,350,141	1,466	22	486	170	788	15,610	2,009	12,739	862
Rate per 100,000 inhabitants		108.6	1.6	36.0	12.6	58.4	1,156.2	148.8	943.5	63.8
Maryland[4]										
Metropolitan statistical area	5,905,671									
Area actually reporting	100.0%	23,755	548	1,700	7,114	14,393	95,548	14,906	70,271	10,371
Cities outside metropolitan areas	51,424									
Area actually reporting	100.0%	349	4	18	53	274	1,323	203	1,051	69
Nonmetropolitan counties	98,707									
Area actually reporting	100.0%	111	1	14	7	89	616	152	435	29
State total	6,055,802	24,215	553	1,732	7,174	14,756	97,487	15,261	71,757	10,469
Rate per 100,000 inhabitants		399.9	9.1	28.6	118.5	243.7	1,609.8	252.0	1,184.9	172.9
Massachusetts										
Metropolitan statistical area	6,864,763									
Area actually reporting	99.2%	21,064	160	1,818	2,995	16,091	71,962	10,234	54,919	6,809
Estimated total	100.0%	21,186	160	1,837	3,012	16,177	72,225	10,289	55,107	6,829
Cities outside metropolitan areas	28,811									
Area actually reporting	100.0%	102	0	14	3	85	377	34	337	6
Nonmetropolitan counties										
Area actually reporting	100.0%	0	0	0	0	0	0	0	0	0
State total	6,893,574	21,288	160	1,851	3,015	16,262	72,602	10,323	55,444	6,835
Rate per 100,000 inhabitants		308.8	2.3	26.9	43.7	235.9	1,053.2	149.7	804.3	99.2
Michigan										
Metropolitan statistical area	8,171,665									
Area actually reporting	97.7%	42,329	712	4,587	4,283	32,747	116,391	19,432	80,101	16,858
Estimated total	100.0%	42,773	715	4,669	4,315	33,074	118,153	19,707	81,403	17,043
Cities outside metropolitan areas	574,930									
Area actually reporting	99.9%	1,702	14	437	83	1,168	7,910	894	6,533	483
Estimated total	100.0%	1,703	14	437	83	1,169	7,921	895	6,542	484
Nonmetropolitan counties	1,219,960									
Area actually reporting	99.0%	3,146	25	955	40	2,126	9,493	2,616	6,023	854
Estimated total	100.0%	3,165	25	959	40	2,141	9,559	2,629	6,072	858
State total	9,966,555	47,641	754	6,065	4,438	36,384	135,633	23,231	94,017	18,385
Rate per 100,000 inhabitants		478.0	7.6	60.9	44.5	365.1	1,360.9	233.1	943.3	184.5
Minnesota										
Metropolitan statistical area	4,414,276									
Area actually reporting	99.9%	13,564	170	1,792	3,773	7,829	103,367	14,521	76,020	12,826
Estimated total	100.0%	13,568	170	1,793	3,773	7,832	103,424	14,527	76,068	12,829
Cities outside metropolitan areas	575,358									
Area actually reporting	99.2%	1,385	11	270	83	1,021	11,045	1,389	8,933	723
Estimated total	100.0%	1,392	11	270	83	1,028	11,145	1,403	9,013	729
Nonmetropolitan counties	667,708									
Area actually reporting	100.0%	738	9	148	21	560	5,643	1,440	3,615	588
State total	5,657,342	15,698	190	2,211	3,877	9,420	120,212	17,370	88,696	14,146
Rate per 100,000 inhabitants		277.5	3.4	39.1	68.5	166.5	2,124.9	307.0	1,567.8	250.0

(Number, percent, rate per 100,000 population.)

Area	Population[1]	Violent crime[2]	Murder and nonnegligent manslaughter	Rape (revised definition)[3]	Robbery	Aggravated assault	Property crime	Burglary	Larceny-theft	Motor vehicle theft
Mississippi										
Metropolitan statistical area	1,441,468									
Area actually reporting	77.5%	3,692	177	410	885	2,220	28,621	5,026	20,558	3,037
Estimated total	100.0%	4,412	186	628	938	2,660	33,213	5,817	23,818	3,578
Cities outside metropolitan areas	555,942									
Area actually reporting	49.0%	1,305	49	119	174	963	9,620	2,583	6,416	621
Estimated total	100.0%	2,370	73	213	310	1,774	18,048	5,038	11,866	1,144
Nonmetropolitan counties	969,376									
Area actually reporting	46.9%	925	32	132	94	667	5,085	1,838	2,691	556
Estimated total	100.0%	1,856	56	307	171	1,322	11,090	3,633	6,096	1,361
State total	2,966,786	8,638	315	1,148	1,419	5,756	62,351	14,488	41,780	6,083
Rate per 100,000 inhabitants		291.2	10.6	38.7	47.8	194.0	2,101.6	488.3	1,408.3	205.0
Missouri										
Metropolitan statistical area	4,621,557									
Area actually reporting	99.3%	28,401	656	2,102	4,317	21,326	125,871	17,644	87,324	20,903
Estimated total	100.0%	28,614	656	2,112	4,346	21,500	126,817	17,778	87,968	21,071
Cities outside metropolitan areas	635,377									
Area actually reporting	95.9%	2,573	35	315	146	2,077	18,815	2,949	14,378	1,488
Estimated total	100.0%	2,654	35	321	147	2,151	19,564	3,070	14,941	1,553
Nonmetropolitan counties	894,614									
Area actually reporting	95.9%	2,027	31	223	80	1,693	8,914	2,347	5,061	1,506
Estimated total	100.0%	2,117	32	228	82	1,775	9,317	2,452	5,300	1,565
State total	6,151,548	33,385	723	2,661	4,575	25,426	155,698	23,300	108,209	24,189
Rate per 100,000 inhabitants		542.7	11.8	43.3	74.4	413.3	2,531.0	378.8	1,759.1	393.2
Montana										
Metropolitan statistical area	386,281									
Area actually reporting	100.0%	2,000	21	235	194	1,550	12,719	1,597	9,723	1,399
Cities outside metropolitan areas	235,155									
Area actually reporting	98.7%	1,729	13	191	47	1,478	5,019	540	3,971	508
Estimated total	100.0%	1,747	13	194	47	1,493	5,089	547	4,027	515
Nonmetropolitan counties	459,141									
Area actually reporting	99.4%	1,323	20	169	38	1,096	5,081	770	3,552	759
Estimated total	100.0%	1,330	20	169	38	1,103	5,109	775	3,572	762
State total	1,080,577	5,077	54	598	279	4,146	22,917	2,919	17,322	2,676
Rate per 100,000 inhabitants		469.8	5.0	55.3	25.8	383.7	2,120.8	270.1	1,603.0	247.6
Nebraska										
Metropolitan statistical area	1,272,351									
Area actually reporting	99.0%	5,058	51	840	689	3,478	28,674	3,136	21,292	4,246
Estimated total	100.0%	5,102	51	846	695	3,510	28,866	3,165	21,422	4,279
Cities outside metropolitan areas	341,322									
Area actually reporting	93.1%	812	10	224	55	523	5,428	774	4,203	451
Estimated total	100.0%	910	10	237	71	592	5,869	855	4,542	472
Nonmetropolitan counties	323,879									
Area actually reporting	86.1%	295	8	63	5	219	1,347	293	868	186
Estimated total	100.0%	461	8	80	33	340	2,256	435	1,524	297
State total	1,937,552	6,473	69	1,163	799	4,442	36,991	4,455	27,488	5,048
Rate per 100,000 inhabitants		334.1	3.6	60.0	41.2	229.3	1,909.2	229.9	1,418.7	260.5
Nevada										
Metropolitan statistical area	2,853,689									
Area actually reporting	100.0%	13,540	155	1,741	2,709	8,935	56,841	10,635	36,142	10,064
Cities outside metropolitan areas	48,735									
Area actually reporting	100.0%	217	11	30	29	147	1,155	273	748	134
Nonmetropolitan counties	235,835									
Area actually reporting	100.0%	688	14	80	47	547	2,466	666	1,442	358
State total	3,138,259	14,445	180	1,851	2,785	9,629	60,462	11,574	38,332	10,556
Rate per 100,000 inhabitants		460.3	5.7	59.0	88.7	306.8	1,926.6	368.8	1,221.4	336.4
New Hampshire										
Metropolitan statistical area	862,794									
Area actually reporting	99.2%	1,274	9	306	203	756	8,897	774	7,500	623
Estimated total	100.0%	1,301	9	310	207	775	9,038	797	7,602	639
Cities outside metropolitan areas	467,654									
Area actually reporting	95.6%	568	1	206	57	304	5,264	497	4,444	323
Estimated total	100.0%	646	1	214	71	360	5,682	563	4,745	374
Nonmetropolitan counties	35,827									
Area actually reporting	92.2%	42	2	17	0	23	238	43	171	24
Estimated total	100.0%	53	2	18	2	31	294	52	211	31

(Number, percent, rate per 100,000 population.)

Area	Population[1]	Violent crime[2]	Murder and nonnegligent manslaughter	Rape (revised definition)[3]	Robbery	Aggravated assault	Property crime	Burglary	Larceny-theft	Motor vehicle theft
State total................	1,366,275	2,000	12	542	280	1,166	15,014	1,412	12,558	1,044
Rate per 100,000 inhabitants		146.4	0.9	39.7	20.5	85.3	1,098.9	103.3	919.1	76.4
New Jersey										
Metropolitan statistical area................	8,882,371									
Area actually reporting................	100.0%	17,353	329	1,277	4,384	11,363	102,875	12,983	79,614	10,278
Cities outside metropolitan areas................	None									
Nonmetropolitan counties	None									
State total................	8,882,371	17,353	329	1,277	4,384	11,363	102,875	12,983	79,614	10,278
Rate per 100,000 inhabitants		195.4	3.7	14.4	49.4	127.9	1,158.2	146.2	896.3	115.7
New Mexico										
Metropolitan statistical area................	1,418,447									
Area actually reporting................	100.0%	11,598	109	809	1,768	8,912	44,460	9,501	27,801	7,158
Cities outside metropolitan areas................	395,987									
Area actually reporting................	94.0%	2,753	29	216	262	2,246	11,207	2,802	7,250	1,155
Estimated total................	100.0%	2,896	32	229	270	2,365	11,968	2,939	7,758	1,271
Nonmetropolitan counties	291,885									
Area actually reporting................	96.0%	1,881	23	131	46	1,681	3,307	1,148	1,592	567
Estimated total................	100.0%	1,899	23	132	48	1,696	3,431	1,225	1,629	577
State total................	2,106,319	16,393	164	1,170	2,086	12,973	59,859	13,665	37,188	9,006
Rate per 100,000 inhabitants		778.3	7.8	55.5	99.0	615.9	2,841.9	648.8	1,765.5	427.6
New York										
Metropolitan statistical area................	17,993,042									
Area actually reporting	99.3%	67,582	783	4,604	17,267	44,928	255,315	29,045	207,497	18,773
Estimated total................	100.0%	67,805	783	4,632	17,310	45,080	257,063	29,270	208,938	18,855
Cities outside metropolitan areas................	492,133									
Area actually reporting	95.3%	1,060	7	208	117	728	7,862	1,192	6,402	268
Estimated total................	100.0%	1,098	7	218	119	754	8,404	1,263	6,858	283
Nonmetropolitan counties	851,601									
Area actually reporting	92.9%	1,361	14	595	56	696	7,158	1,466	5,318	374
Estimated total................	100.0%	1,436	18	618	96	704	7,321	1,470	5,333	518
State total................	19,336,776	70,339	808	5,468	17,525	46,538	272,788	32,003	221,129	19,656
Rate per 100,000 inhabitants		363.8	4.2	28.3	90.6	240.7	1,410.7	165.5	1,143.6	101.7
North Carolina										
Metropolitan statistical area................	8,612,057									
Area actually reporting	88.8%	32,769	561	1,966	5,855	24,387	170,639	31,200	124,252	15,187
Estimated total................	100.0%	36,136	615	2,248	6,444	26,829	191,181	35,707	138,329	17,145
Cities outside metropolitan areas................	588,746									
Area actually reporting	78.1%	3,290	81	207	431	2,571	18,779	4,953	12,715	1,111
Estimated total................	100.0%	4,113	97	245	564	3,207	23,894	6,564	15,955	1,375
Nonmetropolitan counties	1,400,020									
Area actually reporting	84.9%	3,378	113	359	267	2,639	17,352	6,346	9,329	1,677
Estimated total................	100.0%	4,202	140	429	332	3,301	20,951	7,681	11,270	2,000
State total................	10,600,823	44,451	852	2,922	7,340	33,337	236,026	49,952	165,554	20,520
Rate per 100,000 inhabitants		419.3	8.0	27.6	69.2	314.5	2,226.5	471.2	1,561.7	193.6
North Dakota										
Metropolitan statistical area................	382,437									
Area actually reporting................	100.0%	1,273	18	237	110	908	10,531	2,121	7,318	1,092
Cities outside metropolitan areas................	193,373									
Area actually reporting................	100.0%	1,045	12	113	32	888	4,261	734	2,818	709
Nonmetropolitan counties	189,499									
Area actually reporting................	100.0%	200	2	46	9	143	1,464	341	850	273
State total................	765,309	2,518	32	396	151	1,939	16,256	3,196	10,986	2,074
Rate per 100,000 inhabitants		329.0	4.2	51.7	19.7	253.4	2,124.1	417.6	1,435.5	271.0
Ohio[8]										
Metropolitan statistical area................	9,394,238									
Area actually reporting................	90.3%	31,161	764	3,932	7,216	19,249	167,695	29,577	121,075	17,043
Estimated total................	100.0%	32,797	774	4,237	7,522	20,264	183,497	31,741	133,675	18,081
Cities outside metropolitan areas................	1,012,995									
Area actually reporting................	76.4%	1,350	12	338	166	834	14,656	1,943	12,103	610
Estimated total................	100.0%	1,739	13	414	225	1,087	20,824	2,627	17,319	878
Nonmetropolitan counties	1,285,984									
Area actually reporting................	85.0%	1,349	27	342	64	916	10,102	2,441	6,742	919
Estimated total................	100.0%	1,568	33	401	79	1,055	12,042	2,911	8,013	1,118
State total................	11,693,217	36,104	820	5,052	7,826	22,406	216,363	37,279	159,007	20,077
Rate per 100,000 inhabitants		308.8	7.0	43.2	66.9	191.6	1,850.3	318.8	1,359.8	171.7

Area	Population[1]	Violent crime[2]	Murder and nonnegligent manslaughter	Rape (revised definition)[3]	Robbery	Aggravated assault	Property crime	Burglary	Larceny-theft	Motor vehicle theft
Oklahoma										
Metropolitan statistical area	2,660,978									
Area actually reporting	100.0%	13,795	225	1,554	2,028	9,988	77,442	16,896	49,075	11,471
Cities outside metropolitan areas	731,657									
Area actually reporting	99.9%	3,247	38	382	289	2,538	22,973	5,121	15,474	2,378
Estimated total	100.0%	3,250	38	382	289	2,541	22,999	5,128	15,490	2,381
Nonmetropolitan counties	588,148									
Area actually reporting	98.0%	1,185	33	162	33	957	7,110	2,338	3,603	1,169
Estimated total	100.0%	1,210	33	166	34	977	7,264	2,391	3,678	1,195
State total	3,980,783	18,255	296	2,102	2,351	13,506	107,705	24,415	68,243	15,047
Rate per 100,000 inhabitants		458.6	7.4	52.8	59.1	339.3	2,705.6	613.3	1,714.3	378.0
Oregon[8]										
Metropolitan statistical area	3,560,965									
Area actually reporting	96.3%	10,123	96	1,227	1,975	6,825	94,922	11,466	68,855	14,601
Estimated total	100.0%	10,389	96	1,287	2,018	6,988	97,297	11,799	70,580	14,918
Cities outside metropolitan areas	315,863									
Area actually reporting	97.4%	1,020	12	174	134	700	10,030	1,399	7,802	829
Estimated total	100.0%	1,040	12	178	137	713	10,233	1,438	7,957	838
Nonmetropolitan counties	364,679									
Area actually reporting	90.3%	884	15	90	22	757	4,748	1,040	2,945	763
Estimated total	100.0%	951	17	100	25	809	5,252	1,149	3,274	829
State total	4,241,507	12,380	125	1,565	2,180	8,510	112,782	14,386	81,811	16,585
Rate per 100,000 inhabitants		291.9	2.9	36.9	51.4	200.6	2,659.0	339.2	1,928.8	391.0
Pennsylvania[4]										
Metropolitan statistical area	11,346,468									
Area actually reporting	56.3%	26,424	672	1,887	6,619	17,246	93,715	12,118	72,972	8,625
Estimated total	100.0%	45,360	943	3,753	9,972	30,692	187,212	27,994	144,943	14,275
Cities outside metropolitan areas	638,381									
Area actually reporting	63.9%	522	12	91	68	351	3,649	503	3,025	121
Estimated total	100.0%	1,397	16	174	226	981	8,237	1,239	6,364	634
Nonmetropolitan counties	798,405									
Area actually reporting	0.1%	4	0	1	0	3	10	0	10	0
Estimated total	100.0%	3,036	50	301	530	2,155	14,718	2,541	11,612	565
State total	12,783,254	49,793	1,009	4,228	10,728	33,828	210,167	31,774	162,919	15,474
Rate per 100,000 inhabitants		389.5	7.9	33.1	83.9	264.6	1,644.1	248.6	1,274.5	121.0
Puerto Rico										
Metropolitan statistical area	3,159,343									
Area actually reporting	100.0%	4,939	508	142	1,153	3,136	12,937	2,831	8,151	1,955
Cities outside metropolitan areas										
Area actually reporting	100.0%	257	21	6	24	206	304	121	160	23
Total	3,159,343	5,196	529	148	1,177	3,342	13,241	2,952	8,311	1,978
Rate per 100,000 inhabitants		164.5	16.7	4.7	37.3	105.8	419.1	93.4	263.1	62.6
Rhode Island										
Metropolitan statistical area	1,057,125									
Area actually reporting	100.0%	2,440	32	407	336	1,665	13,166	1,763	9,894	1,509
Cities outside metropolitan areas	None									
Nonmetropolitan counties	None									
State total	1,057,125	2,440	32	407	336	1,665	13,166	1,763	9,894	1,509
Rate per 100,000 inhabitants		230.8	3.0	38.5	31.8	157.5	1,245.5	166.8	935.9	142.7
South Carolina										
Metropolitan statistical area	4,482,389									
Area actually reporting	98.9%	22,153	412	1,782	2,722	17,237	119,049	18,299	88,013	12,737
Estimated total	100.0%	22,439	423	1,799	2,751	17,466	120,444	18,534	89,047	12,863
Cities outside metropolitan areas	202,374									
Area actually reporting	95.3%	2,073	56	92	189	1,736	9,021	1,804	6,683	534
Estimated total	100.0%	2,146	59	95	196	1,796	9,391	1,873	6,958	560
Nonmetropolitan counties	533,277									
Area actually reporting	95.2%	2,965	65	184	167	2,549	11,580	2,831	7,514	1,235
Estimated total	100.0%	3,106	67	192	175	2,672	12,152	2,970	7,887	1,295
State total	5,218,040	27,691	549	2,086	3,122	21,934	141,987	23,377	103,892	14,718
Rate per 100,000 inhabitants		530.7	10.5	40.0	59.8	420.3	2,721.1	448.0	1,991.0	282.1
South Dakota										
Metropolitan statistical area	432,981									
Area actually reporting	99.4%	2,270	30	336	223	1,681	11,251	1,970	7,647	1,634
Estimated total	100.0%	2,279	30	336	225	1,688	11,301	1,977	7,684	1,640

(Number, percent, rate per 100,000 population.)

Area	Population[1]	Violent crime[2]	Murder and nonnegligent manslaughter	Rape (revised definition)[3]	Robbery	Aggravated assault	Property crime	Burglary	Larceny-theft	Motor vehicle theft
Cities outside metropolitan areas........................	220,585									
Area actually reporting	96.2%	1,807	7	206	21	1,573	4,399	665	3,278	456
Estimated total	100.0%	1,836	7	209	25	1,595	4,567	691	3,401	475
Nonmetropolitan counties	239,151									
Area actually reporting	85.9%	236	2	43	1	190	921	261	541	119
Estimated total	100.0%	361	3	54	24	280	1,600	368	1,032	200
State total..	892,717	4,476	40	599	274	3,563	17,468	3,036	12,117	2,315
Rate per 100,000 inhabitants		501.4	4.5	67.1	30.7	399.1	1,956.7	340.1	1,357.3	259.3
Tennessee										
Metropolitan statistical area...........................	5,395,999									
Area actually reporting	100.0%	40,585	602	2,198	5,346	32,439	145,547	21,208	106,428	17,911
Cities outside metropolitan areas........................	487,422									
Area actually reporting	100.0%	2,780	27	200	159	2,394	14,532	2,231	11,025	1,276
Nonmetropolitan counties	1,003,413									
Area actually reporting	100.0%	2,963	34	280	70	2,579	11,596	3,040	6,645	1,911
State total..	6,886,834	46,328	663	2,678	5,575	37,412	171,675	26,479	124,098	21,098
Rate per 100,000 inhabitants		672.7	9.6	38.9	81.0	543.2	2,492.8	384.5	1,802.0	306.4
Texas										
Metropolitan statistical area...........................	26,246,546									
Area actually reporting	99.8%	122,935	1,809	12,239	26,282	82,605	613,723	96,741	437,257	79,725
Estimated total	100.0%	123,092	1,809	12,258	26,293	82,732	614,731	96,947	437,942	79,842
Cities outside metropolitan areas........................	1,450,340									
Area actually reporting	96.3%	4,930	65	683	430	3,752	28,072	6,515	19,073	2,484
Estimated total	100.0%	5,023	65	685	432	3,841	28,809	6,732	19,494	2,583
Nonmetropolitan counties	1,663,873									
Area actually reporting	98.8%	2,934	57	561	109	2,207	15,400	5,101	8,476	1,823
Estimated total...	100.0%	2,969	57	566	109	2,237	15,620	5,172	8,597	1,851
State total..	29,360,759	131,084	1,931	13,509	26,834	88,810	659,160	108,851	466,033	84,276
Rate per 100,000 inhabitants		446.5	6.6	46.0	91.4	302.5	2,245.0	370.7	1,587.3	287.0
Utah										
Metropolitan statistical area...........................	2,911,284									
Area actually reporting	92.9%	6,761	82	1,423	1,155	4,101	67,990	7,892	51,407	8,691
Estimated total	100.0%	7,667	91	1,575	1,337	4,664	75,331	8,749	56,842	9,740
Cities outside metropolitan areas........................	156,076									
Area actually reporting	80.7%	311	5	110	13	183	2,097	233	1,654	210
Estimated total	100.0%	390	5	138	16	231	2,592	280	2,041	271
Nonmetropolitan counties	182,519									
Area actually reporting	91.0%	376	6	84	9	277	1,953	362	1,339	252
Estimated total	100.0%	414	6	96	9	303	2,168	415	1,476	277
State total..	3,249,879	8,471	102	1,809	1,362	5,198	80,091	9,444	60,359	10,288
Rate per 100,000 inhabitants		260.7	3.1	55.7	41.9	159.9	2,464.4	290.6	1,857.3	316.6
Vermont										
Metropolitan statistical area...........................	221,248									
Area actually reporting	100.0%	439	5	115	32	287	3,561	362	3,116	83
Cities outside metropolitan areas........................	190,219									
Area actually reporting	100.0%	384	3	64	24	293	2,846	341	2,409	96
Nonmetropolitan counties	211,880									
Area actually reporting	100.0%	258	6	34	8	210	1,179	258	836	85
State total..	623,347	1,081	14	213	64	790	7,586	961	6,361	264
Rate per 100,000 inhabitants		173.4	2.2	34.2	10.3	126.7	1,217.0	154.2	1,020.5	42.4
Virginia										
Metropolitan statistical area...........................	7,542,652									
Area actually reporting	99.9%	15,961	438	1,905	2,814	10,804	112,733	9,615	93,273	9,845
Estimated total	100.0%	15,963	438	1,906	2,814	10,805	112,764	9,621	93,297	9,846
Cities outside metropolitan areas........................	242,932									
Area actually reporting	99.6%	538	22	94	45	377	5,265	581	4,384	300
Estimated total	100.0%	540	22	94	45	379	5,282	584	4,397	301
Nonmetropolitan counties	804,979									
Area actually reporting	100.0%	1,422	64	279	88	991	7,068	1,260	5,102	706
State total..	8,590,563	17,925	524	2,279	2,947	12,175	125,114	11,465	102,796	10,853
Rate per 100,000 inhabitants		208.7	6.1	26.5	34.3	141.7	1,456.4	133.5	1,196.6	126.3
Washington...	6,908,760									
Metropolitan statistical area...........................	99.8%	21,080	269	2,395	5,037	13,379	195,996	36,804	133,204	25,988
Area actually reporting	100.0%	21,102	269	2,398	5,041	13,394	196,238	36,852	133,377	26,009
Estimated total	316,271									

Table 3. Crime in the United States, by State and Area, 2020—*Continued*

(Number, percent, rate per 100,000 population.)

Area	Population[1]	Violent crime[2]	Murder and nonnegligent manslaughter	Rape (revised definition)[3]	Robbery	Aggravated assault	Property crime	Burglary	Larceny-theft	Motor vehicle theft
Cities outside metropolitan areas...............	93.5%	859	11	160	103	585	8,375	1,539	6,061	775
Area actually reporting	100.0%	902	11	169	105	617	8,951	1,699	6,415	837
Estimated total	468,581									
Nonmetropolitan counties	100.0%	592	21	110	37	424	5,034	1,616	2,865	553
Area actually reporting	7,693,612	22,596	301	2,677	5,183	14,435	210,223	40,167	142,657	27,399
State total		293.7	3.9	34.8	67.4	187.6	2,732.4	522.1	1,854.2	356.1
Rate per 100,000 inhabitants										
West Virginia..................................	1,152,948									
Metropolitan statistical area..................	83.1%	3,276	61	543	261	2,411	16,207	3,282	11,446	1,479
Area actually reporting	100.0%	4,091	68	598	313	3,112	18,269	3,640	13,024	1,605
Estimated total	172,139									
Cities outside metropolitan areas........................	61.5%	414	3	48	13	350	1,798	197	1,505	96
Area actually reporting	100.0%	1,094	3	59	15	1,017	3,596	365	3,018	213
Estimated total	459,700									
Nonmetropolitan counties	90.5%	1,094	40	166	40	848	2,939	820	1,688	431
Area actually reporting	100.0%	1,167	46	175	41	905	3,111	872	1,786	453
Estimated total..........................	1,784,787	6,352	117	832	369	5,034	24,976	4,877	17,828	2,271
State total		355.9	6.6	46.6	20.7	282.1	1,399.4	273.3	998.9	127.2
Rate per 100,000 inhabitants										
Wisconsin..................................	4,359,969									
Metropolitan statistical area..................	99.3%	16,356	270	1,541	2,960	11,585	70,961	10,348	52,276	8,337
Area actually reporting	100.0%	16,454	271	1,551	2,977	11,655	71,533	10,430	52,706	8,397
Estimated total	642,656									
Cities outside metropolitan areas........................	96.3%	1,359	11	297	50	1,001	9,127	743	7,900	484
Area actually reporting	100.0%	1,442	11	304	65	1,062	9,585	813	8,235	537
Estimated total	830,030									
Nonmetropolitan counties	97.2%	874	24	156	23	671	5,062	1,426	3,233	403
Area actually reporting	100.0%	965	26	165	39	735	5,536	1,501	3,576	459
State total..................................	5,832,655	18,861	308	2,020	3,081	13,452	86,654	12,744	64,517	9,393
Rate per 100,000 inhabitants		323.4	5.3	34.6	52.8	230.6	1,485.7	218.5	1,106.1	161.0
Wyoming										
Metropolitan statistical area..................	181,286									
Area actually reporting	100.0%	513	7	114	45	347	4,571	547	3,512	512
Cities outside metropolitan areas........................	237,938									
Area actually reporting	96.4%	591	5	166	12	408	3,562	421	2,819	322
Estimated total	100.0%	621	5	167	18	431	3,736	449	2,944	343
Nonmetropolitan counties	163,104									
Area actually reporting	92.0%	210	5	49	3	153	995	205	688	102
Estimated total	100.0%	230	6	52	3	169	1,072	229	734	109
State total..................................	582,328	1,364	18	333	66	947	9,379	1,225	7,190	964
Rate per 100,000 inhabitants		234.2	3.1	57.2	11.3	162.6	1,610.6	210.4	1,234.7	165.5

NOTE: Although arson data are included in the trend and clearance tables, sufficient data are not available to estimate totals for this offense. Therefore, no arson data are published in this table.

[1] Population figures are U.S. Census Bureau provisional estimates as of July 1, 2020.
[2] The violent crime figures include the offenses of murder, rape (revised definition), robbery, and aggravated assault.
[3] The figures shown in this column for the offense of rape (revised definition) were estimated using the revised Uniform Crime Reporting (UCR) definition of rape. See chapter notes for further explanation.
[4] Limited data for 2020 were available for Alabama, Maryland, and Pennsylvania.
[5] Includes offenses reported by the Metro Transit Police and the Arson Investigation Unit of the District of Columbia Fire and Emergency Medical Services.
[6] Because of changes in the state/local agency's reporting practices, figures are not comparable to previous years' data.
[7] The FBI determined that the state did not follow national UCR Program guidelines for reporting an offense. Consequently, those figures are not included in this table. The agency of Rockford submits independently and therefore includes all offenses.
[8] This state's agencies submitted rape data according to the legacy UCR definition of rape.

Table 4. Crime in the United States, by Selected Metropolitan Statistical Area, 2020

(Number, percent, rate per 100,000 population.)

Area	Population	Violent crime	Murder and nonnegligent manslaughter	Rape[1]	Robbery	Aggravated assault	Property crime	Burglary	Larceny-theft	Motor vehicle theft
Abilene, TX M.S.A.	172,211									
Includes Callahan, Jones, and Taylor Counties										
City of Abilene...	124,061	514	3	117	63	331	2,649	435	2,013	201
Total area actually reporting	100.0%	611	6	142	64	399	3,088	568	2,269	251
Rate per 100,000 inhabitants....................		354.8	3.5	82.5	37.2	231.7	1,793.1	329.8	1,317.6	145.8
Akron, OH M.S.A.	702,634									
Includes Portage and Summit Counties										
City of Akron..	197,433	1,797	47	215	268	1,267	6,971	1,288	4,855	828
Total area actually reporting	95.9%	2,599	55	330	347	1,867	14,557	2,315	10,999	1,243
Estimated total......................................	100.0%	2,659	55	359	354	1,891	15,032	2,375	11,389	1,268
Rate per 100,000 inhabitants....................		378.4	7.8	51.1	50.4	269.1	2,139.4	338.0	1,620.9	180.5
Albany, GA M.S.A.[2]	145,715									
Includes Dougherty,[2] Lee,[2] Terrell, and Worth[2] Counties										
City of Albany[2]......................................	71,567	1,234	19	40	132	1,043	3,148	575	2,234	339
Total area actually reporting	96.2%	1,451	23	68	147	1,213	4,200	821	2,897	482
Estimated total......................................	100.0%	1,469	23	70	151	1,225	4,281	837	2,953	491
Rate per 100,000 inhabitants....................		1,008.1	15.8	48.0	103.6	840.7	2,937.9	574.4	2,026.6	337.0
Albany-Lebanon, OR M.S.A.	130,611									
Includes Linn County................................										
City of Albany..	48,329	72	2	12	24	34	1,336	97	1,134	105
City of Lebanon	17,635	23	0	4	1	18	297	23	251	23
Total area actually reporting	100.0%	195	7	34	31	123	2,821	345	2,212	264
Rate per 100,000 inhabitants....................		149.3	5.4	26.0	23.7	94.2	2,159.8	264.1	1,693.6	202.1
Albany-Schenectady-Troy, NY M.S.A.	875,848									
Includes Albany, Rensselaer, Saratoga, Schenectady, and Schoharie Counties										
City of Albany..	96,318	869	16	61	161	631	2,650	422	1,945	283
City of Schenectady.................................	65,176	468	5	26	90	347	1,622	266	1,187	169
City of Troy	49,052	330	9	16	68	237	1,411	263	1,026	122
Total area actually reporting	99.7%	2,382	34	306	432	1,610	14,535	1,782	11,839	914
Estimated total......................................	100.0%	2,386	34	307	433	1,612	14,552	1,785	11,852	915
Rate per 100,000 inhabitants....................		272.4	3.9	35.1	49.4	184.1	1,661.5	203.8	1,353.2	104.5
Albuquerque, NM M.S.A.	923,729									
Includes Bernalillo, Sandoval, Torrance, and Valencia Counties..........										
City of Albuquerque................................	562,065	7,552	80	441	1,439	5,592	28,171	5,075	18,131	4,965
Total area actually reporting	100.0%	9,296	87	566	1,585	7,058	33,754	6,356	21,278	6,120
Rate per 100,000 inhabitants....................		1,006.4	9.4	61.3	171.6	764.1	3,654.1	688.1	2,303.5	662.5
Alexandria, LA M.S.A.	151,268									
Includes Grant and Rapides Parishes.....................										
City of Alexandria....................................	45,986	850	19	15	145	671	3,317	754	2,300	263
Total area actually reporting	82.1%	1,363	21	53	172	1,117	5,534	1,455	3,610	469
Estimated total......................................	100.0%	1,464	22	62	190	1,190	6,079	1,541	4,004	534
Rate per 100,000 inhabitants....................		967.8	14.5	41.0	125.6	786.7	4,018.7	1,018.7	2,647.0	353.0
Amarillo, TX M.S.A.[2]	265,667									
Includes Armstrong, Carson, Oldham,[2] Potter, and Randall Counties										
City of Amarillo......................................	200,296	1,676	15	141	241	1,279	7,369	1,400	4,903	1,066
Total area actually reporting	99.9%	1,787	18	168	249	1,352	8,082	1,561	5,353	1,168
Estimated total......................................	100.0%	1,787	18	168	249	1,352	8,083	1,561	5,354	1,168
Rate per 100,000 inhabitants....................		672.6	6.8	63.2	93.7	508.9	3,042.5	587.6	2,015.3	439.6
Ames, IA M.S.A.[3]	124,033									
Includes Boone[3] and Story Counties.....................										
City of Ames..	67,109	122	0	54	15	53	1,189	218	903	68
Total area actually reporting	94.6%	201	1	64	15	121			1,183	117
Estimated total......................................	100.0%	228	1	67	19	141			1,386	128
Rate per 100,000 inhabitants....................		183.8	0.8	54.0	15.3	113.7			1,117.4	103.2
Anchorage, AK M.S.A.	305,257									
Includes Anchorage Municipality and Matanuska-Susitna Borough										
City of Anchorage....................................	286,388	3,472	18	558	558	2,338	9,872	1,444	7,279	1,149

Table 4. Crime in the United States, by Selected Metropolitan Statistical Area, 2020—*Continued*

(Number, percent, rate per 100,000 population.)

Area	Population	Violent crime	Murder and nonnegligent manslaughter	Rape[1]	Robbery	Aggravated assault	Property crime	Burglary	Larceny-theft	Motor vehicle theft
Total area actually reporting	100.0%	3,576	18	570	566	2,422	10,393	1,488	7,703	1,202
Rate per 100,000 inhabitants		1,171.5	5.9	186.7	185.4	793.4	3,404.7	487.5	2,523.4	393.8
Ann Arbor, MI M.S.A.	368,868									
Includes Washtenaw County										
City of Ann Arbor	120,647	294	1	49	38	206	1,592	153	1,358	81
Total area actually reporting	100.0%	1,521	9	233	134	1,145	4,670	569	3,698	403
Rate per 100,000 inhabitants		412.3	2.4	63.2	36.3	310.4	1,266.0	154.3	1,002.5	109.3
Appleton, WI M.S.A.	239,143									
Includes Calumet and Outagamie Counties										
City of Appleton	72,570	194	1	35	19	139	1,129	125	942	62
Total area actually reporting	97.4%	385	3	83	28	271	2,672	299	2,228	145
Estimated total	100.0%	408	3	85	32	288	2,798	319	2,319	160
Rate per 100,000 inhabitants		170.6	1.3	35.5	13.4	120.4	1,170.0	133.4	969.7	66.9
Asheville, NC M.S.A.	467,076									
Includes Buncombe, Haywood, Henderson, and Madison Counties										
City of Asheville	93,980	761	11	54	153	543	5,395	730	4,142	523
Total area actually reporting	77.1%	1,240	20	105	207	908	10,540	2,170	7,312	1,058
Estimated total	100.0%	1,481	24	135	234	1,088	12,301	2,638	8,439	1,224
Rate per 100,000 inhabitants		317.1	5.1	28.9	50.1	232.9	2,633.6	564.8	1,806.8	262.1
Athens-Clarke County, GA M.S.A.[2]	215,827									
Includes Clarke, Madison,[2] Oconee, and Oglethorpe[2] Counties										
City of Athens-Clarke County[2]	128,152	654	4	105	102	443	3,785	597	2,837	351
Total area actually reporting	80.4%	777	4	117	105	551	4,368	732	3,221	415
Estimated total	100.0%	834	6	123	112	593	4,719	789	3,482	448
Rate per 100,000 inhabitants		386.4	2.8	57.0	51.9	274.8	2,186.5	365.6	1,613.3	207.6
Atlantic City-Hammonton, NJ M.S.A.	262,199									
Includes Atlantic County										
City of Atlantic City	37,550	309	9	28	116	156	1,013	139	785	89
City of Hammonton	13,845	23	0	0	0	23	189	37	145	7
Total area actually reporting	100.0%	665	17	55	183	410	5,054	793	3,978	283
Rate per 100,000 inhabitants		253.6	6.5	21.0	69.8	156.4	1,927.5	302.4	1,517.2	107.9
Austin-Round Rock-Georgetown, TX M.S.A.[2]	2,283,668									
Includes Bastrop, Caldwell,[2] Hays,[2] Travis,[2] and Williamson Counties										
City of Austin	1,000,276	4,671	44	478	1,101	3,048	36,322	4,774	27,481	4,067
City of Round Rock[2]	137,593	185	3	25	55	102	2,282	235	1,954	93
City of Georgetown	84,210	123	4	50	16	53	1,077	148	836	93
City of San Marcos	67,432	283	2	99	32	150	1,419	260	1,017	142
Total area actually reporting	100.0%	7,207	74	995	1,424	4,714	54,045	7,687	40,683	5,675
Rate per 100,000 inhabitants		315.6	3.2	43.6	62.4	206.4	2,366.6	336.6	1,781.5	248.5
Bakersfield, CA M.S.A.	897,941									
Includes Kern County										
City of Bakersfield	388,265	2,007	44	106	604	1,253	15,619	3,134	8,656	3,829
Total area actually reporting	100.0%	6,216	116	331	1,190	4,579	27,890	6,358	13,995	7,537
Rate per 100,000 inhabitants		692.3	12.9	36.9	132.5	509.9	3,106.0	708.1	1,558.6	839.4
Bangor, ME M.S.A.	152,409									
Includes Penobscot County										
City of Bangor	32,179	51	2	7	13	29	1,207	100	1,044	63
Total area actually reporting	100.0%	88	6	12	16	54	2,339	260	1,950	129
Rate per 100,000 inhabitants		57.7	3.9	7.9	10.5	35.4	1,534.7	170.6	1,279.5	84.6
Barnstable Town, MA M.S.A.	211,545									
Includes Barnstable County										
City of Barnstable	44,169	188	0	30	12	146	350	52	281	17
Total area actually reporting	100.0%	635	3	92	28	512	1,730	374	1,288	68
Rate per 100,000 inhabitants		300.2	1.4	43.5	13.2	242.0	817.8	176.8	608.9	32.1
Baton Rouge, LA M.S.A.[2]	855,151									
Includes Ascension, Assumption, East Baton Rouge, East Feliciana, Iberville,[2] Livingston, Pointe Coupee, St. Helena, West Baton Rouge, and West Feliciana Parishes										

(Number, percent, rate per 100,000 population.)

Area	Population	Violent crime	Murder and nonnegligent manslaughter	Rape[1]	Robbery	Aggravated assault	Property crime	Burglary	Larceny-theft	Motor vehicle theft
City of Baton Rouge...............	219,245	2,087	102	55	457	1,473	10,580	1,898	7,854	828
Total area actually reporting	97.8%	4,734	143	218	653	3,720	26,001	3,884	20,343	1,774
Estimated total....................	100.0%	4,839	144	223	662	3,810	26,433	3,977	20,637	1,819
Rate per 100,000 inhabitants................		565.9	16.8	26.1	77.4	445.5	3,091.0	465.1	2,413.3	212.7
Battle Creek, MI M.S.A.................	133,509									
Includes Calhoun County.....................										
City of Battle Creek..................	60,479	540	8	38	30	464	1,569	335	1,066	168
Total area actually reporting	100.0%	886	14	101	48	723	3,170	574	2,326	270
Rate per 100,000 inhabitants................		663.6	10.5	75.7	36.0	541.5	2,374.4	429.9	1,742.2	202.2
Bay City, MI M.S.A.................	102,285									
Includes Bay County.....................										
City of Bay City..................	32,485	276	0	48	25	203	500	104	331	65
Total area actually reporting	100.0%	384	3	90	32	259	1,084	206	760	118
Rate per 100,000 inhabitants................		375.4	2.9	88.0	31.3	253.2	1,059.8	201.4	743.0	115.4
Beaumont-Port Arthur, TX M.S.A.[2]...............	391,609									
Includes Hardin,[2] Jefferson, and Orange[2] Counties......										
City of Beaumont[2]..................	116,766	1,431	20	79	300	1,032	3,863	955	2,546	362
City of Port Arthur[2]..................	54,257	422	7	42	76	297	1,253	346	775	132
Total area actually reporting	99.9%	2,371	35	181	432	1,723	8,028	2,000	5,102	926
Estimated total....................	100.0%	2,372	35	181	432	1,724	8,036	2,002	5,107	927
Rate per 100,000 inhabitants................		605.7	8.9	46.2	110.3	440.2	2,052.0	511.2	1,304.1	236.7
Beckley, WV M.S.A.................	114,718									
Includes Fayette and Raleigh Counties................										
City of Beckley..................	15,762	137	2	8	11	116	905	149	708	48
Total area actually reporting	95.3%	355	7	40	18	290	2,248	467	1,635	146
Estimated total....................	100.0%	433	7	44	22	360	2,269	474	1,645	150
Rate per 100,000 inhabitants................		377.4	6.1	38.4	19.2	313.8	1,977.9	413.2	1,434.0	130.8
Bellingham, WA M.S.A.................	231,784									
Includes Whatcom County.................										
City of Bellingham	93,629	240	0	29	80	131	4,306	610	3,320	376
Total area actually reporting	100.0%	428	5	72	90	261	5,459	885	4,129	445
Rate per 100,000 inhabitants................		184.7	2.2	31.1	38.8	112.6	2,355.2	381.8	1,781.4	192.0
Bend, OR M.S.A.................	201,709									
Includes Deschutes County										
City of Bend..................	103,485	174	0	28	31	115	1,959	201	1,593	165
Total area actually reporting	100.0%	360	0	57	50	253	3,664	397	2,919	348
Rate per 100,000 inhabitants................		178.5	0.0	28.3	24.8	125.4	1,816.5	196.8	1,447.1	172.5
Billings, MT M.S.A.	183,705									
Includes Carbon, Stillwater, and Yellowstone Counties										
City of Billings..................	110,157	939	14	85	125	715	5,249	717	3,715	817
Total area actually reporting	100.0%	1,152	15	103	133	901	6,378	868	4,512	998
Rate per 100,000 inhabitants................		627.1	8.2	56.1	72.4	490.5	3,471.9	472.5	2,456.1	543.3
Binghamton, NY M.S.A.[2].................	235,803									
Includes Broome[2] and Tioga Counties............										
City of Binghamton[2]..................	44,083	372	1	28	50	293	1,775	294	1,380	101
Total area actually reporting	99.0%	669	4	111	79	475	4,818	711	3,875	232
Estimated total....................	100.0%	673	4	111	80	478	4,857	715	3,909	233
Rate per 100,000 inhabitants................		285.4	1.7	47.1	33.9	202.7	2,059.8	303.2	1,657.7	98.8
Bismarck, ND M.S.A.	129,675									
Includes Burleigh, Morton, and Oliver Counties...........										
City of Bismarck..................	74,997	260	0	49	26	185	2,471	343	1,876	252
Total area actually reporting	100.0%	433	4	74	30	325	3,692	610	2,677	405
Rate per 100,000 inhabitants................		333.9	3.1	57.1	23.1	250.6	2,847.1	470.4	2,064.4	312.3
Blacksburg-Christiansburg, VA M.S.A.................	167,909									
Includes Giles, Montgomery, and Pulaski Counties and										
Radford City										
City of Blacksburg..................	44,422	29	0	13	2	14	310	29	266	15
City of Christiansburg..................	22,643	37	0	13	2	22	479	44	424	11
Total area actually reporting	100.0%	313	5	99	20	189	2,476	336	2,013	127
Rate per 100,000 inhabitants................		186.4	3.0	59.0	11.9	112.6	1,474.6	200.1	1,198.9	75.6

Part 2—Crime in the United States, 2020   49

Area	Population	Violent crime	Murder and nonnegligent manslaughter	Rape[1]	Robbery	Aggravated assault	Property crime	Burglary	Larceny-theft	Motor vehicle theft
Bloomington, IL M.S.A.[4]...................	170,810									
Includes McLean County[4]										
City of Bloomington[4]	77,386	314	1	64	23	226		144		70
Total area actually reporting	97.1%	475	1	105	44	325		289		123
Estimated total..............................	100.0%	483	1	106	45	331		299		129
Rate per 100,000 inhabitants.............		282.8	0.6	62.1	26.3	193.8		175.0		75.5
Bloomington, IN M.S.A.[2]...................	170,127									
Includes Monroe[2] and Owen Counties										
City of Bloomington[2]	86,347	480	7	52	67	354	2,079	346	1,595	138
Total area actually reporting	83.8%	547	8	86	77	376	2,792	410	2,180	202
Estimated total..............................	100.0%	586	8	91	79	408	3,072	467	2,372	233
Rate per 100,000 inhabitants.............		344.4	4.7	53.5	46.4	239.8	1,805.7	274.5	1,394.3	137.0
Boise City, ID M.S.A....................	771,135									
Includes Ada, Boise, Canyon, Gem, and Owyhee Counties										
City of Boise	231,223	677	4	170	55	448	3,793	479	3,035	279
Total area actually reporting	99.9%	2,025	14	451	92	1,468	8,952	1,441	6,669	842
Estimated total..............................	100.0%	2,026	14	451	92	1,469	8,958	1,442	6,674	842
Rate per 100,000 inhabitants.............		262.7	1.8	58.5	11.9	190.5	1,161.7	187.0	865.5	109.2
Boston-Cambridge-Newton, MA-NH M.S.A.[2].........	4,885,414									
Includes the Metropolitan Divisions of Boston, MA; Cambridge-Newton-Framingham, MA; and Rockingham County-Strafford County, NH										
City of Boston, MA[2]	697,323	4,354	58	184	919	3,193	13,015	1,698	10,037	1,280
City of Cambridge, MA.....................	119,938	341	1	25	67	248	2,200	202	1,917	81
City of Newton, MA.........................	88,281	48	0	4	8	36	486	51	420	15
City of Framingham, MA...................	74,680	264	2	13	20	229	862	110	625	127
City of Waltham, MA........................	62,339	85	1	10	3	71	385	51	310	24
Total area actually reporting	99.9%	12,392	109	1,062	1,865	9,356	48,632	5,737	38,398	4,497
Estimated total..............................	100.0%	12,399	109	1,063	1,865	9,362	48,653	5,740	38,415	4,498
Rate per 100,000 inhabitants.............		253.8	2.2	21.8	38.2	191.6	995.9	117.5	786.3	92.1
Boston, MA M.D.[2]...................	2,037,005									
Includes Norfolk, Plymouth, and Suffolk Counties....										
Total area actually reporting.............	99.7%	7,583	73	528	1,285	5,697	24,436	3,062	18,980	2,394
Estimated total..............................	100.0%	7,590	73	529	1,285	5,703	24,457	3,065	18,997	2,395
Rate per 100,000 inhabitants.............		372.6	3.6	26.0	63.1	280.0	1,200.6	150.5	932.6	117.6
Cambridge-Newton-Framingham, MA M.D.	2,404,962									
Includes Essex and Middlesex Counties..................										
Total area actually reporting.............	100.0%	4,421	32	401	510	3,478	19,930	2,362	15,778	1,790
Rate per 100,000 inhabitants.............		183.8	1.3	16.7	21.2	144.6	828.7	98.2	656.1	74.4
Rockingham County-Strafford County, NH M.D.	443,447									
Includes Rockingham and Strafford Counties...........										
Total area actually reporting.............	100.0%	388	4	133	70	181	4,266	313	3,640	313
Rate per 100,000 inhabitants.............		87.5	0.9	30.0	15.8	40.8	962.0	70.6	820.8	70.6
Boulder, CO M.S.A....................	327,747									
Includes Boulder County										
City of Boulder...............................	106,598	343	2	31	72	238	4,019	654	2,994	371
Total area actually reporting	100.0%	961	4	177	140	640	9,046	1,328	6,723	995
Rate per 100,000 inhabitants.............		293.2	1.2	54.0	42.7	195.3	2,760.1	405.2	2,051.3	303.6
Bowling Green, KY M.S.A....................	181,430									
Includes Allen, Butler, Edmonson, and Warren Counties										
City of Bowling Green........................	71,861	247	9	56	71	111	3,195	560	2,318	317
Total area actually reporting	100.0%	341	11	80	83	167	4,163	763	2,933	467
Rate per 100,000 inhabitants.............		188.0	6.1	44.1	45.7	92.0	2,294.5	420.5	1,616.6	257.4
Bremerton-Silverdale-Port Orchard, WA M.S.A.	272,867									
Includes Kitsap County........................										
City of Bremerton.............................	41,817	143	1	16	23	103	1,342	224	945	173
City of Port Orchard..........................	14,886	61	0	9	8	44	550	100	380	70
Total area actually reporting	100.0%	597	5	133	57	402	4,887	873	3,496	518
Rate per 100,000 inhabitants.............		218.8	1.8	48.7	20.9	147.3	1,791.0	319.9	1,281.2	189.8

(Number, percent, rate per 100,000 population.)

Area	Population	Violent crime	Murder and nonnegligent manslaughter	Rape[1]	Robbery	Aggravated assault	Property crime	Burglary	Larceny-theft	Motor vehicle theft
Bridgeport-Stamford-Norwalk, CT M.S.A.[3]	928,567									
Includes Fairfield County										
City of Bridgeport	144,350	829	24	47	340	418	2,514	675	1,196	643
City of Stamford[3]	130,425	284	6	26	85	167			1,206	234
City of Norwalk	89,140	143	2	12	21	108	1,222	148	930	144
City of Danbury	85,080	98	4	9	40	45	806	81	643	82
City of Stratford	51,895	53	2	2	31	18	923	105	651	167
Total area actually reporting	100.0%	1,522	40	122	550	810			8,017	1,923
Rate per 100,000 inhabitants		163.9	4.3	13.1	59.2	87.2			863.4	207.1
Brownsville-Harlingen, TX M.S.A.	423,478									
Includes Cameron County										
City of Brownsville	183,627	738	7	83	153	495	3,394	403	2,870	121
City of Harlingen	65,014	269	3	21	67	178	2,437	315	1,999	123
Total area actually reporting	99.7%	1,526	13	176	247	1,090	8,241	1,161	6,692	388
Estimated total	100.0%	1,528	13	176	247	1,092	8,261	1,165	6,705	391
Rate per 100,000 inhabitants		360.8	3.1	41.6	58.3	257.9	1,950.8	275.1	1,583.3	92.3
Buffalo-Cheektowaga, NY M.S.A.[2]	1,119,988									
Includes Erie and Niagara[2] Counties										
City of Buffalo[2]	254,627	2,592	61	53	680	1,798	7,844	1,146	5,508	1,190
City of Cheektowaga Town	76,536	216	1	22	51	142	2,226	273	1,782	171
Total area actually reporting	100.0%	4,237	79	257	1,030	2,871	21,574	2,844	16,547	2,183
Rate per 100,000 inhabitants		378.3	7.1	22.9	92.0	256.3	1,926.3	253.9	1,477.4	194.9
Burlington, NC M.S.A.	171,665									
Includes Alamance County										
City of Burlington	55,003	527	3	43	56	425	2,391	419	1,782	190
Total area actually reporting	100.0%	820	12	65	80	663	4,070	738	2,992	340
Rate per 100,000 inhabitants		477.7	7.0	37.9	46.6	386.2	2,370.9	429.9	1,742.9	198.1
Burlington-South Burlington, VT M.S.A.	221,248									
Includes Chittenden, Franklin, and Grand Isle Counties										
City of Burlington	42,862	151	1	36	16	98	1,032	109	906	17
City of South Burlington	19,690	33	0	5	6	22	608	33	557	18
Total area actually reporting	100.0%	439	5	115	32	287	3,561	362	3,116	83
Rate per 100,000 inhabitants		198.4	2.3	52.0	14.5	129.7	1,609.5	163.6	1,408.4	37.5
California-Lexington Park, MD M.S.A.	114,031									
Includes St. Mary's County										
Total area actually reporting	100.0%	224	8	27	38	151	1,556	255	1,214	87
Rate per 100,000 inhabitants		196.4	7.0	23.7	33.3	132.4	1,364.5	223.6	1,064.6	76.3
Canton-Massillon, OH M.S.A.	396,284									
Includes Carroll and Stark Counties										
City of Canton	70,124	1,002	14	115	154	719	3,411	708	2,350	353
City of Massillon	32,617	56	0	20	10	26	759	95	624	40
Total area actually reporting	98.0%	1,441	19	223	214	985	8,414	1,575	6,157	682
Estimated total	100.0%	1,451	19	225	216	991	8,546	1,591	6,266	689
Rate per 100,000 inhabitants		366.2	4.8	56.8	54.5	250.1	2,156.5	401.5	1,581.2	173.9
Cape Coral-Fort Myers, FL M.S.A.	787,016									
Includes Lee County										
City of Cape Coral	199,503	255	1	18	20	216	2,130	305	1,692	133
City of Fort Myers	90,380	467	9	39	67	352	1,699	193	1,359	147
Total area actually reporting	100.0%	2,100	32	239	304	1,525	8,118	1,180	6,167	771
Rate per 100,000 inhabitants		266.8	4.1	30.4	38.6	193.8	1,031.5	149.9	783.6	98.0
Cape Girardeau, MO-IL M.S.A.[2]	96,785									
Includes Alexander County,[4] IL and Bollinger and Cape Girardeau Counties, MO[2]										
City of Cape Girardeau, MO[2]	40,845	362	4	42	35	281	1,204	179	892	133
Total area actually reporting	97.9%	530	5	59	38	428	1,785	339	1,284	162
Estimated total	100.0%	532	5	59	38	430	1,811	342	1,305	164
Rate per 100,000 inhabitants		549.7	5.2	61.0	39.3	444.3	1,871.2	353.4	1,348.3	169.4
Carson City, NV M.S.A.[2]	56,250									
Includes Carson City[2]										
Total area actually reporting	100.0%	225	1	62	13	149	643	165	396	82
Rate per 100,000 inhabitants		400.0	1.8	110.2	23.1	264.9	1,143.1	293.3	704.0	145.8

Table 4. Crime in the United States, by Selected Metropolitan Statistical Area, 2020—*Continued*

(Number, percent, rate per 100,000 population.)

Area	Population	Violent crime	Murder and nonnegligent manslaughter	Rape[1]	Robbery	Aggravated assault	Property crime	Burglary	Larceny-theft	Motor vehicle theft
Casper, WY M.S.A.[2]	80,625									
Includes Natrona County[2]										
City of Casper..........................	58,244	124	2	59	14	49	1,659	222	1,270	167
Total area actually reporting	100.0%	183	4	71	16	92	1,954	274	1,467	213
Rate per 100,000 inhabitants................		227.0	5.0	88.1	19.8	114.1	2,423.6	339.8	1,819.5	264.2
Cedar Rapids, IA M.S.A...........................	274,312									
Includes Benton, Jones, and Linn Counties.................										
City of Cedar Rapids	134,330	432	11	16	102	303	4,254	832	2,865	557
Total area actually reporting	85.6%	593	12	48	111	422	5,303	1,133	3,486	684
Estimated total..................	100.0%	691	12	71	116	492	5,803	1,278	3,789	736
Rate per 100,000 inhabitants................		251.9	4.4	25.9	42.3	179.4	2,115.5	465.9	1,381.3	268.3
Champaign-Urbana, IL M.S.A.[3,4]	225,728									
Includes Champaign and Piatt Counties[4]										
City of Champaign[4]	89,785	827	9	60	88	670		281		191
City of Urbana[3,4] ..	42,211		2	41	36			137		42
Total area actually reporting	99.0%		12	139	147			613		324
Estimated total..................	100.0%		12	139	147			616		325
Rate per 100,000 inhabitants................			5.3	61.6	65.1			272.9		144.0
Charleston, WV M.S.A.	254,717									
Includes Boone, Clay, Jackson, Kanawha, and Lincoln Counties										
City of Charleston.........................	46,038	424	11	37	51	325	2,122	506	1,423	193
Total area actually reporting	85.3%	1,191	30	137	88	936	5,775	1,297	3,859	619
Estimated total..................	100.0%	1,366	30	149	95	1,092	5,873	1,332	3,910	631
Rate per 100,000 inhabitants................		536.3	11.8	58.5	37.3	428.7	2,305.7	522.9	1,535.0	247.7
Charleston-North Charleston, SC M.S.A.	819,676									
Includes Berkeley, Charleston, and Dorchester Counties										
City of Charleston.........................	139,582	650	17	54	100	479	3,218	326	2,439	453
City of North Charleston	117,503	1,345	38	90	318	899	5,998	651	4,667	680
Total area actually reporting	99.0%	3,607	91	293	648	2,575	20,056	2,492	15,247	2,317
Estimated total..................	100.0%	3,657	93	296	654	2,614	20,333	2,533	15,461	2,339
Rate per 100,000 inhabitants................		446.2	11.3	36.1	79.8	318.9	2,480.6	309.0	1,886.2	285.4
Charlottesville, VA M.S.A.	220,388									
Includes Albemarle, Buckingham, Fluvanna, Greene, and Nelson Counties and Charlottesville City										
City of Charlottesville.........................	47,671	189	5	25	28	131	916	79	765	72
Total area actually reporting	100.0%	415	13	83	47	272	2,849	280	2,376	193
Rate per 100,000 inhabitants................		188.3	5.9	37.7	21.3	123.4	1,292.7	127.0	1,078.1	87.6
Chattanooga, TN-GA M.S.A.[2]	569,147									
Includes Catoosa,2 Dade, and Walker Counties, GA and Hamilton, Marion, and Sequatchie Counties, TN ..										
City of Chattanooga, TN	184,211	2,504	33	182	268	2,021	11,709	1,173	8,435	2,101
Total area actually reporting	86.0%	3,329	40	255	322	2,712	16,606	1,994	11,791	2,821
Estimated total..................	100.0%	3,487	45	270	343	2,829	17,474	2,137	12,414	2,923
Rate per 100,000 inhabitants................		612.7	7.9	47.4	60.3	497.1	3,070.2	375.5	2,181.2	513.6
Cheyenne, WY M.S.A.	100,661									
Includes Laramie County										
City of Cheyenne........................	64,751	244	2	35	27	180	2,186	172	1,768	246
Total area actually reporting	100.0%	330	3	43	29	255	2,617	273	2,045	299
Rate per 100,000 inhabitants................		327.8	3.0	42.7	28.8	253.3	2,599.8	271.2	2,031.6	297.0
Chico, CA M.S.A...........................	216,938									
Includes Butte County										
City of Chico............................	105,355	540	3	56	80	401	2,113	246	1,551	316
Total area actually reporting	100.0%	1,069	12	128	143	786	4,328	833	2,832	663
Rate per 100,000 inhabitants................		492.8	5.5	59.0	65.9	362.3	1,995.0	384.0	1,305.4	305.6
Cincinnati, OH-KY-IN M.S.A.	2,227,744									
Includes Dearborn, Franklin, Ohio, and Union Counties, IN; Boone, Bracken, Campbell, Gallatin, Grant, Kenton, and Pendleton Counties, KY; and Brown, Butler, Clermont, Hamilton, and Warren Counties, OH										

Table 4. Crime in the United States, by Selected Metropolitan Statistical Area, 2020—*Continued*

(Number, percent, rate per 100,000 population.)

Area	Population	Violent crime	Murder and nonnegligent manslaughter	Rape[1]	Robbery	Aggravated assault	Property crime	Burglary	Larceny-theft	Motor vehicle theft
City of Cincinnati, OH................................	304,724	2,721	92	215	750	1,664	11,224	2,322	7,396	1,506
Total area actually reporting	89.1%	4,733	123	656	1,132	2,822	32,917	5,080	24,525	3,312
Estimated total...................................	100.0%	5,250	128	735	1,217	3,170	36,953	5,737	27,573	3,643
Rate per 100,000 inhabitants......................		235.7	5.7	33.0	54.6	142.3	1,658.8	257.5	1,237.7	163.5
Clarksville, TN-KY M.S.A..........................	311,846									
Includes Christian and Trigg Counties, KY and Montgomery and Stewart Counties, TN										
City of Clarksville, TN............................	161,167	983	15	84	78	806	3,615	441	2,765	409
Total area actually reporting	100.0%	1,321	21	133	117	1,050	5,777	893	4,254	630
Rate per 100,000 inhabitants......................		423.6	6.7	42.6	37.5	336.7	1,852.5	286.4	1,364.1	202.0
Cleveland, TN M.S.A.	125,999									
Includes Bradley and Polk Counties										
City of Cleveland.................................	45,994	454	2	21	62	369	2,312	374	1,734	204
Total area actually reporting	100.0%	710	5	39	71	595	3,398	612	2,422	364
Rate per 100,000 inhabitants......................		563.5	4.0	31.0	56.3	472.2	2,696.8	485.7	1,922.2	288.9
Cleveland-Elyria, OH M.S.A.	2,042,966									
Includes Cuyahoga, Geauga, Lake, Lorain, and Medina Counties										
City of Cleveland.................................	379,121	6,281	160	393	1,593	4,135	15,433	3,692	8,800	2,941
City of Elyria....................................	53,677	136	7	21	26	82	785	178	546	61
Total area actually reporting	87.6%	8,616	207	664	2,100	5,645	30,659	5,749	20,511	4,399
Estimated total...................................	100.0%	9,002	210	740	2,175	5,877	34,823	6,261	23,896	4,666
Rate per 100,000 inhabitants......................		440.6	10.3	36.2	106.5	287.7	1,704.5	306.5	1,169.7	228.4
Coeur d'Alene, ID M.S.A.	170,237									
Includes Kootenai County										
City of Coeur d'Alene.............................	53,405	209	1	66	8	134	835	92	701	42
Total area actually reporting	100.0%	343	2	81	16	244	1,807	308	1,403	96
Rate per 100,000 inhabitants......................		201.5	1.2	47.6	9.4	143.3	1,061.5	180.9	824.1	56.4
College Station-Bryan, TX M.S.A.[2]	268,082									
Includes Brazos,[2] Burleson,[2] and Robertson Counties...										
City of College Station............................	120,831	217	2	55	27	133	2,299	321	1,768	210
City of Bryan[2]....................................	87,435	463	7	104	49	303	1,718	280	1,302	136
Total area actually reporting	100.0%	799	10	182	88	519	4,970	835	3,698	437
Rate per 100,000 inhabitants......................		298.0	3.7	67.9	32.8	193.6	1,853.9	311.5	1,379.4	163.0
Colorado Springs, CO M.S.A..................................	752,364									
Includes El Paso and Teller Counties										
City of Colorado Springs..........................	485,083	2,896	36	400	376	2,084	16,394	2,588	11,374	2,432
Total area actually reporting	99.6%	3,655	47	577	440	2,591	19,859	3,100	13,880	2,879
Estimated total...................................	100.0%	3,661	47	578	441	2,595	19,960	3,106	13,958	2,896
Rate per 100,000 inhabitants......................		486.6	6.2	76.8	58.6	344.9	2,653.0	412.8	1,855.2	384.9
Columbia, MO M.S.A.[2]	210,096									
Includes Boone,[2] Cooper, and Howard[2] Counties										
City of Columbia[2]...............................	124,829	552	13	89	58	392	3,326	404	2,478	444
Total area actually reporting	98.2%	739	15	132	71	521	4,522	573	3,366	583
Estimated total...................................	100.0%	769	15	134	75	545	4,635	590	3,440	605
Rate per 100,000 inhabitants......................		366.0	7.1	63.8	35.7	259.4	2,206.1	280.8	1,637.3	288.0
Columbia, SC M.S.A.	847,504									
Includes Calhoun, Fairfield, Kershaw, Lexington, Richland, and Saluda Counties...................										
City of Columbia.................................	131,777	991	19	86	206	680	5,898	728	4,536	634
Total area actually reporting	100.0%	4,729	78	355	644	3,652	27,730	4,335	20,161	3,234
Rate per 100,000 inhabitants......................		558.0	9.2	41.9	76.0	430.9	3,272.0	511.5	2,378.9	381.6
Columbus, OH M.S.A.	2,145,231									
Includes Delaware, Fairfield, Franklin, Hocking, Licking, Madison, Morrow, Perry, Pickaway, and Union Counties										
City of Columbus.................................	911,383	5,064	174	816	1,796	2,278	28,530	5,551	19,874	3,105
Total area actually reporting	93.8%	6,534	191	1,128	2,097	3,118	45,217	7,810	33,179	4,228
Estimated total...................................	100.0%	6,718	192	1,164	2,131	3,231	47,407	8,082	34,972	4,353
Rate per 100,000 inhabitants......................		313.2	9.0	54.3	99.3	150.6	2,209.9	376.7	1,630.2	202.9

Table 4. Crime in the United States, by Selected Metropolitan Statistical Area, 2020—*Continued*

(Number, percent, rate per 100,000 population.)

Area	Population	Violent crime	Murder and nonnegligent manslaughter	Rape[1]	Robbery	Aggravated assault	Property crime	Burglary	Larceny-theft	Motor vehicle theft
Corpus Christi, TX M.S.A.[2]	430,354									
Includes Nueces and San Patricio Counties										
City of Corpus Christi[2]	329,050	2,772	34	232	478	2,028	10,747	2,042	7,824	881
Total area actually reporting	99.9%	3,175	43	278	509	2,345	12,659	2,428	9,202	1,029
Estimated total	100.0%	3,176	43	278	509	2,346	12,668	2,430	9,208	1,030
Rate per 100,000 inhabitants		738.0	10.0	64.6	118.3	545.1	2,943.6	564.7	2,139.6	239.3
Crestview-Fort Walton Beach-Destin, FL M.S.A.	290,040									
Includes Okaloosa and Walton Counties...................										
City of Crestview	25,787	93	4	18	13	58	602	72	457	73
City of Fort Walton Beach	22,871	74	2	13	4	55	462	89	324	49
Total area actually reporting	100.0%	780	10	117	50	603	3,927	601	2,947	379
Rate per 100,000 inhabitants.........................		268.9	3.4	40.3	17.2	207.9	1,354.0	207.2	1,016.1	130.7
Danville, IL M.S.A.[4].........................	74,737									
Includes Vermilion County[4]										
City of Danville[4]	30,208	505	8	10	59	428		399		48
Total area actually reporting	100.0%	785	13	70	87	615		658		170
Rate per 100,000 inhabitants.........................		1,050.3	17.4	93.7	116.4	822.9		880.4		227.5
Davenport-Moline-Rock Island, IA-IL M.S.A.[4]........	377,817									
Includes Henry, Mercer, and Rock Island Counties, IL[4]										
and Scott County, IA...................................										
City of Davenport, IA	101,806	750	10	67	136	537	3,996	912	2,615	469
City of Moline, IL[4]	41,128	204	1	32	25	146		225		76
City of Rock Island, IL[4]..............................	36,981	213	7	8	50	148		139		124
Total area actually reporting	96.5%	1,770	26	221	265	1,258		1,833		934
Estimated total..	100.0%	1,798	26	225	269	1,278		1,866		950
Rate per 100,000 inhabitants.........................		475.9	6.9	59.6	71.2	338.3		493.9		251.4
Decatur, IL M.S.A.[4]..............................	102,740									
Includes Macon County[4]										
City of Decatur[4]	70,175	489	13	41	83	352		621		196
Total area actually reporting	100.0%	540	13	49	84	394		677		214
Rate per 100,000 inhabitants.........................		525.6	12.7	47.7	81.8	383.5		658.9		208.3
Deltona-Daytona Beach-Ormond Beach, FL M.S.A...............................	675,651									
Includes Flagler and Volusia Counties....................										
City of Daytona Beach	70,084	725	14	25	77	609	2,145	274	1,668	203
City of Ormond Beach	44,271	161	1	26	23	111	1,035	166	773	96
City of DeLand..	35,874	188	1	8	16	163	870	111	697	62
Total area actually reporting	100.0%	2,280	26	192	274	1,788	9,815	1,528	7,452	835
Rate per 100,000 inhabitants.........................		337.5	3.8	28.4	40.6	264.6	1,452.7	226.2	1,102.9	123.6
Denver-Aurora-Lakewood, CO M.S.A.....................	2,998,046									
Includes Adams, Arapahoe, Broomfield, Clear Creek,										
Denver, Douglas, Elbert, Gilpin, Jefferson, and Park										
Counties..										
City of Denver..	737,709	6,329	97	670	1,218	4,344	34,294	5,223	20,662	8,409
City of Aurora..	385,720	3,473	39	397	775	2,262	13,079	1,760	7,390	3,929
City of Lakewood.....................................	159,719	903	8	110	219	566	8,050	1,076	5,580	1,394
City of Centennial....................................	112,104	144	1	6	26	111	1,979	317	1,360	302
City of Broomfield....................................	71,795	76	0	15	13	48	2,145	222	1,654	269
City of Commerce City................................	62,164	298	6	73	38	181	2,051	238	1,241	572
Total area actually reporting	99.6%	14,675	183	1,970	2,811	9,711	98,712	13,268	63,475	21,969
Estimated total..	100.0%	14,701	183	1,974	2,816	9,728	99,017	13,307	63,699	22,011
Rate per 100,000 inhabitants.........................		490.4	6.1	65.8	93.9	324.5	3,302.7	443.9	2,124.7	734.2
Des Moines-West Des Moines, IA M.S.A.	709,374									
Includes Dallas, Guthrie, Jasper, Madison, Polk, and										
Warren Counties.......................................										
City of Des Moines....................................	215,290	1,517	33	119	246	1,119	8,400	1,925	5,053	1,422
City of West Des Moines..............................	69,252	93	1	27	7	58	1,140	129	893	118
Total area actually reporting	100.0%	2,402	44	247	295	1,816	14,354	3,006	9,299	2,049
Rate per 100,000 inhabitants.........................		338.6	6.2	34.8	41.6	256.0	2,023.5	423.8	1,310.9	288.8
Detroit-Warren-Dearborn, MI M.S.A.	4,308,550									
Includes the Metropolitan Divisions of Detroit-Dear-										
born-Livonia and Warren-Troy-Farmington Hills										
City of Detroit..	659,616	14,370	328	676	1,848	11,518	21,178	4,361	11,239	5,578

(Number, percent, rate per 100,000 population.)

Area	Population	Violent crime	Murder and nonnegligent manslaughter	Rape[1]	Robbery	Aggravated assault	Property crime	Burglary	Larceny-theft	Motor vehicle theft
City of Warren	133,928	672	12	93	91	476	1,938	348	1,169	421
City of Dearborn	93,507	277	5	25	31	216	1,662	194	1,215	253
City of Livonia	93,342	209	0	26	12	171	1,196	115	979	102
City of Troy	84,441	86	1	9	15	61	732	46	635	51
City of Farmington Hills	80,708	84	0	11	9	64	558	65	439	54
City of Southfield	72,794	288	3	33	35	217	1,309	190	759	360
City of Taylor	60,698	371	1	25	35	310	1,108	182	790	136
City of Pontiac	59,411	840	13	50	88	689	1,096	240	743	113
City of Novi	61,554	60	1	15	3	41	429	21	372	36
Total area actually reporting	100.0%	24,568	452	1,989	2,791	19,336	57,445	9,472	37,647	10,326
Rate per 100,000 inhabitants		570.2	10.5	46.2	64.8	448.8	1,333.3	219.8	873.8	239.7
Detroit-Warren-Dearborn, MI M.S.A.	1,736,289									
Includes Wayne County										
Total area actually reporting	100.0%	18,894	387	1,136	2,247	15,124	35,699	6,526	21,529	7,644
Rate per 100,000 inhabitants		1,088.2	22.3	65.4	129.4	871.1	2,056.1	375.9	1,239.9	440.2
Warren-Troy-Farmington Hills, MI M.D.	2,572,261									
Includes Lapeer, Livingston, Macomb, Oakland, and St. Clair Counties										
Total area actually reporting	100.0%	5,674	65	853	544	4,212	21,746	2,946	16,118	2,682
Rate per 100,000 inhabitants		220.6	2.5	33.2	21.1	163.7	845.4	114.5	626.6	104.3
Dover, DE M.S.A.	183,675									
Includes Kent County										
City of Dover	38,428	329	9	22	24	274	1,549	57	1,412	80
Total area actually reporting	100.0%	813	13	79	58	663	3,404	372	2,829	203
Rate per 100,000 inhabitants		442.6	7.1	43.0	31.6	361.0	1,853.3	202.5	1,540.2	110.5
Dubuque, IA M.S.A.	97,551									
Includes Dubuque County										
City of Dubuque	57,904	231	1	54	26	150	1,165	208	885	72
Total area actually reporting	100.0%	262	1	62	26	173	1,363	267	1,004	92
Rate per 100,000 inhabitants		268.6	1.0	63.6	26.7	177.3	1,397.2	273.7	1,029.2	94.3
Duluth, MN-WI M.S.A.[2]	287,596									
Includes Carlton,[2] Lake,[2] and St. Louis Counties, MN and Douglas County, WI[2]										
City of Duluth, MN	85,555	257	1	33	44	179	3,224	326	2,677	221
Total area actually reporting	100.0%	607	5	93	67	442	6,924	982	5,455	487
Rate per 100,000 inhabitants		211.1	1.7	32.3	23.3	153.7	2,407.5	341.5	1,896.8	169.3
Durham-Chapel Hill, NC M.S.A.	653,860									
Includes Chatham, Durham, Granville, Orange and Person Counties										
City of Durham	284,925	2,447	36	125	626	1,660	10,650	1,906	7,779	965
City of Chapel Hill	64,853	93	0	7	22	64	1,140	198	885	57
Total area actually reporting	100.0%	3,272	53	190	745	2,284	16,350	3,085	11,888	1,377
Rate per 100,000 inhabitants		500.4	8.1	29.1	113.9	349.3	2,500.5	471.8	1,818.1	210.6
Eau Claire, WI M.S.A.	170,028									
Includes Chippewa and Eau Claire Counties										
City of Eau Claire	69,086	191	2	41	38	110	1,927	334	1,494	99
Total area actually reporting	100.0%	326	3	72	42	209	2,951	558	2,227	166
Rate per 100,000 inhabitants		191.7	1.8	42.3	24.7	122.9	1,735.6	328.2	1,309.8	97.6
El Centro, CA M.S.A.	180,129									
Includes Imperial County										
City of El Centro	44,238	158	1	10	30	117	1,003	213	679	111
Total area actually reporting	96.1%	582	7	32	80	463	3,384	851	2,085	448
Estimated total	100.0%	609	7	35	85	482	3,526	873	2,188	465
Rate per 100,000 inhabitants		338.1	3.9	19.4	47.2	267.6	1,957.5	484.7	1,214.7	258.1
Elizabethtown-Fort Knox, KY M.S.A.	154,232									
Includes Hardin, Larue, and Meade Counties										
City of Elizabethtown	30,505	44	3	8	9	24	286	68	182	36
Total area actually reporting	100.0%	155	5	26	25	99	1,286	279	836	171
Rate per 100,000 inhabitants		100.5	3.2	16.9	16.2	64.2	833.8	180.9	542.0	110.9

(Number, percent, rate per 100,000 population.)

Area	Population	Violent crime	Murder and nonnegligent manslaughter	Rape[1]	Robbery	Aggravated assault	Property crime	Burglary	Larceny-theft	Motor vehicle theft
Elmira, NY M.S.A.	82,347									
Includes Chemung County........................										
City of Elmira........................	26,820	59	2	0	25	32	812	87	684	41
Total area actually reporting	100.0%	173	3	32	28	110	1,329	131	1,131	67
Rate per 100,000 inhabitants........................		210.1	3.6	38.9	34.0	133.6	1,613.9	159.1	1,373.5	81.4
El Paso, TX M.S.A.[2]	845,510									
Includes El Paso2 and Hudspeth Counties										
City of El Paso2........................	685,288	2,167	28	261	289	1,589	8,507	847	7,245	415
Total area actually reporting	100.0%	2,611	33	319	321	1,938	9,708	1,042	8,134	532
Rate per 100,000 inhabitants........................		308.8	3.9	37.7	38.0	229.2	1,148.2	123.2	962.0	62.9
Enid, OK M.S.A.	61,092									
Includes Garfield County........................										
City of Enid........................	49,708	233	4	35	15	179	1,420	375	948	97
Total area actually reporting	100.0%	254	4	38	15	197	1,576	430	1,039	107
Rate per 100,000 inhabitants........................		415.8	6.5	62.2	24.6	322.5	2,579.7	703.9	1,700.7	175.1
Evansville, IN-KY M.S.A.[2]	315,160									
Includes Posey, Vanderburgh, and Warrick Counties, IN and Henderson County, KY........................										
City of Evansville2........................	117,747	1,185	10	77	115	983	4,252	626	3,188	438
Total area actually reporting	92.0%	1,563	14	119	140	1,290	6,292	1,011	4,636	645
Estimated total........................	100.0%	1,601	14	123	143	1,321	6,557	1,067	4,817	673
Rate per 100,000 inhabitants........................		508.0	4.4	39.0	45.4	419.2	2,080.5	338.6	1,528.4	213.5
Fairbanks, AK M.S.A.	32,922									
Includes Fairbanks North Star Borough........................										
City of Fairbanks........................	30,832	260	3	24	41	192	1,276	171	908	197
Total area actually reporting	100.0%	277	3	26	42	206	1,367	180	975	212
Rate per 100,000 inhabitants........................		841.4	9.1	79.0	127.6	625.7	4,152.2	546.7	2,961.5	643.9
Fargo, ND-MN M.S.A.	248,368									
Includes Clay County, MN and Cass County, ND........										
City of Fargo, ND........................	126,927	584	7	107	61	409	4,403	1,016	2,922	465
Total area actually reporting	100.0%	871	14	172	82	603	7,027	1,611	4,690	726
Rate per 100,000 inhabitants........................		350.7	5.6	69.3	33.0	242.8	2,829.3	648.6	1,888.3	292.3
Farmington, NM M.S.A.[2]	123,608									
Includes San Juan County										
City of Farmington2........................	44,191	529	1	78	40	410	1,447	295	1,010	142
Total area actually reporting	100.0%	817	4	122	51	640	2,026	447	1,373	206
Rate per 100,000 inhabitants........................		661.0	3.2	98.7	41.3	517.8	1,639.1	361.6	1,110.8	166.7
Fayetteville, NC M.S.A.[2]	531,101									
Includes Cumberland, Harnett,[2] and Hoke Counties										
City of Fayetteville........................	212,033	2,074	30	87	262	1,695	7,210	1,327	5,418	465
Total area actually reporting	89.3%	2,811	44	145	345	2,277	11,555	2,516	8,219	820
Estimated total........................	100.0%	2,938	46	160	360	2,372	12,396	2,752	8,737	907
Rate per 100,000 inhabitants........................		553.2	8.7	30.1	67.8	446.6	2,334.0	518.2	1,645.1	170.8
Flint, MI M.S.A.	402,374									
Includes Genesee County........................										
City of Flint........................	94,842	996	44	67	83	802	1,614	406	1,004	204
Total area actually reporting	100.0%	2,324	75	260	177	1,812	5,823	1,281	3,882	660
Rate per 100,000 inhabitants........................		577.6	18.6	64.6	44.0	450.3	1,447.2	318.4	964.8	164.0
Florence, SC M.S.A.	205,067									
Includes Darlington and Florence Counties.................										
City of Florence........................	38,597	562	12	15	72	463	2,390	322	1,812	256
Total area actually reporting	95.7%	1,708	38	96	174	1,400	7,081	1,335	4,942	804
Estimated total........................	100.0%	1,764	39	100	181	1,444	7,384	1,379	5,177	828
Rate per 100,000 inhabitants........................		860.2	19.0	48.8	88.3	704.2	3,600.8	672.5	2,524.5	403.8
Fond du Lac, WI M.S.A.	103,517									
Includes Fond du Lac County										
City of Fond du Lac........................	43,295	134	1	25	9	99	878	66	776	36
Total area actually reporting	100.0%	181	2	44	10	125	1,187	130	1,003	54
Rate per 100,000 inhabitants........................		174.9	1.9	42.5	9.7	120.8	1,146.7	125.6	968.9	52.2

(Number, percent, rate per 100,000 population.)

Area	Population	Violent crime	Murder and nonnegligent manslaughter	Rape[1]	Robbery	Aggravated assault	Property crime	Burglary	Larceny-theft	Motor vehicle theft
Fort Smith, AR-OK M.S.A.	250,603									
Includes Crawford, Franklin, and Sebastian Counties, AR and Sequoyah County, OK										
City of Fort Smith, AR	88,071	1,031	7	96	106	822	4,871	637	3,716	518
Total area actually reporting	99.1%	1,530	11	188	114	1,217	7,176	1,294	5,166	716
Estimated total	100.0%	1,541	11	190	115	1,225	7,224	1,303	5,199	722
Rate per 100,000 inhabitants		614.9	4.4	75.8	45.9	488.8	2,882.6	519.9	2,074.6	288.1
Fort Wayne, IN M.S.A.	415,629									
Includes Allen and Whitley Counties										
City of Fort Wayne	272,270	1,124	39	97	245	743	6,117	655	4,952	510
Total area actually reporting	94.5%	1,369	41	125	267	936	7,067	800	5,662	605
Estimated total	100.0%	1,392	41	129	269	953	7,266	851	5,782	633
Rate per 100,000 inhabitants		334.9	9.9	31.0	64.7	229.3	1,748.2	204.7	1,391.1	152.3
Fresno, CA M.S.A.	996,752									
Includes Fresno County										
City of Fresno	535,472	3,560	77	148	889	2,446	16,475	3,036	10,789	2,650
Total area actually reporting	100.0%	5,948	94	302	1,169	4,383	24,724	4,955	15,697	4,072
Rate per 100,000 inhabitants		596.7	9.4	30.3	117.3	439.7	2,480.5	497.1	1,574.8	408.5
Gainesville, FL M.S.A.	330,910									
Includes Alachua, Gilchrist, and Levy Counties										
City of Gainesville	135,076	1,042	10	128	209	695	4,297	411	3,400	486
Total area actually reporting	100.0%	2,516	17	271	356	1,872	7,414	1,120	5,513	781
Rate per 100,000 inhabitants		760.3	5.1	81.9	107.6	565.7	2,240.5	338.5	1,666.0	236.0
Gainesville, GA M.S.A.[2]	207,015									
Includes Hall County										
City of Gainesville[2]	44,398	184	0	12	38	134	1,116	140	887	89
Total area actually reporting	100.0%	479	7	58	60	354	2,631	369	2,003	259
Rate per 100,000 inhabitants		231.4	3.4	28.0	29.0	171.0	1,270.9	178.2	967.6	125.1
Glens Falls, NY M.S.A.[2]	123,934									
Includes Warren and Washington Counties										
City of Glens Falls[2]	14,215	10	0	2	0	8	105	7	95	3
Total area actually reporting	98.0%	152	0	94	7	51	898	121	739	38
Estimated total	100.0%	156	0	95	8	53	914	124	751	39
Rate per 100,000 inhabitants		125.9	0.0	76.7	6.5	42.8	737.5	100.1	606.0	31.5
Goldsboro, NC M.S.A.	123,171									
Includes Wayne County										
City of Goldsboro	34,051	397	2	11	46	338	1,709	349	1,272	88
Total area actually reporting	97.7%	585	7	18	65	495	2,959	733	1,941	285
Estimated total	100.0%	593	7	19	65	502	3,094	758	2,045	291
Rate per 100,000 inhabitants		481.4	5.7	15.4	52.8	407.6	2,512.0	615.4	1,660.3	236.3
Grand Forks, ND-MN M.S.A.[2]	100,189									
Includes Polk County, MN2 and Grand Forks County, ND										
City of Grand Forks, ND	56,163	164	4	34	14	112	1,315	210	988	117
Total area actually reporting	100.0%	233	6	47	15	165	1,762	313	1,299	150
Rate per 100,000 inhabitants		232.6	6.0	46.9	15.0	164.7	1,758.7	312.4	1,296.5	149.7
Grand Island, NE M.S.A.	75,484									
Includes Hall, Howard, and Merrick Counties										
City of Grand Island	51,547	216	0	50	17	149	1,258	149	1,015	94
Total area actually reporting	100.0%	257	0	59	17	181	1,383	178	1,091	114
Rate per 100,000 inhabitants		340.5	0.0	78.2	22.5	239.8	1,832.2	235.8	1,445.3	151.0
Grand Junction, CO M.S.A.	154,127									
Includes Mesa County										
City of Grand Junction	64,149	348	3	43	40	262	2,966	385	2,298	283
Total area actually reporting	99.7%	563	3	89	56	415	4,546	749	3,319	478
Estimated total	100.0%	565	3	89	56	417	4,594	751	3,361	482
Rate per 100,000 inhabitants		366.6	1.9	57.7	36.3	270.6	2,980.7	487.3	2,180.7	312.7
Grand Rapids-Kentwood, MI M.S.A.	1,083,395									
Includes Ionia, Kent, Montcalm, and Ottawa Counties										
City of Grand Rapids	202,513	1,443	28	121	192	1,102	3,956	463	2,912	581

Table 4. Crime in the United States, by Selected Metropolitan Statistical Area, 2020—*Continued*

(Number, percent, rate per 100,000 population.)

Area	Population	Violent crime	Murder and nonnegligent manslaughter	Rape[1]	Robbery	Aggravated assault	Property crime	Burglary	Larceny-theft	Motor vehicle theft
City of Kentwood	52,263	229	4	28	26	171	1,207	166	837	204
Total area actually reporting	99.9%	3,789	50	744	380	2,615	13,834	1,780	10,278	1,776
Estimated total	100.0%	3,793	50	745	380	2,618	13,853	1,783	10,293	1,777
Rate per 100,000 inhabitants		350.1	4.6	68.8	35.1	241.6	1,278.7	164.6	950.1	164.0
Grants Pass, OR M.S.A.	87,577									
Includes Josephine County										
City of Grants Pass	38,420	133	0	27	25	81	1,160	131	901	128
Total area actually reporting	100.0%	252	9	40	34	169	1,500	171	1,045	284
Rate per 100,000 inhabitants		287.7	10.3	45.7	38.8	193.0	1,712.8	195.3	1,193.2	324.3
Great Falls, MT M.S.A.	81,529									
Includes Cascade County										
City of Great Falls	58,345	266	0	43	28	195	2,999	293	2,535	171
Total area actually reporting	100.0%	359	0	55	28	276	3,261	355	2,719	187
Rate per 100,000 inhabitants		440.3	0.0	67.5	34.3	338.5	3,999.8	435.4	3,335.0	229.4
Greeley, CO M.S.A.	331,283									
Includes Weld County										
City of Greeley	110,505	470	9	53	78	330	2,722	369	1,961	392
Total area actually reporting	97.3%	1,053	16	174	130	733	6,799	819	4,781	1,199
Estimated total	100.0%	1,074	16	177	134	747	7,165	838	5,076	1,251
Rate per 100,000 inhabitants		324.2	4.8	53.4	40.4	225.5	2,162.8	253.0	1,532.2	377.6
Green Bay, WI M.S.A.	324,478									
Includes Brown, Kewaunee, and Oconto Counties										
City of Green Bay	104,649	552	6	71	45	430	1,600	206	1,279	115
Total area actually reporting	100.0%	730	8	121	52	549	3,216	475	2,554	187
Rate per 100,000 inhabitants		225.0	2.5	37.3	16.0	169.2	991.1	146.4	787.1	57.6
Greensboro-High Point, NC M.S.A.	777,379									
Includes Guilford, Randolph, and Rockingham Counties										
City of Greensboro	299,887	2,704	59	95	581	1,969	10,830	2,212	7,503	1,115
City of High Point	108,114	734	13	27	117	577	3,246	489	2442	315
Total area actually reporting	83.0%	4,124	88	195	790	3,051	18,395	3,617	12,962	1,816
Estimated total	100.0%	4,479	95	230	837	3,317	20,792	4,194	14,558	2,040
Rate per 100,000 inhabitants		576.2	12.2	29.6	107.7	426.7	2,674.6	539.5	1,872.7	262.4
Greenville, NC M.S.A.	182,129									
Includes Pitt County										
City of Greenville	94,372	415	13	26	71	305	2,481	360	2,006	115
Total area actually reporting	99.1%	659	21	33	110	495	3,588	624	2,780	184
Estimated total	100.0%	664	21	34	110	499	3,665	638	2,840	187
Rate per 100,000 inhabitants		364.6	11.5	18.7	60.4	274.0	2,012.3	350.3	1,559.3	102.7
Hanford-Corcoran, CA M.S.A.	151,473									
Includes Kings County										
City of Hanford	58,075	321	5	17	45	254	1,119	155	755	209
City of Corcoran	21,700	112	2	11	12	87	392	82	199	111
Total area actually reporting	100.0%	777	11	63	91	612	2,506	451	1,498	557
Rate per 100,000 inhabitants		513.0	7.3	41.6	60.1	404.0	1,654.4	297.7	989.0	367.7
Harrisonburg, VA M.S.A.	135,962									
Includes Rockingham County and Harrisonburg City										
City of Harrisonburg	53,442	117	1	15	14	87	811	74	688	49
Total area actually reporting	100.0%	207	5	41	16	145	1,335	177	1,065	93
Rate per 100,000 inhabitants		152.2	3.7	30.2	11.8	106.6	981.9	130.2	783.3	68.4
Hartford-East Hartford-Middletown, CT M.S.A.	1,014,700									
Includes Hartford, Middlesex, and Tolland Counties										
City of Hartford	121,749	1,208	23	31	280	874	3,787	430	2,708	649
City of East Hartford	49,720	77	0	12	37	28	1,208	101	886	221
City of Middletown	46,106	38	3	4	7	24	597	62	477	58
Total area actually reporting	100.0%	2,211	37	175	614	1,385	21,196	2,381	16,043	2,772
Rate per 100,000 inhabitants		217.9	3.6	17.2	60.5	136.5	2,088.9	234.7	1,581.1	273.2
Hattiesburg, MS M.S.A.	168,941									
Includes Covington, Forrest, Lamar, and Perry Counties										

(Number, percent, rate per 100,000 population.)

Area	Population	Violent crime	Murder and nonnegligent manslaughter	Rape[1]	Robbery	Aggravated assault	Property crime	Burglary	Larceny-theft	Motor vehicle theft
City of Hattiesburg....................	45,870	171	7	31	27	106	2,418	342	1,904	172
Total area actually reporting	80.6%	306	10	62	41	193	3,377	639	2,480	258
Estimated total........................	100.0%	422	10	102	43	267	3,743	720	2,705	318
Rate per 100,000 inhabitants............		249.8	5.9	60.4	25.5	158.0	2,215.6	426.2	1,601.2	188.2
Hilton Head Island-Bluffton, SC M.S.A.	226,652									
Includes Beaufort and Jasper Counties										
City of Bluffton........................	27,549	25	0	7	2	16	199	38	145	16
Total area actually reporting	91.6%	642	16	60	61	505	3,009	435	2,356	218
Estimated total........................	100.0%	741	22	65	67	587	3,354	516	2,580	258
Rate per 100,000 inhabitants............		326.9	9.7	28.7	29.6	259.0	1,479.8	227.7	1,138.3	113.8
Homosassa Springs, FL M.S.A.	150,189									
Includes Citrus County................										
Total area actually reporting	100.0%	405	7	25	38	335	1,928	334	1,403	191
Rate per 100,000 inhabitants............		269.7	4.7	16.6	25.3	223.1	1,283.7	222.4	934.2	127.2
Hot Springs, AR M.S.A.	99,763									
Includes Garland County................										
City of Hot Springs....................	38,893	287	9	39	43	196	2,276	656	1,431	189
Total area actually reporting	100.0%	582	9	77	53	443	3,575	1,200	2,052	323
Rate per 100,000 inhabitants............		583.4	9.0	77.2	53.1	444.1	3,583.5	1,202.9	2,056.9	323.8
Houston-The Woodlands-Sugar Land, TX M.S.A.[2].	7,180,258									
Includes Austin, Brazoria, Chambers, Fort Bend, Galveston, Harris, Liberty, Montgomery, and Waller Counties										
City of Houston........................	2,346,155	29,474	400	1,137	8,757	19,180	98,043	15,788	67,474	14,781
City of Sugar Land[2]	119,671	68	4	8	20	36	1,277	111	1,077	89
City of Baytown[2]	77,823	338	9	43	85	201	2,917	390	2,106	421
City of Conroe........................	94,451	175	2	35	47	91	2,336	246	1,914	176
City of Galveston[2]	50,751	327	6	80	65	176	1,694	225	1,217	252
Total area actually reporting	99.9%	45,358	662	3,206	12,057	29,433	187,868	28,857	132,143	26,868
Estimated total........................	100.0%	45,368	662	3,208	12,057	29,441	187,935	28,871	132,187	26,877
Rate per 100,000 inhabitants............		631.8	9.2	44.7	167.9	410.0	2,617.4	402.1	1,841.0	374.3
Huntington-Ashland, WV-KY-OH M.S.A.	353,926									
Includes Boyd, Carter, and Greenup Counties, KY; Lawrence County OH; and Cabell, Putnam, and Wayne Counties, WV										
City of Huntington, WV	44,684	368	7	35	69	257	1,642	378	1,083	181
City of Ashland, KY	19,979	41	1	7	7	26	642	105	490	47
Total area actually reporting	87.3%	719	12	153	89	465	4,704	933	3,299	472
Estimated total........................	100.0%	850	14	164	101	571	5,213	1,015	3,697	501
Rate per 100,000 inhabitants............		240.2	4.0	46.3	28.5	161.3	1,472.9	286.8	1,044.6	141.6
Idaho Falls, ID M.S.A.	154,789									
Includes Bonneville, Butte, and Jefferson Counties										
City of Idaho Falls	63,457	291	2	35	18	236	1,152	325	704	123
Total area actually reporting	100.0%	439	4	57	25	353	1,994	534	1,241	219
Rate per 100,000 inhabitants............		283.6	2.6	36.8	16.2	228.1	1,288.2	345.0	801.7	141.5
Iowa City, IA M.S.A.	175,256									
Includes Johnson and Washington Counties...............										
City of Iowa City......................	75,964	151	2	21	16	112	1,335	261	934	140
Total area actually reporting	99.4%	471	3	80	26	362	2,599	501	1,880	218
Estimated total........................	100.0%	475	3	80	27	365	2,623	506	1,896	221
Rate per 100,000 inhabitants............		271.0	1.7	45.6	15.4	208.3	1,496.7	288.7	1,081.8	126.1
Ithaca, NY M.S.A	101,580									
Includes Tompkins County................										
City of Ithaca........................	30,927	98	0	14	31	53	1,157	141	1,000	16
Total area actually reporting	100.0%	163	0	45	35	83	1,924	224	1,660	40
Rate per 100,000 inhabitants............		160.5	0.0	44.3	34.5	81.7	1,894.1	220.5	1,634.2	39.4
Jackson, MI M.S.A.	157,798									
Includes Jackson County................										
City of Jackson........................	32,332	350	7	47	32	264	1,001	173	722	106
Total area actually reporting	100.0%	881	14	170	44	653	2,641	392	1,984	265
Rate per 100,000 inhabitants............		558.3	8.9	107.7	27.9	413.8	1,673.7	248.4	1,257.3	167.9

Table 4. Crime in the United States, by Selected Metropolitan Statistical Area, 2020—*Continued*

(Number, percent, rate per 100,000 population.)

Area	Population	Violent crime	Murder and nonnegligent manslaughter	Rape[1]	Robbery	Aggravated assault	Property crime	Burglary	Larceny-theft	Motor vehicle theft
Jackson, TN M.S.A.	178,525									
Includes Chester, Crockett, Gibson, and Madison Counties										
City of Jackson	67,234	703	12	21	87	583	2,414	361	1,814	239
Total area actually reporting	100.0%	1,115	17	46	106	946	3,840	701	2,750	389
Rate per 100,000 inhabitants		624.6	9.5	25.8	59.4	529.9	2,151.0	392.7	1,540.4	217.9
Jacksonville, FL M.S.A.	1,580,803									
Includes Baker, Clay, Duval, Nassau, and St. Johns Counties										
City of Jacksonville	920,508	6,424	140	456	928	4,900	26,432	3,860	19,602	2,970
Total area actually reporting	100.0%	7,901	156	641	1,085	6,019	34,037	4,996	25,414	3,627
Rate per 100,000 inhabitants		499.8	9.9	40.5	68.6	380.8	2,153.1	316.0	1,607.7	229.4
Jacksonville, NC M.S.A.	199,234									
Includes Onslow County										
City of Jacksonville	71,842	245	3	24	23	195	1,481	263	1,153	65
Total area actually reporting	100.0%	419	4	40	40	335	3,151	720	2,236	195
Rate per 100,000 inhabitants		210.3	2.0	20.1	20.1	168.1	1,581.6	361.4	1,122.3	97.9
Janesville-Beloit, WI M.S.A.	163,558									
Includes Rock County										
City of Janesville	64,682	145	4	31	36	74	1,392	136	1,200	56
City of Beloit	36,921	179	2	23	34	120	1,069	117	878	74
Total area actually reporting	100.0%	381	6	63	75	237	2,916	324	2,427	165
Rate per 100,000 inhabitants		232.9	3.7	38.5	45.9	144.9	1,782.9	198.1	1,483.9	100.9
Jefferson City, MO M.S.A.[2]	151,302									
Includes Callaway,[2] Cole,[2] Moniteau, and Osage Counties										
City of Jefferson City	42,653	109	2	17	16	74	821	70	658	93
Total area actually reporting	97.8%	238	4	44	19	171	2,367	425	1,702	240
Estimated total	100.0%	251	4	45	20	182	2,465	436	1,775	254
Rate per 100,000 inhabitants		165.9	2.6	29.7	13.2	120.3	1,629.2	288.2	1,173.2	167.9
Johnson City, TN M.S.A.	204,189									
Includes Carter, Unicoi, and Washington Counties										
City of Johnson City	66,917	295	3	29	38	225	2,701	285	2,173	243
Total area actually reporting	100.0%	625	6	56	51	512	4,371	567	3,231	573
Rate per 100,000 inhabitants		306.1	2.9	27.4	25.0	250.7	2,140.7	277.7	1,582.4	280.6
Jonesboro, AR M.S.A.	135,377									
Includes Craighead and Poinsett Counties										
City of Jonesboro	79,702	642	12	78	55	497	2,825	1,038	1,576	211
Total area actually reporting	95.8%	871	13	130	63	665	3,847	1,339	2,193	315
Estimated total	100.0%	893	13	132	67	681	3,964	1,358	2,276	330
Rate per 100,000 inhabitants		659.6	9.6	97.5	49.5	503.0	2,928.1	1,003.1	1,681.2	243.8
Joplin, MO M.S.A.[2]	179,903									
Includes Jasper and Newton2 Counties										
City of Joplin	50,935	338	9	49	67	213	3,276	379	2,528	369
Total area actually reporting	100.0%	655	11	98	91	455	6,354	868	4,761	725
Rate per 100,000 inhabitants		364.1	6.1	54.5	50.6	252.9	3,531.9	482.5	2,646.4	403.0
Kahului-Wailuku-Lahaina, HI M.S.A.	167,178									
Includes Maui County										
Total area actually reporting	100.0%	379	5	71	59	244	3,537	496	2,612	429
Rate per 100,000 inhabitants		226.7	3.0	42.5	35.3	146.0	2,115.7	296.7	1,562.4	256.6
Kalamazoo-Portage, MI M.S.A.	265,804									
Includes Kalamazoo County										
City of Kalamazoo	76,411	1,094	14	77	136	867	3,670	737	2,445	488
City of Portage	49,798	111	2	15	10	84	1,340	153	1,098	89
Total area actually reporting	100.0%	1,763	20	175	199	1,369	8,789	1,571	6,144	1,074
Rate per 100,000 inhabitants		663.3	7.5	65.8	74.9	515.0	3,306.6	591.0	2,311.5	404.1
Kankakee, IL M.S.A.[4]	108,899									
Includes Kankakee County[4]										
City of Kankakee[4]	25,863	244	8	23	33	180		112		52
Total area actually reporting	75.7%	340	9	50	41	240		203		93

Table 4. Crime in the United States, by Selected Metropolitan Statistical Area, 2020—*Continued*

(Number, percent, rate per 100,000 population.)

Area	Population	Violent crime	Murder and nonnegligent manslaughter	Rape[1]	Robbery	Aggravated assault	Property crime	Burglary	Larceny-theft	Motor vehicle theft
Estimated total........................	100.0%	387	10	57	52	268		250		120
Rate per 100,000 inhabitants...............		355.4	9.2	52.3	47.8	246.1		229.6		110.2
Kennewick-Richland, WA M.S.A.	303,959									
Includes Benton and Franklin Counties................										
City of Kennewick................	85,526	215	1	38	46	130	2,836	521	2,097	218
City of Richland................	59,370	164	3	33	18	110	1,553	267	1,216	70
Total area actually reporting	100.0%	718	9	116	133	460	6,869	1,323	5,010	536
Rate per 100,000 inhabitants...............		236.2	3.0	38.2	43.8	151.3	2,259.8	435.3	1,648.2	176.3
Killeen-Temple, TX M.S.A.[2,3]	464,991									
Includes Bell, Coryell, and Lampasas Counties[2]										
City of Killeen[2,3]................	154,417	1,033	26	87	159	761			1,851	436
City of Temple................	79,878	297	8	64	29	196	2,098	302	1,460	336
Total area actually reporting	99.6%	1,750	48	216	228	1,258			5,641	1,047
Estimated total................	100.0%	1,754	48	216	228	1,262			5,663	1,052
Rate per 100,000 inhabitants...............		377.2	10.3	46.5	49.0	271.4			1,217.9	226.2
Kingsport-Bristol, TN-VA M.S.A.	306,891									
Includes Hawkins and Sullivan Counties, TN and Scott and Washington Counties and Bristol City, VA										
City of Kingsport, TN................	54,260	372	5	40	28	299	2,426	271	1,856	299
City of Bristol, TN................	27,013	155	3	19	10	123	774	73	617	84
Total area actually reporting	100.0%	1,116	20	144	59	893	6,466	919	4,679	868
Rate per 100,000 inhabitants...............		363.6	6.5	46.9	19.2	291.0	2,106.9	299.5	1,524.6	282.8
Kingston, NY M.S.A.	175,918									
Includes Ulster County................										
City of Kingston................	22,682	85	3	12	17	53	455	55	378	22
Total area actually reporting	92.0%	224	5	64	25	130	1,550	178	1,303	69
Estimated total................	100.0%	246	5	67	29	145	1,846	208	1,561	77
Rate per 100,000 inhabitants...............		139.8	2.8	38.1	16.5	82.4	1,049.4	118.2	887.3	43.8
Knoxville, TN M.S.A.	875,248									
Includes Anderson, Blount, Campbell, Knox, Loudon, Morgan, Roane, and Union Counties................										
City of Knoxville................	188,672	1,528	38	124	241	1,125	7,977	1,080	5,775	1,122
Total area actually reporting	100.0%	3,343	56	326	328	2,633	17,024	2,674	11,953	2,397
Rate per 100,000 inhabitants...............		381.9	6.4	37.2	37.5	300.8	1,945.0	305.5	1,365.7	273.9
Kokomo, IN M.S.A.[2]	82,444									
Includes Howard County[2]										
City of Kokomo[2]................	58,001	437	8	25	38	366	1,152	225	838	89
Total area actually reporting	98.6%	490	8	28	40	414	1,291	267	921	103
Estimated total................	100.0%	498	8	29	42	419	1,313	276	933	104
Rate per 100,000 inhabitants...............		604.0	9.7	35.2	50.9	508.2	1,592.6	334.8	1,131.7	126.1
La Crosse-Onalaska, WI-MN M.S.A.[2]	136,752									
Includes Houston County, MN2 and La Crosse County, WI										
City of La Crosse, WI................	51,211	131	1	34	26	70	2,236	170	1,958	108
City of Onalaska, WI................	19,072	19	0	1	5	13	715	44	655	16
Total area actually reporting	100.0%	213	1	46	31	135	3,421	293	2,975	153
Rate per 100,000 inhabitants...............		155.8	0.7	33.6	22.7	98.7	2,501.6	214.3	2,175.5	111.9
Lafayette, LA M.S.A.	489,998									
Includes Acadia, Iberia, Lafayette, St. Martin, and Vermilion Parishes................										
City of Lafayette................	126,679	712	14	17	147	534	5,725	1,069	4,247	409
Total area actually reporting	84.7%	1,919	37	75	227	1,580	10,679	2,284	7,553	842
Estimated total................	100.0%	2,205	41	104	276	1,784	12,188	2,523	8,644	1,021
Rate per 100,000 inhabitants...............		450.0	8.4	21.2	56.3	364.1	2,487.4	514.9	1,764.1	208.4
Lake Charles, LA M.S.A.[2]	210,851									
Includes Calcasieu and Cameron Parishes................										
City of Lake Charles[2]................	79,077	409	7	31	49	322	2,511	849	1,424	238
Total area actually reporting	95.2%	1,625	19	123	87	1,396	7,839	2,215	4,924	700
Estimated total................	100.0%	1,663	19	127	94	1,423	8,041	2,247	5,070	724
Rate per 100,000 inhabitants...............		788.7	9.0	60.2	44.6	674.9	3,813.6	1,065.7	2,404.5	343.4

Table 4. Crime in the United States, by Selected Metropolitan Statistical Area, 2020—*Continued*

(Number, percent, rate per 100,000 population.)

Area	Population	Violent crime	Murder and nonnegligent manslaughter	Rape[1]	Robbery	Aggravated assault	Property crime	Burglary	Larceny-theft	Motor vehicle theft
Lake Havasu City-Kingman, AZ M.S.A.[2]...........	214,625									
Includes Mohave County..........										
City of Lake Havasu City[2]	56,243	105	0	27	3	75	790	115	619	56
City of Kingman..........	31,351	124	2	9	17	96	1,106	136	868	102
Total area actually reporting..........	100.0%	490	14	50	47	379	4,643	889	3,324	430
Rate per 100,000 inhabitants..........		228.3	6.5	23.3	21.9	176.6	2,163.3	414.2	1,548.7	200.3
Lakeland-Winter Haven, FL M.S.A.	737,548									
Includes Polk County..........										
City of Lakeland..........	113,876	404	12	58	80	254	2,813	320	2,275	218
City of Winter Haven	46,275	171	4	19	12	136	920	125	724	71
Total area actually reporting	100.0%	2,115	40	171	209	1,695	10,002	1,576	7,471	955
Rate per 100,000 inhabitants..........		286.8	5.4	23.2	28.3	229.8	1,356.1	213.7	1,013.0	129.5
Lansing-East Lansing, MI M.S.A.	550,296									
Includes Clinton, Eaton, Ingham, and Shiawassee Counties										
City of Lansing..........	118,651	1,699	16	121	195	1,367	3,565	1,002	1,993	570
City of East Lansing..........	48,098	74	0	17	13	44	817	86	568	163
Total area actually reporting	100.0%	2,741	23	385	259	2,074	9,020	1,795	6,111	1,114
Rate per 100,000 inhabitants..........		498.1	4.2	70.0	47.1	376.9	1,639.1	326.2	1,110.5	202.4
Laredo, TX M.S.A.[2]	278,663									
Includes Webb County[2]										
City of Laredo..........	265,515	859	12	90	156	601	3,836	626	2,994	216
Total area actually reporting	98.3%	924	12	95	158	659	4,093	705	3,146	242
Estimated total..........	100.0%	936	12	96	159	669	4,175	719	3,207	249
Rate per 100,000 inhabitants..........		335.9	4.3	34.5	57.1	240.1	1,498.2	258.0	1,150.9	89.4
Las Vegas-Henderson-Paradise, NV M.S.A.[2]	2,313,970									
Includes Clark County..........										
City of Las Vegas Metropolitan Police Department[2]	1,693,061	8,934	96	1,068	1,707	6,063	37,426	7,057	23,546	6,823
City of Henderson[2]..........	328,056	682	13	104	177	388	4,679	619	3,516	544
Total area actually reporting	100.0%	11,077	127	1,264	2,322	7,364	47,356	8,683	30,109	8,564
Rate per 100,000 inhabitants..........		478.7	5.5	54.6	100.3	318.2	2,046.5	375.2	1,301.2	370.1
Lawton, OK M.S.A.	125,862									
Includes Comanche and Cotton Counties										
City of Lawton..........	92,507	727	14	79	102	532	2,071	632	1,166	273
Total area actually reporting	100.0%	759	16	85	106	552	2,343	723	1,305	315
Rate per 100,000 inhabitants..........		603.0	12.7	67.5	84.2	438.6	1,861.6	574.4	1,036.8	250.3
Lewiston, ID-WA M.S.A.	63,436									
Includes Nez Perce County, ID and Asotin County, WA										
City of Lewiston, ID..........	32,886	61	1	15	4	41	767	135	582	50
Total area actually reporting	100.0%	117	3	27	7	80	1,307	254	968	85
Rate per 100,000 inhabitants..........		184.4	4.7	42.6	11.0	126.1	2,060.3	400.4	1,525.9	134.0
Lewiston-Auburn, ME M.S.A.[2]	108,661									
Includes Androscoggin County[2]										
City of Lewiston..........	36,186	97	2	26	16	53	639	81	519	39
City of Auburn..........	23,455	46	2	18	6	20	518	41	455	22
Total area actually reporting	100.0%	193	4	61	23	105	1,449	169	1,204	76
Rate per 100,000 inhabitants..........		177.6	3.7	56.1	21.2	96.6	1,333.5	155.5	1,108.0	69.9
Lexington-Fayette, KY M.S.A.	521,623									
Includes Bourbon, Clark, Fayette, Jessamine, Scott, and Woodford Counties..........										
City of Lexington	325,851	1,043	28	178	335	502	9,357	1,450	6,870	1,037
Total area actually reporting	100.0%	1,308	31	236	391	650	13,357	2,072	9,824	1,461
Rate per 100,000 inhabitants..........		250.8	5.9	45.2	75.0	124.6	2,560.7	397.2	1,883.4	280.1
Little Rock-North Little Rock-Conway, AR M.S.A...	747,089									
Includes Faulkner, Grant, Lonoke, Perry, Pulaski, and Saline Counties..........										
City of Little Rock..........	197,688	3,657	49	196	376	3,036	9,602	1,527	7,062	1,013
City of North Little Rock..........	66,303	665	20	12	110	523	2,433	366	1,750	317
City of Conway..........	68,599	359	3	45	29	282	1,915	159	1,628	128
Total area actually reporting	100.0%	7,014	98	504	664	5,748	23,746	4,039	17,116	2,591
Rate per 100,000 inhabitants..........		938.8	13.1	67.5	88.9	769.4	3,178.5	540.6	2,291.0	346.8

(Number, percent, rate per 100,000 population.)

Area	Population	Violent crime	Murder and nonnegligent manslaughter	Rape[1]	Robbery	Aggravated assault	Property crime	Burglary	Larceny-theft	Motor vehicle theft
Logan, UT-ID M.S.A.[2]	143,828									
Includes Franklin County, ID and Cache County, UT2										
City of Logan, UT	51,899	100	0	41	6	53	592	82	472	38
Total area actually reporting	91.4%	156	1	73	6	76	993	134	756	103
Estimated total	100.0%	170	1	78	7	84	1,148	158	871	119
Rate per 100,000 inhabitants		118.2	0.7	54.2	4.9	58.4	798.2	109.9	605.6	82.7
Longview, TX M.S.A.[2]	286,379									
Includes Gregg, Harrison, Rusk, and Upshur2 Counties										
City of Longview	81,751	276	10	62	47	157	2,362	461	1,729	172
Total area actually reporting	99.7%	891	23	142	97	629	5,916	1,258	4,062	596
Estimated total	100.0%	893	23	142	97	631	5,930	1,261	4,071	598
Rate per 100,000 inhabitants		311.8	8.0	49.6	33.9	220.3	2,070.7	440.3	1,421.5	208.8
Longview, WA M.S.A.	111,183									
Includes Cowlitz County										
City of Longview	38,629	99	0	25	20	54	1,196	214	846	136
Total area actually reporting	100.0%	208	2	60	26	120	2,224	436	1,527	261
Rate per 100,000 inhabitants		187.1	1.8	54.0	23.4	107.9	2,000.3	392.1	1,373.4	234.7
Los Angeles-Long Beach-Anaheim, CA M.S.A.	13,124,616									
Includes the Metropolitan Divisions of Anaheim-Santa Ana-Irvine and Los Angeles-Long Beach-Glendale										
City of Los Angeles	4,000,587	28,882	351	1,983	8,013	18,535	85,932	13,773	50,990	21,169
City of Long Beach	462,654	2,343	36	242	721	1,344	12,707	2,554	7,373	2,780
City of Anaheim	351,913	1,241	16	133	412	680	8,865	1,229	5,897	1,739
City of Santa Ana	333,107	1,429	15	145	401	868	6,926	1,136	4,078	1,712
City of Irvine	297,069	152	1	36	49	66	4,452	828	3,336	288
City of Glendale	200,168	206	3	14	87	102	3,197	407	2,357	433
City of Torrance	143,421	274	3	44	105	122	2,935	378	2,060	497
City of Pasadena	141,473	414	7	51	118	238	3,021	654	2,015	352
City of Orange	138,846	180	4	14	54	108	2,396	504	1,468	424
City of Costa Mesa	113,317	488	2	64	116	306	3,581	513	2,699	369
City of Burbank	102,419	174	1	12	48	113	2,474	293	1,880	301
City of Carson	91,372	392	8	21	98	265	2,044	253	1,262	529
City of Santa Monica	90,474	541	1	38	167	335	3,852	931	2,530	391
City of Newport Beach	84,448	141	1	29	43	68	1,785	321	1,312	152
City of Tustin	79,795	148	0	13	76	59	2,131	283	1,586	262
City of Gardena	59,385	269	5	18	104	142	1,324	168	686	470
City of Arcadia	58,122	87	2	6	20	59	1,034	265	696	73
City of Fountain Valley	55,345	67	0	6	23	38	1,338	199	998	141
Total area actually reporting	100.0%	62,030	737	4,538	17,385	39,370	274,976	46,244	169,909	58,823
Rate per 100,000 inhabitants		472.6	5.6	34.6	132.5	300.0	2,095.1	352.3	1,294.6	448.2
Anaheim-Santa Ana-Irvine, CA M.D.	3,162,050									
Includes Orange County										
Total area actually reporting	100.0%	7,340	59	777	2,134	4,370	61,066	9,427	42,599	9,040
Rate per 100,000 inhabitants		232.1	1.9	24.6	67.5	138.2	1,931.2	298.1	1,347.2	285.9
Los Angeles-Long Beach-Glendale, CA M.D.	9,962,566									
Includes Los Angeles County										
Total area actually reporting	100.0%	54,690	678	3,761	15,251	35,000	213,910	36,817	127,310	49,783
Rate per 100,000 inhabitants		549.0	6.8	37.8	153.1	351.3	2,147.1	369.6	1,277.9	499.7
Lubbock, TX M.S.A.[2]	324,679									
Includes Crosby, Lubbock, and Lynn2 Counties										
City of Lubbock	262,146	2,852	28	225	431	2,168	10,770	2,296	7,316	1,158
Total area actually reporting	98.3%	2,973	31	251	442	2,249	11,862	2,564	8,015	1,283
Estimated total	100.0%	2,985	31	252	443	2,259	11,956	2,584	8,075	1,297
Rate per 100,000 inhabitants		919.4	9.5	77.6	136.4	695.8	3,682.4	795.9	2,487.1	399.5
Lynchburg, VA M.S.A.	264,579									
Includes Amherst, Appomattox, Bedford, and Campbell Counties and Lynchburg City										
City of Lynchburg	82,871	367	3	36	51	277	1,350	177	1,047	126
Total area actually reporting	100.0%	646	9	84	64	489	3,103	378	2,446	279
Rate per 100,000 inhabitants		244.2	3.4	31.7	24.2	184.8	1,172.8	142.9	924.5	105.5

Table 4. Crime in the United States, by Selected Metropolitan Statistical Area, 2020—*Continued*

(Number, percent, rate per 100,000 population.)

Area	Population	Violent crime	Murder and nonnegligent manslaughter	Rape[1]	Robbery	Aggravated assault	Property crime	Burglary	Larceny-theft	Motor vehicle theft
Macon-Bibb County, GA M.S.A.[2]	229,395									
Includes Bibb,[2] Crawford,[2] Jones,[2] Monroe, and Twiggs[2] Counties										
Total area actually reporting	87.5%	1,529	42	69	212	1,206	5,863	1,008	4,084	771
Estimated total	100.0%	1,624	44	78	222	1,280	6,299	1,088	4,369	842
Rate per 100,000 inhabitants		707.9	19.2	34.0	96.8	558.0	2,745.9	474.3	1,904.6	367.1
Madera, CA M.S.A.	156,466									
Includes Madera County										
City of Madera	66,351	310	4	35	69	202	1,141	200	691	250
Total area actually reporting	100.0%	578	9	61	105	403	2,132	353	1,329	450
Rate per 100,000 inhabitants		369.4	5.8	39.0	67.1	257.6	1,362.6	225.6	849.4	287.6
Madison, WI M.S.A.	671,149									
Includes Columbia, Dane, Green, and Iowa Counties										
City of Madison	262,736	842	10	74	165	593	7,301	1,307	5,346	648
Total area actually reporting	98.3%	1,310	16	157	228	909	11,885	1,914	8,980	991
Estimated total	100.0%	1,354	17	161	236	940	12,117	1,951	9,148	1,018
Rate per 100,000 inhabitants		201.7	2.5	24.0	35.2	140.1	1,805.4	290.7	1,363.0	151.7
Manchester-Nashua, NH M.S.A.	419,347									
Includes Hillsborough County										
City of Manchester	113,018	670	5	73	110	482	2,560	287	2,096	177
City of Nashua	89,671	107	0	54	12	41	818	54	710	54
Total area actually reporting	98.3%	886	5	173	133	575	4,631	461	3,860	310
Estimated total	100.0%	913	5	177	137	594	4,772	484	3,962	326
Rate per 100,000 inhabitants		217.7	1.2	42.2	32.7	141.6	1,138.0	115.4	944.8	77.7
Manhattan, KS M.S.A.[3]	130,281									
Includes Geary, Pottawatomie,[3] and Riley Counties										
Total area actually reporting	96.3%	478	6	65	20	387			1,573	151
Estimated total	100.0%	490	6	67	21	396			1,658	163
Rate per 100,000 inhabitants		376.1	4.6	51.4	16.1	304.0			1,272.6	125.1
Mankato, MN M.S.A.[2]	102,134									
Includes Blue Earth and Nicollet[2] Counties										
City of Mankato	43,276	108	1	30	11	66	1,033	115	855	63
Total area actually reporting	100.0%	191	1	49	15	126	1,479	196	1,187	96
Rate per 100,000 inhabitants		187.0	1.0	48.0	14.7	123.4	1,448.1	191.9	1,162.2	94.0
McAllen-Edinburg-Mission, TX M.S.A.[2]	876,280									
Includes Hidalgo County[2]										
City of McAllen	144,569	123	3	43	23	54	2,791	139	2,603	49
City of Edinburg	103,491	325	6	79	36	204	2,310	281	1,966	63
City of Mission	85,052	132	1	27	14	90	1,304	133	1,096	75
Total area actually reporting	98.1%	2,363	35	419	271	1,638	15,559	2,055	12,658	846
Estimated total	100.0%	2,408	35	424	276	1,673	15,851	2,104	12,877	870
Rate per 100,000 inhabitants		274.8	4.0	48.4	31.5	190.9	1,808.9	240.1	1,469.5	99.3
Medford, OR M.S.A.	221,880									
Includes Jackson County										
City of Medford	84,016	388	2	36	94	256	3,615	296	3,012	307
Total area actually reporting	100.0%	663	3	67	122	471	6,289	698	5,058	533
Rate per 100,000 inhabitants		298.8	1.4	30.2	55.0	212.3	2,834.4	314.6	2,279.6	240.2
Memphis, TN-MS-AR M.S.A.[2]	1,348,509									
Includes Crittenden County, AR; DeSoto, Marshall, Tate, and Tunica2 Counties, MS; and Fayette, Shelby, and Tipton Counties, TN										
City of Memphis, TN	650,937	15,310	289	411	2,131	12,479	36,197	5,831	25,924	4,442
Total area actually reporting	95.3%	18,195	324	605	2,375	14,891	49,358	7,664	35,783	5,911
Estimated total	100.0%	18,324	327	648	2,384	14,965	50,144	7,822	36,321	6,001
Rate per 100,000 inhabitants		1,358.8	24.2	48.1	176.8	1,109.7	3,718.5	580.0	2,693.4	445.0
Merced, CA M.S.A.	277,305									
Includes Merced County										
City of Merced	84,197	672	7	40	133	492	1,949	390	1,132	427
Total area actually reporting	100.0%	1,660	24	84	252	1,300	5,951	1,285	3,320	1,346
Rate per 100,000 inhabitants		598.6	8.7	30.3	90.9	468.8	2,146.0	463.4	1,197.2	485.4

Table 4. Crime in the United States, by Selected Metropolitan Statistical Area, 2020—*Continued*

(Number, percent, rate per 100,000 population.)

Area	Population	Violent crime	Murder and nonnegligent manslaughter	Rape[1]	Robbery	Aggravated assault	Property crime	Burglary	Larceny-theft	Motor vehicle theft
Miami-Fort Lauderdale-Pompano Beach, FL M.S.A.....................	6,216,543									
Includes the Metropolitan Divisions of Fort Lauderdale-Pompano Beach-Sunrise, Miami-Miami Beach-Kendall, and West Palm Beach-Boca Raton-Boynton Beach										
City of Miami................................	476,102	2,645	61	94	610	1,880	13,092	1,453	10,017	1,622
City of Fort Lauderdale..................	184,347	1,158	37	91	321	709	7,662	1,074	5,681	907
City of Pompano Beach..................	113,545	837	19	62	244	512	3,142	434	2,237	471
City of West Palm Beach................	113,268	863	18	76	231	538	3,862	452	2,967	443
City of Boca Raton........................	101,583	206	2	35	67	102	1,996	191	1,573	232
City of Sunrise..............................	96,428	195	3	21	60	111	1,324	96	1,031	197
City of Miami Beach......................	89,017	668	5	62	200	401	5,109	444	4,244	421
City of Deerfield Beach	81,749	285	3	20	59	203	1,603	135	1,273	195
City of Boynton Beach...................	79,913	523	9	20	105	389	1,794	153	1,468	173
City of Delray Beach.....................	70,487	401	5	31	67	298	2,412	245	1,929	238
City of Jupiter..............................	67,054	83	1	10	13	59	701	99	552	50
City of Doral...............................	68,425	63	0	9	8	46	1,238	103	986	149
City of Palm Beach Gardens	58,629	65	1	8	14	42	999	86	871	42
City of Coral Gables......................	50,017	51	0	7	13	31	1,167	127	959	81
Total area actually reporting	99.4%	25,744	463	1,909	5,499	17,873	135,122	13,941	106,055	15,126
Estimated total............................	100.0%	25,920	465	1,921	5,529	18,005	136,292	14,095	106,985	15,212
Rate per 100,000 inhabitants.........		417.0	7.5	30.9	88.9	289.6	2,192.4	226.7	1,721.0	244.7
Fort Lauderdale-Pompano Beach-Deerfield Beach, FL M.D.	1,970,496									
Includes Broward County...............										
Total area actually reporting.........	100.0%	7,058	150	596	1,716	4,596	40,341	4,385	30,940	5,016
Rate per 100,000 inhabitants		358.2	7.6	30.2	87.1	233.2	2,047.3	222.5	1,570.2	254.6
Miami-Miami Beach-Kendall, FL M.D.	2,733,199									
Includes Miami-Dade County...........										
Total area actually reporting.........	98.6%	13,125	224	776	2,687	9,438	66,623	6,400	52,888	7,335
Estimated total...........................	100.0%	13,301	226	788	2,717	9,570	67,793	6,554	53,818	7,421
Rate per 100,000 inhabitants.........		486.6	8.3	28.8	99.4	350.1	2,480.4	239.8	1,969.0	271.5
West Palm Beach-Boca Raton-Boynton Beach, FL M.D.	1,512,848									
Includes Palm Beach County...........										
Total area actually reporting.........	100.0%	5,561	89	537	1,096	3,839	28,158	3,156	22,227	2,775
Rate per 100,000 inhabitants.........		367.6	5.9	35.5	72.4	253.8	1,861.3	208.6	1,469.2	183.4
Midland, MI M.S.A.	82,820									
Includes Midland County										
City of Midland............................	41,526	62	0	18	1	43	328	40	282	6
Total area actually reporting	100.0%	120	1	43	1	75	580	93	461	26
Rate per 100,000 inhabitants.........		144.9	1.2	51.9	1.2	90.6	700.3	112.3	556.6	31.4
Midland, TX M.S.A.	187,186									
Includes Martin and Midland Counties................										
City of Midland............................	150,529	549	10	81	50	408	3,119	404	2,249	466
Total area actually reporting	100.0%	700	13	92	55	540	4,058	532	2,838	688
Rate per 100,000 inhabitants.........		374.0	6.9	49.1	29.4	288.5	2,167.9	284.2	1,516.1	367.5
Milwaukee-Waukesha, WI M.S.A.[2]	1,575,891									
Includes Milwaukee, Ozaukee, Washington, and Waukesha[2] Counties....................										
City of Milwaukee.........................	589,105	9,407	191	431	1,925	6,860	16,074	3,408	8,178	4,488
City of Waukesha..........................	72,421	123	1	17	21	84	595	62	477	56
Total area actually reporting	99.5%	10,678	206	629	2,218	7,625	30,716	4,532	20,659	5,525
Estimated total............................	100.0%	10,688	206	631	2,219	7,632	30,821	4,540	20,751	5,530
Rate per 100,000 inhabitants.........		678.2	13.1	40.0	140.8	484.3	1,955.8	288.1	1,316.8	350.9
Missoula, MT M.S.A.	121,047									
Includes Missoula County...............										
City of Missoula...........................	76,468	376	4	60	32	280	2,745	273	2,285	187
Total area actually reporting	100.0%	489	6	77	33	373	3,080	374	2,492	214
Rate per 100,000 inhabitants.........		404.0	5.0	63.6	27.3	308.1	2,544.5	309.0	2,058.7	176.8

(Number, percent, rate per 100,000 population.)

Area	Population	Violent crime	Murder and nonnegligent manslaughter	Rape[1]	Robbery	Aggravated assault	Property crime	Burglary	Larceny-theft	Motor vehicle theft
Modesto, CA M.S.A....................	549,195									
Includes Stanislaus County......................										
City of Modesto................................	216,560	1,603	16	106	281	1,200	5,340	706	3,533	1,101
Total area actually reporting...............	100.0%	2,823	33	185	587	2,018	10,843	1,825	6,927	2,091
Rate per 100,000 inhabitants...............		514.0	6.0	33.7	106.9	367.4	1,974.3	332.3	1,261.3	380.7
Monroe, LA M.S.A.......................	199,081									
Includes Morehouse, Ouachita, and Union Parishes.....										
City of Monroe	47,119	1,399	19	9	154	1,217	2,883	649	2,042	192
Total area actually reporting...............	91.4%	2,540	22	107	221	2,190	6,930	1,611	4,799	520
Estimated total................................	100.0%	2,605	23	113	233	2,236	7,275	1,665	5,049	561
Rate per 100,000 inhabitants...............		1,308.5	11.6	56.8	117.0	1,123.2	3,654.3	836.3	2,536.2	281.8
Morristown, TN M.S.A....................	143,413									
Includes Grainger, Hamblen, and Jefferson Counties ...										
City of Morristown............................	30,330	258	1	12	22	223	1,290	177	998	115
Total area actually reporting...............	100.0%	519	2	39	30	448	2,686	473	1,900	313
Rate per 100,000 inhabitants...............		361.9	1.4	27.2	20.9	312.4	1,872.9	329.8	1,324.8	218.3
Mount Vernon-Anacortes, WA M.S.A....................	130,213									
Includes Skagit County......................										
City of Mount Vernon	36,513	70	1	9	13	47	1,109	142	857	110
City of Anacortes.............................	17,735	15	0	2	7	6	398	43	327	28
Total area actually reporting...............	100.0%	192	2	20	36	134	3,153	467	2,436	250
Rate per 100,000 inhabitants...............		147.5	1.5	15.4	27.6	102.9	2,421.4	358.6	1,870.8	192.0
Muskegon, MI M.S.A.	173,165									
Includes Muskegon County......................										
City of Muskegon	36,391	254	5	8	20	221	1,004	174	740	90
Total area actually reporting...............	100.0%	714	10	97	58	549	3,581	486	2,841	254
Rate per 100,000 inhabitants...............		412.3	5.8	56.0	33.5	317.0	2,068.0	280.7	1,640.6	146.7
Napa, CA M.S.A.	136,475									
Includes Napa County......................										
City of Napa	78,237	267	0	44	36	187	1,320	272	883	165
Total area actually reporting...............	100.0%	539	1	65	59	414	2,306	522	1,511	273
Rate per 100,000 inhabitants...............		394.9	0.7	47.6	43.2	303.4	1,689.7	382.5	1,107.2	200.0
Naples-Marco Island, FL M.S.A....................	391,365									
Includes Collier County......................										
City of Naples	22,388	21	1	4	1	15	276	26	223	27
City of Marco Island...........................	18,121	15	0	3	1	11	103	13	75	15
Total area actually reporting...............	100.0%	876	6	68	122	680	3,806	416	3,039	351
Rate per 100,000 inhabitants...............		223.8	1.5	17.4	31.2	173.8	972.5	106.3	776.5	89.7
Nashville-Davidson–Murfreesboro–Franklin, TN M.S.A....................	1,969,367									
Includes Cannon, Cheatham, Davidson, Dickson, Macon, Maury, Robertson, Rutherford, Smith, Sumner, Trousdale, Williamson, and Wilson Counties										
City of Metropolitan Nashville Police Department........	688,013	7,951	113	385	1,742	5,711	28,023	3,745	21,238	3,040
City of Murfreesboro..........................	151,769	740	11	91	101	537	3,772	362	3,113	297
City of Franklin	85,722	195	1	17	14	163	792	58	685	49
Total area actually reporting...............	100.0%	12,137	152	757	2,097	9,131	46,329	6,307	35,206	4,816
Rate per 100,000 inhabitants...............		616.3	7.7	38.4	106.5	463.7	2,352.5	320.3	1,787.7	244.5
New Bern, NC M.S.A.	123,955									
Includes Craven, Jones, and Pamlico Counties............										
City of New Bern	30,047	190	4	11	21	154	930	199	701	30
Total area actually reporting...............	89.0%	421	11	32	39	339	2,366	589	1,640	137
Estimated total................................	100.0%	451	11	35	42	363	2,666	657	1,850	159
Rate per 100,000 inhabitants...............		363.8	8.9	28.2	33.9	292.8	2,150.8	530.0	1,492.5	128.3
New Haven-Milford, CT M.S.A.[2]...................	799,461									
Includes New Haven County......................										
City of New Haven............................	130,299	922	21	29	336	536	4,575	547	3,267	761
City of Milford2	54,968	33	0	3	25	5	1,107	109	884	114
Total area actually reporting...............	100.0%	2,049	49	164	745	1,091	17,342	1,843	12,726	2,773
Rate per 100,000 inhabitants...............		256.3	6.1	20.5	93.2	136.5	2,169.2	230.5	1,591.8	346.9

(Number, percent, rate per 100,000 population.)

Area	Population	Violent crime	Murder and nonnegligent manslaughter	Rape[1]	Robbery	Aggravated assault	Property crime	Burglary	Larceny-theft	Motor vehicle theft
New Orleans-Metairie, LA M.S.A.[2]	1,275,017									
Includes Jefferson, Orleans, Plaquemines, St. Bernard, St. Charles,[2] St. James, St. John the Baptist, and St. Tammany Parishes										
City of New Orleans	393,779	5,215	201	712	1,106	3,196	17,876	1,994	12,358	3,524
Total area actually reporting	95.3%	7,698	272	899	1,464	5,063	33,569	3,915	25,120	4,534
Estimated total	100.0%	7,960	277	924	1,504	5,255	35,121	4,145	26,290	4,686
Rate per 100,000 inhabitants		624.3	21.7	72.5	118.0	412.2	2,754.6	325.1	2,061.9	367.5
Niles, MI M.S.A.	152,517									
Includes Berrien County										
City of Niles	11,102	74	0	16	11	47	328	42	225	61
Total area actually reporting	100.0%	1,013	8	130	58	817	2,882	566	2,030	286
Rate per 100,000 inhabitants		664.2	5.2	85.2	38.0	535.7	1,889.6	371.1	1,331.0	187.5
North Port-Sarasota-Bradenton, FL M.S.A.	850,904									
Includes Manatee and Sarasota Counties										
City of North Port	72,389	117	3	27	6	81	743	88	634	21
City of Sarasota	59,002	349	1	32	59	257	1,622	227	1,271	124
City of Bradenton	60,688	306	4	25	46	231	1,322	108	1,115	99
City of Venice	24,366	16	0	2	5	9	346	56	274	16
Total area actually reporting	100.0%	2,854	22	321	373	2,138	12,831	1,711	10,194	926
Rate per 100,000 inhabitants		335.4	2.6	37.7	43.8	251.3	1,507.9	201.1	1,198.0	108.8
Norwich-New London, CT M.S.A.	173,802									
Includes New London County										
City of Norwich	38,576	134	3	14	28	89	542	114	350	78
City of New London	26,776	67	0	7	24	36	500	79	333	88
Total area actually reporting	100.0%	313	4	42	66	201	2,210	302	1,635	273
Rate per 100,000 inhabitants		180.1	2.3	24.2	38.0	115.6	1,271.6	173.8	940.7	157.1
Ocala, FL M.S.A.	368,501									
Includes Marion County										
City of Ocala	61,275	413	3	55	61	294	1,936	161	1,663	112
Total area actually reporting	100.0%	1,557	19	184	136	1,218	6,012	1,141	4,289	582
Rate per 100,000 inhabitants		422.5	5.2	49.9	36.9	330.5	1,631.5	309.6	1,163.9	157.9
Ocean City, NJ M.S.A.	91,384									
Includes Cape May County										
City of Ocean City	10,893	8	0	1	2	5	334	39	287	8
Total area actually reporting	100.0%	154	0	19	25	110	1,856	237	1,559	60
Rate per 100,000 inhabitants		168.5	0.0	20.8	27.4	120.4	2,031.0	259.3	1,706.0	65.7
Odessa, TX M.S.A.[2]	169,268									
Includes Ector County										
City of Odessa[2]	126,288	1,020	13	107	106	794	3,163	586	2,113	464
Total area actually reporting	100.0%	1,180	19	109	160	892	5,005	859	3,270	876
Rate per 100,000 inhabitants		697.1	11.2	64.4	94.5	527.0	2,956.8	507.5	1,931.8	517.5
Ogden-Clearfield, UT M.S.A.[2]	692,112									
Includes Box Elder,[2] Davis, Morgan, and Weber Counties										
City of Ogden	88,309	446	4	79	75	288	2,915	375	2,151	389
City of Clearfield	32,358	69	1	13	10	45	525	60	413	52
Total area actually reporting	100.0%	1,197	14	354	140	689	11,454	1,580	8,686	1,188
Rate per 100,000 inhabitants		172.9	2.0	51.1	20.2	99.6	1,654.9	228.3	1,255.0	171.6
Oklahoma City, OK M.S.A.[2]	1,427,075									
Includes Canadian, Cleveland, Grady, Lincoln, Logan, McClain, and Oklahoma Counties										
City of Oklahoma City[2]	663,661	4,818	63	559	817	3,379	25,853	5,849	16,222	3,782
Total area actually reporting	100.0%	6,719	111	842	1,032	4,734	41,616	8,847	27,156	5,613
Rate per 100,000 inhabitants		470.8	7.8	59.0	72.3	331.7	2,916.2	619.9	1,902.9	393.3
Olympia-Lacey-Tumwater, WA M.S.A.	294,061									
Includes Thurston County										
City of Olympia	53,571	268	1	24	69	174	1,753	271	1,284	198
City of Lacey	53,826	83	0	13	21	49	1,386	160	1,099	127
City of Tumwater	24,493	63	0	10	13	40	613	94	453	66

Table 4. Crime in the United States, by Selected Metropolitan Statistical Area, 2020—*Continued*

(Number, percent, rate per 100,000 population.)

Area	Population	Violent crime	Murder and nonnegligent manslaughter	Rape[1]	Robbery	Aggravated assault	Property crime	Burglary	Larceny-theft	Motor vehicle theft
Total area actually reporting	100.0%	657	3	73	127	454	5,636	990	4,029	617
Rate per 100,000 inhabitants		223.4	1.0	24.8	43.2	154.4	1,916.6	336.7	1,370.1	209.8
Omaha-Council Bluffs, NE-IA M.S.A.	954,892									
Includes Harrison, Mills, and Pottawattamie Counties, IA and Cass, Douglas, Sarpy, Saunders, and Washington Counties, NE										
City of Omaha, NE	480,297	3,032	37	351	464	2,180	15,247	1,521	10,697	3,029
City of Council Bluffs, IA	62,144	574	0	36	68	470	2,976	408	2,127	441
Total area actually reporting	99.6%	4,093	44	526	570	2,953	21,718	2,423	15,293	4,002
Estimated total	100.0%	4,103	44	527	574	2,958	21,780	2,431	15,337	4,012
Rate per 100,000 inhabitants		429.7	4.6	55.2	60.1	309.8	2,280.9	254.6	1,606.2	420.2
Orlando-Kissimmee-Sanford, FL M.S.A.	2,658,987									
Includes Lake, Orange, Osceola, and Seminole Counties										
City of Orlando	293,363	2,524	31	169	507	1,817	11,158	1,198	8,812	1,148
City of Kissimmee	74,337	318	4	29	32	253	1,707	206	1,359	142
City of Sanford	62,342	511	3	38	84	386	1,396	210	1,084	102
Total area actually reporting	100.0%	11,347	158	1,118	1,919	8,152	49,514	7,138	37,606	4,770
Rate per 100,000 inhabitants		426.7	5.9	42.0	72.2	306.6	1,862.1	268.4	1,414.3	179.4
Oshkosh-Neenah, WI M.S.A.	172,301									
Includes Winnebago County										
City of Oshkosh	67,080	187	4	48	12	123	1,239	138	1,036	65
City of Neenah	26,390	57	1	12	5	39	315	21	282	12
Total area actually reporting	98.6%	322	6	75	21	220	2,233	360	1,772	101
Estimated total	100.0%	332	6	76	23	227	2,283	368	1,808	107
Rate per 100,000 inhabitants		192.7	3.5	44.1	13.3	131.7	1,325.0	213.6	1,049.3	62.1
Owensboro, KY M.S.A.	119,839									
Includes Daviess, Hancock, and McLean Counties										
City of Owensboro	60,430	161	5	41	45	70	2,326	404	1,638	284
Total area actually reporting	100.0%	197	6	53	51	87	2,793	539	1,903	351
Rate per 100,000 inhabitants		164.4	5.0	44.2	42.6	72.6	2,330.6	449.8	1,588.0	292.9
Oxnard-Thousand Oaks-Ventura, CA M.S.A.	839,861									
Includes Ventura County										
City of Oxnard	210,064	743	8	81	274	380	4,323	638	2,907	778
City of Thousand Oaks	126,823	76	1	21	23	31	1,315	189	1,027	99
City of Ventura	109,295	328	2	31	94	201	3,086	460	2,354	272
City of Camarillo	70,424	53	0	16	17	20	817	100	661	56
Total area actually reporting	100.0%	1,686	20	224	494	948	13,083	1,909	9,616	1,558
Rate per 100,000 inhabitants		200.7	2.4	26.7	58.8	112.9	1,557.8	227.3	1,145.0	185.5
Palm Bay-Melbourne-Titusville, FL M.S.A.	606,953									
Includes Brevard County										
City of Palm Bay	116,897	328	3	59	39	227	1,770	241	1,380	149
City of Melbourne	83,806	757	8	74	86	589	2,531	393	1,987	151
City of Titusville	46,919	295	5	24	51	215	1,081	199	764	118
Total area actually reporting	100.0%	2,288	30	225	298	1,735	10,662	1,629	8,161	872
Rate per 100,000 inhabitants		377.0	4.9	37.1	49.1	285.9	1,756.6	268.4	1,344.6	143.7
Panama City, FL M.S.A.	174,857									
Includes Bay County										
City of Panama City	34,672	303	4	38	29	232	1,453	252	1,059	142
Total area actually reporting	99.4%	843	11	93	67	672	4,603	771	3,451	381
Estimated total	100.0%	847	11	93	68	675	4,626	775	3,467	384
Rate per 100,000 inhabitants		484.4	6.3	53.2	38.9	386.0	2,645.6	443.2	1,982.8	219.6
Parkersburg-Vienna, WV M.S.A.	88,918									
Includes Wirt and Wood Counties										
City of Parkersburg	29,096	106	2	29	23	52	1,269	265	911	93
City of Vienna	10,049	9	0	1	1	7	348	10	331	7
Total area actually reporting	100.0%	257	2	56	25	174	2,013	380	1,476	157
Rate per 100,000 inhabitants		289.0	2.2	63.0	28.1	195.7	2,263.9	427.4	1,660.0	176.6
Pensacola-Ferry Pass-Brent, FL M.S.A.	507,320									
Includes Escambia and Santa Rosa Counties										
City of Pensacola	53,083	327	5	26	52	244	1,543	191	1,272	80

(Number, percent, rate per 100,000 population.)

Area	Population	Violent crime	Murder and nonnegligent manslaughter	Rape[1]	Robbery	Aggravated assault	Property crime	Burglary	Larceny-theft	Motor vehicle theft
Total area actually reporting	100.0%	2,180	38	271	395	1,476	9,849	1,911	7,084	854
Rate per 100,000 inhabitants		429.7	7.5	53.4	77.9	290.9	1,941.4	376.7	1,396.4	168.3
Peoria, IL M.S.A.[4]	396,798									
Includes Fulton,[4] Marshall,[4] Peoria,[4] Stark,[4] Tazewell,[4] and Woodford Counties										
City of Peoria[4]	109,924	1,084	14	72	196	802		652		430
Total area actually reporting	91.7%	1,633	22	191	227	1,193		1,380		685
Estimated total	100.0%	1,689	23	200	237	1,229		1,439		719
Rate per 100,000 inhabitants		425.7	5.8	50.4	59.7	309.7		362.7		181.2
Phoenix-Mesa-Chandler, AZ M.S.A.[2]	5,064,185									
Includes Maricopa and Pinal Counties										
City of Phoenix	1,708,960	13,646	187	1,068	3,278	9,113	51,089	7,406	36,254	7,429
City of Mesa[2]	527,361	1,960	19	235	380	1,326	9,737	1,597	7,124	1,016
City of Chandler	264,071	543	9	123	104	307	4,898	505	3,956	437
City of Scottsdale	263,006	470	7	109	97	257	4,945	683	3,963	299
City of Tempe	199,935	1,100	8	155	248	689	7,124	960	5,464	700
City of Casa Grande[2]	59,822	338	1	23	38	276	1,200	150	947	103
Total area actually reporting	90.5%	22,455	288	2,145	4,722	15,300	107,047	15,453	79,187	12,407
Estimated total	100.0%	23,512	314	2,250	4,749	16,199	112,293	16,684	82,568	13,041
Rate per 100,000 inhabitants		464.3	6.2	44.4	93.8	319.9	2,217.4	329.5	1,630.4	257.5
Pine Bluff, AR M.S.A	86,540									
Includes Cleveland, Jefferson, and Lincoln Counties										
City of Pine Bluff	40,718	746	23	27	59	637	1,990	414	1,323	253
Total area actually reporting	100.0%	950	24	55	70	801	2,638	578	1,710	350
Rate per 100,000 inhabitants		1,097.8	27.7	63.6	80.9	925.6	3,048.3	667.9	1,976.0	404.4
Pittsfield, MA M.S.A.	123,599									
Includes Berkshire County										
City of Pittsfield	41,865	341	1	35	34	271	664	232	369	63
Total area actually reporting	91.7%	509	1	56	49	403	1,350	369	884	97
Estimated total	100.0%	533	1	60	53	419	1,401	380	919	102
Rate per 100,000 inhabitants		431.2	0.8	48.5	42.9	339.0	1,133.5	307.4	743.5	82.5
Pocatello, ID M.S.A.	96,729									
Includes Bannock and Power Counties										
City of Pocatello	56,900	206	0	12	11	183	1,223	291	822	110
Total area actually reporting	100.0%	260	0	14	11	235	1,747	349	1,233	165
Rate per 100,000 inhabitants		268.8	0.0	14.5	11.4	242.9	1,806.1	360.8	1,274.7	170.6
Portland-South Portland, ME M.S.A.[2]	542,906									
Includes Cumberland, Sagadahoc, and York Counties[2]										
City of Portland	66,229	129	0	28	34	67	1,143	94	991	58
City of South Portland	25,593	32	1	4	10	17	402	24	346	32
Total area actually reporting	100.0%	516	1	163	80	272	5,524	582	4,641	301
Rate per 100,000 inhabitants		95.0	0.2	30.0	14.7	50.1	1,017.5	107.2	854.8	55.4
Portland-Vancouver-Hillsboro, OR-WA M.S.A.[3]	2,511,480									
Includes Clackamas, Columbia, Multnomah,[3] Washington, and Yamhill Counties, OR and Clark and Skamania Counties, WA										
City of Portland, OR	662,941	3,465	53	262	807	2,343	31,416	3,759	21,287	6,370
City of Vancouver, WA	186,440	884	5	137	167	575	6,709	1,065	4,448	1,196
City of Hillsboro, OR	111,146	257	2	55	46	154	2,147	212	1,695	240
City of Beaverton, OR	100,085	235	1	38	47	149	2,197	255	1,693	249
City of Tigard, OR	56,377	107	1	14	24	68	1,472	161	1,170	141
Total area actually reporting	99.5%			1,029	1,505	5,104	67,067	8,584	46,657	11,826
Estimated total	100.0%			1,032	1,507	5,116	67,267	8,607	46,815	11,845
Rate per 100,000 inhabitants				41.1	60.0	203.7	2,678.4	342.7	1,864.0	471.6
Port St. Lucie, FL M.S.A.	495,563									
Includes Martin and St. Lucie Counties										
City of Port St. Lucie	206,450	264	5	35	40	184	1,666	189	1,381	96
Total area actually reporting	100.0%	1,170	23	170	167	810	5,459	679	4,362	418
Rate per 100,000 inhabitants		236.1	4.6	34.3	33.7	163.5	1,101.6	137.0	880.2	84.3

Table 4. Crime in the United States, by Selected Metropolitan Statistical Area, 2020—*Continued*

(Number, percent, rate per 100,000 population.)

Area	Population	Violent crime	Murder and nonnegligent manslaughter	Rape[1]	Robbery	Aggravated assault	Property crime	Burglary	Larceny-theft	Motor vehicle theft
Prescott Valley-Prescott, AZ M.S.A.	239,151									
Includes Yavapai County										
City of Prescott Valley	47,459	80	0	21	10	49	374	39	317	18
City of Prescott	44,835	168	0	31	3	134	657	129	494	34
Total area actually reporting	100.0%	581	8	72	24	477	2,910	490	2,195	225
Rate per 100,000 inhabitants		242.9	3.3	30.1	10.0	199.5	1,216.8	204.9	917.8	94.1
Providence-Warwick, RI-MA M.S.A.	1,621,159									
Includes Bristol County, MA and Bristol, Kent, Newport, Providence, and Washington Counties, RI										
City of Providence, RI	179,603	873	17	66	183	607	4,337	602	3,191	544
City of Warwick, RI	80,605	66	0	21	7	38	993	92	823	78
Total area actually reporting	99.5%	4,620	41	644	610	3,325	18,780	2,756	13,972	2,052
Estimated total	100.0%	4,630	41	645	611	3,333	18,808	2,760	13,995	2,053
Rate per 100,000 inhabitants		285.6	2.5	39.8	37.7	205.6	1,160.2	170.2	863.3	126.6
Pueblo, CO M.S.A.[5]	168,374									
Includes Pueblo County[5]										
City of Pueblo	113,002	1,181	16	199	198	768	5,233	896	3,399	938
Total area actually reporting	100.0%	1,216	18	199	208	791		1,112		1,078
Rate per 100,000 inhabitants		722.2	10.7	118.2	123.5	469.8		660.4		640.2
Punta Gorda, FL M.S.A.	191,879									
Includes Charlotte County										
City of Punta Gorda	20,766	14	0	0	2	12	272	14	241	17
Total area actually reporting	100.0%	292	1	32	21	238	1,651	221	1,302	128
Rate per 100,000 inhabitants		152.2	0.5	16.7	10.9	124.0	860.4	115.2	678.6	66.7
Racine, WI M.S.A.[2]	196,239									
Includes Racine County[2]										
City of Racine	76,573	414	2	36	86	290	1,381	321	916	144
Total area actually reporting	100.0%	540	3	54	101	382	2,437	444	1,788	205
Rate per 100,000 inhabitants		275.2	1.5	27.5	51.5	194.7	1,241.9	226.3	911.1	104.5
Raleigh-Cary, NC M.S.A.	1,422,373									
Includes Franklin, Johnston, and Wake Counties										
City of Raleigh	480,964	1,886	21	165	467	1,233	9,716	1,298	7,060	1,358
City of Cary	172,079	115	1	13	25	76	1,627	194	1,323	110
Total area actually reporting	99.3%	3,144	47	276	668	2,153	21,023	3,118	15,791	2,114
Estimated total	100.0%	3,180	47	280	673	2,180	21,397	3,194	16,068	2,135
Rate per 100,000 inhabitants		223.6	3.3	19.7	47.3	153.3	1,504.3	224.6	1,129.7	150.1
Rapid City, SD M.S.A.	143,884									
Includes Meade and Pennington Counties										
City of Rapid City	78,492	673	13	108	104	448	3,137	657	2,014	466
Total area actually reporting	100.0%	957	15	211	115	616	4,275	887	2,804	584
Rate per 100,000 inhabitants		665.1	10.4	146.6	79.9	428.1	2,971.1	616.5	1,948.8	405.9
Redding, CA M.S.A.	178,587									
Includes Shasta County										
City of Redding	92,895	513	5	67	94	347	2,323	596	1,529	198
Total area actually reporting	100.0%	977	12	99	126	740	3,430	936	2,028	466
Rate per 100,000 inhabitants		547.1	6.7	55.4	70.6	414.4	1,920.6	524.1	1,135.6	260.9
Reno, NV M.S.A.[2]	483,469									
Includes Storey and Washoe Counties										
City of Reno[2]	259,168	1,460	17	281	286	876	5,564	1,105	3,486	973
Total area actually reporting	100.0%	2,238	27	415	374	1,422	8,842	1,787	5,637	1,418
Rate per 100,000 inhabitants		462.9	5.6	85.8	77.4	294.1	1,828.9	369.6	1,165.9	293.3
Richmond, VA M.S.A.	1,303,052									
Includes Amelia, Charles City, Chesterfield, Dinwiddie, Goochland, Hanover, Henrico, King and Queen, King William, New Kent, Powhatan, Prince George, and Sussex Counties and Colonial Heights, Hopewell, Petersburg, and Richmond Cities										
City of Richmond	233,350	814	66	20	274	454	6,816	771	5,434	611
Total area actually reporting	100.0%	2,811	129	268	605	1,809	23,905	2,229	19,789	1,887
Rate per 100,000 inhabitants		215.7	9.9	20.6	46.4	138.8	1,834.5	171.1	1,518.7	144.8

(Number, percent, rate per 100,000 population.)

Area	Population	Violent crime	Murder and nonnegligent manslaughter	Rape[1]	Robbery	Aggravated assault	Property crime	Burglary	Larceny-theft	Motor vehicle theft
Riverside-San Bernardino-Ontario, CA M.S.A.	4,651,426									
Includes Riverside and San Bernardino Counties										
City of Riverside	334,370	1,491	20	152	394	925	9,980	1,639	6,456	1,885
City of San Bernardino	216,365	3,033	68	134	730	2,101	6,059	1,201	3,149	1,709
City of Ontario	187,464	686	10	83	195	398	3,994	641	2,296	1,057
City of Corona	171,848	240	1	36	86	117	3,610	677	2,160	773
City of Temecula	116,442	148	0	12	67	69	2,262	368	1,537	357
City of Chino	96,309	335	3	31	77	224	2,075	274	1,493	308
City of Redlands	71,820	238	6	51	69	112	1,865	323	1,289	253
City of Palm Desert	53,811	125	0	5	28	92	1,564	278	1,105	181
Total area actually reporting	100.0%	20,054	335	1,296	4,281	14,142	92,307	17,140	54,945	20,222
Rate per 100,000 inhabitants		431.1	7.2	27.9	92.0	304.0	1,984.5	368.5	1,181.3	434.7
Roanoke, VA M.S.A.	313,488									
Includes Botetourt, Craig, Franklin, and Roanoke Counties and Roanoke and Salem Cities										
City of Roanoke	99,335	448	15	38	90	305	3,809	412	3,048	349
Total area actually reporting	100.0%	821	25	79	130	587	6,607	656	5,357	594
Rate per 100,000 inhabitants		261.9	8.0	25.2	41.5	187.2	2,107.6	209.3	1,708.8	189.5
Rochester, MN M.S.A.[2]	222,817									
Includes Dodge,[2] Fillmore,[2] Olmsted, and Wabasha Counties										
City of Rochester	120,336	300	5	74	44	177	2,314	332	1,828	154
Total area actually reporting	98.7%	414	6	110	47	251	2,984	522	2,248	214
Estimated total	100.0%	418	6	111	47	254	3,041	528	2,296	217
Rate per 100,000 inhabitants		187.6	2.7	49.8	21.1	114.0	1,364.8	237.0	1,030.4	97.4
Rochester, NY M.S.A.[2]	1,061,736									
Includes Livingston, Monroe,[2] Ontario, Orleans, Wayne, and Yates Counties										
City of Rochester	205,199	1,680	48	86	418	1,128	6,887	1,389	4,583	915
Total area actually reporting	94.0%	2,644	54	374	562	1,654	16,302	2,594	12,284	1,424
Estimated total	100.0%	2,782	54	388	587	1,753	17,338	2,725	13,135	1,478
Rate per 100,000 inhabitants		262.0	5.1	36.5	55.3	165.1	1,633.0	256.7	1,237.1	139.2
Rockford, IL M.S.A.[4]	332,940									
Includes Boone and Winnebago4 Counties										
City of Rockford	144,795	2,101	30	102	238	1,731	4,104	742	2,968	394
Total area actually reporting	84.0%	2,432	34	180	280	1,938		1,000		510
Estimated total	100.0%	2,566	36	199	297	2,034		1,132		578
Rate per 100,000 inhabitants		770.7	10.8	59.8	89.2	610.9		340.0		173.6
Sacramento-Roseville-Folsom, CA M.S.A.	2,364,420									
Includes El Dorado, Placer, Sacramento, and Yolo Counties										
City of Sacramento	519,050	3,547	42	125	879	2,501	14,248	2,834	8,903	2,511
City of Roseville	144,128	277	4	18	87	168	2,843	318	2,245	280
City of Folsom	82,427	83	0	13	21	49	1,198	223	911	64
City of Rancho Cordova	76,292	322	6	13	73	230	1,555	302	1,107	146
City of West Sacramento	54,068	211	3	22	82	104	1,505	209	1,083	213
Total area actually reporting	100.0%	8,945	113	639	2,069	6,124	47,650	8,796	32,420	6,434
Rate per 100,000 inhabitants		378.3	4.8	27.0	87.5	259.0	2,015.3	372.0	1,371.2	272.1
Saginaw, MI M.S.A.	188,889									
Includes Saginaw County										
City of Saginaw	47,767	1,029	24	57	62	886	720	225	388	107
Total area actually reporting	100.0%	1,501	33	141	93	1,234	2,410	512	1,671	227
Rate per 100,000 inhabitants		794.6	17.5	74.6	49.2	653.3	1,275.9	271.1	884.6	120.2
Salem, OR M.S.A.	436,715									
Includes Marion and Polk Counties										
City of Salem	176,632	698	2	28	148	520	6,698	678	4,911	1,109
Total area actually reporting	99.0%	1,139	7	74	224	834	12,365	1,341	8,935	2,089
Estimated total	100.0%	1,177	7	104	225	841	12,462	1,349	9,015	2,098
Rate per 100,000 inhabitants		269.5	1.6	23.8	51.5	192.6	2,853.6	308.9	2,064.3	480.4
Salinas, CA M.S.A.	431,704									
Includes Monterey County										
City of Salinas	155,984	866	8	69	233	556	3,481	790	1,779	912

Table 4. Crime in the United States, by Selected Metropolitan Statistical Area, 2020—*Continued*

(Number, percent, rate per 100,000 population.)

Area	Population	Violent crime	Murder and nonnegligent manslaughter	Rape[1]	Robbery	Aggravated assault	Property crime	Burglary	Larceny-theft	Motor vehicle theft
Total area actually reporting............................	100.0%	1,480	14	175	342	949	7,728	1,463	4,736	1,529
Rate per 100,000 inhabitants............................		342.8	3.2	40.5	79.2	219.8	1,790.1	338.9	1,097.0	354.2
Salt Lake City, UT M.S.A.[2]................................	1,246,234									
Includes Salt Lake and Tooele[2] Counties....................										
City of Salt Lake City................................	202,187	1,865	17	277	487	1,084	14,865	1,545	11,128	2,192
Total area actually reporting............................	99.9%	4,784	60	835	961	2,928	47,548	5,350	35,415	6,783
Estimated total..	100.0%	4,785	60	835	961	2,929	47,566	5,352	35,429	6,785
Rate per 100,000 inhabitants............................		384.0	4.8	67.0	77.1	235.0	3,816.8	429.5	2,842.9	544.4
San Angelo, TX M.S.A.[2]................................	122,608									
Includes Irion, Sterling, and Tom Green[2] Counties........										
City of San Angelo..	101,860	357	7	65	41	244	3,039	475	2,242	322
Total area actually reporting............................	100.0%	397	8	80	41	268	3,259	542	2,365	352
Rate per 100,000 inhabitants............................		323.8	6.5	65.2	33.4	218.6	2,658.1	442.1	1,928.9	287.1
San Antonio-New Braunfels, TX M.S.A.[2]...............	2,591,157									
Includes Atascosa, Bandera, Bexar,[2] Comal, Guadalupe, Kendall, Medina,[2] and Wilson[2] Counties............										
City of San Antonio[2].....................................	1,573,189	11,569	130	1,187	2,163	8,089	57,057	7,919	42,158	6,980
City of New Braunfels.....................................	78,610	219	6	10	25	178	1,230	206	866	158
Total area actually reporting............................	99.9%	13,741	170	1,555	2,391	9,625	72,724	10,939	53,056	8,729
Estimated total..	100.0%	13,749	170	1,556	2,392	9,631	72,783	10,951	53,095	8,737
Rate per 100,000 inhabitants............................		530.6	6.6	60.1	92.3	371.7	2,808.9	422.6	2,049.1	337.2
San Diego-Chula Vista-Carlsbad, CA M.S.A.............	3,331,816									
Includes San Diego County................................										
City of San Diego..	1,437,608	5,303	56	485	1,207	3,555	24,321	3,324	16,044	4,953
City of Chula Vista.......................................	278,027	916	10	63	302	541	3,257	476	2,021	760
City of Carlsbad..	116,516	224	3	24	35	162	1,841	256	1,428	157
City of Poway..	49,479	53	0	4	16	33	366	84	245	37
Total area actually reporting............................	100.0%	11,517	114	967	2,527	7,909	49,471	7,301	32,863	9,307
Rate per 100,000 inhabitants............................		345.7	3.4	29.0	75.8	237.4	1,484.8	219.1	986.3	279.3
San Francisco-Oakland-Berkeley, CA M.S.A............	4,729,308									
Includes the Metropolitan Divisions of Oakland-Berkeley-Livermore, San Francisco-San Mateo-Redwood City, and San Rafael										
City of San Francisco.....................................	881,514	4,796	48	198	2,388	2,162	38,737	7,452	25,319	5,966
City of Oakland...	437,923	5,653	102	362	2,479	2,710	22,622	2,537	13,373	6,712
City of Berkeley..	122,346	537	6	47	274	210	5,535	797	3,933	805
City of San Mateo..	105,246	274	4	41	71	158	2,306	523	1,493	290
City of Livermore...	91,200	164	1	38	47	78	1,526	164	1,166	196
City of Redwood City.....................................	86,983	187	1	38	58	90	1,489	240	970	279
City of Pleasanton..	83,164	94	1	11	40	42	1,188	161	937	90
City of San Ramon..	76,502	54	0	11	22	21	796	104	636	56
City of Walnut Creek......................................	70,849	91	0	3	27	61	2,063	264	1,582	217
City of South San Francisco...............................	68,260	155	1	15	58	81	1,560	157	1,155	248
City of San Rafael..	58,512	229	0	26	67	136	1,912	260	1,152	500
Total area actually reporting............................	100.0%	20,814	253	1,504	8,440	10,617	142,267	20,761	92,931	28,575
Rate per 100,000 inhabitants............................		440.1	5.3	31.8	178.5	224.5	3,008.2	439.0	1,965.0	604.2
Oakland-Berkeley-Livermore, CA M.D................	2,826,657									
Includes Alameda and Contra Costa Counties.........										
Total area actually reporting............................	100.0%	13,515	187	967	5,307	7,054	81,991	10,295	52,093	19,603
Rate per 100,000 inhabitants............................		478.1	6.6	34.2	187.7	249.6	2,900.6	364.2	1,842.9	693.5
San Francisco-San Mateo-Redwood City, CA M.D.....	1,645,756									
Includes San Francisco and San Mateo Counties......										
Total area actually reporting............................	100.0%	6,676	65	485	3,010	3,116	55,003	9,668	37,150	8,185
Rate per 100,000 inhabitants............................		405.6	3.9	29.5	182.9	189.3	3,342.1	587.5	2,257.3	497.3
San Rafael, CA M.D.................................	256,895									
Includes Marin County....................................										
Total area actually reporting............................	100.0%	623	1	52	123	447	5,273	798	3,688	787
Rate per 100,000 inhabitants............................		242.5	0.4	20.2	47.9	174.0	2,052.6	310.6	1,435.6	306.4
San Jose-Sunnyvale-Santa Clara, CA M.S.A...........	1,987,878									
Includes San Benito and Santa Clara Counties............										
City of San Jose..	1,029,542	4,375	40	566	1,185	2,584	23,847	4,045	12,737	7,065

(Number, percent, rate per 100,000 population.)

Area	Population	Violent crime	Murder and nonnegligent manslaughter	Rape[1]	Robbery	Aggravated assault	Property crime	Burglary	Larceny-theft	Motor vehicle theft
City of Sunnyvale	154,133	229	2	32	61	134	3,178	516	2,276	386
City of Santa Clara	131,976	206	1	39	85	81	3,301	432	2,314	555
City of Mountain View	83,745	144	0	9	52	83	2,177	422	1,566	189
City of Milpitas	86,416	111	2	16	40	53	2,103	277	1,516	310
City of Palo Alto	65,459	81	1	12	39	29	1,931	242	1,570	119
City of Cupertino	59,343	69	0	9	26	34	830	196	581	53
Total area actually reporting	100.0%	6,306	56	826	1,723	3,701	44,263	7,338	26,867	10,058
Rate per 100,000 inhabitants		317.2	2.8	41.6	86.7	186.2	2,226.6	369.1	1,351.5	506.0
San Luis Obispo-Paso Robles, CA M.S.A.	281,778									
Includes San Luis Obispo County										
City of San Luis Obispo	47,722	207	1	39	28	139	1,620	284	1,219	117
City of Paso Robles	32,428	53	3	2	8	40	363	35	295	33
Total area actually reporting	100.0%	816	7	93	79	637	4,610	868	3,381	361
Rate per 100,000 inhabitants		289.6	2.5	33.0	28.0	226.1	1,636.0	308.0	1,199.9	128.1
Santa Cruz-Watsonville, CA M.S.A.	271,608									
Includes Santa Cruz County										
City of Santa Cruz	65,073	309	2	33	76	198	2,237	267	1,734	236
City of Watsonville	54,151	299	4	27	44	224	1,132	167	655	310
Total area actually reporting	100.0%	970	12	104	172	682	6,155	905	4,252	998
Rate per 100,000 inhabitants		357.1	4.4	38.3	63.3	251.1	2,266.1	333.2	1,565.5	367.4
Santa Maria-Santa Barbara, CA M.S.A	444,547									
Includes Santa Barbara County										
City of Santa Maria	108,140	834	2	81	179	572	2,472	328	1,114	1,030
City of Santa Barbara	91,692	389	2	60	84	243	2,188	217	1,748	223
Total area actually reporting	100.0%	1,824	8	227	341	1,248	8,827	1,178	5,812	1,837
Rate per 100,000 inhabitants		410.3	1.8	51.1	76.7	280.7	1,985.6	265.0	1,307.4	413.2
Santa Rosa-Petaluma, CA M.S.A.	490,455									
Includes Sonoma County										
City of Santa Rosa	176,932	913	4	110	135	664	2,838	542	1,875	421
City of Petaluma	60,806	255	2	25	33	195	756	90	597	69
Total area actually reporting	100.0%	2,212	10	239	266	1,697	6,412	1,272	4,408	732
Rate per 100,000 inhabitants		451.0	2.0	48.7	54.2	346.0	1,307.4	259.4	898.8	149.2
Seattle-Tacoma-Bellevue, WA M.S.A.	4,030,255									
Includes the Metropolitan Divisions of Seattle-Bellevue-Kent and Tacoma-Lakewood										
City of Seattle	771,517	4,832	52	301	1,471	3,008	37,593	10,427	22,255	4,911
City of Tacoma	220,123	1,856	28	127	435	1,266	12,123	1,987	7,967	2,169
City of Bellevue	150,548	175	4	19	68	84	4,526	597	3,641	288
City of Kent	133,883	470	8	78	184	200	5,393	1,054	3,378	961
City of Everett	112,439	379	4	37	98	240	3,654	515	2,436	703
City of Renton	102,856	348	6	37	108	197	4,342	498	3,063	781
City of Auburn	82,779	362	10	40	121	191	3,394	584	2,150	660
City of Redmond	74,154	74	0	12	19	43	1,742	207	1,443	92
City of Lakewood	61,432	381	4	32	72	273	2,620	445	1,721	454
Total area actually reporting	100.0%	13,692	181	1,253	3,767	8,491	127,233	24,849	83,956	18,428
Rate per 100,000 inhabitants		339.7	4.5	31.1	93.5	210.7	3,156.9	616.6	2,083.1	457.2
Seattle-Bellevue-Kent, WA M.D.	3,115,239									
Includes King and Snohomish Counties										
Total area actually reporting	100.0%	9,720	128	943	2,934	5,715	97,577	19,512	64,595	13,470
Rate per 100,000 inhabitants		312.0	4.1	30.3	94.2	183.5	3,132.2	626.3	2,073.5	432.4
Tacoma-Lakewood, WA M.D.	915,016									
Includes Pierce County										
Total area actually reporting	100.0%	3,972	53	310	833	2,776	29,656	5,337	19,361	4,958
Rate per 100,000 inhabitants		434.1	5.8	33.9	91.0	303.4	3,241.0	583.3	2,115.9	541.8
Sebastian-Vero Beach, FL M.S.A.	162,048									
Includes Indian River County										
City of Sebastian	26,626	21	0	4	3	14	155	12	132	11
City of Vero Beach	17,776	34	0	1	6	27	250	37	190	23
Total area actually reporting	100.0%	219	3	14	28	174	1,880	187	1,513	180
Rate per 100,000 inhabitants		135.1	1.9	8.6	17.3	107.4	1,160.2	115.4	933.7	111.1
Sebring-Avon Park, FL M.S.A.	106,784									
Includes Highlands County										

Table 4. Crime in the United States, by Selected Metropolitan Statistical Area, 2020—*Continued*

(Number, percent, rate per 100,000 population.)

Area	Population	Violent crime	Murder and nonnegligent manslaughter	Rape[1]	Robbery	Aggravated assault	Property crime	Burglary	Larceny-theft	Motor vehicle theft
City of Sebring........................	10,664	79	3	8	15	53	389	69	302	18
Total area actually reporting	100.0%	296	8	29	39	220	1,889	333	1,405	151
Rate per 100,000 inhabitants...............		277.2	7.5	27.2	36.5	206.0	1,769.0	311.8	1,315.7	141.4
Sheboygan, WI M.S.A.[2]...............	115,218									
Includes Sheboygan County[2]										
City of Sheboygan	47,814	157	1	33	15	108	832	97	702	33
Total area actually reporting	100.0%	209	1	55	15	138	1,364	134	1,169	61
Rate per 100,000 inhabitants...............		181.4	0.9	47.7	13.0	119.8	1,183.8	116.3	1,014.6	52.9
Sherman-Denison, TX M.S.A.[2].............	137,545									
Includes Grayson County[2]										
City of Sherman[2].....................	44,611	197	6	34	24	133	1,095	222	769	104
City of Denison[2]......................	25,858	113	1	23	9	80	484	124	276	84
Total area actually reporting	98.4%	388	9	74	40	265	2,027	445	1,331	251
Estimated total........................	100.0%	392	9	74	40	269	2,064	453	1,355	256
Rate per 100,000 inhabitants...............		285.0	6.5	53.8	29.1	195.6	1,500.6	329.3	985.1	186.1
Shreveport-Bossier City, LA M.S.A.[2].............	392,827									
Includes Bossier, Caddo, and De Soto Parishes............										
City of Shreveport.....................	185,588	1,713	69	125	235	1,284	8,907	1,516	6,690	701
City of Bossier City[2]..................	68,869	609	8	52	77	472	3,201	400	2,472	329
Total area actually reporting	99.5%	2,675	85	196	336	2,058	14,056	2,363	10,505	1,188
Estimated total........................	100.0%	2,683	85	196	338	2,064	14,095	2,369	10,533	1,193
Rate per 100,000 inhabitants...............		683.0	21.6	49.9	86.0	525.4	3,588.1	603.1	2,681.3	303.7
Sierra Vista-Douglas, AZ M.S.A..............	125,923									
Includes Cochise County										
City of Sierra Vista	42,800	82	1	4	12	65	888	85	764	39
City of Douglas........................	16,044	17	0	1	1	15	395	67	311	17
Total area actually reporting	91.0%	190	8	8	20	154	1,876	340	1,403	133
Estimated total........................	100.0%	310	8	15	33	254	2,598	479	1,925	194
Rate per 100,000 inhabitants...............		246.2	6.4	11.9	26.2	201.7	2,063.2	380.4	1,528.7	154.1
Sioux City, IA-NE-SD M.S.A..............	144,522									
Includes Woodbury County, IA; Dakota and Dixon Counties, NE; and Union County, SD.........										
City of Sioux City, IA..................	82,628	477	9	61	75	332	2,682	479	1,933	270
Total area actually reporting	94.8%	595	9	72	79	435	3,245	552	2,357	336
Estimated total........................	100.0%	619	9	76	79	455	3,326	569	2,409	348
Rate per 100,000 inhabitants...............		428.3	6.2	52.6	54.7	314.8	2,301.4	393.7	1,666.9	240.8
Sioux Falls, SD M.S.A..............	273,001									
Includes Lincoln, McCook, Minnehaha, and Turner Counties										
City of Sioux Falls.....................	187,370	1,120	13	97	102	908	5,867	684	4,259	924
Total area actually reporting	99.3%	1,297	15	124	107	1,051	6,856	1,075	4,745	1,036
Estimated total........................	100.0%	1,304	15	124	109	1,056	6,891	1,080	4,771	1,040
Rate per 100,000 inhabitants...............		477.7	5.5	45.4	39.9	386.8	2,524.2	395.6	1,747.6	381.0
South Bend-Mishawaka, IN-MI M.S.A.[2].............	323,697									
Includes St. Joseph County, IN and Cass County, MI....										
City of South Bend, IN	102,119	1,765	28	78	238	1,421	3,741	659	2,511	571
City of Mishawaka, IN[2].................	50,610	80	0	15	6	59	1,207	131	935	141
Total area actually reporting	87.1%	2,031	29	132	266	1,604	6,675	1,221	4,527	927
Estimated total........................	100.0%	2,121	30	149	274	1,668	7,031	1,302	4,773	956
Rate per 100,000 inhabitants...............		655.2	9.3	46.0	84.6	515.3	2,172.1	402.2	1,474.5	295.3
Spartanburg, SC M.S.A..............	324,314									
Includes Spartanburg and Union Counties............										
City of Spartanburg	37,469	536	4	29	94	409	2,286	434	1,595	257
Total area actually reporting	99.8%	1,642	9	90	173	1,370	7,919	1,700	5,275	944
Estimated total........................	100.0%	1,643	9	90	173	1,371	7,935	1,703	5,286	946
Rate per 100,000 inhabitants...............		506.6	2.8	27.8	53.3	422.7	2,446.7	525.1	1,629.9	291.7
Spokane-Spokane Valley, WA M.S.A..............	572,842									
Includes Spokane and Stevens Counties............										
City of Spokane.....................	223,524	1,341	19	187	280	855	11,514	1,745	8,666	1,103
City of Spokane Valley.................	102,366	342	3	28	77	234	4,370	691	3,339	340
Total area actually reporting	100.0%	2,005	30	282	393	1,300	19,927	3,277	14,863	1,787
Rate per 100,000 inhabitants...............		350.0	5.2	49.2	68.6	226.9	3,478.6	572.1	2,594.6	312.0

(Number, percent, rate per 100,000 population.)

Area	Population	Violent crime	Murder and nonnegligent manslaughter	Rape[1]	Robbery	Aggravated assault	Property crime	Burglary	Larceny-theft	Motor vehicle theft
Springfield, IL M.S.A.[4]	205,389									
Includes Menard and Sangamon[4] Counties										
City of Springfield[4]	113,912	1,078	11	101	195	771		937		254
Total area actually reporting	94.1%	1,357	12	133	215	997		1,223		357
Estimated total	100.0%	1,369	12	134	215	1,008		1,257		366
Rate per 100,000 inhabitants		666.5	5.8	65.2	104.7	490.8		612.0		178.2
Springfield, MA M.S.A.	693,972									
Includes Franklin, Hampden and Hampshire Counties										
City of Springfield	153,084	1,480	18	70	350	1,042	3,730	618	2,616	496
Total area actually reporting	97.5%	3,163	28	272	536	2,327	10,694	1,671	7,988	1,035
Estimated total	100.0%	3,216	28	280	546	2,362	10,788	1,695	8,050	1,043
Rate per 100,000 inhabitants		463.4	4.0	40.3	78.7	340.4	1,554.5	244.2	1,160.0	150.3
Springfield, MO M.S.A.[2]	473,913									
Includes Christian, Dallas, Greene, Polk, and Webster Counties										
City of Springfield[2]	168,856	2,545	22	178	375	1,970	11,738	1,795	8,639	1,304
Total area actually reporting	97.9%	2,943	26	230	398	2,289	15,370	2,496	11,237	1,637
Estimated total	100.0%	2,993	26	232	405	2,330	15,647	2,533	11,433	1,681
Rate per 100,000 inhabitants		631.6	5.5	49.0	85.5	491.7	3,301.7	534.5	2,412.5	354.7
Springfield, OH M.S.A.	133,456									
Includes Clark County										
City of Springfield	58,696	338	8	52	107	171	3,014	619	2,060	335
Total area actually reporting	94.1%	391	9	57	110	215	3,741	767	2,611	363
Estimated total	100.0%	401	9	59	112	221	3,872	784	2,719	369
Rate per 100,000 inhabitants		300.5	6.7	44.2	83.9	165.6	2,901.3	587.5	2,037.4	276.5
Staunton, VA M.S.A.	123,568									
Includes Augusta County and Staunton and Waynesboro Cities										
City of Staunton	25,048	45	2	10	6	27	549	54	469	26
Total area actually reporting	100.0%	231	4	63	15	149	1,812	256	1,438	118
Rate per 100,000 inhabitants		186.9	3.2	51.0	12.1	120.6	1,466.4	207.2	1,163.7	95.5
St. George, UT M.S.A.	182,066									
Includes Washington County										
City of St. George	91,673	148	3	42	10	93	1,025	148	772	105
Total area actually reporting	98.4%	290	5	73	13	199	2,038	268	1,583	187
Estimated total	100.0%	294	5	74	13	202	2,118	273	1,652	193
Rate per 100,000 inhabitants		161.5	2.7	40.6	7.1	110.9	1,163.3	149.9	907.4	106.0
St. Joseph, MO-KS M.S.A.	124,927									
Includes Doniphan County, KS and Andrew, Buchanan, and DeKalb Counties, MO										
City of St. Joseph, MO	74,680	414	3	122	47	242	3,843	576	2,711	556
Total area actually reporting	99.4%	518	4	143	48	323	4,407	695	3,052	660
Estimated total	100.0%	521	4	143	48	326	4,424	698	3,063	663
Rate per 100,000 inhabitants		417.0	3.2	114.5	38.4	261.0	3,541.3	558.7	2,451.8	530.7
St. Louis, MO-IL M.S.A.[2,4]	2,802,055									
Includes Bond, Calhoun, Clinton,[4] Jersey,[4] Macoupin,[4] Madison,[4] Monroe,[4] and St. Clair Counties, IL and Franklin, Jefferson,[2] Lincoln,[2] St. Charles,[2] St. Louis,[2] and Warren Counties and St. Louis City, MO										
City of St. Louis, MO	298,422	6,017	263	234	1,242	4,278	17,399	2,552	11,626	3,221
City of St. Charles, MO	71,563	192	3	19	27	143	1,368	145	1,022	201
Total area actually reporting	95.2%	13,647	399	937	2,183	10,128		8,827		10,171
Estimated total	100.0%	13,925	402	974	2,218	10,331		9,130		10,327
Rate per 100,000 inhabitants		497.0	14.3	34.8	79.2	368.7		325.8		368.6
Stockton, CA M.S.A.	763,250									
Includes San Joaquin County										
City of Stockton	314,981	4,023	56	189	909	2,869	9,391	1,533	6,362	1,496
Total area actually reporting	100.0%	5,517	84	264	1,281	3,888	17,805	2,817	12,091	2,897
Rate per 100,000 inhabitants		722.8	11.0	34.6	167.8	509.4	2,332.8	369.1	1,584.1	379.6
Sumter, SC M.S.A.	140,399									
Includes Clarendon and Sumter Counties										

Table 4. Crime in the United States, by Selected Metropolitan Statistical Area, 2020—*Continued*

(Number, percent, rate per 100,000 population.)

Area	Population	Violent crime	Murder and nonnegligent manslaughter	Rape[1]	Robbery	Aggravated assault	Property crime	Burglary	Larceny-theft	Motor vehicle theft
City of Sumter	39,542	491	10	9	45	427	1,459	211	1,179	69
Total area actually reporting	99.4%	1,138	28	49	88	973	3,831	738	2,809	284
Estimated total	100.0%	1,140	28	49	89	974	3,852	742	2,824	286
Rate per 100,000 inhabitants		812.0	19.9	34.9	63.4	693.7	2,743.6	528.5	2,011.4	203.7
Syracuse, NY M.S.A.	642,895									
Includes Madison, Onondaga, and Oswego Counties										
City of Syracuse	142,011	1,192	32	96	222	842	4,009	1,032	2,463	514
Total area actually reporting	100.0%	1,953	35	297	315	1,306	10,985	1,874	8,039	1,072
Rate per 100,000 inhabitants		303.8	5.4	46.2	49.0	203.1	1,708.7	291.5	1,250.4	166.7
Tallahassee, FL M.S.A.	388,159									
Includes Gadsden, Jefferson, Leon, and Wakulla Counties										
City of Tallahassee	196,012	1,516	24	196	238	1,058	5,786	1,067	4,159	560
Total area actually reporting	97.8%	2,119	35	253	280	1,551	8,391	1,684	5,889	818
Estimated total	100.0%	2,157	35	256	285	1,581	8,643	1,728	6,075	840
Rate per 100,000 inhabitants		555.7	9.0	66.0	73.4	407.3	2,226.7	445.2	1,565.1	216.4
Tampa-St. Petersburg-Clearwater, FL M.S.A.	3,234,443									
Includes Hernando, Hillsborough, Pasco, and Pinellas Counties										
City of Tampa	407,350	2,119	41	101	325	1,652	5,561	925	3,993	643
City of St. Petersburg	267,690	1,772	15	110	275	1,372	6,841	887	5,315	639
City of Clearwater	117,859	460	0	92	87	281	2,232	249	1,850	133
City of Largo	85,594	332	4	38	60	230	1,810	154	1,505	151
City of Pinellas Park	54,114	187	0	32	47	108	1,788	185	1,484	119
Total area actually reporting	100.0%	10,159	130	1,076	1,525	7,428	44,114	5,914	34,203	3,997
Rate per 100,000 inhabitants		314.1	4.0	33.3	47.1	229.7	1,363.9	182.8	1,057.5	123.6
The Villages, FL M.S.A.	137,110									
Includes Sumter County										
Total area actually reporting	100.0%	279	3	22	20	234	967	191	666	110
Rate per 100,000 inhabitants		203.5	2.2	16.0	14.6	170.7	705.3	139.3	485.7	80.2
Toledo, OH M.S.A.	639,977									
Includes Fulton, Lucas, Ottawa, and Wood Counties										
City of Toledo	271,237	2,729	53	213	493	1,970	7,849	1,777	5,064	1,008
Total area actually reporting	92.0%	3,052	56	296	542	2,158	12,195	2,219	8,783	1,193
Estimated total	100.0%	3,108	56	306	552	2,194	12,956	2,337	9,383	1,236
Rate per 100,000 inhabitants		485.6	8.8	47.8	86.3	342.8	2,024.4	365.2	1,466.1	193.1
Trenton-Princeton, NJ M.S.A.	367,006									
Includes Mercer County										
City of Trenton	82,909	969	40	50	262	617	1,733	412	1,038	283
City of Princeton	31,458	11	0	0	3	8	196	19	161	16
Total area actually reporting	100.0%	1,316	41	101	343	831	4,910	846	3,587	477
Rate per 100,000 inhabitants		358.6	11.2	27.5	93.5	226.4	1,337.9	230.5	977.4	130.0
Tucson, AZ M.S.A.[2]	1,060,180									
Includes Pima County[2]										
City of Tucson	550,448	3,843	61	463	978	2,341	19,931	2,097	15,956	1,878
Total area actually reporting	100.0%	5,020	86	545	1,169	3,220	29,948	3,407	24,023	2,518
Rate per 100,000 inhabitants		473.5	8.1	51.4	110.3	303.7	2,824.8	321.4	2,265.9	237.5
Tulsa, OK M.S.A.[2]	1,005,482									
Includes Creek, Okmulgee, Osage, Pawnee, Rogers,[2] Tulsa, and Wagoner Counties										
City of Tulsa	402,166	4,555	72	378	741	3,364	20,557	4,407	12,246	3,904
Total area actually reporting	100.0%	5,947	94	565	873	4,415	31,267	6,704	19,185	5,378
Rate per 100,000 inhabitants		591.5	9.3	56.2	86.8	439.1	3,109.7	666.7	1,908.0	534.9
Twin Falls, ID M.S.A.[3]	113,458									
Includes Jerome and Twin Falls[3] Counties										
City of Twin Falls	50,872	259	2	36	7	214	892	100	754	38
Total area actually reporting	100.0%	435	3	71	11	350			994	90
Rate per 100,000 inhabitants		383.4	2.6	62.6	9.7	308.5			876.1	79.3
Tyler, TX M.S.A.	234,573									
Includes Smith County										
City of Tyler	108,139	472	6	53	69	344	3,296	523	2,563	210

Table 4. Crime in the United States, by Selected Metropolitan Statistical Area, 2020—*Continued*

(Number, percent, rate per 100,000 population.)

Area	Population	Violent crime	Murder and nonnegligent manslaughter	Rape[1]	Robbery	Aggravated assault	Property crime	Burglary	Larceny-theft	Motor vehicle theft
Total area actually reporting	100.0%	869	18	104	94	653	5,092	994	3,632	466
Rate per 100,000 inhabitants		370.5	7.7	44.3	40.1	278.4	2,170.8	423.7	1,548.3	198.7
Utica-Rome, NY M.S.A.[2]	287,148									
Includes Herkimer and Oneida Counties										
City of Utica[2]	59,483	298	1	23	70	204	2,017	267	1,636	114
City of Rome[2]	31,978	65	0	8	7	50	570	70	457	43
Total area actually reporting	95.0%	625	4	138	95	388	4,594	598	3,768	228
Estimated total	100.0%	644	4	142	99	399	4,684	615	3,837	232
Rate per 100,000 inhabitants		224.3	1.4	49.5	34.5	139.0	1,631.2	214.2	1,336.2	80.8
Valdosta, GA M.S.A.[2]	147,899									
Includes Brooks,[2] Echols, Lanier,[2] and Lowndes[2] Counties										
City of Valdosta[2]	56,628	220	6	13	43	158	1,848	222	1,530	96
Total area actually reporting	96.2%	433	8	57	62	306	3,201	477	2,475	249
Estimated total	100.0%	472	9	60	68	335	3,380	503	2,608	269
Rate per 100,000 inhabitants		319.1	6.1	40.6	46.0	226.5	2,285.3	340.1	1,763.4	181.9
Vallejo, CA M.S.A.	447,025									
Includes Solano County										
City of Vallejo	122,326	1,212	27	134	315	736	4,078	1,811	1,200	1,067
Total area actually reporting	100.0%	2,350	40	275	589	1,446	10,689	2,751	5,695	2,243
Rate per 100,000 inhabitants		525.7	8.9	61.5	131.8	323.5	2,391.1	615.4	1,274.0	501.8
Victoria, TX M.S.A.	100,050									
Includes Goliad and Victoria Counties										
City of Victoria	67,407	311	2	34	42	233	1,823	354	1,345	124
Total area actually reporting	100.0%	449	6	58	54	331	2,205	491	1,552	162
Rate per 100,000 inhabitants		448.8	6.0	58.0	54.0	330.8	2,203.9	490.8	1,551.2	161.9
Vineland-Bridgeton, NJ M.S.A.	148,593									
Includes Cumberland County										
City of Vineland	59,288	227	3	17	34	173	1,239	198	1,000	41
City of Bridgeton	24,032	234	2	11	82	139	737	158	534	45
Total area actually reporting	100.0%	669	8	39	154	468	3,192	593	2,446	153
Rate per 100,000 inhabitants		450.2	5.4	26.2	103.6	315.0	2,148.1	399.1	1,646.1	103.0
Virginia Beach-Norfolk-Newport News, VA-NC M.S.A.[2]	1,773,594									
Includes Camden, Currituck and Gates2 Counties, NC and Gloucester, Isle of Wight, James City, Mathews, Southampton, and York Counties and Chesapeake, Franklin, Hampton, Newport News, Norfolk, Poquoson, Portsmouth, Suffolk, Virginia Beach, and Williamsburg Cities, VA										
City of Virginia Beach, VA	450,858	445	17	60	124	244	6,816	499	5,693	624
City of Norfolk, VA	242,516	1,543	49	103	259	1,132	6,591	519	5,282	790
City of Newport News, VA	178,896	1,119	25	67	104	923	3,648	416	2,896	336
City of Hampton, VA	134,082	357	24	33	95	205	3,338	301	2,765	272
City of Portsmouth, VA	94,205	867	34	26	222	585	4,277	465	3,314	498
Total area actually reporting	100.0%	6,239	183	465	1,014	4,577	34,571	3,117	28,200	3,254
Rate per 100,000 inhabitants		351.8	10.3	26.2	57.2	258.1	1,949.2	175.7	1,590.0	183.5
Visalia, CA M.S.A.	464,150									
Includes Tulare County										
City of Visalia	135,733	555	8	106	142	299	3,077	610	2,049	418
Total area actually reporting	100.0%	1,699	29	206	356	1,108	9,400	1,828	5,770	1,802
Rate per 100,000 inhabitants		366.0	6.2	44.4	76.7	238.7	2,025.2	393.8	1,243.1	388.2
Waco, TX M.S.A.	275,324									
Includes Falls and McLennan Counties										
City of Waco	140,870	905	14	80	142	669	4,854	870	3,568	416
Total area actually reporting	98.5%	1,264	16	156	178	914	7,013	1,319	5,084	610
Estimated total	100.0%	1,274	16	158	179	921	7,078	1,332	5,127	619
Rate per 100,000 inhabitants		462.7	5.8	57.4	65.0	334.5	2,570.8	483.8	1,862.2	224.8
Walla Walla, WA M.S.A.	60,767									
Includes Walla Walla County										
City of Walla Walla	32,944	83	0	21	11	51	749	126	573	50

Table 4. Crime in the United States, by Selected Metropolitan Statistical Area, 2020—*Continued*

(Number, percent, rate per 100,000 population.)

Area	Population	Violent crime	Murder and nonnegligent manslaughter	Rape[1]	Robbery	Aggravated assault	Property crime	Burglary	Larceny-theft	Motor vehicle theft
Total area actually reporting	100.0%	129	1	26	14	88	1,267	255	920	92
Rate per 100,000 inhabitants		212.3	1.6	42.8	23.0	144.8	2,085.0	419.6	1,514.0	151.4
Watertown-Fort Drum, NY M.S.A.[2]	108,426									
Includes Jefferson County[2]										
City of Watertown	24,624	181	0	40	21	120	967	158	766	43
Total area actually reporting	100.0%	271	0	73	22	176	1,749	254	1,432	63
Rate per 100,000 inhabitants		249.9	0.0	67.3	20.3	162.3	1,613.1	234.3	1,320.7	58.1
Wausau-Weston, WI M.S.A.	163,196									
Includes Lincoln and Marathon Counties										
City of Wausau	38,492	174	0	26	14	134	560	66	435	59
Total area actually reporting	100.0%	399	3	74	20	302	1,487	227	1,144	116
Rate per 100,000 inhabitants		244.5	1.8	45.3	12.3	185.1	911.2	139.1	701.0	71.1
Wenatchee, WA M.S.A.	121,320									
Includes Chelan and Douglas Counties										
City of Wenatchee	34,525	67	0	16	6	45	570	72	448	50
Total area actually reporting	100.0%	141	1	30	16	94	1,392	239	1,029	124
Rate per 100,000 inhabitants		116.2	0.8	24.7	13.2	77.5	1,147.4	197.0	848.2	102.2
Wheeling, WV-OH M.S.A.	137,859									
Includes Belmont County, OH and Marshall and Ohio Counties, WV										
City of Wheeling, WV	26,222	330	1	31	28	270	582	180	361	41
Total area actually reporting	86.0%	525	2	82	31	410	1,140	279	782	79
Estimated total	100.0%	585	2	86	36	461	1,423	317	1,011	95
Rate per 100,000 inhabitants		424.3	1.5	62.4	26.1	334.4	1,032.2	229.9	733.4	68.9
Wichita Falls, TX M.S.A.[2]	150,700									
Includes Archer, Clay, and Wichita Counties										
City of Wichita Falls[2]	104,673	405	9	83	76	237	3,222	626	2,318	278
Total area actually reporting	95.5%	512	9	91	82	330	3,721	768	2,618	335
Estimated total	100.0%	544	9	95	83	357	3,864	809	2,702	353
Rate per 100,000 inhabitants		361.0	6.0	63.0	55.1	236.9	2,564.0	536.8	1,793.0	234.2
Wilmington, NC M.S.A.	302,620									
Includes New Hanover and Pender Counties										
City of Wilmington	125,794	791	22	66	143	560	3,204	595	2,410	199
Total area actually reporting	80.1%	1,001	24	100	172	705	5,181	881	4,026	274
Estimated total	100.0%	1,126	26	115	186	799	6,058	1,127	4,568	363
Rate per 100,000 inhabitants		372.1	8.6	38.0	61.5	264.0	2,001.9	372.4	1,509.5	120.0
Winchester, VA-WV M.S.A.	141,877									
Includes Frederick County and Winchester City, VA and Hampshire County, WV										
City of Winchester, VA	28,279	72	2	21	10	39	586	56	495	35
Total area actually reporting	99.7%	209	5	44	16	144	1,628	185	1,316	127
Estimated total	100.0%	214	5	44	16	149	1,629	185	1,317	127
Rate per 100,000 inhabitants		150.8	3.5	31.0	11.3	105.0	1,148.2	130.4	928.3	89.5
Worcester, MA-CT M.S.A.	871,848									
Includes Windham County, CT and Worcester County, MA										
City of Worcester, MA	184,850	1,169	10	40	210	909	3,695	667	2,581	447
Total area actually reporting	98.1%	2,620	13	257	320	2,030	8,486	1,447	6,118	921
Estimated total	100.0%	2,648	13	262	322	2,051	8,555	1,460	6,169	926
Rate per 100,000 inhabitants		303.7	1.5	30.1	36.9	235.2	981.2	167.5	707.6	106.2
Yakima, WA M.S.A.	250,785									
Includes Yakima County										
City of Yakima	93,862	639	9	22	100	508	3,220	599	2,115	506
Total area actually reporting	95.5%	944	21	69	161	693	6,593	1,372	4,175	1,046
Estimated total	100.0%	966	21	72	165	708	6,835	1,420	4,348	1,067
Rate per 100,000 inhabitants		385.2	8.4	28.7	65.8	282.3	2,725.4	566.2	1,733.8	425.5
Yuba City, CA M.S.A.	174,855									
Includes Sutter and Yuba Counties										
City of Yuba City	67,165	242	4	29	70	139	1,850	264	1,275	311
Total area actually reporting	100.0%	715	7	70	139	499	4,266	727	2,500	1,039
Rate per 100,000 inhabitants		408.9	4.0	40.0	79.5	285.4	2,439.7	415.8	1,429.8	594.2

Table 4. Crime in the United States, by Selected Metropolitan Statistical Area, 2020—*Continued*

(Number, percent, rate per 100,000 population.)

Area	Population	Violent crime	Murder and nonnegligent manslaughter	Rape[1]	Robbery	Aggravated assault	Property crime	Burglary	Larceny-theft	Motor vehicle theft
Yuma, AZ M.S.A.	216,821									
Includes Yuma County										
City of Yuma..	99,096	498	11	39	43	405	1,927	330	1,412	185
Total area actually reporting	100.0%	717	20	68	54	575	3,235	653	2,184	398
Rate per 100,000 inhabitants........................		330.7	9.2	31.4	24.9	265.2	1,492.0	301.2	1,007.3	183.6
Aguadilla-Isabela, Puerto Rico M.S.A.	286,064									
Includes Aguada, Aguadilla, Anasco, Isabela, Lares, Moca, Rincon, San Sebastian, and Utuado Municipios.										
Total area actually reporting	100.0%	372	20	16	31	305	802	234	509	59
Rate per 100,000 inhabitants........................		130.0	7.0	5.6	10.8	106.6	280.4	81.8	177.9	20.6
Arecibo, Puerto Rico M.S.A.	173,218									
Includes Arecibo, Camuy, Hatillo, and Quebradillas Municipios....................................										
Total area actually reporting	100.0%	249	24	6	31	188	470	150	274	46
Rate per 100,000 inhabitants........................		143.7	13.9	3.5	17.9	108.5	271.3	86.6	158.2	26.6
Guayama, Puerto Rico M.S.A.	72,240									
Includes Arroyo, Guayama, and Patillas Municipios										
Total area actually reporting	100.0%	178	11	9	29	129	235	82	148	5
Rate per 100,000 inhabitants........................		246.4	15.2	12.5	40.1	178.6	325.3	113.5	204.9	6.9
Mayagüez, Puerto Rico M.S.A.	93,412									
Includes Hormigueros, Las Marias, and Mayaguez Municipios....................................										
Total area actually reporting	100.0%	105	16	7	9	73	214	64	134	16
Rate per 100,000 inhabitants........................		112.4	17.1	7.5	9.6	78.1	229.1	68.5	143.5	17.1
Ponce, Puerto Rico M.S.A.	211,465									
Includes Adjuntas, Juana Diaz, Ponce, and Villalba Municipios....................................										
Total area actually reporting	100.0%	287	20	8	91	168	743	166	509	68
Rate per 100,000 inhabitants........................		135.7	9.5	3.8	43.0	79.4	351.4	78.5	240.7	32.2
San Germán, Puerto Rico M.S.A.	120,280									
Includes Cabo Rojo, Lajas, Sabana Grande, and San German Municipios....................................										
Total area actually reporting	100.0%	100	9	3	10	78	185	63	109	13
Rate per 100,000 inhabitants........................		83.1	7.5	2.5	8.3	64.8	153.8	52.4	90.6	10.8
San Juan-Bayamón-Caguas, Puerto Rico M.S.A.	2,002,906									
Includes Aguas Buenas, Aibonito, Barceloneta, Barranquitas, Bayamon, Caguas, Canovanas, Carolina, Catano, Cayey, Ceiba, Ciales, Cidra, Comerio, Corozal, Dorado, Fajardo, Florida, Guaynabo, Gurabo, Humacao, Juncos, Las Piedras, Loiza, Luquillo, Manati, Maunabo, Morovis, Naguabo, Naranjito, Orocovis, Rio Grande, San Juan, San Lorenzo, Toa Alta, Toa Baja, Trujillo Alto, Vega Alta, Vega Baja, and Yabucoa Municipios....................................										
Total area actually reporting	100.0%	3,510	400	91	934	2,085	10,114	2,011	6,362	1,741
Rate per 100,000 inhabitants........................		175.2	20.0	4.5	46.6	104.1	505.0	100.4	317.6	86.9
Yauco, Puerto Rico M.S.A.	84,112									
Includes Guanica, Guayanilla, Penuelas, and Yauco Municipios....................................										
Total area actually reporting	100.0%	138	8	2	18	110	174	61	106	7
Rate per 100,000 inhabitants........................		164.1	9.5	2.4	21.4	130.8	206.9	72.5	126.0	8.3

[1]The figures shown in this column for the offense of rape were reported using only the revised Uniform Crime Reporting (UCR) definition of rape. See the chapter notes for further explanation.
[2]Because of changes in the state/local agency's reporting practices, figures are not comparable to previous years' data.
[3]The FBI determined that the agency's data were overreported. Consequently, those data are not included in this table.
[4]The FBI determined that the state did not follow national UCR Program guidelines for reporting an offense. Consequently, those figures are not included in this table.
[5]The FBI determined that the agency's data were underreported. Consequently, those data are not included in this table.

Table 5. Offense Analysis, United States, 2016–2020

(Number.)

Classification	2016	2017	2018	2019[1]	2020
Murder	17,413	17,294	16,374	16,669	21,570
Rape[2]	132,414	135,666	143,765	143,224	126,430
Robbery[3]	332,797	320,596	281,278	268,483	243,600
By location					
Street/highway	129,337	119,180	102,149	94,263	77,984
Commercial house	50,785	49,654	45,148	44,210	41,139
Gas or service station	9,708	9,603	8,863	8,570	8,804
Convenience store	20,656	21,048	19,647	18,346	18,039
Residence	55,102	51,260	45,408	42,885	42,637
Bank	5,914	5,441	4,461	3,841	2,669
Miscellaneous	61,296	64,410	55,602	56,368	52,328
Burglary[3]	1,516,405	1,397,045	1,235,013	1,118,096	1,035,314
By location					
Residence (dwelling)	1,054,470	939,509	808,611	702,700	575,049
Residence, night	311,805	285,358	257,085	238,720	220,533
Residence, day	543,930	474,495	408,349	354,525	280,183
Residence, unknown	198,735	179,656	143,178	109,455	74,333
Nonresidence (store, office, etc.)	461,935	457,536	426,402	415,396	460,265
Nonresidence, night	199,741	200,859	190,817	191,731	221,126
Nonresidence, day	159,630	157,375	151,091	153,010	175,367
Nonresidence, unknown	102,564	99,302	84,493	70,654	63,772
Larceny-theft (except motor vehicle theft)[3]	5,644,835	5,513,000	5,232,167	5,152,267	4,606,324
By type					
Pocket-picking	27,648	31,026	27,326	29,865	18,910
Purse-snatching	22,671	21,961	20,113	18,810	14,101
Shoplifting	1,179,137	1,144,948	1,116,664	1,128,275	964,196
From motor vehicles (except accessories)	1,477,587	1,477,684	1,410,567	1,397,708	1,268,031
Motor vehicle accessories	415,590	407,017	324,298	330,039	393,091
Bicycles	184,546	174,803	157,042	156,013	158,157
From buildings	605,765	586,612	534,418	504,601	390,286
From coin-operated machines	12,349	12,014	11,511	11,475	8,809
All others	1,719,542	1,656,937	1,630,232	1,575,481	1,390,743
By value					
Over $200	2,561,619	2,529,654	2,445,915	2,439,300	2,219,999
$50 to $200	1,221,246	1,169,612	1,120,011	1,093,554	931,647
Under $50	1,861,970	1,813,734	1,666,185	1,619,413	1,454,678
Motor vehicle theft	767,290	772,943	751,904	724,872	810,400

[1]The crime figures have been adjusted.
[2]The figures shown for this offense of rape were estimated using the revised Uniform Crime Reporting (UCR) definition of rape. See chapter notes for more detail.
[3]Because of rounding, the number of offenses may not add to the total.

Table 6. Crime Trends, by Population Group, 2019–2020

(Number, percent change.)

Population group	Violent crime	Murder and nonnegligent manslaughter	Rape[1]	Robbery	Aggravated assault	Property crime	Burglary	Larceny-theft	Motor vehicle theft	Arson	Number of agencies	Estimated population, 2020
Total, All Agencies												
2019	1,099,647	14,440	127,821	238,036	719,350	5,977,531	968,856	4,327,744	650,351	30,580	13,827	294,203,623
2020	1,147,914	18,623	111,947	215,106	802,238	5,563,304	893,344	3,906,065	726,283	37,612		
Percent change	4.4	29.0	-12.4	-9.6	11.5	-6.9	-7.8	-9.7	11.7	23.0		
Total, Cities												
2019	882,969	11,195	95,780	209,835	566,159	4,799,777	727,290	3,528,095	520,810	23,582	9,985	200,688,039
2020	922,257	14,794	82,808	189,624	635,031	4,457,179	679,313	3,162,763	585,754	29,349		
Percent change	4.4	32.1	-13.5	-9.6	12.2	-7.1	-6.6	-10.4	12.5	24.5		
Group I (250,000 and over)												
2019	431,053	5,837	36,083	119,853	269,280	1,794,877	280,025	1,263,441	242,884	8,527	84	60,095,451
2020	454,913	7,833	30,592	109,133	307,355	1,672,010	268,045	1,122,909	270,136	10,920		
Percent change	5.5	34.2	-15.2	-8.9	14.1	-6.8	-4.3	-11.1	11.2	28.1		
1,000,000 and over (Group I subset)												
2019	185,593	1,987	14,984	55,642	112,980	646,333	100,111	453,510	90,773	1,939	11	27,146,381
2020	192,910	2,779	12,140	51,754	126,237	611,719	96,553	409,536	102,979	2,651		
Percent change	3.9	39.9	-19.0	-7.0	11.7	-5.4	-3.6	-9.7	13.4	36.7		
500,000 to 999,999 (Group I subset)												
2019	134,189	2,136	10,004	36,403	85,646	601,095	94,854	424,586	78,525	3,130	23	16,076,918
2020	143,079	2,764	8,408	31,758	100,149	552,774	91,945	373,324	83,597	3,908		
Percent change	6.6	29.4	-16.0	-12.8	16.9	-8.0	-3.1	-12.1	6.5	24.9		
250,000 to 499,999 (Group I subset)												
2019	111,271	1,714	11,095	27,808	70,654	547,449	85,060	385,345	73,586	3,458	50	16,872,152
2020	118,924	2,290	10,044	25,621	80,969	507,517	79,547	340,049	83,560	4,361		
Percent change	6.9	33.6	-9.5	-7.9	14.6	-7.3	-6.5	-11.8	13.6	26.1		
Group II (100,000 to 249,999)												
2019	140,351	1,857	15,917	33,730	88,847	844,224	125,334	616,880	97,847	4,163	223	32,301,225
2020	148,026	2,502	14,018	30,139	101,367	793,009	117,723	559,645	110,199	5,442		
Percent change	5.5	34.7	-11.9	-10.6	14.1	-6.1	-6.1	-9.3	12.6	30.7		
Group III (50,000 to 99,999)												
2019	107,242	1,226	12,891	24,427	68,698	705,455	102,260	530,921	68,854	3,420	475	33,149,178
2020	111,601	1,551	11,562	21,473	77,015	662,747	93,319	485,558	79,762	4,108		
Percent change	4.1	26.5	-10.3	-12.1	12.1	-6.1	-8.7	-8.5	15.8	20.1		
Group IV (25,000 to 49,999)												
2019	76,663	906	10,933	14,756	50,068	549,474	80,610	420,821	45,423	2,620	831	28,909,214
2020	80,251	1,150	9,841	13,670	55,590	510,310	73,590	381,353	52,087	3,280		
Percent change	4.7	26.9	-10.0	-7.4	11.0	-7.1	-8.7	-9.4	14.7	25.2		
Group V (10,000 to 24,999)												
2019	66,763	782	10,273	10,292	45,416	491,918	75,598	376,751	37,260	2,309	1,645	26,337,532
2020	68,750	1,039	9,001	9,539	49,171	458,635	68,695	344,088	43,119	2,733		
Percent change	3.0	32.9	-12.4	-7.3	8.3	-6.8	-9.1	-8.7	15.7	18.4		
Group VI (under 10,000)												
2019	60,897	587	9,683	6,777	43,850	413,829	63,463	319,281	28,542	2,543	6,727	19,895,439
2020	58,716	719	7,794	5,670	44,533	360,468	57,941	269,210	30,451	2,866		
Percent change	-3.6	22.5	-19.5	-16.3	1.6	-12.9	-8.7	-15.7	6.7	12.7		
Metropolitan Counties												
2019	170,794	2,391	23,214	26,110	119,079	955,842	177,543	668,556	104,641	5,102	1,697	71,020,687
2020	177,270	2,807	21,133	23,373	129,957	894,680	156,865	617,695	114,150	5,970		
Percent change	3.8	17.4	-9.0	-10.5	9.1	-6.4	-11.6	-7.6	9.1	17.0		
Nonmetropolitan Counties[2]												
2019	45,884	854	8,827	2,091	34,112	221,912	64,023	131,093	24,900	1,896	2,145	22,494,897
2020	48,387	1,022	8,006	2,109	37,250	211,445	57,166	125,607	26,379	2,293		
Percent change	5.5	19.7	-9.3	0.9	9.2	-4.7	10.7	-4.2	5.9	20.9		
Suburban Areas[3]												
2019	294,113	3,691	41,756	49,027	199,639	1,908,002	309,769	1,406,493	182,277	9,463	7,430	125,892,017
2020	300,262	4,429	37,220	43,886	214,727	1,765,243	277,444	1,273,709	202,906	11,184		
Percent change	2.1	20.0	-10.9	-10.5	7.6	-7.5	-10.4	-9.4	11.3	18.2		

[1] The figures shown in this column for the offense of rape were reported using only the revised Uniform Crime Reporting definition of rape. See chapter notes for more detail.

[2] Includes state police agencies that report aggregately for the entire state.

[3] Suburban areas include law enforcement agencies in cities with less than 50,000 inhabitants and county law enforcement agencies that are within a Metropolitan Statistical Area. Suburban areas exclude all metropolitan agencies associated with a principal city. The agencies associated with suburban areas also appear in other groups within this table.

Table 7. Rate: Number of Crimes Per 100,000 Population, by Population Group, 2020

(Number, rate.)

Population group	Violent crime		Murder and nonnegligent manslaughter		Rape[1]		Robbery		Aggravated assault	
	Number of offenses known	Rate	Number of offenses known	Rate	Number of offenses known	Rate	Number of offenses known	Rate	Number of offenses known	Rate
Total, All Agencies....................................	1,106,727	404.5	17,597	6.4	107,907	39.4	207,636	75.9	773,587	282.9
Total, Cities...	894,132	469.4	14,108	7.4	80,176	42.1	185,379	97.4	614,469	322.7
Group I (250,000 and over).........................	444,979	753.7	7,575	12.8	30,208	51.2	108,259	183.4	298,937	506.3
1,000,000 and over (Group I subset)........	192,910	710.6	2,779	10.2	12,140	44.7	51,754	190.6	126,237	465.0
500,000 to 999,999 (Group I subset).......	137,376	874.7	2,556	16.3	8,593	54.7	29,848	190.1	96,379	613.7
250,000 to 499,999 (Group I subset).......	114,693	708.5	2,240	13.8	9,475	58.5	26,657	164.7	76,321	471.4
Group II (100,000 to 249,999)...................	146,782	471.6	2,384	7.7	13,803	44.3	29,435	94.6	101,160	325.0
Group III (50,000 to 99,999)......................	109,725	347.2	1,469	4.6	11,324	35.8	20,896	66.2	76,036	240.6
Group IV (25,000 to 49,999)......................	74,413	279.0	1,050	3.9	9,100	34.1	12,706	47.6	51,557	193.6
Group V (10,000 to 24,999)	65,196	266.8	993	4.1	8,597	35.2	8,998	36.9	46,608	191.1
Group VI (under 10,000)............................	53,037	301.4	637	3.6	7,144	40.6	5,085	28.9	40,171	228.3
Metropolitan Counties	166,369	265.0	2,516	4.0	19,838	31.6	20,189	32.2	123,826	197.2
Nonmetropolitan Counties[2]	46,226	227.5	973	4.8	7,893	38.9	2,068	10.2	35,292	173.7
Suburban Areas[3]	271,751	250.4	3,888	3.6	33,299	30.7	37,638	34.7	196,926	181.5

(Number, rate.)

Population group	Property crime		Burglary		Larceny-theft		Motor vehicle theft	
	Number of offenses known	Rate	Number of offenses known	Rate	Number of offenses known	Rate	Number of offenses known	Rate
Total, All Agencies...	5,304,354	1,938.9	858,592	315.0	3,740,519	1,422.6	705,243	257.8
Total, Cities	4,293,456	2,254.0	658,718	347.1	3,059,998	1,686.7	574,740	301.8
Group I (250,000 and over).........................	1,635,354	2,769.9	264,458	447.9	1,103,756	1,958.9	267,140	452.5
1,000,000 and over (Group I subset)	609,068	2,243.6	96,553	355.7	409,536	1,674.8	102,979	379.3
500,000 to 999,999 (Group I subset)	547,124	3,483.7	91,506	582.6	372,525	2,372.0	83,093	529.1
250,000 to 499,999 (Group I subset)	479,162	2,959.8	76,399	471.9	321,695	1,987.1	81,068	500.8
Group II (100,000 to 249,999).....................	772,260	2,481.1	114,538	371.4	547,196	1,797.4	110,526	355.1
Group III (50,000 to 99,999)	640,987	2,028.1	92,111	291.9	470,968	1,551.6	77,908	246.5
Group IV (25,000 to 49,999)........................	475,556	1,782.8	68,387	258.2	357,646	1,435.0	49,523	185.7
Group V (10,000 to 24,999)	435,899	1,784.1	65,472	269.2	329,152	1,448.8	41,275	169.0
Group VI (under 10,000)...............................	333,400	1,894.4	53,752	306.3	251,280	1,510.9	28,368	161.2
Metropolitan Counties	809,432	1,289.1	144,818	231.6	559,531	906.9	105,083	167.4
Nonmetropolitan Counties[2]	201,466	991.7	55,056	272.2	120,990	610.5	25,420	125.2
Suburban Areas[3]	1,616,701	1,489.8	251,026	231.3	1,181,850	1,089.1	183,825	169.4

NOTE: Due to a system upgrade, the rates in this table are now caculated using aggregate popualtion for each individual offense. The agency counts and population are provided for each individual offense.
[1]The figures shown in this column for the offense of rape were reported using only the revised Uniform Crime Reporting definition of rape. See the chapter notes for further explanation.
[2]Includes state police agencies that report aggregately for the entire state.
[3]Suburban areas include law enforcement agencies in cities with less than 50,000 inhabitants and county law enforcement agencies that are within a Metropolitan Statistical Area. Suburban areas exclude all metropolitan agencies associated with a principal city. The agencies associated with suburban areas also appear in other groups within this table.

Table 8. Offense Analysis, Number and Percent Change, 2019–2020

(Number, percent, dollars; 12,751 agencies; 2020 estimated population 277,124,125.)

Classification	Number of offenses, 2020	Percent change from 2019	Percent distribution[1]	Average value (dollars)
Murder	16,896	+28.4	NA	X
Rape[2]	105,273	-12.1	NA	X
Robbery	198,877	-9.9	100.0%	1,834
By location				
Street/highway..	63,667	-15.2	32.0%	1,719
Commercial house	33,586	-9.1	16.9%	1,497
Gas or service station	7,188	8.3	3.6%	1,469
Convenience store...	14,727	0.8	7.4%	1,005
Residence..	34,809	-1.6	17.5%	2,236
Bank	2,179	-29.9	1.1%	4,339
Miscellaneous...	42,721	-12.8	21.5%	2,161
Burglary	859,572	-7.5	100.0%	2,692
By location				
Residence (dwelling)...	477,436	-58.8	55.5%	7,937
Residence, night..	183,098	-7.7	21.3%	2,140
Residence, day...	232,623	-21.4	27.1%	2,321
Residence, unknown..	61,715	-29.7	7.2%	3,477
Nonresidence (store, office, etc.)..........................	382,136	19.7	44.5%	9,779
Nonresidence, night..	183,590	14.9	21.4%	2,974
Nonresidence, day...	145,599	12.1	16.9%	2,822
Nonresidence, unknown..................................	52,947	-7.3	6.2%	3,982
Larceny-theft (except motor vehicle theft)........................	3,800,545	-9.6	100.0%	1,482
By type				
Pocket-picking..	15,602	-40.2	0.4%	1,233
Purse-snatching..	11,634	-21.5	0.3%	634
Shoplifting	795,530	-14.8	20.9%	306
From motor vehicles (except accessories)	1,046,216	-7.0	27.5%	1,053
Motor vehicle accessories	324,328	19.4	8.5%	873
Bicycles	130,491	1.7	3.4%	724
From buildings	322,014	-22.6	8.5%	1,616
From coin-operated machines	7,268	-19.4	0.2%	816
All others	1,147,462	-10.4	30.2%	2,926
By value				
Over $200...	1,831,657	-7.8	48.2%	3,026
$50 to $200..	768,675	-12.7	20.2%	101
Under $50...	1,200,213	-10.2	31.6%	10
Motor Vehicle Theft..	692,517	11.7	NA	9,166

NA = Not available.
X = Not applicable.
[1]Because of rounding, the percentages may not add to 100.0.
[2]The figures shown in this column for the offense of rape were reported using only the revised Uniform Crime Reporting definition of rape. See the chapter notes for further explanation.

Table 9. Property Stolen and Recovered, by Type and Value, 2020

(Dollars, percent; 12,903 agencies; 2020 estimated population 275,056,054.)

Type of property	Value of property (dollars)		Percent recovered
	Stolen	Recovered	
Total	$13,808,565,134	$4,298,423,601	31.1
Currency, notes, etc.	1,245,350,575	31,941,249	2.6
Jewelry and precious metals............................	837,911,482	25,033,119	3.0
Clothing and furs..	340,253,807	19,232,176	5.7
Locally stolen motor vehicles..........................	6,452,048,172	3,640,955,256	56.4
Office equipment...	303,766,541	17,763,680	5.8
Televisions, radios, stereos, etc.	207,809,902	9,497,929	4.6
Firearms..	135,177,366	14,248,649	10.5
Household goods...	275,789,411	107,637,809	39.0
Consumable goods..	152,385,338	11,958,702	7.8
Livestock...	11,743,047	1,162,991	9.9
Miscellaneous	3,846,329,493	418,992,041	10.9

Table 10. Number and Percent of Offenses Cleared by Arrest or Exceptional Means, by Population Group, 2020

(Number, percent.)

Population group	Violent crime	Murder and nonnegligent manslaughter	Rape[1]	Robbery	Aggravated assault	Property crime	Burglary	Larceny-theft	Motor vehicle theft	Arson[2]	Number of agencies	Estimated population, 2020
Total, All Agencies												
Offenses known	1,137,525	18,109	110,095	209,643	799,678	5,670,244	898,176	4,004,124	727,045	40,899	13,804	288,224,102
Percent cleared by arrest..............	41.7	54.4	30.6	28.8	46.4	14.6	14.0	15.1	12.3	21.5		
Total Cities												
Offenses known	902,091	14,168	80,482	183,590	623,851	4,528,049	677,169	3,236,517	582,325	32,038	9,871	193,856,641
Percent cleared by arrest..............	39.5	52.3	28.5	27.8	44.0	14.4	13.5	15.1	11.2	20.7		
Group I (250,000 and over)												
Offenses known	438,385	7,303	29,775	105,215	296,092	1,693,877	267,123	1,146,402	266,470	13,882	84	58,292,525
Percent cleared by arrest..............	32.3	47.3	25.6	23.8	35.7	9.2	10.8	8.9	8.7	14.0		
1,000,000 and over (Group I subset)												
Offenses known	166,327	2,008	10,794	43,885	109,640	595,381	87,910	409,536	92,926	5,009	10	24,452,783
Percent cleared by arrest..............	30.9	48.9	25.0	23.0	34.3	7.5	9.7	7.0	7.6	9.7		
500,000 to 999,999 (Group I subset)												
Offenses known	151,635	3,005	9,031	34,116	105,483	590,900	99,666	396,817	89,984	4,433	24	16,967,590
Percent cleared by arrest..............	33.2	44.9	28.2	24.1	36.3	9.3	10.9	8.7	9.4	16.7		
250,000 to 499,999 (Group I subset)												
Offenses known	120,423	2,290	9,950	27,214	80,969	507,596	79,547	340,049	83,560	4,440	50	16,872,152
Percent cleared by arrest..............	33.1	49.0	23.9	24.8	36.6	11.0	11.9	11.2	9.3	16.1		
Group II (100,000 to 249,999)												
Offenses known	147,671	2,482	13,834	29,726	101,629	799,322	117,152	564,511	112,380	5,279	218	31,572,750
Percent cleared by arrest..............	41.1	55.5	28.6	29.9	45.7	13.0	13.2	13.4	10.8	24.9		
Group III (50,000 to 99,999)												
Offenses known	111,246	1,534	11,399	21,076	77,237	674,088	93,809	496,226	79,971	4,082	459	32,114,069
Percent cleared by arrest..............	47.4	57.8	32.9	33.9	52.9	16.5	15.1	17.3	12.2	27.3		
Group IV (25,000 to 49,999)												
Offenses known	77,198	1,103	9,268	13,026	53,801	515,758	71,974	390,166	50,481	3,137	786	27,406,287
Percent cleared by arrest..............	46.3	58.0	29.8	34.2	51.9	18.9	15.3	20.2	13.7	24.2		
Group V (10,000 to 24,999)												
Offenses known	67,169	996	8,511	8,956	48,706	470,604	68,457	357,439	42,035	2,673	1,572	25,072,927
Percent cleared by arrest..............	49.4	62.3	29.6	35.9	55.1	21.8	16.8	23.4	16.3	26.4		
Group VI (under 10,000)												
Offenses known	60,422	750	7,695	5,591	46,386	374,400	58,654	281,773	30,988	2,985	6,752	19,398,083
Percent cleared by arrest..............	52.8	58.5	30.5	39.7	58.0	21.4	18.3	22.1	20.7	26.8		
Metropolitan Counties												
Offenses known	185,468	2,907	21,380	23,863	137,318	920,546	161,052	635,640	117,370	6,484	1,731	71,573,154
Percent cleared by arrest..............	50.3	61.8	37.2	35.4	54.6	15.5	15.6	15.3	15.7	23.7		
Nonmetropolitan Counties												
Offenses known	49,966	1,034	8,233	2,190	38,509	221,649	59,955	131,967	27,350	2,377	2,202	22,794,307
Percent cleared by arrest..............	50.8	62.1	34.3	37.8	54.8	15.1	15.2	13.6	20.7	26.2		
Suburban Areas[3]												
Offenses known	303,760	4,450	36,426	43,096	219,788	1,803,833	278,407	1,310,538	203,377	11,511	7,275	123,406,306
Percent cleared by arrest..............	50.1	60.7	34.4	35.7	55.3	17.5	15.9	18.2	15.1	24.2		

[1]The figures shown in this column for the offense of rape were reported using only the revised Uniform Crime Reporting definition of rape.
[2]Not all agencies submit reports for arson to the FBI. As a result, the number of reports the FBI uses to compute the percent of offenses cleared for arson is less than the number it uses to compute the percent of offenses cleared for all other offenses.
[3]Suburban area includes law enforcement agencies in cities with less than 50,000 inhabitants and county law enforcement agencies that are within a Metropolitan Statistical Area. Suburban area excludes all metropolitan agencies associated with a principal city. The agencies associated with suburban areas also appear in other groups within this table.

Table 11. Estimated Number of Arrests, 2020

(Number.)

Offense	Arrests
Total[1]	7,632,473
Violent crime[2]	482,408
Murder and nonnegligent manslaughter	12,444
Rape[3]	20,872
Robbery	67,903
Aggravated assault	381,189
Property crime[2]	871,370
Burglary	149,352
Larceny-theft	629,024
Motor vehicle theft	83,219
Arson	9,775
Other assaults	906,980
Forgery and counterfeiting	32,499
Fraud	79,518
Embezzlement	9,393
Stolen property; buying, receiving, possessing	88,316
Vandalism	173,774
Weapons; carrying, possessing, etc.	166,197
Prostitution and commercialized vice	16,770
Sex offenses (except forcible rape and prostitution)	31,793
Drug abuse violations	1,155,610
Gambling	1,625
Offenses against the family and children	59,396
Driving under the influence	778,906
Liquor laws	104,201
Drunkenness	194,249
Disorderly conduct	225,804
Vagrancy	13,653
All other offenses (except traffic)	2,228,332
Suspicion	363
Curfew and loitering law violations	11,679

[1] Does not include suspicion.
[2] Violent crimes are offenses of murder and nonnegligent manslaughter, rape, robbery, and aggravated assault. Property crimes are offenses of burglary, larceny-theft, motor vehicle theft, and arson.
[3] The rape figures in this table are an aggregate total of the data submitted using both the revised and legacy Uniform Crime Reporting definitions.

Table 12. Number and Rate of Arrests, by Geographic Region, 2020

(Number, rate per 100,000 inhabitants.)

Offense charged	United States total (10,466 agencies; population 228,864,358)		Northeast (2,015 agencies; population 32,300,146)		Midwest (2,844 agencies; population 44,977,955)		South (3,791 agencies; population 78,729,908)		West (1,816 agencies; population 72,856,349)	
	Total	Rate	Total	Rate	Total	Rate	Total	Rate	Total	Rate
Total[1]	5,291,886	2,312.2	565,777	1,751.6	1,052,926	2,341.0	1,895,649	2,407.8	1,777,534	2,439.8
Violent crime[2]	338,443	147.9	29,952	92.7	57,087	126.9	98,867	125.6	152,537	209.4
Murder and nonnegligent manslaughter	8,701	3.8	609	1.9	1,684	3.7	3,606	4.6	2,802	3.8
Rape[3]	14,462	6.3	1,739	5.4	3,452	7.7	4,574	5.8	4,697	6.4
Robbery	48,035	21.0	5,008	15.5	6,850	15.2	14,277	18.1	21,900	30.1
Aggravated assault	267,245	116.8	22,596	70.0	45,101	100.3	76,410	97.1	123,138	169.0
Property crime[2]	611,731	267.3	71,184	220.4	121,082	269.2	224,668	285.4	194,797	267.4
Burglary	104,535	45.7	10,424	32.3	15,139	33.7	34,876	44.3	44,096	60.5
Larceny-theft	442,016	193.1	55,952	173.2	95,879	213.2	170,187	216.2	119,998	164.7
Motor vehicle theft	58,326	25.5	4,156	12.9	9,078	20.2	17,945	22.8	27,147	37.3
Arson	6,854	3.0	652	2.0	986	2.2	1,660	2.1	3,556	4.9
Other assaults	633,704	276.9	81,111	251.1	134,078	298.1	230,240	292.4	188,275	258.4
Forgery and counterfeiting	22,559	9.9	2,903	9.0	4,406	9.8	9,278	11.8	5,972	8.2
Fraud	54,756	23.9	5,680	17.6	12,259	27.3	23,234	29.5	13,583	18.6
Embezzlement	6,592	2.9	411	1.3	1,411	3.1	3,192	4.1	1,578	2.2
Stolen property; buying, receiving, possessing	61,868	27.0	6,679	20.7	12,453	27.7	18,839	23.9	23,897	32.8
Vandalism	121,403	53.0	19,369	60.0	22,704	50.5	29,776	37.8	49,554	68.0
Weapons; carrying, possessing, etc.	115,832	50.6	8,927	27.6	27,124	60.3	36,955	46.9	42,826	58.8
Prostitution and commercialized vice	11,754	5.1	688	2.1	791	1.8	2,849	3.6	7,426	10.2
Sex offenses (except forcible rape and prostitution)	22,065	9.6	2,748	8.5	3,495	7.8	4,483	5.7	11,339	15.6
Drug abuse violations	801,546	350.2	91,969	284.7	131,965	293.4	302,931	384.8	274,681	377.0
Gambling	1,191	0.5	121	0.4	39	0.1	316	0.4	715	1.0
Offenses against the family and children	40,498	17.7	6,342	19.6	7,891	17.5	15,779	20.0	10,486	14.4
Driving under the influence	531,846	232.4	55,264	171.1	118,960	264.5	162,960	207.0	194,662	267.2
Liquor laws	70,875	31.0	4,657	14.4	28,061	62.4	16,554	21.0	21,603	29.7
Drunkenness	135,744	59.3	3,287	10.2	13,518	30.1	77,483	98.4	41,456	56.9
Disorderly conduct	156,502	68.4	24,078	74.5	55,086	122.5	41,543	52.8	35,795	49.1
Vagrancy	9,795	4.3	453	1.4	1,626	3.6	2,744	3.5	4,972	6.8
All other offenses (except traffic)	1,534,972	670.7	149,693	463.4	296,119	658.4	590,122	749.6	499,038	685.0
Suspicion	238	0.1	57	0.2	18	*	17	*	146	0.2
Curfew and loitering law violations	8,210	3.6	261	0.8	2,771	6.2	2,836	3.6	2,342	3.2

* = Less than one-tenth of 1 percent.
[1]Does not include suspicion.
[2]Violent crimes are offenses of murder and nonnegligent manslaughter, rape, robbery, and aggravated assault. Property crimes are offenses of burglary, larceny-theft, motor vehicle theft, and arson.
[3]The rape figures in this table are aggregate totals of the data submitted based on both the legacy and revised Uniform Crime Reporting definitions.

Table 13. Number and Rate of Arrests, by Population Group, 2020

(Number, rate per 100,000 inhabitants.)

Offense charged	Total (10,466 agencies; population 228,864,358)		Total cities (7,634 cities; population 159,832,632)		Group I (72 cities, 250,000 and over; population 44,271,326)		Group II (189 cities, 100,000 to 249,999; population 27,356,047)		Group III (398 cities, 50,000 to 99,999; population 27,901,884)		Group IV (664 cities, 25,000 to 49,999; population 23,023,304)	
	Total	Rate	Total	Rate	Total	Rate	Total	Rate	Total	Rate	Total	Rate
Total[2]	5,291,886	2,312.2	3,851,077	2,409.4	924,243	2,087.7	653,477	2,388.8	638,180	2,287.2	517,766	2,248.9
Violent crime[3]	338,443	147.9	267,047	167.1	99,537	224.8	52,274	191.1	43,245	155.0	26,233	113.9
Murder and nonnegligent man-slaughter	8,701	3.8	6,510	4.1	2,877	6.5	1,354	4.9	828	3.0	537	2.3
Rape[4]	14,462	6.3	10,360	6.5	3,214	7.3	1,767	6.5	1,699	6.1	1,251	5.4
Robbery.....................................	48,035	21.0	41,569	26.0	18,541	41.9	7,707	28.2	6,468	23.2	3,936	17.1
Aggravated assault	267,245	116.8	208,608	130.5	74,905	169.2	41,446	151.5	34,250	122.8	20,509	89.1
Property crime[3]	611,731	267.3	506,199	316.7	114,060	257.6	85,923	314.1	87,236	312.7	76,071	330.4
Burglary.....................................	104,535	45.7	80,714	50.5	24,305	54.9	15,073	55.1	13,191	47.3	10,173	44.2
Larceny-theft	442,016	193.1	375,128	234.7	72,545	163.9	60,638	221.7	66,049	236.7	60,701	263.7
Motor vehicle theft	58,326	25.5	44,997	28.2	15,633	35.3	9,138	33.4	7,094	25.4	4,575	19.9
Arson..	6,854	3.0	5,360	3.4	1,577	3.6	1,074	3.9	902	3.2	622	2.7
Other assaults............................	633,704	276.9	490,395	306.8	140,917	318.3	86,010	314.4	82,501	295.7	63,697	276.7
Forgery and counterfeiting............	22,559	9.9	17,093	10.7	2,872	6.5	2,933	10.7	3,137	11.2	2,562	11.1
Fraud..	54,756	23.9	40,644	25.4	7,754	17.5	5,888	21.5	6,964	25.0	6,085	26.4
Embezzlement	6,592	2.9	5,322	3.3	1,515	3.4	794	2.9	981	3.5	850	3.7
Stolen property; buying, receiving, possessing	61,868	27.0	46,638	29.2	14,083	31.8	8,560	31.3	8,596	30.8	6,018	26.1
Vandalism..................................	121,403	53.0	96,164	60.2	27,373	61.8	16,463	60.2	16,242	58.2	12,267	53.3
Weapons; carrying, possessing, etc.	115,832	50.6	88,908	55.6	35,855	81.0	15,984	58.4	12,559	45.0	8,707	37.8
Prostitution and commercialized vice..	11,754	5.1	10,617	6.6	7,381	16.7	1,651	6.0	712	2.6	468	2.0
Sex offenses (except forcible rape and prostitution).........................	22,065	9.6	16,162	10.1	5,040	11.4	2,780	10.2	2,818	10.1	1,974	8.6
Drug abuse violations...................	801,546	350.2	561,935	351.6	112,526	254.2	103,839	379.6	101,925	365.3	77,694	337.5
Gambling...................................	1,191	0.5	861	0.5	322	0.7	236	0.9	177	0.6	32	0.1
Offenses against the family and children	40,498	17.7	26,519	16.6	6,291	14.2	3,527	12.9	3,386	12.1	3,781	16.4
Driving under the influence...........	531,846	232.4	311,168	194.7	66,656	150.6	46,421	169.7	48,732	174.7	44,414	192.9
Liquor laws	70,875	31.0	53,701	33.6	6,728	15.2	6,517	23.8	6,470	23.2	7,642	33.2
Drunkenness...............................	135,744	59.3	115,065	72.0	16,215	36.6	23,564	86.1	19,891	71.3	14,789	64.2
Disorderly conduct	156,502	68.4	128,297	80.3	22,438	50.7	19,143	70.0	19,679	70.5	19,059	82.8
Vagrancy....................................	9,795	4.3	8,813	5.5	2,742	6.2	2,705	9.9	1,188	4.3	892	3.9
All other offenses (except traffic)....	1,534,972	670.7	1,052,267	658.4	232,421	525.0	167,283	611.5	170,432	610.8	143,434	623.0
Suspicion	238	0.1	200	0.1	3	*	0	0.0	12	*	16	0.1
Curfew and loitering law violations	8,210	3.6	7,262	4.5	1,517	3.4	982	3.6	1,309	4.7	1,097	4.8

Table 13. Number and Rate of Arrests, by Population Group, 2020—*Continued*

(Number, rate per 100,000 inhabitants.)

Offense charged	Group V (1,351 cities, 10,000 to 24,999; population 21,468,840)		Group VI (4,960 cities, under 10,000; population 15,811,231)		Metropolitan counties (1,195 agencies; population 50,082,964)		Nonmetropolitan counties (1,637 agencies; population 18,948,762)		Suburban areas[1] (5,475 agencies; population 94,124,752)	
	Total	Rate	Total	Rate	Total	Rate	Total	Rate	Total	Rate
Total[2]	558,011	2,599.2	559,400	3,538.0	983,370	1,963.5	457,439	2,414.1	1,964,322	2,086.9
Violent crime[3]	24,695	115.0	21,063	133.2	54,143	108.1	17,253	91.1	97,976	104.1
Murder and nonnegligent manslaughter.	532	2.5	382	2.4	1,554	3.1	637	3.4	2,282	2.4
Rape[4]	1,305	6.1	1,124	7.1	2,733	5.5	1,369	7.2	4,929	5.2
Robbery.....................	2,902	13.5	2,015	12.7	5,390	10.8	1,076	5.7	11,687	12.4
Aggravated assault	19,956	93.0	17,542	110.9	44,466	88.8	14,171	74.8	79,078	84.0
Property crime[3]	82,959	386.4	59,950	379.2	81,314	162.4	24,218	127.8	218,927	232.6
Burglary.....................	9,834	45.8	8,138	51.5	16,654	33.3	7,167	37.8	33,777	35.9
Larceny-theft.....................	67,948	316.5	47,247	298.8	53,892	107.6	12,996	68.6	164,967	175.3
Motor vehicle theft	4,553	21.2	4,004	25.3	9,729	19.4	3,600	19.0	18,095	19.2
Arson.....................	624	2.9	561	3.5	1,039	2.1	455	2.4	2,088	2.2
Other assaults.....................	62,775	292.4	54,495	344.7	102,954	205.6	40,355	213.0	212,497	225.8
Forgery and counterfeiting.....................	2,627	12.2	2,962	18.7	4,244	8.5	1,222	6.4	9,273	9.9
Fraud.....................	6,056	28.2	7,897	49.9	10,675	21.3	3,437	18.1	23,240	24.7
Embezzlement.....................	696	3.2	486	3.1	979	2.0	291	1.5	2,275	2.4
Stolen property; buying, receiving, possessing.....................	5,412	25.2	3,969	25.1	11,739	23.4	3,491	18.4	22,898	24.3
Vandalism.....................	12,616	58.8	11,203	70.9	19,020	38.0	6,219	32.8	39,983	42.5
Weapons; carrying, possessing, etc.	8,244	38.4	7,559	47.8	20,177	40.3	6,747	35.6	36,425	38.7
Prostitution and commercialized vice.......	284	1.3	121	0.8	1,054	2.1	83	0.4	1,689	1.8
Sex offenses (except forcible rape and prostitution).....................	1,840	8.6	1,710	10.8	4,333	8.7	1,570	8.3	7,889	8.4
Drug abuse violations.....................	81,110	377.8	84,841	536.6	162,238	323.9	77,373	408.3	317,731	337.6
Gambling.....................	59	0.3	35	0.2	273	0.5	57	0.3	359	0.4
Offenses against the family and children.	4,064	18.9	5,470	34.6	8,915	17.8	5,064	26.7	15,426	16.4
Driving under the influence.....................	51,461	239.7	53,484	338.3	140,244	280.0	80,434	424.5	235,930	250.7
Liquor laws.....................	10,203	47.5	16,141	102.1	9,189	18.3	7,985	42.1	27,056	28.7
Drunkenness.....................	15,990	74.5	24,616	155.7	14,141	28.2	6,538	34.5	39,762	42.2
Disorderly conduct.....................	22,277	103.8	25,701	162.5	18,076	36.1	10,129	53.5	55,216	58.7
Vagrancy.....................	659	3.1	627	4.0	803	1.6	179	0.9	2,126	2.3
All other offenses (except traffic).............	162,716	757.9	175,981	1,113.0	318,146	635.2	164,559	868.4	594,985	632.1
Suspicion.....................	54	0.3	115	0.7	3	*	35	0.2	122	0.1
Curfew and loitering law violations.........	1,268	5.9	1,089	6.9	713	1.4	235	1.2	2,659	2.8

* = Less than one-tenth of one percent.
[1] Suburban areas include law enforcement agencies in cities with less than 50,000 inhabitants and county law enforcement agencies that are within a Metropolitan Statistical Area. Suburban areas exclude all metropolitan agencies associated with a principal city. The agencies associated with suburban areas also appear in other groups within this table.
[2] Does not include suspicion.
[3] Violent crimes are offenses of murder and nonnegligent manslaughter, forcible rape, robbery, and aggravated assault. Property crimes are offenses of burglary, larceny-theft, motor vehicle theft, and arson.
[4] The rape figures in this table are aggregate totals of the data submitted based on both the legacy and revised Uniform Crime Reporting definitions.

Table 14. Ten-Year Arrest Trends, 2011 and 2020

(Number, percent change; 8,708 agencies; 2020 estimated population 180,606,800; 2011 estimated population 170,682,854.)

Offense charged	Total, all ages 2011	Total, all ages 2020	Total, all ages Percent change	Under 18 years of age 2011	Under 18 years of age 2020	Under 18 years of age Percent change	18 years of age and over 2011	18 years of age and over 2020	18 years of age and over Percent change
Total[1]	6,440,166	4,136,575	-35.8	768,471	240,121	-68.8	5,671,695	3,896,454	-31.3
Violent crime[2]	267,941	247,966	-7.5	31,103	17,730	-43.0	236,838	230,236	-2.8
Murder and nonnegligent manslaughter ...	5,095	6,135	+20.4	376	456	+21.3	4,719	5,679	+20.3
Rape[3]	10,230	11,006	NA	1,557	1,661		8,673	9,345	NA
Robbery	48,155	32,700	-32.1	9,965	5,595	-43.9	38,190	27,105	-29.0
Aggravated assault	204,461	198,125	-3.1	19,205	10,018	-47.8	185,256	188,107	+1.5
Property crime[2]	878,975	490,655	-44.2	183,084	42,776	-76.6	695,891	447,879	-35.6
Burglary	160,004	81,350	-49.2	33,098	8,251	-75.1	126,906	73,099	-42.4
Larceny-theft	680,688	359,412	-47.2	140,780	27,417	-80.5	539,908	331,995	-38.5
Motor vehicle theft	32,157	44,419	+38.1	6,454	6,387	-1.0	25,703	38,032	+48.0
Arson	6,126	5,474	-10.6	2,752	721	-73.8	3,374	4,753	+40.9
Other assaults	650,128	484,992	-25.4	98,892	39,639	-59.9	551,236	445,353	-19.2
Forgery and counterfeiting	36,910	18,761	-49.2	848	285	-66.4	36,062	18,476	-48.8
Fraud	92,521	44,734	-51.6	2,973	1,517	-49.0	89,548	43,217	-51.7
Embezzlement	9,016	5,358	-40.6	224	270	+20.5	8,792	5,088	-42.1
Stolen property; buying, receiving, possessing	53,257	48,649	-8.7	7,828	4,304	-45.0	45,429	44,345	-2.4
Vandalism	125,018	92,761	-25.8	36,960	13,680	-63.0	88,058	79,081	-10.2
Weapons; carrying, possessing, etc.	75,788	82,728	+9.2	14,392	5,666	-60.6	61,396	77,062	+25.5
Prostitution and commercialized vice	16,099	5,081	-68.4	310	39	-87.4	15,789	5,042	-68.1
Sex offenses (except forcible rape and prostitution)	35,350	17,104	-51.6	6,840	2,229	-67.4	28,510	14,875	-47.8
Drug abuse violations	759,311	645,454	-15.0	77,623	24,723	-68.1	681,688	620,731	-8.9
Gambling	1,523	888	-41.7	91	31	-65.9	1,432	857	-40.2
Offenses against the family and children ...	67,172	31,872	-52.6	1,923	1,368	-28.9	65,249	30,504	-53.2
Driving under the influence	626,737	375,190	-40.1	5,690	3,090	-45.7	621,047	372,100	-40.1
Liquor laws	257,232	58,057	-77.4	52,527	10,732	-79.6	204,705	47,325	-76.9
Drunkenness	297,165	110,581	-62.8	7,033	1,262	-82.1	290,132	109,319	-62.3
Disorderly conduct	277,249	127,096	-54.2	67,460	14,470	-78.6	209,789	112,626	-46.3
Vagrancy	10,490	6,631	-36.8	536	145	-72.9	9,954	6,486	-34.8
All other offenses (except traffic)	1,873,768	1,235,290	-34.1	143,618	49,438	-65.6	1,730,150	1,185,852	-31.5
Suspicion	225	156	-30.7	22	21	-4.5	203	135	-33.5
Curfew and loitering law violations	28,516	6,727	-76.4	28,516	6,727	-76.4	NA	NA	NA

NA = Not available.
[1] Does not include suspicion.
[2] Violent crimes are offenses of murder and nonnegligent manslaughter, rape, robbery, and aggravated assault. Property crimes are offenses of burglary, larceny-theft, motor vehicle theft, and arson.
[3] The 2011 rape figures are based on the legacy definition, and the 2020 rape figures are aggregate totals based on both the legacy and revised Uniform Crime Reporting definitions. For this reason, a percent change is not provided.

Table 15. Five-Year Arrest Trends, by Age, 2016 and 2020

(Number, percent change; 9,329 agencies; 2020 estimated population 200,962,238; 2016 estimated population 196,853,348.)

| | Number of persons arrested | | | | | | | | |
| | Total, all ages | | | Under 18 years of age | | | 18 years of age and over | | |
Offense charged	2016	2020	Percent change	2016	2020	Percent change	2016	2020	Percent change
Total[1]	6,479,915	4,768,317	-26.4	512,375	267,338	-47.8	5,967,540	4,500,979	-24.6
Violent crime[2]	306,674	292,029	-4.8	28,750	20,918	-27.2	277,924	271,111	-2.5
Murder and nonnegligent manslaughter	6,585	7,250	+10.1	460	535	+16.3	6,125	6,715	+9.6
Rape[3]	13,839	12,609	-8.9	2,152	1,812	-15.8	11,687	10,797	-7.6
Robbery	53,164	40,083	-24.6	9,759	6,957	-28.7	43,405	33,126	-23.7
Aggravated assault	233,086	232,087	-0.4	16,379	11,614	-29.1	216,707	220,473	+1.7
Property crime[2]	829,059	551,243	-33.5	112,981	47,291	-58.1	716,078	503,952	-29.6
Burglary	128,847	93,195	-27.7	19,778	9,433	-52.3	109,069	83,762	-23.2
Larceny-theft	644,576	401,887	-37.7	83,553	29,845	-64.3	561,023	372,042	-33.7
Motor vehicle theft	50,192	49,965	-0.5	8,174	7,237	-11.5	42,018	42,728	+1.7
Arson	5,444	6,196	+13.8	1,476	776	-47.4	3,968	5,420	+36.6
Other assaults	654,284	563,102	-13.9	76,185	44,961	-41.0	578,099	518,141	-10.4
Forgery and counterfeiting	34,923	20,762	-40.5	737	304	-58.8	34,186	20,458	-40.2
Fraud	78,230	49,721	-36.4	2,498	1,658	-33.6	75,732	48,063	-36.5
Embezzlement	10,236	6,166	-39.8	333	285	-14.4	9,903	5,881	-40.6
Stolen property; buying, receiving, possessing	60,363	57,208	-5.2	6,556	5,220	-20.4	53,807	51,988	-3.4
Vandalism	121,150	109,530	-9.6	24,312	15,005	-38.3	96,838	94,525	-2.4
Weapons; carrying, possessing, etc.	91,760	99,827	+8.8	11,092	6,630	-40.2	80,668	93,197	+15.5
Prostitution and commercialized vice	18,795	8,492	-54.8	294	74	-74.8	18,501	8,418	-54.5
Sex offenses (except forcible rape and prostitution)	29,938	20,310	-32.2	5,085	2,542	-50.0	24,853	17,768	-28.5
Drug abuse violations	956,732	726,791	-24.0	60,401	26,608	-55.9	896,331	700,183	-21.9
Gambling	1,197	997	-16.7	77	38	-50.6	1,120	959	-14.4
Offenses against the family and children	56,169	36,340	-35.3	2,341	1,436	-38.7	53,828	34,904	-35.2
Driving under the influence	614,726	474,472	-22.8	3,962	3,598	-9.2	610,764	470,874	-22.9
Liquor laws	142,435	65,069	-54.3	23,444	11,435	-51.2	118,991	53,634	-54.9
Drunkenness	219,596	125,293	-42.9	3,055	1,408	-53.9	216,541	123,885	-42.8
Disorderly conduct	207,631	143,595	-30.8	36,665	15,961	-56.5	170,966	127,634	-25.3
Vagrancy	14,185	9,189	-35.2	502	184	-63.3	13,683	9,005	-34.2
All other offenses (except traffic)	2,015,881	1,400,889	-30.5	97,154	54,490	-43.9	1,918,727	1,346,399	-29.8
Suspicion	313	189	-39.6	25	23	-8.0	288	166	-42.4
Curfew and loitering law violations	15,951	7,292	-54.3	15,951	7,292	-54.3	NA	NA	NA

NA = Not available.
[1]Does not include suspicion.
[2]Violent crimes are offenses of murder and nonnegligent manslaughter, rape, robbery, and aggravated assault. Property crimes are offenses of burglary, larceny-theft, motor vehicle theft, and arson.
[3]The rape figures in this table are aggregate totals of the data submitted based on both the legacy and revised Uniform Crime Reporting definitions.

Table 16. Current Year Over Previous Year Arrest Trends, 2019–2020

(Number, percent change; 9,245 agencies; 2020 estimated population 199,329,726; 2019 estimated population 198,464,294.)

| | Number of persons arrested | | | | | | | | | | | |
| | Total, all ages | | | Under 15 years of age | | | Under 18 years of age | | | 18 years of age and over | | |
Offense charged	2019	2020	Percent change	2019	2020	Percent change	2019	2020	Percent change	2019	2020	Percent change
Total[1]	5,945,932	4,620,603	-22.3	133,506	76,275	-42.9	415,981	263,317	-36.7	5,529,951	4,357,286	-21.2
Violent crime[2]	303,843	291,290	-4.1	8,882	5,761	-35.1	28,961	21,370	-26.2	274,882	269,920	-1.8
Murder and nonnegligent manslaughter ...	6,424	7,509	+16.9	50	59	+18.0	510	570	+11.8	5,914	6,939	+17.3
Rape[3]	14,601	12,742	-12.7	1,122	784	-30.1	2,524	1,832	-27.4	12,077	10,910	-9.7
Robbery	46,622	41,145	-11.7	2,038	1,543	-24.3	9,664	7,368	-23.8	36,958	33,777	-8.6
Aggravated assault	236,196	229,894	-2.7	5,672	3,375	-40.5	16,263	11,600	-28.7	219,933	218,294	-0.7
Property crime[2]	686,252	542,450	-21.0	22,677	13,623	-39.9	75,353	47,383	-37.1	610,899	495,067	-19.0
Burglary	103,980	91,817	-11.7	4,119	3,041	-26.2	12,807	9,561	-25.3	91,173	82,256	-9.8
Larceny-theft	527,116	394,234	-25.2	15,731	8,007	-49.1	53,216	29,599	-44.4	473,900	364,635	-23.1
Motor vehicle theft	49,783	50,257	+1.0	2,240	2,146	-4.2	8,281	7,430	-10.3	41,502	42,827	+3.2
Arson	5,373	6,142	+14.3	587	429	-26.9	1,049	793	-24.4	4,324	5,349	+23.7
Other assaults	613,181	553,284	-9.8	31,927	17,000	-46.8	73,463	43,819	-40.4	539,718	509,465	-5.6
Forgery and counterfeiting	28,784	20,156	-30.0	89	47	-47.2	557	305	-45.2	28,227	19,851	-29.7
Fraud	70,458	48,575	-31.1	553	433	-21.7	2,323	1,672	-28.0	68,135	46,903	-31.2
Embezzlement	9,056	5,928	-34.5	17	9	-47.1	365	287	-21.4	8,691	5,641	-35.1
Stolen property; buying, receiving, possessing	57,805	55,940	-3.2	1,254	1,138	-9.3	5,914	5,388	-8.9	51,891	50,552	-2.6
Vandalism	110,704	106,599	-3.7	8,454	5,826	-31.1	19,353	14,652	-24.3	91,351	91,947	+0.7
Weapons; carrying, possessing, etc.	94,199	99,430	+5.6	2,844	1,298	-54.4	9,830	6,774	-31.1	84,369	92,656	+9.8
Prostitution and commercialized vice	12,360	6,864	-44.5	22	6	-72.7	102	36	-64.7	12,258	6,828	-44.3
Sex offenses (except forcible rape and prostitution)	24,572	19,085	-22.3	1,999	1,206	-39.7	4,141	2,473	-40.3	20,431	16,612	-18.7
Drug abuse violations	927,890	709,607	-23.5	9,337	3,978	-57.4	47,811	25,971	-45.7	880,079	683,636	-22.3
Gambling	1,286	945	-26.5	9	7	-22.2	71	37	-47.9	1,215	908	-25.3
Offenses against the family and children ...	49,486	35,667	-27.9	632	429	-32.1	1,730	1,346	-22.2	47,756	34,321	-28.1
Driving under the influence	576,138	465,982	-19.1	79	50	-36.7	3,208	3,500	+9.1	572,930	462,482	-19.3
Liquor laws	95,438	62,473	-34.5	2,296	1,355	-41.0	14,824	10,998	-25.8	80,614	51,475	-36.1
Drunkenness	182,242	114,892	-37.0	295	228	-22.7	2,022	1,292	-36.1	180,220	113,600	-37.0
Disorderly conduct	180,812	138,200	-23.6	13,856	6,076	-56.1	31,733	15,310	-51.8	149,079	122,890	-17.6
Vagrancy	11,593	8,531	-26.4	62	44	-29.0	229	186	-18.8	11,364	8,345	-26.6
All other offenses (except traffic)	1,900,410	1,327,322	-30.2	25,073	15,231	-39.3	84,568	53,135	-37.2	1,815,842	1,274,187	-29.8
Suspicion	182	179	-1.6	2	7	+250.0	6	25	+316.7	176	154	-12.5
Curfew and loitering law violations	9,423	7,383	-21.6	3,149	2,530	-19.7	9,423	7,383	-21.6	NA	NA	NA

NA = Not available.
[1] Does not include suspicion.
[2] Violent crimes are offenses of murder and nonnegligent manslaughter, rape, robbery, and aggravated assault. Property crimes are offenses of burglary, larceny-theft, motor vehicle theft, and arson.
[3] The rape figures in this table are aggregate totals of the data submitted based on both the legacy and revised Uniform Crime Reporting definitions.

Table 17. Full-Time Law Enforcement Employees,[1] by Region and Geographic Division and Population Group, 2020

(Number, rate per 1,000 inhabitants.)

Region/geographic division	Total (10,293 cities; population 198,498,223	Group I (86 cities, 250,000 and over; population 63,000,994)	Group II (212 cities, 100,000 to 249,999; population 30,779,686)	Group III (430 cities, 50,000 to 99,999; population 29,997,046)	Group IV (789 cities, 25,000 to 49,999; population 27,195,395)	Group V (1,681 cities, 10,000 to 24,999; population 26,678,434)
Total, United States						
Number of employees	569,097	206,548	64,935	61,530	57,759	62,007
Average number of employees per 1,000 inhabitants	2.9	3.3	2.1	2.1	2.1	2.3
Northeast						
Number of employees	156,175	64,592	8,085	15,054	17,682	19,244
Average number of employees per 1,000 inhabitants	3.6	5.5	2.9	2.4	2.2	2.2
New England						
Number of employees	34,492	2,715	4,388	6,069	7,399	7,365
Average number of employees per 1,000 inhabitants	2.6	3.9	2.9	2.3	2.2	2.3
Middle Atlantic						
Number of employees	121,683	61,877	3,697	8,985	10,283	11,879
Average number of employees per 1,000 inhabitants	3.9	5.6	2.9	2.5	2.1	2.1
Midwest						
Number of employees	97,840	34,713	7,983	10,636	12,445	13,740
Average number of employees per 1,000 inhabitants	2.6	3.6	1.9	1.8	1.9	2.1
East North Central						
Number of employees	67,105	28,583	4,413	6,883	9,312	8,477
Average number of employees per 1,000 inhabitants	2.7	4.0	1.9	1.9	1.9	2.0
West North Central						
Number of employees	30,735	6,130	3,570	3,753	3,133	5,263
Average number of employees per 1,000 inhabitants	2.4	2.6	1.9	1.6	1.8	2.1
South						
Number of employees	197,564	54,447	28,857	20,952	18,948	22,117
Average number of employees per 1,000 inhabitants	3.2	2.8	2.4	2.4	2.6	2.9
South Atlantic						
Number of employees	90,405	23,428	13,555	11,509	9,179	9,829
Average number of employees per 1,000 inhabitants	3.5	3.4	2.6	2.6	2.7	3.1
East South Central						
Number of employees	36,272	6,538	5,126	2,747	4,442	4,999
Average number of employees per 1,000 inhabitants	3.6	2.8	3.1	2.5	2.7	3.0
West South Central						
Number of employees	70,887	24,481	10,176	6,696	5,327	7,289
Average number of employees per 1,000 inhabitants	2.7	2.3	2.1	2.1	2.3	2.6
West						
Number of employees	117,518	52,796	20,010	14,888	8,684	6,906
Average number of employees per 1,000 inhabitants	2.2	2.4	1.7	1.6	1.7	2.0
Mountain						
Number of employees	42,385	18,894	5,783	4,585	3,422	2,460
Average number of employees per 1,000 inhabitants	2.5	2.4	2.0	1.9	1.8	2.3
Pacific						
Number of employees	75,133	33,902	14,227	10,303	5,262	4,446
Average number of employees per 1,000 inhabitants	2.1	2.4	1.6	1.5	1.7	1.9

Table 17. Full-Time Law Enforcement Employees,[1] by Region and Geographic Division and Population Group, 2020—*Continued*

(Number, rate per 1,000 inhabitants.)

Region/geographic division	Group VI (7,095 cities, under 10,000; population 20,846,668)	Total city agencies	2020 estimated city population	County[2] (3,084 agencies; population 93,625,066)	Total city and county agencies	2020 estimated total agency population	Suburban areas[3] (7,147 agencies; population 124,916,229)
Total, United States							
Number of employees	116,318	10,293	198,498,223	436,682	13,377	292,123,289	469,639
Average number of employees per 1,000 inhabitants	5.6			4.7			3.8
Northeast							
Number of employees	31,518	2,530	43,951,402				
Average number of employees per 1,000 inhabitants	5.1						
New England							
Number of employees	6,556	807	13,067,841				
Average number of employees per 1,000 inhabitants	3.7						
Middle Atlantic							
Number of employees	24,962	1,723	30,883,561				
Average number of employees per 1,000 inhabitants	5.6						
Midwest							
Number of employees	18,323	2,439	38,130,123				
Average number of employees per 1,000 inhabitants	3.5						
East North Central							
Number of employees	9,437	1,336	25,111,109				
Average number of employees per 1,000 inhabitants	3.3						
West North Central							
Number of employees	8,886	1,103	13,019,014				
Average number of employees per 1,000 inhabitants	3.8						
South							
Number of employees	52,243	3,963	62,648,093				
Average number of employees per 1,000 inhabitants	7.2						
South Atlantic							
Number of employees	22,905	1,646	26,109,579				
Average number of employees per 1,000 inhabitants	8.0						
East South Central							
Number of employees	12,420	958	10,192,793				
Average number of employees per 1,000 inhabitants	6.8						
West South Central							
Number of employees	16,918	1,359	26,345,721				
Average number of employees per 1,000 inhabitants	6.5						
West							
Number of employees	14,234	1,361	53,768,605				
Average number of employees per 1,000 inhabitants	6.6						
Mountain							
Number of employees	7,241	600	17,194,281				
Average number of employees per 1,000 inhabitants	6.7						
Pacific							
Number of employees	6,993	761	36,574,324				
Average number of employees per 1,000 inhabitants	6.6						

[1] Full-time law enforcement employees include civilians.
[2] The designation county is a combination of both metropolitan and nonmetropolitan counties.
[3] Suburban areas include law enforcement agencies in cities with less than 50,000 inhabitants and county law enforcement agencies that are within a Metropolitan Statistical Area. Suburban areas exclude all metropolitan agencies associated with a principal city. The agencies associated with suburban areas also appear in other groups within this table.

Table 18. Full-Time Law Enforcement Officers, by Region, Geographic Division, and Population Group, 2020

(Number, rate per 1,000 inhabitants.)

Region/geographic division	Total (10,293 cities; population 198,498,223	Group I (86 cities, 250,000 and over; population 63,000,994)	Group II (212 cities, 100,000 to 249,999; population 30,779,686)	Group III (430 cities, 50,000 to 99,999; population 29,997,046)	Group IV (789 cities, 25,000 to 49,999; population 27,195,395)	Group V (1,681 cities, 10,000 to 24,999; population 26,678,434)
Total						
Number of officers	442,266	158,544	49,681	47,902	46,218	50,478
Average number of officers per 1,000 inhabitants	2.2	2.5	1.6	1.6	1.7	1.9
Northeast						
Number of officers	122,737	46,326	6,908	12,525	14,916	16,438
Average number of officers per 1,000 inhabitants	2.8	4.0	2.5	2.0	1.8	1.8
New England						
Number of officers	28,138	2,132	3,733	5,125	6,149	5,929
Average number of officers per 1,000 inhabitants	2.2	3.1	2.5	2.0	1.9	1.9
Middle Atlantic						
Number of officers	94,599	44,194	3,175	7,400	8,767	10,509
Average number of officers per 1,000 inhabitants	3.1	4.0	2.5	2.0	1.8	1.8
Midwest						
Number of officers	81,692	30,043	6,570	8,686	9,951	11,470
Average number of officers per 1,000 inhabitants	2.1	3.1	1.6	1.5	1.5	1.7
East North Central						
Number of officers	56,966	25,129	3,689	5,607	7,431	7,131
Average number of officers per 1,000 inhabitants	2.3	3.5	1.6	1.5	1.5	1.7
West North Central						
Number of officers	24,726	4,914	2,881	3,079	2,520	4,339
Average number of officers per 1,000 inhabitants	1.9	2.1	1.5	1.3	1.5	1.7
South						
Number of officers	152,739	42,941	21,847	16,212	15,013	17,416
Average number of officers per 1,000 inhabitants	2.4	2.2	1.8	1.9	2.0	2.3
South Atlantic						
Number of officers	70,345	18,010	10,385	8,946	7,380	7,838
Average number of officers per 1,000 inhabitants	2.7	2.6	2.0	2.0	2.1	2.5
East South Central						
Number of officers	28,351	5,187	3,951	2,196	3,570	4,034
Average number of officers per 1,000 inhabitants	2.8	2.2	2.4	2.0	2.2	2.4
West South Central						
Number of officers	54,043	19,744	7,511	5,070	4,063	5,544
Average number of officers per 1,000 inhabitants	2.1	1.9	1.5	1.6	1.7	2.0
West						
Number of officers	85,098	39,234	14,356	10,479	6,338	5,154
Average number of officers per 1,000 inhabitants	1.6	1.8	1.2	1.1	1.2	1.5
Mountain						
Number of officers	30,858	13,972	4,359	3,264	2,607	1,840
Average number of officers per 1,000 inhabitants	1.8	1.8	1.5	1.3	1.4	1.7
Pacific						
Number of officers	54,240	25,262	9,997	7,215	3,731	3,314
Average number of officers per 1,000 inhabitants	1.5	1.8	1.1	1.1	1.2	1.4

Table 18. Full-Time Law Enforcement Officers, by Region, Geographic Division, and Population Group, 2020—*Continued*

(Number, rate per 1,000 inhabitants.)

Region/geographic division	Group VI (7,095 cities, under 10,000; population 20,846,668)	Total city agencies	2020 estimated city population	County[1] (3,084 agencies; population 93,625,066)	Total city and county agencies	2020 estimated total agency population	Suburban areas[2] (7,147 agencies; population 124,916,229)
Total							
Number of officers	89,443	10,293	198,498,223	254,378	13,377	292,123,289	305,724
Average number of officers per 1,000 inhabitants	4.3			2.7			2.4
Northeast							
Number of officers	25,624	2,530	43,951,402				
Average number of officers per 1,000 inhabitants	4.1						
New England							
Number of officers	5,070	807	13,067,841				
Average number of officers per 1,000 inhabitants	2.9						
Middle Atlantic							
Number of officers	20,554	1,723	30,883,561				
Average number of officers per 1,000 inhabitants	4.6						
Midwest							
Number of officers	14,972	2,439	38,130,123				
Average number of officers per 1,000 inhabitants	2.9						
East North Central							
Number of officers	7,979	1,336	25,111,109				
Average number of officers per 1,000 inhabitants	2.8						
West North Central							
Number of officers	6,993	1,103	13,019,014				
Average number of officers per 1,000 inhabitants	3.0						
South							
Number of officers	39,310	3,963	62,648,093				
Average number of officers per 1,000 inhabitants	5.4						
South Atlantic							
Number of officers	17,786	1,646	26,109,579				
Average number of officers per 1,000 inhabitants	6.2						
East South Central							
Number of officers	9,413	958	10,192,793				
Average number of officers per 1,000 inhabitants	5.1						
West South Central							
Number of officers	12,111	1,359	26,345,721				
Average number of officers per 1,000 inhabitants	4.7						
West							
Number of officers	9,537	1,361	53,768,605				
Average number of officers per 1,000 inhabitants	4.4						
Mountain							
Number of officers	4,816	600	17,194,281				
Average number of officers per 1,000 inhabitants	4.4						
Pacific							
Number of officers	4,721	761	36,574,324				
Average number of officers per 1,000 inhabitants	4.4						

[1] The designation county is a combination of both metropolitan and nonmetropolitan counties.
[2] Suburban areas include law enforcement agencies in cities with less than 50,000 inhabitants and county law enforcement agencies that are within a Metropolitan Statistical Area. Suburban areas exclude all metropolitan agencies associated with a principal city. The agencies associated with suburban areas also appear in other groups within this table.

Table 19. Full-Time Law Enforcement Employees, by Selected State and City, 2020

(Number.)

State/city	Population	Total law enforcement employees	Total officers	Total civilians
ALABAMA				
Abbeville	2,545	10	9	1
Adamsville	4,257	25	14	11
Addison	714	3	3	0
Alabaster	33,750	79	63	16
Albertville	21,769	67	45	22
Alexander City	14,251	68	53	15
Aliceville	2,230	6	5	1
Altoona	910	5	5	0
Andalusia	8,643	35	28	7
Anniston	21,112	89	82	7
Arab	8,416	35	26	9
Ardmore	1,495	9	5	4
Argo	4,377	7	7	0
Arley	344	2	2	0
Ashford	2,184	4	4	0
Ashland	1,880	9	8	1
Ashville	2,380	4	4	0
Athens	28,039	57	46	11
Atmore	8,997	34	25	9
Attalla	5,742	28	22	6
Auburn	67,814	139	130	9
Baker Hill	249	4	3	1
Bay Minette	9,482	30	22	8
Bayou La Batre	2,466	18	13	5
Bear Creek	1,068	2	2	0
Berry	1,090	4	4	0
Bessemer	26,347	157	112	45
Birmingham	209,081	1,034	828	206
Blountsville	1,668	5	5	0
Boaz	9,730	33	22	11
Brantley	764	5	4	1
Brent	4,725	7	7	0
Brewton	5,189	33	24	9
Bridgeport	2,282	10	6	4
Brighton	2,757	14	8	6
Brilliant	870	1	1	0
Brookside	1,325	16	12	4
Brookwood	1,851	6	6	0
Brundidge	1,884	10	6	4
Calera	15,093	43	34	9
Camden	1,739	11	9	2
Camp Hill	944	5	5	0
Carrollton	935	3	3	0
Cedar Bluff	1,823	6	6	0
Centre	3,547	14	13	1
Centreville	2,591	6	6	0
Chatom	1,171	3	3	0
Cherokee	1,004	1	1	0
Chickasaw	5,661	20	20	0
Childersburg	4,804	20	18	2
Citronelle	3,856	20	11	9
Clanton	8,812	26	25	1
Clayton	2,831	4	4	0
Clio	1,263	4	4	0
Coaling	1,663	4	4	0
Coffeeville	319	3	3	0
Collinsville	2,012	8	4	4
Columbia	737	2	2	0
Columbiana	4,596	15	11	4
Coosada	1,307	7	6	1
Cordova	1,825	6	4	2
Cottonwood	1,252	3	3	0
Courtland	585	2	2	0
Creola	2,049	9	4	5
Crossville	1,856	5	5	0
Cullman	16,134	58	51	7
Dadeville	3,035	16	15	1
Daleville	5,080	22	16	6
Daphne	27,496	89	59	30
Dauphin Island	1,347	16	8	8

(Number.)

State/city	Population	Total law enforcement employees	Total officers	Total civilians
Decatur	54,295	152	133	19
Demopolis	6,525	26	22	4
Dora	1,890	12	8	4
Dothan	69,265	235	164	71
Double Springs	1,056	7	7	0
Douglas	782	5	5	0
East Brewton	2,343	21	10	11
Eclectic	1,016	9	8	1
Elba	3,796	17	12	5
Elberta	1,775	11	10	1
Enterprise	28,569	74	58	16
Eufaula	11,568	55	34	21
Eutaw	2,570	8	7	1
Evergreen	3,482	25	19	6
Excel	623	2	2	0
Fairfield	10,512	5	4	1
Fairhope	23,517	64	41	23
Falkville	1,254	8	6	2
Fayette	4,239	12	12	0
Flomaton	1,388	12	7	5
Florala	1,898	8	8	0
Florence	40,936	137	110	27
Foley	21,036	93	65	28
Fort Deposit	1,136	3	3	0
Fort Payne	14,071	35	35	0
Frisco City	1,137	2	2	0
Fultondale	9,391	35	28	7
Fyffe	1,048	5	5	0
Gadsden	34,791	126	97	29
Gantt	215	6	4	2
Gardendale	14,198	41	31	10
Geneva	4,273	13	12	1
Georgiana	1,594	8	5	3
Geraldine	897	6	6	0
Gilbertown	191	3	2	1
Glencoe	5,063	10	9	1
Goodwater	1,298	8	4	4
Gordo	1,600	4	4	0
Gordon	325	1	1	0
Grant	918	2	2	0
Greensboro	2,245	9	9	0
Greenville	7,318	29	26	3
Grove Hill	1,717	7	6	1
Guin	2,264	7	7	0
Gulf Shores	12,985	71	50	21
Guntersville	8,606	46	35	11
Gurley	809	6	6	0
Hackleburg	1,234	4	4	0
Haleyville	4,115	16	11	5
Hamilton	6,575	16	14	2
Hanceville	3,494	11	9	2
Harpersville	1,734	9	8	1
Hartford	2,574	15	11	4
Hartselle	14,486	29	28	1
Hayneville	769	5	4	1
Headland	4,733	31	16	15
Heflin	3,400	12	11	1
Helena	20,279	35	30	5
Henagar	2,364	13	9	4
Highland Lake	410	6	6	0
Hillsboro	518	2	2	0
Hokes Bluff	4,254	9	9	0
Hollywood	982	5	5	0
Homewood	25,407	118	81	37
Hoover	86,321	219	182	37
Hueytown	15,235	44	35	9
Huntsville	202,884	662	450	212
Ider	717	7	3	4
Irondale	12,949	39	32	7
Jackson	4,583	24	20	4
Jacksons Gap	827	2	2	0

(Number.)

State/city	Population	Total law enforcement employees	Total officers	Total civilians
Jacksonville	12,475	34	27	7
Jasper	13,327	70	46	24
Jemison	2,678	13	12	1
Killen	951	4	4	0
Kimberly	3,660	6	6	0
Kinsey	2,274	1	1	0
Kinston	548	2	1	1
LaFayette	2,901	14	13	1
Lake View	2,756	3	3	0
Lanett	6,117	31	29	2
Leeds	12,068	31	30	1
Leesburg	1,014	3	3	0
Leighton	754	4	3	1
Level Plains	1,994	5	5	0
Lexington	706	4	4	0
Lincoln	6,843	20	18	2
Linden	1,856	7	7	0
Lineville	2,231	11	7	4
Lipscomb	2,132	9	4	5
Littleville	990	7	5	2
Livingston	3,240	10	7	3
Louisville	456	2	2	0
Loxley	3,235	25	16	9
Luverne	2,737	13	11	2
Lynn	633	1	1	0
Madison	52,573	109	78	31
Maplesville	699	7	7	0
Margaret	5,222	7	7	0
Marion	3,067	5	5	0
McIntosh	213	8	8	0
McKenzie	488	3	3	0
Mentone	369	2	2	0
Midfield	4,967	18	14	4
Midland City	2,377	4	4	0
Millbrook	15,993	56	40	16
Millport	973	1	1	0
Millry	492	1	1	0
Mobile	243,900	747	495	252
Monroeville	5,638	29	23	6
Montevallo	6,784	20	16	4
Montgomery	197,755	569	485	84
Moody	13,220	28	27	1
Morris	2,176	5	5	0
Moulton	3,217	11	11	0
Moundville	2,463	11	10	1
Mountain Brook	20,281	69	56	13
Mount Vernon	1,487	5	4	1
Munford	1,344	1	1	0
Muscle Shoals	14,737	28	26	2
Napier Field	343	3	2	1
New Brockton	1,275	6	5	1
New Hope	2,927	6	6	0
New Site	759	2	2	0
Newton	1,450	10	8	2
Newville	509	1	1	0
North Courtland	619	1	1	0
Northport	26,372	75	57	18
Notasulga	808	8	3	5
Oakman	718	1	1	0
Odenville	3,915	10	10	0
Ohatchee	1,153	6	6	0
Oneonta	6,576	27	26	1
Opelika	31,437	111	89	22
Opp	6,361	29	21	8
Orange Beach	6,329	75	49	26
Owens Crossroads	2,206	4	4	0
Oxford	21,191	71	69	2
Ozark	14,215	39	32	7
Parrish	932	2	2	0
Pelham	24,188	82	66	16
Pell City	14,195	42	40	2

(Number.)

State/city	Population	Total law enforcement employees	Total officers	Total civilians
Phenix City	36,883	104	80	24
Pickensville	575	1	1	0
Piedmont	4,501	22	16	6
Pine Hill	840	5	5	0
Pleasant Grove	9,551	20	15	5
Powell	968	4	4	0
Prattville	36,162	87	80	7
Priceville	3,940	7	7	0
Prichard	21,305	56	35	21
Ragland	1,731	4	4	0
Rainbow City	9,610	37	23	14
Rainsville	5,138	14	10	4
Ranburne	397	3	2	1
Red Bay	3,077	13	9	4
Red Level	477	2	2	0
Reform	1,537	6	6	0
River Falls	536	3	3	0
Riverside	2,395	5	5	0
Roanoke	5,894	28	23	5
Robertsdale	6,961	28	16	12
Rogersville	1,250	6	6	0
Russellville	9,723	31	27	4
Samson	1,844	7	7	0
Saraland	14,751	58	46	12
Sardis City	1,783	5	5	0
Satsuma	6,195	18	14	4
Scottsboro	14,398	69	42	27
Selma	16,876	58	42	16
Sheffield	8,886	31	29	2
Shorter	388	6	5	1
Silverhill	1,238	7	6	1
Skyline	837	1	1	0
Slocomb	1,890	11	11	0
Snead	838	13	13	0
Somerville	774	4	4	0
Southside	8,957	19	13	6
Spanish Fort	9,511	28	24	4
Springville	4,325	11	11	0
Steele	1,094	3	3	0
Stevenson	1,941	7	5	2
St. Florian	708	4	4	0
Sulligent	1,825	6	6	0
Summerdale	1,804	12	11	1
Sylacauga	11,955	40	39	1
Sylvania	1,897	3	3	0
Talladega	15,398	47	43	4
Tallassee	4,482	27	20	7
Tarrant	6,080	26	20	6
Taylor	2,437	5	4	1
Thomasville	3,799	21	21	0
Thorsby	2,063	6	6	0
Town Creek	1,032	2	2	0
Trafford	615	1	1	0
Triana	1,026	3	3	0
Trinity	2,490	7	7	0
Troy	19,041	80	62	18
Trussville	22,961	78	65	13
Tuscaloosa	102,391	354	283	71
Tuscumbia	8,446	28	21	7
Tuskegee	7,973	29	18	11
Union Springs	3,365	21	12	9
Uniontown	2,181	6	5	1
Valley	9,101	29	27	2
Valley Head	548	2	2	0
Vance	1,672	5	5	0
Vernon	1,835	9	9	0
Vestavia Hills	34,489	102	99	3
Wadley	710	5	5	0
Warrior	3,214	17	10	7
Weaver	3,060	11	8	3
Wedowee	791	10	9	1

State/city	Population	Total law enforcement employees	Total officers	Total civilians
West Blocton	1,248	1	1	0
Wetumpka	8,562	33	30	3
Winfield	4,497	14	13	1
Woodstock	1,663	5	5	0
York	2,208	4	4	0
ALASKA				
Anchorage	286,388	592	425	167
Bethel	6,642	24	11	13
Bristol Bay Borough	817	9	4	5
Cordova	2,161	10	4	6
Craig	1,268	10	5	5
Dillingham	2,364	20	8	12
Fairbanks	30,832	38	33	5
Haines	2,524	10	5	5
Homer	6,028	22	12	10
Hoonah	794	9	5	4
Juneau	31,925	83	48	35
Kenai	7,885	27	17	10
Ketchikan	8,307	38	25	13
Klawock	790	2	2	0
Kodiak	5,778	39	16	23
Kotzebue	3,249	18	10	8
Nome	3,900	17	10	7
North Pole	2,090	13	11	2
North Slope Borough	9,836	76	45	31
Palmer	7,641	24	14	10
Petersburg	3,259	14	8	6
Sand Point	1,073	6	5	1
Seward	2,806	22	9	13
Sitka	8,420	26	14	12
Skagway	1,206	9	3	6
Soldotna	4,782	17	14	3
Unalaska	4,439	23	12	11
Valdez	3,841	12	12	0
Wasilla	11,228	30	26	4
Whittier	203	5	5	0
Wrangell	2,508	11	5	6
ARIZONA				
Apache Junction	43,385	101	65	36
Avondale	89,338	198	133	65
Benson	4,854	22	15	7
Bisbee	5,184	20	14	6
Buckeye	83,608	130	96	34
Bullhead City	41,035	101	67	34
Camp Verde	11,223	35	22	13
Casa Grande	59,822	99	80	19
Chandler	264,071	472	318	154
Chino Valley	12,564	31	26	5
Clarkdale	4,433	9	8	1
Clifton	3,761	10	4	6
Colorado City	4,838	13	9	4
Coolidge	13,277	40	27	13
Cottonwood	12,380	52	29	23
Douglas	16,044	42	28	14
Eagar	4,944	8	6	2
El Mirage	36,221	69	51	18
Eloy	19,981	36	26	10
Flagstaff	76,107	149	104	45
Florence	27,571	34	25	9
Fredonia	1,275	3	3	0
Gilbert	259,629	422	289	133
Glendale	255,468	548	400	148
Globe	7,328	27	23	4
Goodyear	89,607	154	115	39
Hayden	976	5	5	0
Holbrook	5,088	13	11	2
Huachuca City	1,723	7	5	2
Jerome	456	5	5	0
Kearny	2,193	12	8	4

(Number.)

State/city	Population	Total law enforcement employees	Total officers	Total civilians
Kingman	31,351	64	47	17
Lake Havasu City	56,243	109	71	38
Mammoth	1,709	4	4	0
Marana	50,942	124	96	28
Maricopa	53,165	84	67	17
Mesa	527,361	1,268	828	440
Miami	1,774	12	7	5
Nogales	20,026	63	46	17
Oro Valley	46,634	122	96	26
Page	7,546	30	19	11
Paradise Valley	14,859	45	34	11
Parker	3,224	12	10	2
Patagonia	870	3	3	0
Payson	15,869	44	25	19
Peoria	178,486	297	197	100
Phoenix	1,708,960	3,903	2,939	964
Pima	2,580	5	5	0
Pinetop-Lakeside	4,490	18	14	4
Prescott	44,835	90	75	15
Prescott Valley	47,459	95	72	23
Quartzsite	3,772	12	11	1
Safford	10,033	24	21	3
Sahuarita	32,053	59	49	10
San Luis	35,574	59	37	22
Scottsdale	263,006	613	379	234
Sedona	10,373	43	24	19
Show Low	11,527	51	30	21
Sierra Vista	42,800	84	66	18
Snowflake-Taylor	10,384	16	14	2
Somerton	16,811	27	19	8
South Tucson	5,723	17	16	1
Springerville	1,979	8	6	2
St. Johns	3,514	10	7	3
Superior	3,212	10	9	1
Surprise	144,620	199	140	59
Tempe	199,935	487	346	141
Thatcher	5,242	12	11	1
Tolleson	7,470	46	30	16
Tombstone	1,294	9	7	2
Tucson	550,448	1,087	855	232
Wellton	3,062	7	6	1
Wickenburg	7,041	25	20	5
Willcox	3,509	18	11	7
Williams	3,271	21	11	10
Winslow	9,298	43	23	20
Yuma	99,096	227	137	90
ARKANSAS				
Alexander	3,524	10	10	0
Alma	5,904	19	15	4
Altus	726	1	1	0
Amity	681	3	1	2
Arkadelphia	10,732	29	23	6
Ashdown	4,367	14	12	2
Ash Flat	1,099	6	6	0
Atkins	3,040	9	8	1
Augusta	1,917	5	5	0
Austin	4,401	4	4	0
Bald Knob	2,864	14	8	6
Barling	5,076	10	10	0
Batesville	10,938	26	25	1
Bay	1,823	4	4	0
Beebe	8,268	23	17	6
Bella Vista	29,138	52	36	16
Benton	37,542	77	68	9
Bentonville	57,575	115	83	32
Berryville	5,577	16	14	2
Blytheville	13,239	53	36	17
Booneville	3,765	13	9	4
Bradford	734	2	2	0
Brinkley	2,531	15	9	6

(Number.)

State/city	Population	Total law enforcement employees	Total officers	Total civilians
Bryant	21,497	57	46	11
Bull Shoals	1,945	7	4	3
Cabot	26,593	54	43	11
Caddo Valley	637	5	4	1
Camden	10,605	36	18	18
Cammack Village	713	4	4	0
Caraway	1,283	3	3	0
Carlisle	2,149	9	5	4
Cave Springs	5,888	9	9	0
Centerton	17,220	24	22	2
Charleston	2,462	5	5	0
Cherokee Village	4,657	8	7	1
Cherry Valley	576	1	1	0
Clarendon	1,330	3	3	0
Clarksville	9,829	23	19	4
Clinton	2,505	8	7	1
Conway	68,599	162	118	44
Corning	3,018	10	6	4
Cotter	949	3	3	0
Crossett	4,723	26	17	9
Damascus	382	1	1	0
Danville	2,391	6	5	1
Dardanelle	4,520	17	11	6
Decatur	1,801	5	5	0
De Queen	6,526	17	14	3
Des Arc	1,568	6	6	0
DeWitt	2,976	13	8	5
Diamond City	802	1	1	0
Diaz	1,196	3	3	0
Dover	1,446	5	5	0
Dumas	3,984	16	12	4
Dyer	901	1	1	0
Earle	2,156	3	3	0
El Dorado	17,523	67	51	16
Elkins	3,588	10	10	0
England	2,673	12	8	4
Etowah	313	1	1	0
Eudora	1,866	6	4	2
Eureka Springs	2,110	18	13	5
Fairfield Bay	2,173	17	7	10
Farmington	7,575	18	18	0
Fayetteville	89,252	171	125	46
Flippin	1,319	7	7	0
Fordyce	3,646	11	7	4
Forrest City	13,656	38	29	9
Fort Smith	88,071	193	148	45
Gassville	2,168	4	4	0
Gentry	4,086	12	10	2
Gillett	680	2	1	1
Glenwood	2,117	4	4	0
Gosnell	3,066	6	6	0
Gravette	3,558	12	11	1
Greenbrier	5,779	14	9	5
Green Forest	2,760	14	12	2
Greenland	1,416	4	4	0
Greenwood	9,449	20	18	2
Greers Ferry	853	5	4	1
Gurdon	2,069	5	4	1
Guy	792	2	2	0
Hamburg	2,574	7	6	1
Hampton	1,251	4	4	0
Hardy	765	5	5	0
Harrisburg	2,309	7	5	2
Harrison	13,096	45	34	11
Haskell	4,667	8	8	0
Hazen	1,331	7	6	1
Heber Springs	6,880	17	16	1
Helena-West Helena	10,086	28	15	13
Higginson	737	1	1	0
Highfill	641	4	4	0
Highland	1,113	3	3	0

(Number.)

State/city	Population	Total law enforcement employees	Total officers	Total civilians
Hope	9,543	35	25	10
Hot Springs	38,893	137	100	37
Hughes	1,193	4	3	1
Huntsville	2,585	10	8	2
Jacksonville	28,217	67	56	11
Johnson	3,781	9	8	1
Jonesboro	79,702	178	163	15
Judsonia	1,991	4	3	1
Kensett	1,613	3	3	0
Lake City	2,720	4	4	0
Lakeview	718	2	2	0
Lake Village	2,155	13	7	6
Lamar	1,734	3	3	0
Lavaca	2,441	3	3	0
Leachville	1,835	5	4	1
Lead Hill	265	1	1	0
Lewisville	1,097	2	2	0
Lincoln	2,503	6	6	0
Little Flock	2,816	7	7	0
Little Rock	197,688	736	560	176
Lonoke	4,178	16	12	4
Lowell	9,825	27	21	6
Luxora	1,011	1	1	0
Magnolia	11,434	24	22	2
Malvern	10,966	23	21	2
Mammoth Spring	959	2	2	0
Mansfield	1,090	4	4	0
Marianna	3,325	23	13	10
Marion	12,285	34	29	5
Marked Tree	2,405	14	8	6
Marmaduke	1,265	4	4	0
Marshall	1,330	4	4	0
Marvell	892	7	4	3
Maumelle	18,307	49	37	12
Mayflower	2,418	9	8	1
McCrory	1,464	6	5	1
McGehee	3,631	25	13	12
McRae	667	1	1	0
Mena	5,461	14	13	1
Menifee	319	2	1	1
Mineral Springs	1,142	4	3	1
Monette	1,602	3	3	0
Monticello	9,348	29	21	8
Morrilton	6,631	27	24	3
Mountainburg	612	1	1	0
Mountain Home	12,582	38	31	7
Mountain View	2,875	11	10	1
Mulberry	1,697	4	4	0
Murfreesboro	1,576	3	3	0
Nashville	4,360	17	16	1
Newport	7,423	24	18	6
North Little Rock	66,303	218	185	33
Ola	1,203	4	3	1
Osceola	6,527	34	24	10
Ozark	3,583	13	11	2
Paragould	29,288	57	51	6
Paris	3,345	13	8	5
Patterson	385	1	1	0
Pea Ridge	6,398	16	15	1
Perryville	1,457	5	5	0
Piggott	3,494	7	7	0
Pine Bluff	40,718	134	111	23
Plumerville	768	2	2	0
Pocahontas	6,647	18	17	1
Pottsville	3,390	9	7	2
Prairie Grove	7,058	16	16	0
Prescott	2,957	12	6	6
Quitman	714	4	4	0
Ravenden	448	1	1	0
Redfield	1,540	7	6	1
Rogers	70,194	154	116	38

State/city	Population	Total law enforcement employees	Total officers	Total civilians
Rose Bud	488	4	3	1
Russellville	29,266	61	55	6
Salem	1,679	4	4	0
Searcy	23,742	72	53	19
Shannon Hills	4,098	5	5	0
Sheridan	4,963	30	16	14
Sherwood	31,636	100	76	24
Siloam Springs	17,332	54	39	15
Springdale	85,146	205	146	59
Stamps	1,442	1	1	0
Star City	2,005	6	5	1
St. Charles	210	1	1	0
Stuttgart	8,402	30	22	8
Sulphur Springs	530	3	3	0
Swifton	726	2	2	0
Texarkana	29,622	86	75	11
Trumann	6,934	26	19	7
Tuckerman	1,663	4	4	0
Turrell	549	1	1	0
Tyronza	717	2	2	0
Van Buren	23,779	64	50	14
Vilonia	4,719	8	8	0
Waldron	3,344	10	9	1
Walnut Ridge	5,023	8	8	0
Ward	5,517	12	11	1
Warren	5,546	23	14	9
Weiner	669	1	1	0
West Fork	2,688	7	6	1
West Memphis	24,205	95	75	20
White Hall	4,904	19	17	2
Wilson	805	1	1	0
Wynne	7,682	22	20	2
CALIFORNIA				
Alameda	78,047	105	72	33
Albany	19,830	31	22	9
Alhambra	83,817	124	81	43
Alturas	2,535	8	8	0
Anaheim	351,913	556	402	154
Anderson	10,705	27	19	8
Angels Camp	3,974	7	6	1
Antioch	112,481	166	120	46
Arcadia	58,122	89	63	26
Arcata	18,516	38	25	13
Arroyo Grande	18,054	25	22	3
Arvin	22,149	24	16	8
Atascadero	30,266	38	28	10
Atherton	7,162	28	20	8
Atwater	29,704	33	23	10
Auburn	14,293	27	20	7
Avenal	13,321	19	17	2
Azusa	50,373	80	53	27
Bakersfield	388,265	588	403	185
Baldwin Park	75,233	84	63	21
Banning	31,392	42	26	16
Barstow	24,041	58	41	17
Bear Valley	121	6	5	1
Beaumont	52,884	56	41	15
Bell	35,526	41	30	11
Bell Gardens	42,008	67	45	22
Belmont	27,063	44	32	12
Belvedere	2,107	6	6	0
Benicia	28,374	49	31	18
Berkeley	122,346	254	163	91
Beverly Hills	33,776	226	134	92
Bishop	3,733	19	11	8
Blythe	19,590	30	20	10
Brawley	26,363	40	26	14
Brea	43,705	100	57	43
Brentwood	66,061	95	64	31
Brisbane	4,716	17	14	3

(Number.)

State/city	Population	Total law enforcement employees	Total officers	Total civilians
Broadmoor	4,176	8	7	1
Buena Park	81,901	130	87	43
Burbank	102,419	230	147	83
Burlingame	31,126	59	39	20
Calexico	39,957	39	24	15
California City	14,286	25	14	11
Calistoga	5,255	16	11	5
Campbell	41,921	73	42	31
Capitola	10,020	27	21	6
Carlsbad	116,516	180	128	52
Carmel	3,825	21	14	7
Cathedral City	55,417	67	47	20
Central Marin	34,593	44	40	4
Ceres	49,028	63	47	16
Chico	105,355	144	94	50
Chino	96,309	165	114	51
Chowchilla	18,278	30	20	10
Chula Vista	278,027	342	243	99
Citrus Heights	88,314	130	83	47
Claremont	36,422	62	38	24
Clayton	12,420	13	11	2
Clearlake	15,268	39	21	18
Cloverdale	8,660	21	13	8
Clovis	116,809	165	98	67
Coalinga	17,061	24	17	7
Colma	1,495	24	18	6
Colton	55,117	76	52	24
Colusa	6,042	10	9	1
Concord	130,074	178	135	43
Corcoran	21,700	31	17	14
Corning	7,714	21	13	8
Corona	171,848	209	142	67
Coronado	23,750	70	47	23
Costa Mesa	113,317	190	129	61
Cotati	7,426	17	12	5
Covina	47,413	80	58	22
Crescent City	6,706	13	12	1
Culver City	39,218	144	110	34
Cypress	49,124	60	45	15
Daly City	106,855	127	98	29
Davis	69,853	88	56	32
Delano	53,625	68	50	18
Del Rey Oaks	1,657	10	10	0
Desert Hot Springs	29,074	33	26	7
Dinuba	24,807	46	33	13
Dixon	20,967	31	26	5
Dos Palos	5,594	16	11	5
Downey	111,054	160	116	44
East Palo Alto	29,439	45	37	8
El Cajon	103,035	176	120	56
El Centro	44,238	63	43	20
El Cerrito	25,725	46	38	8
Elk Grove	177,331	242	135	107
El Monte	115,690	157	118	39
El Segundo	16,605	73	53	20
Emeryville	12,328	54	37	17
Escalon	7,625	13	12	1
Escondido	152,446	208	151	57
Etna	716	4	4	0
Eureka	26,656	71	46	25
Exeter	10,501	18	17	1
Fairfax	7,530	16	11	5
Fairfield	118,491	179	117	62
Farmersville	10,716	17	16	1
Ferndale	1,350	8	8	0
Firebaugh	8,377	17	12	5
Folsom	82,427	102	75	27
Fontana	216,553	297	186	111
Fort Bragg	7,289	19	14	5
Fortuna	12,283	24	18	6
Foster City	34,291	52	37	15

Table 19. Full-Time Law Enforcement Employees, by Selected State and City, 2020—*Continued*

(Number.)

State/city	Population	Total law enforcement employees	Total officers	Total civilians
Fountain Valley	55,345	77	58	19
Fowler	6,929	12	12	0
Fremont	244,259	301	195	106
Fresno	535,472	1,026	788	238
Fullerton	139,011	181	121	60
Galt	26,867	44	31	13
Gardena	59,385	104	82	22
Garden Grove	171,698	236	171	65
Gilroy	60,269	90	60	30
Glendale	200,168	354	225	129
Glendora	51,676	78	48	30
Gonzales	8,321	13	10	3
Grass Valley	12,811	32	26	6
Greenfield	17,643	30	24	6
Gridley	7,320	17	11	6
Grover Beach	13,491	26	19	7
Guadalupe	7,865	15	13	2
Gustine	5,922	9	7	2
Hanford	58,075	86	60	26
Hawthorne	86,269	137	92	45
Hayward	160,891	287	174	113
Healdsburg	11,907	23	16	7
Hemet	86,058	104	70	34
Hercules	26,524	26	22	4
Hermosa Beach	19,300	64	35	29
Hillsborough	11,447	35	26	9
Hollister	41,438	39	31	8
Huntington Beach	200,128	321	199	122
Huntington Park	57,442	82	54	28
Huron	7,343	8	6	2
Imperial	18,528	24	21	3
Indio	93,219	112	70	42
Inglewood	107,986	249	191	58
Ione	8,674	9	9	0
Irvine	297,069	319	218	101
Irwindale	1,449	34	27	7
Jackson	4,861	10	9	1
Kensington	5,077	10	10	0
Kerman	15,478	27	23	4
King City	14,214	18	16	2
Kingsburg	12,182	21	18	3
Laguna Beach	22,834	98	54	44
La Habra	60,672	98	68	30
Lakeport	5,035	12	11	1
Lake Shastina	2,561	3	3	0
La Mesa	59,488	92	66	26
La Palma	15,415	26	19	7
La Verne	32,073	52	37	15
Lemoore	26,980	40	32	8
Lincoln	48,887	32	24	8
Lindsay	13,668	18	17	1
Livermore	91,200	125	88	37
Livingston	15,115	25	16	9
Lodi	68,207	100	71	29
Lompoc	42,915	60	35	25
Long Beach	462,654	1,174	809	365
Los Alamitos	11,400	23	19	4
Los Altos	30,203	45	32	13
Los Angeles	4,000,587	12,863	9,863	3,000
Los Banos	41,631	71	43	28
Los Gatos	30,271	59	39	20
Madera	66,351	97	69	28
Mammoth Lakes	8,236	19	15	4
Manhattan Beach	35,190	99	60	39
Manteca	84,929	101	73	28
Marina	23,147	36	28	8
Martinez	38,543	46	33	13
Marysville	12,519	27	17	10
McFarland	15,858	14	11	3
Mendota	11,531	16	14	2
Menifee	96,837	80	58	22

(Number.)

State/city	Population	Total law enforcement employees	Total officers	Total civilians
Menlo Park	35,002	57	42	15
Merced	84,197	132	94	38
Mill Valley	14,297	26	20	6
Milpitas	86,416	121	82	39
Modesto	216,560	302	203	99
Monrovia	36,302	71	44	27
Montclair	40,473	61	36	25
Montebello	61,895	93	70	23
Monterey	28,209	65	48	17
Monterey Park	59,609	106	75	31
Moraga	17,986	13	11	2
Morgan Hill	46,925	58	38	20
Morro Bay	10,577	19	17	2
Mountain View	83,745	132	88	44
Mount Shasta	3,261	12	8	4
Murrieta	117,639	151	100	51
Napa	78,237	112	69	43
National City	61,710	114	82	32
Nevada City	3,156	10	8	2
Newark	49,934	75	51	24
Newman	11,965	14	12	2
Newport Beach	84,448	217	137	80
Novato	55,926	75	54	21
Oakdale	23,926	31	22	9
Oakland	437,923	1,056	740	316
Oceanside	176,616	299	208	91
Ontario	187,464	337	258	79
Orange	138,846	218	150	68
Orange Cove	10,334	11	10	1
Orland	7,878	14	11	3
Oroville	20,983	37	21	16
Oxnard	210,064	325	227	98
Pacifica	38,677	34	31	3
Pacific Grove	15,451	32	21	11
Palm Springs	48,952	147	97	50
Palo Alto	65,459	123	80	43
Palos Verdes Estates	13,255	26	17	9
Paradise	4,072	24	16	8
Parlier	15,734	22	18	4
Pasadena	141,473	358	233	125
Paso Robles	32,428	50	35	15
Petaluma	60,806	96	57	39
Piedmont	11,184	30	20	10
Pinole	19,350	43	26	17
Pismo Beach	8,226	31	19	12
Pittsburg	73,673	103	85	18
Placentia	51,260	68	48	20
Placerville	11,255	26	18	8
Pleasant Hill	35,032	56	43	13
Pleasanton	83,164	109	78	31
Pomona	151,982	244	152	92
Porterville	59,757	100	68	32
Port Hueneme	21,949	30	20	10
Red Bluff	14,590	36	23	13
Redding	92,895	142	101	41
Redlands	71,820	117	84	33
Redondo Beach	66,729	143	85	58
Redwood City	86,983	116	84	32
Reedley	25,800	45	30	15
Rialto	104,004	141	106	35
Richmond	111,367	200	145	55
Ridgecrest	29,120	49	31	18
Rio Dell	3,347	5	5	0
Rio Vista	10,020	14	12	2
Ripon	16,616	32	22	10
Riverside	334,370	522	379	143
Rocklin	70,219	84	60	24
Rohnert Park	43,572	97	71	26
Roseville	144,128	196	136	60
Ross	2,454	8	8	0
Sacramento	519,050	1,012	684	328

State/city	Population	Total law enforcement employees	Total officers	Total civilians
Salinas	155,984	200	150	50
San Bernardino	216,365	334	239	95
San Bruno	42,997	57	42	15
Sand City	407	11	10	1
San Diego	1,437,608	2,424	1,846	578
San Fernando	24,399	40	27	13
San Francisco	881,514	2,992	2,239	753
San Gabriel	39,927	64	51	13
Sanger	25,457	40	35	5
San Jose	1,029,542	1,631	1,170	461
San Leandro	89,239	130	89	41
San Luis Obispo	47,722	84	59	25
San Marino	13,042	34	26	8
San Mateo	105,246	151	108	43
San Pablo	31,164	83	56	27
San Rafael	58,512	89	64	25
San Ramon	76,502	83	67	16
Santa Ana	333,107	594	366	228
Santa Barbara	91,692	199	131	68
Santa Clara	131,976	216	145	71
Santa Cruz	65,073	115	83	32
Santa Maria	108,140	181	133	48
Santa Monica	90,474	373	212	161
Santa Paula	29,861	42	31	11
Santa Rosa	176,932	252	174	78
Sausalito	7,080	25	19	6
Scotts Valley	11,777	24	17	7
Seal Beach	23,873	52	37	15
Seaside	33,822	44	32	12
Sebastopol	7,697	21	15	6
Selma	24,982	44	32	12
Shafter	20,799	41	28	13
Sierra Madre	10,779	21	16	5
Signal Hill	11,467	44	32	12
Simi Valley	125,742	165	124	41
Soledad	26,000	21	17	4
Sonora	4,860	17	10	7
South Gate	93,336	123	77	46
South Lake Tahoe	22,286	53	37	16
South Pasadena	25,299	50	34	16
South San Francisco	68,260	109	79	30
Stallion Springs	2,488	4	4	0
St. Helena	6,134	17	11	6
Stockton	314,981	663	468	195
Suisun City	29,842	33	21	12
Sunnyvale	154,133	289	217	72
Susanville	14,740	19	16	3
Sutter Creek	2,634	5	5	0
Taft	9,274	22	12	10
Tehachapi	12,873	27	17	10
Tiburon	9,098	17	13	4
Torrance	143,421	298	194	104
Tracy	96,067	142	92	50
Truckee	16,800	40	25	15
Tulare	66,207	113	67	46
Tulelake	975	2	2	0
Turlock	74,183	111	76	35
Tustin	79,795	141	90	51
Ukiah	15,992	43	27	16
Union City	74,625	86	69	17
Upland	77,511	102	71	31
Vacaville	101,616	171	116	55
Vallejo	122,326	163	111	52
Ventura	109,295	186	131	55
Vernon	110	55	44	11
Visalia	135,733	216	150	66
Walnut Creek	70,849	117	80	37
Watsonville	54,151	87	69	18
Weed	2,699	14	8	6
West Covina	104,989	133	90	43
Westminster	90,741	123	89	34

(Number.)

State/city	Population	Total law enforcement employees	Total officers	Total civilians
Westmorland	2,256	3	3	0
West Sacramento	54,068	95	71	24
Wheatland	3,916	8	8	0
Whittier	85,074	169	120	49
Williams	5,443	12	10	2
Willits	4,887	12	8	4
Winters	7,397	11	9	2
Woodlake	7,697	12	11	1
Woodland	61,123	81	66	15
Yreka	7,489	21	13	8
Yuba City	67,165	88	64	24
COLORADO				
Alamosa	9,669	29	25	4
Arvada	122,983	242	185	57
Aspen	7,478	36	25	11
Ault	1,913	6	5	1
Aurora	385,720	906	770	136
Avon	6,526	21	19	2
Basalt	4,195	11	10	1
Bayfield	2,731	9	8	1
Black Hawk	129	34	23	11
Blue River	929	4	4	0
Boulder	106,598	264	176	88
Breckenridge	4,991	25	21	4
Brighton	42,536	110	79	31
Broomfield	71,795	222	115	107
Brush	5,413	15	10	5
Buena Vista	2,902	8	7	1
Burlington	3,043	7	3	4
Calhan	840	4	4	0
Canon City	16,761	45	37	8
Carbondale	6,955	15	12	3
Castle Rock	71,150	113	82	31
Cedaredge	2,301	5	4	1
Centennial	112,104	173	143	30
Center	2,266	18	6	12
Cherry Hills Village	6,722	28	23	5
Collbran	699	3	3	0
Colorado Springs	485,083	1,018	725	293
Columbine Valley	1,528	6	6	0
Commerce City	62,164	135	105	30
Cortez	8,764	51	28	23
Craig	8,975	25	20	5
Crested Butte	1,751	9	8	1
Cripple Creek	1,261	20	11	9
Dacono	6,285	17	13	4
De Beque	520	5	5	0
Del Norte	1,556	4	3	1
Delta	9,011	24	18	6
Denver	737,709	1,818	1,552	266
Dillon	974	9	8	1
Dinosaur	331	3	3	0
Durango	19,220	63	50	13
Eagle	7,043	13	12	1
Eaton	5,911	12	10	2
Edgewater	5,353	18	18	0
Elizabeth	1,591	10	9	1
Empire	307	3	2	1
Englewood	35,464	106	76	30
Erie	28,198	44	37	7
Estes Park	6,480	36	22	14
Evans	21,515	38	35	3
Fairplay	797	3	3	0
Federal Heights	12,983	40	25	15
Firestone	17,013	37	30	7
Florence	3,952	13	11	2
Fort Collins	173,274	323	222	101
Fort Lupton	8,421	24	19	5
Fort Morgan	11,471	32	25	7
Fountain	31,297	59	51	8

(Number.)

State/city	Population	Total law enforcement employees	Total officers	Total civilians
Fowler	1,136	5	4	1
Fraser/Winter Park	2,438	11	10	1
Frederick	14,712	29	24	5
Frisco	3,231	12	9	3
Fruita	13,574	19	16	3
Garden City	269	4	4	0
Georgetown	1,121	3	3	0
Glendale	5,243	40	27	13
Glenwood Springs	9,976	26	19	7
Golden	20,981	61	45	16
Granby	2,174	10	8	2
Grand Junction	64,149	214	111	103
Greeley	110,505	212	155	57
Green Mountain Falls	730	1	1	0
Greenwood Village	15,945	84	63	21
Gunnison	6,736	20	15	5
Gypsum	7,479	4	4	0
Haxtun	899	2	2	0
Hayden	1,999	6	4	2
Holyoke	2,195	4	4	0
Hotchkiss	929	4	4	0
Hudson	2,817	8	6	2
Hugo	782	2	2	0
Idaho Springs	1,793	12	9	3
Ignacio	914	8	8	0
Johnstown	15,932	27	24	3
Kersey	1,704	5	4	1
Lafayette	31,457	47	36	11
La Junta	6,859	19	10	9
Lakeside	8	5	4	1
Lakewood	159,719	408	295	113
Lamar	7,625	20	14	6
La Salle	2,389	6	6	0
La Veta	813	1	1	0
Leadville	2,900	9	6	3
Limon	1,960	6	5	1
Littleton	48,805	99	74	25
Lochbuie	7,653	13	10	3
Log Lane Village	852	2	2	0
Lone Tree	13,423	58	49	9
Longmont	98,545	227	156	71
Louisville	21,101	37	31	6
Loveland	80,302	159	108	51
Mancos	1,440	4	4	0
Manitou Springs	5,435	18	15	3
Manzanola	415	3	2	1
Mead	4,897	11	9	2
Meeker	2,231	6	5	1
Milliken	8,509	15	11	4
Monte Vista	4,104	15	13	2
Montrose	19,864	61	41	20
Monument	8,361	22	19	3
Morrison	425	9	8	1
Mountain View	540	10	9	1
Mountain Village	1,439	10	7	3
Mount Crested Butte	883	9	8	1
Nederland	1,543	4	4	0
New Castle	5,289	10	9	1
Northglenn	39,161	78	62	16
Oak Creek	966	3	3	0
Olathe	1,834	5	5	0
Ouray	1,037	5	5	0
Pagosa Springs	2,127	7	6	1
Palisade	2,745	10	9	1
Palmer Lake	3,048	2	2	0
Paonia	1,470	6	5	1
Parachute	1,121	5	4	1
Parker	59,245	105	67	38
Platteville	3,905	9	8	1
Pueblo	113,002	265	208	57
Rangely	2,254	12	6	6

(Number.)

State/city	Population	Total law enforcement employees	Total officers	Total civilians
Ridgway	1,057	3	3	0
Rifle	9,747	24	19	5
Rocky Ford	3,798	10	5	5
Salida	6,183	21	18	3
Severance	7,040	9	8	1
Sheridan	6,246	35	34	1
Silt	3,222	7	5	2
Silverthorne	5,021	19	16	3
Simla	643	1	1	0
Snowmass Village	2,723	12	9	3
South Fork	422	3	3	0
Springfield	1,366	4	3	1
Steamboat Springs	13,345	39	26	13
Sterling	14,459	27	21	6
Telluride	2,508	14	10	4
Thornton	144,156	311	236	75
Timnath	6,289	11	9	2
Trinidad	8,114	36	23	13
Vail	5,450	61	28	33
Westminster	113,941	267	193	74
Wheat Ridge	31,451	106	86	20
Wiggins	1,201	2	2	0
Windsor	32,169	50	43	7
Woodland Park	7,969	34	25	9
Wray	2,345	7	6	1
Yuma	3,475	9	8	1
CONNECTICUT				
Ansonia	18,586	52	42	10
Avon	18,289	41	31	10
Berlin	20,497	53	41	12
Bethel	19,932	52	39	13
Bloomfield	21,294	56	43	13
Branford	27,886	60	48	12
Bridgeport	144,350	409	364	45
Bristol	59,886	142	117	25
Brookfield	17,031	44	34	10
Canton	10,249	20	15	5
Cheshire	28,897	60	47	13
Clinton	12,890	36	27	9
Coventry	12,404	21	16	5
Cromwell	13,822	37	27	10
Danbury	85,080	154	149	5
Darien	21,840	63	51	12
Derby	12,281	35	33	2
East Hampton	12,783	20	18	2
East Hartford	49,720	155	118	37
East Haven	28,498	58	54	4
East Lyme	18,391	34	26	8
Easton	7,522	20	15	5
East Windsor	11,723	35	25	10
Enfield	43,551	117	95	22
Fairfield	62,311	107	100	7
Farmington	25,512	58	44	14
Glastonbury	34,487	76	59	17
Granby	11,531	21	16	5
Greenwich	63,012	177	150	27
Groton	8,861	33	26	7
Groton Long Point	506	5	5	0
Groton Town	28,890	82	65	17
Guilford	22,106	42	35	7
Hamden	60,440	122	96	26
Hartford	121,749	458	430	28
Ledyard	14,575	31	22	9
Madison	18,004	41	30	11
Manchester	57,510	145	113	32
Meriden	59,238	127	116	11
Middlebury	7,819	14	12	2
Middletown	46,106	136	112	24
Milford	54,968	130	108	22
Monroe	19,427	53	44	9

(Number.)

State/city	Population	Total law enforcement employees	Total officers	Total civilians
Naugatuck	31,024	69	58	11
New Britain	72,412	163	155	8
New Canaan	20,281	53	47	6
New Haven	130,299	375	325	50
Newington	29,957	63	50	13
New London	26,776	84	68	16
New Milford	26,668	59	46	13
Newtown	27,924	47	44	3
North Branford	14,115	28	22	6
North Haven	23,639	61	49	12
Norwalk	89,140	202	175	27
Norwich	38,576	101	87	14
Old Saybrook	10,042	30	22	8
Orange	13,922	53	43	10
Plainfield	15,095	26	17	9
Plainville	17,519	49	40	9
Plymouth	11,529	22	20	2
Portland	9,242	13	12	1
Putnam	9,370	20	15	5
Redding	9,112	23	16	7
Ridgefield	24,990	46	41	5
Rocky Hill	20,160	47	35	12
Seymour	16,426	43	40	3
Shelton	41,302	50	44	6
Simsbury	25,614	46	36	10
Southington	43,906	88	69	19
South Windsor	26,213	58	44	14
Stamford	130,425	288	263	25
Stonington	18,563	48	37	11
Stratford	51,895	108	103	5
Suffield	15,820	25	19	6
Thomaston	7,497	27	16	11
Torrington	33,796	82	73	9
Trumbull	35,632	88	77	11
Vernon	29,379	64	50	14
Wallingford	44,236	95	74	21
Waterbury	107,263	333	287	46
Waterford	18,664	54	49	5
Watertown	21,475	49	40	9
West Hartford	62,911	146	124	22
West Haven	54,516	135	127	8
Weston	10,258	18	17	1
Westport	28,728	77	63	14
Wethersfield	25,936	61	47	14
Willimantic	17,737	49	44	5
Wilton	18,375	46	43	3
Winchester	10,536	25	22	3
Windsor	28,692	58	45	13
Windsor Locks	12,894	35	27	8
Wolcott	16,573	33	25	8
Woodbridge	8,725	31	23	8
DELAWARE				
Bethany Beach	1,268	11	10	1
Blades	1,479	3	3	0
Bridgeville	2,409	7	7	0
Camden	3,562	10	9	1
Cheswold	1,718	4	4	0
Clayton	3,577	10	9	1
Dagsboro	943	3	3	0
Delaware City	1,844	4	3	1
Delmar	1,850	13	12	1
Dewey Beach	407	11	9	2
Dover	38,428	123	92	31
Ellendale	442	1	1	0
Elsmere	5,851	12	11	1
Felton	1,429	3	3	0
Fenwick Island	453	7	7	0
Frederica	859	2	2	0
Georgetown	7,698	23	21	2
Greenwood	1,159	4	3	1

(Number.)

State/city	Population	Total law enforcement employees	Total officers	Total civilians
Harrington	3,646	11	10	1
Laurel	4,431	19	18	1
Lewes	3,378	12	11	1
Middletown	23,385	45	38	7
Milford	11,994	48	35	13
Millsboro	4,613	18	16	2
Milton	3,066	9	8	1
Newark	33,752	90	73	17
New Castle	5,420	18	17	1
Newport	1,035	6	6	0
Ocean View	2,231	12	11	1
Rehoboth Beach	1,573	29	18	11
Seaford	8,145	35	28	7
Selbyville	2,585	9	8	1
Smyrna	12,011	33	25	8
South Bethany	540	6	6	0
Wilmington	70,100	349	293	56
Wyoming	1,577	3	3	0
DISTRICT OF COLUMBIA				
Washington	712,816	4,466	3,766	700
FLORIDA				
Alachua	9,998	37	28	9
Altamonte Springs	44,440	112	95	17
Apopka	54,842	139	104	35
Arcadia	8,392	22	18	4
Atlantic Beach	14,012	39	26	13
Atlantis	2,144	16	11	5
Auburndale	17,046	45	37	8
Aventura	37,114	124	88	36
Bal Harbour Village	2,992	36	24	12
Bartow	20,507	55	35	20
Bay Harbor Islands	5,821	25	21	4
Belleair	4,297	17	15	2
Belle Isle	7,392	20	18	2
Belleview	5,168	17	15	2
Biscayne Park	3,063	10	10	0
Blountstown	2,435	20	14	6
Boca Raton	101,583	314	214	100
Bonifay	2,698	6	5	1
Bowling Green	2,882	6	6	0
Boynton Beach	79,913	194	134	60
Bradenton	60,688	152	119	33
Bradenton Beach	1,292	10	10	0
Cape Coral	199,503	337	255	82
Casselberry	29,080	63	53	10
Cedar Key	719	3	3	0
Chiefland	2,181	14	12	2
Clearwater	117,859	336	237	99
Clermont	39,932	87	80	7
Clewiston	8,125	22	16	6
Cocoa	18,769	93	62	31
Cocoa Beach	11,763	58	39	19
Coconut Creek	62,220	140	105	35
Coral Gables	50,017	268	178	90
Coral Springs	135,027	307	216	91
Crestview	25,787	43	38	5
Cross City	1,711	5	5	0
Dade City	7,444	31	23	8
Davenport	6,516	15	14	1
Davie	107,988	262	186	76
Daytona Beach	70,084	287	231	56
Daytona Beach Shores	4,656	38	29	9
DeFuniak Springs	7,200	27	20	7
DeLand	35,874	75	58	17
Delray Beach	70,487	235	162	73
Doral	68,425	196	145	51
Dunnellon	1,852	10	9	1
Eatonville	2,223	14	12	2
Edgewater	24,166	37	31	6

(Number.)

State/city	Population	Total law enforcement employees	Total officers	Total civilians
El Portal	2,397	9	9	0
Eustis	21,642	51	37	14
Fernandina Beach	13,383	40	35	5
Flagler Beach	5,195	18	15	3
Florida City	11,826	44	34	10
Fort Lauderdale	184,347	674	517	157
Fort Myers	90,380	310	233	77
Fort Pierce	46,574	143	114	29
Fort Walton Beach	22,871	61	50	11
Fruitland Park	12,021	21	20	1
Gainesville	135,076	367	268	99
Golden Beach	934	27	19	8
Graceville	2,109	9	9	0
Green Cove Springs	8,783	28	21	7
Groveland	17,622	52	37	15
Gulf Breeze	7,037	29	20	9
Gulfport	12,378	34	30	4
Gulf Stream	995	13	13	0
Haines City	26,719	68	54	14
Havana	1,703	14	10	4
Hialeah	234,235	350	277	73
Hialeah Gardens	23,667	61	43	18
Hillsboro Beach	2,027	19	15	4
Holly Hill	12,440	25	21	4
Hollywood	156,434	407	319	88
Holmes Beach	4,360	23	17	6
Homestead	70,538	146	113	33
Howey-in-the-Hills	1,191	6	6	0
Indialantic	2,929	18	12	6
Indian Creek Village	89	13	9	4
Indian Harbour Beach	8,602	28	20	8
Indian River Shores	4,363	26	22	4
Indian Shores	3,787	13	12	1
Interlachen	1,471	3	3	0
Jacksonville	920,508	3,078	1,789	1,289
Jacksonville Beach	23,894	86	67	19
Jasper	4,127	6	6	0
Jay	646	8	7	1
Juno Beach	3,710	15	13	2
Jupiter	67,054	140	111	29
Jupiter Inlet Colony	459	4	4	0
Jupiter Island	942	23	18	5
Kenneth City	5,131	15	14	1
Key Biscayne	12,898	47	36	11
Key Colony Beach	804	4	4	0
Kissimmee	74,337	226	148	78
Lady Lake	16,255	33	28	5
Lake Alfred	6,425	18	13	5
Lake City	12,403	53	38	15
Lake Clarke Shores	3,653	11	10	1
Lake Hamilton	1,530	9	7	2
Lake Helen	2,822	7	6	1
Lakeland	113,876	351	239	112
Lake Mary	17,947	54	46	8
Lake Placid	2,498	10	8	2
Lake Wales	17,075	52	45	7
Lantana	12,825	37	30	7
Largo	85,594	164	133	31
Lauderhill	72,421	145	114	31
Lawtey	725	3	3	0
Leesburg	24,063	88	64	24
Lighthouse Point	11,373	40	32	8
Live Oak	6,985	22	19	3
Longboat Key	7,342	21	18	3
Longwood	15,793	48	43	5
Lynn Haven	20,733	50	37	13
Madison	2,735	16	15	1
Maitland	17,863	61	53	8
Manalapan	473	16	14	2
Marco Island	18,121	36	32	4
Margate	59,449	147	113	34

State/city	Population	Total law enforcement employees	Total officers	Total civilians
Marianna	5,644	21	16	5
Mascotte	6,468	14	12	2
Medley	888	54	40	14
Melbourne	83,806	221	145	76
Melbourne Beach	3,321	11	10	1
Melbourne Village	698	4	4	0
Miami	476,102	1,737	1,317	420
Miami Beach	89,017	500	416	84
Miami Gardens	110,284	261	212	49
Miami Shores	10,358	46	39	7
Miami Springs	13,925	57	46	11
Midway	2,995	5	4	1
Milton	10,728	27	20	7
Miramar	143,470	283	203	80
Monticello	2,397	14	8	6
Mount Dora	14,801	63	47	16
Naples	22,388	101	68	33
Neptune Beach	7,285	30	22	8
New Port Richey	16,954	58	42	16
New Smyrna Beach	28,380	60	45	15
Niceville	16,345	37	29	8
North Bay Village	8,165	35	26	9
North Miami	63,109	149	118	31
North Miami Beach	43,273	137	104	33
North Palm Beach	13,255	37	32	5
North Port	72,389	158	121	37
Oakland	3,193	13	12	1
Ocala	61,275	290	187	103
Ocean Ridge	1,976	23	18	5
Ocoee	49,877	110	87	23
Okeechobee	5,833	30	22	8
Opa Locka	15,962	52	44	8
Orange City	12,454	30	26	4
Orange Park	8,864	35	26	9
Orlando	293,363	1,074	806	268
Ormond Beach	44,271	85	65	20
Oviedo	42,903	77	71	6
Palatka	10,436	35	32	3
Palm Bay	116,897	212	151	61
Palm Beach	8,891	94	65	29
Palm Beach Gardens	58,629	178	122	56
Palmetto	13,873	48	34	14
Palm Springs	25,451	61	43	18
Panama City	34,672	120	85	35
Panama City Beach	12,703	87	67	20
Parker	4,241	11	10	1
Pembroke Pines	175,757	331	235	96
Pensacola	53,083	180	134	46
Perry	6,865	22	20	2
Pinellas Park	54,114	125	108	17
Plantation	95,669	253	164	89
Plant City	40,330	83	66	17
Ponce Inlet	3,340	14	12	2
Port Orange	65,828	109	83	26
Port Richey	2,963	22	15	7
Port St. Lucie	206,450	310	242	68
Punta Gorda	20,766	55	37	18
Quincy	6,707	36	25	11
Riviera Beach	35,798	151	110	41
Rockledge	28,614	66	50	16
Sanford	62,342	155	139	16
Sanibel	7,511	36	23	13
Sarasota	59,002	224	175	49
Satellite Beach	11,252	34	24	10
Sea Ranch Lakes	626	11	7	4
Sebastian	26,626	57	41	16
Sebring	10,664	39	33	6
Sewall's Point	2,252	10	9	1
Shalimar	850	5	4	1
Sneads	1,771	7	6	1
South Daytona	13,176	33	27	6

State/city	Population	Total law enforcement employees	Total officers	Total civilians
South Miami	11,933	57	50	7
Springfield	8,542	28	24	4
Starke	5,415	18	16	2
St. Augustine Beach	7,101	22	20	2
St. Cloud	56,828	137	93	44
St. Petersburg	267,690	776	557	219
Stuart	16,347	61	45	16
Sunny Isles Beach	21,907	65	52	13
Sunrise	96,428	236	181	55
Surfside	5,659	37	31	6
Sweetwater	21,109	57	51	6
Tallahassee	196,012	459	366	93
Tampa	407,350	1,181	926	255
Tavares	18,221	32	29	3
Temple Terrace	26,890	68	51	17
Tequesta	6,193	20	19	1
Titusville	46,919	129	86	43
Treasure Island	6,946	23	19	4
Trenton	2,179	3	2	1
Umatilla	3,910	9	8	1
Valparaiso	5,449	17	12	5
Venice	24,366	68	50	18
Vero Beach	17,776	76	57	19
Village of Pinecrest	19,255	69	47	22
Virginia Gardens	2,380	8	7	1
Wauchula	4,773	18	15	3
Welaka	718	1	1	0
West Melbourne	25,020	57	51	6
West Miami	9,154	26	21	5
West Palm Beach	113,268	390	292	98
White Springs	765	2	2	0
Wildwood	7,568	40	36	4
Wilton Manors	12,885	47	33	14
Winter Garden	47,484	104	77	27
Winter Haven	46,275	113	81	32
Winter Park	31,183	103	74	29
Winter Springs	37,788	64	50	14
Zephyrhills	16,772	51	36	15
GEORGIA				
Abbeville	2,654	7	6	1
Acworth	23,085	67	48	19
Adairsville	4,998	18	16	2
Alamo	3,340	4	4	0
Alapaha	676	2	1	1
Albany	71,567	196	162	34
Alma	3,370	17	15	2
Alpharetta	68,326	120	108	12
Alto	1,200	5	2	3
Americus	14,910	41	32	9
Aragon	1,344	9	4	5
Arcade	1,991	3	3	0
Athens-Clarke County	128,152	273	215	58
Atlanta	515,945	2,015	1,548	467
Attapulgus	423	2	1	1
Auburn	7,730	20	16	4
Austell	7,245	33	23	10
Avondale Estates	3,149	15	15	0
Bainbridge	12,006	50	37	13
Ball Ground	2,290	5	5	0
Barnesville	6,653	18	18	0
Bartow	246	1	1	0
Baxley	4,655	12	11	1
Blackshear	3,535	20	17	3
Blairsville	646	8	7	1
Blakely	4,521	16	14	2
Bloomingdale	2,691	17	15	2
Blue Ridge	1,474	8	8	0
Blythe	709	3	3	0
Boston	1,317	5	5	0
Bowdon	2,107	8	7	1

(Number.)

State/city	Population	Total law enforcement employees	Total officers	Total civilians
Braselton	13,758	19	18	1
Braswell	384	2	1	1
Bremen	6,685	21	19	2
Brookhaven	56,248	86	72	14
Brooklet	1,870	5	4	1
Brunswick	16,365	61	56	5
Buchanan	1,184	9	8	1
Buena Vista	2,037	4	4	0
Butler	1,739	7	7	0
Byron	5,304	28	25	3
Cairo	9,340	26	23	3
Calhoun	17,387	52	44	8
Camilla	4,981	21	18	3
Canon	790	1	1	0
Canton	31,416	61	53	8
Carrollton	27,609	85	70	15
Cartersville	21,995	57	47	10
Cave Spring	1,061	3	3	0
Cecil	283	3	2	1
Cedartown	10,020	36	32	4
Centerville	7,960	20	17	3
Chamblee	30,716	77	63	14
Chatsworth	4,290	18	17	1
Chickamauga	3,258	7	7	0
Clarkston	12,697	15	15	0
Claxton	2,185	15	10	5
Cleveland	4,251	17	16	1
Cochran	4,984	12	11	1
Cohutta	637	4	4	0
College Park	15,204	109	82	27
Columbus	195,998	487	386	101
Conyers	16,368	83	61	22
Coolidge	529	3	3	0
Cordele	10,451	27	18	9
Cornelia	4,741	20	18	2
Covington	14,330	61	48	13
Cumming	6,669	22	20	2
Dallas	14,280	34	24	10
Dalton	33,723	99	86	13
Darien	1,920	10	10	0
Dawson	4,073	14	8	6
Decatur	26,473	59	47	12
Demorest	2,157	11	7	4
Dillard	378	4	3	1
Doerun	732	5	4	1
Donalsonville	2,445	10	9	1
Doraville	10,329	57	40	17
Douglas	11,696	39	34	5
Douglasville	34,409	110	95	15
Dublin	15,849	71	59	12
Duluth	29,946	74	57	17
Dunwoody	49,687	74	61	13
East Ellijay	571	7	7	0
Eastman	5,018	16	14	2
Eatonton	6,753	23	16	7
Edison	1,380	5	4	1
Elberton	4,303	25	23	2
Ellaville	1,872	4	4	0
Ellijay	1,725	12	11	1
Emerson	1,610	9	8	1
Enigma	1,352	6	4	2
Eton	903	4	4	0
Euharlee	4,393	12	11	1
Fairburn	17,220	54	43	11
Fayetteville	18,202	62	54	8
Fitzgerald	8,611	32	24	8
Flowery Branch	8,671	18	16	2
Folkston	5,072	7	7	0
Forest Park	20,202	85	64	21
Forsyth	4,160	20	18	2
Fort Oglethorpe	10,072	29	26	3

State/city	Population	Total law enforcement employees	Total officers	Total civilians
Fort Valley	8,877	35	23	12
Franklin	968	8	8	0
Franklin Springs	1,222	2	2	0
Gainesville	44,398	117	101	16
Garden City	8,716	42	35	7
Glennville	5,004	11	9	2
Gordon	1,841	11	6	5
Grantville	3,322	14	13	1
Gray	3,273	14	13	1
Greensboro	3,299	20	16	4
Greenville	842	8	6	2
Griffin	22,773	81	72	9
Grovetown	15,650	31	22	9
Guyton	2,297	5	5	0
Hagan	962	4	3	1
Hahira	3,060	11	9	2
Hampton	8,201	20	18	2
Hartwell	4,445	27	22	5
Hazlehurst	4,126	13	11	2
Helen	565	12	11	1
Hephzibah	3,933	7	7	0
Hiawassee	916	5	5	0
Hinesville	33,316	95	82	13
Hiram	4,301	20	17	3
Hogansville	3,138	20	15	5
Holly Springs	16,345	39	38	1
Homeland	943	7	7	0
Homerville	2,340	10	8	2
Irwinton	552	2	2	0
Jackson	5,259	15	13	2
Jacksonville	132	1	1	0
Jasper	4,009	19	17	2
Jefferson	12,349	26	24	2
Jesup	9,807	33	31	2
Johns Creek	85,408	86	77	9
Jonesboro	4,994	32	20	12
Kennesaw	34,481	69	59	10
Kingston	684	2	1	1
LaGrange	30,406	105	86	19
Lake City	2,855	17	15	2
Lakeland	3,273	11	9	2
Lavonia	2,204	14	14	0
Lawrenceville	31,256	92	68	24
Leesburg	3,073	13	13	0
Leslie	367	4	3	1
Lilburn	12,941	34	29	5
Lithonia	2,374	7	6	1
Locust Grove	8,575	29	26	3
Loganville	13,187	34	32	2
Lookout Mountain	1,571	7	7	0
Louisville	2,187	6	6	0
Ludowici	2,355	10	6	4
Lyons	4,218	20	16	4
Madison	4,236	12	11	1
Manchester	3,942	19	14	5
Marietta	61,348	178	132	46
Marshallville	1,206	2	2	0
Maysville	2,135	3	3	0
McDonough	27,338	54	48	6
McIntyre	601	5	5	0
McRae-Helena	8,246	12	11	1
Metter	3,927	13	12	1
Midville	252	1	1	0
Midway	2,059	6	4	2
Milledgeville	18,751	58	41	17
Millen	2,730	11	11	0
Milton	40,368	44	38	6
Monroe	13,761	50	47	3
Montezuma	2,903	12	10	2
Morrow	7,327	24	22	2
Moultrie	14,199	41	37	4
Mount Airy	1,268	5	1	4

(Number.)

State/city	Population	Total law enforcement employees	Total officers	Total civilians
Mount Zion	1,825	7	6	1
Nahunta	1,152	4	4	0
Nashville	4,839	17	12	5
Newington	261	1	1	0
Newnan	42,658	101	86	15
Norcross	16,778	60	36	24
Norman Park	961	2	2	0
Oakwood	4,180	21	20	1
Ocilla	3,759	13	13	0
Oglethorpe	1,138	6	5	1
Omega	1,231	6	5	1
Oxford	2,372	4	4	0
Palmetto	4,890	17	14	3
Peachtree City	36,421	69	64	5
Pearson	2,035	6	5	1
Pelham	3,420	13	11	2
Pembroke	2,685	10	9	1
Pendergrass	576	2	2	0
Perry	18,417	49	41	8
Pine Lake	757	4	4	0
Pine Mountain	1,430	11	10	1
Pooler	26,634	65	57	8
Port Wentworth	10,281	39	28	11
Powder Springs	15,971	31	29	2
Remerton	1,074	9	8	1
Richmond Hill	14,437	39	33	6
Rincon	10,525	19	17	2
Ringgold	3,646	9	8	1
Rochelle	1,096	7	5	2
Rockmart	4,458	22	20	2
Rome	36,747	91	81	10
Roswell	95,396	185	138	47
Sandersville	5,346	21	15	6
Sandy Springs	111,219	160	141	19
Smyrna	57,317	140	93	47
Snellville	20,282	57	45	12
Social Circle	4,583	16	15	1
South Fulton	100,658	156	138	18
Sparks	2,010	3	3	0
Sparta	1,213	12	7	5
Springfield	4,281	10	9	1
Stapleton	388	2	2	0
Statesboro	33,498	91	77	14
Stone Mountain	6,332	19	18	1
Summerville	4,215	16	14	2
Suwanee	21,633	51	39	12
Swainsboro	7,577	25	23	2
Sylvania	2,449	11	8	3
Sylvester	5,732	30	25	5
Tallapoosa	3,186	12	10	2
Temple	4,832	16	13	3
Thomaston	8,711	29	25	4
Thunderbolt	2,634	9	7	2
Toccoa	8,312	32	31	1
Tunnel Hill	911	3	3	0
Twin City	1,696	2	2	0
Tybee Island	3,072	38	25	13
Tyrone	7,575	16	16	0
Union City	22,744	65	59	6
Valdosta	56,628	162	138	24
Vidalia	10,398	39	28	11
Villa Rica	16,296	52	43	9
Warner Robins	78,508	156	113	43
Warwick	383	5	3	2
Waycross	13,363	64	51	13
Waynesboro	5,308	30	23	7
Winder	18,376	42	34	8
Woodstock	34,252	64	55	9
HAWAII				
Honolulu	966,438	2,516	2,005	511

(Number.)

State/city	Population	Total law enforcement employees	Total officers	Total civilians
IDAHO				
Aberdeen	1,975	5	5	0
American Falls	4,298	10	8	2
Ashton	1,042	2	2	0
Bellevue	2,471	2	2	0
Blackfoot	12,036	30	27	3
Boise	231,223	373	288	85
Bonners Ferry	2,652	7	7	0
Buhl	4,544	9	8	1
Caldwell	59,987	89	75	14
Chubbuck	15,773	35	22	13
Coeur d'Alene	53,405	114	92	22
Cottonwood	944	1	1	0
Emmett	7,114	15	14	1
Filer	2,980	5	5	0
Fruitland	5,505	16	12	4
Garden City	12,084	36	28	8
Gooding	3,429	9	7	2
Grangeville	3,246	6	6	0
Hailey	8,778	13	12	1
Heyburn	3,489	8	7	1
Homedale	2,730	6	5	1
Idaho City	470	1	1	0
Idaho Falls	63,457	134	89	45
Jerome	12,120	23	20	3
Kellogg	2,136	8	8	0
Ketchum	2,872	11	10	1
Kimberly	4,146	9	8	1
Lewiston	32,886	68	46	22
McCall	3,677	13	11	2
Meridian	119,203	154	124	30
Middleton	8,877	10	9	1
Montpelier	2,533	4	3	1
Moscow	25,918	41	34	7
Mountain Home	14,597	33	29	4
Nampa	101,411	185	128	57
Orofino	3,088	6	5	1
Osburn	1,557	2	2	0
Parma	2,167	5	5	0
Payette	7,753	16	14	2
Pinehurst	1,627	2	2	0
Pocatello	56,900	128	91	37
Ponderay	1,170	8	7	1
Post Falls	37,317	70	47	23
Preston	5,592	9	8	1
Priest River	1,911	6	5	1
Rathdrum	9,449	18	15	3
Rexburg	29,865	41	32	9
Rigby	4,332	8	7	1
Rupert	5,927	13	12	1
Salmon	3,171	9	9	0
Sandpoint	9,111	24	20	4
Shelley	4,470	8	8	0
Shoshone	1,504	6	6	0
Soda Springs	3,020	7	7	0
Spirit Lake	2,610	7	6	1
St. Anthony	3,552	6	6	0
Sun Valley	1,495	12	11	1
Twin Falls	50,872	94	75	19
Weiser	5,364	13	10	3
Wilder	1,858	4	4	0
ILLINOIS				
Abingdon	3,026	6	6	0
Addison	36,411	127	63	64
Albers	1,130	2	1	1
Algonquin	30,990	51	44	7
Alsip	18,646	44	41	3
Alton	26,027	81	58	23
Amboy	2,301	2	2	0
Antioch	14,141	29	26	3

(Number.)

State/city	Population	Total law enforcement employees	Total officers	Total civilians
Arlington Heights	74,706	128	101	27
Ashland	1,176	1	1	0
Assumption	1,055	2	2	0
Aurora	197,709	352	291	61
Aviston	2,153	1	1	0
Bannockburn	1,508	7	7	0
Barrington	10,205	27	23	4
Barrington Hills	4,185	20	16	4
Belleville	40,537	93	72	21
Bellwood	18,629	43	39	4
Bensenville	18,009	36	32	4
Bethany	1,227	2	2	0
Bloomingdale	21,746	55	43	12
Bolingbrook	74,665	128	112	16
Bourbonnais	19,551	27	26	1
Bradley	15,251	37	34	3
Bridgeview	16,056	32	32	0
Buffalo Grove	40,380	74	58	16
Burr Ridge	10,782	31	27	4
Cambridge	2,069	1	1	0
Campton Hills	11,092	7	7	0
Carbondale	24,933	73	57	16
Carlinville	5,434	18	13	5
Carlyle	3,174	8	7	1
Carpentersville	37,201	61	57	4
Cary	18,036	26	25	1
Centralia	12,123	32	24	8
Champaign	89,785	134	113	21
Channahon	13,312	29	27	2
Chatham	13,152	21	15	6
Chenoa	3,110	4	4	0
Chicago	2,693,598	13,562	12,727	835
Chicago Heights	29,207	86	74	12
Chicago Ridge	13,885	37	32	5
Chillicothe	6,004	12	12	0
Cicero	80,420	179	154	25
Clarendon Hills	8,787	14	13	1
Collinsville	24,261	61	43	18
Cortland	4,421	6	6	0
Crest Hill	20,328	31	29	2
Crete	7,996	20	18	2
Crystal Lake	39,726	76	67	9
Danville	30,208	74	62	12
Deerfield	18,692	55	41	14
DeKalb	42,710	71	57	14
Des Plaines	58,950	102	89	13
Downers Grove	49,070	84	67	17
Dupo	3,845	8	8	0
Du Quoin	5,624	14	10	4
Dwight	3,955	10	9	1
Earlville	1,575	4	3	1
East Dundee	3,260	13	12	1
East Moline	20,573	38	35	3
Edwardsville	25,327	59	44	15
Effingham	12,531	40	25	15
Elburn	6,043	9	8	1
Elgin	111,127	238	184	54
Elk Grove Village	32,290	97	83	14
Elmhurst	47,034	87	66	21
Elmwood Park	24,011	41	35	6
Elwood	2,220	11	10	1
Evanston	73,352	168	119	49
Evergreen Park	19,070	74	56	18
Fairfield	4,914	13	9	4
Fairview Heights	16,217	49	45	4
Farmer City	1,927	5	5	0
Farmington	2,200	6	6	0
Flora	4,829	18	12	6
Flossmoor	9,123	25	20	5
Fox Lake	10,426	33	28	5
Frankfort	19,551	36	33	3

(Number.)

State/city	Population	Total law enforcement employees	Total officers	Total civilians
Freeport	23,583	56	39	17
Galena	3,131	11	10	1
Geneva	21,831	44	35	9
Genoa	5,244	7	6	1
Gibson City	3,214	8	7	1
Glencoe	8,837	42	36	6
Glendale Heights	33,539	68	50	18
Glen Ellyn	27,704	47	39	8
Glenwood	8,685	26	23	3
Golf	493	1	1	0
Granite City	27,982	70	57	13
Greenfield	979	2	2	0
Gurnee	30,281	96	62	34
Hanover Park	37,350	81	58	23
Havana	2,954	14	9	5
Henning	232	1	1	0
Herscher	1,494	3	3	0
Hickory Hills	13,672	38	27	11
Highland	9,819	26	19	7
Hillside	7,902	33	24	9
Hinckley	2,048	3	3	0
Hodgkins	1,979	23	21	2
Homewood	18,636	43	38	5
Hoopeston	4,972	19	10	9
Hopedale	820	1	1	0
Huntley	27,566	41	36	5
Island Lake	8,014	14	13	1
Itasca	9,944	23	20	3
Jacksonville	18,515	37	33	4
Joliet	147,324	317	254	63
Kankakee	25,863	66	62	4
Kenilworth	2,471	9	8	1
Kingston	1,170	2	2	0
Kirkland	1,727	2	2	0
La Grange	15,295	29	25	4
Lake Bluff	5,548	16	14	2
Lake Forest	19,452	43	37	6
Lake in the Hills	28,598	47	39	8
Lake Zurich	19,895	47	30	17
Lansing	27,297	73	56	17
Lemont	17,432	27	22	5
Lincoln	13,417	29	27	2
Lincolnshire	7,962	27	25	2
Lindenhurst	14,174	14	12	2
Lisle	23,351	48	37	11
Litchfield	6,668	16	15	1
Lombard	44,392	74	62	12
Loves Park	23,303	39	37	2
Lovington	1,016	2	2	0
Lyons	10,332	19	16	3
Mackinaw	1,878	3	3	0
Manteno	8,980	20	19	1
Maple Park	1,371	1	1	0
Marissa	1,788	4	3	1
Markham	12,289	33	31	2
Marseilles	4,804	10	9	1
Matteson	19,494	54	36	18
McHenry	27,061	78	46	32
Metropolis	5,881	18	13	5
Midlothian	14,294	32	29	3
Milan	4,969	16	15	1
Milledgeville	943	2	2	0
Minier	1,183	2	2	0
Moline	41,128	87	81	6
Monee	5,054	16	15	1
Montgomery	19,783	36	32	4
Monticello	5,532	9	7	2
Morris	15,216	31	27	4
Morrison	3,966	8	8	0
Morton	16,267	22	18	4
Mount Carmel	6,971	17	12	5

(Number.)

State/city	Population	Total law enforcement employees	Total officers	Total civilians
Mount Pulaski	1,454	2	2	0
Mount Zion	5,788	12	10	2
Mundelein	31,053	79	51	28
Murphysboro	7,345	23	15	8
Naperville	149,137	264	174	90
Neoga	1,598	3	3	0
New Athens	1,865	4	4	0
New Lenox	27,230	43	37	6
Niles	28,839	69	55	14
Normal	54,677	89	81	8
North Pekin	1,540	6	6	0
North Riverside	6,402	25	23	2
Oak Brook	8,029	49	41	8
Oakbrook Terrace	2,097	25	21	4
Oak Park	52,435	134	109	25
Oakwood Hills	2,023	4	3	1
O'Fallon	29,672	63	47	16
Orion	1,791	2	2	0
Orland Park	57,993	128	98	30
Oswego	36,934	60	49	11
Ottawa	17,983	52	36	16
Palatine	67,358	139	106	33
Palestine	1,263	2	2	0
Palos Heights	12,520	30	27	3
Palos Hills	17,013	33	30	3
Palos Park	4,723	11	10	1
Pana	5,327	13	8	5
Park Ridge	36,888	68	54	14
Pawnee	2,628	3	3	0
Pekin	31,834	61	53	8
Peoria	109,924	224	203	21
Peoria Heights	5,748	16	14	2
Petersburg	2,202	5	5	0
Plano	11,755	25	23	2
Polo	2,153	5	5	0
Pontiac	11,184	21	19	2
Princeton	7,420	18	16	2
Prophetstown	1,924	4	4	0
Prospect Heights	15,845	26	22	4
Richmond	1,908	5	5	0
River Forest	10,776	29	27	2
River Grove	9,843	30	26	4
Riverton	3,430	10	10	0
Riverwoods	3,550	7	7	0
Rochelle	8,998	30	21	9
Rochester	3,709	9	9	0
Rockdale	1,901	6	6	0
Rockford	144,795	332	289	43
Rock Island	36,981	99	75	24
Round Lake	18,069	29	26	3
Roxana	1,423	5	4	1
Salem	6,921	24	17	7
San Jose	589	2	2	0
Savanna	2,769	7	7	0
Shiloh	13,701	21	20	1
Silvis	7,470	20	17	3
Skokie	62,462	151	109	42
South Barrington	5,044	22	19	3
South Beloit	7,594	14	13	1
South Elgin	25,084	39	35	4
South Holland	21,218	49	46	3
Springfield	113,912	257	229	28
Spring Grove	5,698	8	7	1
Spring Valley	5,081	12	11	1
St. Charles	32,949	67	57	10
St. Elmo	1,397	3	3	0
Sterling	14,361	34	27	7
Streator	13,019	26	22	4
Sumner	2,959	2	2	0
Sycamore	18,413	30	28	2
Taylorville	10,264	20	20	0

State/city	Population	Total law enforcement employees	Total officers	Total civilians
Thayer	651	1	1	0
Trenton	2,576	5	5	0
University Park	6,861	18	16	2
Urbana	42,211	70	58	12
Vandalia	6,647	12	12	0
Vernon Hills	26,693	65	40	25
Villa Park	21,421	45	36	9
Waterloo	10,645	19	18	1
Watseka	4,713	12	11	1
Wauconda	13,488	27	25	2
Waukegan	85,739	188	146	42
West Chicago	26,768	46	41	5
West Dundee	8,215	20	18	2
Westmont	24,416	40	35	5
Wheaton	52,706	83	68	15
Wheeling	38,753	84	55	29
White Hall	2,309	10	6	4
Willow Springs	5,606	10	9	1
Winfield	9,693	19	16	3
Winnetka	12,328	32	26	6
Wood Dale	13,588	43	34	9
Woodstock	25,283	42	39	3
Worth	10,430	27	25	2
Yorkville	21,052	33	30	3
INDIANA				
Anderson	54,623	113	95	18
Angola	8,748	23	19	4
Auburn	13,560	26	23	3
Austin	4,100	9	9	0
Bargersville	8,342	13	12	1
Bedford	13,192	39	31	8
Bluffton	10,173	32	20	12
Brownsburg	27,621	57	51	6
Carmel	103,100	153	128	25
Cedar Lake	13,372	20	18	2
Chesterton	14,203	26	22	4
Columbus	48,505	22	21	1
Crawfordsville	16,137	45	40	5
Cumberland	6,097	18	16	2
Danville	10,247	20	18	2
Dyer	15,932	35	32	3
Edinburgh	4,603	13	12	1
Ellettsville	6,804	12	11	1
Elwood	8,372	18	17	1
Evansville	117,747	310	283	27
Fairmount	2,749	7	6	1
Fort Wayne	272,270	538	474	64
Franklin	25,825	60	54	6
Gas City	5,732	11	11	0
Goshen	34,409	72	64	8
Greenfield	23,273	45	41	4
Greenwood	60,460	71	63	8
Hammond	74,966	241	204	37
Hartford City	5,606	11	10	1
Highland	22,165	43	37	6
Hobart	27,791	78	67	11
Huntingburg	6,182	15	14	1
Huntington	17,096	36	33	3
Indianapolis	890,672	2,656	2,086	570
Jasper	15,790	31	23	8
Kendallville	9,897	28	19	9
Lafayette	72,040	184	132	52
La Porte	21,515	46	42	4
Lawrence	49,865	81	61	20
Lebanon	16,097	42	40	2
Linton	5,179	15	9	6
Mount Vernon	6,471	15	15	0
Muncie	67,760	109	95	14
Munster	22,357	46	41	5
Nappanee	6,864	21	18	3

(Number.)

State/city	Population	Total law enforcement employees	Total officers	Total civilians
New Haven	16,044	31	23	8
New Palestine	2,615	7	7	0
New Whiteland	6,332	8	7	1
Noblesville	66,127	99	89	10
North Webster	1,170	5	5	0
Pittsboro	3,698	9	8	1
Plainfield	36,239	65	59	6
Porter	4,832	14	11	3
Richmond	35,192	82	72	10
Roseland	636	4	3	1
Schererville	28,454	67	52	15
Shelbyville	19,451	58	45	13
Shirley	892	2	2	0
South Bend	102,119	272	224	48
Speedway	12,235	50	35	15
St. John	19,289	25	23	2
Terre Haute	60,604	141	132	9
Valparaiso	34,139	63	57	6
Walkerton	2,269	10	6	4
Washington	12,612	28	21	7
West Lafayette	52,104	65	46	19
Winchester	4,634	13	13	0
Zionsville	28,824	37	35	2
IOWA				
Ackley	1,488	2	2	0
Adel	5,696	12	11	1
Albia	3,670	7	6	1
Algona	5,380	14	10	4
Altoona	19,804	37	35	2
Ames	67,109	79	55	24
Anamosa	5,536	9	8	1
Ankeny	70,301	72	62	10
Asbury	5,909	5	5	0
Atlantic	6,465	13	12	1
Audubon	1,871	4	4	0
Belle Plaine	2,430	5	5	0
Belmond	2,252	5	5	0
Bettendorf	36,926	51	45	6
Bloomfield	2,683	6	5	1
Blue Grass	1,686	4	3	1
Boone	12,355	18	17	1
Burlington	24,622	50	44	6
Camanche	4,356	9	9	0
Carlisle	4,341	9	8	1
Carroll	9,800	16	15	1
Carter Lake	3,784	11	10	1
Cedar Falls	40,675	67	66	1
Cedar Rapids	134,330	282	219	63
Centerville	5,425	17	10	7
Charles City	7,269	21	14	7
Cherokee	4,826	7	6	1
Clarinda	5,343	9	8	1
Clarion	2,695	6	6	0
Clear Lake	7,526	22	15	7
Clinton	24,905	53	47	6
Clive	17,447	33	29	4
Colfax	2,061	4	4	0
Coralville	22,699	37	33	4
Council Bluffs	62,144	134	115	19
Creston	7,701	16	12	4
Davenport	101,806	189	167	22
Dayton	769	1	1	0
Decorah	7,516	14	13	1
Denison	8,234	20	13	7
Des Moines	215,290	464	367	97
DeWitt	5,178	11	10	1
Dubuque	57,904	110	102	8
Durant	1,864	4	4	0
Dyersville	4,357	7	7	0
Dysart	1,307	2	2	0

Table 19. Full-Time Law Enforcement Employees, by Selected State and City, 2020—*Continued*

(Number.)

State/city	Population	Total law enforcement employees	Total officers	Total civilians
Eagle Grove	3,388	5	5	0
Eldora	2,599	5	5	0
Eldridge	6,991	10	9	1
Emmetsburg	3,661	7	6	1
Estherville	5,595	11	11	0
Evansdale	4,742	8	7	1
Fairfield	10,538	20	13	7
Forest City	4,013	9	8	1
Fort Dodge	23,755	44	40	4
Fort Madison	10,239	19	17	2
Glenwood	5,402	11	10	1
Gowrie	944	1	1	0
Grinnell	9,104	13	11	2
Grundy Center	2,666	5	5	0
Hampton	4,176	8	7	1
Harlan	4,732	9	8	1
Hawarden	2,434	4	4	0
Hiawatha	7,465	16	16	0
Humboldt	4,577	6	6	0
Huxley	4,124	6	6	0
Independence	6,141	11	9	2
Indianola	16,154	24	21	3
Iowa City	75,964	103	81	22
Iowa Falls	5,034	14	10	4
Jefferson	4,075	7	7	0
Johnston	23,252	35	30	5
Keokuk	10,091	27	23	4
Knoxville	7,155	15	13	2
Lake City	1,633	3	3	0
Lansing	928	3	3	0
Le Claire	3,990	8	7	1
Le Mars	10,110	17	15	2
Leon	1,808	3	3	0
Lisbon	2,259	2	2	0
Manchester	4,965	16	10	6
Maquoketa	5,966	18	11	7
Marengo	2,460	3	3	0
Marion	40,968	60	46	14
Marshalltown	26,564	42	37	5
Mason City	26,811	45	39	6
Mechanicsville	1,127	1	1	0
Monticello	3,891	8	7	1
Mount Pleasant	8,670	16	14	2
Mount Vernon	4,463	7	6	1
Muscatine	23,616	43	39	4
Nevada	6,662	11	9	2
New Hampton	3,389	6	6	0
Newton	15,176	32	27	5
North Liberty	20,294	24	22	2
Norwalk	12,313	20	19	1
Oelwein	5,846	14	10	4
Ogden	1,972	2	2	0
Onawa	2,739	5	5	0
Orange City	6,195	7	7	0
Osage	3,548	7	6	1
Osceola	5,275	12	11	1
Oskaloosa	11,505	16	14	2
Ottumwa	24,293	50	38	12
Pella	10,225	24	18	6
Perry	7,669	19	12	7
Pleasant Hill	10,158	22	20	2
Polk City	5,165	7	7	0
Postville	2,034	4	4	0
Prairie City	1,723	2	2	0
Princeton	953	1	1	0
Red Oak	5,230	12	10	2
Rock Valley	3,899	6	6	0
Sac City	2,051	4	4	0
Sergeant Bluff	5,226	9	8	1
Sheldon	5,069	6	6	0
Shenandoah	4,786	10	9	1

(Number.)

State/city	Population	Total law enforcement employees	Total officers	Total civilians
Sigourney	2,013	2	1	1
Sioux Center	7,669	8	8	0
Sioux City	82,628	150	125	25
Spencer	10,922	30	20	10
Spirit Lake	5,189	11	10	1
State Center	1,432	2	2	0
Storm Lake	10,282	24	20	4
Story City	3,307	5	5	0
Tama	2,717	6	6	0
Tipton	3,224	7	6	1
Toledo	2,123	6	6	0
University Heights	1,025	5	5	0
Urbandale	44,959	60	51	9
Van Meter	1,324	2	2	0
Vinton	5,056	10	9	1
Walcott	1,636	3	3	0
Washington	7,227	12	11	1
Waterloo	67,200	128	119	9
Waukee	25,590	30	26	4
Waukon	3,594	5	4	1
Waverly	10,234	15	14	1
Webster City	7,630	19	12	7
West Branch	2,510	4	4	0
West Burlington	2,878	10	10	0
West Des Moines	69,252	102	89	13
West Liberty	3,768	6	6	0
Williamsburg	3,175	7	7	0
Wilton	2,828	4	4	0
Windsor Heights	4,798	13	12	1
Winterset	5,403	8	8	0
KANSAS				
Abilene	6,133	17	14	3
Altamont	1,012	3	3	0
Andover	13,592	34	26	8
Anthony	2,051	4	3	1
Arkansas City	11,589	31	27	4
Arma	1,413	5	5	0
Atchison	10,421	25	24	1
Attica	550	1	1	0
Augusta	9,339	32	25	7
Baldwin City	4,720	13	11	2
Basehor	6,742	17	15	2
Baxter Springs	3,915	9	8	1
Bel Aire	8,490	11	10	1
Belle Plaine	1,543	5	5	0
Beloit	3,604	8	7	1
Benton	869	2	2	0
Blue Rapids	955	2	2	0
Bonner Springs	7,955	26	23	3
Buhler	1,272	3	3	0
Burden	525	2	2	0
Burlingame	898	2	2	0
Burlington	2,530	9	7	2
Burrton	855	2	2	0
Caldwell	978	3	3	0
Caney	1,943	11	6	5
Canton	689	1	1	0
Carbondale	1,362	3	3	0
Cedar Vale	501	1	1	0
Chanute	9,034	20	18	2
Chapman	1,332	3	3	0
Chase	434	1	1	0
Cheney	2,174	6	6	0
Cherokee	708	1	1	0
Cherryvale	2,114	6	5	1
Chetopa	1,007	4	4	0
Claflin	596	1	1	0
Clay Center	3,944	8	7	1
Clearwater	2,559	7	6	1
Coffeyville	9,171	32	24	8

(Number.)

State/city	Population	Total law enforcement employees	Total officers	Total civilians
Colby	5,365	19	13	6
Coldwater	727	1	1	0
Columbus	3,025	9	8	1
Colwich	1,483	3	3	0
Conway Springs	1,212	4	4	0
Council Grove	2,112	8	7	1
Derby	25,229	57	48	9
Dodge City	27,066	54	42	12
Eastborough	729	6	6	0
Edwardsville	4,503	18	17	1
El Dorado	12,924	23	20	3
Elkhart	1,714	3	3	0
Ellinwood	1,923	5	5	0
Ellis	2,004	4	4	0
Ellsworth	2,943	7	6	1
Elwood	1,188	3	3	0
Emporia	24,564	48	41	7
Eudora	6,440	12	12	0
Fairway	3,970	9	9	0
Fredonia	2,199	7	6	1
Frontenac	3,382	10	7	3
Galena	2,832	10	8	2
Galva	876	1	1	0
Garden City	26,360	86	60	26
Gardner	22,370	39	34	5
Garnett	3,216	7	7	0
Girard	2,659	7	6	1
Goddard	4,840	13	12	1
Goodland	4,397	9	8	1
Grandview Plaza	1,503	8	7	1
Great Bend	14,864	34	30	4
Hays	20,769	8	7	1
Haysville	11,395	29	23	6
Herington	2,241	8	7	1
Hesston	3,744	8	7	1
Hiawatha	3,103	11	10	1
Highland	992	1	1	0
Hill City	1,403	4	4	0
Hillsboro	2,796	5	5	0
Hoisington	2,446	7	6	1
Holcomb	2,070	2	1	1
Holton	3,196	6	6	0
Holyrood	411	1	1	0
Hoxie	1,193	2	2	0
Hugoton	3,724	8	6	2
Hutchinson	40,186	96	65	31
Independence	8,405	26	19	7
Inman	1,328	4	4	0
Iola	5,220	18	17	1
Junction City	21,242	69	45	24
Kanopolis	448	1	1	0
Kechi	2,015	5	4	1
Kingman	2,807	7	7	0
Kiowa	921	1	1	0
La Cygne	1,116	2	2	0
Lake Quivira	936	1	1	0
Lansing	12,023	17	16	1
Larned	3,632	6	6	0
Lawrence	99,368	169	143	26
Leavenworth	36,023	72	55	17
Leawood	35,054	81	60	21
Lebo	882	1	1	0
Lenexa	56,508	135	87	48
Liberal	19,028	48	38	10
Lindsborg	3,273	8	7	1
Little River	519	1	1	0
Louisburg	4,590	12	11	1
Lyndon	1,017	1	1	0
Lyons	3,478	7	6	1
Macksville	528	1	1	0
Marion	1,759	5	5	0

State/city	Population	Total law enforcement employees	Total officers	Total civilians
Marquette	594	1	1	0
Marysville	3,265	9	8	1
McLouth	845	1	1	0
McPherson	13,053	40	32	8
Meade	1,502	4	3	1
Medicine Lodge	1,816	4	4	0
Merriam	11,087	36	31	5
Minneapolis	1,885	5	5	0
Mission	9,979	30	27	3
Mission Hills	3,555	3	3	0
Moran	505	1	1	0
Mound City	676	1	1	0
Moundridge	1,869	4	4	0
Mount Hope	800	2	2	0
Mulberry	521	1	1	0
Mulvane	6,528	21	14	7
Neodesha	2,239	8	7	1
Newton	18,830	42	38	4
North Newton	1,761	4	4	0
Oakley	2,077	9	5	4
Oberlin	1,691	5	5	0
Olathe	142,228	211	184	27
Osage City	2,795	7	7	0
Oswego	1,663	5	5	0
Ottawa	12,212	28	23	5
Overland Park	198,036	325	257	68
Oxford	994	3	3	0
Paola	5,730	21	15	6
Parsons	9,373	29	21	8
Peabody	1,090	2	2	0
Pleasanton	1,157	3	3	0
Prairie Village	22,390	61	47	14
Pratt	6,460	20	15	5
Roeland Park	6,683	17	15	2
Rose Hill	3,972	9	8	1
Russell	4,412	9	8	1
Salina	46,400	108	81	27
Scott City	3,738	13	8	5
Sedgwick	1,654	2	2	0
Seneca	2,083	4	4	0
Shawnee	66,208	109	89	20
Smith Center	1,559	2	2	0
Spearville	785	1	1	0
Spring Hill	7,572	13	12	1
Sterling	2,195	5	5	0
St. George	1,049	2	2	0
St. Marys	2,656	6	6	0
Topeka	125,024	330	285	45
Troy	954	1	1	0
Ulysses	5,546	11	10	1
Valley Center	7,383	18	16	2
WaKeeney	1,751	5	5	0
Wamego	4,769	13	8	5
Wathena	1,287	2	2	0
Wellington	7,608	19	16	3
Wellsville	1,773	6	5	1
Westwood	1,657	8	7	1
Winfield	11,900	27	22	5
Yates Center	1,311	4	4	0
KENTUCKY				
Adairville	883	1	1	0
Alexandria	9,861	21	17	4
Anchorage	2,431	14	10	4
Ashland	19,979	51	48	3
Auburn	1,384	2	2	0
Augusta	1,143	2	2	0
Bancroft	514	1	1	0
Bardstown	13,330	34	31	3
Beattyville	1,212	6	6	0
Beaver Dam	3,578	6	6	0

(Number.)

State/city	Population	Total law enforcement employees	Total officers	Total civilians
Bellefonte	816	5	5	0
Bellevue	5,695	12	11	1
Berea	16,311	38	33	5
Bloomfield	1,071	1	1	0
Bowling Green	71,861	159	120	39
Brandenburg	2,898	5	5	0
Burkesville	1,456	10	6	4
Burnside	844	5	5	0
Calvert City	2,497	8	7	1
Carrollton	3,763	15	14	1
Catlettsburg	1,734	7	7	0
Cave City	2,439	9	9	0
Central City	5,703	12	12	0
Clay	1,087	2	2	0
Clay City	1,090	3	3	0
Cloverport	1,152	1	1	0
Coal Run Village	1,501	4	3	1
Cold Spring	6,641	14	14	0
Columbia	4,609	16	15	1
Corbin	7,190	30	24	6
Covington	40,324	121	110	11
Danville	16,826	31	29	2
Dayton	5,639	12	11	1
Eddyville	2,544	3	3	0
Edgewood	8,776	17	17	0
Edmonton	1,593	7	7	0
Elizabethtown	30,505	80	60	20
Elkton	2,127	8	7	1
Elsmere	8,618	15	15	0
Eminence	2,591	6	6	0
Erlanger	23,441	46	44	2
Eubank	331	1	1	0
Falmouth	2,091	8	7	1
Flatwoods	7,041	12	12	0
Florence	33,397	68	66	2
Fort Mitchell	8,249	13	13	0
Fort Thomas	16,273	31	23	8
Fort Wright	5,752	14	14	0
Frankfort	27,803	59	57	2
Franklin	9,072	24	23	1
Georgetown	35,702	82	57	25
Glasgow	14,537	45	37	8
Grayson	3,870	11	10	1
Greenville	4,174	12	11	1
Guthrie	1,408	3	3	0
Hardinsburg	2,338	5	5	0
Harlan	1,480	15	10	5
Harrodsburg	8,553	25	18	7
Hawesville	991	1	1	0
Heritage Creek	1,139	11	11	0
Highland Heights	7,069	12	11	1
Hillview	9,311	20	20	0
Hodgenville	3,251	8	8	0
Hopkinsville	30,532	103	69	34
Hustonville	368	1	1	0
Hyden	328	1	1	0
Independence	28,957	36	34	2
Indian Hills	2,978	8	8	0
Irvine	2,279	5	5	0
Jackson	1,913	12	8	4
Jamestown	1,791	4	4	0
Jeffersontown	27,700	67	54	13
Jenkins	1,899	4	4	0
Junction City	2,312	3	3	0
La Grange	9,142	17	15	2
Lakeside Park-Crestview Hills	6,134	13	12	1
Lancaster	3,873	12	12	0
Lawrenceburg	11,565	21	14	7
Lebanon	5,726	25	17	8
Leitchfield	6,880	21	20	1
Lewisburg	803	1	1	0

State/city	Population	Total law enforcement employees	Total officers	Total civilians
Lexington	325,851	670	580	90
Louisa	2,313	6	6	0
Louisville Metro	673,730	1,388	1,124	264
Loyall	592	2	2	0
Ludlow	4,499	12	11	1
Madisonville	18,494	59	46	13
Manchester	1,274	11	11	0
Marion	2,821	9	6	3
Martin	547	2	2	0
Mayfield	9,791	26	25	1
Maysville	8,695	36	26	10
Middlesboro	8,968	26	21	5
Middletown	7,910	17	16	1
Millersburg	779	2	2	0
Monticello	5,966	9	9	0
Morehead	7,644	28	19	9
Morganfield	3,350	5	5	0
Mount Sterling	7,268	23	21	2
Mount Washington	14,964	27	25	2
Muldraugh	991	3	3	0
Murray	19,499	48	40	8
Newport	14,874	44	40	4
Nicholasville	31,191	74	67	7
Oak Grove	7,299	16	16	0
Olive Hill	1,548	8	7	1
Owensboro	60,430	125	93	32
Owingsville	1,580	5	5	0
Paducah	24,850	97	69	28
Paintsville	3,964	9	8	1
Park Hills	2,983	8	8	0
Pewee Valley	1,585	1	1	0
Pikeville	6,501	32	23	9
Pineville	1,709	7	7	0
Pioneer Village	2,967	5	5	0
Pippa Passes	671	7	1	6
Powderly	735	3	2	1
Prestonsburg	3,500	18	13	5
Prospect	4,929	8	7	1
Providence	2,979	5	5	0
Radcliff	22,950	45	34	11
Ravenna	554	1	1	0
Richmond	36,691	70	61	9
Russell	3,208	12	12	0
Russell Springs	2,661	10	9	1
Russellville	7,125	25	24	1
Science Hill	696	3	3	0
Scottsville	4,576	26	16	10
Sebree	1,523	1	1	0
Shelbyville	16,863	31	30	1
Shepherdsville	12,567	38	36	2
Shively	15,735	36	30	6
Simpsonville	2,974	10	10	0
Smiths Grove	807	1	1	0
Somerset	11,622	52	47	5
Southgate	4,039	8	8	0
South Shore	1,050	1	1	0
Springfield	2,980	15	8	7
Stamping Ground	819	2	2	0
Stanton	2,701	8	8	0
St. Matthews	18,162	43	37	6
Tompkinsville	2,242	10	7	3
Trenton	374	1	1	0
Vanceburg	1,393	5	5	0
Versailles	26,899	35	34	1
Villa Hills	7,478	14	14	0
Vine Grove	6,596	11	11	0
Warsaw	1,705	4	4	0
West Buechel	1,277	11	11	0
West Point	870	3	3	0
Whitesburg	1,813	6	5	1
Wilder	3,058	10	10	0

(Number.)

State/city	Population	Total law enforcement employees	Total officers	Total civilians
Williamstown	3,907	7	6	1
Wilmore	6,496	9	8	1
Winchester	18,570	47	31	16
LOUISIANA				
Abbeville	12,018	37	34	3
Alexandria	45,986	159	127	32
Baker	13,122	36	34	2
Basile	1,779	9	8	1
Bastrop	9,889	22	22	0
Bernice	1,583	3	3	0
Berwick	4,365	14	13	1
Bossier City	68,869	200	161	39
Breaux Bridge	8,149	29	26	3
Broussard	13,299	37	33	4
Carencro	9,668	30	28	2
Church Point	4,336	16	16	0
Crowley	12,515	38	32	6
De Ridder	10,583	27	26	1
Dixie Inn	261	2	2	0
Erath	2,031	11	7	4
Eunice	9,751	40	29	11
Gonzales	11,092	48	43	5
Haughton	3,278	14	13	1
Iowa	3,184	18	14	4
Jennings	9,737	27	21	6
Kaplan	4,402	20	14	6
Kinder	2,357	15	11	4
Lafayette	126,679	327	275	52
Lake Charles	79,077	174	140	34
Mansfield	4,587	22	16	6
Marksville	5,299	24	17	7
Minden	11,711	29	28	1
Monroe	47,119	158	123	35
Opelousas	15,820	58	45	13
Patterson	5,758	25	25	0
Pineville	14,079	77	69	8
Plaquemine	6,479	29	20	9
Port Allen	4,695	21	20	1
Rayne	7,997	24	23	1
Rayville	3,450	10	10	0
Ruston	21,846	49	37	12
Scott	8,696	30	28	2
Springhill	4,720	19	14	5
Sterlington	3,135	3	3	0
Sulphur	20,029	65	52	13
Tallulah	6,596	13	7	6
Thibodaux	14,418	62	42	20
Tickfaw	772	5	5	0
Vidalia	3,765	33	25	8
Ville Platte	6,991	24	17	7
Welsh	3,227	14	14	0
Westlake	4,997	17	14	3
West Monroe	12,134	64	49	15
Winnfield	4,201	22	14	8
Youngsville	15,654	34	30	4
MAINE				
Ashland	1,208	3	3	0
Auburn	23,455	59	52	7
Augusta	18,653	56	45	11
Baileyville	1,439	5	5	0
Bangor	32,179	97	81	16
Bar Harbor	7,716	28	20	8
Bath	8,322	24	19	5
Belfast	6,681	17	16	1
Berwick	7,944	13	12	1
Biddeford	21,530	84	57	27
Boothbay Harbor	2,219	9	8	1
Brewer	8,988	23	21	2
Bridgton	5,459	10	9	1

(Number.)

State/city	Population	Total law enforcement employees	Total officers	Total civilians
Brunswick	20,566	47	32	15
Bucksport	4,927	13	10	3
Buxton	8,360	14	8	6
Calais	2,993	7	7	0
Camden	4,776	12	11	1
Cape Elizabeth	9,340	15	14	1
Caribou	7,532	15	14	1
Carrabassett Valley	788	1	1	0
Clinton	3,340	4	4	0
Cumberland	8,327	14	12	2
Damariscotta	2,144	6	5	1
Dexter	3,687	6	6	0
Dover-Foxcroft	4,018	5	5	0
East Millinocket	2,922	5	5	0
Eastport	1,258	1	1	0
Eliot	6,990	8	7	1
Ellsworth	8,231	22	19	3
Fairfield	6,531	12	12	0
Falmouth	12,444	28	19	9
Farmington	7,764	12	11	1
Fort Fairfield	3,263	2	2	0
Fort Kent	3,831	9	4	5
Freeport	8,637	18	16	2
Fryeburg	3,452	5	5	0
Gardiner	5,639	14	13	1
Gorham	18,167	25	22	3
Gouldsboro	1,742	2	2	0
Greenville	1,599	3	3	0
Hallowell	2,382	5	5	0
Hampden	7,428	11	11	0
Holden	3,106	4	4	0
Houlton	5,713	15	10	5
Islesboro	560	1	1	0
Jay	4,600	8	7	1
Kennebunk	11,719	26	23	3
Kennebunkport	3,671	18	13	5
Kittery	9,855	29	22	7
Lewiston	36,186	93	80	13
Limestone	2,159	3	3	0
Lincoln	4,838	6	5	1
Lisbon	9,004	18	13	5
Livermore Falls	3,154	6	6	0
Machias	2,007	3	3	0
Madawaska	3,704	7	6	1
Mechanic Falls	2,974	6	6	0
Mexico	2,624	5	5	0
Milbridge	1,288	1	1	0
Millinocket	4,226	7	6	1
Milo	2,279	3	3	0
Monmouth	4,139	4	4	0
Newport	3,272	6	6	0
North Berwick	4,744	9	8	1
Norway	4,989	10	9	1
Oakland	6,317	11	10	1
Ogunquit	932	12	11	1
Old Orchard Beach	9,061	25	22	3
Old Town	7,388	16	15	1
Orono	10,851	15	14	1
Oxford	4,095	8	7	1
Paris	5,149	9	8	1
Phippsburg	2,274	1	1	0
Pittsfield	3,971	7	6	1
Portland	66,229	203	148	55
Presque Isle	8,937	19	14	5
Rangeley	1,153	3	3	0
Richmond	3,477	4	4	0
Rockland	7,151	19	17	2
Rockport	3,367	6	6	0
Rumford	5,735	13	12	1
Sabattus	5,054	9	8	1
Saco	20,133	47	31	16

(Number.)

State/city	Population	Total law enforcement employees	Total officers	Total civilians
Sanford..	21,272	43	39	4
Scarborough...	21,237	59	39	20
Searsport..	2,635	3	3	0
Skowhegan..	8,202	17	16	1
South Berwick...	7,605	11	10	1
South Portland..	25,593	62	53	9
Southwest Harbor..	1,795	8	4	4
Thomaston..	2,741	5	5	0
Topsham..	8,891	15	14	1
Veazie...	1,823	4	4	0
Waldoboro..	5,070	7	7	0
Washburn..	1,526	2	2	0
Waterville..	16,654	41	30	11
Wells	10,803	33	24	9
Westbrook...	19,256	43	39	4
Wilton	3,944	4	4	0
Windham...	18,720	30	27	3
Winslow...	7,599	11	10	1
Winter Harbor...	511	1	1	0
Winthrop...	5,983	14	9	5
Wiscasset..	3,767	4	3	1
Yarmouth..	8,617	15	14	1
York..	13,377	37	26	11
MARYLAND				
Aberdeen...	16,140	54	41	13
Annapolis..	39,315	146	115	31
Baltimore..	588,594	2,940	2,465	475
Baltimore City Sheriff..		183	122	61
Bel Air...	10,116	41	31	10
Berlin..	4,914	19	14	5
Berwyn Heights...	3,269	11	10	1
Bladensburg..	9,455	34	23	11
Boonsboro...	3,677	5	4	1
Bowie..	59,008	80	63	17
Brentwood...	3,485	4	3	1
Brunswick..	6,562	16	16	0
Cambridge...	12,239	42	39	3
Capitol Heights..	4,537	13	11	2
Centreville...	5,026	11	11	0
Chestertown..	5,027	12	11	1
Cheverly..	6,456	16	13	3
Chevy Chase Village...	2,067	17	11	6
Colmar Manor..	1,459	5	4	1
Cottage City..	1,361	5	4	1
Crisfield...	2,548	14	10	4
Cumberland...	19,122	63	48	15
Delmar..	3,384	13	12	1
Denton..	4,525	13	12	1
District Heights..	6,010	10	9	1
Edmonston..	1,497	6	5	1
Elkton...	15,639	45	39	6
Fairmount Heights	1,530	1	1	0
Federalsburg..	2,653	10	9	1
Forest Heights...	2,574	8	7	1
Frederick..	73,042	192	146	46
Frostburg..	8,451	21	17	4
Fruitland..	5,362	23	20	3
Glenarden..	6,177	18	16	2
Greenbelt...	23,342	62	47	15
Greensboro..	1,874	5	5	0
Hagerstown...	40,136	108	91	17
Hampstead..	6,410	10	9	1
Havre de Grace..	14,132	42	31	11
Hurlock..	2,015	11	10	1
Hyattsville...	18,305	61	44	17
Landover Hills..	1,642	6	5	1
La Plata...	9,728	21	20	1
Laurel	25,704	82	64	18
Luke..	59	1	1	0
Manchester..	4,855	7	6	1

(Number.)

State/city	Population	Total law enforcement employees	Total officers	Total civilians
Morningside	1,286	9	8	1
Mount Airy	9,476	10	8	2
Mount Rainier	8,126	19	14	5
New Carrollton	12,990	31	19	12
North East	3,648	11	10	1
Oakland	1,806	2	2	0
Ocean City	6,926	130	104	26
Ocean Pines	11,710	19	15	4
Perryville	4,428	12	11	1
Pocomoke City	4,078	24	17	7
Princess Anne	3,535	12	11	1
Ridgely	1,659	5	5	0
Rising Sun	2,780	5	5	0
Riverdale Park	7,229	30	23	7
Rock Hall	1,270	3	3	0
Salisbury	33,233	111	82	29
Seat Pleasant	4,761	29	24	5
Smithsburg	2,972	4	3	1
Snow Hill	2,043	7	7	0
St. Michaels	1,041	10	9	1
Sykesville	3,960	8	7	1
Takoma Park	17,831	61	40	21
Taneytown	6,824	16	14	2
Thurmont	6,977	15	12	3
University Park	2,639	8	7	1
Upper Marlboro	675	4	3	1
Westminster	18,654	55	45	10
MASSACHUSETTS				
Abington	17,306	33	30	3
Acton	23,728	54	43	11
Acushnet	10,604	24	20	4
Adams	7,959	18	17	1
Agawam	28,533	66	53	13
Amesbury	17,578	39	33	6
Amherst	40,061	55	37	18
Andover	36,534	69	50	19
Aquinnah	322	4	4	0
Arlington	45,582	82	68	14
Ashburnham	6,344	16	12	4
Ashby	3,217	8	7	1
Ashfield	1,715	2	2	0
Ashland	17,842	31	25	6
Athol	11,682	26	19	7
Attleboro	45,181	97	82	15
Auburn	16,736	50	38	12
Avon	4,561	20	15	5
Ayer	8,237	30	20	10
Barnstable	44,169	138	111	27
Barre	5,568	10	9	1
Becket	1,709	4	4	0
Bedford	14,135	35	28	7
Belchertown	15,148	26	20	6
Bellingham	17,331	34	26	8
Belmont	26,136	60	47	13
Berkley	6,864	13	13	0
Berlin	3,266	11	10	1
Bernardston	2,086	3	3	0
Beverly	42,229	73	69	4
Billerica	43,473	81	63	18
Blackstone	9,269	22	18	4
Bolton	5,455	13	12	1
Boston	697,323	2,715	2,132	583
Bourne	19,657	51	43	8
Boxborough	5,856	19	13	6
Boxford	8,328	9	9	0
Boylston	4,728	14	10	4
Braintree	37,278	98	82	16
Brewster	9,714	29	24	5
Bridgewater	8,107	45	43	2
Brockton	99,171	211	187	24

Table 19. Full-Time Law Enforcement Employees, by Selected State and City, 2020—*Continued*

(Number.)

State/city	Population	Total law enforcement employees	Total officers	Total civilians
Brookfield	3,442	5	5	0
Brookline	59,057	187	137	50
Buckland	1,845	2	2	0
Burlington	28,960	68	61	7
Cambridge	119,938	312	271	41
Canton	24,015	45	45	0
Carlisle	5,267	15	10	5
Carver	12,197	22	17	5
Charlton	13,720	24	18	6
Chatham	5,935	27	21	6
Chelmsford	35,369	62	57	5
Chelsea	39,995	115	107	8
Cheshire	3,118	1	1	0
Chicopee	54,918	125	121	4
Clinton	13,967	36	26	10
Cohasset	8,653	20	19	1
Concord	18,952	42	33	9
Dalton	6,500	9	8	1
Danvers	27,517	57	45	12
Dartmouth	33,986	86	71	15
Dedham	25,217	58	54	4
Deerfield	4,976	10	9	1
Dennis	13,760	51	44	7
Dighton	8,026	15	14	1
Douglas	9,054	18	14	4
Dover	6,176	17	16	1
Dracut	31,708	44	41	3
Dudley	11,745	16	15	1
Dunstable	3,410	9	8	1
Duxbury	16,561	33	31	2
East Bridgewater	15,103	31	22	9
East Brookfield	2,200	4	4	0
Eastham	4,874	23	17	6
Easthampton	15,804	35	29	6
East Longmeadow	16,181	28	25	3
Easton	25,176	46	36	10
Edgartown	4,374	20	19	1
Essex	3,812	11	10	1
Everett	46,765	125	117	8
Fairhaven	16,014	37	31	6
Fall River	89,136	272	221	51
Falmouth	30,769	60	56	4
Fitchburg	40,443	92	77	15
Foxborough	18,539	41	39	2
Framingham	74,680	147	129	18
Franklin	34,281	55	53	2
Freetown	9,401	19	19	0
Gardner	20,629	51	32	19
Georgetown	8,783	18	13	5
Gill	1,464	2	2	0
Gloucester	30,445	67	60	7
Goshen	1,059	2	2	0
Grafton	18,908	24	20	4
Granby	6,297	15	11	4
Great Barrington	6,928	18	17	1
Greenfield	17,239	47	34	13
Groton	11,337	26	19	7
Groveland	6,856	13	11	2
Hadley	5,352	22	16	6
Halifax	8,207	11	10	1
Hamilton	8,038	18	13	5
Hanson	11,367	24	23	1
Hardwick	3,047	5	5	0
Harwich	12,068	34	28	6
Haverhill	64,015	117	100	17
Hingham	25,816	49	47	2
Hinsdale	1,899	5	4	1
Holbrook	11,035	23	22	1
Holden	19,412	39	24	15
Holland	2,473	2	2	0
Holliston	14,986	30	25	5

(Number.)

State/city	Population	Total law enforcement employees	Total officers	Total civilians
Holyoke	40,002	128	113	15
Hopedale	5,924	17	13	4
Hopkinton	18,806	36	26	10
Hudson	19,839	44	33	11
Hull	10,850	27	24	3
Ipswich	14,097	29	25	4
Kingston	14,481	32	24	8
Lakeville	12,053	24	19	5
Lancaster	8,040	12	11	1
Lanesboro	2,924	6	6	0
Lawrence	79,997	181	158	23
Leicester	11,329	21	20	1
Lenox	4,930	10	10	0
Leominster	41,598	92	76	16
Leverett	1,836	3	3	0
Lexington	33,138	61	45	16
Lincoln	7,092	18	13	5
Littleton	10,326	28	20	8
Longmeadow	15,640	27	25	2
Lowell	110,876	310	232	78
Ludlow	21,171	52	40	12
Lunenburg	11,874	17	16	1
Lynn	94,223	195	177	18
Lynnfield	13,093	27	21	6
Malden	60,231	110	101	9
Mansfield	24,484	46	37	9
Marblehead	20,525	39	30	9
Marion	5,396	15	15	0
Marlborough	39,498	81	67	14
Mashpee	14,180	44	35	9
Mattapoisett	6,659	20	20	0
Maynard	11,420	27	21	6
Medfield	13,034	25	19	6
Medway	13,534	26	25	1
Melrose	27,975	44	43	1
Mendon	6,232	17	14	3
Methuen	50,810	101	84	17
Middleboro	26,606	48	44	4
Middleton	10,189	17	16	1
Millbury	13,949	59	49	10
Millis	8,339	23	18	5
Millville	3,247	6	5	1
Milton	27,600	60	52	8
Montague	8,185	22	17	5
Nahant	3,505	13	12	1
Nantucket	11,484	56	38	18
Natick	36,200	70	54	16
Needham	31,586	59	50	9
New Bedford	94,886	291	248	43
Newburyport	18,288	37	32	5
Newton	88,281	194	149	45
Norfolk	12,068	23	21	2
North Adams	12,620	36	24	12
Northampton	28,428	66	59	7
North Andover	31,341	52	38	14
North Attleboro	29,280	62	45	17
Northborough	15,105	28	20	8
Northbridge	16,699	26	18	8
Northfield	2,950	3	3	0
North Reading	15,886	35	32	3
Norton	19,932	35	34	1
Norwell	11,605	26	23	3
Norwood	29,791	72	61	11
Oak Bluffs	4,677	19	17	2
Oakham	1,953	1	1	0
Orleans	5,745	28	22	6
Oxford	13,967	29	22	7
Palmer	12,200	29	22	7
Paxton	4,953	17	16	1
Peabody	52,975	102	85	17
Pelham	1,312	2	2	0

(Number.)

State/city	Population	Total law enforcement employees	Total officers	Total civilians
Pembroke	19,211	32	31	1
Pepperell	12,114	17	16	1
Petersham	1,244	2	2	0
Pittsfield	41,865	107	86	21
Plymouth	64,199	144	128	16
Plympton	3,105	9	8	1
Princeton	3,477	7	6	1
Provincetown	2,947	24	18	6
Quincy	94,519	258	224	34
Randolph	32,052	64	59	5
Raynham	14,512	38	30	8
Reading	25,417	59	44	15
Rehoboth	12,406	32	26	6
Revere	52,930	106	100	6
Rockland	18,652	34	31	3
Rockport	7,279	17	16	1
Rowley	6,509	17	12	5
Salem	43,154	103	92	11
Salisbury	9,630	26	15	11
Sandwich	20,008	44	34	10
Saugus	28,397	82	67	15
Scituate	19,655	34	33	1
Seekonk	15,927	40	38	2
Sharon	19,011	34	30	4
Sheffield	3,115	5	5	0
Shelburne	1,830	3	3	0
Sherborn	4,335	15	14	1
Shirley	7,632	13	11	2
Shrewsbury	38,656	59	45	14
Somerset	18,024	38	33	5
Somerville	81,552	155	122	33
Southampton	6,213	13	9	4
Southborough	10,202	25	20	5
Southbridge	16,805	49	38	11
South Hadley	17,613	33	28	5
Southwick	9,732	24	18	6
Spencer	11,896	23	18	5
Springfield	153,084	622	474	148
Stockbridge	1,884	7	6	1
Stoneham	24,329	45	37	8
Stoughton	29,067	69	58	11
Stow	7,266	12	10	2
Sturbridge	9,585	27	20	7
Sudbury	19,778	41	30	11
Sunderland	3,622	6	5	1
Sutton	9,600	19	15	4
Swampscott	15,391	29	28	1
Swansea	16,854	39	34	5
Templeton	8,110	14	9	5
Tewksbury	31,237	71	62	9
Tisbury	4,108	15	13	2
Topsfield	6,668	12	11	1
Townsend	9,515	14	13	1
Truro	1,997	17	12	5
Uxbridge	14,202	26	19	7
Wakefield	27,114	48	47	1
Walpole	25,273	55	44	11
Waltham	62,339	212	148	64
Wareham	23,619	52	43	9
Warren	5,203	7	6	1
Watertown	36,201	79	67	12
Webster	16,876	32	30	2
Wellesley	28,687	57	42	15
Wellfleet	2,707	20	15	5
Wenham	5,296	11	10	1
Westborough	19,138	37	35	2
West Brookfield	3,715	6	6	0
Westfield	41,072	84	80	4
Westford	25,011	52	48	4
Westminster	8,038	18	14	4
Weston	12,146	36	26	10

(Number.)

State/city	Population	Total law enforcement employees	Total officers	Total civilians
Westport	16,003	32	29	3
West Tisbury	2,919	10	9	1
Westwood	16,578	37	29	8
Weymouth	58,090	117	98	19
Wilbraham	14,690	28	27	1
Williamsburg	2,464	1	1	0
Williamstown	7,397	14	12	2
Wilmington	23,437	54	50	4
Winchendon	10,908	21	15	6
Winchester	22,827	49	40	9
Winthrop	18,561	31	30	1
Woburn	40,142	84	79	5
Worcester	184,850	492	442	50
Wrentham	12,112	23	22	1
Yarmouth	23,015	75	61	14
MICHIGAN				
Adrian	20,540	32	30	2
Adrian Township	6,237	2	2	0
Akron	372	1	1	0
Albion	8,381	20	19	1
Allegan	5,023	9	8	1
Allen Park	26,809	42	38	4
Alma	8,839	17	14	3
Almont	2,809	7	7	0
Alpena	9,900	18	16	2
Ann Arbor	120,647	145	118	27
Argentine Township	6,473	5	5	0
Armada	1,714	2	2	0
Auburn Hills	25,149	55	50	5
Augusta	900	9	6	3
Bad Axe	2,893	7	7	0
Bangor	1,827	6	6	0
Baraga	1,935	2	2	0
Baroda-Lake Township	3,890	6	5	1
Barryton	353	1	1	0
Barry Township	3,531	4	4	0
Bath Township	13,167	13	12	1
Battle Creek	60,479	123	103	20
Bay City	32,485	58	52	6
Beaverton	1,177	4	4	0
Belding	5,741	7	7	0
Bellaire	1,064	2	2	0
Belleville	3,887	8	7	1
Bellevue	1,305	2	2	0
Benton Harbor	9,710	30	29	1
Benton Township	14,251	27	21	6
Berkley	15,410	37	29	8
Berrien Springs-Oronoko Township	8,894	9	8	1
Beverly Hills	10,363	27	23	4
Big Rapids	10,355	20	18	2
Birch Run	1,468	6	5	1
Birmingham	21,536	44	33	11
Blackman Township	37,034	41	40	1
Blissfield	3,259	7	6	1
Bloomfield Hills	4,012	25	22	3
Bloomfield Township	42,059	81	65	16
Boyne City	3,729	7	6	1
Breckenridge	1,267	1	1	0
Bridgeport Township	9,736	9	8	1
Bridgman	2,204	5	5	0
Brighton	7,679	18	16	2
Bronson	2,298	4	4	0
Brown City	1,242	1	1	0
Brownstown Township	32,255	37	30	7
Buchanan	4,242	9	8	1
Buena Vista Township	8,047	13	12	1
Burton	28,427	38	36	2
Cadillac	10,513	17	16	1
Cambridge Township	5,679	4	4	0
Canton Township	94,128	102	93	9

(Number.)

State/city	Population	Total law enforcement employees	Total officers	Total civilians
Capac	1,832	2	2	0
Carleton	2,354	4	3	1
Caro	3,959	7	7	0
Carrollton Township	5,599	6	6	0
Carson City	1,111	1	1	0
Caseville	730	2	2	0
Caspian-Gaastra	1,162	1	1	0
Cass City	2,260	4	4	0
Cassopolis	1,692	5	5	0
Center Line	8,162	25	20	5
Central Lake	938	1	1	0
Charlevoix	2,486	8	7	1
Charlotte	9,091	16	15	1
Cheboygan	4,668	9	9	0
Chelsea	5,471	14	10	4
Chesaning	2,221	2	1	1
Chesterfield Township	47,059	59	45	14
Chikaming Township	3,078	7	6	1
Chocolay Township	5,918	5	4	1
Clare	3,071	7	7	0
Clawson	11,846	19	18	1
Clayton Township	7,057	7	6	1
Clay Township	8,886	23	18	5
Clinton	2,285	4	4	0
Clinton Township	100,884	103	94	9
Clio	2,482	4	4	0
Coldwater	12,076	20	18	2
Coleman	1,199	2	2	0
Coloma Township	6,319	10	7	3
Colon	1,155	3	3	0
Columbia Township	7,350	7	7	0
Constantine	2,110	6	5	1
Corunna	3,327	3	3	0
Covert Township	2,891	9	9	0
Croswell	2,269	5	5	0
Crystal Falls	1,354	1	1	0
Davison	4,848	6	5	1
Davison Township	19,197	22	20	2
Dearborn	93,507	230	186	44
Dearborn Heights	55,105	105	81	24
Decatur	1,724	5	5	0
Denton Township	5,421	4	4	0
Detroit	659,616	3,149	2,528	621
DeWitt	4,844	7	6	1
DeWitt Township	15,756	16	15	1
Dowagiac	5,648	14	13	1
Dryden Township	4,724	4	4	0
Dundee	4,681	5	5	0
Durand	3,818	5	5	0
East Grand Rapids	12,105	30	28	2
East Jordan	2,348	5	5	0
East Lansing	48,098	60	51	9
Eastpointe	32,046	47	42	5
Eaton Rapids	5,248	10	9	1
Eau Claire	594	1	1	0
Ecorse	9,576	19	19	0
Elk Rapids	1,613	5	5	0
Elkton	743	1	1	0
Emmett Township	11,611	16	14	2
Erie Township	4,308	4	3	1
Escanaba	12,111	44	32	12
Essexville	3,257	8	8	0
Evart	1,879	3	3	0
Fair Haven Township	1,038	1	1	0
Farmington	10,503	24	23	1
Farmington Hills	80,708	135	99	36
Fennville	1,433	5	5	0
Fenton	11,369	18	15	3
Ferndale	20,048	49	39	10
Flat Rock	10,019	20	18	2
Flint	94,842	117	95	22

(Number.)

State/city	Population	Total law enforcement employees	Total officers	Total civilians
Flint Township	30,178	48	41	7
Flushing	7,827	10	10	0
Flushing Township	10,133	9	8	1
Forsyth Township	6,182	10	8	2
Fowlerville	2,895	6	5	1
Frankenmuth	5,595	9	7	2
Frankfort	1,291	3	3	0
Franklin	3,256	11	11	0
Fraser	14,480	30	29	1
Fremont	4,077	9	8	1
Fruitport Township	14,476	10	10	0
Gagetown	360	1	1	0
Gaines Township	6,103	1	1	0
Galien	527	2	1	1
Garden City	26,282	38	35	3
Garfield Township	850	1	1	0
Gaylord	3,692	12	11	1
Genesee Township	20,325	21	18	3
Gerrish Township	2,946	6	6	0
Gibraltar	4,505	10	9	1
Gladstone	4,670	11	10	1
Gladwin	2,887	5	5	0
Grand Beach/Michiana	463	5	5	0
Grand Blanc	7,831	18	16	2
Grand Blanc Township	36,498	48	41	7
Grand Haven	11,126	33	30	3
Grand Ledge	7,908	16	16	0
Grand Rapids	202,513	360	291	69
Grandville	15,913	27	25	2
Grant	883	2	2	0
Grayling	1,848	6	5	1
Green Oak Township	19,154	19	17	2
Greenville	8,415	17	15	2
Grosse Ile Township	10,114	23	17	6
Grosse Pointe	5,127	21	21	0
Grosse Pointe Farms	9,077	37	32	5
Grosse Pointe Park	10,998	38	33	5
Grosse Pointe Shores	2,786	18	18	0
Grosse Pointe Woods	15,269	37	31	6
Hamburg Township	21,867	19	18	1
Hampton Township	9,354	10	10	0
Hamtramck	21,514	38	33	5
Hancock	4,487	10	10	0
Harbor Beach	1,575	4	4	0
Harbor Springs	1,207	7	6	1
Harper Woods	13,679	31	27	4
Hart	2,064	5	5	0
Hartford	2,582	5	5	0
Hastings	7,307	17	15	2
Hazel Park	16,340	43	37	6
Hesperia	927	3	3	0
Highland Park	10,680	12	11	1
Hillsdale	7,972	14	12	2
Holland	33,228	67	58	9
Holly	6,157	10	10	0
Home Township	1,370	1	1	0
Houghton	7,760	14	13	1
Howell	9,620	20	18	2
Hudson	2,200	3	3	0
Huntington Woods	6,268	17	16	1
Huron Township	16,288	29	22	7
Imlay City	3,567	10	9	1
Inkster	24,173	39	29	10
Ionia	11,153	17	15	2
Iron Mountain	7,274	15	14	1
Iron River	2,807	4	4	0
Ironwood	4,816	11	11	0
Ishpeming	6,410	12	11	1
Ishpeming Township	3,513	1	1	0
Jackson	32,332	52	43	9
Jonesville	2,210	3	3	0

(Number.)

State/city	Population	Total law enforcement employees	Total officers	Total civilians
Kalamazoo	76,411	258	235	23
Kalamazoo Township	24,562	36	32	4
Kalkaska	2,103	5	5	0
Keego Harbor	3,431	5	5	0
Kentwood	52,263	90	70	20
Kingsford	4,931	19	19	0
Kingston	406	1	1	0
Kinross Township	7,439	2	2	0
Laingsburg	1,285	1	1	0
Lake Angelus	308	1	1	0
Lake Linden	942	1	1	0
Lake Odessa	2,043	4	4	0
Lake Orion	3,206	4	4	0
Lakeview	1,002	3	3	0
L'Anse	1,824	4	4	0
Lansing	118,651	250	199	51
Lansing Township	8,254	16	15	1
Lapeer	8,505	22	19	3
Lathrup Village	4,090	11	10	1
Laurium	1,889	4	4	0
Lawton	1,800	4	4	0
Leslie	1,903	4	4	0
Lexington	1,114	3	3	0
Lincoln Park	36,140	53	46	7
Lincoln Township	14,587	13	12	1
Linden	3,934	5	5	0
Litchfield	1,327	2	2	0
Livonia	93,342	157	118	39
Lowell	4,216	6	5	1
Ludington	8,111	16	14	2
Luna Pier	1,392	1	1	0
Mackinac Island	469	8	8	0
Mackinaw City	794	6	6	0
Madison Heights	29,906	62	48	14
Madison Township	8,229	5	5	0
Mancelona	1,364	1	1	0
Manistee	6,103	12	12	0
Manistique	2,923	8	8	0
Manton	1,588	1	1	0
Marine City	4,038	5	4	1
Marlette	1,755	4	4	0
Marquette	20,957	38	33	5
Marshall	6,954	15	15	0
Marysville	9,643	16	14	2
Mason	8,480	13	12	1
Mattawan	1,981	6	6	0
Mayville	878	3	3	0
Melvindale	10,199	23	23	0
Memphis	1,174	1	1	0
Mendon	848	1	1	0
Menominee	7,971	16	15	1
Meridian Township	43,598	37	34	3
Metamora Township	4,283	5	5	0
Metro Police Authority of Genesee County	19,883	29	26	3
Midland	41,682	52	50	2
Milan	6,065	17	12	5
Milford	17,038	21	19	2
Millington	989	2	2	0
Monroe	19,433	42	36	6
Montague	2,361	4	4	0
Montrose Township	7,431	9	8	1
Morenci	2,139	7	7	0
Morrice	908	2	2	0
Mount Morris	2,822	5	5	0
Mount Morris Township	20,207	29	25	4
Mount Pleasant	24,668	34	28	6
Munising	2,188	4	4	0
Muskegon	36,391	83	74	9
Muskegon Heights	10,724	25	22	3
Muskegon Township	18,022	15	14	1
Napoleon Township	6,767	5	5	0

(Number.)

State/city	Population	Total law enforcement employees	Total officers	Total civilians
Nashville	1,691	1	1	0
Negaunee	4,520	9	9	0
Newaygo	2,076	7	7	0
New Baltimore	12,377	25	15	10
New Buffalo	1,866	7	7	0
New Era	439	1	1	0
Niles	11,102	28	17	11
Northfield Township	8,720	11	10	1
North Muskegon	3,793	8	8	0
Northville	5,956	14	13	1
Northville Township	29,434	47	34	13
Norton Shores	24,742	35	33	2
Norway	2,736	6	6	0
Novi	61,554	93	70	23
Oak Park	29,432	61	48	13
Olivet	1,782	2	2	0
Ontwa Township-Edwardsburg	6,602	9	8	1
Orchard Lake	2,483	9	8	1
Oscoda Township	6,741	13	12	1
Otsego	3,997	6	5	1
Ovid	1,616	2	2	0
Owosso	14,363	17	17	0
Oxford	3,570	13	9	4
Paw Paw	3,351	9	8	1
Pentwater	847	2	2	0
Perry	2,084	4	4	0
Petoskey	5,767	19	18	1
Pigeon	1,111	2	2	0
Pinckney	2,419	6	6	0
Pittsfield Township	39,400	40	39	1
Plainwell	3,774	9	8	1
Pleasant Ridge	2,423	5	5	0
Plymouth	9,159	17	16	1
Plymouth Township	26,988	43	28	15
Portage	49,798	78	59	19
Port Austin	618	2	2	0
Port Huron	28,602	62	54	8
Portland	3,955	6	6	0
Potterville	2,765	2	2	0
Prairieville Township	3,534	2	2	0
Quincy	1,614	3	3	0
Raisin Township	7,784	4	4	0
Reading	1,040	2	2	0
Redford Township	46,510	67	59	8
Reed City	2,388	4	4	0
Reese	1,355	2	2	0
Richfield Township, Genesee County	8,292	11	9	2
Richfield Township, Roscommon County	3,653	4	4	0
Richland	841	4	4	0
Richland Township, Saginaw County	3,904	4	4	0
Richmond	5,856	13	10	3
River Rouge	7,369	27	19	8
Riverview	11,986	22	21	1
Rochester	13,362	30	22	8
Rockford	6,472	11	10	1
Rockwood	3,145	9	8	1
Rogers City	2,636	6	6	0
Romeo	3,607	10	7	3
Romulus	23,533	55	42	13
Roosevelt Park	3,793	5	5	0
Roseville	46,983	70	67	3
Rothbury	448	1	1	0
Royal Oak	59,506	112	78	34
Saginaw	47,767	63	55	8
Saginaw Township	38,971	48	43	5
Saline	9,400	17	13	4
Sandusky	2,503	6	5	1
Saugatuck-Douglas	2,322	5	4	1
Sault Ste. Marie	13,340	25	23	2
Schoolcraft	1,554	3	3	0
Scottville	1,211	2	2	0

(Number.)

State/city	Population	Total law enforcement employees	Total officers	Total civilians
Sebewaing	1,618	2	2	0
Shelby	2,008	2	2	0
Shelby Township	81,416	101	76	25
Shepherd	1,484	2	2	0
Somerset Township	4,520	3	3	0
Southfield	72,794	149	124	25
Southgate	28,848	42	37	5
South Haven	4,341	23	18	5
South Lyon	11,877	17	16	1
South Rockwood	1,655	2	2	0
Sparta	4,429	5	5	0
Spring Arbor Township	7,838	2	2	0
Springport Township	2,156	2	2	0
Stanton	1,423	1	1	0
St. Charles	1,880	1	1	0
St. Clair	5,259	8	8	0
St. Clair Shores	58,898	88	84	4
Sterling Heights	132,745	171	150	21
St. Ignace	2,311	5	5	0
St. Johns	7,954	12	11	1
St. Joseph	8,313	24	22	2
St. Joseph Township	9,638	12	11	1
St. Louis	7,244	8	7	1
Stockbridge	1,253	2	2	0
Sturgis	10,831	24	19	5
Sumpter Township	9,348	18	16	2
Sylvan Lake	1,869	5	5	0
Tawas	4,492	5	4	1
Taylor	60,698	93	79	14
Tecumseh	8,392	15	14	1
Thetford Township	6,605	1	1	0
Thomas Township	11,411	9	8	1
Three Oaks	1,537	3	3	0
Three Rivers	7,604	17	15	2
Tittabawassee Township	10,009	7	6	1
Traverse City	15,855	33	30	3
Trenton	18,085	34	33	1
Troy	84,441	149	103	46
Tuscarora Township	2,904	9	8	1
Ubly	779	1	1	0
Unadilla Township	3,468	3	3	0
Union City	1,561	5	5	0
Utica	5,149	19	15	4
Van Buren Township	28,355	56	40	16
Vassar	2,525	5	5	0
Vernon	767	1	1	0
Vicksburg	3,554	6	6	0
Walker	25,020	41	37	4
Walled Lake	7,142	6	6	0
Warren	133,928	234	198	36
Waterford Township	72,735	79	61	18
Watersmeet Township	1,350	1	1	0
Watervliet	1,639	3	3	0
Wayland	4,241	7	6	1
Wayne	16,734	26	23	3
West Bloomfield Township	65,711	110	80	30
West Branch	2,042	5	5	0
Westland	81,244	95	77	18
White Cloud	1,385	2	2	0
Whitehall	2,846	8	8	0
White Lake Township	31,505	38	29	9
White Pigeon	1,526	4	4	0
Williamston	3,976	7	6	1
Wixom	14,110	23	20	3
Wolverine Lake	4,835	7	7	0
Woodhaven	12,427	31	29	2
Wyandotte	24,757	46	35	11
Wyoming	76,071	100	86	14
Yale	1,861	4	4	0
Ypsilanti	20,240	35	31	4
Zeeland	5,540	11	10	1
Zilwaukee	1,516	1	1	0

Table 19. Full-Time Law Enforcement Employees, by Selected State and City, 2020—*Continued*

(Number.)

State/city	Population	Total law enforcement employees	Total officers	Total civilians
MINNESOTA				
Aitkin	1,969	7	6	1
Akeley	444	1	1	0
Albany	2,787	4	3	1
Albert Lea	17,599	29	26	3
Alexandria	13,978	27	24	3
Annandale	3,549	6	5	1
Anoka	17,593	39	29	10
Appleton	1,316	3	3	0
Apple Valley	55,846	59	51	8
Arlington	2,136	5	4	1
Atwater	1,117	1	1	0
Audubon	520	1	1	0
Austin	25,267	37	34	3
Avon	1,613	4	3	1
Babbitt	1,485	5	5	0
Bagley	1,409	3	3	0
Barnesville	2,606	5	5	0
Battle Lake	935	3	3	0
Baxter	8,447	16	15	1
Bayport	3,799	6	6	0
Becker	4,997	8	7	1
Belgrade/Brooten	1,535	3	3	0
Belle Plaine	7,243	12	10	2
Bemidji	15,567	37	34	3
Benson	3,022	7	6	1
Big Lake	11,355	16	13	3
Blackduck	839	2	2	0
Blaine	66,588	81	66	15
Blooming Prairie	1,930	3	3	0
Bloomington	85,159	145	119	26
Blue Earth	3,087	5	5	0
Bovey	782	2	2	0
Braham	1,819	5	5	0
Brainerd	13,417	27	22	5
Breckenridge	3,148	8	8	0
Breezy Point	2,424	7	6	1
Breitung Township	611	2	2	0
Brooklyn Center	30,744	58	47	11
Brooklyn Park	80,897	134	99	35
Brownton	716	1	1	0
Buffalo	16,550	21	17	4
Buffalo Lake	680	2	2	0
Burnsville	61,445	85	75	10
Caledonia	2,741	6	5	1
Callaway	230	1	1	0
Cambridge	9,302	15	14	1
Canby	1,658	3	3	0
Cannon Falls	4,046	8	6	2
Centennial Lakes	11,704	18	16	2
Champlin	25,517	31	26	5
Chaska	27,353	32	26	6
Chatfield	2,834	5	5	0
Chisholm	4,835	12	11	1
Clara City	1,267	2	2	0
Clearbrook	521	1	1	0
Cloquet	11,995	23	21	2
Cold Spring/Richmond	5,791	11	10	1
Coleraine	1,972	2	2	0
Columbia Heights	21,291	32	25	7
Coon Rapids	63,162	74	63	11
Corcoran	6,352	10	9	1
Cottage Grove	37,940	47	41	6
Crookston	7,749	17	15	2
Crosby	2,316	9	8	1
Crosslake	2,378	6	6	0
Crystal	22,987	40	34	6
Danube	453	1	1	0
Dawson/Boyd	1,540	3	3	0
Dayton	6,958	10	8	2
Deephaven	3,963	8	7	1

(Number.)

State/city	Population	Total law enforcement employees	Total officers	Total civilians
Deer River	929	4	4	0
Deerwood	532	3	3	0
Detroit Lakes	9,352	19	17	2
Dilworth	4,469	8	7	1
Duluth	85,555	177	152	25
Dundas	1,679	3	3	0
Eagan	66,618	86	73	13
Eagle Lake	3,172	3	3	0
East Grand Forks	8,526	25	23	2
East Range	3,558	8	8	0
Eden Prairie	65,353	93	70	23
Eden Valley	1,039	1	1	0
Edina	53,422	77	56	21
Elko New Market	4,855	5	5	0
Elk River	25,467	42	33	9
Ely	3,344	8	7	1
Emily	843	2	2	0
Eveleth	3,553	11	10	1
Fairfax	1,120	2	2	0
Fairmont	9,964	20	18	2
Faribault	23,958	43	35	8
Farmington	23,318	28	25	3
Fergus Falls	13,834	28	23	5
Floodwood	521	3	2	1
Foley	2,678	4	4	0
Forest Lake	21,230	28	25	3
Frazee	1,395	3	3	0
Fridley	27,892	51	43	8
Fulda	1,197	2	2	0
Gaylord	2,196	4	4	0
Gilbert	1,779	7	6	1
Glencoe	5,532	9	8	1
Glenwood	2,617	6	5	1
Glyndon	1,370	4	4	0
Golden Valley	22,060	43	31	12
Goodhue	1,177	2	2	0
Goodview	4,119	5	4	1
Grand Rapids	11,253	23	20	3
Granite Falls	2,677	7	6	1
Hallock	914	1	1	0
Hastings	22,959	34	30	4
Hawley	2,213	5	5	0
Hector	1,039	3	3	0
Henderson	934	2	2	0
Henning	809	2	2	0
Hermantown	9,661	18	15	3
Hibbing	15,802	29	26	3
Hill City	580	1	1	0
Hokah	543	1	1	0
Hopkins	18,568	38	30	8
Houston	963	2	2	0
Howard Lake	2,155	3	3	0
Hutchinson	13,966	34	22	12
International Falls	5,747	12	12	0
Inver Grove Heights	35,861	45	40	5
Isanti	6,219	11	10	1
Isle	801	4	4	0
Janesville	2,251	4	4	0
Jordan	6,514	12	10	2
Kasson	6,549	9	8	1
Keewatin	1,008	3	3	0
La Crescent	5,016	9	8	1
Lake City	5,129	11	10	1
Lake Crystal	2,482	3	3	0
Lakefield	1,605	3	3	0
Lake Park	794	2	2	0
Lakes Area	10,000	15	13	2
Lake Shore	1,064	2	2	0
Lakeville	68,688	69	60	9
Le Center	2,517	3	3	0
Lester Prairie	1,724	3	3	0

(Number.)

State/city	Population	Total law enforcement employees	Total officers	Total civilians
Le Sueur	4,058	8	7	1
Lewiston	1,539	2	2	0
Lino Lakes	22,337	28	25	3
Litchfield	6,641	11	10	1
Little Falls	8,682	17	15	2
Long Prairie	3,284	6	6	0
Lonsdale	4,269	8	7	1
Madelia	2,247	4	4	0
Madison Lake	1,192	1	1	0
Mankato	43,276	64	56	8
Maple Grove	73,939	79	66	13
Mapleton	2,189	3	3	0
Maplewood	41,096	60	55	5
Marshall	13,466	25	22	3
Medina	6,952	12	11	1
Melrose	3,663	6	5	1
Menahga	1,302	3	3	0
Mendota Heights	11,373	21	20	1
Milaca	2,927	7	6	1
Minneapolis	435,116	974	833	141
Minneota	1,352	1	1	0
Minnesota Lake	634	1	1	0
Minnetonka	54,561	63	55	8
Minnetrista	10,738	17	13	4
Montevideo	5,009	12	11	1
Montgomery	3,061	8	7	1
Moorhead	44,132	67	53	14
Moose Lake	2,815	5	5	0
Morgan	834	1	1	0
Morris	5,339	10	8	2
Motley	658	2	2	0
Mounds View	13,421	23	21	2
Mountain Lake	2,029	4	4	0
Nashwauk	948	4	4	0
New Brighton	22,843	35	29	6
New Hope	20,970	39	29	10
New Prague	8,374	12	10	2
New Richland	1,179	2	2	0
New Ulm	13,181	22	22	0
New York Mills	1,220	3	3	0
Nisswa	2,112	6	6	0
North Branch	10,841	14	12	2
Northfield	20,820	29	24	5
North Mankato	14,008	16	15	1
North St. Paul	12,591	19	17	2
Oakdale	27,990	39	31	8
Oak Park Heights	5,071	10	9	1
Olivia	2,316	5	5	0
Onamia	862	3	3	0
Orono	20,387	31	27	4
Ortonville	1,767	4	4	0
Osakis	1,745	3	3	0
Osseo	2,775	8	7	1
Owatonna	25,720	40	36	4
Parkers Prairie	996	2	2	0
Park Rapids	4,280	12	11	1
Paynesville	2,530	5	5	0
Pelican Rapids	2,563	5	5	0
Pequot Lakes	2,315	7	6	1
Perham	3,724	7	6	1
Pierz	1,362	2	2	0
Pike Bay	1,706	1	1	0
Pine River	925	3	3	0
Plainview	3,293	8	7	1
Plymouth	80,843	96	79	17
Preston	1,285	3	3	0
Princeton	4,728	14	12	2
Prior Lake	27,748	34	30	4
Proctor	3,025	8	7	1
Ramsey	28,205	30	27	3
Red Wing	16,304	32	27	5

State/city	Population	Total law enforcement employees	Total officers	Total civilians
Redwood Falls	4,930	14	12	2
Renville	1,178	3	3	0
Rice	1,404	2	2	0
Richfield	36,493	55	46	9
Robbinsdale	14,437	29	23	6
Rochester	120,336	209	145	64
Rogers	13,769	23	20	3
Roseau	2,677	6	5	1
Rosemount	25,597	28	25	3
Roseville	36,675	58	49	9
Rushford	1,692	3	3	0
Sartell	19,262	23	20	3
Sauk Centre	4,528	8	7	1
Sauk Rapids	14,300	18	17	1
Savage	33,020	45	35	10
Sebeka	661	2	2	0
Shakopee	42,076	58	46	12
Sherburn	1,082	4	4	0
Silver Bay	1,750	5	5	0
Slayton	1,956	5	4	1
Sleepy Eye	3,331	7	7	0
South Lake Minnetonka	12,867	19	16	3
South St. Paul	20,053	35	30	5
Springfield	1,989	5	5	0
Spring Grove	1,258	3	3	0
Spring Lake Park	6,978	14	11	3
St. Anthony	9,095	23	20	3
Staples	2,999	8	7	1
Starbuck	1,267	4	4	0
St. Charles	3,760	7	7	0
St. Cloud	68,751	135	109	26
St. Francis	7,997	15	12	3
Stillwater	19,736	27	22	5
St. James	4,380	9	8	1
St. Joseph	7,448	11	10	1
St. Louis Park	49,058	69	56	13
St. Paul	309,859	763	621	142
St. Paul Park	5,374	8	8	0
St. Peter	12,041	20	14	6
Thief River Falls	8,849	17	15	2
Tracy	2,068	3	3	0
Trimont	695	1	1	0
Truman	1,034	2	2	0
Twin Valley	748	2	2	0
Two Harbors	3,506	9	8	1
Tyler	1,062	2	2	0
Verndale	567	2	2	0
Virginia	8,337	24	24	0
Wabasha	2,468	9	8	1
Wadena	4,108	10	9	1
Waite Park	7,812	21	18	3
Walker	932	3	3	0
Walnut Grove	799	1	1	0
Warroad	1,795	6	5	1
Waseca	8,805	20	18	2
Waterville	1,894	4	4	0
Wayzata	6,602	16	14	2
Wells	2,152	5	5	0
Westbrook	700	1	1	0
West Concord	766	1	1	0
West Hennepin	5,995	12	10	2
West St. Paul	20,007	35	31	4
Wheaton	1,275	3	3	0
White Bear Lake	26,036	35	31	4
Willmar	19,901	39	35	4
Windom	4,358	10	9	1
Winnebago	1,330	3	3	0
Winona	26,487	43	39	4
Winsted	2,230	4	4	0
Winthrop	1,340	3	3	0
Woodbury	74,110	79	68	11

(Number.)

State/city	Population	Total law enforcement employees	Total officers	Total civilians
Worthington	13,131	35	24	11
Wyoming	8,095	10	9	1
Zumbrota	3,526	6	6	0
MISSISSIPPI				
Aberdeen	5,163	19	14	5
Ackerman	1,438	5	5	0
Amory	6,740	28	21	7
Batesville	7,193	53	41	12
Bay Springs	1,645	8	7	1
Biloxi	46,433	179	126	53
Booneville	8,472	28	21	7
Brandon	24,545	47	34	13
Brookhaven	11,886	45	35	10
Bruce	1,805	6	6	0
Byram	11,418	41	28	13
Canton	12,103	31	19	12
Carthage	4,753	22	16	6
Charleston	1,836	10	10	0
Clarksdale	14,591	39	31	8
Cleveland	10,944	55	46	9
Clinton	24,349	75	56	19
Coldwater	1,518	5	5	0
Collins	2,409	28	20	8
Crenshaw	841	2	2	0
Decatur	1,692	5	5	0
D'Iberville	14,298	37	34	3
Drew	1,576	1	1	0
Durant	2,220	8	4	4
Edwards	1,000	3	3	0
Ellisville	4,573	10	8	2
Eupora	1,985	8	7	1
Fayette	1,420	7	5	2
Flora	1,859	10	9	1
Florence	4,536	19	16	3
Flowood	9,564	62	48	14
Forest	5,517	20	16	4
Fulton	3,984	11	11	0
Gautier	18,479	40	28	12
Gloster	860	7	4	3
Grenada	12,131	38	32	6
Gulfport	72,142	211	158	53
Hattiesburg	45,870	166	103	63
Hazlehurst	3,699	21	13	8
Hernando	16,675	53	42	11
Hollandale	2,264	12	6	6
Holly Springs	7,799	22	18	4
Horn Lake	27,404	60	43	17
Houston	3,405	4	2	2
Indianola	8,877	28	20	8
Inverness	851	3	3	0
Iuka	2,926	12	9	3
Kosciusko	6,652	21	21	0
Laurel	18,317	65	46	19
Leland	3,694	20	14	6
Lexington	1,425	11	11	0
Long Beach	16,161	46	31	15
Louisville	5,917	21	20	1
Lucedale	3,179	21	15	6
Madison	25,831	92	71	21
Magee	4,062	42	32	10
Mendenhall	2,374	8	5	3
Meridian	35,855	89	69	20
Morton	3,509	11	11	0
Moss Point	13,315	34	25	9
Natchez	14,497	46	38	8
New Augusta	597	1	1	0
Newton	3,133	16	14	2
Ocean Springs	17,917	48	34	14
Okolona	2,577	9	9	0
Olive Branch	39,566	103	84	19

State/city	Population	Total law enforcement employees	Total officers	Total civilians
Oxford	28,866	91	79	12
Pascagoula	21,633	69	49	20
Pass Christian	6,527	27	20	7
Pearl	26,596	80	60	20
Petal	10,652	30	26	4
Philadelphia	7,036	32	23	9
Picayune	10,826	39	26	13
Pickens	979	4	4	0
Poplarville	2,901	8	8	0
Purvis	2,416	14	11	3
Quitman	2,089	8	8	0
Raymond	2,142	11	10	1
Richland	7,276	48	35	13
Ridgeland	24,080	84	58	26
Rolling Fork	1,908	11	10	1
Ruleville	2,512	16	16	0
Sandersville	728	15	15	0
Shelby	1,920	7	2	5
Southaven	56,573	156	123	33
Starkville	25,854	66	57	9
Stonewall	963	8	8	0
Summit	1,555	7	6	1
Sunflower	960	2	2	0
Terry	1,246	2	2	0
Tupelo	38,383	124	110	14
Union	1,888	8	7	1
Utica	890	2	2	0
Vicksburg	21,420	63	49	14
Water Valley	3,242	10	9	1
Waveland	6,287	20	19	1
Waynesboro	4,779	10	10	0
West Point	10,314	34	30	4
Wiggins	4,555	21	15	6
Winona	3,861	8	8	0
Yazoo City	10,806	19	14	5
MISSOURI				
Adrian	1,588	4	4	0
Advance	1,335	3	3	0
Annapolis	341	1	1	0
Arbyrd	457	1	1	0
Arcadia	555	3	3	0
Arnold	21,115	62	54	8
Ashland	3,996	8	7	1
Aurora	7,441	24	17	7
Auxvasse	977	6	6	0
Ava	2,852	12	7	5
Ballwin	30,044	56	45	11
Bel-Nor	1,391	8	8	0
Belton	23,698	61	39	22
Berkeley	8,809	34	27	7
Birch Tree	646	1	1	0
Bonne Terre	7,135	10	10	0
Boonville	8,450	28	21	7
Bourbon	1,579	5	5	0
Bowling Green	5,617	12	10	2
Branson	11,745	68	48	20
Branson West	443	14	14	0
Breckenridge Hills	4,548	18	16	2
Brentwood	7,957	29	28	1
Bridgeton	11,521	65	57	8
Brookfield	4,179	12	10	2
Buckner	3,016	8	7	1
Buffalo	3,092	8	7	1
California	4,429	8	7	1
Calverton Park	1,266	12	9	3
Cameron	9,618	24	16	8
Campbell	1,788	8	8	0
Canalou	297	1	1	0
Carl Junction	8,366	16	11	5
Caruthersville	5,268	14	13	1

(Number.)

State/city	Population	Total law enforcement employees	Total officers	Total civilians
Cassville	3,293	10	10	0
Centralia	4,298	13	9	4
Charleston	5,422	18	12	6
Chesterfield	47,544	112	98	14
Chillicothe	9,735	27	18	9
Clarkton	1,138	2	2	0
Clayton	16,837	54	45	9
Clever	2,842	7	6	1
Columbia	124,829	195	158	37
Country Club Hills	1,244	7	7	0
Country Club Village	2,501	1	1	0
Crestwood	11,829	30	24	6
Creve Coeur	18,716	52	47	5
Crocker	1,030	3	3	0
Crystal City	4,685	22	16	6
Cuba	3,286	16	15	1
Delta	423	1	1	0
De Soto	6,341	28	19	9
Dexter	7,807	26	18	8
Diamond	912	2	2	0
Doniphan	1,907	10	6	4
East Prairie	2,922	9	4	5
Edgar Springs	193	1	1	0
Edmundson	828	11	10	1
Eldon	4,721	13	12	1
El Dorado Springs	3,617	12	8	4
Ellisville	9,927	25	24	1
Ellsinore	427	2	2	0
Excelsior Springs	11,802	32	23	9
Farmington	19,446	32	30	2
Fayette	2,689	7	7	0
Ferguson	20,454	39	34	5
Flordell Hills	799	8	8	0
Florissant	50,812	118	92	26
Fordland	852	1	1	0
Forsyth	2,570	7	6	1
Fredericktown	3,984	15	14	1
Frontenac	3,839	22	21	1
Fulton	12,578	30	24	6
Galena	437	1	1	0
Gideon	960	2	2	0
Grain Valley	14,722	28	23	5
Granby	2,080	4	4	0
Grandview	24,898	66	52	14
Hamilton	1,671	5	5	0
Hannibal	17,299	45	34	11
Hardin	533	1	1	0
Harrisonville	10,083	29	23	6
Hartville	605	2	2	0
Hayti	2,458	5	5	0
Hazelwood	25,051	78	59	19
Herculaneum	4,216	9	8	1
Hermann	2,332	12	6	6
Higginsville	4,589	22	10	12
Highlandville	1,066	1	1	0
Hillsdale	1,549	12	11	1
Holden	2,234	7	7	0
Holts Summit	5,157	12	10	2
Houston	2,081	8	8	0
Howardville	333	2	1	1
Independence	116,648	257	176	81
Ironton	1,381	8	8	0
Jackson	14,955	30	29	1
Jasper	976	2	2	0
Jefferson City	42,653	124	88	36
Kansas City	499,335	1,241	989	252
Kearney	11,164	17	16	1
Kennett	10,005	40	30	10
Kirkwood	27,834	88	60	28
Knob Noster	2,792	8	7	1
Ladue	8,627	34	29	5

State/city	Population	Total law enforcement employees	Total officers	Total civilians
La Grange	888	5	5	0
Lake Lafayette	337	1	1	0
Lake Lotawana	2,129	7	6	1
Lake Ozark	1,856	16	11	5
Lakeshire	1,384	10	10	0
Lake St. Louis	17,136	42	34	8
Lake Tapawingo	718	4	3	1
Lake Winnebago	1,285	7	7	0
La Plata	1,302	4	4	0
Laurie	969	4	4	0
Leadington	622	1	1	0
Lee's Summit	100,268	192	140	52
Lexington	4,513	10	8	2
Licking	3,070	5	5	0
Lincoln	1,194	4	4	0
Linn	1,610	5	5	0
Lone Jack	1,357	9	8	1
Louisiana	3,191	6	5	1
Malden	3,851	15	13	2
Manchester	18,072	39	35	4
Mansfield	1,240	5	5	0
Maplewood	8,096	35	33	2
Marble Hill	1,461	5	4	1
Marionville	2,175	2	2	0
Marshall	12,817	31	24	7
Marshfield	7,667	12	11	1
Maryland Heights	26,901	112	77	35
Memphis	1,835	3	3	0
Merriam Woods	1,858	5	5	0
Mexico	11,517	29	28	1
Milan	1,755	4	4	0
Miner	930	10	10	0
Moline Acres	2,338	18	17	1
Monett	9,150	23	21	2
Morehouse	854	1	1	0
Moscow Mills	3,620	8	8	0
Mound City	1,026	2	2	0
Mountain View	2,641	8	7	1
Mount Vernon	4,502	11	11	0
Neosho	12,077	29	27	2
New Franklin	1,054	3	3	0
New London	987	2	2	0
Nixa	22,924	39	33	6
Normandy	7,405	26	25	1
Northwoods	4,350	16	15	1
Oakland	1,366	88	60	28
Odessa	5,238	11	10	1
Old Monroe	290	2	1	1
Olivette	7,829	23	22	1
Oregon	756	1	1	0
Oronogo	2,700	4	4	0
Orrick	800	2	2	0
Osage Beach	4,696	25	23	2
Overland	15,497	51	45	6
Ozark	20,788	39	36	3
Palmyra	3,597	9	8	1
Peculiar	5,582	9	8	1
Perry	696	1	1	0
Pevely	6,020	21	15	6
Piedmont	1,879	6	6	0
Pierce City	1,311	2	2	0
Pilot Grove	760	1	1	0
Pineville	808	4	4	0
Platte City	4,987	12	12	0
Platte Woods	407	4	4	0
Pleasant Hill	8,744	20	13	7
Pleasant Valley	3,042	27	14	13
Poplar Bluff	16,927	54	42	12
Puxico	842	1	1	0
Queen City	628	1	1	0
Qulin	456	1	1	0

(Number.)

State/city	Population	Total law enforcement employees	Total officers	Total civilians
Raymore	22,545	39	26	13
Raytown	28,922	48	34	14
Reeds Spring	863	3	3	0
Republic	17,174	25	21	4
Rich Hill	1,309	2	2	0
Richland	1,785	5	5	0
Richmond	5,638	12	10	2
Richmond Heights	8,831	37	36	1
Riverside	3,574	36	27	9
Riverview	2,820	13	12	1
Rogersville	3,960	10	10	0
Rolla	20,522	58	35	23
Salem	4,915	18	13	5
Salisbury	1,513	4	3	1
Sarcoxie	1,548	3	3	0
Savannah	5,240	6	5	1
Scott City	4,458	18	13	5
Sedalia	21,639	60	43	17
Seligman	841	4	4	0
Senath	1,595	3	3	0
Seneca	2,392	6	6	0
Seymour	2,021	7	7	0
Shrewsbury	6,074	23	21	2
Sikeston	15,987	66	48	18
Smithville	11,097	20	19	1
Southwest City	954	3	3	0
Springfield	168,856	404	329	75
St. Ann	12,586	67	46	21
Steele	1,861	4	4	0
St. John	6,318	23	22	1
St. Joseph	74,680	169	128	41
St. Louis	298,422	1,659	1,262	397
Stover	1,094	3	3	0
Strasburg	142	2	2	0
St. Robert	6,485	27	19	8
Sullivan	7,128	26	19	7
Summersville	489	3	3	0
Sunset Hills	8,445	32	25	7
Thayer	2,121	13	8	5
Town and Country	11,142	30	29	1
Troy	13,089	25	23	2
Truesdale	905	1	1	0
Union	12,195	26	24	2
University City	34,045	91	70	21
Van Buren	795	5	5	0
Velda City	1,355	7	4	3
Verona	599	2	2	0
Versailles	2,477	17	16	1
Viburnum	648	3	3	0
Vienna	591	2	2	0
Vinita Park	10,951	42	40	2
Walnut Grove	794	2	2	0
Warrensburg	20,591	31	26	5
Warrenton	8,450	27	23	4
Warson Woods	1,892	6	6	0
Washington	14,092	32	29	3
Waynesville	5,338	27	25	2
Weatherby Lake	2,115	15	15	0
Webb City	12,264	27	23	4
Webster Groves	22,798	48	46	2
Wellington	804	3	3	0
Wellsville	1,153	3	3	0
Weston	1,834	4	4	0
Willow Springs	2,090	12	10	2
Winona	1,289	1	1	0
Woodson Terrace	4,032	20	18	2
Wright City	4,458	15	14	1
MONTANA				
Baker	1,907	4	4	0
Belgrade	9,762	23	19	4

(Number.)

State/city	Population	Total law enforcement employees	Total officers	Total civilians
Billings	110,157	184	156	28
Boulder	1,287	3	3	0
Bozeman	51,460	69	60	9
Bridger	760	3	3	0
Chinook	1,260	4	4	0
Colstrip	2,249	11	7	4
Columbia Falls	6,023	11	10	1
Columbus	2,100	4	4	0
Conrad	2,458	5	5	0
Cut Bank	3,075	9	7	2
Deer Lodge	2,822	6	6	0
Dillon	4,318	11	10	1
East Helena	2,113	4	4	0
Ennis	1,012	1	1	0
Eureka	1,407	4	4	0
Fairview	867	3	3	0
Fort Benton	1,429	4	4	0
Glasgow	3,326	10	6	4
Glendive	4,908	15	10	5
Great Falls	58,345	127	87	40
Hamilton	4,970	15	14	1
Havre	9,820	26	20	6
Helena	33,629	69	47	22
Hot Springs	587	2	2	0
Kalispell	25,125	51	41	10
Laurel	6,732	20	14	6
Lewistown	5,772	24	13	11
Libby	2,797	6	6	0
Livingston	7,892	14	14	0
Manhattan	1,955	4	4	0
Miles City	8,250	17	16	1
Missoula	76,468	144	116	28
Plains	1,149	2	2	0
Polson	5,115	16	15	1
Red Lodge	2,324	7	7	0
Ronan City	2,141	6	6	0
Sidney	6,279	12	11	1
Stevensville	2,100	4	3	1
Thompson Falls	1,439	4	4	0
Troy	966	4	4	0
West Yellowstone	1,388	11	5	6
Whitefish	8,523	20	17	3
Wolf Point	2,744	8	6	2
NEBRASKA				
Albion	1,576	6	3	3
Alliance	8,051	23	15	8
Aurora	4,554	11	10	1
Bayard	1,071	4	4	0
Beatrice	12,238	36	22	14
Bellevue	53,761	106	93	13
Bennington	1,527	3	3	0
Blair	7,919	18	16	2
Boys Town	545	14	14	0
Broken Bow	3,492	8	7	1
Burwell	1,157	2	2	0
Central City	2,867	7	6	1
Chadron	5,366	18	11	7
Columbus	23,597	43	36	7
Crete	7,009	13	13	0
Emerson	787	1	1	0
Falls City	4,094	13	9	4
Fremont	26,381	41	35	6
Gering	8,086	19	17	2
Gordon	1,512	8	6	2
Gothenburg	3,432	7	6	1
Grand Island	51,547	101	84	17
Harvard	959	2	2	0
Hastings	24,638	53	39	14
Holdrege	5,399	17	10	7
Imperial	2,053	4	4	0

(Number.)

State/city	Population	Total law enforcement employees	Total officers	Total civilians
Kearney	34,201	73	57	16
Kimball	2,359	4	4	0
Laurel	911	1	1	0
La Vista	17,228	45	39	6
Lexington	10,103	21	19	2
Lincoln	292,600	481	342	139
Madison	2,390	3	3	0
McCook	7,543	23	16	7
Milford	2,090	3	3	0
Minden	2,954	6	6	0
Mitchell	1,614	4	4	0
Morrill	885	2	2	0
Nebraska City	7,292	15	14	1
Neligh	1,488	3	3	0
Norfolk	24,467	58	40	18
North Platte	23,523	62	40	22
Ogallala	4,472	10	9	1
Omaha	480,297	1,012	867	145
O'Neill	3,565	8	7	1
Ord	2,069	4	4	0
Papillion	20,512	50	46	4
Pierce	1,724	3	3	0
Plattsmouth	6,435	17	14	3
Ralston	7,422	15	14	1
Ravenna	1,357	2	2	0
Schuyler	6,312	11	9	2
Scottsbluff	15,665	35	31	4
Scribner	793	1	1	0
Seward	7,242	13	11	2
Sidney	6,049	13	11	2
South Sioux City	12,746	28	27	1
St. Paul	2,336	4	4	0
Superior	1,791	2	2	0
Sutton	1,427	2	2	0
Tekamah	1,696	5	5	0
Tilden	927	1	1	0
Valentine	2,704	6	5	1
Valley	2,948	5	5	0
Wahoo	4,550	7	7	0
Waterloo	922	4	4	0
Wayne	5,658	11	6	5
West Point	3,273	7	5	2
Wymore	1,324	2	2	0
York	7,854	17	15	2
NEVADA				
Boulder City	16,346	48	35	13
Carlin	2,268	7	5	2
Elko	20,697	45	38	7
Fallon	8,648	40	27	13
Henderson	328,056	654	463	191
Las Vegas Metropolitan Police Department	1,693,061	5,716	4,115	1,601
Lovelock	1,822	5	2	3
Mesquite	20,290	49	36	13
Reno	259,168	469	339	130
Sparks	106,664	159	108	51
West Wendover	4,258	21	12	9
Winnemucca	7,786	28	23	5
Yerington	3,256	7	6	1
NEW HAMPSHIRE				
Alexandria	1,618	1	1	0
Allenstown	4,462	11	10	1
Alstead	1,938	2	2	0
Alton	5,343	14	12	2
Amherst	11,414	20	19	1
Antrim	2,697	7	6	1
Ashland	2,053	5	5	0
Atkinson	7,196	9	8	1
Auburn	5,662	12	10	2
Barnstead	4,762	4	4	0

(Number.)

State/city	Population	Total law enforcement employees	Total officers	Total civilians
Barrington	9,358	14	13	1
Bartlett	2,807	4	4	0
Bedford	22,788	53	40	13
Belmont	7,342	17	14	3
Bennington	1,518	2	2	0
Berlin	10,140	31	23	8
Bethlehem	2,579	6	6	0
Boscawen	4,032	8	7	1
Bow	8,032	13	12	1
Bradford	1,714	3	3	0
Brentwood	4,525	4	3	1
Bristol	3,102	10	9	1
Brookline	5,506	9	8	1
Campton	3,297	9	7	2
Canaan	3,894	6	5	1
Candia	3,970	8	7	1
Canterbury	2,475	3	3	0
Carroll	745	4	4	0
Center Harbor	1,099	5	4	1
Charlestown	5,010	11	7	4
Chester	5,334	9	8	1
Chesterfield	3,630	5	4	1
Chichester	2,726	5	5	0
Claremont	12,887	27	21	6
Colebrook	2,121	5	5	0
Concord	43,737	93	81	12
Conway	10,269	30	22	8
Danville	4,581	5	5	0
Deerfield	4,576	9	8	1
Deering	1,978	2	2	0
Derry	33,555	69	56	13
Dover	32,480	76	49	27
Dublin	1,538	4	3	1
Dunbarton	2,894	5	5	0
Durham	16,510	20	17	3
East Kingston	2,428	6	5	1
Effingham	1,479	1	1	0
Enfield	4,526	8	7	1
Epping	7,115	16	15	1
Epsom	4,787	7	6	1
Exeter	15,448	32	24	8
Farmington	7,003	15	14	1
Fitzwilliam	2,367	4	3	1
Franconia	1,105	4	4	0
Franklin	8,711	25	17	8
Freedom	1,593	2	2	0
Fremont	4,764	6	5	1
Gilford	7,258	26	20	6
Gilmanton	3,779	6	5	1
Goffstown	18,098	45	30	15
Gorham	2,587	10	6	4
Grantham	2,942	6	5	1
Greenland	4,194	10	9	1
Hampstead	8,654	9	9	0
Hampton	15,570	42	35	7
Hampton Falls	2,437	4	4	0
Hancock	1,657	3	3	0
Hanover	11,498	28	17	11
Haverhill	4,551	7	6	1
Henniker	5,039	9	8	1
Hillsborough	6,001	23	15	8
Hinsdale	3,893	9	6	3
Holderness	2,106	7	6	1
Hollis	8,040	18	15	3
Hooksett	14,668	40	29	11
Hopkinton	5,781	6	5	1
Hudson	25,748	67	51	16
Jackson	863	4	4	0
Jaffrey	5,258	12	11	1
Keene	22,707	51	40	11
Kensington	2,107	6	5	1

(Number.)

State/city	Population	Total law enforcement employees	Total officers	Total civilians
Kingston	6,500	7	6	1
Laconia	16,669	54	45	9
Lancaster	3,229	9	7	2
Lebanon	13,709	46	33	13
Lee	4,601	9	8	1
Lincoln	1,771	16	10	6
Lisbon	1,577	3	3	0
Litchfield	8,682	14	12	2
Littleton	5,862	15	13	2
Londonderry	26,812	69	56	13
Loudon	5,675	6	5	1
Lyme	1,671	2	2	0
Madison	2,618	4	4	0
Manchester	113,018	279	225	54
Marlborough	2,078	2	2	0
Mason	1,438	3	3	0
Meredith	6,484	17	13	4
Merrimack	26,602	52	39	13
Middleton	1,845	4	4	0
Milford	16,561	32	27	5
Milton	4,633	7	6	1
Mont Vernon	2,686	4	4	0
Moultonborough	4,198	9	8	1
Nashua	89,671	233	174	59
New Boston	5,966	10	9	1
Newbury	2,246	5	5	0
New Castle	981	4	4	0
New Durham	2,715	5	5	0
Newfields	1,744	5	4	1
New Hampton	2,231	5	4	1
Newington	821	12	11	1
New Ipswich	5,425	6	5	1
New London	4,300	14	9	5
Newmarket	9,192	20	13	7
Newport	6,342	16	11	5
Newton	4,969	7	6	1
Northfield	4,956	9	8	1
North Hampton	4,513	13	12	1
Northumberland	2,123	3	3	0
Northwood	4,321	9	8	1
Nottingham	5,182	9	8	1
Orford	1,308	1	1	0
Ossipee	4,389	10	9	1
Pelham	14,373	30	23	7
Pembroke	7,212	14	12	2
Peterborough	6,736	14	12	2
Pittsburg	815	2	2	0
Pittsfield	4,126	6	6	0
Plainfield	2,404	2	2	0
Plaistow	7,738	22	15	7
Plymouth	6,850	18	11	7
Portsmouth	22,032	84	65	19
Raymond	10,583	24	16	8
Rindge	6,100	9	8	1
Rochester	31,762	72	57	15
Rollinsford	2,596	4	4	0
Rye	5,495	11	10	1
Salem	29,943	79	63	16
Sanbornton	3,000	7	6	1
Sandown	6,620	8	7	1
Sandwich	1,362	2	2	0
Seabrook	8,871	30	25	5
Somersworth	12,005	34	27	7
South Hampton	829	2	2	0
Springfield	1,344	2	2	0
Strafford	4,242	6	6	0
Stratham	7,521	12	11	1
Sugar Hill	579	2	2	0
Sunapee	3,501	6	5	1
Swanzey	7,219	12	11	1
Tamworth	3,101	3	3	0

State/city	Population	Total law enforcement employees	Total officers	Total civilians
Thornton	2,541	7	6	1
Tilton...	3,546	20	16	4
Troy	2,100	2	2	0
Tuftonboro...	2,425	4	4	0
Wakefield	5,799	14	12	2
Warner	2,931	5	4	1
Washington	1,101	1	1	0
Waterville Valley.......................................	240	6	6	0
Weare..	9,124	12	11	1
Webster	1,962	2	2	0
Whitefield..	2,200	7	6	1
Wilton	3,801	7	7	0
Winchester	4,213	9	8	1
Windham	15,017	28	21	7
Wolfeboro	6,433	19	13	6
Woodstock	1,364	6	6	0
NEW JERSEY				
Aberdeen Township	19,471	49	42	7
Absecon	8,856	30	24	6
Allendale	6,751	20	15	5
Allenhurst..	482	13	9	4
Allentown..	1,770	7	6	1
Alpine..	1,845	12	12	0
Andover Township	5,826	17	12	5
Asbury Park	15,331	93	89	4
Atlantic City..	37,550	224	190	34
Atlantic Highlands....................................	4,348	19	14	5
Audubon	8,608	18	17	1
Avalon	1,225	28	21	7
Avon-by-the-Sea	1,771	12	12	0
Barnegat Township	23,998	55	53	2
Barrington	6,601	17	15	2
Bay Head	979	10	9	1
Bayonne...	65,013	247	184	63
Beach Haven...	1,210	13	12	1
Beachwood...	11,357	22	20	2
Bedminster Township	7,963	18	16	2
Belleville..	36,533	101	96	5
Bellmawr	11,318	22	21	1
Belmar...	5,518	30	24	6
Belvidere	2,548	7	6	1
Bergenfield	27,347	51	43	8
Berkeley Heights Township..........................	13,371	30	27	3
Berkeley Township	42,168	92	70	22
Berlin...	7,517	19	18	1
Berlin Township...	5,721	19	18	1
Bernards Township.....................................	27,130	41	38	3
Bernardsville...	7,593	26	20	6
Beverly...	2,472	8	8	0
Blairstown Township	5,665	9	8	1
Bloomfield..	50,221	150	126	24
Bloomingdale..	8,098	20	19	1
Bogota...	8,342	20	15	5
Boonton	8,977	25	23	2
Boonton Township	4,228	13	13	0
Bordentown City..	3,778	14	14	0
Bordentown Township	11,974	25	23	2
Bound Brook...	10,174	31	25	6
Bradley Beach	4,131	22	18	4
Branchburg Township	14,526	29	27	2
Brick Township..	76,326	211	141	70
Bridgeton...	24,032	74	61	13
Bridgewater Township................................	44,006	81	73	8
Brielle	4,656	17	16	1
Brigantine..	8,566	45	35	10
Brooklawn..	1,892	8	8	0
Burlington City..	9,849	37	33	4
Burlington Township	22,595	56	47	9
Butler...	7,643	17	16	1
Byram Township..	7,880	14	14	0

(Number.)

State/city	Population	Total law enforcement employees	Total officers	Total civilians
Caldwell	7,938	18	18	0
Camden County Police Department	73,127	423	386	37
Cape May	3,401	27	22	5
Carlstadt	6,126	28	26	2
Carney's Point Township	7,632	20	19	1
Carteret	23,444	74	64	10
Cedar Grove Township	12,483	31	30	1
Chatham	8,586	25	21	4
Chatham Township	10,071	24	22	2
Cherry Hill Township	71,220	164	135	29
Chesilhurst	1,615	10	9	1
Chesterfield Township	7,557	12	11	1
Chester Township	7,640	24	23	1
Cinnaminson Township	16,429	28	28	0
Clark Township	16,026	47	36	11
Clayton	8,790	16	15	1
Clementon	4,950	12	12	0
Cliffside Park	26,400	44	43	1
Clifton	85,058	194	158	36
Clinton	2,684	10	10	0
Clinton Township	12,465	24	23	1
Closter	8,511	21	20	1
Collingswood	13,864	31	27	4
Colts Neck Township	9,786	27	26	1
Cranbury Township	4,086	22	21	1
Cranford Township	24,186	66	52	14
Cresskill	8,672	29	24	5
Deal	715	22	18	4
Delanco Township	4,448	13	12	1
Delaware Township	4,410	8	7	1
Delran Township	16,444	32	28	4
Demarest	4,884	16	16	0
Denville Township	16,400	42	33	9
Deptford Township	30,275	73	67	6
Dover	17,654	43	39	4
Dumont	17,507	40	32	8
Dunellen	7,192	19	19	0
Eastampton Township	6,156	20	19	1
East Brunswick Township	47,573	106	83	23
East Greenwich Township	10,834	22	21	1
East Hanover Township	10,881	38	34	4
East Newark	2,614	7	7	0
East Orange	64,320	243	192	51
East Rutherford	9,767	39	38	1
East Windsor Township	27,265	48	43	5
Eatontown	12,124	49	37	12
Edgewater	13,573	31	29	2
Edgewater Park Township	8,618	17	15	2
Edison Township	99,584	231	184	47
Egg Harbor City	4,031	15	14	1
Egg Harbor Township	42,110	133	86	47
Elizabeth	129,518	407	312	95
Elk Township	4,168	12	11	1
Elmer	1,299	2	2	0
Elmwood Park	19,994	54	49	5
Emerson	7,610	25	22	3
Englewood	28,514	101	77	24
Englewood Cliffs	5,351	22	21	1
Englishtown	1,921	7	7	0
Essex Fells	2,083	13	13	0
Evesham Township	45,148	88	79	9
Ewing Township	36,325	97	77	20
Fairfield Township, Essex County	7,468	43	39	4
Fair Haven	5,696	13	13	0
Fair Lawn	32,910	69	60	9
Fairview	14,209	36	33	3
Fanwood	7,732	17	16	1
Far Hills	903	6	6	0
Flemington	4,577	15	15	0
Florence Township	12,527	31	29	2
Florham Park	11,455	38	32	6

(Number.)

State/city	Population	Total law enforcement employees	Total officers	Total civilians
Fort Lee	38,921	112	93	19
Franklin	4,684	17	16	1
Franklin Lakes	11,166	33	26	7
Franklin Township, Gloucester County	16,226	41	37	4
Franklin Township, Hunterdon County	3,557	6	6	0
Franklin Township, Somerset County	66,138	124	103	21
Freehold Borough	11,643	34	30	4
Freehold Township	34,456	72	68	4
Frenchtown	1,347	3	2	1
Galloway Township	35,444	83	63	20
Garfield	31,908	68	59	9
Garwood	4,360	20	16	4
Gibbsboro	2,210	9	9	0
Glassboro	20,461	55	50	5
Glen Ridge	7,574	29	23	6
Glen Rock	11,705	25	23	2
Gloucester City	11,182	38	36	2
Gloucester Township	63,755	150	128	22
Green Brook Township	7,004	23	22	1
Greenwich Township, Gloucester County	4,777	17	16	1
Greenwich Township, Warren County	5,415	12	12	0
Guttenberg	11,100	29	26	3
Hackettstown	9,316	20	19	1
Haddonfield	11,274	25	22	3
Haddon Heights	7,527	16	15	1
Haddon Township	14,510	27	25	2
Haledon	8,280	20	20	0
Hamburg	3,110	9	8	1
Hamilton Township, Atlantic County	25,654	82	56	26
Hamilton Township, Mercer County	86,805	202	168	34
Hammonton	13,845	36	30	6
Hanover Township	14,290	39	32	7
Harding Township	3,750	15	14	1
Hardyston Township	7,744	23	17	6
Harrington Park	4,730	11	11	0
Harrison	20,937	50	41	9
Harrison Township	13,178	24	23	1
Harvey Cedars	345	9	9	0
Hasbrouck Heights	11,988	31	29	2
Haworth	3,391	13	12	1
Hawthorne	18,728	39	33	6
Hazlet Township	19,593	45	42	3
High Bridge	3,385	7	7	0
Highland Park	13,666	35	28	7
Highlands	4,682	16	15	1
Hightstown	5,273	14	13	1
Hillsborough Township	40,210	63	54	9
Hillsdale	10,308	25	20	5
Hillside Township	21,995	74	64	10
Hi-Nella	856	12	12	0
Hoboken	52,902	148	133	15
Ho-Ho-Kus	4,058	20	16	4
Holland Township	5,074	8	7	1
Holmdel Township	16,726	51	43	8
Hopatcong	14,086	35	29	6
Hopewell Township	17,641	38	29	9
Howell Township	52,048	129	114	15
Independence Township	5,386	10	9	1
Irvington	54,306	201	144	57
Island Heights	1,685	7	7	0
Jackson Township	58,120	110	90	20
Jamesburg	5,878	21	16	5
Jefferson Township	20,626	42	34	8
Jersey City	263,273	1,284	1,005	279
Keansburg	9,582	42	33	9
Kearny	41,037	114	108	6
Kenilworth	8,211	32	27	5
Keyport	6,951	22	20	2
Kinnelon	9,859	17	16	1
Lacey Township	29,524	56	42	14
Lakehurst	2,718	12	10	2

(Number.)

State/city	Population	Total law enforcement employees	Total officers	Total civilians
Lakewood Township	108,023	189	148	41
Lambertville	3,788	12	10	2
Laurel Springs	1,860	7	7	0
Lavallette	1,868	14	12	2
Lawnside	2,872	10	9	1
Lawrence Township, Mercer County	32,282	67	60	7
Lebanon Township	6,055	11	10	1
Leonia	9,033	22	19	3
Lincoln Park	10,051	30	24	6
Linden	42,515	184	140	44
Lindenwold	17,206	47	44	3
Linwood	6,612	18	17	1
Little Egg Harbor Township	21,928	55	43	12
Little Falls Township	14,463	34	28	6
Little Ferry	10,736	30	25	5
Little Silver	5,761	20	15	5
Livingston Township	30,372	87	70	17
Lodi	24,343	50	47	3
Logan Township	5,847	23	22	1
Long Beach Township	3,075	47	35	12
Long Branch	30,175	118	94	24
Long Hill Township	8,389	25	23	2
Longport	846	12	12	0
Lopatcong Township	8,419	17	16	1
Lower Alloways Creek Township	1,660	12	12	0
Lower Township	21,177	57	51	6
Lumberton Township	12,153	26	24	2
Lyndhurst Township	23,169	55	52	3
Madison	17,850	35	27	8
Magnolia	4,259	12	12	0
Mahwah Township	26,201	60	51	9
Manalapan Township	39,353	62	58	4
Manasquan	5,796	22	17	5
Manchester Township	43,856	123	74	49
Mansfield Township, Burlington County	8,527	16	15	1
Mansfield Township, Warren County	7,325	16	15	1
Mantoloking	245	11	10	1
Mantua Township	14,769	29	27	2
Manville	10,116	26	23	3
Maple Shade Township	18,402	38	34	4
Maplewood Township	25,531	75	63	12
Margate City	5,813	37	28	9
Marlboro Township	39,593	115	89	26
Matawan	8,613	25	24	1
Maywood	9,610	26	22	4
Medford Lakes	3,888	11	10	1
Medford Township	23,433	39	35	4
Mendham	4,825	15	14	1
Mendham Township	5,632	16	15	1
Merchantville	3,688	16	14	2
Metuchen	14,639	34	29	5
Middlesex Borough	13,669	32	29	3
Middle Township	18,093	66	55	11
Middletown Township	65,170	118	108	10
Midland Park	7,214	18	17	1
Millburn Township	20,053	64	58	6
Milltown	6,967	19	16	3
Millville	27,272	87	76	11
Monmouth Beach	3,235	10	9	1
Monroe Township, Gloucester County	36,893	68	64	4
Monroe Township, Middlesex County	45,653	87	66	21
Montclair	38,621	130	107	23
Montgomery Township	23,268	40	34	6
Montvale	8,643	26	24	2
Montville Township	20,982	42	37	5
Moonachie	2,700	22	19	3
Moorestown Township	20,491	36	31	5
Morris Plains	6,335	19	17	2
Morristown	19,337	61	57	4
Morris Township	22,100	54	49	5
Mountain Lakes	4,224	14	13	1

State/city	Population	Total law enforcement employees	Total officers	Total civilians
Mountainside	6,902	26	21	5
Mount Arlington	5,944	16	15	1
Mount Ephraim	4,573	14	13	1
Mount Holly Township	9,546	27	24	3
Mount Laurel Township	41,179	82	75	7
Mount Olive Township	28,973	60	50	10
Mullica Township	5,825	15	14	1
Neptune City	4,573	19	18	1
Neptune Township	27,320	88	76	12
Netcong	3,116	13	12	1
Newark	282,242	1,407	1,062	345
New Brunswick	55,701	164	146	18
New Hanover Township	7,859	3	3	0
New Milford	16,417	43	41	2
New Providence	13,741	27	25	2
Newton	8,008	27	22	5
North Arlington	15,695	39	31	8
North Bergen Township	60,567	136	116	20
North Brunswick Township	41,383	98	81	17
North Caldwell	6,666	21	16	5
Northfield	7,979	23	22	1
North Haledon	8,382	28	22	6
North Hanover Township	7,443	11	10	1
North Plainfield	21,279	53	45	8
Northvale	4,955	14	14	0
North Wildwood	3,731	37	29	8
Norwood	5,792	17	16	1
Nutley Township	28,408	83	70	13
Oakland	12,929	34	28	6
Oaklyn	3,942	17	16	1
Ocean City	10,893	82	66	16
Ocean Gate	2,042	12	11	1
Oceanport	5,708	16	15	1
Ocean Township, Monmouth County	26,462	74	61	13
Ocean Township, Ocean County	9,184	31	21	10
Ogdensburg	2,237	6	6	0
Old Bridge Township	65,537	122	101	21
Old Tappan	5,904	14	13	1
Oradell	8,137	24	23	1
Orange City	30,541	163	134	29
Palisades Park	20,818	42	39	3
Palmyra	7,114	17	16	1
Paramus	26,222	125	101	24
Park Ridge	8,688	21	20	1
Parsippany-Troy Hills Township	51,317	128	99	29
Passaic	69,610	194	159	35
Paterson	144,947	430	403	27
Paulsboro	5,820	21	19	2
Peapack-Gladstone	2,606	9	8	1
Pemberton Borough	1,315	6	6	0
Pemberton Township	26,875	43	38	5
Pennington	2,575	6	6	0
Pennsauken Township	35,698	96	89	7
Penns Grove	4,721	15	14	1
Pennsville Township	12,315	23	21	2
Pequannock Township	14,887	36	31	5
Perth Amboy	51,384	141	122	19
Phillipsburg	14,136	38	37	1
Pine Beach	2,192	7	6	1
Pine Hill	10,427	24	21	3
Pine Valley	11	6	6	0
Piscataway Township	56,870	95	77	18
Pitman	8,701	19	18	1
Plainfield	50,333	142	121	21
Plainsboro Township	22,847	48	36	12
Pleasantville	20,135	71	65	6
Plumsted Township	8,598	15	14	1
Pohatcong Township	3,158	16	15	1
Point Pleasant	18,842	40	31	9
Point Pleasant Beach	4,543	31	25	6
Pompton Lakes	10,961	29	24	5

(Number.)

State/city	Population	Total law enforcement employees	Total officers	Total civilians
Princeton	31,458	55	51	4
Prospect Park	5,834	19	18	1
Rahway	30,157	87	76	11
Ramsey	14,904	41	34	7
Randolph Township	25,311	41	35	6
Raritan	7,888	22	21	1
Raritan Township	22,402	41	38	3
Readington Township	15,813	25	23	2
Red Bank	11,929	45	39	6
Ridgefield	11,171	30	28	2
Ridgefield Park	12,904	44	37	7
Ridgewood	25,036	50	45	5
Ringwood	12,177	26	21	5
Riverdale	4,198	22	17	5
River Edge	11,431	27	24	3
Riverside Township	7,788	18	18	0
Riverton	2,676	6	6	0
River Vale Township	10,007	24	23	1
Robbinsville Township	14,628	37	29	8
Rochelle Park Township	5,566	26	22	4
Rockaway	6,250	16	15	1
Rockaway Township	26,046	61	50	11
Roseland	5,829	25	24	1
Roselle	21,867	66	53	13
Roselle Park	13,604	36	34	2
Roxbury Township	22,439	45	42	3
Rumson	6,675	21	16	5
Runnemede	8,273	19	18	1
Rutherford	18,307	43	41	2
Saddle Brook Township	13,533	35	33	2
Saddle River	3,170	23	18	5
Salem	4,661	19	17	2
Sayreville	44,282	103	88	15
Scotch Plains Township	24,313	52	49	3
Sea Bright	1,325	17	11	6
Sea Girt	1,758	13	12	1
Sea Isle City	2,019	28	22	6
Seaside Heights	2,917	28	25	3
Seaside Park	1,541	13	12	1
Secaucus	22,535	89	74	15
Ship Bottom	1,156	12	10	2
Shrewsbury	4,082	20	16	4
Somerdale	5,511	16	15	1
Somers Point	10,108	38	30	8
Somerville	12,084	33	31	2
South Amboy	9,235	34	28	6
South Bound Brook	4,526	14	13	1
South Brunswick Township	45,877	106	82	24
South Hackensack Township	2,438	24	21	3
South Orange Village	16,732	52	46	6
South Plainfield	24,100	72	58	14
South River	15,731	40	31	9
South Toms River	3,701	13	12	1
Sparta Township	18,467	44	32	12
Spotswood	8,216	29	25	4
Springfield Township, Burlington County	3,241	11	10	1
Springfield Township, Union County	17,639	49	45	4
Spring Lake	2,894	14	14	0
Spring Lake Heights	4,502	15	15	0
Stafford Township	28,029	72	55	1/
Stanhope	3,275	9	8	1
Stone Harbor	804	19	17	2
Stratford	6,937	14	14	0
Summit	21,917	51	47	4
Surf City	1,203	10	10	0
Teaneck Township	40,290	108	93	15
Tenafly	14,427	40	34	6
Tewksbury Township	5,754	13	12	1
Tinton Falls	17,388	44	42	2
Toms River Township	94,561	207	162	45
Totowa	10,777	32	28	4

State/city	Population	Total law enforcement employees	Total officers	Total civilians
Trenton	82,909	323	255	68
Tuckerton	3,396	14	13	1
Union Beach	5,210	21	17	4
Union City	68,055	199	162	37
Union Township	58,613	187	135	52
Upper Saddle River	8,199	21	17	4
Ventnor City	9,815	50	37	13
Vernon Township	21,819	41	33	8
Verona	13,368	35	29	6
Vineland	59,288	153	120	33
Voorhees Township	29,130	62	52	10
Waldwick	10,156	26	21	5
Wallington	11,499	24	23	1
Wall Township	25,489	87	71	16
Wanaque	11,828	28	23	5
Warren Township	15,689	37	30	7
Washington Township, Bergen County	9,171	26	21	5
Washington Township, Gloucester County	47,551	92	84	8
Washington Township, Morris County	18,086	30	29	1
Washington Township, Warren County	6,323	30	28	2
Watchung	6,018	36	30	6
Waterford Township	10,675	26	25	1
Wayne Township	53,162	146	118	28
Weehawken Township	14,874	66	55	11
Westampton Township	8,632	26	23	3
West Amwell Township	2,728	6	6	0
West Caldwell Township	10,841	31	26	5
West Deptford Township	20,878	45	42	3
Westfield	29,389	74	61	13
West Long Branch	7,860	22	21	1
West Milford Township	26,310	52	45	7
West New York	52,977	133	120	13
West Orange	47,666	112	98	14
Westville	4,123	14	13	1
West Wildwood	545	6	6	0
West Windsor Township	27,944	61	49	12
Westwood	11,079	31	26	5
Wharton	6,343	23	21	2
Wildwood	4,908	51	41	10
Wildwood Crest	3,024	28	25	3
Willingboro Township	32,048	71	63	8
Winfield Township	1,504	9	9	0
Winslow Township	38,460	80	74	6
Woodbridge Township	100,119	263	203	60
Woodbury	9,744	30	27	3
Woodbury Heights	2,949	8	7	1
Woodcliff Lake	5,845	20	19	1
Woodland Park	12,653	32	27	5
Woodlynne	2,906	8	6	2
Wood-Ridge	9,489	28	24	4
Woodstown	3,429	10	9	1
Woolwich Township	13,278	29	28	1
Wyckoff Township	16,950	27	27	0
NEW MEXICO				
Artesia	12,451	45	25	20
Capitan	1,425	4	3	1
Clovis	38,326	75	50	25
Cuba	760	5	4	1
Dexter	1,241	6	5	1
Farmington	44,191	164	124	40
Hobbs	39,751	131	89	42
Las Vegas	12,799	54	43	11
Los Alamos	19,581	72	34	38
Los Lunas	16,170	69	34	35
Magdalena	872	3	3	0
Moriarty	1,846	10	9	1
Mountainair	866	6	5	1
Peralta	3,576	14	13	1
Roswell	47,451	94	72	22
Santa Clara	1,746	4	3	1

State/city	Population	Total law enforcement employees	Total officers	Total civilians
San Ysidro	202	3	2	1
Springer	892	1	1	0
Sunland Park	18,437	25	20	5
Tatum	833	9	4	5
Texico	1,061	2	2	0
NEW YORK				
Addison Town and Village	2,458	3	3	0
Akron Village	2,852	1	1	0
Albany	96,318	371	295	76
Albion Village	5,698	13	12	1
Alfred Village	3,970	5	5	0
Altamont Village	1,664	1	1	0
Amherst Town	121,304	183	155	28
Amityville Village	9,387	22	21	1
Amsterdam	17,675	42	38	4
Arcade Village	1,919	6	6	0
Ardsley Village	4,515	19	19	0
Asharoken Village	644	3	3	0
Attica Village	2,389	5	5	0
Avon Village	3,272	5	5	0
Baldwinsville Village	7,895	13	12	1
Ballston Spa Village	5,204	4	4	0
Batavia	14,278	36	33	3
Bath Village	5,438	11	10	1
Beacon	13,984	36	33	3
Bedford Town	17,672	43	38	5
Bethlehem Town	35,039	53	38	15
Blooming Grove Town	11,822	17	15	2
Bolivar Village	968	1	1	0
Brant Town	2,056	1	1	0
Briarcliff Manor Village	8,126	20	20	0
Bronxville Village	6,422	23	21	2
Buffalo	254,627	927	752	175
Cairo Town	6,390	2	2	0
Cambridge Village	1,803	3	3	0
Camden Village	2,151	2	2	0
Camillus Town and Village	24,098	28	24	4
Canajoharie Village	2,122	5	5	0
Canandaigua	10,112	27	25	2
Canastota Village	4,518	6	6	0
Canisteo Village	2,120	3	3	0
Canton Village	6,516	11	10	1
Carmel Town	34,093	39	32	7
Carthage Village	3,250	4	4	0
Catskill Village	3,787	16	14	2
Cayuga Heights Village	3,589	7	6	1
Cazenovia Village	2,851	6	5	1
Central Square Village	1,740	4	4	0
Centre Island Village	409	6	6	0
Cheektowaga Town	76,536	156	119	37
Chester Town	8,095	15	15	0
Chester Village	4,108	15	14	1
Chittenango Village	4,826	2	1	1
Clayton Village	1,816	2	2	0
Cobleskill Village	4,323	11	11	0
Coeymans Town	7,247	3	2	1
Cohoes	16,746	34	31	3
Colchester Town	1,947	2	2	0
Colonie Town	79,082	144	109	35
Corning	10,469	25	21	4
Cornwall-on-Hudson Village	2,911	3	3	0
Cornwall Town	9,538	11	9	2
Cortland	18,615	46	44	2
Cuba Town	3,059	5	5	0
Deerpark Town	7,732	4	4	0
Delhi Village	2,935	5	5	0
Depew Village	14,965	33	27	6
DeWitt Town	24,947	46	43	3
Dobbs Ferry Village	11,037	29	27	2
Dolgeville Village	2,055	4	4	0

State/city	Population	Total law enforcement employees	Total officers	Total civilians
Dryden Village	2,066	4	4	0
Dunkirk	11,673	38	37	1
East Aurora-Aurora Town	13,748	21	16	5
Eastchester Town	19,991	50	48	2
East Fishkill Town	29,578	33	26	7
East Greenbush Town	16,186	33	24	9
East Hampton Town	19,927	92	65	27
East Hampton Village	1,140	29	24	5
Eden Town	7,602	2	1	1
Ellicott Town	4,981	13	13	0
Ellicottville	1,563	4	4	0
Elmira	26,820	79	70	9
Elmira Heights Village	3,774	9	9	0
Elmira Town	5,529	4	4	0
Elmsford Village	5,279	24	21	3
Evans Town	16,061	25	19	6
Fallsburg Town	12,264	21	21	0
Florida Village	2,931	1	1	0
Fort Edward Village	3,256	5	5	0
Fort Plain Village	2,212	3	3	0
Frankfort Town	4,752	3	3	0
Fredonia Village	10,205	18	14	4
Freeport Village	42,962	112	100	12
Fulton City	11,017	36	35	1
Garden City Village	22,465	65	51	14
Geddes Town	10,002	18	16	2
Geneseo Village	8,130	9	9	0
Geneva	12,569	35	33	2
Glen Cove	27,186	58	53	5
Glens Falls	14,215	32	30	2
Glenville Town	21,609	25	24	1
Gloversville	14,656	37	34	3
Goshen Town	8,938	6	6	0
Goshen Village	5,361	21	18	3
Gouverneur Village	3,637	8	5	3
Granville Village	2,428	6	6	0
Great Neck Estates Village	2,892	17	14	3
Greene Village	1,400	1	1	0
Greenwich Village	1,708	1	1	0
Greenwood Lake Village	3,080	4	4	0
Groton Village	2,211	1	1	0
Guilderland Town	34,103	53	37	16
Hamburg Town	46,513	64	62	2
Hamburg Village	9,744	14	13	1
Hamilton Village	4,077	5	5	0
Harriman Village	2,455	7	7	0
Harrison Town	29,110	79	68	11
Hastings-on-Hudson Village	7,853	21	21	0
Hempstead Village	55,230	142	113	29
Herkimer Village	7,212	19	19	0
Holley Village	1,669	1	1	0
Homer Village	3,081	5	4	1
Horseheads Village	6,325	10	10	0
Hudson Falls Village	7,029	12	12	0
Hunter Town	2,620	3	3	0
Huntington Bay Village	1,436	4	4	0
Hyde Park Town	20,766	20	16	4
Ilion Village	7,613	18	17	1
Irondequoit Town	49,889	58	48	10
Irvington Village	6,478	23	23	0
Ithaca	30,927	69	61	8
Jamestown	28,842	70	60	10
Johnstown	8,183	24	23	1
Kenmore Village	14,968	29	25	4
Kensington Village	1,193	6	6	0
Kent Town	13,123	23	18	5
Kings Point Village	5,315	21	19	2
Kingston	22,682	74	69	5
Lackawanna	17,674	51	44	7
Lake Placid Village	2,339	16	14	2
Lake Success Village	3,161	27	24	3

(Number.)

State/city	Population	Total law enforcement employees	Total officers	Total civilians
Lakewood-Busti	7,125	11	10	1
Lancaster Town	37,633	65	50	15
Larchmont Village	6,112	25	23	2
Le Roy Village	4,246	7	7	0
Lewisboro Town	12,533	3	3	0
Liberty Village	4,182	19	17	2
Little Falls	4,604	12	11	1
Liverpool Village	2,191	4	4	0
Lloyd Town	10,484	12	10	2
Lockport	20,212	49	47	2
Lowville Village	3,297	6	6	0
Lynbrook Village	19,441	58	50	8
Macedon Town and Village	8,856	7	6	1
Malone Village	5,566	13	13	0
Malverne Village	8,482	22	22	0
Mamaroneck Town	12,017	37	36	1
Mamaroneck Village	19,154	58	50	8
Manlius Town	24,139	38	34	4
Marlborough Town	8,579	11	8	3
Massena Village	10,123	24	19	5
Maybrook Village	3,773	3	3	0
Mechanicville	5,018	10	10	0
Medina Village	5,613	13	12	1
Menands Village	3,850	14	11	3
Middleport Village	1,733	3	3	0
Middletown	28,194	79	68	11
Mohawk Village	2,507	4	4	0
Monroe Village	8,609	22	18	4
Montgomery Town	9,222	14	11	3
Montgomery Village	4,617	4	4	0
Monticello Village	6,338	22	20	2
Moriah Town	4,437	2	2	0
Mount Morris Village	2,765	3	3	0
Mount Pleasant Town	26,966	55	47	8
Mount Vernon	67,339	225	164	61
Newark Village	8,784	14	14	0
New Berlin Town	1,507	1	1	0
Newburgh	28,095	74	62	12
Newburgh Town	31,691	56	45	11
New Castle Town	17,824	41	38	3
New Paltz Town and Village	14,040	24	21	3
New Windsor Town	27,980	62	50	12
New York	8,300,377	50,083	34,018	16,065
New York Mills Village	3,200	4	4	0
Niagara Falls	47,474	154	137	17
Niskayuna Town	22,428	31	29	2
North Castle Town	12,266	34	32	2
North Greenbush Town	12,264	20	18	2
Northport Village	7,258	21	17	4
Norwich	6,474	20	20	0
Ocean Beach Village	83	4	4	0
Ogdensburg	10,364	26	22	4
Old Brookville Village	2,196	34	26	8
Old Westbury Village	4,603	30	25	5
Olean	13,334	41	34	7
Oneida	10,849	28	24	4
Oneonta City	13,904	28	22	6
Orchard Park Town	29,653	47	36	11
Ossining Village	24,786	65	57	8
Oswego City	17,138	54	47	7
Owego Village	3,846	4	3	1
Oxford Village	1,372	2	2	0
Oyster Bay Cove Village	4,300	14	14	0
Peekskill	24,371	61	51	10
Pelham Manor Village	5,535	24	23	1
Pelham Village	6,956	29	26	3
Penn Yan Village	4,900	13	12	1
Perry Village	3,471	3	3	0
Plattsburgh City	19,460	48	42	6
Pleasantville Village	7,280	23	21	2
Port Chester Village	29,181	60	58	2

(Number.)

State/city	Population	Total law enforcement employees	Total officers	Total civilians
Port Dickinson Village	1,513	5	4	1
Port Jervis	8,526	31	30	1
Portville Village	941	1	1	0
Port Washington	19,391	68	60	8
Poughkeepsie	30,480	115	89	26
Poughkeepsie Town	38,934	95	80	15
Pound Ridge Town	5,133	2	1	1
Quogue Village	1,019	15	14	1
Rensselaer City	9,149	35	28	7
Riverhead Town	33,461	94	79	15
Rochester	205,199	810	711	99
Rockville Centre Village	24,604	65	56	9
Rome	31,978	69	67	2
Rosendale Town	5,755	2	2	0
Rotterdam Town	30,071	44	40	4
Rye	15,692	41	37	4
Rye Brook Village	9,542	28	27	1
Sag Harbor Village	2,296	13	12	1
Salamanca	5,360	18	18	0
Sands Point Village	2,919	20	20	0
Saranac Lake Village	5,177	12	12	0
Saugerties Town	18,956	28	24	4
Scarsdale Village	17,953	44	39	5
Schenectady	65,176	174	150	24
Schodack Town	11,617	9	8	1
Scotia Village	7,631	14	13	1
Shandaken Town	2,921	4	4	0
Shawangunk Town	13,782	3	3	0
Shelter Island Town	2,419	11	10	1
Sherrill	2,964	3	3	0
Sidney Village	3,553	8	8	0
Skaneateles Village	2,466	2	2	0
Sleepy Hollow Village	10,064	27	27	0
Solvay Village	6,196	14	13	1
Southampton Town	51,162	144	99	45
Southampton Village	3,330	48	33	15
South Glens Falls Village	3,647	5	5	0
Southold Town	19,957	65	48	17
Suffern Village	11,037	25	21	4
Syracuse	142,011	493	422	71
Tarrytown Village	11,383	37	33	4
Tonawanda	14,700	34	28	6
Tonawanda Town	56,503	147	100	47
Troy	49,052	137	127	10
Trumansburg Village	1,709	1	1	0
Tuckahoe Village	6,554	26	23	3
Tupper Lake Village	3,420	8	8	0
Tuxedo Park Village	598	4	3	1
Tuxedo Town	2,969	6	6	0
Ulster Town	12,626	28	24	4
Walden Village	6,666	15	12	3
Wappingers Falls Village	5,540	4	2	2
Warsaw Village	3,225	5	5	0
Warwick Town	18,459	35	30	5
Washingtonville Village	5,755	16	15	1
Waterford Town and Village	8,466	11	9	2
Waterloo Village	4,842	9	8	1
Watertown	24,624	65	62	3
Watervliet	9,863	23	22	1
Watkins Glen Village	1,874	5	5	0
Waverly Village	4,083	11	10	1
Webb Town	1,779	6	6	0
Weedsport Village	1,695	1	1	0
Wellsville Village	4,343	12	11	1
Westfield Village	2,941	6	6	0
Westhampton Beach Village	1,806	16	14	2
West Seneca Town	45,278	73	60	13
White Plains	58,240	211	201	10
Whitesboro Village	3,595	5	5	0
Whitestown Town	8,948	7	7	0
Windham Town	1,672	1	1	0

(Number.)

State/city	Population	Total law enforcement employees	Total officers	Total civilians
Woodbury Town	11,133	25	20	5
Woodstock Town	5,754	10	10	0
Yonkers	200,816	688	607	81
Yorktown Town	36,284	67	58	9
Yorkville Village	2,556	3	3	0
NORTH CAROLINA				
Aberdeen	8,189	29	27	2
Ahoskie	4,733	14	12	2
Albemarle	16,287	48	41	7
Andrews	1,854	5	5	0
Angier	5,533	15	15	0
Apex	62,320	114	95	19
Archdale	11,521	31	25	6
Asheboro	25,994	84	76	8
Asheville	93,980	252	202	50
Atlantic Beach	1,513	17	16	1
Ayden	5,155	23	19	4
Badin	1,973	5	5	0
Bailey	561	2	2	0
Bakersville	443	1	1	0
Bald Head Island	185	26	25	1
Banner Elk	1,160	9	8	1
Beaufort	4,481	19	18	1
Beech Mountain	325	14	10	4
Belhaven	1,567	6	5	1
Belmont	12,848	45	39	6
Benson	3,995	17	16	1
Bessemer City	5,605	15	14	1
Bethel	1,614	4	4	0
Beulaville	1,292	6	6	0
Biltmore Forest	1,424	16	12	4
Biscoe	1,713	9	8	1
Black Creek	770	3	3	0
Black Mountain	8,197	23	19	4
Bladenboro	1,599	6	6	0
Blowing Rock	1,334	15	13	2
Boiling Spring Lakes	6,396	14	14	0
Boiling Springs	4,523	10	10	0
Boone	19,975	47	36	11
Boonville	1,139	3	3	0
Brevard	7,954	27	23	4
Bridgeton	438	1	1	0
Broadway	1,295	4	4	0
Bryson City	1,455	7	6	1
Bunn	390	3	2	1
Burgaw	4,182	15	15	0
Burlington	55,003	176	133	43
Burnsville	1,642	8	8	0
Butner	7,887	38	32	6
Candor	815	4	4	0
Canton	4,364	20	15	5
Cape Carteret	2,069	7	7	0
Carolina Beach	6,479	27	26	1
Carrboro	21,377	38	35	3
Carthage	2,582	11	10	1
Cary	174,441	212	174	38
Caswell Beach	435	4	4	0
Chadbourn	1,698	7	6	1
Chapel Hill	64,853	120	95	25
Charlotte-Mecklenburg[1]	958,358	2,320	1,749	571
Cherryville	6,110	19	14	5
China Grove	4,227	13	13	0
Chocowinity	789	3	3	0
Claremont	1,414	8	8	0
Clayton	26,087	49	46	3
Cleveland	874	4	4	0
Clinton	8,431	28	24	4
Coats	2,545	7	7	0
Columbus	998	9	8	1
Concord	98,411	205	184	21

State/city	Population	Total law enforcement employees	Total officers	Total civilians
Conover	8,567	28	25	3
Conway	718	2	2	0
Cooleemee	984	1	1	0
Cornelius	30,904	75	57	18
Cramerton	4,491	13	13	0
Creedmoor	4,669	19	15	4
Dallas	4,835	15	13	2
Davidson	13,313	23	21	2
Dobson	1,534	8	8	0
Drexel	1,851	5	5	0
Duck	398	12	11	1
Dunn	9,763	47	42	5
Durham	284,925	679	507	172
East Bend	599	2	2	0
East Spencer	1,552	8	8	0
Eden	14,799	45	42	3
Edenton	4,575	19	17	2
Elizabeth City	17,652	71	61	10
Elizabethtown	3,349	17	16	1
Elkin	4,009	22	18	4
Elon	12,609	21	20	1
Emerald Isle	3,698	20	18	2
Enfield	2,247	7	6	1
Erwin	5,227	11	10	1
Fair Bluff	874	4	4	0
Fairmont	2,585	9	9	0
Farmville	4,775	24	19	5
Fayetteville	212,033	528	372	156
Fletcher	8,508	17	16	1
Forest City	7,130	33	31	2
Four Oaks	2,291	8	8	0
Foxfire Village	1,057	3	3	0
Franklin	4,130	19	18	1
Franklinton	2,267	9	6	3
Fremont	1,260	4	4	0
Fuquay-Varina	32,091	55	48	7
Garner	32,093	72	63	9
Garysburg	904	2	2	0
Gaston	1,007	4	4	0
Gastonia	77,918	189	166	23
Gibsonville	7,437	19	18	1
Glen Alpine	1,482	4	4	0
Goldsboro	34,051	101	89	12
Graham	15,801	42	39	3
Granite Falls	4,654	18	14	4
Granite Quarry	3,018	9	9	0
Greensboro	299,887	746	643	103
Greenville	94,372	243	195	48
Grifton	2,689	7	7	0
Hamlet	6,302	17	15	2
Havelock	19,722	36	28	8
Haw River	2,563	8	8	0
Henderson	14,861	47	39	8
Hendersonville	14,275	56	42	14
Hertford	2,109	8	7	1
Hickory	41,300	143	112	31
Highlands	988	14	13	1
High Point	113,727	288	243	45
Hillsborough	7,226	27	25	2
Holden Beach	674	8	8	0
Holly Ridge	3,077	11	10	1
Holly Springs	39,600	78	63	15
Hope Mills	15,924	36	31	5
Hot Springs	579	1	1	0
Hudson	3,703	15	14	1
Huntersville	59,470	100	92	8
Indian Beach	119	5	5	0
Jackson	448	1	1	0
Jacksonville	71,842	149	120	29
Jefferson	1,526	6	6	0
Jonesville	2,207	9	8	1

(Number.)

State/city	Population	Total law enforcement employees	Total officers	Total civilians
Kannapolis	51,837	104	78	26
Kenansville	839	3	3	0
Kenly	1,612	7	7	0
Kernersville	24,835	83	64	19
Kill Devil Hills	7,407	35	29	6
King	6,860	26	23	3
Kings Mountain	11,015	42	33	9
Kinston	19,862	82	70	12
Kitty Hawk	3,606	18	16	2
Knightdale	18,735	33	30	3
Kure Beach	2,107	14	13	1
Lake Lure	1,152	10	9	1
Lake Royale	2,506	12	8	4
Lake Waccamaw	1,393	5	5	0
Landis	3,144	10	10	0
Laurel Park	2,350	8	8	0
Laurinburg	14,905	42	40	2
Leland	24,967	41	38	3
Lenoir	17,880	67	51	16
Lexington	18,933	63	53	10
Liberty	2,658	10	9	1
Lilesville	479	1	1	0
Lillington	3,710	15	14	1
Lincolnton	11,300	35	31	4
Littleton	582	3	3	0
Locust	3,275	15	15	0
Long View	4,936	16	16	0
Louisburg	3,641	17	16	1
Lowell	3,738	8	8	0
Lumberton	20,370	92	83	9
Madison	2,103	15	15	0
Maggie Valley	1,247	12	11	1
Magnolia	953	2	2	0
Maiden	3,456	20	19	1
Manteo	1,471	9	8	1
Marion	7,861	25	23	2
Marshall	912	4	4	0
Mars Hill	1,949	6	6	0
Marshville	2,825	9	9	0
Matthews	33,860	74	58	16
Maxton	2,335	10	6	4
Mayodan	2,372	15	15	0
Maysville	925	2	2	0
Mebane	16,894	38	34	4
Micro	548	2	2	0
Middlesex	826	5	5	0
Mint Hill	28,209	39	36	3
Misenheimer	760	5	5	0
Mocksville	5,274	18	17	1
Monroe	35,836	100	87	13
Montreat	889	5	5	0
Mooresville	39,692	110	82	28
Morehead City	9,729	44	41	3
Morganton	16,550	90	56	34
Morrisville	30,264	41	39	2
Mount Airy	10,186	44	33	11
Mount Gilead	1,138	7	7	0
Mount Holly	16,575	41	32	9
Mount Olive	4,573	16	15	1
Murfreesboro	2,978	8	7	1
Murphy	1,661	11	10	1
Nags Head	2,999	25	23	2
Nashville	5,549	18	17	1
Navassa	2,423	1	1	0
New Bern	30,047	111	85	26
Newland	684	5	5	0
Newport	4,646	10	10	0
Newton	13,204	41	32	9
Newton Grove	564	3	3	0
Norlina	1,039	3	3	0
North Topsail Beach	743	14	12	2

State/city	Population	Total law enforcement employees	Total officers	Total civilians
Northwest....................................	791	3	3	0
North Wilkesboro........................	4,192	25	24	1
Norwood.....................................	2,457	9	9	0
Oakboro.....................................	1,918	8	8	0
Oak Island..................................	8,581	26	24	2
Ocean Isle Beach........................	680	14	13	1
Old Fort.....................................	926	4	4	0
Oriental.....................................	857	2	2	0
Oxford.......................................	8,934	31	23	8
Parkton.....................................	437	2	2	0
Pembroke..................................	2,940	17	14	3
Pikeville....................................	674	4	4	0
Pilot Mountain...........................	1,406	9	8	1
Pinebluff...................................	1,658	3	3	0
Pinehurst...................................	16,837	28	23	5
Pine Knoll Shores........................	1,325	9	9	0
Pine Level..................................	2,059	5	5	0
Pinetops....................................	1,220	12	7	5
Pineville....................................	9,214	50	39	11
Pink Hill....................................	503	1	1	0
Pittsboro...................................	4,440	13	12	1
Plymouth...................................	3,311	14	13	1
Polkton.....................................	2,491	2	2	0
Princeton...................................	1,423	5	5	0
Raeford.....................................	4,990	18	16	2
Raleigh......................................	482,264	822	695	127
Ramseur....................................	1,689	5	5	0
Randleman.................................	4,114	15	15	0
Ranlo..	3,694	12	11	1
Red Springs................................	3,282	16	15	1
Reidsville..................................	13,936	52	45	7
Richlands...................................	1,726	7	7	0
River Bend.................................	3,016	6	6	0
Roanoke Rapids..........................	14,178	40	36	4
Robbins.....................................	1,233	6	6	0
Robersonville.............................	1,328	6	6	0
Rockingham...............................	8,567	38	36	2
Rockwell....................................	2,164	8	8	0
Rocky Mount..............................	53,520	183	145	38
Rolesville..................................	9,304	21	20	1
Rose Hill...................................	1,617	6	6	0
Rowland.....................................	987	6	5	1
Roxboro.....................................	8,304	38	33	5
Rutherfordton............................	4,077	14	14	0
Salisbury...................................	34,045	84	76	8
Saluda......................................	695	4	4	0
Sanford.....................................	30,299	95	72	23
Scotland Neck............................	1,819	9	8	1
Seagrove...................................	229	1	1	0
Selma..	7,218	21	20	1
Seven Devils..............................	217	6	6	0
Shallotte...................................	4,457	16	15	1
Sharpsburg................................	2,012	9	8	1
Shelby.......................................	19,994	86	73	13
Siler City...................................	8,267	22	16	6
Smithfield..................................	13,215	40	36	4
Snow Hill...................................	1,503	7	7	0
Southern Pines...........................	14,924	46	38	8
Southern Shores.........................	2,986	13	12	1
Southport...................................	4,102	12	12	0
Sparta.......................................	1,721	6	6	0
Spencer.....................................	3,256	12	12	0
Spindale....................................	4,192	9	9	0
Spring Hope...............................	1,309	7	7	0
Spring Lake................................	12,062	31	28	3
Spruce Pine................................	2,133	11	11	0
Stallings....................................	16,426	23	21	2
Stanfield....................................	1,555	5	5	0
Stanley......................................	3,788	12	11	1
Stantonsburg..............................	778	4	4	0
Star..	846	4	4	0

(Number.)

State/city	Population	Total law enforcement employees	Total officers	Total civilians
Statesville	27,879	100	76	24
Stoneville	1,252	5	5	0
St. Pauls	2,285	19	14	5
Sugar Mountain	197	5	5	0
Sunset Beach	4,092	15	15	0
Surf City	2,537	23	22	1
Swansboro	3,425	13	12	1
Sylva	2,757	14	14	0
Tabor City	4,181	11	10	1
Tarboro	10,629	33	27	6
Taylorsville	2,167	12	12	0
Taylortown	867	2	2	0
Thomasville	26,631	71	65	6
Topsail Beach	434	9	8	1
Trent Woods	4,005	6	6	0
Troutman	2,806	15	15	0
Troy	3,194	11	10	1
Tryon	1,613	9	7	2
Valdese	4,416	12	11	1
Vanceboro	961	4	4	0
Vass	799	4	4	0
Wadesboro	5,221	29	24	5
Wagram	771	1	1	0
Wake Forest	47,738	100	82	18
Wallace	3,859	20	16	4
Walnut Creek	862	4	3	1
Warrenton	826	5	4	1
Warsaw	3,086	14	12	2
Washington	9,459	43	32	11
Waxhaw	18,222	31	27	4
Waynesville	10,174	46	35	11
Weaverville	4,065	17	16	1
Weldon	1,452	8	8	0
Wendell	8,951	18	16	2
West Jefferson	1,313	9	9	0
Whispering Pines	3,451	8	7	1
Whitakers	698	2	2	0
White Lake	764	6	6	0
Whiteville	5,293	29	26	3
Wilkesboro	3,440	24	22	2
Williamston	5,145	23	20	3
Wilmington	125,794	327	253	74
Wilson	49,486	130	114	16
Wilson's Mills	2,815	7	7	0
Windsor	3,353	9	9	0
Wingate	4,741	5	5	0
Winston-Salem	250,021	669	498	171
Winterville	10,010	20	19	1
Woodfin	6,767	15	14	1
Woodland	693	1	1	0
Wrightsville Beach	2,563	22	20	2
Yadkinville	2,865	14	13	1
Youngsville	1,402	11	10	1
Zebulon	6,104	21	20	1
NORTH DAKOTA				
Belfield	1,039	1	1	0
Berthold	483	1	1	0
Beulah	3,141	6	5	1
Bismarck	74,997	159	129	30
Bowman	1,594	4	3	1
Burlington	1,218	2	2	0
Carrington	1,971	4	4	0
Cavalier	1,226	3	3	0
Devils Lake	7,339	21	19	2
Dickinson	23,801	61	41	20
Ellendale	1,232	2	2	0
Emerado	451	1	1	0
Fargo	126,927	204	181	23
Grafton	4,143	10	9	1
Grand Forks	56,163	106	91	15

State/city	Population	Total law enforcement employees	Total officers	Total civilians
Harvey	1,630	4	4	0
Hazen	2,298	5	5	0
Jamestown	15,044	33	29	4
Kenmare	1,013	2	2	0
Killdeer	1,202	5	5	0
Lamoure	883	1	1	0
Lincoln	4,006	6	6	0
Lisbon	2,041	4	4	0
Mandan	23,221	45	38	7
Medora	131	2	2	0
Minot	48,108	110	83	27
Napoleon	747	1	1	0
New Town	2,677	5	5	0
Northwood	890	2	2	0
Oakes	1,685	3	3	0
Powers Lake	285	2	2	0
Ray	945	1	1	0
Rolette	592	1	1	0
Rolla	1,249	4	4	0
Rugby	2,561	3	3	0
Stanley	2,868	4	4	0
Steele	711	1	1	0
Surrey	1,452	2	2	0
Thompson	1,025	1	1	0
Tioga	1,348	7	5	2
Valley City	6,288	17	14	3
Wahpeton	7,731	18	16	2
Watford City	9,309	27	21	6
West Fargo	38,561	78	65	13
Williston	31,046	87	74	13
Wishek	880	2	2	0
OHIO				
Ada	5,500	8	8	0
Amherst	12,244	31	23	8
Andover	1,090	3	3	0
Archbold	4,319	11	11	0
Ashland	20,247	37	30	7
Aurora	16,430	37	29	8
Bainbridge Township	11,442	26	22	4
Barberton	25,890	42	41	1
Bath Township, Summit County	9,635	30	23	7
Bay Village	15,135	26	22	4
Beavercreek	48,029	66	50	16
Beaver Township	6,358	14	10	4
Bedford	12,383	39	34	5
Bellefontaine	13,240	37	30	7
Bellville	1,933	6	6	0
Belpre	6,381	16	11	5
Bethel	2,823	6	5	1
Bluffton	4,054	9	9	0
Boardman	38,625	79	59	20
Bowling Green	31,621	52	39	13
Brunswick	34,948	50	38	12
Butler Township	7,816	19	18	1
Cambridge	10,243	29	23	6
Canal Fulton	5,406	11	10	1
Canton	70,124	208	167	41
Carey	3,541	15	12	3
Catawba Island Township	3,522	5	5	0
Celina	10,427	21	16	5
Centerville	23,670	56	41	15
Chagrin Falls	3,921	14	13	1
Cincinnati	304,724	1,124	1,005	119
Circleville	14,113	29	20	9
Clayton	13,219	19	18	1
Clearcreek Township	16,312	17	16	1
Cleveland	379,121	1,788	1,546	242
Clyde	6,141	20	16	4
Colerain Township	59,307	64	54	10
Columbiana	6,233	17	14	3

(Number.)

State/city	Population	Total law enforcement employees	Total officers	Total civilians
Columbus	911,383	2,277	1,897	380
Columbus Grove	2,071	3	3	0
Covington	2,720	7	6	1
Danville	1,012	4	4	0
Defiance	16,576	32	28	4
Delaware	42,064	63	55	8
Dublin	49,954	113	70	43
East Cleveland	16,859	44	42	2
East Liverpool	10,539	22	17	5
Eaton	8,118	16	15	1
Elida	1,795	3	2	1
Elmore	1,391	4	4	0
Englewood	13,435	26	19	7
Evendale	2,725	22	20	2
Fairborn	33,951	72	49	23
Fairfax	1,701	11	10	1
Fairfield	42,558	80	61	19
Fairfield Township	22,978	24	22	2
Fayette	1,237	5	5	0
Findlay	41,237	82	64	18
Forest Park	18,571	43	36	7
Fort Loramie	1,527	2	2	0
Fort Recovery	1,458	3	3	0
Genoa Township	28,758	28	26	2
Germantown	5,517	12	11	1
German Township, Montgomery County	2,894	6	6	0
Greenhills	3,563	11	10	1
Green Springs	1,300	2	2	0
Greenville	12,549	30	23	7
Groveport	5,649	25	24	1
Harrison	12,133	24	21	3
Heath	11,015	27	19	8
Hilliard	37,585	75	63	12
Hinckley Township	8,117	14	13	1
Hiram	1,135	3	3	0
Holland	1,650	9	9	0
Howland Township	16,318	19	19	0
Hubbard	7,370	13	13	0
Huber Heights	38,158	72	52	20
Hudson	22,234	35	29	6
Hunting Valley	716	11	11	0
Ironton	10,469	16	15	1
Jackson Township, Mahoning County	1,999	7	7	0
Jamestown	2,148	5	5	0
Kent	29,732	59	42	17
Kirtland Hills	644	8	7	1
Lancaster	40,700	78	62	16
Lockland	3,440	14	14	0
Lordstown	3,241	13	9	4
Loudonville	2,614	7	7	0
Louisville	9,370	13	13	0
Lyndhurst	13,291	35	28	7
Macedonia	12,098	33	24	9
Madeira	9,303	15	14	1
Madison Township, Franklin County	19,828	17	16	1
Mansfield	46,476	115	79	36
Mariemont	3,524	10	10	0
Maumee	13,605	50	38	12
Medina	25,882	50	39	11
Medina Township	9,105	10	10	0
Mentor-on-the-Lake	7,385	14	9	5
Miamisburg	20,140	37	35	2
Miami Township, Clermont County	42,931	45	42	3
Middletown	48,814	127	88	39
Mifflin Township	2,609	6	6	0
Milan	1,330	3	3	0
Milford	6,872	21	19	2
Milton Township	2,415	5	5	0
Minerva Park	1,326	10	9	1
Minster	2,818	8	7	1
Mogadore	3,816	8	8	0

(Number.)

State/city	Population	Total law enforcement employees	Total officers	Total civilians
Monroeville	1,345	5	5	0
Montgomery	10,929	25	22	3
Napoleon	8,148	22	17	5
Navarre	1,804	6	6	0
Newark	50,625	86	76	10
New Boston	2,080	12	8	4
New Bremen	2,959	7	7	0
Newcomerstown	3,728	9	6	3
New London	2,347	5	5	0
Newtown	2,671	9	8	1
Niles	18,070	40	35	5
North Olmsted	31,176	59	46	13
North Randall	983	10	10	0
North Ridgeville	34,972	46	40	6
Northwood	5,458	23	18	5
Norton	11,951	17	16	1
Norwalk	16,843	32	25	7
Oberlin	8,178	23	17	6
Orrville	8,427	17	16	1
Ottawa	4,346	8	8	0
Ottoville	962	2	2	0
Oxford Township	2,210	3	3	0
Peninsula	554	3	3	0
Perkins Township	11,636	21	20	1
Perrysburg Township	13,011	31	24	7
Perry Township, Columbiana County	4,259	4	4	0
Perry Township, Franklin County	3,761	12	11	1
Perry Township, Stark County	28,005	27	24	3
Pierce Township	11,789	19	18	1
Plain City	4,628	12	11	1
Poland Township	11,772	12	12	0
Port Clinton	6,159	21	16	5
Portsmouth	20,151	52	41	11
Powell	13,593	22	20	2
Reynoldsburg	38,600	84	67	17
Rockford	1,102	2	2	0
Rocky River	19,951	38	34	4
Rossford	6,587	17	16	1
Russell Township	5,199	11	10	1
Salem	11,538	23	23	0
Salineville	1,209	2	2	0
Seaman	891	2	2	0
Sebring	4,163	12	7	5
Seven Hills	11,561	18	17	1
Shaker Heights	26,859	79	64	15
Sharonville	13,712	51	40	11
Shawnee Hills	837	4	4	0
Shawnee Township	12,044	18	13	5
Sidney	20,372	47	36	11
Silver Lake	2,491	9	8	1
South Russell	3,736	9	9	0
Spencerville	2,154	4	4	0
Springboro	19,109	35	31	4
Springfield	58,696	134	124	10
Springfield Township, Hamilton County	35,947	51	45	6
Springfield Township, Mahoning County	6,352	10	10	0
St. Henry	2,568	3	3	0
St. Marys	8,142	21	16	5
Stow	34,781	51	42	9
Strasburg	2,697	5	5	0
Strongsville	44,623	87	68	19
Sugarcreek	2,236	9	9	0
Sugarcreek Township	8,484	19	17	2
Sylvania	19,337	38	31	7
Sylvania Township	29,711	62	44	18
Tallmadge	17,517	30	26	4
Tiffin	17,543	38	28	10
Toledo	271,237	682	609	73
Trenton	13,281	22	17	5
Troy	26,407	45	42	3
Uhrichsville	5,304	9	9	0

(Number.)

State/city	Population	Total law enforcement employees	Total officers	Total civilians
Union Township, Clermont County	48,733	63	49	14
University Heights	12,711	32	29	3
Upper Sandusky	6,423	17	13	4
Urbana	11,351	18	18	0
Valley View, Cuyahoga County	1,992	20	18	2
Vandalia	14,968	39	30	9
Van Wert	10,659	28	20	8
Wadsworth	24,324	40	31	9
Warren	38,462	72	67	5
Wells Township	2,624	5	5	0
West Carrollton	12,833	22	20	2
West Salem	1,513	1	1	0
West Union	3,152	5	4	1
Whitehall	19,014	63	49	14
Whitehouse	4,932	11	11	0
Wickliffe	12,743	39	29	10
Williamsburg	2,579	6	6	0
Willoughby	23,058	56	42	14
Wooster	26,424	47	43	4
Worthington	14,822	37	33	4
Xenia	27,095	69	44	25
Zanesville	25,136	96	57	39
OKLAHOMA				
Achille	545	3	2	1
Ada	17,278	37	34	3
Adair	809	4	4	0
Allen	925	4	3	1
Altus	18,184	51	39	12
Alva	4,944	10	10	0
Amber	487	2	2	0
Anadarko	6,473	19	18	1
Antlers	2,308	16	6	10
Apache	1,387	3	3	0
Arcadia	273	1	1	0
Ardmore	24,718	63	44	19
Arkoma	1,889	4	2	2
Atoka	3,019	17	16	1
Barnsdall	1,140	4	4	0
Bartlesville	36,183	82	62	20
Beaver	1,387	1	1	0
Beggs	1,233	5	3	2
Bennington	370	2	2	0
Bernice	581	1	1	0
Bethany	19,239	35	26	9
Big Cabin	248	1	1	0
Binger	628	1	1	0
Bixby	28,840	43	32	11
Blackwell	6,508	22	14	8
Blanchard	9,090	15	10	5
Boise City	1,067	2	2	0
Bokchito	694	6	5	1
Bokoshe	496	3	2	1
Boley	1,173	2	2	0
Boswell	679	3	3	0
Bristow	4,196	15	11	4
Broken Arrow	111,488	201	148	53
Broken Bow	4,081	18	12	6
Burns Flat	1,885	4	4	0
Cache	2,810	4	3	1
Caddo	1,115	4	4	0
Calera	2,393	11	10	1
Calvin	273	2	1	1
Caney	197	4	3	1
Canton	585	3	3	0
Carnegie	1,636	8	4	4
Carney	620	2	2	0
Cashion	879	2	2	0
Catoosa	6,930	18	16	2
Cement	472	1	1	0
Chandler	3,084	11	8	3

State/city	Population	Total law enforcement employees	Total officers	Total civilians
Chattanooga	451	2	1	1
Checotah	3,069	13	10	3
Chelsea	1,899	4	4	0
Cherokee	1,489	3	3	0
Chickasha	16,478	37	28	9
Choctaw	12,850	21	17	4
Chouteau	2,090	10	9	1
Claremore	18,757	45	38	7
Clayton	782	8	4	4
Cleveland	3,112	8	8	0
Clinton	9,094	26	17	9
Coalgate	1,774	6	6	0
Colbert	1,264	3	2	1
Colcord	852	6	5	1
Collinsville	7,441	20	11	9
Comanche	1,547	6	6	0
Commerce	2,502	5	5	0
Cordell	2,715	5	4	1
Covington	534	1	1	0
Coweta	10,109	23	15	8
Crescent	1,577	7	5	2
Cushing	7,592	24	16	8
Cyril	1,006	2	2	0
Davenport	806	2	2	0
Davis	2,921	10	8	2
Del City	21,750	51	38	13
Depew	479	2	2	0
Dewar	848	3	3	0
Dewey	3,381	12	10	2
Dibble	868	4	3	1
Dickson	1,252	4	3	1
Disney	302	1	1	0
Drumright	2,827	6	6	0
Duncan	22,226	67	48	19
Durant	19,007	41	36	5
Earlsboro	623	3	2	1
Edmond	95,571	154	117	37
Eldorado	402	1	1	0
Elgin	3,313	5	5	0
Elk City	11,571	35	26	9
Elmore City	712	5	4	1
El Reno	20,348	49	34	15
Enid	49,708	113	85	28
Erick	993	1	1	0
Eufaula	2,849	11	10	1
Fairfax	1,253	3	1	2
Fairland	1,028	3	2	1
Fairview	2,596	9	5	4
Fletcher	1,138	2	2	0
Forest Park	1,077	4	2	2
Fort Gibson	3,936	15	14	1
Fort Towson	487	2	2	0
Frederick	3,504	8	6	2
Gans	299	1	1	0
Garber	805	1	1	0
Geary	1,263	12	6	6
Geronimo	1,208	1	1	0
Glenpool	14,319	32	24	8
Goodwell	1,267	4	4	0
Gore	948	5	4	1
Grandfield	922	1	1	0
Granite	1,946	4	4	0
Grove	7,210	30	21	9
Guthrie	11,829	38	26	12
Guymon	10,939	22	17	5
Haileyville	745	3	3	0
Harrah	6,681	11	10	1
Hartshorne	1,944	4	3	1
Haskell	1,922	8	8	0
Healdton	2,671	4	4	0
Heavener	3,286	9	8	1

(Number.)

State/city	Population	Total law enforcement employees	Total officers	Total civilians
Hennessey	2,233	9	5	4
Henryetta	5,527	15	11	4
Hinton	3,221	6	6	0
Hobart	3,393	12	7	5
Holdenville	5,470	11	10	1
Hollis	1,853	9	5	4
Hominy	3,370	8	4	4
Hooker	1,835	2	2	0
Howe	787	2	2	0
Hugo	5,067	25	16	9
Hulbert	581	4	3	1
Hydro	933	3	3	0
Idabel	6,827	25	20	5
Inola	1,804	6	5	1
Jay	2,546	14	9	5
Jenks	24,639	35	24	11
Jennings	353	1	1	0
Jones	3,225	6	6	0
Kansas	801	5	5	0
Kellyville	1,146	2	2	0
Keota	547	2	2	0
Kiefer	2,053	5	5	0
Kingfisher	4,939	14	14	0
Kingston	1,683	7	7	0
Kiowa	670	8	6	2
Konawa	1,186	5	5	0
Krebs	1,933	9	7	2
Lahoma	617	1	1	0
Langley	821	4	4	0
Langston	1,872	3	2	1
Laverne	1,327	1	1	0
Lawton	92,507	208	170	38
Lexington	2,188	9	5	4
Lindsay	2,770	16	9	7
Locust Grove	1,392	9	8	1
Lone Grove	5,153	11	7	4
Luther	1,829	7	6	1
Madill	4,063	12	11	1
Mangum	2,667	11	6	5
Mannford	3,207	11	7	4
Marietta	2,785	8	8	0
Marlow	4,393	14	9	5
Maud	1,061	3	3	0
Maysville	1,202	6	5	1
McAlester	17,752	41	39	2
McCurtain	500	4	3	1
McLoud	4,767	11	10	1
Medford	932	3	3	0
Medicine Park	460	2	2	0
Meeker	1,140	5	5	0
Miami	13,032	33	32	1
Midwest City	57,730	125	99	26
Minco	1,650	5	5	0
Moore	62,840	95	90	5
Mooreland	1,165	4	3	1
Morris	1,414	3	3	0
Mounds	1,273	1	1	0
Mountain View	729	2	2	0
Muldrow	3,228	13	8	5
Muskogee	36,884	92	84	8
Mustang	23,658	37	26	11
Newcastle	11,038	30	22	8
Newkirk	2,155	6	6	0
Nichols Hills	3,966	24	16	8
Nicoma Park	2,473	6	5	1
Ninnekah	1,052	4	3	1
Noble	7,117	18	13	5
Norman	126,480	230	164	66
North Enid	928	3	3	0
Nowata	3,533	8	6	2
Oilton	1,014	3	3	0

(Number.)

State/city	Population	Total law enforcement employees	Total officers	Total civilians
Okarche	1,344	6	5	1
Okeene	1,131	2	2	0
Okemah	3,120	14	9	5
Oklahoma City	663,661	1,443	1,161	282
Okmulgee	11,627	21	18	3
Olustee	549	1	1	0
Oologah	1,179	5	5	0
Owasso	37,815	84	62	22
Paoli	613	2	2	0
Pauls Valley	6,111	18	14	4
Pawhuska	3,386	17	9	8
Pawnee	2,096	5	5	0
Perkins	2,815	8	8	0
Perry	4,807	18	12	6
Piedmont	8,931	12	10	2
Pocola	4,128	12	8	4
Ponca City	23,484	65	46	19
Pond Creek	831	2	2	0
Porum	698	4	4	0
Poteau	8,899	35	27	8
Prague	2,365	14	9	5
Pryor Creek	9,361	38	29	9
Purcell	6,445	23	20	3
Quinton	978	4	4	0
Ramona	546	5	4	1
Rattan	295	2	2	0
Ringling	946	1	1	0
Roland	3,998	11	8	3
Rush Springs	1,259	5	5	0
Salina	1,393	7	6	1
Sallisaw	8,448	30	22	8
Sand Springs	20,026	44	31	13
Sapulpa	21,394	53	43	10
Savanna	641	8	6	2
Sawyer	312	3	2	1
Sayre	4,500	12	6	6
Seiling	855	1	1	0
Seminole	6,994	12	11	1
Shady Point	996	1	1	0
Shattuck	1,247	1	1	0
Shawnee	31,606	89	72	17
Skiatook	8,135	23	19	4
Snyder	1,265	3	3	0
South Coffeyville	729	5	5	0
Spavinaw	428	1	1	0
Spencer	3,973	5	3	2
Sperry	1,354	4	4	0
Spiro	2,157	4	4	0
Sportsmen Acres	307	1	1	0
Stigler	2,680	14	9	5
Stillwater	50,831	118	74	44
Stilwell	4,070	18	12	6
Stratford	1,525	4	4	0
Stringtown	401	5	5	0
Stroud	2,701	11	7	4
Sulphur	5,055	12	10	2
Tahlequah	16,936	46	40	6
Talala	279	1	1	0
Talihina	1,078	8	5	3
Tecumseh	6,652	13	10	3
Texhoma	898	2	2	0
Thackerville	520	2	1	1
The Village	9,632	29	23	6
Thomas	1,200	1	1	0
Tipton	750	1	1	0
Tishomingo	3,085	9	7	2
Tonkawa	2,956	13	8	5
Tryon	502	2	1	1
Tulsa	402,166	1,034	819	215
Tupelo	300	3	3	0
Tushka	388	3	3	0

(Number.)

State/city	Population	Total law enforcement employees	Total officers	Total civilians
Tuttle	7,768	19	13	6
Tyrone	738	2	1	1
Union City	2,221	8	7	1
Valley Brook	770	7	7	0
Valliant	736	4	4	0
Velma	592	2	2	0
Verden	538	4	2	2
Verdigris	4,669	7	6	1
Vian	1,356	6	6	0
Vici	705	1	1	0
Vinita	5,264	21	15	6
Wagoner	9,283	21	16	5
Walters	2,334	5	5	0
Warner	1,584	4	4	0
Warr Acres	10,140	30	25	5
Washington	605	4	2	2
Watonga	2,820	10	7	3
Watts	312	3	2	1
Waukomis	1,297	2	2	0
Waynoka	912	4	4	0
Weatherford	12,155	40	25	15
Webbers Falls	590	4	4	0
Weleetka	949	9	6	3
Wellston	772	3	3	0
West Siloam Springs	862	12	11	1
Westville	1,542	9	5	4
Wetumka	1,193	12	6	6
Wewoka	3,202	5	5	0
Wilburton	2,512	7	6	1
Wilson	1,692	4	4	0
Wister	1,058	3	3	0
Woodward	12,143	23	19	4
Wright City	732	3	2	1
Wyandotte	323	11	9	2
Wynnewood	2,201	6	5	1
Yale	1,222	7	4	3
Yukon	28,735	69	52	17
OREGON				
Albany	55,926	89	56	33
Ashland	21,419	36	29	7
Astoria	10,076	27	16	11
Aumsville	4,249	8	7	1
Baker City	9,808	16	15	1
Bandon	3,161	9	6	3
Beaverton	100,085	176	131	45
Bend	103,485	131	97	34
Black Butte		8	7	1
Boardman	3,811	13	12	1
Brookings	6,495	23	15	8
Burns	2,794	4	4	0
Canby	18,074	30	26	4
Cannon Beach	1,777	10	7	3
Carlton	2,202	4	4	0
Central Point	19,032	33	27	6
Coburg	1,187	5	4	1
Columbia City	2,030	2	2	0
Coos Bay	16,403	36	24	12
Coquille	3,944	7	6	1
Corvallis	59,375	109	73	36
Cottage Grove	10,556	32	17	15
Dallas	17,265	15	10	5
Eagle Point	9,681	12	11	1
Enterprise	2,002	4	4	0
Eugene	174,513	317	197	120
Florence	9,228	23	16	7
Forest Grove	26,065	35	30	5
Gearhart	1,662	3	3	0
Gervais	2,795	6	5	1
Gladstone	12,418	18	15	3
Gold Beach	2,310	8	6	2

(Number.)

State/city	Population	Total law enforcement employees	Total officers	Total civilians
Grants Pass	38,420	92	57	35
Gresham	109,767	155	127	28
Hermiston	17,896	33	28	5
Hillsboro	111,146	185	135	50
Hines	1,543	4	4	0
Hood River	7,863	14	13	1
Hubbard	3,615	7	6	1
Independence	10,477	20	15	5
Jacksonville	2,912	6	5	1
John Day	1,663	5	4	1
Junction City	6,333	16	10	6
Keizer	40,087	47	40	7
King City	4,512	7	6	1
Klamath Falls	22,693	38	34	4
La Grande	13,674	30	18	12
Lake Oswego	40,171	67	41	26
Lebanon	17,635	40	27	13
Lincoln City	9,275	38	24	14
Madras	7,140	11	10	1
Malin	835	7	7	0
Manzanita	668	4	4	0
McMinnville	35,040	48	42	6
Medford	84,016	165	114	51
Milton-Freewater	7,075	16	11	5
Milwaukie	21,040	42	37	5
Molalla	9,351	18	16	2
Monmouth	10,708	15	14	1
Mount Angel	3,647	8	6	2
Myrtle Creek	3,493	9	7	2
Myrtle Point	2,564	6	5	1
Newberg-Dundee	24,081	47	33	14
Newport	10,950	28	21	7
North Bend	9,778	24	17	7
Nyssa	3,176	7	7	0
Oakridge	3,389	6	5	1
Ontario	10,952	29	24	5
Oregon City	37,892	52	44	8
Pendleton	16,804	27	23	4
Philomath	5,805	10	9	1
Phoenix	4,680	11	9	2
Pilot Rock	1,510	2	2	0
Portland	662,941	1,132	873	259
Port Orford	1,155	5	5	0
Prineville	10,919	31	21	10
Rainier	2,021	6	5	1
Redmond	33,198	54	43	11
Reedsport	4,111	15	10	5
Rockaway Beach	1,429	3	3	0
Rogue River	2,355	8	6	2
Roseburg	23,551	43	38	5
Salem	176,632	336	189	147
Sandy	11,598	19	15	4
Scappoose	7,666	11	10	1
Seaside	6,938	27	19	8
Sherwood	20,052	28	24	4
Silverton	10,782	19	16	3
Springfield	63,666	93	60	33
Stanfield	2,119	4	4	0
Stayton	8,364	13	12	1
St. Helens	13,818	22	19	3
Sunriver	1,393	13	12	1
Sutherlin	8,223	18	14	4
Sweet Home	10,099	21	14	7
Talent	6,671	9	7	2
The Dalles	15,849	28	25	3
Tigard	56,377	83	67	16
Tillamook	5,392	11	8	3
Toledo	3,665	13	7	6
Tualatin	28,030	47	40	7
Turner	2,153	2	2	0
Umatilla	7,366	15	13	2

(Number.)

State/city	Population	Total law enforcement employees	Total officers	Total civilians
Vernonia	2,294	6	5	1
Warrenton	5,823	14	12	2
West Linn	26,916	34	30	4
Winston	5,528	12	10	2
Woodburn	26,521	41	32	9
Yamhill	1,187	6	3	3
PENNSYLVANIA				
Abington Township, Montgomery County	55,310	108	90	18
Adams Township, Butler County	14,255	17	17	0
Adams Township, Cambria County	5,474	5	5	0
Akron	4,029	3	3	0
Alburtis	2,669	4	4	0
Aldan	4,160	7	5	2
Aliquippa	8,780	15	14	1
Allegheny Township, Blair County	6,490	10	9	1
Allegheny Township, Westmoreland County	7,993	11	10	1
Allegheny Valley Regional	3,241	2	2	0
Allentown	121,818	234	214	20
Altoona	43,090	71	63	8
Ambler	6,498	14	13	1
Ambridge	6,553	10	10	0
Amity Township	13,237	15	14	1
Annville Township	5,087	6	5	1
Apollo	1,510	1	1	0
Archbald	7,033	7	7	0
Ashland	2,664	2	2	0
Ashley	2,715	3	3	0
Aspinwall	2,682	5	5	0
Aston Township	16,753	22	20	2
Athens	3,170	4	4	0
Athens Township	5,053	11	10	1
Avalon	4,518	5	5	0
Avoca	2,625	3	3	0
Avonmore Boro	945	2	1	1
Baden	3,853	3	3	0
Baldwin Borough	19,508	25	24	1
Baldwin Township	1,931	5	5	0
Bally	1,267	2	2	0
Bangor	5,224	7	7	0
Beaver	4,238	11	10	1
Beaver Falls	9,418	17	16	1
Beaver Meadows	831	2	1	1
Bedford	2,660	5	5	0
Bedminster Township	7,300	8	7	1
Bell Acres	1,365	5	5	0
Bellefonte	6,247	11	10	1
Bellevue	8,002	14	13	1
Bellwood	1,741	3	3	0
Bensalem Township	60,517	129	102	27
Bentleyville	2,469	1	1	0
Berlin	1,925	2	2	0
Bern Township	6,984	12	12	0
Bernville	945	1	1	0
Berwick	9,839	17	16	1
Bethel Park	32,350	45	37	8
Bethel Township, Berks County	4,176	6	5	1
Bethlehem	75,909	167	153	14
Bethlehem Township	24,403	36	35	1
Bigler Township Regional	1,224	1	1	0
Biglerville	1,221	2	2	0
Birdsboro	5,145	8	7	1
Birmingham Township	4,200	3	3	0
Blairsville	3,196	5	5	0
Blair Township	4,475	5	5	0
Blakely	6,173	9	9	0
Blawnox	1,382	3	3	0
Bloomsburg Town	13,700	22	17	5
Bonneauville	1,841	1	1	0
Brackenridge	3,122	4	4	0
Bradford	8,150	19	19	0

State/city	Population	Total law enforcement employees	Total officers	Total civilians
Bradford Township	4,560	5	5	0
Branch Township	1,730	2	2	0
Brecknock Township, Berks County	4,701	5	5	0
Brentwood	9,228	16	14	2
Briar Creek Township	2,926	5	5	0
Bridgeport	4,571	9	8	1
Bridgeville	4,883	9	8	1
Bridgewater	840	4	3	1
Brighton Township	8,270	12	12	0
Bristol	9,560	15	13	2
Bristol Township	53,355	61	54	7
Brookhaven	8,052	8	7	1
Brownsville	2,211	3	3	0
Bryn Athyn	1,408	4	4	0
Buckingham Township	20,255	22	20	2
Buffalo Township	7,407	8	8	0
Buffalo Valley Regional	12,699	16	15	1
Bushkill Township	8,655	16	15	1
Butler	12,792	25	24	1
Butler Township, Butler County	16,384	23	21	2
Butler Township, Luzerne County	10,023	11	10	1
Butler Township, Schuylkill County	5,539	5	5	0
Caernarvon Township, Berks County	4,191	8	7	1
California	6,653	9	8	1
Caln Township	14,323	19	18	1
Cambria Township	5,651	3	3	0
Cambridge Springs	2,677	3	3	0
Camp Hill	7,906	14	13	1
Canonsburg	8,734	18	17	1
Canton	1,850	3	3	0
Carbondale	8,329	9	9	0
Carlisle	19,249	34	32	2
Carmichaels	438	1	1	0
Carnegie	7,787	14	13	1
Carrolltown	777	2	2	0
Carroll Township, Washington County	5,420	3	3	0
Carroll Township, York County	6,583	13	13	0
Carroll Valley	3,949	3	2	1
Castle Shannon	8,205	14	13	1
Catasauqua	6,617	10	9	1
Catawissa	1,457	5	5	0
Cecil Township	13,262	26	25	1
Center Township	11,423	19	18	1
Centerville	3,125	3	3	0
Central Berks Regional	13,624	21	20	1
Central Bucks Regional	15,526	30	26	4
Chambersburg	21,247	34	31	3
Charleroi Regional	6,418	11	11	0
Chartiers Township	8,134	14	14	0
Cheltenham Township	37,159	81	74	7
Chester	34,007	83	81	2
Chester Township	4,086	12	12	0
Chippewa Township	7,901	9	8	1
Churchill	2,909	7	7	0
Clairton	6,513	14	14	0
Clarion	5,766	9	8	1
Clarks Summit	6,218	5	5	0
Clearfield	5,801	7	7	0
Cleona	2,235	4	4	0
Clifton Heights	6,702	12	11	1
Clymer	1,256	2	2	0
Coaldale	2,125	4	4	0
Coal Township	10,192	12	11	1
Coatesville	13,068	31	27	4
Cochranton	1,070	2	2	0
Collegeville	5,183	8	8	0
Collier Township	8,348	19	18	1
Collingdale	8,795	11	10	1
Colonial Regional	18,309	27	25	2
Columbia	10,351	22	19	3
Conemaugh Township, Cambria County	1,806	1	1	0

(Number.)

State/city	Population	Total law enforcement employees	Total officers	Total civilians
Conemaugh Township, Somerset County	6,799	6	6	0
Conewago Township, Adams County	7,243	11	10	1
Conewango Township	3,312	4	4	0
Conneaut Lake Regional	4,745	4	4	0
Connellsville	7,247	15	15	0
Conshohocken	8,069	21	19	2
Conway	2,055	5	5	0
Conyngham	1,862	3	3	0
Coopersburg	2,588	7	7	0
Coplay	3,222	6	5	1
Coraopolis	5,400	14	10	4
Cornwall	4,406	7	6	1
Corry	6,165	10	9	1
Coudersport	2,389	3	3	0
Courtdale	715	9	9	0
Covington Township	2,271	3	3	0
Crafton	6,157	10	9	1
Cranberry Township	32,051	34	31	3
Crescent Township	2,539	6	6	0
Cresson	1,537	2	2	0
Cresson Township	2,487	1	1	0
Croyle Township	2,202	1	1	0
Cumberland Township, Adams County	6,267	12	12	0
Cumberland Township, Greene County	6,108	6	6	0
Cumru Township	15,512	27	26	1
Curwensville	2,369	4	3	1
Dallas	2,787	6	6	0
Dallas Township	9,304	13	12	1
Dalton	1,183	3	3	0
Danville	4,642	9	8	1
Darby	10,703	14	13	1
Darby Township	9,281	14	13	1
Darlington Township	1,863	1	1	0
Delmont	2,510	5	5	0
Derry	2,494	3	3	0
Derry Township, Dauphin County	25,313	41	39	2
Donegal Township	3,252	2	2	0
Donora	4,539	5	5	0
Dormont	8,247	14	13	1
Douglass Township, Berks County	3,622	6	6	0
Douglass Township, Montgomery County	10,588	14	12	2
Downingtown	7,898	22	18	4
Doylestown Township	17,368	22	20	2
Dublin Borough	2,130	2	2	0
DuBois	7,319	14	13	1
Duncansville	1,155	2	2	0
Dunmore	12,837	21	20	1
Dupont	2,679	2	2	0
Duquesne	5,556	16	16	0
Duryea	4,845	2	2	0
East Berlin	1,548	3	1	2
East Brandywine Township	9,346	17	15	2
East Cocalico Township	10,713	16	15	1
East Coventry Township	6,760	8	7	1
East Deer Township	1,430	1	1	0
East Earl Township	6,934	6	6	0
Eastern Adams Regional	7,425	5	5	0
Eastern Pike Regional	4,614	11	10	1
East Fallowfield Township	7,568	7	7	0
East Franklin Township	3,817	1	1	0
East Greenville	2,942	3	3	0
East Hempfield Township	24,831	37	33	4
East Lampeter Township	17,103	41	38	3
East Lansdowne	2,671	5	4	1
East Marlborough Township	7,608	2	2	0
East Norriton Township	14,010	29	28	1
Easton	27,232	65	60	5
East Pennsboro Township	21,556	23	22	1
East Pikeland Township	7,574	11	11	0
Easttown Township	10,652	14	13	1
East Vincent Township	7,402	7	7	0

(Number.)

State/city	Population	Total law enforcement employees	Total officers	Total civilians
East Whiteland Township	13,106	22	21	1
Ebensburg	3,023	5	5	0
Economy	9,108	14	13	1
Eddystone	2,412	10	9	1
Edgewood	2,991	8	8	0
Edgeworth	1,643	5	4	1
Edinboro	5,422	8	8	0
Edwardsville	4,709	6	6	0
Elizabeth	1,965	1	1	0
Elizabethtown	11,436	18	16	2
Elizabeth Township	12,916	12	12	0
Ellwood City	7,227	11	10	1
Emmaus	11,498	20	18	2
Emporium	1,790	2	2	0
Ephrata	13,920	34	31	3
Erie	94,842	194	173	21
Etna	3,294	7	6	1
Evans City-Seven Fields Regional	4,417	5	5	0
Everett	1,707	3	3	0
Exeter	5,532	3	3	0
Exeter Township, Berks County	25,815	35	33	2
Exeter Township, Luzerne County	2,352	5	5	0
Fairview Township, Luzerne County	4,514	7	7	0
Fairview Township, York County	17,709	20	18	2
Falls Township, Bucks County	33,465	62	55	7
Farrell	4,541	16	15	1
Fawn Township	2,288	1	1	0
Ferguson Township	19,646	24	22	2
Ferndale	1,479	2	2	0
Findlay Township	6,140	25	18	7
Fleetwood	4,105	9	8	1
Folcroft	6,633	13	12	1
Ford City	2,741	3	3	0
Forest City	1,725	2	2	0
Forest Hills	6,272	9	9	0
Forks Township	15,879	23	22	1
Forty Fort	4,028	5	5	0
Forward Township	3,260	1	1	0
Fountain Hill	4,708	11	10	1
Fox Chapel	5,062	11	11	0
Frackville	3,590	5	5	0
Franconia Township	13,400	11	10	1
Franklin	5,956	25	15	10
Franklin Park	15,042	19	17	2
Franklin Township, Beaver County	3,811	4	4	0
Franklin Township, Carbon County	4,169	4	4	0
Frazer Township	1,116	2	2	0
Freedom Township	3,318	3	3	0
Freemansburg	2,627	3	3	0
Freeport	1,663	2	2	0
Galeton	1,070	1	1	0
Gallitzin	1,738	2	2	0
Geistown	2,250	3	3	0
German Township	4,747	3	3	0
Gettysburg	7,738	11	10	1
Gilpin Township	2,379	2	2	0
Girard	2,892	4	4	0
Glassport	4,296	9	9	0
Glenolden	7,165	9	8	1
Granville Township	4,974	10	8	2
Greenfield Township	2,008	1	1	0
Greenfield Township, Blair County	3,943	3	3	0
Greensburg	14,030	32	26	6
Green Tree	4,882	10	10	0
Greenville	5,202	10	9	1
Grove City	7,702	11	10	1
Hamburg	4,369	7	6	1
Hampden Township	31,034	26	25	1
Hampton Township	18,161	20	19	1
Hanover	15,767	26	24	2
Hanover Township, Luzerne County	10,797	18	18	0

State/city	Population	Total law enforcement employees	Total officers	Total civilians
Harmar Township.........................	3,006	8	8	0
Harmony Township.......................	2,974	11	11	0
Harrisburg..................................	49,244	159	129	30
Harrison Township.......................	10,211	14	13	1
Harveys Lake..............................	2,773	5	5	0
Hastings....................................	1,142	2	2	0
Hatboro.....................................	7,516	18	15	3
Hatfield Township........................	21,246	30	28	2
Haverford Township......................	49,638	76	70	6
Hazleton....................................	24,726	41	39	2
Hegins Township.........................	3,346	2	2	0
Heidelberg.................................	1,203	4	4	0
Hellam Township.........................	8,626	12	12	0
Hellertown.................................	5,825	10	10	0
Hemlock Township.......................	2,261	9	9	0
Hempfield Township, Mercer County...	3,535	8	7	1
Hermitage..................................	15,368	34	31	3
Highspire...................................	2,370	5	5	0
Hilltown Township.......................	15,911	19	17	2
Hollidaysburg.............................	5,664	11	9	2
Homer City.................................	1,576	1	1	0
Homestead.................................	3,144	11	10	1
Honesdale..................................	4,257	5	5	0
Honey Brook...............................	1,763	1	1	0
Hopewell Township......................	12,583	17	16	1
Horsham Township.......................	26,522	47	40	7
Hughestown................................	1,348	1	1	0
Hughesville................................	2,019	3	3	0
Hummelstown..............................	4,857	7	6	1
Huntingdon................................	6,920	12	12	0
Independence Township, Beaver County...	2,323	2	2	0
Indiana.....................................	13,084	20	19	1
Indiana Township.........................	7,109	10	10	0
Indian Lake................................	376	2	2	0
Ingram......................................	3,185	4	4	0
Irwin..	3,718	3	3	0
Jackson Township, Butler County......	4,325	11	10	1
Jackson Township, Cambria County...	3,967	3	3	0
Jackson Township, Luzerne County...	4,662	7	7	0
Jeannette...................................	9,011	14	13	1
Jefferson Hills Borough..................	11,152	20	19	1
Jefferson Township, Mercer County...	1,794	2	2	0
Jenkins Township.........................	4,569	5	5	0
Jenkintown.................................	4,419	16	14	2
Jim Thorpe.................................	4,644	9	8	1
Johnsonburg...............................	2,271	3	3	0
Johnstown..................................	20,390	42	38	4
Kane...	3,419	4	4	0
Kennedy Township........................	8,159	12	10	2
Kennett Square............................	6,219	14	11	3
Kennett Township.........................	8,387	10	9	1
Kidder Township..........................	1,938	7	7	0
Kingston....................................	12,774	21	19	2
Kingston Township........................	6,887	13	13	0
Kiskiminetas Township...................	4,440	2	2	0
Kline Township............................	1,353	1	1	0
Knox..	1,061	2	2	0
Kulpmont...................................	2,736	3	3	0
Kutztown...................................	5,090	14	12	2
Lake City...................................	2,835	3	3	0
Lancaster...................................	59,264	161	143	18
Lancaster Township, Butler County...	2,802	4	4	0
Langhorne Borough......................	1,576	1	1	0
Lansdale....................................	17,173	32	25	7
Lansdowne.................................	10,650	18	16	2
Lansford....................................	3,789	6	6	0
Latimore Township.......................	2,711	1	1	0
Latrobe.....................................	7,777	15	14	1
Laureldale.................................	3,911	5	5	0
Lawrence Park Township.................	3,718	8	8	0
Lawrence Township, Clearfield County...	7,507	11	10	1

State/city	Population	Total law enforcement employees	Total officers	Total civilians
Lebanon	25,925	41	38	3
Leechburg	1,972	3	3	0
Leetsdale	1,152	5	5	0
Leet Township	1,579	4	4	0
Lehighton	5,293	11	10	1
Lehigh Township, Northampton County	10,425	13	12	1
Lehman Township	3,491	6	6	0
Lewistown	8,102	14	13	1
Liberty	2,443	1	1	0
Liberty Township, Adams County	1,270	1	1	0
Limerick Township	19,441	31	29	2
Lincoln	1,017	3	2	1
Linesville	970	1	1	0
Lititz	9,499	15	14	1
Littlestown	4,518	9	9	0
Lock Haven	9,011	16	14	2
Locust Township	1,375	5	5	0
Logan Township	12,185	18	16	2
Lower Allen Township	20,535	25	22	3
Lower Burrell	11,006	18	17	1
Lower Chichester Township	3,474	5	5	0
Lower Frederick Township	4,936	4	4	0
Lower Gwynedd Township	11,506	19	18	1
Lower Heidelberg Township	6,259	11	10	1
Lower Makefield Township	32,830	42	39	3
Lower Merion Township	60,353	146	130	16
Lower Moreland Township	13,125	31	26	5
Lower Paxton Township	50,230	65	58	7
Lower Pottsgrove Township	12,156	22	20	2
Lower Providence Township	27,030	33	31	2
Lower Salford Township	15,593	21	19	2
Lower Saucon Township	10,845	16	15	1
Lower Southampton Township	19,205	34	32	2
Lower Swatara Township	9,001	18	16	2
Lower Windsor Township	7,597	11	10	1
Luzerne	2,808	3	3	0
Luzerne Township	5,898	1	1	0
Lykens	1,768	1	1	0
Macungie	3,190	4	4	0
Mahanoy Township	3,174	7	6	1
Mahoning Township, Carbon County	4,232	6	5	1
Mahoning Township, Lawrence County	2,835	2	2	0
Mahoning Township, Montour County	4,137	8	7	1
Malvern	3,510	8	7	1
Manheim	4,848	18	17	1
Manheim Township	40,811	77	65	12
Manor	3,360	4	4	0
Manor Township, Armstrong County	4,019	3	3	0
Manor Township, Lancaster County	21,177	21	19	2
Mansfield	2,847	5	5	0
Marcus Hook	2,403	6	5	1
Marion Township, Beaver County	864	2	2	0
Marlborough Township	3,404	4	4	0
Marple Township	24,015	34	31	3
Martinsburg	1,824	3	3	0
Marysville	2,562	2	2	0
Masontown	3,257	4	4	0
Mayfield	1,683	2	2	0
McAdoo	2,141	3	3	0
McCandless	28,151	31	29	2
McDonald Borough	2,040	6	5	1
McKeesport	20,647	43	40	3
McKees Rocks	5,830	10	9	1
McSherrystown	3,096	5	5	0
Meadville	12,579	27	22	5
Mechanicsburg	8,992	18	16	2
Media	5,724	16	15	1
Mercer	1,865	4	4	0
Mercersburg	1,530	2	2	0
Meshoppen	1,411	2	2	0
Meyersdale	2,002	5	5	0

(Number.)

State/city	Population	Total law enforcement employees	Total officers	Total civilians
Middleburg..	1,267	4	3	1
Middlesex Township, Butler County........................	5,839	4	4	0
Middlesex Township, Cumberland County....................	7,455	13	12	1
Middletown...	9,669	11	11	0
Middletown Township..................................	44,918	63	58	5
Midland..	2,451	4	4	0
Mifflinburg..	3,470	8	7	1
Mifflin County Regional...............................	16,897	14	14	0
Milford..	978	2	2	0
Millbourne...	1,160	1	1	0
Millcreek Township, Erie County........................	52,329	78	61	17
Millcreek Township, Lebanon County.....................	5,842	2	2	0
Millersburg..	2,515	3	2	1
Millersville..	8,385	15	13	2
Millvale..	3,646	7	7	0
Milton...	6,563	9	8	1
Minersville...	4,131	6	6	0
Mohnton...	3,021	3	3	0
Monaca..	5,387	11	11	0
Monessen..	7,186	13	12	1
Monongahela...	9,749	8	7	1
Monroeville..	27,275	56	46	10
Montgomery Township.................................	26,315	45	36	9
Montoursville..	4,375	7	6	1
Montrose..	1,462	5	5	0
Moon Township.......................................	25,575	38	30	8
Moore Township......................................	9,456	12	11	1
Moosic...	5,845	9	9	0
Morrisville...	8,499	11	11	0
Morton..	2,672	5	5	0
Moscow..	2,037	2	2	0
Mount Carmel..	5,709	9	9	0
Mount Carmel Township...............................	2,959	7	7	0
Mount Holly Springs..................................	2,055	4	4	0
Mount Joy...	8,378	12	11	1
Mount Lebanon.......................................	31,799	54	43	11
Mount Oliver...	3,267	10	10	0
Mount Pleasant.......................................	4,199	3	3	0
Mount Pleasant Township..............................	3,517	5	5	0
Mount Union...	2,327	4	4	0
Muhlenberg Township.................................	20,417	30	28	2
Muncy...	2,404	3	3	0
Muncy Township......................................	1,202	2	2	0
Munhall...	10,965	26	24	2
Murrysville..	19,537	23	21	2
Nanticoke...	10,296	12	11	1
Nanty Glo...	2,445	2	2	0
Narberth..	4,342	10	6	4
Nazareth..	5,698	6	5	1
Neshannock Township.................................	9,163	8	8	0
Nesquehoning..	3,240	5	5	0
Nether Providence Township...........................	13,788	15	14	1
Newberry Township...................................	15,989	19	17	2
New Bethlehem.......................................	2,686	3	3	0
New Brighton..	8,627	9	9	0
New Britain Township.................................	11,568	14	13	1
New Castle...	21,445	40	37	3
New Cumberland......................................	7,289	10	9	1
New Hanover Township................................	13,483	12	11	1
New Holland...	5,472	15	15	0
New Hope..	2,530	10	9	1
New Kensington......................................	12,205	26	22	4
Newport Township....................................	5,340	5	5	0
New Sewickley Township...............................	7,136	11	10	1
Newtown...	2,238	6	6	0
Newtown Township, Bucks County.......................	22,723	33	29	4
Newtown Township, Delaware County....................	14,150	22	20	2
Newville...	1,349	4	4	0
New Wilmington......................................	2,170	5	5	0
Norristown...	34,339	81	68	13
Northampton...	9,867	15	13	2

(Number.)

State/city	Population	Total law enforcement employees	Total officers	Total civilians
Northampton Township	39,103	49	43	6
North Belle Vernon	1,844	2	2	0
North Braddock	4,648	1	1	0
North Catasauqua	2,829	4	4	0
North Cornwall Township	7,972	10	9	1
North Coventry Township	7,969	13	12	1
North East, Erie County	4,006	7	7	0
Northeastern Regional	11,992	13	12	1
Northern Berks Regional	13,537	14	13	1
Northern Cambria Borough	3,471	3	3	0
Northern Lancaster County Regional	41,322	35	31	4
Northern Regional	36,504	42	40	2
Northern York County Regional	86,465	64	60	4
North Fayette Township	14,913	25	21	4
North Hopewell Township	2,768	2	2	0
North Huntingdon Township	30,350	34	28	6
North Lebanon Township	12,272	14	12	2
North Londonderry Township	8,658	10	9	1
North Middleton Township	11,886	11	10	1
North Sewickley Township	5,357	1	1	0
North Strabane Township	14,596	26	25	1
Northumberland	3,587	6	6	0
North Versailles Township	11,992	24	19	5
North Wales	3,268	5	5	0
North Woodbury	2,589	2	2	0
Norwood	5,898	7	6	1
Oakmont	6,568	7	7	0
O'Hara Township	8,788	17	16	1
Ohio Township	7,209	20	18	2
Ohioville	3,264	2	2	0
Oil City	9,521	17	16	1
Old Forge	7,849	7	7	0
Old Lycoming Township	4,907	10	9	1
Olyphant	5,008	7	7	0
Orangeville Area	3,568	1	1	0
Orwigsburg	2,936	6	6	0
Oxford	5,640	10	9	1
Palmerton	5,326	10	9	1
Palmer Township	21,506	37	35	2
Palmyra	7,616	12	11	1
Parkesburg	4,040	8	7	1
Parkside	2,330	1	1	0
Parks Township	2,545	2	2	0
Patterson Township	4,125	4	4	0
Patton	1,581	2	2	0
Patton Township	15,874	22	20	2
Penbrook	2,982	7	7	0
Penndel	2,140	1	1	0
Penn Hills	40,636	52	49	3
Pennridge Regional	10,946	12	11	1
Penn Township, Butler County	4,858	5	4	1
Penn Township, Westmoreland County	19,275	24	22	2
Penn Township, York County	16,737	25	22	3
Perkasie	8,765	19	17	2
Perryopolis	1,653	2	2	0
Peters Township	22,137	26	25	1
Philadelphia	1,586,666	7,140	6,359	781
Phoenixville	17,024	32	31	1
Pine Creek Township	3,222	2	2	0
Pine Grove	2,056	2	2	0
Pitcairn	3,144	2	2	0
Pittsburgh	298,608	1,036	998	38
Pittston Township	3,359	6	6	0
Plains Township	9,636	20	20	0
Pleasant Hills	8,001	20	18	2
Plum	27,082	29	27	2
Plumstead Township	14,730	18	16	2
Plymouth Township, Montgomery County	17,645	52	45	7
Pocono Mountain Regional	43,250	48	43	5
Pocono Township	11,091	20	19	1
Point Township	3,582	6	6	0

(Number.)

State/city	Population	Total law enforcement employees	Total officers	Total civilians
Polk	763	2	2	0
Portage	2,357	2	2	0
Port Allegany	1,982	3	3	0
Port Vue	3,635	2	2	0
Pottstown	22,626	58	44	14
Pottsville	13,384	24	23	1
Prospect Park	6,496	9	8	1
Pulaski Township, Lawrence County	3,207	2	2	0
Punxsutawney	5,678	10	9	1
Pymatuning Township	3,004	10	7	3
Quakertown	8,762	24	21	3
Quarryville	2,774	5	5	0
Raccoon Township	2,884	4	4	0
Radnor Township	31,910	46	42	4
Ralpho Township	4,184	6	6	0
Rankin	2,018	1	1	0
Reading	88,412	186	162	24
Reading Township	5,902	2	2	0
Redstone Township	4,136	2	2	0
Renovo	1,202	1	1	0
Reserve Township	3,212	6	6	0
Reynoldsville	2,635	2	2	0
Rice Township	3,570	6	6	0
Richland Township, Bucks County	13,357	18	16	2
Richland Township, Cambria County	11,715	21	20	1
Ridgway	3,717	8	7	1
Ridley Park	7,070	10	10	0
Ridley Township	31,242	35	32	3
Riverside	1,845	3	3	0
Roaring Brook Township	1,989	2	2	0
Roaring Spring	2,421	3	3	0
Robeson Township	7,457	5	5	0
Robinson Township, Allegheny County	13,904	29	28	1
Rochester	3,416	8	7	1
Rochester Township	2,617	3	3	0
Rockledge	2,529	5	5	0
Ross Township	30,403	44	43	1
Rostraver Township	10,970	18	17	1
Royalton	1,036	1	1	0
Royersford	4,753	9	8	1
Rural Valley	807	1	1	0
Rush Township	3,241	1	1	0
Sadsbury Township, Chester County	4,174	4	4	0
Salem Township, Luzerne County	4,189	7	7	0
Salisbury Township	13,985	21	19	2
Sandy Lake	621	1	1	0
Sandy Township	10,422	13	12	1
Saxonburg	1,429	2	2	0
Saxton	676	3	3	0
Sayre	6,334	13	11	2
Schuylkill Haven	5,069	8	8	0
Schuylkill Township, Chester County	8,626	13	11	2
Scottdale	4,066	6	6	0
Scott Township, Allegheny County	16,362	22	21	1
Scott Township, Columbia County	5,048	8	8	0
Scott Township, Lackawanna County	4,729	4	4	0
Scranton	76,719	153	140	13
Selinsgrove	5,931	6	5	1
Sewickley Heights	806	3	3	0
Shaler Township	27,612	28	26	2
Shamokin	6,908	10	10	0
Shamokin Dam	1,709	3	3	0
Sharon	12,820	31	30	1
Sharon Hill	5,690	12	11	1
Sharpsburg	3,304	6	6	0
Sharpsville	4,038	6	6	0
Shenandoah	4,727	6	6	0
Shenango Township, Lawrence County	7,080	8	8	0
Shenango Township, Mercer County	3,648	11	11	0
Shillington	5,322	7	6	1
Shinglehouse	1,046	1	1	0

(Number.)

State/city	Population	Total law enforcement employees	Total officers	Total civilians
Shippensburg	5,570	11	10	1
Shippingport	187	2	2	0
Shiremanstown	1,629	2	2	0
Silver Spring Township	18,910	24	23	1
Sinking Spring	4,119	7	6	1
Slate Belt Regional	12,530	21	20	1
Slatington	4,316	6	6	0
Slippery Rock	3,518	4	4	0
Smethport	1,517	2	2	0
Smith Township	4,341	5	5	0
Solebury Township	8,537	18	16	2
Somerset	5,810	8	7	1
Souderton	7,134	7	6	1
South Abington Township	8,872	11	10	1
South Beaver Township	2,637	4	4	0
South Buffalo Township	2,506	2	2	0
South Coatesville	1,472	2	2	0
South Connellsville Borough	1,853	1	1	0
Southern Chester County Regional	16,477	20	18	2
Southern Regional York County	12,864	16	15	1
South Fayette Township	16,123	21	20	1
South Fork	833	1	1	0
South Greensburg	1,983	2	2	0
South Heidelberg Township	12,368	14	14	0
South Park Township	13,650	16	15	1
South Pymatuning Township	2,494	4	4	0
South Strabane Township	9,439	21	20	1
Southwest Greensburg	2,004	11	11	0
Southwest Regional, Fayette County	2,620	1	1	0
Southwest Regional, Washington County	130	1	1	0
South Whitehall Township	20,042	41	39	2
Spring City	3,301	3	3	0
Springdale	3,275	4	4	0
Springettsbury Township	26,884	32	29	3
Springfield Township, Bucks County	5,032	4	4	0
Springfield Township, Delaware County	24,276	39	34	5
Springfield Township, Montgomery County	19,901	31	29	2
Spring Garden Township	13,293	24	20	4
Spring Township, Berks County	27,717	29	28	1
Spring Township, Centre County	8,120	9	8	1
State College	58,471	65	55	10
St. Clair Boro	2,811	5	5	0
Steelton	5,959	15	14	1
St. Marys City	12,177	16	15	1
Stockertown	926	1	1	0
Stoneboro	973	1	1	0
Stonycreek Township	2,558	4	4	0
Stowe Township	6,095	11	10	1
Strasburg	3,053	5	5	0
Stroud Area Regional	35,441	56	47	9
Sugarcreek	4,861	2	2	0
Summerhill Township	2,236	2	2	0
Summit Hill	2,946	5	5	0
Summit Township	2,101	1	1	0
Sunbury	9,306	10	8	2
Susquehanna Regional	8,433	16	14	2
Susquehanna Township, Dauphin County	25,233	44	40	4
Swarthmore	6,364	8	8	0
Swatara Township	26,820	53	50	3
Sweden Township	812	1	1	0
Swissvale	8,609	15	15	0
Swoyersville	4,997	5	5	0
Sykesville	1,110	1	1	0
Tamaqua	6,617	10	9	1
Tarentum	4,347	10	10	0
Tatamy	1,173	2	2	0
Taylor	5,876	8	8	0
Throop	3,875	8	8	0
Tiadaghton Valley Regional	7,512	11	11	0
Tilden Township	3,622	4	4	0
Tinicum Township, Bucks County	3,948	3	3	0

(Number.)

State/city	Population	Total law enforcement employees	Total officers	Total civilians
Tinicum Township, Delaware County..........................	4,113	18	16	2
Tioga..	645	2	1	1
Titusville...	5,112	11	11	0
Towamencin Township..	18,536	25	23	2
Towanda...	2,797	6	6	0
Trafford..	3,019	5	5	0
Tredyffrin Township...	29,401	47	42	5
Troy..	1,224	2	2	0
Tullytown...	2,176	5	4	1
Tulpehocken Township..	3,477	3	3	0
Tunkhannock...	1,683	3	3	0
Tunkhannock Township, Wyoming County........................	5,998	8	8	0
Turtle Creek..	5,116	5	5	0
Tyrone..	5,105	9	7	2
Union City..	3,096	4	3	1
Uniontown...	9,653	21	20	1
Union Township, Lawrence County.............................	4,817	11	11	0
Upland..	3,327	8	7	1
Upper Allen Township..	20,655	24	23	1
Upper Burrell Township......................................	2,201	2	2	0
Upper Chichester Township...................................	16,987	24	23	1
Upper Darby Township..	82,947	128	116	12
Upper Dublin Township.......................................	26,658	42	37	5
Upper Gwynedd Township......................................	15,850	24	21	3
Upper Macungie Township.....................................	25,811	32	29	3
Upper Makefield Township....................................	8,646	17	16	1
Upper Merion Township.......................................	33,595	86	70	16
Upper Moreland Township.....................................	24,031	43	37	6
Upper Nazareth Township.....................................	7,161	10	9	1
Upper Perkiomen...	3,856	4	4	0
Upper Pottsgrove Township...................................	5,799	9	9	0
Upper Providence Township, Delaware County..................	10,479	16	15	1
Upper Providence Township, Montgomery County................	24,725	29	27	2
Upper Saucon Township.......................................	17,603	25	23	2
Upper Southampton Township..................................	14,934	25	22	3
Upper St. Clair Township....................................	19,791	35	28	7
Upper Uwchlan Township......................................	11,887	12	12	0
Upper Yoder Township..	4,989	6	6	0
Uwchlan Township..	18,924	24	23	1
Valley Township...	7,884	7	7	0
Vernon Township...	5,341	4	4	0
Verona..	2,401	4	3	1
Versailles..	1,455	2	2	0
Walnutport..	2,089	4	4	0
Warminster Township...	32,300	47	43	4
Warren..	8,979	18	16	2
Warrington Township...	24,689	37	36	1
Warwick Township, Bucks County..............................	14,725	18	17	1
Washington Township, Fayette County.........................	3,575	4	4	0
Washington Township, Franklin County........................	14,853	12	10	2
Washington Township, Westmoreland County....................	7,023	9	9	0
Washington, Washington County...............................	13,371	33	31	2
Watsontown..	2,241	6	6	0
Waverly Township..	1,676	3	3	0
Waynesboro..	10,921	21	19	2
Waynesburg..	3,941	8	8	0
Weatherly...	2,451	4	4	0
Wellsboro...	3,223	7	7	0
Wesleyville...	3,093	8	7	1
West Brandywine Township....................................	7,474	10	9	1
West Caln Township..	9,120	4	4	0
West Chester..	20,211	57	44	13
West Conshohocken...	1,445	13	12	1
West Deer Township..	12,009	15	14	1
West Earl Township..	8,457	8	7	1
West Fallowfield Township...................................	2,592	2	2	0
West Goshen Township..	23,100	36	32	4
West Hazleton...	4,342	5	5	0
West Hempfield Township.....................................	16,808	22	21	1
West Hills Regional...	9,793	12	11	1
West Homestead..	1,857	13	12	1

State/city	Population	Total law enforcement employees	Total officers	Total civilians
West Lampeter Township	16,036	19	17	2
West Mahanoy Township	2,693	3	3	0
West Manchester Township	18,808	32	28	4
West Manheim Township	8,765	11	11	0
West Mead Township	4,994	2	2	0
West Mifflin	19,632	40	33	7
West Newton	2,462	2	2	0
West Norriton Township	15,608	30	27	3
West Penn Township	4,278	2	2	0
West Pikeland Township	4,071	4	4	0
West Pike Run	1,525	1	1	0
West Pittston	4,746	3	3	0
West Pottsgrove Township	3,836	6	6	0
West Reading	4,298	17	15	2
West Sadsbury Township	2,504	5	5	0
West Shore Regional	7,696	13	12	1
Westtown-East Goshen Regional	32,317	32	29	3
West View	6,489	11	10	1
West Vincent Township	6,081	7	6	1
West Whiteland Township	19,923	29	27	2
Whitehall	13,352	24	19	5
Whitehall Township	27,953	52	47	5
White Haven Borough	1,100	1	1	0
Whitemarsh Township	18,453	42	36	6
White Oak	7,398	14	13	1
Whitpain Township	19,279	37	29	8
Wiconisco Township	1,204	1	1	0
Wilkes-Barre	40,683	83	79	4
Wilkes-Barre Township	2,875	15	14	1
Wilkinsburg	15,230	26	24	2
Wilkins Township	6,109	12	12	0
Williamsburg	1,169	2	2	0
Williamsport	28,055	50	46	4
Willistown Township	11,071	18	16	2
Wilson	7,797	15	14	1
Windber	3,780	3	2	1
Womelsdorf	2,912	3	3	0
Woodward Township	2,361	2	2	0
Wright Township	5,625	7	6	1
Wyoming	3,004	4	4	0
Wyomissing	10,658	21	20	1
Yardley	2,522	5	5	0
Yeadon	11,502	18	17	1
York	43,940	109	92	17
York Area Regional	56,505	51	46	5
Youngsville	1,600	2	2	0
Zelienople	3,580	9	8	1
Zerbe Township	1,743	1	1	0
RHODE ISLAND				
Barrington	15,986	32	25	7
Bristol	21,748	49	40	9
Burrillville	16,904	32	25	7
Central Falls	19,530	46	38	8
Charlestown	7,803	25	20	5
Coventry	34,740	81	57	24
Cranston	81,313	178	148	30
Cumberland	35,357	51	42	9
East Greenwich	13,084	38	31	7
East Providence	47,542	110	92	18
Foster	4,747	13	9	4
Glocester	10,358	21	16	5
Hopkinton	8,025	19	14	5
Jamestown	5,493	19	14	5
Johnston	29,458	78	65	13
Lincoln	22,029	43	35	8
Little Compton	3,463	14	10	4
Middletown	15,817	40	36	4
Narragansett	15,248	51	38	13
Newport	24,202	100	83	17
New Shoreham	1,025	11	5	6

(Number.)

State/city	Population	Total law enforcement employees	Total officers	Total civilians
North Kingstown	26,221	60	52	8
North Providence	32,652	68	61	7
North Smithfield	12,616	33	26	7
Pawtucket	72,017	171	140	31
Portsmouth	17,162	39	36	3
Providence	179,603	510	420	90
Richmond	7,724	16	14	2
Scituate	10,739	24	15	9
Smithfield	21,893	54	40	14
South Kingstown	30,238	67	52	15
Tiverton	15,604	40	27	13
Warren	10,469	30	25	5
Warwick	80,605	201	165	36
Westerly	22,277	66	51	15
West Greenwich	6,399	19	13	6
West Warwick	28,831	58	48	10
Woonsocket	41,693	113	100	13
SOUTH CAROLINA				
Abbeville	4,990	20	19	1
Aiken	31,007	117	87	30
Allendale	2,870	6	6	0
Anderson	27,815	144	106	38
Atlantic Beach	459	5	4	1
Aynor	1,025	6	6	0
Bamberg	3,147	10	8	2
Barnwell	4,241	17	15	2
Batesburg-Leesville	5,419	31	26	5
Beaufort	13,561	50	45	5
Belton	4,488	14	13	1
Bennettsville	7,591	29	27	2
Bethune	352	1	1	0
Blacksburg	1,885	11	11	0
Blackville	2,166	8	7	1
Bluffton	27,549	63	57	6
Bonneau	490	4	2	2
Bowman	880	4	2	2
Branchville	946	3	2	1
Burnettown	2,762	2	2	0
Calhoun Falls	1,892	4	4	0
Camden	7,264	33	29	4
Cameron	396	1	1	0
Campobello	601	11	10	1
Cayce	14,117	83	56	27
Central	5,407	12	11	1
Chapin	1,657	6	6	0
Charleston	139,582	505	409	96
Cheraw	5,529	29	23	6
Chesnee	969	6	5	1
Chester	5,354	21	19	2
Chesterfield	1,409	5	5	0
Clemson	17,951	42	31	11
Clover	6,693	22	17	5
Columbia	131,777	431	343	88
Conway	27,120	59	52	7
Coward	773	1	1	0
Cowpens	2,450	9	7	2
Darlington	5,895	35	32	3
Denmark	2,876	10	9	1
Dillon	6,261	25	23	2
Due West	1,200	5	5	0
Duncan	3,679	23	22	1
Easley	21,512	58	48	10
Edgefield	4,816	10	10	0
Edisto Beach	405	7	7	0
Ehrhardt	476	2	1	1
Elgin	1,616	7	5	2
Elloree	635	3	3	0
Estill	1,838	7	6	1
Eutawville	288	2	2	0
Florence	38,597	91	78	13

(Number.)

State/city	Population	Total law enforcement employees	Total officers	Total civilians
Folly Beach	2,676	23	17	6
Forest Acres	10,283	33	26	7
Fort Lawn	885	3	2	1
Fort Mill	23,966	65	56	9
Fountain Inn	10,820	33	25	8
Gaffney	12,631	38	34	4
Gaston	1,706	3	3	0
Georgetown	8,697	34	29	5
Gifford	260	5	2	3
Goose Creek	44,522	88	65	23
Great Falls	1,866	5	5	0
Greeleyville	375	1	1	0
Greenville	72,014	249	206	43
Greenwood	23,422	54	49	5
Greer	34,320	79	59	20
Hampton	2,474	14	13	1
Hanahan	28,143	32	30	2
Hardeeville	7,970	27	25	2
Harleyville	702	2	2	0
Hartsville	7,519	40	38	2
Holly Hill	1,168	6	6	0
Honea Path	3,857	15	13	2
Irmo	12,639	26	23	3
Isle of Palms	4,385	27	18	9
Iva	1,335	9	9	0
Jackson	1,812	4	3	1
Johnsonville	1,484	7	6	1
Johnston	2,382	9	9	0
Jonesville	831	3	3	0
Kingstree	3,035	9	6	3
Lake City	6,477	22	22	0
Lake View	752	3	3	0
Landrum	2,713	13	11	2
Lane	446	4	1	3
Latta	1,275	9	8	1
Laurens	8,830	32	26	6
Lexington	22,592	64	61	3
Liberty	3,143	15	10	5
Loris	2,804	14	11	3
Lyman	3,768	13	13	0
Manning	3,869	20	19	1
Marion	6,268	19	16	3
Mauldin	25,662	59	47	12
McColl	1,949	7	6	1
McCormick	2,310	6	6	0
Moncks Corner	12,580	33	29	4
Mount Pleasant	94,704	175	158	17
Mullins	4,196	21	16	5
Myrtle Beach	35,658	304	203	101
Newberry	10,181	27	25	2
New Ellenton	2,164	2	2	0
Nichols	332	1	1	0
Ninety Six	2,042	8	8	0
North	702	5	5	0
North Augusta	24,139	92	65	27
North Charleston	117,503	396	321	75
North Myrtle Beach	17,183	147	80	67
Orangeburg	12,529	68	38	30
Pageland	2,629	14	10	4
Pamplico	1,219	3	3	0
Pawleys Island	109	5	4	1
Pelion	714	2	2	0
Port Royal	13,553	26	25	1
Prosperity	1,295	4	4	0
Quinby	922	1	1	0
Ridgeland	3,788	14	13	1
Ridge Spring	749	2	2	0
Ridgeville	1,678	1	1	0
Rock Hill	76,016	201	152	49
Salley	417	1	1	0
Saluda	3,610	9	8	1

(Number.)

State/city	Population	Total law enforcement employees	Total officers	Total civilians
Scranton	863	2	1	1
Seneca	8,581	44	30	14
Simpsonville	24,960	55	44	11
South Congaree	2,504	7	6	1
Spartanburg	37,469	143	120	23
Springdale	2,745	12	11	1
Springfield	479	3	3	0
St. George	2,217	12	10	2
St. Matthews	1,901	7	6	1
Sullivans Island	1,939	12	10	2
Summerton	921	5	5	0
Summerville	53,711	140	116	24
Sumter	39,542	155	111	44
Surfside Beach	4,608	22	17	5
Swansea	974	3	3	0
Tega Cay	11,813	34	26	8
Travelers Rest	5,435	22	16	6
Trenton	199	1	1	0
Union	7,565	28	25	3
Wagener	841	2	2	0
Walhalla	4,498	14	13	1
Walterboro	5,387	33	31	2
Ware Shoals	2,152	7	7	0
Wellford	2,754	10	8	2
West Columbia	18,143	63	53	10
West Pelzer	954	4	3	1
West Union	337	3	3	0
Whitmire	1,455	4	3	1
Williamston	4,294	19	18	1
Winnsboro	3,144	18	17	1
Woodruff	4,457	11	10	1
York	8,486	40	34	6
SOUTH DAKOTA				
Aberdeen	28,494	58	49	9
Alcester	749	2	2	0
Avon	590	1	1	0
Belle Fourche	5,712	13	11	2
Beresford	2,028	5	5	0
Box Elder	10,402	19	18	1
Brandon	10,205	14	13	1
Brookings	24,682	47	35	12
Burke	584	1	1	0
Canton	3,615	6	6	0
Centerville	870	2	2	0
Chamberlain	2,364	6	6	0
Clark	1,053	2	2	0
Deadwood	1,293	18	15	3
Eagle Butte	1,349	1	1	0
Elk Point	1,860	5	5	0
Faith	410	1	1	0
Flandreau	2,314	8	7	1
Freeman	1,272	2	2	0
Gettysburg	1,070	2	2	0
Groton	1,477	4	4	0
Hot Springs	3,477	9	7	2
Huron	13,469	25	25	0
Jefferson	507	2	2	0
Kadoka	724	1	1	0
Kimball	670	1	1	0
Lead	2,923	7	6	1
Lennox	2,520	5	5	0
Madison	7,357	14	13	1
Martin	1,042	3	3	0
Menno	615	1	1	0
Milbank	3,077	7	7	0
Miller	1,318	4	4	0
Mitchell	15,726	23	21	2
Mobridge	3,442	16	8	8
Murdo	432	2	2	0
North Sioux City	2,975	9	8	1

(Number.)

State/city	Population	Total law enforcement employees	Total officers	Total civilians
Parkston	1,473	2	2	0
Philip	764	2	2	0
Pierre	13,888	40	25	15
Platte	1,261	2	2	0
Rapid City	78,492	171	134	37
Scotland	800	2	2	0
Sioux Falls	187,370	308	273	35
Sisseton	2,392	7	7	0
Spearfish	11,902	32	21	11
Springfield	1,915	2	2	0
Sturgis	6,955	18	15	3
Summerset	2,769	4	4	0
Tea	6,340	8	8	0
Tripp	621	1	1	0
Tyndall	1,017	2	2	0
Vermillion	10,969	20	19	1
Wagner	1,544	6	6	0
Watertown	22,248	54	36	18
Webster	1,709	5	5	0
Whitewood	984	5	4	1
Winner	2,813	12	12	0
Yankton	14,712	31	30	1
TENNESSEE				
Adamsville	2,161	8	7	1
Alamo	2,268	4	4	0
Alcoa	10,174	54	46	8
Alexandria	1,017	4	3	1
Algood	4,584	15	15	0
Ardmore	1,221	9	5	4
Ashland City	4,785	18	16	2
Athens	14,059	33	31	2
Atoka	9,632	23	22	1
Baileyton	454	3	3	0
Bartlett	59,714	158	121	37
Baxter	1,551	7	7	0
Bean Station	3,098	7	6	1
Belle Meade	2,854	21	15	6
Bells	2,439	3	3	0
Benton	1,268	7	6	1
Berry Hill	505	18	14	4
Big Sandy	519	1	1	0
Blaine	1,861	4	4	0
Bluff City	1,667	8	8	0
Bolivar	4,892	27	24	3
Bradford	970	4	4	0
Brentwood	43,454	80	63	17
Brighton	2,911	7	7	0
Bristol	27,013	88	69	19
Brownsville	9,340	39	35	4
Bruceton	1,387	2	2	0
Burns	1,467	1	1	0
Calhoun	501	3	3	0
Camden	3,637	18	13	5
Carthage	2,343	12	8	4
Caryville	2,130	6	6	0
Celina	1,412	8	6	2
Centerville	3,533	18	15	3
Chapel Hill	1,548	7	6	1
Charleston	703	2	2	0
Chattanooga	184,211	573	470	103
Church Hill	6,655	10	9	1
Clarksville	161,167	368	304	64
Cleveland	45,994	124	105	19
Clifton	2,651	5	5	0
Clinton	10,111	43	33	10
Collegedale	11,750	25	24	1
Collierville	51,677	140	107	33
Collinwood	940	4	4	0
Columbia	41,013	94	83	11
Cookeville	35,119	93	72	21

(Number.)

State/city	Population	Total law enforcement employees	Total officers	Total civilians
Coopertown	4,621	5	4	1
Cornersville	1,307	2	2	0
Covington	8,818	33	32	1
Cowan	1,650	3	3	0
Cross Plains	1,841	1	1	0
Crossville	11,885	45	42	3
Cumberland City	306	2	2	0
Dandridge	3,229	12	11	1
Dayton	7,367	18	18	0
Decatur	1,668	6	6	0
Decaturville	862	1	1	0
Decherd	2,374	13	12	1
Dickson	15,680	66	59	7
Dover	1,562	5	5	0
Dresden	2,921	9	8	1
Dunlap	5,214	13	12	1
Dyer	2,195	7	6	1
Dyersburg	16,226	68	60	8
Eagleville	779	4	4	0
East Ridge	21,202	48	44	4
Elizabethton	13,432	46	42	4
Elkton	522	2	2	0
Englewood	1,535	6	5	1
Erin	1,274	5	4	1
Erwin	5,901	17	16	1
Estill Springs	2,035	6	6	0
Ethridge	488	5	4	1
Etowah	3,495	13	12	1
Fairview	9,300	22	22	0
Fayetteville	7,077	29	27	2
Franklin	85,722	135	123	12
Friendship	662	1	1	0
Gainesboro	960	6	3	3
Gallatin	44,584	97	86	11
Gallaway	644	2	1	1
Gatlinburg	3,846	47	45	2
Germantown	39,264	130	107	23
Gibson	383	3	2	1
Gleason	1,368	5	5	0
Goodlettsville	16,896	55	41	14
Gordonsville	1,249	7	6	1
Grand Junction	267	3	3	0
Graysville	1,587	4	4	0
Greenbrier	6,896	16	15	1
Greeneville	14,875	56	54	2
Greenfield	2,074	7	6	1
Halls	2,047	8	8	0
Harriman	6,110	20	19	1
Henderson	6,361	16	16	0
Hendersonville	58,901	141	125	16
Henry	448	1	1	0
Hohenwald	3,822	17	16	1
Hollow Rock	677	2	1	1
Hornbeak	467	1	1	0
Humboldt	8,116	31	26	5
Huntingdon	3,818	17	13	4
Huntland	841	4	4	0
Jacksboro	2,060	6	5	1
Jackson	67,234	239	202	37
Jamestown	2,123	9	9	0
Jasper	3,459	8	8	0
Jefferson City	8,188	31	29	2
Jellico	2,148	4	3	1
Johnson City	67,293	168	139	29
Jonesborough	5,675	23	18	5
Kenton	1,185	2	2	0
Kimball	1,452	9	9	0
Kingsport	54,260	152	112	40
Kingston	5,998	13	12	1
Kingston Springs	2,726	8	7	1
Knoxville	188,672	495	371	124

State/city	Population	Total law enforcement employees	Total officers	Total civilians
Lafayette	5,428	23	16	7
La Follette	6,606	27	21	6
La Vergne	36,067	73	58	15
Lawrenceburg	11,093	39	34	5
Lebanon	37,832	128	100	28
Lenoir City	9,404	29	27	2
Lewisburg	12,515	31	30	1
Lexington	7,915	34	28	6
Livingston	4,046	23	18	5
Lookout Mountain	1,892	21	16	5
Loretto	1,780	5	5	0
Loudon	5,953	16	15	1
Madisonville	5,031	21	18	3
Manchester	11,145	38	34	4
Martin	10,380	37	27	10
Maryville	30,006	63	57	6
Mason	1,525	4	4	0
Maynardville	2,435	4	4	0
McEwen	1,731	5	5	0
McKenzie	5,323	21	16	5
McMinnville	13,783	40	36	4
Medina	4,365	10	9	1
Memphis	650,937	2,563	2,064	499
Metropolitan Nashville Police Department	688,013	1,917	1,419	498
Middleton	627	3	3	0
Milan	7,585	33	26	7
Millersville	6,811	13	11	2
Millington	10,626	39	31	8
Minor Hill	532	2	2	0
Monteagle	1,231	7	6	1
Monterey	2,906	10	9	1
Morristown	30,330	86	81	5
Moscow	553	4	4	0
Mountain City	2,429	9	9	0
Mount Carmel	5,284	9	8	1
Mount Juliet	38,685	79	63	16
Mount Pleasant	4,934	20	14	6
Munford	6,134	18	18	0
Murfreesboro	151,769	324	265	59
Newbern	3,289	11	11	0
New Johnsonville	1,868	6	5	1
New Market	1,379	5	4	1
Newport	6,880	32	28	4
New Tazewell	2,707	10	10	0
Niota	735	3	2	1
Nolensville	10,665	15	14	1
Norris	1,603	5	5	0
Oakland	8,558	21	19	2
Oak Ridge	29,139	82	64	18
Obion	1,032	2	2	0
Oliver Springs	3,416	14	10	4
Oneida	3,696	15	10	5
Paris	10,047	39	27	12
Parsons	2,283	8	8	0
Petersburg	571	1	1	0
Pigeon Forge	6,311	76	58	18
Pikeville	1,756	3	3	0
Piperton	2,057	8	8	0
Pittman Center	578	4	4	0
Plainview	2,160	2	2	0
Pleasant View	4,874	8	8	0
Portland	13,208	36	32	4
Pulaski	7,571	26	23	3
Puryear	662	1	1	0
Red Bank	11,861	25	23	2
Red Boiling Springs	1,135	4	4	0
Ridgely	1,605	5	3	2
Ripley	7,686	32	26	6
Rockwood	5,410	15	14	1
Rocky Top	1,774	9	6	3
Rogersville	4,368	18	13	5

State/city	Population	Total law enforcement employees	Total officers	Total civilians
Rossville	1,003	7	7	0
Rutherford	1,058	5	4	1
Rutledge	1,362	3	3	0
Savannah	6,928	23	21	2
Scotts Hill	978	3	3	0
Selmer	4,289	19	17	2
Sevierville	17,395	76	60	16
Sharon	911	2	1	1
Shelbyville	22,306	55	45	10
Signal Mountain	8,644	17	15	2
Smithville	4,929	15	14	1
Smyrna	52,984	109	86	23
Soddy-Daisy	13,697	35	28	7
Somerville	3,282	12	11	1
South Carthage	1,408	4	4	0
South Fulton	2,195	9	8	1
South Pittsburg	3,022	8	8	0
Sparta	4,960	15	13	2
Spencer	1,700	2	2	0
Spring City	1,850	8	7	1
Springfield	17,372	41	37	4
Spring Hill	45,765	64	60	4
St. Joseph	833	1	1	0
Surgoinsville	1,755	1	1	0
Sweetwater	5,904	20	19	1
Tazewell	2,281	7	7	0
Tellico Plains	915	5	5	0
Tiptonville	3,920	7	7	0
Townsend	467	4	4	0
Tracy City	1,391	4	4	0
Trenton	4,168	20	14	6
Trimble	609	1	1	0
Troy	1,313	5	5	0
Tullahoma	19,664	34	29	5
Tusculum	2,692	2	2	0
Unicoi	3,592	4	4	0
Union City	10,263	40	30	10
Vonore	1,559	9	9	0
Wartburg	924	6	6	0
Wartrace	700	2	1	1
Watertown	1,528	6	6	0
Waverly	4,154	14	13	1
Waynesboro	2,417	7	7	0
Westmoreland	2,421	10	8	2
White Bluff	3,706	5	5	0
White House	12,936	26	23	3
White Pine	2,353	11	10	1
Whiteville	4,436	8	7	1
Whitwell	1,731	5	5	0
Winchester	9,029	25	23	2
Woodbury	2,919	10	10	0
TEXAS				
Abernathy	2,694	5	5	0
Abilene	124,061	275	211	64
Addison	16,778	71	60	11
Alamo	20,078	46	34	12
Alamo Heights	8,807	34	21	13
Alba	550	2	2	0
Alice	18,634	36	27	9
Allen	108,218	207	144	63
Alpine	5,978	20	12	8
Alton	18,632	28	22	6
Alvarado	4,626	19	17	2
Alvin	27,015	78	50	28
Amarillo	200,296	416	354	62
Andrews	14,487	19	18	1
Angleton	19,500	51	35	16
Anna	16,036	20	19	1
Anthony	5,389	17	16	1
Aransas Pass	8,414	42	28	14

Table 19. Full-Time Law Enforcement Employees, by Selected State and City, 2020—*Continued*

(Number.)

State/city	Population	Total law enforcement employees	Total officers	Total civilians
Archer City	1,687	2	2	0
Arcola	2,811	8	8	0
Argyle	4,527	14	12	2
Arlington	402,700	876	682	194
Arp	1,037	8	7	1
Athens	12,757	32	24	8
Atlanta	5,451	16	11	5
Aubrey	5,274	15	15	0
Austin	1,000,276	2,290	1,738	552
Azle	13,660	41	30	11
Baird	1,485	2	2	0
Balch Springs	25,189	53	36	17
Balcones Heights	3,362	25	17	8
Ballinger	3,629	9	7	2
Bangs	1,518	3	3	0
Bartonville	1,810	5	5	0
Bastrop	9,479	25	21	4
Bay City	17,505	57	35	22
Bayou Vista	1,644	6	6	0
Baytown	77,823	217	164	53
Beaumont	116,766	320	261	59
Bedford	49,274	125	76	49
Bee Cave	7,255	20	19	1
Beeville	12,788	31	23	8
Bellaire	19,210	57	41	16
Bellmead	10,835	28	18	10
Bells	1,528	4	4	0
Bellville	4,233	12	11	1
Belton	23,435	48	35	13
Benbrook	23,766	51	40	11
Bertram	1,491	6	6	0
Beverly Hills	1,984	13	7	6
Big Sandy	1,418	4	4	0
Big Spring	28,294	49	38	11
Bishop	3,048	10	6	4
Blanco	2,103	10	9	1
Blue Mound	2,450	13	8	5
Boerne	19,342	62	42	20
Bogata	1,053	5	5	0
Bonham	10,416	29	20	9
Borger	12,318	29	27	2
Bovina	1,768	3	3	0
Bowie	5,103	21	15	6
Boyd	1,557	6	6	0
Brady	5,280	12	11	1
Brazoria	3,059	12	8	4
Breckenridge	5,386	18	12	6
Bremond	971	3	3	0
Brenham	18,106	42	37	5
Bridge City	7,864	22	16	6
Bridgeport	6,732	24	15	9
Brookshire	5,948	23	18	5
Brookside Village	1,583	4	4	0
Brownfield	9,324	29	24	5
Brownsboro	1,309	4	4	0
Brownsville	183,627	312	225	87
Brownwood	18,367	61	38	23
Bryan	87,435	183	153	30
Buda	18,531	25	22	3
Bullard	3,900	12	11	1
Bulverde	5,370	17	16	1
Burkburnett	11,321	23	17	6
Burleson	49,660	90	65	25
Burnet	6,455	21	19	2
Cactus	3,250	12	9	3
Caddo Mills	1,739	7	7	0
Caldwell	4,403	11	10	1
Cameron	5,458	14	10	4
Canton	3,895	20	15	5
Canyon	16,263	29	26	3
Carrollton	141,745	222	169	53

(Number.)

State/city	Population	Total law enforcement employees	Total officers	Total civilians
Carthage	6,395	21	15	6
Castroville	3,159	9	8	1
Cedar Hill	48,352	91	70	21
Cedar Park	82,653	130	94	36
Celina	18,165	33	30	3
Center	5,157	30	22	8
Chandler	3,233	8	8	0
Childress	6,039	11	10	1
Chillicothe	669	1	1	0
Cibolo	32,777	41	37	4
Cisco	3,774	10	8	2
Clarksville	3,042	5	5	0
Cleburne	31,486	68	52	16
Cleveland	8,285	30	20	10
Clifton	3,446	8	7	1
Clint	1,137	3	3	0
Clute	11,742	39	26	13
Clyde	3,838	10	9	1
Coleman	4,230	8	8	0
College Station	120,831	201	142	59
Colleyville	27,602	48	43	5
Collinsville	2,000	4	4	0
Colorado City	3,827	10	6	4
Comanche	4,183	12	11	1
Combes	3,002	7	7	0
Commerce	9,876	20	16	4
Conroe	94,451	186	142	44
Coppell	41,807	68	59	9
Copperas Cove	33,333	68	50	18
Corinth	22,367	37	32	5
Corpus Christi	329,050	626	425	201
Corsicana	23,914	53	39	14
Crandall	4,147	16	16	0
Crane	3,722	14	8	6
Crockett	6,327	17	15	2
Crosbyton	1,599	3	3	0
Crowley	16,909	38	24	14
Crystal City	7,158	17	10	7
Cuero	8,237	15	14	1
Cumby	800	5	5	0
Cuney	140	1	1	0
Daingerfield	2,362	7	6	1
Dalhart	8,349	19	15	4
Dallas	1,363,028	3,646	3,137	509
Dalworthington Gardens	2,382	17	12	5
Danbury	1,765	1	1	0
Dawson	800	2	2	0
Dayton	8,510	28	19	9
Decatur	7,220	34	29	5
Deer Park	33,631	94	63	31
De Kalb	1,584	4	4	0
De Leon	2,193	4	4	0
Del Rio	35,733	77	54	23
Denison	25,858	68	52	16
Denton	144,569	229	185	44
Denver City	4,964	16	10	6
DeSoto	53,515	97	68	29
Devine	4,883	14	11	3
Diboll	5,182	17	12	5
Dickinson	21,364	46	30	16
Dilley	4,559	13	12	1
Dimmitt	4,065	7	5	2
Donna	16,400	48	35	13
Double Oak	3,089	8	8	0
Dublin	3,546	9	8	1
Dumas	13,729	30	23	7
Duncanville	38,847	71	61	10
Eagle Lake	3,793	9	8	1
Early	3,205	10	8	2
Eastland	3,836	13	11	2
Edinburg	103,491	215	156	59

(Number.)

State/city	Population	Total law enforcement employees	Total officers	Total civilians
Edna	5,813	10	8	2
El Campo	11,523	41	27	14
Electra	2,723	13	8	5
Elgin	10,567	26	22	4
El Paso	685,288	1,455	1,189	266
Elsa	7,274	24	18	6
Emory	1,368	5	4	1
Encinal	595	2	2	0
Ennis	20,557	44	34	10
Euless	57,881	137	89	48
Everman	6,220	20	16	4
Fairfield	2,885	14	10	4
Fair Oaks Ranch	10,497	25	22	3
Falfurrias	4,797	10	8	2
Farmers Branch	51,078	99	76	23
Farmersville	3,668	11	9	2
Fate	16,917	21	19	2
Ferris	3,042	15	10	5
Flatonia	1,436	8	8	0
Floresville	8,247	21	19	2
Flower Mound	80,907	145	96	49
Floydada	2,641	6	6	0
Forest Hill	13,058	29	21	8
Forney	29,366	46	31	15
Fort Stockton	8,429	31	20	11
Fort Worth	929,509	2,085	1,667	418
Franklin	1,649	5	5	0
Frankston	1,164	5	5	0
Fredericksburg	11,604	38	31	7
Freeport	12,144	47	32	15
Freer	2,651	9	6	3
Friendswood	40,795	80	58	22
Frisco	212,626	310	212	98
Fulshear	14,094	26	24	2
Fulton	1,502	1	1	0
Gainesville	16,986	55	41	14
Galena Park	10,740	25	19	6
Galveston	50,751	198	148	50
Ganado	2,062	3	3	0
Garden Ridge	4,235	12	11	1
Garland	241,845	477	354	123
Gatesville	12,394	33	21	12
Georgetown	84,210	120	88	32
George West	2,575	12	10	2
Giddings	5,126	17	12	5
Gilmer	5,171	19	15	4
Gladewater	6,333	20	15	5
Glenn Heights	13,662	22	15	7
Godley	1,423	6	6	0
Gonzales	7,568	26	18	8
Granbury	11,080	48	42	6
Grand Prairie	196,990	413	274	139
Grand Saline	3,178	11	10	1
Granger	1,514	2	2	0
Granite Shoals	5,096	14	11	3
Grapevine	56,343	147	93	54
Greenville	29,209	69	50	19
Gregory	1,886	7	7	0
Groesbeck	4,244	9	9	0
Groves	15,412	22	20	2
Gun Barrel City	6,269	20	14	6
Gunter	1,696	5	5	0
Hallettsville	2,645	9	8	1
Hallsville	4,382	6	6	0
Haltom City	44,037	78	72	6
Hamilton	3,005	8	7	1
Hamlin	2,010	10	5	5
Harker Heights	33,091	67	53	14
Harlingen	65,014	169	125	44
Haskell	3,136	6	5	1
Hawkins	1,328	3	3	0

(Number.)

State/city	Population	Total law enforcement employees	Total officers	Total civilians
Hawley	622	2	2	0
Hearne	4,345	18	12	6
Heath	9,584	25	24	1
Hedwig Village	2,643	23	17	6
Helotes	10,301	31	30	1
Hemphill	1,243	4	4	0
Hempstead	8,699	21	17	4
Henderson	13,093	41	33	8
Hewitt	15,092	38	28	10
Hickory Creek	4,979	12	12	0
Highland Park	9,160	70	57	13
Highland Village	16,848	42	29	13
Hillsboro	8,480	34	25	9
Hitchcock	8,023	18	16	2
Hollywood Park	3,370	18	17	1
Hondo	9,506	27	23	4
Honey Grove	1,745	5	5	0
Hooks	2,706	7	7	0
Horizon City	19,973	41	23	18
Horseshoe Bay	4,085	25	21	4
Houston	2,346,155	6,223	5,212	1,011
Howe	3,442	8	7	1
Hudson	5,035	4	4	0
Hudson Oaks	2,587	12	11	1
Hughes Springs	1,704	4	4	0
Humble	15,901	75	60	15
Huntington	2,110	6	6	0
Huntsville	42,648	68	59	9
Hurst	38,796	119	71	48
Hutchins	5,941	26	18	8
Hutto	29,590	48	44	4
Idalou	2,308	4	4	0
Indian Lake	883	3	3	0
Ingleside	10,296	33	22	11
Ingram	1,859	8	7	1
Iowa Colony	3,686	9	9	0
Iowa Park	6,334	17	10	7
Irving	242,976	574	376	198
Italy	1,928	8	7	1
Itasca	1,743	6	6	0
Jacinto City	10,455	26	20	6
Jacksboro	4,372	11	10	1
Jacksonville	14,843	44	29	15
Jamaica Beach	1,089	6	6	0
Jarrell	1,953	6	6	0
Jasper	7,543	28	21	7
Jefferson	1,896	7	5	2
Jersey Village	7,921	26	24	2
Jones Creek	2,079	5	5	0
Jonestown	2,139	10	9	1
Josephine	2,182	5	5	0
Joshua	8,319	13	11	2
Jourdanton	4,467	10	9	1
Junction	2,387	9	7	2
Karnes City	3,419	9	8	1
Katy	22,797	82	66	16
Keller	48,117	82	50	32
Kemah	2,046	18	13	5
Kemp	1,259	6	6	0
Kempner	1,145	3	2	1
Kenedy	3,357	15	14	1
Kennedale	8,881	23	19	4
Kerens	1,519	5	5	0
Kermit	6,583	18	14	4
Kerrville	23,912	65	46	19
Kilgore	15,016	51	37	14
Killeen	154,417	285	235	50
Kingsville	25,195	71	45	26
Kirby	8,805	23	17	6
Knox City	1,118	2	2	0
Kountze	2,104	7	6	1

(Number.)

State/city	Population	Total law enforcement employees	Total officers	Total civilians
Kress	677	1	1	0
Kyle	51,306	82	53	29
Lacy-Lakeview	6,748	20	12	8
La Feria	7,232	20	15	5
Lago Vista	7,740	25	18	7
La Grange	4,680	13	12	1
La Grulla	1,710	9	8	1
Laguna Vista	3,183	9	9	0
La Joya	4,326	17	12	5
Lake City	534	1	1	0
Lake Dallas	8,174	16	13	3
Lake Jackson	27,265	63	47	16
Lakeport	998	4	4	0
Lakeside	1,603	7	7	0
Lakeview, Harrison County	6,231	14	13	1
Lake Worth	4,921	33	26	7
La Marque	17,656	39	32	7
Lamesa	9,119	27	20	7
Lampasas	8,132	32	22	10
Lancaster	39,587	63	59	4
La Porte	35,102	103	79	24
Laredo	265,515	602	509	93
La Vernia	1,481	9	9	0
League City	110,518	163	116	47
Leander	68,571	84	64	20
Leon Valley	12,453	50	46	4
Levelland	13,502	35	24	11
Lewisville	110,800	219	165	54
Liberty	9,418	26	15	11
Liberty Hill	3,345	15	14	1
Lindale	6,675	25	17	8
Linden	1,908	6	5	1
Little Elm	57,482	81	73	8
Live Oak	16,910	45	34	11
Livingston	5,240	29	22	7
Log Cabin	779	4	4	0
Lone Star	1,472	6	5	1
Longview	81,751	214	170	44
Lorena	1,762	10	8	2
Los Indios	1,063	2	2	0
Lubbock	262,146	557	446	111
Lufkin	35,007	96	76	20
Lumberton	13,195	21	18	3
Lyford	2,531	3	3	0
Lytle	3,135	9	8	1
Madisonville	4,715	13	10	3
Magnolia	2,193	16	14	2
Manor	15,569	32	27	5
Mansfield	74,360	158	103	55
Manvel	13,971	28	22	6
Marble Falls	7,157	35	22	13
Marfa	1,589	5	5	0
Marion	1,262	3	3	0
Marlin	5,539	14	10	4
Marshall	22,755	65	49	16
Mathis	4,694	13	9	4
McAllen	144,569	428	286	142
McGregor	5,368	16	10	6
McKinney	208,335	287	218	69
Meadows Place	4,587	17	16	1
Melissa	13,424	14	14	0
Memorial Villages	12,375	46	33	13
Mercedes	16,699	41	33	8
Merkel	2,620	6	5	1
Mesquite	141,325	319	227	92
Mexia	7,329	18	16	2
Midland	150,529	243	152	91
Midlothian	34,962	95	66	29
Milford	749	3	3	0
Mineola	4,797	19	12	7
Mineral Wells	15,057	46	33	13

(Number.)

State/city	Population	Total law enforcement employees	Total officers	Total civilians
Mission	85,052	203	159	44
Missouri City	76,476	130	102	28
Monahans	7,924	20	15	5
Mont Belvieu	6,954	25	16	9
Montgomery	1,488	13	12	1
Morgans Point Resort	4,738	9	9	0
Moulton	901	4	4	0
Mount Pleasant	15,974	46	33	13
Muleshoe	5,005	13	7	6
Murphy	20,798	35	24	11
Mustang Ridge	999	5	5	0
Nacogdoches	32,873	86	57	29
Naples	1,307	3	3	0
Nash	3,938	9	9	0
Nassau Bay	3,968	15	14	1
Natalia	1,610	4	4	0
Navasota	8,104	27	19	8
Nederland	17,413	41	27	14
New Boston	4,588	19	14	5
New Braunfels	94,751	172	137	35
Newton	2,359	4	4	0
Nixon	2,560	7	7	0
Nocona	2,999	6	5	1
Nolanville	6,048	11	10	1
Northeast	3,485	13	12	1
Northlake	3,582	18	16	2
North Richland Hills	71,520	187	113	74
Oak Ridge	256	3	1	2
Oak Ridge North	3,171	17	17	0
Odessa	126,288	198	137	61
Olmos Park	2,492	14	13	1
Olney	3,080	9	7	2
Omaha	975	3	3	0
Onalaska	3,006	8	8	0
Orange	18,064	58	42	16
Ore City	1,238	4	4	0
Overton	2,498	9	6	3
Ovilla	4,247	11	10	1
Oyster Creek	1,203	12	9	3
Palacios	4,516	13	9	4
Palestine	17,625	43	28	15
Palmer	2,136	11	10	1
Palmhurst	2,753	16	13	3
Palm Valley	1,232	5	5	0
Pampa	16,975	37	25	12
Panhandle	2,298	4	4	0
Pantego	2,533	16	11	5
Paris	24,801	69	46	23
Parker	5,364	12	11	1
Pasadena	151,421	373	282	91
Patton Village	2,228	8	8	0
Pearland	126,111	235	174	61
Pearsall	10,783	20	16	4
Pecos	10,667	53	23	30
Pelican Bay	2,064	9	8	1
Penitas	4,756	20	18	2
Perryton	8,486	22	13	9
Pflugerville	67,559	121	85	36
Pharr	80,098	162	125	37
Pilot Point	4,582	11	11	0
Pinehurst	1,963	8	6	2
Pineland	795	3	3	0
Pittsburg	4,717	12	10	2
Plainview	19,926	37	30	7
Plano	290,786	557	380	177
Pleasanton	11,006	30	23	7
Ponder	2,521	7	6	1
Port Aransas	4,362	28	19	9
Port Arthur	54,257	151	116	35
Port Isabel	6,244	21	16	5
Portland	17,468	49	34	15

(Number.)

State/city	Population	Total law enforcement employees	Total officers	Total civilians
Port Lavaca	11,817	23	17	6
Port Neches	12,616	25	22	3
Poteet	3,535	11	10	1
Pottsboro	2,528	10	8	2
Prairie View	7,126	13	12	1
Premont	2,531	6	6	0
Presidio	3,836	4	4	0
Primera	5,250	10	9	1
Princeton	15,031	27	25	2
Prosper	27,250	50	37	13
Queen City	1,432	5	5	0
Quitman	1,854	7	7	0
Rancho Viejo	2,462	8	8	0
Ranger	2,469	4	3	1
Raymondville	10,833	23	14	9
Red Oak	13,801	31	28	3
Refugio	2,718	9	7	2
Reno, Lamar County	3,364	6	5	1
Reno, Parker County	3,294	7	7	0
Richardson	124,190	255	165	90
Richland Hills	7,971	22	19	3
Richmond	12,630	40	28	12
Richwood	4,044	10	10	0
Riesel	1,040	3	3	0
Rio Grande City	14,587	45	33	12
Rio Hondo	2,744	7	7	0
River Oaks	7,653	22	16	6
Roanoke	9,862	39	29	10
Robinson	12,087	32	23	9
Robstown	11,238	31	22	9
Rockdale	5,503	15	10	5
Rockport	10,672	34	27	7
Rockwall	46,867	100	79	21
Rollingwood	1,607	9	9	0
Roma	11,559	34	26	8
Roman Forest	2,058	11	10	1
Rosenberg	39,162	107	83	24
Round Rock	137,593	244	172	72
Rowlett	68,810	127	92	35
Royse City	15,388	25	21	4
Runaway Bay	1,612	5	5	0
Rusk	5,606	13	12	1
Sachse	26,799	46	32	14
Saginaw	24,822	51	39	12
Salado	2,393	5	5	0
San Angelo	101,860	198	165	33
San Antonio	1,573,189	3,087	2,379	708
San Benito	24,237	50	41	9
San Diego	4,196	6	5	1
San Elizario	9,070	3	3	0
Sanger	8,953	16	14	2
San Juan	37,337	59	43	16
San Marcos	67,432	150	109	41
Santa Fe	13,577	29	22	7
Schertz	43,315	97	61	36
Schulenburg	2,920	9	8	1
Seabrook	14,415	42	32	10
Seagoville	17,120	36	26	10
Sealy	6,484	26	23	3
Seguin	30,513	79	57	22
Selma	12,013	32	28	4
Seven Points	1,532	10	6	4
Seymour	2,532	7	4	3
Shallowater	2,586	5	5	0
Shavano Park	4,098	19	18	1
Shenandoah	3,098	26	25	1
Sherman	44,611	91	67	24
Silsbee	6,613	23	17	6
Sinton	5,324	12	11	1
Slaton	5,864	19	13	6
Socorro	34,626	58	36	22

(Number.)

State/city	Population	Total law enforcement employees	Total officers	Total civilians
Somerset	2,000	4	4	0
Somerville	1,475	3	2	1
Sonora	2,765	7	5	2
Sour Lake	1,937	7	5	2
South Houston	17,485	44	31	13
Southlake	33,083	78	70	8
South Padre Island	2,772	37	27	10
Southside Place	1,902	12	8	4
Splendora	2,337	15	13	2
Springtown	3,254	15	11	4
Spring Valley	4,389	24	18	6
Spur	1,186	3	2	1
Stafford	17,423	71	54	17
Stamford	2,921	7	6	1
Stanton	3,061	6	6	0
Stephenville	21,777	56	34	22
Stinnett	1,759	4	4	0
Stratford	2,062	3	2	1
Sugar Land	119,671	194	166	28
Sullivan City	4,186	16	10	6
Sulphur Springs	16,322	39	28	11
Sunrise Beach Village	806	5	5	0
Sunset Valley	675	14	13	1
Surfside Beach	591	21	18	3
Sweeny	3,716	8	8	0
Sweetwater	10,419	31	25	6
Tatum	1,384	6	6	0
Teague	3,511	7	6	1
Temple	79,878	185	146	39
Tenaha	1,145	3	3	0
Terrell	19,204	64	42	22
Terrell Hills	5,512	17	17	0
Texarkana	36,303	92	80	12
Texas City	50,660	114	88	26
The Colony	45,419	104	74	30
Thrall	993	2	2	0
Three Rivers	1,960	10	9	1
Tioga	1,081	4	4	0
Tomball	11,901	61	43	18
Tool	2,310	8	4	4
Trophy Club	13,053	24	20	4
Tulia	4,618	15	8	7
Tye	1,345	7	6	1
Tyler	108,139	230	185	45
Universal City	21,162	37	27	10
University Park	25,253	55	39	16
Uvalde	16,027	55	39	16
Van	2,753	10	10	0
Van Alstyne	4,557	17	11	6
Venus	4,570	13	13	0
Vernon	10,253	28	21	7
Vidor	10,370	31	21	10
Waco	140,870	348	253	95
Waelder	1,141	3	3	0
Wake Village	5,309	10	9	1
Waller	3,654	15	13	2
Wallis	1,309	8	8	0
Watauga	24,588	47	36	11
Waxahachie	39,039	92	73	19
Weatherford	34,522	82	63	19
Webster	11,545	63	45	18
Weimar	2,235	8	7	1
Weslaco	42,184	100	76	24
West	3,008	9	9	0
West Columbia	3,823	20	13	7
West Lake Hills	3,310	15	14	1
West Orange	3,199	12	10	2
Westover Hills	688	16	11	5
West University Place	15,700	33	24	9
Westworth	2,790	18	13	5
Wharton	8,612	35	25	10

State/city	Population	Total law enforcement employees	Total officers	Total civilians
Whitehouse	9,047	16	15	1
White Oak	6,303	20	16	4
White Settlement	18,051	42	32	10
Whitewright	1,734	4	4	0
Wichita Falls	104,673	292	203	89
Willis	7,166	21	19	2
Willow Park	6,096	16	15	1
Wills Point	3,667	9	8	1
Wilmer	4,919	21	16	5
Windcrest	5,930	37	26	11
Wink	1,039	3	3	0
Winnsboro	3,302	18	12	6
Wolfforth	5,735	13	12	1
Woodsboro	1,399	2	2	0
Woodville	2,411	10	9	1
Woodway	9,089	42	32	10
Wortham	988	4	4	0
Wylie	54,460	77	64	13
Yoakum	5,956	19	12	7
UTAH				
Alta	378	8	4	4
American Fork/Cedar Hills	44,093	49	43	6
Aurora	1,056	1	1	0
Big Water	515	1	1	0
Blanding	3,663	6	5	1
Bluffdale	17,826	14	14	0
Bountiful	44,129	56	36	20
Brian Head	94	5	5	0
Brigham City	19,792	33	27	6
Cedar City	35,486	45	39	6
Centerville	17,855	24	19	5
Clearfield	32,358	43	31	12
Clinton	22,725	20	18	2
Cottonwood Heights	33,871	47	39	8
Draper	49,326	60	44	16
East Carbon	1,574	4	4	0
Enoch	7,340	12	7	5
Ephraim	7,450	8	7	1
Fairview	1,371	1	1	0
Farmington	26,256	26	23	3
Fountain Green	1,177	1	1	0
Grantsville	12,468	17	15	2
Harrisville	7,029	11	10	1
Heber	17,849	29	24	5
Helper	2,094	5	4	1
Herriman	56,312	42	37	5
Hildale	2,911	13	10	3
Hurricane	19,776	31	28	3
Kamas	2,328	2	2	0
Kanab	4,993	8	7	1
Kaysville	32,959	35	32	3
La Verkin	4,491	6	5	1
Layton	79,240	114	83	31
Lehi	72,654	61	56	5
Lindon	11,218	17	15	2
Logan	51,899	85	53	32
Lone Peak	30,191	27	22	5
Mantua	1,000	2	1	1
Mapleton	11,068	11	10	1
Moab	5,362	23	15	8
Moroni	1,566	1	1	0
Mount Pleasant	3,561	4	4	0
Murray	49,169	90	76	14
Naples	2,126	5	4	1
Nephi	6,498	13	10	3
North Ogden	20,960	26	20	6
North Park	16,529	13	10	3
North Salt Lake	21,540	29	23	6
Ogden	88,309	166	129	37
Orem	98,902	123	91	32

(Number.)

State/city	Population	Total law enforcement employees	Total officers	Total civilians
Park City	8,632	37	32	5
Parowan	3,208	6	6	0
Payson	20,498	27	24	3
Perry	5,335	8	7	1
Pleasant Grove	38,803	32	28	4
Pleasant View	11,212	11	10	1
Price	8,291	18	15	3
Provo	117,041	228	198	30
Richfield	7,925	18	15	3
Riverdale	8,876	22	19	3
Riverton	45,095	39	35	4
Roosevelt	7,359	13	12	1
Roy	39,849	43	39	4
Salem	8,902	12	11	1
Salina	2,624	4	4	0
Salt Lake City	202,187	644	523	121
Sandy	97,091	142	110	32
Santa Clara/Ivins	18,229	16	13	3
Santaquin/Genola	14,933	14	12	2
Saratoga Springs	35,623	30	26	4
Smithfield	12,317	11	10	1
South Jordan	80,090	65	60	5
South Ogden	17,266	27	22	5
South Salt Lake	25,816	77	64	13
Spanish Fork	41,605	42	38	4
Spring City	1,090	1	1	0
Springdale	641	9	8	1
Springville	33,728	41	30	11
St. George	91,673	163	115	48
Stockton	688	4	3	1
Sunset	5,387	8	7	1
Syracuse	32,343	26	24	2
Tooele	36,527	44	37	7
Tremonton Garland	11,995	17	15	2
Vernal	10,606	22	20	2
Washington	30,622	39	28	11
Wellington	1,612	9	8	1
West Bountiful	5,861	11	10	1
West Jordan	117,955	146	121	25
West Valley	135,887	262	217	45
Willard	1,979	3	3	0
Woods Cross	11,625	18	17	1
VERMONT				
Barre	8,471	27	20	7
Barre Town	7,698	8	7	1
Bellows Falls	2,946	7	6	1
Bennington	14,879	33	25	8
Berlin	2,770	9	8	1
Bradford	2,691	2	2	0
Brandon	3,710	7	6	1
Brattleboro	11,256	33	21	12
Brighton	1,161	1	1	0
Bristol	3,835	3	3	0
Burlington	42,862	121	86	35
Canaan	916	1	1	0
Castleton	4,490	5	5	0
Chester	3,011	6	5	1
Colchester	17,129	37	29	8
Dover	1,052	7	6	1
Essex	22,156	32	26	6
Fair Haven	2,536	4	4	0
Hardwick	2,846	9	9	0
Hartford	9,515	28	19	9
Hinesburg	4,540	10	5	5
Killington	750	2	2	0
Ludlow	1,854	9	5	4
Lyndonville	1,160	3	3	0
Manchester	4,206	13	9	4
Middlebury	8,813	18	16	2
Milton	10,882	17	16	1

(Number.)

State/city	Population	Total law enforcement employees	Total officers	Total civilians
Montpelier	7,321	26	17	9
Morristown	5,532	10	10	0
Newport	4,222	16	12	4
Northfield	6,560	6	5	1
Norwich	3,409	5	4	1
Pittsford	2,766	1	1	0
Richmond	4,123	3	3	0
Royalton	2,881	2	2	0
Rutland	14,930	47	34	13
Rutland Town	4,117	4	4	0
Shelburne	7,706	19	11	8
South Burlington	19,690	47	39	8
Springfield	8,859	20	14	6
St. Albans	6,788	34	24	10
St. Johnsbury	7,112	17	11	6
Stowe	4,444	12	12	0
Swanton	6,569	7	6	1
Thetford	2,525	3	3	0
Vergennes	2,577	8	8	0
Weathersfield	2,727	2	2	0
Williston	10,247	21	16	5
Wilmington	1,787	8	6	2
Windsor	3,272	8	7	1
Winhall	726	8	7	1
Winooski	7,341	18	14	4
Woodstock	2,907	7	6	1
VIRGINIA				
Abingdon	7,828	27	24	3
Alexandria	161,525	423	314	109
Altavista	3,401	14	13	1
Amherst	2,174	6	6	0
Ashland	7,947	27	25	2
Bedford	6,601	25	21	4
Berryville	4,393	10	9	1
Big Stone Gap	5,080	14	13	1
Blacksburg	44,422	75	65	10
Blackstone	3,299	15	12	3
Bluefield	4,780	23	20	3
Bowling Green	1,182	1	1	0
Bridgewater	6,204	9	9	0
Bristol	16,640	67	50	17
Broadway	4,010	5	5	0
Brookneal	1,096	1	1	0
Buena Vista	6,459	17	16	1
Burkeville	396	1	1	0
Cape Charles	1,020	10	10	0
Cedar Bluff	989	4	4	0
Charlottesville	47,671	126	101	25
Chase City	2,201	10	9	1
Chatham	1,422	2	2	0
Chesapeake	247,118	514	371	143
Chilhowie	1,690	6	6	0
Chincoteague	2,868	14	10	4
Christiansburg	22,643	69	62	7
Clarksville	1,159	6	5	1
Clifton Forge	3,455	10	9	1
Clintwood	1,267	3	3	0
Coeburn	1,824	9	8	1
Colonial Beach	3,628	11	10	1
Colonial Heights	17,360	58	54	4
Covington	5,490	23	14	9
Crewe	2,109	6	5	1
Culpeper	19,131	49	41	8
Damascus	772	4	4	0
Danville	39,704	131	116	15
Dayton	1,648	5	5	0
Dublin	2,590	8	7	1
Dumfries	6,038	11	10	1
Eastville	337	4	4	0
Elkton	2,923	5	4	1

State/city	Population	Total law enforcement employees	Total officers	Total civilians
Emporia	5,282	37	26	11
Exmore	1,362	7	7	0
Fairfax City	24,161	83	59	24
Falls Church	14,877	48	32	16
Farmville	7,806	28	26	2
Franklin	7,896	24	17	7
Fredericksburg	29,592	86	64	22
Front Royal	15,387	51	37	14
Galax	6,275	37	24	13
Gate City	1,850	5	5	0
Glade Spring	1,400	2	2	0
Glasgow	1,102	1	1	0
Glen Lyn	96	1	1	0
Gordonsville	1,641	7	7	0
Gretna	1,181	3	3	0
Grottoes	2,881	6	6	0
Grundy	887	5	5	0
Halifax	1,203	5	5	0
Hampton	134,082	426	325	101
Harrisonburg	53,442	123	101	22
Haymarket	1,699	5	5	0
Haysi	463	1	1	0
Herndon	24,739	39	26	13
Hillsville	2,654	16	15	1
Honaker	1,306	2	2	0
Hopewell	22,498	80	62	18
Hurt	1,215	2	2	0
Independence	886	2	2	0
Jonesville	919	3	3	0
Kenbridge	1,190	3	3	0
Kilmarnock	1,384	6	6	0
La Crosse	572	1	1	0
Lawrenceville	983	6	6	0
Lebanon	3,118	13	12	1
Leesburg	55,070	99	82	17
Lexington	7,487	19	16	3
Louisa	1,753	6	6	0
Luray	4,842	14	13	1
Lynchburg	82,871	197	157	40
Manassas	41,386	124	92	32
Manassas Park	17,839	36	28	8
Marion	5,515	22	21	1
Martinsville	12,417	50	45	5
Middleburg	854	7	6	1
Middletown	1,411	5	4	1
Mount Jackson	2,126	6	6	0
Narrows	1,942	6	6	0
New Market	2,261	6	6	0
Newport News	178,896	623	449	174
Norfolk	242,516	807	656	151
Norton	3,975	23	16	7
Occoquan	1,104	2	2	0
Onancock	1,206	6	6	0
Onley	498	5	5	0
Orange	5,140	17	15	2
Parksley	804	1	1	0
Pearisburg	2,619	8	8	0
Pembroke	1,078	3	3	0
Pennington Gap	1,705	6	6	0
Petersburg	31,195	107	86	21
Pocahontas	348	1	1	0
Poquoson	12,275	28	24	4
Portsmouth	94,205	249	199	50
Pound	907	4	4	0
Pulaski	8,674	32	28	4
Purcellville	10,485	16	14	2
Radford	18,450	52	38	14
Remington	665	1	1	0
Rich Creek	738	1	1	0
Richlands	5,172	25	20	5
Richmond	233,350	1,048	846	202

State/city	Population	Total law enforcement employees	Total officers	Total civilians
Roanoke	99,335	274	228	46
Rocky Mount	4,718	22	20	2
Rural Retreat	1,444	1	1	0
Salem	25,326	86	62	24
Saltville	1,885	7	7	0
Shenandoah	2,327	7	6	1
Smithfield	8,518	24	20	4
South Boston	7,528	29	27	2
South Hill	4,322	22	20	2
Stanley	1,672	5	5	0
Staunton	25,048	63	48	15
Stephens City	2,091	1	1	0
St. Paul	840	6	6	0
Strasburg	6,703	19	18	1
Suffolk	92,881	233	178	55
Tappahannock	2,397	11	10	1
Tazewell	4,088	17	16	1
Timberville	2,710	6	6	0
Victoria	1,615	4	4	0
Vienna	16,570	49	39	10
Vinton	8,117	22	21	1
Virginia Beach	450,858	925	744	181
Warrenton	10,073	28	27	1
Warsaw	1,485	4	4	0
Waverly	1,932	12	7	5
Waynesboro	22,801	53	43	10
Weber City	1,200	5	4	1
West Point	3,250	10	9	1
Williamsburg	15,086	42	40	2
Winchester	28,279	98	73	25
Windsor	2,774	7	7	0
Wintergreen	165	16	12	4
Wise	4,381	12	11	1
Woodstock	5,279	20	18	2
Wytheville	7,890	25	22	3
WASHINGTON				
Aberdeen	16,744	50	36	14
Airway Heights	10,010	22	20	2
Algona	3,228	9	7	2
Anacortes	17,735	30	24	6
Arlington	20,825	35	30	5
Asotin	1,293	1	1	0
Auburn	82,779	134	114	20
Bainbridge Island	25,561	27	23	4
Battle Ground	21,669	27	23	4
Bellevue	150,548	213	173	40
Bellingham	93,629	180	118	62
Black Diamond	4,858	12	10	2
Blaine	5,717	16	14	2
Bonney Lake	21,584	38	31	7
Bothell	48,323	95	67	28
Bremerton	41,817	68	55	13
Brewster	2,355	6	5	1
Brier	7,055	8	7	1
Buckley	5,663	12	10	2
Burien	51,879	70	48	22
Burlington	9,321	29	23	6
Camas	24,979	33	29	4
Carnation	2,345	2	2	0
Castle Rock	2,319	5	4	1
Centralia	17,867	38	27	11
Chehalis	7,700	22	17	5
Cheney	12,741	23	16	7
Chewelah	2,685	6	5	1
Clarkston	7,387	16	14	2
Cle Elum	3,023	9	8	1
Clyde Hill	3,432	10	9	1
Colfax	2,881	3	3	0
College Place	9,374	16	13	3
Colville	4,845	11	9	2

(Number.)

State/city	Population	Total law enforcement employees	Total officers	Total civilians
Connell	5,725	8	7	1
Cosmopolis	1,664	6	5	1
Coulee Dam	1,078	2	2	0
Covington	21,613	25	19	6
Des Moines	32,652	43	33	10
Dupont	9,668	14	12	2
Duvall	8,275	14	13	1
East Wenatchee	14,336	22	19	3
Eatonville	3,058	6	5	1
Edgewood	13,553	14	13	1
Edmonds	42,934	65	55	10
Ellensburg	21,448	34	26	8
Elma	3,357	10	8	2
Enumclaw	12,315	34	19	15
Ephrata	8,184	18	15	3
Everett	112,439	238	197	41
Everson	4,551	7	6	1
Federal Way	97,071	160	129	31
Ferndale	15,337	23	20	3
Fife	10,301	38	29	9
Fircrest	6,869	9	9	0
Forks	3,918	8	4	4
Garfield	610	1	1	0
Gig Harbor	11,216	20	18	2
Goldendale	3,516	11	9	2
Grand Coulee	2,054	8	8	0
Grandview	11,099	22	19	3
Granger	3,898	8	8	0
Hoquiam	8,647	25	23	2
Issaquah	40,659	56	34	22
Kalama	2,852	8	7	1
Kelso	12,476	31	27	4
Kenmore	23,397	20	15	5
Kennewick	85,526	114	99	15
Kent	133,883	207	151	56
Kettle Falls	1,641	5	4	1
Kirkland	94,470	150	109	41
Kittitas	1,513	3	3	0
La Center	3,459	8	7	1
Lacey	53,826	64	49	15
Lake Forest Park	13,604	23	20	3
Lake Stevens	34,600	41	33	8
Lakewood	61,432	108	95	13
Langley	1,155	3	3	0
Liberty Lake	11,410	14	13	1
Long Beach	1,508	7	6	1
Longview	38,629	69	57	12
Lynden	15,625	21	17	4
Lynnwood	39,517	97	66	31
Mabton	2,265	3	3	0
Maple Valley	27,736	24	18	6
Marysville	71,522	103	74	29
Mattawa	4,790	6	5	1
McCleary	1,777	5	5	0
Medina	3,324	11	9	2
Mercer Island	26,268	35	30	5
Mill Creek	21,214	26	21	5
Milton	8,413	13	13	0
Monroe	20,065	41	31	10
Montesano	4,059	8	7	1
Morton	1,207	3	3	0
Moses Lake	24,524	46	38	8
Mountlake Terrace	21,504	35	27	8
Mount Vernon	36,513	53	39	14
Moxee	4,177	7	6	1
Mukilteo	21,573	33	26	7
Napavine	2,025	5	4	1
Newcastle	12,523	14	11	3
Newport	2,205	5	4	1
Normandy Park	6,633	11	10	1
Oak Harbor	23,721	39	28	11
Ocean Shores	6,604	12	10	2

Table 19. Full-Time Law Enforcement Employees, by Selected State and City, 2020—*Continued*

(Number.)

State/city	Population	Total law enforcement employees	Total officers	Total civilians
Odessa	892	2	2	0
Olympia	53,571	105	72	33
Omak	4,776	10	8	2
Oroville	1,671	6	5	1
Orting	8,848	11	9	2
Othello	8,509	23	16	7
Pacific	7,243	12	11	1
Palouse	1,084	2	2	0
Pasco	76,970	92	82	10
Port Angeles	20,364	54	32	22
Port Orchard	14,886	25	20	5
Port Townsend	9,914	17	13	4
Poulsbo	11,401	22	20	2
Prosser	6,451	17	15	2
Pullman	35,071	44	29	15
Puyallup	42,974	86	65	21
Quincy	8,183	28	21	7
Raymond	3,009	7	6	1
Reardan	615	1	1	0
Redmond	74,154	122	85	37
Renton	102,856	153	120	33
Richland	59,370	77	60	17
Ridgefield	9,835	12	11	1
Ritzville	1,651	4	4	0
Roy	827	2	2	0
Royal City	2,247	3	3	0
Ruston	856	5	5	0
Sammamish	66,878	39	31	8
SeaTac	29,282	63	45	18
Seattle	771,517	1,900	1,341	559
Sedro Woolley	12,189	24	20	4
Selah	8,170	17	14	3
Sequim	7,768	24	20	4
Shelton	10,749	22	19	3
Shoreline	57,472	72	52	20
Snohomish	10,269	19	17	2
Snoqualmie	13,987	27	23	4
Soap Lake	1,609	7	6	1
South Bend	1,706	5	4	1
Spokane	223,524	422	342	80
Spokane Valley	102,366	130	106	24
Stanwood	7,410	13	11	2
Steilacoom	6,436	10	9	1
Sumas	1,561	7	6	1
Sumner	10,544	25	20	5
Sunnyside	16,888	43	25	18
Tacoma	220,123	383	341	42
Tenino	1,886	5	4	1
Tieton	1,323	2	2	0
Toledo	777	3	2	1
Toppenish	8,792	16	11	5
Tukwila	20,483	82	66	16
Tumwater	24,493	40	33	7
Twisp	970	3	3	0
Union Gap	6,206	19	16	3
University Place	34,339	17	16	1
Vancouver	186,440	264	218	46
Walla Walla	32,944	77	47	30
Wapato	5,003	9	7	2
Warden	2,825	5	4	1
Washougal	16,334	24	20	4
Wenatchee	34,525	54	43	11
Westport	2,102	8	7	1
West Richland	15,464	24	20	4
White Salmon	2,732	7	6	1
Winlock	1,436	3	3	0
Winthrop	480	3	2	1
Woodinville	13,547	19	15	4
Woodland	6,612	12	10	2
Yakima	93,862	173	133	40
Yelm	9,799	17	15	2
Zillah	3,152	9	8	1

(Number.)

State/city	Population	Total law enforcement employees	Total officers	Total civilians
WEST VIRGINIA				
Alderson	1,119	4	4	0
Anmoore	729	2	2	0
Ansted	1,294	2	2	0
Athens	883	1	1	0
Barboursville	4,291	24	22	2
Barrackville	1,277	1	1	0
Beckley	15,762	62	46	16
Belington	1,900	3	3	0
Belle	1,112	3	3	0
Benwood	1,262	9	6	3
Berkeley Springs	593	2	2	0
Bethlehem	2,302	5	5	0
Bluefield	9,543	33	28	5
Bradshaw	265	1	1	0
Bramwell	334	2	2	0
Bridgeport	8,924	37	33	4
Buckhannon	5,373	12	11	1
Burnsville	473	1	1	0
Cameron	833	2	2	0
Cedar Grove	898	1	1	0
Ceredo	1,260	7	4	3
Chapmanville	1,080	4	4	0
Charleston	46,038	181	158	23
Charles Town	6,123	19	16	3
Chesapeake	1,399	2	2	0
Chester	2,347	6	5	1
Clarksburg	15,092	44	40	4
Clendenin	1,087	5	5	0
Danville	593	2	2	0
Davy	329	1	1	0
Delbarton	489	2	2	0
Dunbar	7,010	13	12	1
East Bank	860	1	1	0
Eleanor	1,594	1	1	0
Elkins	6,970	13	12	1
Fairmont	18,352	38	33	5
Fairview	403	1	1	0
Fayetteville	2,695	13	12	1
Follansbee	2,682	7	7	0
Fort Gay	684	3	3	0
Gary	770	1	1	0
Gassaway	839	1	1	0
Gauley Bridge	547	1	1	0
Gilbert	381	2	2	0
Glen Dale	1,355	6	6	0
Glenville	1,422	2	1	1
Grafton	4,963	9	8	1
Grant Town	592	1	1	0
Granville	3,767	14	14	0
Hamlin	1,038	3	2	1
Harpers Ferry/Bolivar	1,301	3	2	1
Harrisville	1,654	1	1	0
Hartford City	592	1	1	0
Hinton	2,324	6	5	1
Huntington	44,684	96	93	3
Hurricane	6,446	20	18	2
Iaeger	236	1	1	0
Kenova	2,931	14	10	4
Kermit	344	1	1	0
Keyser	4,863	12	8	4
Kimball	149	1	1	0
Kingwood	3,057	3	3	0
Lewisburg	3,803	15	13	2
Logan	1,439	11	8	3
Mabscott	1,248	2	2	0
Madison	2,631	8	7	1
Man	617	2	2	0
Mannington	2,018	4	4	0
Marlinton	952	1	1	0
Marmet	1,352	5	5	0

State/city	Population	Total law enforcement employees	Total officers	Total civilians
Martinsburg	17,479	54	43	11
Mason	932	5	4	1
Masontown	537	2	1	1
Matewan	416	2	1	1
McMechen	1,677	4	4	0
Milton	2,547	11	10	1
Monongah	1,161	1	1	0
Montgomery	1,494	7	6	1
Moorefield	2,403	10	9	1
Morgantown	30,775	83	71	12
Moundsville	8,175	20	16	4
Mount Hope	1,260	4	3	1
Mullens	1,299	3	3	0
New Cumberland	997	2	1	1
New Haven	1,455	3	3	0
New Martinsville	5,092	14	10	4
Nitro	6,314	20	19	1
Nutter Fort	1,502	5	5	0
Oak Hill	8,017	20	16	4
Oceana	1,185	4	4	0
Paden City	2,306	5	4	1
Parkersburg	29,096	82	74	8
Parsons	1,383	1	1	0
Pennsboro	989	1	1	0
Petersburg	2,684	1	1	0
Philippi	3,293	6	6	0
Piedmont	794	1	1	0
Pineville	564	3	3	0
Point Pleasant	4,032	7	7	0
Pratt	551	3	2	1
Princeton	5,627	23	21	2
Rainelle	1,524	2	1	1
Ranson	5,341	19	17	2
Ravenswood	3,621	12	10	2
Reedsville	606	1	1	0
Rhodell	159	2	1	1
Richwood	1,834	3	3	0
Ripley	3,151	12	11	1
Rivesville	900	1	1	0
Romney	1,680	6	5	1
Ronceverte	1,660	6	6	0
Rupert	888	1	1	0
Salem	1,515	4	4	0
Shepherdstown	1,887	6	5	1
Shinnston	2,093	9	8	1
Sistersville	1,275	4	4	0
Sophia	1,220	5	5	0
South Charleston	11,898	49	46	3
Spencer	2,011	6	5	1
St. Albans	9,802	27	24	3
Star City	1,969	7	6	1
St. Marys	1,763	5	4	1
Stonewood	1,704	2	2	0
Summersville	3,243	17	16	1
Sutton	987	1	1	0
Sylvester	134	1	1	0
Terra Alta	1,501	2	2	0
Triadelphia	756	1	1	0
Vienna	10,049	24	20	4
War	668	3	3	0
Wayne	1,563	1	1	0
Webster Springs	652	5	4	1
Weirton	18,111	38	34	4
Welch	1,577	6	5	1
Wellsburg	2,502	6	5	1
West Liberty	1,418	1	1	0
West Logan	357	1	1	0
West Milford	604	2	2	0
Weston	3,831	8	6	2
Westover	4,192	13	12	1
West Union	796	1	1	0
Wheeling	26,222	79	68	11

(Number.)

State/city	Population	Total law enforcement employees	Total officers	Total civilians
White Hall	667	5	5	0
White Sulphur Springs	2,343	8	7	1
Whitesville	419	2	2	0
Williamson	2,625	6	5	1
Williamstown	2,864	8	7	1
Winfield	2,357	5	5	0
WISCONSIN				
Adams	1,884	3	3	0
Albany	990	3	3	0
Algoma	3,035	5	5	0
Altoona	8,009	15	14	1
Amery	2,799	6	6	0
Antigo	7,719	18	15	3
Appleton	74,255	139	112	27
Arcadia	3,051	4	4	0
Argyle	807	1	1	0
Ashland	7,804	40	19	21
Ashwaubenon	17,183	57	52	5
Athens	1,075	1	1	0
Bangor	1,452	3	3	0
Baraboo	12,175	34	29	5
Barneveld	1,253	1	1	0
Barron	3,308	6	6	0
Bayfield	470	3	3	0
Bayside	4,322	13	13	0
Beaver Dam	16,426	36	32	4
Belleville	2,473	7	6	1
Beloit	36,921	79	69	10
Beloit Town	7,741	14	12	2
Berlin	5,369	11	10	1
Big Bend	1,487	3	3	0
Birchwood	426	1	1	0
Black River Falls	3,449	6	5	1
Blair	1,340	2	2	0
Blanchardville	787	1	1	0
Bloomer	3,500	8	7	1
Bloomfield	6,363	8	8	0
Blue Mounds	1,001	1	1	0
Boscobel	3,118	6	6	0
Boyceville	1,131	2	2	0
Brillion	3,067	8	8	0
Brodhead	3,242	12	8	4
Brookfield	39,252	101	85	16
Brookfield Township	6,564	15	14	1
Brown Deer	11,808	33	30	3
Brownsville	584	1	1	0
Burlington	11,025	23	22	1
Butler	1,793	9	8	1
Caledonia	25,323	37	35	2
Campbellsport	1,807	2	2	0
Campbell Township	4,296	5	5	0
Cashton	1,113	1	1	0
Cedarburg	11,621	28	20	8
Chenequa	606	10	8	2
Chetek	2,083	5	4	1
Chilton	3,851	16	8	8
Chippewa Falls	14,437	27	23	4
Cleveland	1,450	2	2	0
Clinton	2,139	10	5	5
Clintonville	4,372	15	11	4
Colby-Abbotsford	4,185	9	8	1
Colfax	1,157	2	2	0
Columbus	5,134	11	9	2
Cornell	1,401	3	3	0
Cottage Grove	7,233	15	13	2
Crandon	1,787	4	3	1
Cross Plains	4,362	7	6	1
Cuba City	2,023	4	4	0
Cudahy	18,064	42	32	10
Cumberland	2,096	7	7	0
Darlington	2,325	10	5	5

State/city	Population	Total law enforcement employees	Total officers	Total civilians
Deforest	10,901	21	18	3
Delavan	9,836	25	23	2
Delavan Town	5,337	13	12	1
Durand	1,786	4	4	0
Eagle River	1,615	7	6	1
Eagle Village	2,177	2	2	0
East Troy	4,313	8	8	0
Eau Claire	69,086	128	91	37
Edgar	1,438	1	1	0
Edgerton	5,655	11	10	1
Eleva	664	1	1	0
Elkhart Lake	1,022	3	3	0
Elkhorn	10,014	17	15	2
Elk Mound	882	2	1	1
Ellsworth	3,320	10	5	5
Elm Grove	6,160	23	16	7
Elroy	1,289	3	3	0
Evansville	5,489	11	10	1
Everest Metropolitan	17,361	33	29	4
Fall Creek	1,286	2	2	0
Fall River	1,744	2	2	0
Fennimore	2,449	12	6	6
Fitchburg	31,483	64	52	12
Fond du Lac	43,295	78	69	9
Fontana	1,747	8	7	1
Fort Atkinson	12,425	26	20	6
Fox Lake	1,442	4	3	1
Fox Point	6,522	18	17	1
Fox Valley Metro	22,737	28	26	2
Franklin	35,814	76	59	17
Frederic	1,084	2	2	0
Galesville	1,606	4	4	0
Geneva Town	5,045	8	7	1
Genoa City	2,978	7	6	1
Germantown	20,133	40	32	8
Gillett	1,285	3	3	0
Gilman	390	1	1	0
Glendale	12,714	46	40	6
Grafton	11,738	27	21	6
Grand Chute	23,579	39	33	6
Grand Rapids	7,393	8	6	2
Grantsburg	1,275	3	3	0
Green Bay	104,649	219	181	38
Greendale	14,141	38	29	9
Greenfield	37,237	79	60	19
Green Lake	968	6	3	3
Hales Corners	7,548	17	16	1
Hammond	1,882	4	3	1
Hartford	15,573	31	27	4
Hartford Township	3,561	1	1	0
Hartland	9,343	19	17	2
Hazel Green	1,216	2	2	0
Highland	825	1	1	0
Hobart-Lawrence	16,178	13	12	1
Holmen	10,135	14	13	1
Horicon	3,644	8	7	1
Hortonville	2,936	7	6	1
Hudson	14,255	31	28	3
Hurley	1,425	7	6	1
Independence	1,299	3	3	0
Iron Ridge	887	1	1	0
Iron River	1,135	3	3	0
Jackson	7,247	12	11	1
Janesville	64,682	114	103	11
Jefferson	7,986	17	14	3
Juneau	2,653	5	4	1
Kaukauna	16,357	27	26	1
Kenosha	100,005	212	199	13
Kewaskum	4,290	8	8	0
Kewaunee	2,838	6	6	0
Kiel	3,805	8	7	1
Kohler	2,053	9	8	1

(Number.)

State/city	Population	Total law enforcement employees	Total officers	Total civilians
Kronenwetter	8,181	9	8	1
La Crosse	51,211	119	99	20
Ladysmith	3,097	8	8	0
La Farge	761	1	1	0
Lake Delton	2,994	46	21	25
Lake Geneva	8,157	34	25	9
Lake Hallie	6,777	11	10	1
Lake Mills	6,013	12	10	2
Lancaster	3,682	6	6	0
Lena	537	1	1	0
Linn Township	2,405	6	6	0
Lodi	3,096	13	6	7
Lomira	2,453	5	4	1
Luxemburg	2,576	1	1	0
Madison	262,736	617	505	112
Manawa	1,262	3	3	0
Manitowoc	32,458	73	63	10
Maple Bluff	1,310	5	5	0
Marathon City	1,505	3	3	0
Marinette	10,497	28	24	4
Marion	1,170	4	4	0
Markesan	1,394	4	4	0
Marshall Village	3,998	10	9	1
Marshfield	18,403	47	39	8
Mauston	4,348	10	9	1
Mayville	4,862	9	8	1
McFarland	9,161	19	17	2
Medford	4,274	10	9	1
Menasha	17,910	38	31	7
Menomonee Falls	38,290	131	59	72
Menomonie	16,582	31	26	5
Mequon	24,527	49	38	11
Merrill	8,984	25	22	3
Middleton	20,322	48	38	10
Milton	5,636	13	11	2
Milwaukee	589,105	2,190	1,752	438
Mineral Point	2,461	6	6	0
Minocqua	4,422	15	10	5
Mishicot	1,383	3	3	0
Mondovi	2,542	4	4	0
Monona	8,245	26	21	5
Monroe	10,538	32	25	7
Montello	1,464	3	2	1
Monticello	1,200	3	3	0
Mosinee	4,080	8	7	1
Mount Horeb	7,579	13	13	0
Mount Pleasant	27,125	61	55	6
Mukwonago	8,137	22	15	7
Mukwonago Town	8,168	7	6	1
Muscoda	1,234	3	3	0
Muskego	25,237	44	34	10
Neenah	26,390	50	40	10
Neillsville	2,403	6	5	1
Nekoosa	2,405	7	7	0
New Berlin	39,703	80	66	14
New Glarus	2,148	4	4	0
New Holstein	3,088	7	6	1
New Lisbon	2,546	4	4	0
New London	7,070	19	17	2
New Richmond	9,535	19	18	1
Niagara	1,535	3	3	0
North Fond du Lac	5,089	11	9	2
North Hudson	3,815	6	5	1
Norwalk	630	1	1	0
Oak Creek	36,502	116	61	55
Oconomowoc	17,116	30	23	7
Oconomowoc Town	8,743	12	11	1
Oconto	4,548	9	9	0
Oconto Falls	2,785	6	6	0
Omro	3,590	8	7	1
Onalaska	19,072	30	28	2
Oregon	10,718	21	18	3

State/city	Population	Total law enforcement employees	Total officers	Total civilians
Osceola	2,556	6	5	1
Oshkosh	67,080	108	94	14
Osseo	1,673	4	4	0
Palmyra	1,753	6	6	0
Park Falls	2,207	6	6	0
Pepin	775	1	1	0
Peshtigo	3,329	6	6	0
Pewaukee Village	8,102	19	18	1
Phillips	1,322	5	5	0
Pittsville	819	2	2	0
Plainfield	833	1	1	0
Platteville	12,184	28	20	8
Pleasant Prairie	21,181	43	33	10
Plover	13,201	23	20	3
Plymouth	8,762	16	16	0
Portage	10,408	26	22	4
Port Edwards	1,757	3	3	0
Port Washington	11,982	24	19	5
Poynette	2,507	5	4	1
Prairie du Chien	5,539	13	12	1
Prescott	4,299	11	10	1
Pulaski	3,742	9	8	1
Racine	76,573	216	185	31
Reedsburg	9,549	28	22	6
Rhinelander	7,629	17	15	2
Rice Lake	8,526	18	18	0
Richland Center	4,918	13	11	2
Rio	1,038	4	2	2
Ripon	7,854	20	14	6
Ripon Town	1,380	1	1	0
River Falls	16,141	26	23	3
River Hills	1,571	11	11	0
Rome Town	2,755	7	7	0
Rosendale	1,028	1	1	0
Rothschild	5,268	14	12	2
Sauk Prairie	4,650	17	15	2
Saukville	4,431	14	12	2
Seymour	3,454	6	6	0
Sharon	1,552	5	4	1
Shawano	8,896	22	20	2
Sheboygan	47,814	101	82	19
Sheboygan Falls	7,938	17	15	2
Shiocton	912	3	2	1
Shorewood	13,133	28	24	4
Shorewood Hills	2,058	9	7	2
Shullsburg	1,188	1	1	0
Siren	771	4	3	1
Slinger	5,621	13	12	1
Somerset	2,951	6	5	1
South Milwaukee	20,626	39	33	6
Sparta	9,865	23	21	2
Spencer	1,874	4	4	0
Spooner	2,557	8	7	1
Spring Green	1,643	2	2	0
Spring Valley	1,348	2	2	0
Stanley	3,722	5	5	0
St. Croix Falls	2,037	7	6	1
Stevens Point	25,790	48	44	4
St. Francis	9,733	22	21	1
Stoughton	13,164	29	23	6
Strum	1,087	2	2	0
Sturgeon Bay	8,913	24	22	2
Sturtevant	6,659	13	12	1
Summit	5,087	11	11	0
Sun Prairie	35,272	76	55	21
Superior	25,845	59	54	5
Theresa	1,199	4	2	2
Thiensville	3,116	8	7	1
Thorp	1,610	3	3	0
Three Lakes	2,112	5	5	0
Tomah	9,418	22	20	2
Tomahawk	3,111	9	8	1

(Number.)

State/city	Population	Total law enforcement employees	Total officers	Total civilians
Town of East Troy	4,060	7	6	1
Town of Madison	6,920	14	13	1
Trempealeau	1,680	3	3	0
Twin Lakes	6,230	18	13	5
Two Rivers	10,970	28	25	3
Verona	13,548	27	25	2
Viroqua	4,407	11	9	2
Walworth	2,828	19	18	1
Washburn	2,028	5	5	0
Waterford Town	6,526	14	7	7
Waterloo	3,332	7	6	1
Watertown	23,437	54	40	14
Waukesha	72,421	154	122	32
Waunakee	14,280	23	21	2
Waupaca	5,953	26	25	1
Waupun	11,184	18	16	2
Wausau	38,492	86	77	9
Wautoma	2,135	10	5	5
Wauwatosa	48,265	118	94	24
Webster	616	15	15	0
West Allis	59,778	153	121	32
West Bend	31,603	67	50	17
Westby	2,259	4	4	0
Westfield	1,268	2	2	0
West Milwaukee	4,081	25	20	5
West Salem	5,037	10	9	1
Whitefish Bay	13,734	23	22	1
Whitehall	1,570	4	4	0
Whitewater	14,952	34	24	10
Wild Rose	680	4	2	2
Williams Bay	2,646	8	7	1
Wind Point	1,692	1	1	0
Winneconne	2,497	6	5	1
Wisconsin Dells	3,025	20	15	5
Wisconsin Rapids	17,524	41	37	4
Woodruff	1,975	6	5	1
WYOMING				
Afton	2,055	4	4	0
Buffalo	4,573	19	10	9
Casper	58,244	154	99	55
Cheyenne	64,751	122	103	19
Cody	9,816	25	22	3
Diamondville	759	2	2	0
Douglas	6,394	17	14	3
Evanston	11,563	32	27	5
Evansville	3,005	11	9	2
Gillette	32,093	81	53	28
Glenrock	2,568	13	7	6
Green River	11,691	30	25	5
Greybull	1,837	6	5	1
Hanna	762	2	2	0
Jackson	10,668	32	26	6
Kemmerer	2,760	6	6	0
Lander	7,441	19	17	2
Laramie	32,913	69	44	25
Lusk	1,521	6	6	0
Mills	4,040	20	15	5
Moorcroft	1,092	4	3	1
Newcastle	3,383	17	8	9
Pine Bluffs	1,158	2	2	0
Powell	6,165	22	16	6
Rawlins	8,434	25	14	11
Riverton	10,772	42	30	12
Rock Springs	22,615	44	36	8
Saratoga	1,607	7	4	3
Sheridan	17,991	43	26	17
Thermopolis	2,738	12	7	5
Torrington	6,623	24	17	7
Wheatland	3,445	10	9	1
Worland	4,975	12	12	0

[1] The employee data presented in this table for Charlotte-Mecklenburg represent only Charlotte-Mecklenburg Police Department and exclude Mecklenburg County Sheriff's Office.

Table 20. Murder Victims, by Race, Ethnicity, and Sex, 2020

(Number.)

Race	Total	Sex		
		Male	Female	Unknown
Total	17,754	14,146	3,573	35
White	7,029	5,123	1,904	2
Black...	9,913	8,469	1,440	4
Other race	497	340	157	0
Unknown race	315	214	72	29
Hispanic or Latino[1]........................	2,847	2,377	470	0
Not Hispanic or Latino[1]	11,347	8,993	2,350	4
Unknown[1]......................................	1,985	1,581	379	25

[1]Not all agencies provide ethnicity data, therefore the race and ethnicity totals will not equal.

Table 20A. Murder Victims, by Age, Sex, Race, and Ethnicity, 2020

(Number; percent; single victim/single offender.)

Age	Total	Sex			Race				Ethnicity		
		Male	Female	Unknown	White	Black or African American	Other[1]	Unknown	Hispanic/ Latino	Not Hispanic/ Latino	Unknown
Total	17,754	14,146	3,573	35	7,029	9,913	497	315	2,847	11,347	1,985
Percent distribution[2]	1.0	0.8	0.2	0.0	0.4	0.6	0.0	0.0	0.2	0.7	0.1
Under 18[3]..........................	1,472	1,092	378	2	591	807	34	40	275	882	167
Under 22[3]..........................	3,701	3,004	693	4	1,289	2,276	64	72	685	2,262	429
18 and over[3]......................	16,146	12,966	3,160	20	6,397	9,045	459	245	2,559	10,396	1,777
Infant (under 1).................	137	87	49	1	64	63	4	6	18	84	21
1 to 4	239	132	107	0	104	118	11	6	39	144	28
5 to 8	115	59	56	0	55	51	6	3	12	80	12
9 to 12	115	85	30	0	59	48	6	2	18	73	15
13 to 16	484	401	83	0	176	289	5	14	107	284	46
17 to 19	1,474	1,271	200	3	497	937	14	26	294	876	176
20 to 24	2,858	2,421	437	0	855	1,894	68	41	487	1,811	336
25 to 29	2,836	2,395	439	2	844	1,896	69	27	424	1,873	291
30 to 34	2,334	1,946	386	2	840	1,392	70	32	382	1,492	250
35 to 39	1,894	1,523	370	1	805	992	67	30	337	1,231	204
40 to 44	1,320	1,055	265	0	612	659	34	15	237	820	149
45 to 49	980	736	241	3	470	456	33	21	169	610	110
50 to 54	782	566	209	7	392	343	27	20	111	515	73
55 to 59	724	528	196	0	388	300	26	10	79	480	80
60 to 64	521	377	144	0	297	190	22	12	51	364	59
65 to 69	337	224	113	0	202	116	11	8	33	224	41
70 to 74	194	118	76	0	129	52	8	5	19	123	26
75 and over	274	134	137	3	199	56	12	7	17	194	27
Unknown...........................	136	88	35	13	41	61	4	30	13	69	41

[1]Includes American Indian or Alaska Native, Asian, Native Hawaiian or Other Pacific Islander.
[2]Because of rounding, the percentages may not add to 100.0.
[3]Does not include unknown ages.

Table 21. Murder Offenders, by Age, Sex, Race, and Ethnicity, 2020

(Number; percent; single victim/single offender.)

Age	Total	Sex			Race				Ethnicity[1]		
		Male	Female	Unknown	White	Black or African American	Other[2]	Unknown	Hispanic/ Latino	Not Hispanic/ Latino	Unknown
Total	20,982	13,023	1,735	6,224	5,844	8,142	404	6,592	1,991	7,964	11,005
Percent distribution[3]	1.0	0.6	0.1	0.3	0.3	0.4	0.0	0.3	0.1	0.4	0.5
Under 18[4]..............................	1,119	1,028	89	2	408	668	24	19	210	567	342
Under 22[4]..............................	3,877	3,493	352	32	1,309	2,405	80	83	618	2,052	1,207
18 and over[4]...........................	12,919	11,184	1,614	121	5,332	6,900	376	311	1,739	7,069	4,090
Infant (under 1).............................	0	0	0	0	0	0	0	0	0	0	0
1 to 4	1	0	0	1	0	0	0	1	0	0	1
5 to 8	4	3	1	0	0	4	0	0	0	3	1
9 to 12	18	15	3	0	7	9	2	0	1	7	10
13 to 16	604	559	45	0	218	363	11	12	119	307	178
17 to 19	1,836	1,678	150	8	621	1,146	43	26	306	981	549
20 to 24	3,025	2,652	348	25	1,001	1,880	66	78	433	1,653	939
25 to 29	2,575	2,241	319	15	905	1,525	90	55	347	1,412	812
30 to 34	1,789	1,526	245	18	768	921	59	41	265	949	570
35 to 39	1,337	1,119	208	10	661	608	41	27	200	734	400
40 to 44	935	800	133	2	461	427	29	18	118	497	318
45 to 49	534	446	79	9	282	221	18	13	63	312	158
50 to 54	452	378	67	7	244	182	10	16	42	249	160
55 to 59	407	348	38	21	220	145	16	26	27	219	161
60 to 64	234	195	39	0	152	74	7	1	15	147	70
65 to 69	120	107	13	0	80	34	2	4	5	72	41
70 to 74	61	53	8	0	43	15	3	0	6	38	16
75 and over	106	92	7	7	77	14	3	12	2	56	48
Unknown....................................	6,944	811	32	6,101	104	574	4	6,262	42	328	6,573

[1] Not all agencies provide ethnicity data, therefore the race and ethnicity totals will not equal.
[2] Includes American Indian or Alaska Native, Asian, Native Hawaiian or Other Pacific Islander.
[3] Because of rounding, the percentages may not add to 100.0.
[4] Does not include unknown ages.

Table 22. Murder, by Victim/Offender Situations, 2020

(Number; percent.)

Situation	Total	Percent distribution (may not add to 100.0 due to rounding)
Total	17,754	100.0
Single victim/single offender	8,608	48.5
Single victim/unknown offender or offenders......................	4,651	26.2
Single victim/multiple offenders	2,465	13.9
Multiple victims/single offender......................	1,205	6.8
Multiple victims/multiple offenders......................	383	2.2
Multiple victims/unknown offender or offenders........................	442	2.5

Table 23. Murder Age of Victim, by Age of Offender, 2020

(Number; single victim/single offender.)

Age of victim	Total	Age of offender		
		Under 18 years	18 years and over	Unknown
Total	7,869	346	7,176	347
Under 18	586	106	450	30
18 and over	7,233	237	6,682	314
Unknown	50	3	44	3

Note: This table is based on incidents where some information about the offender is known by law enforcement; therefore, when the offender age, sex, and race are all reported as unknown, these data are excluded from the table.

Table 24. Murder, Race, Ethnicity, and Sex of Victim by Race, Ethnicity, and Sex of Offender, 2020

(Number; single victim/single offender.)

Victim characteristic	Total	Sex			Race				Ethnicity		
		Male	Female	Unknown	White	Black or African American	Other[1]	Unknown	Hispanic/ Latino	Not Hispanic/ Latino	Unknown
Race											
White	3,709	2,904	664	53	88	3,325	355	29	931	1,723	1,055
Black or African American	3,740	354	3,210	25	151	3,311	341	88	140	2,431	1,169
Other race1	288	71	36	174	7	234	53	1	17	187	84
Unknown	138	71	28	8	31	126	7	5	28	40	70
Sex											
Male	5,830	2,348	3,077	176	229	5,156	566	108	869	3,217	1,744
Female	2,035	1,050	857	83	45	1,835	188	12	247	1,160	628
Unknown	10	2	4	1	3	5	2	3	0	4	6
Ethnicity											
Hispanic or Latino	1,206	934	221	13	38	1,119	73	14	746	276	184
Not Hispanic or Latino	5,038	1,869	2,857	182	130	4,458	508	72	285	3,834	919
Unknown	1,631	597	860	65	109	1,419	175	37	85	271	1,275

NOTE: This table is based on incidents where some information about the offender is known by law enforcement; therefore, when the offender age, sex, race, and ethnicity are all reported as unknown, these data are excluded from the table.
[1]Includes American Indian or Alaska Native, Asian, Native Hawaiian or Other Pacific Islander.

Table 25. Murder Victims, by Weapons, 2016–2020

(Number.)

Weapons	2016	2017	2018	2019	2020
Total	15,367	15,220	14,486	14,391	17,754
Total firearms	10,403	11,020	10,484	10,537	13,620
Handguns	6,783	7,054	6,699	6,543	8,017
Rifles	300	389	304	375	454
Shotguns	247	263	238	215	203
Other guns	172	178	164	51	112
Firearms, type not stated	2,901	3,136	3,079	3,353	4,834
Knives or cutting instruments	1,562	1,605	1,539	1,525	1,732
Blunt objects (clubs, hammers, etc.)	466	476	454	413	392
Personal weapons (hands, fists, feet, etc.)[1]	670	717	715	639	657
Poison	12	15	6	16	16
Explosives	1	0	4	2	4
Fire	78	93	78	85	106
Narcotics	119	114	101	108	113
Drowning	9	8	9	7	5
Strangulation	97	90	75	66	58
Asphyxiation	93	112	93	94	71
Other weapons or weapons not stated	1,857	970	928	899	980

NOTE: The Uniform Crime Reporting Technical Refresh enables updating of prior years' crime data; therefore, data presented in this table may not match previously published data.
[1]Pushed is included in personal weapons.

Table 26. Murder, Types of Weapon,[1] by Region, 2020

(Number.)

Region	All weapons[2]	Firearms	Knives or cutting instruments	Unknown or other dangerous weapons	Personal weapons (hands, feet, fists, etc.)[3]
Total	100.0	76.7	9.8	9.8	3.7
Northeast..........................	100.0	70.3	15.9	8.9	4.9
Midwest............................	100.0	79.4	7.6	10.0	3.1
South...............................	100.0	80.4	7.7	8.7	3.2
West.................................	100.0	69.4	13.4	12.3	4.9

[1]Guam and U.S. Virgin Islands totals are not included in this table.
[2]Because of rounding, the percentages may not add to 100.0.
[3]Pushed is included in personal weapons.

Table 27. Justifiable Homicide by Weapon, Law Enforcement,[1] 2016–2020

(Number.)

Year	Total	Total firearms	Handguns	Rifles	Shotguns	Firearms, type not stated	Knives or cutting instruments	Other dangerous weapons	Personal weapons
2016........................	440	432	313	51	5	63	2	5	1
2017........................	445	437	284	57	2	94	3	4	1
2018........................	425	421	288	54	4	75	1	2	1
2019........................	362	355	260	34	3	58	2	3	2
2020........................	303	298	207	33	2	56	1	4	0

NOTE: The Uniform Crime Reporting Technical Refresh enables updating of prior years' crime data; therefore, data presented in this table may not match previously published data.
[1]The killing of a felon by a law enforcement officer in the line of duty.

Table 28. Justifiable Homicide by Weapon, Private Citizen,[1] 2016–2020

(Number.)

Year	Total	Total firearms	Handguns	Rifles	Shotguns	Firearms, type not stated	Knives or cutting instruments	Other dangerous weapons	Personal weapons
2016........................	334	278	201	11	9	57	34	8	14
2017........................	370	314	238	7	8	61	36	8	12
2018........................	375	317	229	6	10	72	33	13	12
2019........................	414	359	253	17	9	80	33	9	13
2020........................	405	343	250	13	12	68	45	7	10

NOTE: The Uniform Crime Reporting Technical Refresh enables updating of prior years' crime data; therefore, data presented in this table may not match previously published data.
[1]The killing of a felon, during the commission of a felony, by a private citizen.

Table 29. Robbery, Types of Weapons Used, Percent Distribution by Region, 2020

(Percent.)

Region	Total all weapons[1]	Armed			Strong- arm
		Firearms	Knives or cutting instruments	Other weapons	
Total	100.0	37.3	9.1	11.1	42.6
Northeast..........................	100.0	23.0	14.2	10.8	52.0
Midwest	100.0	43.6	5.8	9.7	40.9
South	100.0	49.4	7.3	9.4	33.9
West.................................	100.0	27.6	10.2	13.6	48.5

[1]Because of rounding, the percentages may not add to 100.0.

Table 30. Aggravated Assault, Types of Weapons Used, Percent Distribution by Region, 2020

(Percent.)

Region	Total all weapons[1]	Firearms	Knives or cutting instruments	Other weapons (clubs, blunt objects, etc.)	Personal weapons (hands, fists, feet, etc.)
Total	100.0	34.9	16.4	28.5	20.2
Northeast..	100.0	16.4	24.6	31.9	27.1
Midwest	100.0	38.3	14.0	27.2	20.5
South...	100.0	44.5	15.4	26.4	13.8
West..	100.0	25.2	16.3	31.2	27.3

[1]Because of rounding, the percentages may not add to 100.0.

Table 31. Larceny-Theft, Percent Distribution by Region, 2020

(Percent.)

Region	Larceny theft								
	Total (may not sum to 100.0 due to rounding)	Pocket-picking	Purse-snatching	Shoplifting	From motor vehicles (except accessories)	Motor vehicle accessories	Bicycles	From buildings	From coin-operated machines	All others
Total	100.0	0.4	0.3	20.8	27.8	8.6	3.5	8.4	0.2	30.1
Northeast................................	100.0	0.7	0.3	24.9	21.2	6.4	5.1	15.2	0.1	26.1
Midwest	100.0	0.5	0.4	22.0	22.2	8.3	2.6	9.8	0.2	34.1
South......................................	100.0	0.4	0.2	21.7	28.0	7.7	2.5	6.7	0.2	32.5
West.......................................	100.0	0.4	0.4	17.4	32.7	10.6	4.7	7.6	0.2	25.9

Table 32. Motor Vehicle Theft, Percent Distribution by Region, 2020

(Percent.)

Region	Motor vehicle theft			
	Total (may not sum to 100.0 due to rounding)	Autos	Trucks and buses	Other vehicles
Total	100.0	74.0	16.9	9.1
Northeast.......................................	100.0	86.5	3.4	10.1
Midwest	100.0	83.9	8.4	7.7
South...	100.0	70.7	18.9	10.4
West..	100.0	71.0	20.5	8.5

Table 33. Arson Rate, by Population Group, 2020

(Number; rate; 11,862 agencies; 2020 estimated population 257,801,745; rate per 100,000 inhabitants.)

Population group	Rate
Total, All Agencies..	15.3
Total, cities..	17.8
Group I (250,000 and over)..	29.6
1,000,000 and over	30.0
500,000 to 999,999	30.8
250,000 to 499,999	28.2
Group II (100,000 to 249,999)	17.1
Group III (50,000 to 99,999)	12.6
Group IV (25,000 to 49,999)...	11.3
Group V (10,000 to 24,999)	10.9
Group VI (Under 10,000)	15.1
Metropolitan counties..	9.3
Nonmetropolitan counties..	11.1
Suburban areas[1]...	9.5

[1]Suburban areas include law enforcement agencies in cities with less than 50,000 inhabitants and county law enforcement agencies that are within a Metropolitan Statistical Area. Suburban areas exclude all metropolitan agencies associated with a principal city. The agencies associated with suburban areas also appear in other groups within this table.

Table 34. Arson, by Type of Property, 2020

(Number; percent, dollars; 14,055 agencies; 2020 estimated population 284,773,056.)

Property classification	Number of arson offenses	Percent distribution[1]	Percent not in use	Average damage	Total clearances	Percent of arsons cleared[2]	Percent of clearances under 18
Total	39,851	100.0	4.1	$30,537	8,418	21.1	11.5
Total structure	15,079	37.8	11.0	$72,403	3,865	25.6	12.6
Single occupancy residential	6,030	15.1	10.0	$30,773	1,459	24.2	10.8
Other residential	2,601	6.5	5.4	$54,755	807	31.0	9.8
Storage	851	2.1	11.6	$17,079	167	19.6	16.2
Industrial/manufacturing	164	0.4	24.4	$114,881	46	28.0	15.2
Other commercial	2,149	5.4	15.5	$70,886	554	25.8	7.0
Community/public	1,275	3.2	18.1	$433,164	391	30.7	26.3
Other structure	2,009	5.0	10.2	$12,841	441	22.0	16.8
Total mobile	9,523	23.9	0.0	$9,309	1,013	10.6	6.6
Motor vehicles	8,898	22.3	0.0	$8,925	908	10.2	6.3
Other mobile	625	1.6	0.0	$14,780	105	16.8	9.5
Other	15,249	38.3	0.0	$2,395	3,540	23.2	11.8

[1]Because of rounding, the percentages may not add to 100.0.
[2]Includes arsons cleared by arrest or exceptional means.

Table 35. Offenses Known to Law Enforcement, by Selected Federal Agency, 2020

(Number.)

Agency and unit/office	Violent crime	Murder and nonnegligent manslaughter	Rape	Robbery	Aggravated assault	Property crime	Burglary	Larceny- theft	Motor vehicle theft	Arson
Board of Governors of the Federal Reserve System and the Consumer Financial Protection Bureau, Office of Inspector General	0	0	0	0	0	0	0	0	0	0
Corporation for National and Community Service, Office of Inspector General	0	0	0	0	0	0	0	0	0	0
Export-Import Bank of the United States, Office of Inspector General	0	0	0	0	0	0	0	0	0	0
Federal Emergency Management Agency	0	0	0	0	0	0	0	0	0	0
National Institue of Health	0	0	0	0	0	54	12	42	0	0
National Security Agency Police	0	0	0	0	0	0	0	0	0	0
Peace Corps, Office of Inspector General	0	0	0	0	0	0	0	0	0	0
Tennessee Valley Authority, Office of Inspector General	0	0	0	0	0	2	0	2	0	0
United States Agency for International Development, Office of Inspector General	0	0	0	0	0	2	0	2	0	0
United States Department of Agriculture, Office of Inspector General	0	0	0	0	0	0	0	0	0	0
United States Department of Defense										
Defense Intelligence Agency	0	0	0	0	0	2	0	2	0	0
Pentagon Force Protection Agency	1	1	0	0	0	31	0	30	0	1
United States Department of Education, Office of Inspector General	0	0	0	0	0	0	0	0	0	0
United States Department of the Interior										
Bureau of Indian Affairs[1]										
Bureau of Land Management	24	0	0	1	23	511	3	455	31	22
Bureau of Reclamation	0	0	0	0	0	1	0	1	0	0
Fish and Wildlife Service	13	5	1	0	7	119	30	63	7	19
National Park Service	208	16	75	12	105	3,231	325	2,572	308	26
United States Department of Justice, Office of Inspector General	3	0	3	0	0	5	0	5	0	0
United States Election Assistance Commission, Office of Inspector General	0	0	0	0	0	0	0	0	0	0
United States Environmental Protection Agency, Office of Inspector General	0	0	0	0	0	0	0	0	0	0
United States Federal Deposit Insurance Corporation, Office of Inspector General	0	0	0	0	0	2	0	2	0	0
United States Nuclear Regulatory Commission, Office of Inspector General	0	0	0	0	0	0	0	0	0	0

[1]The Bureau of Indian Affairs submits these statistics to the FBI Uniform Crime Reporting Program on a monthly basis throughout the calendar year and can be found in Table 11 of *Crime in the United States, 2020.*

Table 36. Full-Time Law Enforcement Employees, by Selected Federal Agency, 2020

(Number.)

Agency and unit/office	Total law enforcement employees	Total officers	Total civilians
National Institutes of Health	100	72	28
United States Dept. of the Interior			
Bureau of Land Management	282	266	16
Bureau of Reclamation	130	130	0
Fish and Wildlife Service	3,335	3,335	0
National Park Service	2,700	2,642	58

Table 37. Human Trafficking, Offenses and Clearances by Participating State, 2020

(Number.)

State	Commercial sex acts			Involuntary servitude			Total		
	Offenses	Total cleared	Clearances under 18	Offenses	Total cleared	Clearances under 18	Offenses	Total cleared	Clearances under 18
Alabama	0	0	0	0	0	0	0	0	0
Alaska	3	1	0	1	0	0	4	1	0
Arizona	28	15	0	0	0	0	28	15	0
Arkansas	1	0	0	1	0	0	2	0	0
California[1]	0	0	0	0	0	0	0	0	0
Colorado	29	8	0	1	0	0	30	8	0
Connecticut	9	3	0	1	0	0	10	3	0
Delaware	4	3	0	2	0	0	6	3	0
Florida	134	46	2	3	0	0	137	46	2
Georgia	180	52	0	34	12	0	214	64	0
Hawaii	0	0	0	0	0	0	0	0	0
Idaho	1	0	0	1	0	0	2	0	0
Illinois	14	0	0	9	0	0	23	0	0
Indiana	32	2	1	8	0	0	40	2	1
Kansas[1]	0	0	0	0	0	0	0	0	0
Kentucky	17	7	1	2	7	0	19	14	1
Louisiana	9	6	0	3	3	0	12	9	0
Maine	3	1	0	0	0	0	3	1	0
Maryland	14	10	0	1	0	0	15	10	0
Massachusetts	23	5	0	5	1	0	28	6	0
Michigan	44	25	0	5	1	0	49	26	0
Minnesota	79	17	0	12	1	0	91	18	0
Mississippi	0	0	0	0	0	0	0	0	0
Missouri	37	14	0	3	2	0	40	16	0
Montana	4	1	0	0	0	0	4	1	0
Nebraska	0	2	0	1	0	0	1	2	0
Nevada	198	119	1	5	3	0	203	122	1
New Hampshire	4	1	0	3	0	0	7	1	0
New Jersey	7	6	1	1	1	0	8	7	1
New Mexico	2	1	0	2	0	0	4	1	0
New York	0	0	0	0	0	0	0	0	0
North Carolina	23	7	1	33	7	0	56	14	1
North Dakota	9	1	0	2	1	0	11	2	0
Ohio	15	2	0	2	0	0	17	2	0
Oklahoma	15	11	0	3	1	0	18	12	0
Oregon	22	10	0	2	0	0	24	10	0
Pennsylvania	5	0	0	2	2	0	7	2	0
Puerto Rico	0	0	0	0	0	0	1	0	0
Rhode Island	3	0	0	0	0	0	3	0	0
South Carolina	17	5	0	6	0	0	23	5	0
South Dakota	2	0	0	0	0	0	2	0	0
Tennessee	38	13	0	2	0	0	40	13	0
Texas	352	106	5	132	95	8	484	201	13
Utah	58	43	0	8	0	0	66	43	0
Vermont	1	0	0	0	0	0	1	0	0
Virginia	46	26	0	14	10	0	60	36	0
Washington	63	30	0	15	1	0	78	31	0
West Virginia	59	20	1	0	0	0	59	20	1
Wisconsin	87	31	0	4	4	0	91	35	0
Wyoming	2	2	0	0	0	0	2	2	0

[1]Data submitted through the Bureau of Indian Affairs.

Table 38. Human Trafficking Arrests, by Age and Participating State, 2020

(Number.)

State	Juvenile		Adult	
	Male	Female	Male	Female
Arizona				
Commercial sex acts	0	0	1	0
Involuntary servitude..........................	0	0	0	0
Colorado				
Commercial sex acts	0	0	4	1
Involuntary servitude..........................	0	0	0	0
Connecticut				
Commercial sex acts	0	0	1	0
Involuntary servitude..........................	0	0	0	0
Georgia				
Commercial sex acts	2	1	31	2
Involuntary servitude..........................	0	0	1	0
Indiana				
Commercial sex acts	0	1	0	0
Involuntary servitude..........................	0	0	3	1
Kentucky				
Commercial sex acts	0	0	1	0
Involuntary servitude..........................	0	0	2	0
Louisiana				
Commercial sex acts	0	0	3	1
Involuntary servitude..........................	1	3	3	1
Maine				
Commercial sex acts	0	0	0	1
Involuntary servitude..........................	0	0	0	0
Maryland				
Commercial sex acts	0	0	6	1
Involuntary servitude..........................	0	0	0	0
Massachusetts				
Commercial sex acts	0	0	1	2
Involuntary servitude..........................	0	0	1	1
Michigan				
Commercial sex acts	0	0	18	1
Involuntary servitude..........................	0	0	0	0
Minnesota				
Commercial sex acts	0	0	13	1
Involuntary servitude..........................	0	0	1	0
Missouri				
Commercial sex acts	0	0	3	0
Involuntary servitude..........................	0	0	0	0
Nebraska				
Commercial sex acts	0	0	2	0
Involuntary servitude..........................	0	0	0	0
Nevada				
Commercial sex acts	1	1	17	2
Involuntary servitude..........................	0	0	1	0
New Jersey				
Commercial sex acts	0	0	22	1
Involuntary servitude..........................	0	0	0	6
New Mexico				
Commercial sex acts	0	0	1	1
Involuntary servitude..........................	0	0	0	0
North Carolina				
Commercial sex acts	0	0	0	0
Involuntary servitude..........................	0	0	1	1

(Number.)

State	Juvenile		Adult	
	Male	Female	Male	Female
Ohio				
Commercial sex acts	0	0	4	4
Involuntary servitude...........................	0	0	0	0
Oklahoma				
Commercial sex acts	0	0	1	2
Involuntary servitude...........................	0	0	0	0
Pennsylvania				
Commercial sex acts	0	0	2	0
Involuntary servitude...........................	0	0	0	2
South Carolina				
Commercial sex acts	0	0	4	0
Involuntary servitude...........................	0	0	0	0
South Dakota				
Commercial sex acts	0	0	1	1
Involuntary servitude...........................	0	0	0	0
Tennessee				
Commercial sex acts	0	0	6	5
Involuntary servitude...........................	0	0	0	0
Texas				
Commercial sex acts	3	0	36	4
Involuntary servitude...........................	8	1	17	7
Utah				
Commercial sex acts	0	0	25	0
Involuntary servitude...........................	0	0	1	0
Virginia				
Commercial sex acts	0	0	8	1
Involuntary servitude...........................	0	0	2	0
Washington				
Commercial sex acts	0	0	15	0
Involuntary servitude...........................	0	0	1	0
West Virginia				
Commercial sex acts	0	0	13	0
Involuntary servitude...........................	0	0	0	0
Wisconsin				
Commercial sex acts	1	0	18	1
Involuntary servitude...........................	0	0	14	9
Wyoming				
Commercial sex acts	0	0	1	1
Involuntary servitude...........................	1	2	0	0

Table 39. Human Trafficking Arrests, by Race and Participating State, 2020

(Number.)

State	Juvenile						Adult					
	White	Black or African American	American Indian/ Alaska Native	Asian	Native Hawaiian/ Other Pacific Islander	Total	White	Black or African American	American Indian/ Alaska Native	Asian	Native Hawaiian/ Other Pacific Islander	Total
Arizona												
Commercial sex acts	0	0	0	0	0	0	1	0	0	0	0	1
Involuntary servitude	0	0	0	0	0	0	0	0	0	0	0	0
Colorado												
Commercial sex acts	0	0	0	0	0	0	3	2	0	0	0	5
Involuntary servitude	0	0	0	0	0	0	0	0	0	0	0	0
Connecticut												
Commercial sex acts	0	0	0	0	0	0	1	0	0	0	0	1
Involuntary servitude	0	0	0	0	0	0	0	0	0	0	0	0
Georgia												
Commercial sex acts	3	0	0	0	0	3	23	9	0	1	0	33
Involuntary servitude	0	0	0	0	0	0	0	1	0	0	0	1
Indiana												
Commercial sex acts	2	0	0	0	0	2	0	0	0	0	0	0
Involuntary servitude	0	0	0	0	0	0	4	0	0	0	0	4
Kentucky												
Commercial sex acts	0	0	0	0	0	0	1	0	0	0	0	1
Involuntary servitude	0	0	0	0	0	0	1	1	0	0	0	2
Louisiana												
Commercial sex acts	0	0	0	0	0	0	0	4	0	0	0	4
Involuntary servitude	0	4	0	0	0	4	1	3	0	0	0	4
Maine												
Commercial sex acts	0	0	0	0	0	0	1	0	0	0	0	1
Involuntary servitude	0	0	0	0	0	0	0	0	0	0	0	0
Maryland												
Commercial sex acts	0	0	0	0	0	0	1	6	0	0	0	7
Involuntary servitude	0	0	0	0	0	0	0	0	0	0	0	0
Massachusetts												
Commercial sex acts	0	0	0	0	0	0	2	0	0	1	0	3
Involuntary servitude	0	0	0	0	0	0	0	0	0	2	0	2
Michigan												
Commercial sex acts	0	0	0	0	0	0	10	6	0	0	0	16
Involuntary servitude	0	0	0	0	0	0	0	0	0	0	0	0
Minnesota												
Commercial sex acts	0	0	0	0	0	0	4	9	0	1	0	14
Involuntary servitude	0	0	0	0	0	0	0	1	0	0	0	1
Missouri												
Commercial sex acts	0	0	0	0	0	0	6	0	0	0	0	6
Involuntary servitude	0	0	0	0	0	0	0	0	0	0	0	0
Nebraska												
Commercial sex acts	0	0	0	0	0	0	1	1	0	0	0	2
Involuntary servitude	0	0	0	0	0	0	0	0	0	0	0	0
Nevada												
Commercial sex acts	1	1	0	0	0	2	5	14	0	0	0	19
Involuntary servitude	0	0	0	0	0	0	1	0	0	0	0	1
New Jersey												
Commercial sex acts	0	0	0	0	0	0	12	11	0	0	0	23
Involuntary servitude	0	0	0	0	0	0	5	1	0	0	0	6
New Mexico												
Commercial sex acts	0	0	0	0	0	0	0	2	0	0	0	2
Involuntary servitude	0	0	0	0	0	0	0	0	0	0	0	0

(Number.)

State	Juvenile						Adult					
	White	Black or African American	American Indian/ Alaska Native	Asian	Native Hawaiian/ Other Pacific Islander	Total	White	Black or African American	American Indian/ Alaska Native	Asian	Native Hawaiian/ Other Pacific Islander	Total
North Carolina												
Commercial sex acts	0	0	0	0	0	0	0	0	0	0	0	0
Involuntary servitude	0	0	0	0	0	0	1	1	0	0	0	2
Ohio												
Commercial sex acts	0	0	0	0	0	0	5	3	0	0	1	9
Involuntary servitude	0	0	0	0	0	0	0	0	0	0	0	0
Oklahoma												
Commercial sex acts	5	1	0	0	0	6	18	1	2	0	0	21
Involuntary servitude	0	0	0	0	0	0	0	0	0	0	0	0
Pennsylvania												
Commercial sex acts	0	0	0	0	0	0	1	1	0	0	0	2
Involuntary servitude	0	0	0	0	0	0	2	0	0	0	0	2
South Carolina												
Commercial sex acts	0	0	0	0	0	0	0	4	0	0	0	4
Involuntary servitude	0	0	0	0	0	0	0	0	0	0	0	0
South Dakota												
Commercial sex acts	0	0	0	0	0	0	0	0	2	0	0	2
Involuntary servitude	0	0	0	0	0	0	0	0	0	0	0	0
Tennessee												
Commercial sex acts	0	0	0	0	0	0	6	5	0	0	0	11
Involuntary servitude	0	0	0	0	0	0	0	0	0	0	0	0
Texas												
Commercial sex acts	2	1	0	0	0	3	23	17	0	0	0	40
Involuntary servitude	9	0	0	0	0	9	19	3	0	0	0	22
Utah												
Commercial sex acts	0	0	0	0	0	0	21	1	0	1	0	23
Involuntary servitude	0	0	0	0	0	0	0	1	0	0	0	1
Virginia												
Commercial sex acts	0	0	0	0	0	0	2	7	0	0	0	9
Involuntary servitude	0	0	0	0	0	0	0	1	0	1	0	2
Washington												
Commercial sex acts	0	0	0	0	0	0	6	7	0	1	0	14
Involuntary servitude	0	0	0	0	0	0	0	1	0	0	0	1
West Virginia												
Commercial sex acts	0	0	0	0	0	0	11	0	0	0	0	11
Involuntary servitude	0	0	0	0	0	0	0	0	0	0	0	0
Wisconsin												
Commercial sex acts	1	0	0	0	0	1	0	19	0	0	0	19
Involuntary servitude	0	0	0	0	0	0	17	5	1	0	0	23
Wyoming												
Commercial sex acts	0	0	0	0	0	0	10	2	0	0	0	12
Involuntary servitude	1	0	2	0	0	3	0	0	0	0	0	0

Table 40. Human Trafficking Arrests, by Ethnicity and Participating State, 2020

(Number.)

State	Juvenile			Adult		
	Hispanic or Latino	Not Hispanic or Latino	Total	Hispanic or Latino	Not Hispanic or Latino	Total
Arizona						
Commercial sex acts	0	0	0	0	1	1
Involuntary servitude...........................	0	0	0	0	0	0
Colorado						
Commercial sex acts	0	0	0	0	5	5
Involuntary servitude...........................	0	0	0	0	0	0
Connecticut						
Commercial sex acts	0	0	0	0	1	1
Involuntary servitude...........................	0	0	0	0	0	0
Georgia						
Commercial sex acts	1	2	3	4	24	28
Involuntary servitude...........................	0	0	0	0	0	0
Indiana						
Commercial sex acts	0	2	2	0	0	0
Involuntary servitude...........................	0	0	0	4	0	4
Kentucky						
Commercial sex acts	0	0	0	0	1	1
Involuntary servitude...........................	0	0	0	0	2	2
Louisiana						
Commercial sex acts	0	0	0	0	1	1
Involuntary servitude...........................	0	0	0	0	0	0
Maine						
Commercial sex acts	0	0	0	0	1	1
Involuntary servitude...........................	0	0	0	0	0	0
Maryland						
Commercial sex acts	0	0	0	0	7	7
Involuntary servitude...........................	0	0	0	0	0	0
Massachusetts						
Commercial sex acts	0	0	0	1	2	3
Involuntary servitude...........................	0	0	0	0	2	2
Minnesota						
Commercial sex acts	0	0	0	3	11	14
Involuntary servitude...........................	0	0	0	0	0	0
Missouri						
Commercial sex acts	0	0	0	0	6	6
Involuntary servitude...........................	0	0	0	0	0	0
Nevada						
Commercial sex acts	1	1	2	0	18	18
Involuntary servitude...........................	0	0	0	1	0	1
New Jersey						
Commercial sex acts	0	0	0	5	18	23
Involuntary servitude...........................	0	0	0	3	3	6
New Mexico						
Commercial sex acts	0	0	0	0	2	2
Involuntary servitude...........................	0	0	0	0	0	0
North Carolina						
Commercial sex acts	0	0	0	0	0	0
Involuntary servitude...........................	0	0	0	0	2	2
Ohio						
Commercial sex acts	0	0	0	0	4	4
Involuntary servitude...........................	0	0	0	0	0	0
Oklahoma						
Commercial sex acts	0	6	6	0	21	21
Involuntary servitude...........................	0	0	0	0	0	0

Table 40. Human Trafficking Arrests, by Ethnicity and Participating State, 2020—*Continued*

(Number.)

State	Juvenile			Adult		
	Hispanic or Latino	Not Hispanic or Latino	Total	Hispanic or Latino	Not Hispanic or Latino	Total
Pennsylvania						
Commercial sex acts	0	0	0	0	2	2
Involuntary servitude............................	0	0	0	0	2	2
South Carolina						
Commercial sex acts	0	0	0	0	4	4
Involuntary servitude............................	0	0	0	0	0	0
South Dakota						
Commercial sex acts	0	0	0	0	2	2
Involuntary servitude............................	0	0	0	0	0	0
Tennessee						
Commercial sex acts	0	0	0	1	10	11
Involuntary servitude............................	0	0	0	0	0	0
Texas						
Commercial sex acts	1	2	3	14	33	47
Involuntary servitude............................	9	0	9	17	7	24
Virginia						
Commercial sex acts	0	0	0	0	9	9
Involuntary servitude............................	0	0	0	0	2	2
Washington						
Commercial sex acts	0	0	0	1	10	11
Involuntary servitude............................	0	0	0	0	1	1
West Virginia						
Commercial sex acts	0	0	0	1	11	12
Involuntary servitude............................	0	0	0	0	0	0
Wisconsin						
Commercial sex acts	0	1	1	0	13	13
Involuntary servitude............................	0	0	0	0	3	3
Wyoming						
Commercial sex acts	0	0	0	0	12	12
Involuntary servitude............................	0	3	3	0	0	0

NOTE: Not all agencies provide ethnicity data; therefore, the race and ethnicity totals will not equal.

Table 41. Cargo Theft by Participating State, by Incidents and Stolen/Recovered Values, 2020

(Number; dollars; percent.)

State	Number of agencies reporting an incident	Number of incidents reported	Value of property		Percent recovered
			Stolen	Recovered	
Total	189	1,118	$28,967,583	$7,366,202	25.4
Alaska...	3	6	$34,653	$16,251	46.9
Arizona..	1	1	$0	$0	
Arkansas..	3	3	$3,857	$0	0.0
Colorado	10	18	$353,149	$1,487	0.4
Delaware	3	5	$104,088	$0	0.0
Florida..	26	113	$13,072,422	$3,765,173	28.8
Georgia	11	21	$465,195	$120,737	26.0
Indiana	1	1	$2,000	$0	0.0
Kentucky	2	3	$101,244	$0	0.0
Michigan...	23	61	$974,733	$181,060	18.6
Minnesota	1	1	$190,000	$0	0.0
Mississippi..	5	25	$100,928	$19,287	19.1
Montana...	1	1	$8,250	$0	0.0
Nebraska	2	2	$1,105	$0	0.0
Nevada	2	5	$451,502	$150,000	33.2
New Jersey..	15	25	$1,592,863	$415,950	26.1
New Mexico.......................................	3	4	$9,187	$200	2.2
Ohio...	4	4	$19,762	$0	0.0
Oklahoma...	1	1	$1,000	$0	0.0
Oregon...	1	1	$6,694	$6,694	100.0
Rhode Island.....................................	2	2	$125,439	$0	0.0
South Dakota.....................................	1	1	$40	$0	0.0
Tennessee	4	381	$1,493,055	$475,919	31.9
Texas..	54	422	$9,792,124	$2,208,434	22.6
Utah...	1	1	$10	$10	100.0
Vermont	1	1	$5,000	$5,000	100.0
Virginia...	8	9	$59,283	$0	0.0

Table 42. Cargo Theft Property Stolen and Recovered, by Type of Value, 2020

(Dollars; percent.)

| Type of property | Value of property | | Percent recovered |
	Stolen	Recovered	
Total	$28,967,583	$7,366,202	25.4
Alcohol....................................	481,561	300	0.1
Automobile.............................	604,802	360,452	59.6
Bicycles..................................	103,125	0	0.0
Building materials	234,834	0	0.0
Camping, hunting, fishing equipment, supplies....	301	0	0.0
Chemicals................................	16,634	0	0.0
Clothes, furs	203,284	7,595	3.7
Collections, collectibles	1,910	0	0.0
Computer hardware, software	219,551	10,408	4.7
Consumable goods..................	3,960,158	315,134	8.0
Credit, debit cards[1]	0	0	
Documents, personal or business[1]	0	0	
Drug equipment	3,600,000	0	0.0
Drugs, narcotics......................	1,102	0	0.0
Farm equipment	75	0	0.0
Firearms..................................	7,559	0	0.0
Fuel..	37,374	0	0.0
Gambling equipment...............	1	0	0.0
Household goods.....................	2,256,534	96,874	4.3
Identity documents[1]	0	0	
Identity intangibles[1]	0	0	
Industrial equipment...............	245,180	0	0.0
Jewelry, precious metals..........	65,256	499	0.8
Lawn, yard, garden equipment..........................	41,235	1	*
Logging equipment..................	30,000	0	0.0
Medical, medical lab equipment.........................	3,619,283	2,661,394	73.5
Merchandise............................	3,010,104	97,851	3.3
Metals, non-Precious................	35,002	1	*
Money.....................................	237,987	0	0.0
Negotiable instruments...........	8,251	0	0.0
Nonnegotiable instruments[1]	0	0	
Office equipment.....................	33,201	950	2.9
Other.......................................	2,156,915	588,565	27.3
Other motor vehicles...............	332,502	150,000	45.1
Pending inventory....................	52	1	1.9
Pets..	300	0	0.0
Photographic, optical equipment	1	1	100.0
Portable electronic communications....................	1,000,234	1,800	0.2
Purse, wallet	7,966	50	0.6
Radio, TV, VCR.........................	295,012	16,827	5.7
Recordings...............................	3,594	300	8.3
Recreational/ Sports Equipment..........................	12,050	0	0.0
Structure, storage	4,500	4,500	100.0
Tools.......................................	543,685	55	*
Trailers	1,902,556	1,105,186	58.1
Trucks.....................................	2,802,648	1,936,145	69.1
Vehicle parts...........................	841,263	11,312	1.3
Weapons-Other	10,001	1	*

* = Less than one-tenth of 1 percent.
[1]According to Uniform Crime Reporting guidelines, the value of property stolen and/or recovered must be zero for this property description.

Table 43. Cargo Theft, by Location, 2020

(Number.)

Type of property	Total at location
Air, bus, train terminal	28
Amusement park	1
Auto dealership new, used	2
Bank, savings and loan	1
Church, synagogue, temple, mosque	1
Commercial, office building	76
Construction site	5
Convenience store	41
Department, discount store	13
Dock, wharf, freight, modal terminal	42
Drug store, doctor's office, hospital	4
Field, woods	23
Government, public building	5
Grocery, supermarket	10
Highway, road, alley, street, sidewalk	220
Hotel, motel, etc.	10
Industrial site	25
Liquor store	6
Parking, drop lot, garage	437
Park, playground	3
Rental storage facility	7
Residence, home	34
Rest area	4
Restaurant	5
School, college, university	1
Service, gas station	73
Shopping mall	1
Specialty store	14
Other, unknown	77

Table 44. Cargo Theft, by Victim Type, 2020

(Number.)

Victim type	Total victims
Business..........	907
Government..........	6
Individual..........	227
Other..........	8
Society/public..........	1
Unknown..........	22

Table 45. Cargo Theft, by Offense, 2020

(Number.)

Type of property	Total at location
Grand total of offenses	1,192
Cargo theft applicable offenses	
All other larceny..........	294
Burglary..........	71
Credit card, automated teller machine fraud..........	2
Embezzlement..........	27
False pretenses, swindle, confidence game..........	3
Motor vehicle theft..........	123
Robbery..........	13
Theft from building..........	19
Theft from motor vehicle..........	615
Total cargo theft applicable offenses..........	1167
Other offenses occurring with cargo offenses	
Aggravated assault..........	2
Counterfeiting, forgery..........	1
Destruction of property..........	16
Drug, narcotic violations..........	1
Simple assault..........	2
Stolen property offense..........	2
Theft of motor vehicle parts or accessories..........	1
Total other offenses occurring with cargo offense..........	25

METHODOLOGY

Submitting Uniform Crime Reporting (UCR) program data to the Federal Bureau of Investigation (FBI) is a collective effort on the part of city, county, state, tribal, and federal law enforcement agencies to present a nationwide view of crime. Law enforcement agencies in 46 states and the District of Columbia voluntarily contribute crime data to the UCR program through their respective state UCR programs. For those states that do not have a state program, local agencies submit crime statistics directly to the FBI. The state UCR programs function as liaisons between local agencies and the FBI. Many states have mandatory reporting requirements, and many state programs collect data beyond the scope of the UCR program to address crime problems specific to their particular jurisdictions. In most cases, state programs also provide direct and frequent service to participating law enforcement agencies, make information readily available for statewide use, and help streamline the national program's operations.

Readers should use caution in interpreting data, especially as compared to previous years, due to the conditions imposed by the COVID-19 pandemic.

A NOTE REGARDING RAPE

In 2013, the FBI UCR Program initiated collection of rape data under a revised definition within the Summary Reporting System. Previously, offense data for forcible rape was collected under the legacy UCR definition: the carnal knowledge of a female forcibly and against her will. Beginning with the 2013 data year, the term "forcible" was removed from the offense title, and the definition was changed. The revised UCR definition of rape is: Penetration, no matter how slight, of the vagina or anus with any body part or object, or oral penetration by a sex organ of another person, without the consent of the victim. Attempts or assaults to commit rape are also included; however, statutory rape and incest are excluded. For more information, please see https://ucr.fbi.gov/crime-in-the-u.s/2013/crime-in-the-u.s.-2013/rape-addendum/rape_addendum_final.

CRITERIA FOR STATE UCR PROGRAMS

The criteria established for state programs ensure consistency and comparability in the data submitted to the national program, as well as regular and timely reporting. These criteria are:

1. A UCR Program must conform to the FBI UCR Program's submission standards, definitions, specifications, and required deadlines.

2. A UCR Program must establish data integrity procedures and have personnel assigned to assist contributing agencies in quality assurance practices and crime reporting procedures. Data integrity procedures should include crime trend assessments, offense classification verification, and technical specification validation.

3. A UCR Program's submissions must cover more than 50 percent of the law enforcement agencies within its established reporting domain and be willing to cover any and all UCR-contributing agencies that wish to use the UCR Program from within its domain. (An agency wishing to become a UCR Program must be willing to report for all of the agencies within the state.)

4. A UCR Program must furnish the FBI UCR Program with all of the UCR data collected by the law enforcement agencies within its domain.

These requirements do not prohibit the state from gathering other statistical data beyond the national collection.

DATA COMPLETENESS AND QUALITY

National program staff members contact the state UCR program in connection with crime-reporting matters and, when necessary and approved by the state, they contact individual contributors within the state. To fulfill its responsibilities in connection with the UCR program, the FBI reviews and edits individual agency reports for completeness and quality. Upon request, they conduct training programs within the state on law enforcement record-keeping and crime-reporting procedures. The FBI conducts an audit of each state's UCR data collection procedures once every three years, in accordance with audit standards established by the federal government. Should circumstances develop in which the state program does not comply with the aforementioned requirements, the national program may institute a direct collection of data from law enforcement agencies within the state.

REPORTING PROCEDURES

Offenses known and value of property: Law enforcement agencies tabulate the number of Part I offenses reported based on records of all reports of crime received from victims, officers who discover infractions, or other sources, and submit these reports each month to the FBI directly or through their state UCR programs. Part I offenses include murder and nonnegligent manslaughter, forcible rape, robbery, aggravated assault, burglary, larceny-theft, motor vehicle theft, and arson. Each month, law enforcement agencies also submit to the FBI the value of property stolen and recovered in connection with the offenses and detailed information pertaining to criminal homicide.

Unfounded offenses and clearances: When, through investigation, an agency determines that complaints of crimes are unfounded or false, the agency eliminates that offense from its crime tally through an entry on the monthly report. The report also provides the total number of actual Part I offenses, the number of offenses cleared, and the number of clearances that involve only offenders under the age of 18. (Law enforcement can clear crimes in one of two ways: by the arrest of at least one person who is charged and turned over to the court for prosecution or by exceptional means—when some element beyond law enforcement's control precludes the arrest of a known offender.)

Persons arrested: In addition to reporting Part I offenses each month, law enforcement agencies also provide data on the age, sex, and race of persons arrested for Part I and Part II offenses. Part II offenses encompass all crimes, except traffic violations, that are not classified as Part I offenses.

Officers killed or assaulted: Each month, law enforcement agencies also report information to the UCR program regarding law enforcement officers killed or assaulted, and each year they report the number of full-time sworn and civilian law enforcement personnel employed as of October 31.

EDITING PROCEDURES

The UCR program thoroughly examines each report it receives for arithmetical accuracy and for deviations in crime data from month to month and from present to past years that may indicate errors. UCR staff members compare an agency's monthly reports with its previous submissions and with reports from similar agencies to identify any unusual fluctuations in the agency's crime count. Considerable variations in crime levels may indicate modified records procedures, incomplete reporting, or changes in the jurisdiction's geopolitical structure.

Evaluation of trends: Data reliability is a high priority of the FBI, which brings any deviations or arithmetical adjustments to the attention of state UCR programs or the submitting agencies. Typically, FBI staff members study the monthly reports to evaluate periodic trends prepared for individual reporting units. Any significant increase or decrease becomes the subject of a special inquiry. Changes in crime reporting procedures or annexations that affect an agency's jurisdiction can influence the level of reported crime. When this occurs, the FBI excludes the figures for specific crime categories or totals, if necessary, from the trend tabulations.

Training for contributors: In addition to the evaluation of trends, the FBI provides training seminars and instructional materials on crime reporting procedures to assist contributors in complying with UCR standards. Throughout the country, representatives from the national program coordinate with representatives of state programs and law enforcement personnel and hold training sessions to explain the purpose of the program, the rules of uniform classification and scoring, and the methods of assembling the information for reporting. When an individual agency has specific problems with compiling its crime statistics and its remedial efforts are unsuccessful, personnel from the FBI's Criminal Justice Information Services Division may visit the contributor to aid in resolving the problems.

UCR Handbook: The national UCR program publishes the *Uniform Crime Reporting (UCR) Handbook* (revised 2004), which details procedures for classifying and scoring offenses and serves as the contributing agencies' basic resource for preparing reports. The national staff also produces letters to UCR contributors, state program bulletins, and UCR newsletters as needed. These publications provide policy updates and new information, as well as clarification of reporting issues.

The final responsibility for data submissions rests with the individual contributing law enforcement agency. Although the FBI makes every effort through its editing procedures, training practices, and correspondence to ensure the validity of the data it receives, the accuracy of the statistics depends primarily on the adherence of each contributor to the established standards of reporting. Deviations from these established standards that cannot be resolved by the national UCR program may be brought to the attention of the Criminal Justice Information Systems Committees of the International Association of Chiefs of Police and the National Sheriffs' Association.

NIBRS CONVERSION

Thirty-three state programs are certified to provide their UCR data in the expanded National Incident-Based Reporting System (NIBRS) format. For presentation in this book, the NIBRS data were converted to the historical Summary Reporting System data. The UCR program staff constructed the NIBRS database to allow for such conversion so that UCR's long-running time series could continue.

CRIME TRENDS

By showing fluctuations from year to year, trend statistics offer the data user an added perspective from which to study crime. Percent change tabulations in this publication are computed only for reporting agencies that provided comparable data for the periods under consideration. The FBI excludes from the trend calculations all figures except those received for common months from common agencies. Also excluded are unusual fluctuations of data that the FBI determines are the result of such variables as improved records procedures, annexations, and so on.

CAUTION TO USERS

Data users should exercise care in making any direct comparison between data in this publication and those in prior issues of *Crime in the United States*. Because of differing levels of participation from year to year and reporting problems that require the FBI to estimate crime counts for certain contributors, some data may not be comparable. In addition, this publication may contain updates to data provided in prior years' publications.

For information about the FBI's caution against ranking, including warnings about variables affecting crime and characteristics of jurisdictions, please see https://ucr.fbi.gov/ucr-statistics-their-proper-use.

OFFENSE ESTIMATION

Some tables in this publication contain statistics for the entire United States. Because not all law enforcement agencies provide data for complete reporting periods, the FBI includes estimated crime numbers in these presentations. The FBI estimates data for three areas: Metropolitan Statistical Areas (MSAs), cities outside MSAs, and nonmetropolitan counties; and computes estimates for participating agencies that do not provide 12 months of complete data. For agencies supplying 3 to 11 months of data, the national UCR program estimates for the missing data by following a standard estimation procedure using the data provided by the agency. If an agency has supplied less than 3 months of data, the FBI computes estimates by using the known crime figures of similar areas within a state and assigning the same proportion of crime volumes to nonreporting agencies. The estimation process considers the following: population size covered by the agency; type of jurisdiction; for example, police department versus sheriff's office; and geographic location.

ESTIMATION OF STATE-LEVEL DATA

In response to various circumstances, the FBI calculates estimated offense totals for certain states. For example, some states do not provide forcible rape figures in accordance with UCR guidelines. In addition, problems at the state level have, at times, resulted in no useable data. Also, the conversion of the National Incident-Based Reporting System (NIBRS) data to summary data has contributed to the need for unique estimation procedures.

EXPANDED OFFENSE TABLES

Expanded offense data are the details of the various offenses that the Uniform Crime Reporting Program collects beyond the count of how many crimes law enforcement agencies report. These details may include the type of weapon used in a crime, the type or value of items stolen, and so forth. Expanded homicide data provide supplemental details about murders such as the age, sex, and race of both the victim and the offender, the weapon used in the homicide, the circumstances surrounding the offense, and the relationship of the victim to the offender. In addition, expanded data includes trends (e.g., 2-year comparisons) and rates per 100,000 inhabitants.

Expanded offense data, including expanded homicide data, are information collected in addition to the reports of the number of crimes known. As a result, law enforcement agencies can report an offense without providing the supplemental data about that offense.

FEDERAL CRIME DATA

In past years, these agencies' data were included in various tables in *Crime in the United States*. *Federal Crime Data* signals the move to presenting federal data in a way more attuned with local, state, and tribal UCR data. Included are the federal agencies that have submitted traditional UCR data for some time.

A few agencies, such as the National Institutes of Health (NIH) and several agencies within the U.S. Department of the Interior (DOI), investigate and police in ways similar to local or state authorities. These federal agencies have long reported data to the UCR Program. However, other federal agencies, the FBI included, found it more difficult to fit into the UCR model. This annual report was originally designed as a stepping stone to finding ways to provide a similar transparency and access to federal crime data that the UCR Program has brought to local, state, and tribal crime data for nearly 90 years. The arrest data from the FBI, ATF, and USMS have all been mapped to correspond to the UCR's National Incident-Based Reporting System (NIBRS) offense codes. This makes the overlay of federal data with local and state data much easier.

COMPARABILITY OF FEDERAL DATA TO STATE AND LOCAL DATA

The best approach to viewing the federal data offered is to use it to gain an overall impression of the intensity of certain types of offenses within a specific area by overlaying the federal arrests in conjunction with the local and state information. As developments in the data collection continue to occur, more details will become available from federal agencies, and these impressions will become more sharply focused.

Federal crime data are often different from local and state data, not only in their collection, but also in their generation. The UCR Program has built its traditional data collection on three triggering events that are common to local and state agencies. Offense information begins with either, first, a complaint of a victim/citizen or, second, the observation of a crime in progress by a law enforcement officer. A third trigger for data is when an arrest is made and information related to that occurrence is reported.

For federal agencies, the initiation of investigation may be prompted in different ways. Many crimes, such as human trafficking and hate crime and their associated data, are brought to the attention of the FBI in much the same fashion:

- Reports from victims
- Liaison with other law enforcement agencies
- Information about victims (e.g., human trafficking, hate crime) brought to the FBI by nongovernmental organizations
- Reports from the media

The decision to handle a crime as a federal investigation or as a local investigation is determined on a case-by-case basis. Some of the factors that enter into the decision for federal agencies to pursue an investigation are the available evidence, the availability of resources at the local level, and, in the case of hate crime, statutory provisions that determine whether the U.S. Attorney will accept the case as a federal one. In addition, some states do not have a hate crime statute under which to pursue a case.

Why Federal Numbers Are Smaller Than Those of Other UCR Agencies

As mentioned previously, federal investigations, by nature, often begin under different circumstances and proceed and conclude on different timeframes than investigations conducted by local and state agencies. Just as federal agencies often do not have traditional offenses known to report, they also typically do not have a number of offenses to report until a case has been built and an arrest or indictment has occurred. Perhaps most impactful on the federal numbers is the fact that federal agencies often play a collaborative role with local and state agencies in crime investigations. Because the UCR Program has the "most local reporting" rule, which specifies that the agency involved that is the most local jurisdiction should report the incident to the UCR Program, investigations and arrests that federal authorities have worked on often are reported by city, county, state, or tribal agencies.

HUMAN TRAFFICKING

As state participation has grown, the UCR Program has seen an increase in human trafficking data submissions. The program will continue efforts to expand, gather, and make available information regarding human trafficking incidents.

Trafficking Victims Protection Act

In January 2013, the national UCR Program began collecting offense and arrest data regarding human trafficking as authorized by the William Wilberforce Trafficking Victims Protection Reauthorization Act of 2008. The act requires the FBI to collect human trafficking offense data and to make distinctions between prostitution, assisting or promoting prostitution, and purchasing prostitution.

To comply with the Wilberforce Act, the national UCR Program created two additional offenses in the Summary Reporting System (SRS) and the National Incident-Based Reporting System (NIBRS) through which the UCR Program collects both offense and arrest data. The definitions for these offenses are:

- **Human Trafficking/Commercial Sex Acts:** inducing a person by force, fraud, or coercion to participate in commercial sex acts, or in which the person induced to perform such act(s) has not attained 18 years of age.
- **Human Trafficking/Involuntary Servitude:** obtaining of a person(s) through recruitment, harboring, transportation, or provision, and subjecting such persons by force, fraud, or coercion into involuntary servitude, peonage, debt bondage, or slavery (not to include commercial sex acts).

The data in the tables included in this report reflect the offenses and arrests recorded by state and local law enforcement agencies (LEAs) that currently have the ability to report the data to the national UCR Program. As such, they should not be interpreted as a definitive statement of the level or characteristics of human trafficking as a whole. The data declaration pages, which will help the user better understand the data, and the methodology used for the four following tables are located in the Data Declarations and Methodology section near the end of this report. In addition, a question-and-answer section about human trafficking data is provided as a supplement to this report.

Note: Regarding the data reported to the UCR Program, it is important to note that these data represent only one view of a complex issue—the law enforcement perspective. However, due to the nature of human trafficking, many of these crimes are never reported to the local, state, tribal, and federal LEAs that investigate them. In addition to the law enforcement facet in fighting these crimes, there are victim service organizations whose mission it is to serve the needs of the victims of human trafficking. In order to have the complete picture of human trafficking, it would be necessary to gather information from all of these sources.

Tables include the states that have added human trafficking offenses to their data collection and the number of agencies per state participating in the UCR Program. Even though a state program included human trafficking, the individual agencies in that state may or may not have added it to their collections. Indiana, Mississippi, and portions of Ohio have no UCR state program to manage the collection of UCR data within the state. Each law enforcement agency is responsible for reporting its crime data directly to the FBI.

For UCR purposes, juveniles are individuals under the age of 18 years. Adults are 18 years of age or older.

The data used in creating these tables were from law enforcement agencies submitting one or more human trafficking incidents for at least 1 month of the calendar year. Also included are zero data for states which have incorporated human trafficking offenses in their data collection where no 2016 human trafficking incidents were reported to the FBI UCR Program.

The published data, therefore, do not necessarily represent reports from each participating agency for all 12 months of the calendar year. When the FBI determines that an agency's data collection methodology does not comply with national UCR guidelines, the figure(s) for that agency's offense(s) will not be included in the table, and the discrepancy will be explained in a footnote.

CARGO THEFT

The FBI's Uniform Crime Reporting (UCR) Program collects cargo theft data to inform the law enforcement community, state and federal legislators, academia, and the public at large about this particular crime. The data can be used to create awareness and to measure the impact cargo theft has on the economy and potential threats to national security. Often cargo theft offenses are part of larger criminal schemes and have been found to be components of organized crime rings, drug trafficking, and funding for terrorism. The UCR collection of cargo theft data is new with only 4 years of data published, but the number of agencies reporting cargo theft incidents has increased each year. As more agencies participate, future versions of this cargo theft report will depict a more complete account of the occurrences of cargo theft in the United States.

Due to the significant economic impact cargo theft has on the United States economy, and the potential for use by terrorist organizations, Congress mandated H.R. 3199, the USA Patriot Improvement and Reauthorization Act of 2005 on March 9, 2006. It required the Attorney General to "take the steps necessary to ensure that reports of cargo theft collected by Federal, State, and local officials are reflected as a separate category in the Uniform Crime Reporting System, or any successor system, by no later than December 31, 2006." In response to this mandate, the Criminal Justice Information Services (CJIS) Advisory Policy Board approved a definition for collecting

cargo theft in December 2006. Creation of the data specifications required to capture cargo theft data in the UCR's Summary Reporting System as well as the National Incident-Based Reporting System were finalized in 2010 with the first publication of cargo theft data in 2013.

Cargo theft is defined as "The criminal taking of any cargo including, but not limited to, goods, chattels, money, or baggage that constitutes, in whole or in part, a commercial shipment of freight moving in commerce, from any pipeline system, railroad car, motor truck, or other vehicle, or from any tank or storage facility, station house, platform, or depot, or from any vessel or wharf, or from any aircraft, air terminal, airport, aircraft terminal or air navigation facility, or from any intermodal container, intermodal chassis, trailer, container freight station, warehouse, freight distribution facility, or freight consolidation facility. For purposes of this definition, cargo shall be deemed as moving in commerce at all points between the point of origin and the final destination, regardless of any temporary stop while awaiting transshipment or otherwise."

This definition was developed, not as a legal description for prosecutorial purposes, but to capture the essence of the national cargo theft problem in the United States. The legal elements of knowledge and intent were intentionally omitted.

Participation in the UCR Program is voluntary, and agencies or states may choose not to participate. Participation in the cargo theft data has remained steady; however, several factors have been identified having a direct impact on this important data collection:

- States may not have the resources required to make the necessary technical changes or to align their local and state statutes with federal requirements.
- States may not have the necessary resources to conduct data quality checks on reported incidents associated with cargo theft, which could result in inaccurate data.
- States may not have adequate resources to train participants on how to recognize and properly record cargo theft incidents.
- States may not perceive cargo theft as a priority or a significant problem within their states and make decisions based on their immediate needs regarding resource allocation.

Quality data concerning cargo theft can help us better understand this crime and the threats associated with it. As more agencies choose to report their incidents, the FBI's UCR Program will be able to provide more information about cargo theft on a national scale. For additional information on the UCR Program's collection of cargo theft incidents, visit https://le.fbi. gov/informational-tools/ucr/ucr-technical-specifications-user-manuals-and-data-tools.

Tables present by state the total number of agencies that submitted data about cargo theft incidents, the number of incidents reported, the reported value of stolen property, the value and percentage of recovered property for each submitting state.

Data used were from all law enforcement agencies submitting one or more cargo theft incidents for at least 1 month of the calendar year. The published data, therefore, do not necessarily represent reports from each participating agency for all 12 months of the calendar year. Based on UCR guidelines, the property descriptions of credit/debit cards, nonnegotiable instruments, documents/personal or business, and identity-intangible, must be submitted with zero value for stolen and/or recovered. In the Cargo Theft Program, the victim of a cargo theft may be an individual, a business, an institution, or society as a whole. The UCR Program counted one for each victim type reported in an incident.

Because cargo theft has been defined as "the criminal **taking of** any cargo . . . ," there are specific crimes against property that apply to cargo theft. The applicable crimes against property include:

120 = Robbery
23D = Theft from building
23F = Theft from motor vehicle
23H = All other larceny
26A = False pretenses, swindle, confidence game
26B = Credit card, automatic teller machine fraud
26C = Impersonation
26E = Wire fraud
210 = Extortion, blackmail
220 = Burglary, breaking & entering
240 = Motor vehicle theft
270 = Embezzlement
510 = Bribery

In addition, cargo theft is not considered an offense by itself; all offenses that happen within a cargo theft incident are to be reported. Cargo theft data are derived by capturing the additional element of "theft of cargo" in incidents that contain any of the applicable offenses.

PART 3

Criminal Victimization, 2020

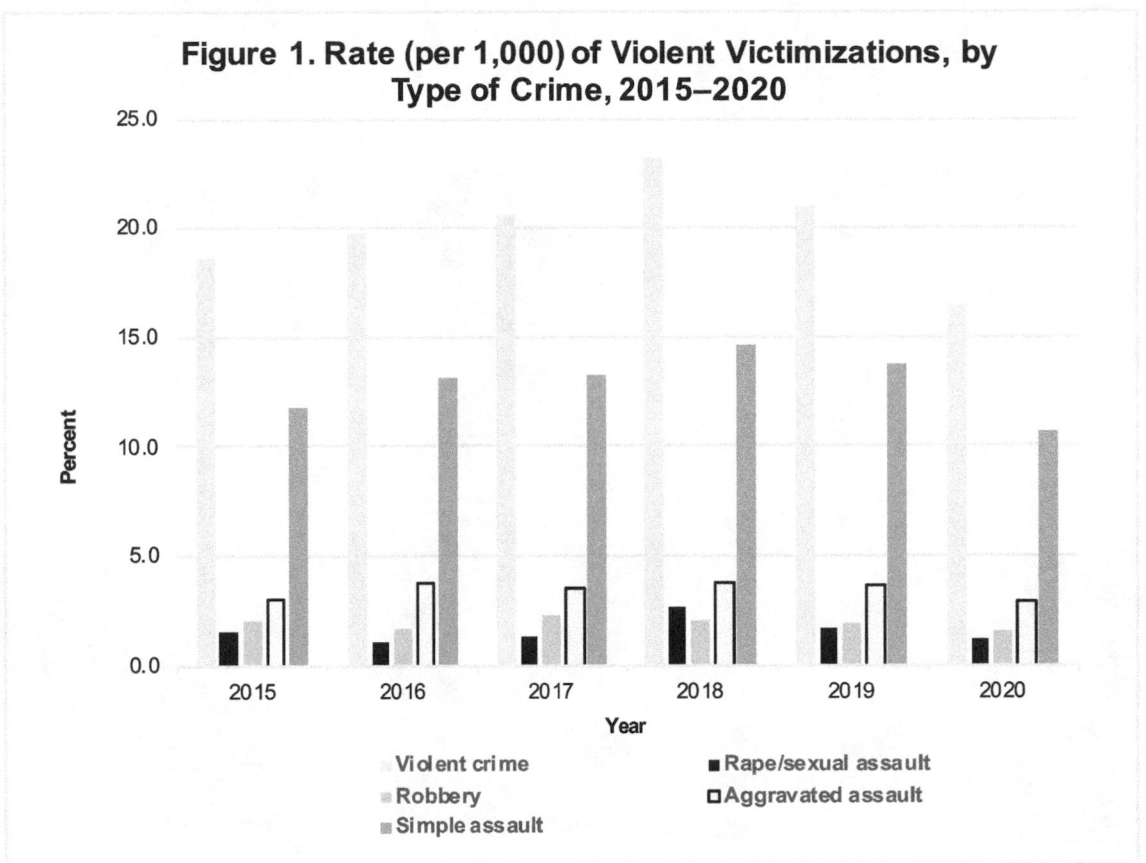

Figure 1. Rate (per 1,000) of Violent Victimizations, by Type of Crime, 2015–2020

- Between 2019 and 2020, there was a decline of approximately 22 percent in the total rate of violent victimization; the rate for persons age 12 and older fell from 21.0 to 16.4 victimizations per 1,000 persons.

- The rate of simple assault declined from 13.7 per 1,000 in 2019 to 10.7 per 1,000 persons in 2020, and the rate of aggravated assault declined from 3.7 to 2.9 per 1,000 persons.

- From 2019 to 2020, 17 percent fewer intimate partner victimizations were reported to police.

- The rate of violent victimization in urban areas—based on the NCVS's new classifications of urban, suburban, and rural areas—declined in suburban areas but did not change in rural areas from 2019 to 2020.

- There were 131,490 fewer firearm victimizations in 2020 than in 2019.

Table 1. Number and Rate of Violent Victimizations, by Type of Crime, 2016–2020

(Number; percent.)

Type of violent crime	2016 Number	2016 Rate per 1,000[1]	2017 Number	2017 Rate per 1,000[1]	2018 Number	2018 Rate per 1,000[1]	2019 Number	2019 Rate per 1,000[1]	2020* Number	2020* Rate per 1,000[1]
Violent Crime[2]	5,353,820[A]	19.7[A]	5,612,670[A]	20.6[A]	6,385,520[A]	23.2[A]	5,813,410[A]	21.0[A]	4,558,150	16.4
Rape/sexual assault[3]	298,410	1.1	393,980	1.4	734,630[A]	2.7[A]	459,310	1.7	319,950	1.2
Robbery..................	458,810	1.7	613,840[A]	2.3[A]	573,100	2.1	534,420	1.9	437,260	1.6
Assault..................	4,596,600[A]	16.9[A]	4,604,850[A]	16.9[A]	5,077,790[A]	18.4[A]	4,819,680[A]	17.4[A]	3,800,950	13.7
Aggravated assault..................	1,040,580[A]	3.8[A]	993,170[B]	3.6[B]	1,058,040[A]	3.8[A]	1,019,490[B]	3.7[B]	812,180	2.9
Simple assault	3,556,020[A]	13.1[A]	3,611,680[A]	13.3[A]	4,019,750[A]	14.6[A]	3,800,190[A]	13.7[A]	2,988,770	10.7
Violent crime excluding simple assault[4]	1,797,790	6.6[B]	2,000,990[A]	7.3[A]	2,365,770[A]	8.6[A]	2,013,220[A]	7.3[A]	1,569,390	5.6
Selected Characteristics of Violent Crime										
Domestic violence[5]..................	1,068,120	3.9	1,237,960[A]	4.5[A]	1,333,050[A]	4.8[A]	1,164,540[B]	4.2[B]	856,750	3.1
Intimate partner violence[6]..................	597,200	2.2	666,310[B]	2.4[B]	847,230[A]	3.1[A]	695,060[B]	2.5[B]	484,830	1.7
Stranger violence	2,082,410	7.7	2,034,100	7.5	2,493,750	9.1[A]	2,254,740	8.1	1,973,200	7.1

NOTE: Details may not sum to totals due to rounding. Categories of violent crime include rape or sexual assault, robbery, aggravated assault, and simple assault, and they include threatened, attempted, and completed occurrences of those crimes.
* = Comparison year.
A = Significant difference from comparison year at the 95% confidence level.
B = Significant difference from comparison year at the 90% confidence level.
[1]Rate is per 1,000 persons age 12 years or older.
[2]Includes rape or sexual assault, robbery, aggravated assault, and simple assault. Excludes homicide because the National Crime Victimization Survey (NCVS) is based on interviews with victims.
[3]See Methodology for details on the measurement of rape or sexual assault in the NCVS.
[4]Includes rape or sexual assault, robbery, and aggravated assault.
[5]Includes the subset of violent victimizations that were committed by intimate partners or family members.
[6]Includes the subset of violent victimizations that were committed by current or former spouses, boyfriends, or girlfriends.

Table 2. Number and Rate of Property Victimizations, by Type of Crime, 2016–2020

(Number; rate.)

Type of property crime	2016 Number	2016 Rate per 1,000[1]	2017 Number	2017 Rate per 1,000[1]	2018 Number	2018 Rate per 1,000[1]	2019 Number	2019 Rate per 1,000[1]	2020* Number	2020* Rate per 1,000[1]
Total[2]	15,815,310	118.6[A]	13,340,220[A]	108.4[A]	13,502,840[A]	108.2[A]	12,818,000[A]	101.4[A]	12,085,170	94.5
Burglary/trespassing[3]..................	3,160,450	23.7[A]	2,538,170[A]	20.6[A]	2,639,620[A]	21.1[A]	2,178,400[A]	17.2[A]	1,741,250	13.6
Burglary[4]..................	2,205,180	16.5[A]	1,688,890[A]	13.7[A]	1,867,620[A]	15.0[A]	1,484,730[A]	11.7[A]	1,210,640	9.5
Trespassing[5]..................	955,270	7.2[A]	849,280[A]	6.9[A]	772,000[A]	6.2[A]	693,670[A]	5.5[A]	530,610	4.1
Motor vehicle theft	618,330	4.6	516,810	4.2	534,010	4.3	495,670	3.9	545,810	4.3
Other theft[6]..................	12,036,530	90.3[A]	10,285,240	83.6[A]	10,329,210[B]	82.7[A]	10,143,930	80.2	9,798,110	76.6

NOTE: Details may not sum to totals due to rounding. Categories include threatened, attempted, and completed crimes. The National Crime Victimization Survey (NCVS) household weighting adjustment was updated for 2017 onward, which decreased the estimated number of households and the number of households experiencing property crime by about 8%. As a result, the number of property crimes for 2016 should not be compared to 2017, 2018, 2019, or 2020. Property crime rates are unaffected by this change.
* = Comparison year.
A = Significant difference from comparison year at the 95% confidence level.
B = Significant difference from comparison year at the 90% confidence level.
[1]Rate is per 1,000 households.
[2]Includes burglary or trespassing, motor vehicle theft, and other theft.
[3]Includes unlawful or forcible entry or attempted entry of places, including a permanent residence, other residence (e.g., a hotel room or vacation residence), or other structure (e.g., a garage or shed). Includes victimizations where the offender stole, attempted to steal, or did not attempt to steal. Excludes trespassing on land.
[4]Includes only crimes where the offender committed or attempted a theft.
[5]Includes crimes where the offender did not commit or attempt a theft. Excludes trespassing on land.
[6]Includes other unlawful taking or attempted unlawful taking of property or cash without personal contact with the victim.

Table 3. Rates of Crime Reported and Not Reported to Police in the Uniform Crime Reporting Program and in the National Crime Victimization Survey, 2019 and 2020

(Rate.)

Type of crime	Reported to police		Not reported to police	
	2019	2020*	2019	2020*
Violent crime[1]..	8.6[A]	6.6	12.1[A]	9.5
Rape/sexual assault[2]..	0.6	0.3	1.0	0.8
Robbery..	0.9	0.9	1.0	0.7
Assault..	7.1[A]	5.5	10.0[A]	7.9
Aggravated assault..	1.9	1.7	1.7	1.2
Simple assault	5.2[A]	3.8	8.3[B]	6.7
Violent crime excluding simple assault[3]..............	3.4[B]	2.8	3.7[A]	2.8
Selected characteristics of violent crime				
Domestic violence[4]...	2.2[A]	1.3	1.9	1.8
Intimate partner violence[5]...................................	1.5[A]	0.7	1.0	1.0
Stranger violence..	3.3	3.1	4.8[A]	3.8
Property crime..	33.0	31.2	67.2[A]	62.0
Burglary/trespassing[6]..	8.3[A]	5.9	8.7	7.6
Burglary[7]..	6.0[A]	4.2	5.7	5.3
Trespassing[8]..	2.3[A]	1.7	3.0[B]	2.4
Motor vehicle theft...	3.1	3.2	0.8	1.0
Other theft[9]...	21.5	22.1	57.7[A]	53.3

NOTE: Rates are per 1,000 persons age 12 or older for violent crime and per 1,000 households for property crime. Categories of violent crime include rape or sexual assault, robbery, aggravated assault, and simple assault, and they include threatened, attempted, and completed occurrences of those crimes.
* = Comparison year.
A = Significant difference from comparison year at the 95% confidence level.
B = Significant difference from comparison year at the 90% confidence level.
[1]Excludes homicide because the National Crime Victimization Survey (NCVS) is based on interviews with victims.
[2]See Methodology for details on the measurement of rape or sexual assault in the NCVS.
[3]Includes rape or sexual assault, robbery, and aggravated assault.
[4]Includes the subset of violent victimizations that were committed by intimate partners or family members.
[5]Includes the subset of violent victimizations that were committed by current or former spouses, boyfriends, or girlfriends.
[6]Includes unlawful or forcible entry or attempted entry of places, including a permanent residence, other residence (e.g., a hotel room or vacation residence), or other structure (e.g., a garage or shed). Includes victimizations where the offender stole, attempted to steal, or did not attempt to steal. Excludes trespassing on land.
[7]Includes only crimes where the offender committed or attempted a theft.
[8]Includes crimes where the offender did not commit or attempt a theft. Excludes trespassing on land.
[9]Includes other unlawful taking or attempted unlawful taking of property or cash without personal contact with the victim.

Table 4. Rate of Crime Reported to Police in the Uniform Crime Reporting Program and National Crime Victimization Survey, 2019 and 2020

(Rate.)

Type of crime	2019 UCR rate per 1,000 residents[1]	Rate per 1,000 persons age 12 or older	
		2019 NVCS	2020 NVCS
Violent crime excluding simple assault..........................	3.79	3.38	2.78
Murder...	0.05	X	X
Rape/sexual assault[2]..	0.43	0.56	0.26
Robbery	0.82	0.90	0.85
Aggravated assault..	2.50	1.92	1.66

Type of crime	2019 UCR rate per 1,000 residents[1]	Rate per 1,000 households	
		2019 NVCS	2020 NVCS
Property crime..	21.10	33.00	31.19
Burglary[3]..	3.41	6.03	4.18
Motor vehicle theft..	2.20	3.12	3.18

NOTE: National Crime Victimization Survey (NCVS) and Uniform Crime Reporting (UCR) program crime rates are calculated differently. UCR crime rates are normally reported per 100,000 persons but were recalculated for this report to align with the reporting of NCVS crime rates per 1,000.
X = Not applicable.
[1]Includes crimes against persons age 11 or younger, persons who are homeless, persons who are institutionalized, and crimes against commercial establishments. These populations are out of sample for the NCVS.
[2]The NCVS estimate includes sexual assault. The UCR estimate excludes sexual assault and is based on the program's revised definition of rape.
[3]The UCR defines burglary as forcible entry, unlawful entry where no force is used, or attempted forcible entry of a structure to commit a felony or theft. The NCVS defines burglary as the unlawful or forcible entry or attempted entry of places, including a permanent residence, other residence (e.g., a hotel room or vacation residence), or other structure (e.g., a garage or shed) where there was a completed or attempted theft.

Table 5. Percent of Victimization Reported to Police, by Type of Crime, 2019 and 2020

(Percent.)

Type of crime	2019	2020*
Violent crime[1]	40.9	40.2
Rape/sexual assault[2]	33.9	22.9
Robbery	46.6	54.3
Assault	40.9	40.0
Aggravated assault	52.1	57.0
Simple assault	37.9	35.4
Violent crime excluding simple assault[3]	46.5	49.3
Selected characteristics of violent crime		
Domestic violence[4]	52.2	41.1
Intimate partner violence[5]	58.4[B]	41.4
Stranger violence	39.9	43.9
Property crime	32.5	33.0
Burglary/trespassing[6]	48.5[B]	43.4
Burglary[7]	51.4[A]	44.2
Trespassing[8]	42.2	41.5
Motor vehicle theft	79.5	74.6
Other theft[9]	26.8[B]	28.9

NOTE: Categories of violent crime include rape or sexual assault, robbery, aggravated assault, and simple assault, and they include threatened, attempted, and completed occurrences of those crimes.
* = Comparison year.
A = Significant difference from comparison year at the 95% confidence level.
B = Significant difference from comparison year at the 90% confidence level.
[1]Excludes homicide because the National Crime Victimization Survey (NCVS) is based on interviews with victims.
[2]See Methodology for details on the measurement of rape or sexual assault in the NCVS.
[3]Includes rape or sexual assault, robbery, and aggravated assault.
[4]Includes the subset of violent victimizations that were committed by intimate partners or family members.
[5]Includes the subset of violent victimizations that were committed by current or former spouses, boyfriends, or girlfriends.
[6]Includes unlawful or forcible entry or attempted entry of places, including a permanent residence, other residence (e.g., a hotel room or vacation residence), or other structure (e.g., a garage or shed). Includes victimizations where the offender stole, attempted to steal, or did not attempt to steal. Excludes trespassing on land.
[7]Includes only crimes where the offender committed or attempted a theft.
[8]Includes crimes where the offender did not commit or attempt a theft. Excludes trespassing on land.
[9]Includes other unlawful taking or attempted unlawful taking of property or cash without personal contact with the victim.

Table 6. Rate of Violent Victimization, by Type of Crime and Demographic Characteristics of Victims, 2019 and 2020

(Rate.)

Victim demographic characteristic	Total violent crime[1]		Violent crime excluding simple assault[2]	
	2019	2020*	2019	2020*
Total	21.0[A]	16.4	7.3[A]	5.6
Sex				
Male	21.2[A]	16.6	7.5[A]	5.1
Female	20.8[A]	16.2	7.0	6.2
Race/Ethnicity				
White[3]	21.0[A]	16.2	6.5[B]	5.3
Black[3]	18.7	17.5	7.0	7.5
Hispanic	21.3[B]	15.9	10.2[A]	5.5
Asian/Native Hawaiian/Other Pacific Islander[4]	8.5	7.5	2.7	1.8
Other[3,4]	72.7	49	21.5	18.7
Age				
12 to 17 years	35.2[A]	17.4	11.0	5.7
18 to 24 years	37.2	29.6	16.0	11.8
25 to 34 years	25.0	21.4	8.9	9.0
35 to 49 years	19.5	18.3	6.7	5.5
50 to 64 years	18.9[A]	14.6	5.6[B]	4.0
65 years and over	6.0	4.5	1.9	1.6
Martial Status				
Never married	31.2[A]	23.9	11.9[B]	9.4
Married	11.5[B]	9.3	3.0[B]	2.2
Widow/widower	10.7[B]	6.8	4.9	2.8
Divorced	28.5	24.1	10.7	7.7
Separated	64.1	42.1	19.5	18.9
Household Income				
Less than $25,000	37.8[A]	27.4	14.2	11.4
$25,000 to $49,999	19.7	17.2	7.5	5.8
$50,000 to $99,999	16.6	14.4	5.5	5.0
$100,000 to $199,999	16.2[A]	11.8	3.9	3.4
$200,000 or more	18.0	13.3	7.0!	2.8

NOTE: Rates are per 1,000 persons age 12 or older. Includes threatened, attempted, and completed occurrences of those crimes.
* = Comparison group.
A = Significant difference from comparison group at the 90% confidence level.
B = Significant difference from comparison group at the 95% confidence level.
! = Interpret estimate with caution. Estimate is based on 10 or fewer sample cases or coefficient of variation is greater than 50%.
[1]Includes rape or sexual assault, robbery, aggravated assault, and simple assault. Excludes homicide because the National Crime Victimization Survey is based on interviews with victims.
[2]Includes rape or sexual assault, robbery, and aggravated assault.
[3]Excludes persons of Hispanic/Latino origin (e.g., "White" refers to non-Hispanic White persons and "Black" refers to non-Hispanic Black persons).
[4]Includes American Indians and Alaska Natives and persons of two or more races.

Table 7. Rate of Victimization, by Type of Crime and Location of Residence, 2019 and 2020

(Rate.[1])

Location of residence	Violent crime[2]		Violent crime excluding simple assault[3]		Property crime[4]	
	2019	2020*	2019	2020*	2019	2020*
Urban[5]......................	21.1	19.0	8.0	7.7	153.0	158.9
Suburban[6]...................	22.3[A]	16.8	5.6[A]	5.6	100.8[A]	90.5
Rural[7]......................	16.3	13.4	4.5	4.5	68.1	65.6

* = Comparison year.
A = Significant difference from comparison year at the 90% confidence level.
[1]Rate is per 1,000 persons age 12 or older for violent crime and per 1,000 households for property crime.
[2]Includes rape or sexual assault, robbery, aggravated assault, and simple assault. Excludes homicide because the National Crime Victimization Survey (NCVS) is based on interviews with victims.
[3]Includes rape or sexual assault, robbery, and aggravated assault.
[4]Includes burglary, residential trespassing, motor-vehicle theft, and other theft.
[5]All census blocks within cities or U.S. Census Bureau-designated places that meet certain criteria based on their population and density. See Methodology in Criminal Victimization, 2019 (NCJ 255113, BJS, September 2020).
[6]All other census blocks not classified as urban or rural.
[7]All census blocks not in Census Bureau-defined urbanized areas or urban clusters.

Table 8. Firearm Violence, 2019 and 2020

(Number; rate; percent.)

Type of crime	2019	2020*
Total violent victimizations.........................	5,813,410[A]	4,558,150
Firearm victimizations.............................	481,950[A]	350,460
Rate of firearm victimization[1]....................	1.7[A]	1.3
Firearm victimizations reported to police		
Number.................................	290,790[A]	212,470
Percent.................................	60.3	60.6

NOTE: Includes violent crimes in which the offender possessed, showed, or used a firearm.
* = Comparison year.
A = Significant difference from comparison year at the 95% confidence level.
[1]Rate is per 1,000 persons age 12 or older. See appendix table 11 for person populations.

METHODOLOGY

Data are from the Bureau of Justice Statistics' (BJS) National Crime Victimization Survey (NCVS), which collects information on nonfatal crimes against persons age 12 or older from a nationally representative sample of U.S. households. The NCVS measures violent crimes, which include rape or sexual assault, robbery, aggravated assault, and simple assault. Property crimes include household burglary, motor vehicle theft, and theft. The survey also measures personal larceny, which includes pickpocketing and purse snatching. Unless otherwise noted, findings in this report are significant at the 95 percent confidence level. For additional estimates excluded from this report, see the NCVS Victimization Analysis Tool (NVAT) on the BJS Web site.

The NCVS is a self-reported survey administered annually from January 1 to December 31. Annual NCVS estimates are based on the number and characteristics of crimes respondents experienced during the prior 6 months, not including the month in which they were interviewed. Therefore, the 2020 survey covers crimes experienced from July 1, 2019, to November 30, 2020, and March 15, 2020, is the middle of the reference period. Crimes are classified by the year of the survey and not by the year of the crime.

NCVS data can be used to produce:

- **Prevalence estimates**: The number or percentage of unique persons who were crime victims, or of unique households that experienced crime.

- **Victimization estimates**: The total number of times that people or households were victimized by crime. For personal crimes, the number of victimizations is the number of victims of that crime. Each crime against a household is counted as having a single victim—the affected household.

- **Incident estimates**: The number of specific criminal acts involving one or more victims.

COVID-19 AND ITS IMPACT

In a typical year, the National Crime Victimization Survey (NCVS) is administered from January 1 through December 31 to persons age 12 or older from a nationally representative sample of U.S. households. Selected households remain in the sample for 3.5 years, and eligible persons in these households are interviewed every 6 months, for a total of seven interviews. All new households entering the panel (incoming sample) are interviewed in person (personal visits). Households that have already been interviewed at least once (returning sample) are interviewed either in person or over the phone.

Due to increasing risks related to COVID-19, the Bureau of Justice Statistics (BJS), in coordination with the U.S. Census Bureau, suspended all incoming sample interviews and shifted all returning sample interviews to telephone calls starting in mid-March 2020. In July 2020, modified personal visits resumed in some geographic areas for returning sample households, based on applicable federal, state, and local guidance at that time. These modifications allowed field representatives (FRs) to leave survey information at respondents' doors and to classify vacant or abandoned properties. Without the FR's visit, these households would have been misclassified as non-respondents. In October 2020, personal visits resumed for both incoming and returning sample households, under modified procedures and subject to federal, state, and local guidance. Interviews were primarily conducted over the phone through the end of 2020.

The household response rate dropped from an average of 71 percent during 2019 to 63 percent in May 2020, before rising to 72 percent in September 2020. Response rates remained steady in the last quarter of 2020, such that the overall unweighted household response rate was 67 percent in 2020.

To address the impact of these modified field operations due to COVID-19, BJS, in collaboration with the U.S. Census Bureau, examined the 2020 data to determine what adjustments were needed to ensure comparability with past and future years of NCVS data. To inform this process, a series of simulations using 2019 NCVS data were developed to assess differences related to changes in the field operations. As a result of this analysis, several adjustments were applied to the 2020 NCVS data:

- Weights for the incoming sample in the first and fourth quarters of 2020 were doubled to compensate for the suppressed incoming sample in the second and third quarters.

- Household weights for the types of group quarters included in the NCVS were controlled to match historical values.

- Household control weights were developed to weight household distributions by sample type.

For more information on the 2020 response rates and weighting adjustments, see the *Source and Accuracy Statement for the 2020 National Crime Victimization Survey* in the NCVS 2020 Codebook (https://www.icpsr.umich.edu/web/NACJD/series/95) and the most recent version of the *National Crime Victimization Survey, 2016: Technical Documentation* (NCJ 251442, BJS, December 2017).

NCVS Methods of Variance Estimation

For surveys with complex sample designs, such as the NCVS, several methods can be used to estimate the magnitude of sampling error associated with an estimate. In previous reports, BJS has used both generalized variance function (GVF) parameters and direct-variance estimation for generating standard errors and testing statistically significant differences between NCVS estimates. Compared to GVFs, direct-variance estimation is generally considered more accurate in approximating the true variance.

This year's bulletin presents tables 1 and 2 using the Balanced Repeated Replication (BRR) method, a form of direct-variance estimation, and continues to present other victimization and incidence estimates using GVFs (except for totals in tables 4, 9, 24, and 25 that are also presented in tables 1 and 2, and statistics in table 12 that are based on the new classification of urban, suburban, and rural areas). The Taylor Series Linearization (TSL) method, another form of direct-variance estimation, continues to be used to generate standard errors for prevalence estimates. BJS has an active research program on direct-variance estimation that seeks to improve the quality and accuracy of NCVS estimates.

NCVS AND UCR

The Bureau of Justice Statistics' National Crime Victimization Survey (NCVS) measures crime reported and not reported to police. The Uniform Crime Reporting (UCR) program, administered by the Federal Bureau of Investigation (FBI), measures only crime recorded by police.

In 2018, the UCR reported that 3.7 total violent crimes (including murder and non-negligent manslaughter, rape, robbery, and aggravated assault) per 1,000 residents and 22.0 property crimes (including burglary and motor-vehicle theft) per 1,000 residents were known to law enforcement. The 2018 NCVS estimated that 4.3 violent crimes excluding simple assault per 1,000 persons age 12 or older, and 36.9 property crimes per 1,000 households, were reported to law enforcement. The 2019 NCVS estimated that 3.4 violent crimes excluding simple assault per 1,000 persons age 12 or older, and 33.0 property crimes per 1,000 households, were reported to law enforcement.

Because the NCVS and the UCR measure an overlapping, but not identical, set of offenses and use different approaches in measuring them, complete congruity should not be expected between estimates from these two sources. Restricting the NCVS to violent crime reported to police, and excluding simple assault, keeps the measures as similar as possible. However, significant methodological and definitional differences remain between how these violent crimes are measured in the NCVS and the UCR:

The UCR includes murder, non-negligent manslaughter, and commercial crimes (including burglary of commercial establishments), while the NCVS excludes those crime types.

The UCR excludes sexual assault, which the NCVS includes.

The UCR property-crime rates are per person, while the NCVS's are per household. (There were 2.2 persons age 12 or older per household in 2019.) Moreover, because the number of households may not grow at the same rate each year as the total population, trend data for rates of property crimes measured by the two programs may not be entirely comparable.

NCVS estimates are based on interviews with a nationally representative sample of persons in U.S. households. UCR estimates are based on counts of crimes recorded by law enforcement agencies and are weighted to compensate for incomplete reporting.

The NCVS does not measure crimes against persons who are homeless or who live in institutions (e.g., nursing homes and correctional institutions) or on military bases. Also, it does not measure crimes against children age 11 or younger. The UCR measures crimes against all U.S. residents, including crimes against children age 11 or younger. In some states mandatory reporting laws require that persons report certain crimes against youth. Due to these factors, the age distribution of crimes measured in the UCR differs from that of the NCVS.

Taken together, these two measures of crime provide a more comprehensive picture of crime in the U.S. For additional information about the differences between the NCVS and UCR, see *The Nation's Two Crime Measures*(NCJ 246832, BJS, September 2014).

Classification of Urban, Suburban, and Rural Areas in the National Crime Victimization Survey

This year, the Bureau of Justice Statistics (BJS) provides new classifications of urban, suburban, and rural areas for the National Crime Victimization Survey (NCVS), with the goal of presenting a more accurate picture of where criminal victimizations occur.

Historically, the NCVS has classified areas as urban, suburban, or rural based on the following definitions:

- **Urban**: within a principal city of a Metropolitan Statistical Area (MSA)

- **Suburban**: within an MSA but not within a principal city of the MSA

- **Rural**: outside of an MSA

These definitions are straightforward, but they suffer from two main shortcomings:

1. Metropolitan statistical areas are based on entire counties, and counties almost always contain both rural and non-rural areas. Yet the NCVS's historical definitions classify each county as being either entirely rural (if not part of an MSA) or entirely non-rural (if part of an MSA). For example, California's San Bernardino County, which includes much of the Mojave Desert and covers more than twice as much land as the state of Maryland, is classified as containing no rural areas under the NCVS's historical definitions. This is because San Bernardino County is part of the Riverside-San Bernardino-Ontario MSA, and the NCVS's historical definitions do not classify any part of an MSA as being rural. On the other hand, Colorado's La Plata County, home of Durango, is classified under the historical definitions as being entirely rural, because it is not part of an MSA. This is true even though the Census Bureau says that, as of 2010, 40 percent of La Plata County's population lived in non-rural areas. Similarly, Casmalia, Calif. had a 2010 population of 138 people and is surrounded by undeveloped land. Because it is located within a county (Santa Barbara) that is designated as an MSA (the Santa Maria-Santa Barbara MSA), the NCVS's historical definitions classify Casmalia as suburban. Meanwhile, Bozeman, Mont., with a 2010 population of 37,280—270 times that of Casmalia—is classified by the NCVS's historical definitions as rural, because it is located in a county that is not part of an MSA.

2. The Office of Management and Budget (OMB) designates principal cities (of which there are anywhere from 1 to nearly 20 in a given MSA) as being among "the more significant places in each Metropolitan and Micropolitan Statistical Area . . . in terms of population and employment." The principal city designation is not necessarily indicative of urban status, nor is it intended to be. Yet the NCVS's historical definitions classify all principal cities of MSAs as urban, and all other places as not urban. As a result, Union City, N.J., located just across the Hudson River from Midtown Manhattan, is classified by the NCVS's historical definitions as suburban, due to its not being defined as a principal city. Union City had a 2010 population density of 51,918 people per square mile, more than three times the population density of San Francisco (17,180). Meanwhile, Rome, N.Y., which had a 2010 population density of 451 people per square mile—less than 1 percent that of Union City—is classified by the historical definitions as urban. The same is true for Yuma, Ariz., Hilton Head Island, S.C., and Foley, Ala. None of these had a population density in 2010 that was even 2 percent that of Union City, yet all are classified as urban under the NCVS's historical definitions, while Union City is classified as suburban.

These are not isolated examples. Weighted housing-unit density (discussed more below) is essentially a measure of how closely people live to one another. Based on the 2010 Census of Population and Housing and 2013 OMB principal-city designations, 506 of the 674 principal cities in the United States (75 percent) had weighted housing-unit densities below that of the U.S. as a whole. In other words, three-quarters of the places classified by the historical definitions as urban were *less* densely developed than the areas where most U.S. residents lived.

A New Definition

BJS's new NCVS definition of urban is based on the notion that urban places are those that are densely populated, are at the center of a major metropolitan area, or some combination of these. BJS's specific criteria is that a place is urban if it is:

- The main city or Census-designated place (i.e., the first place listed) in a 500,000-person (Census-designated) "urbanized area," with a weighted housing-unit density within its city limits of at least 3,000 housing units per square mile. In other words, the primary city in a large "urbanized area" qualifies as urban if it meets the weighted-housing-unit-density threshold of 3,000 housing units per square mile. (The overall weighted housing-unit density for the U.S. is 2,396, based on the 2010 Census.)

- A named city or Census-designated place in a 500,000-person (Census-designated) "urbanized area," with a weighted housing-unit density of at least 4,000 housing units per square mile within its city limits. In other words, a city that is prominent enough to be included by the Census Bureau in the name of a large "urbanized area" (for example, Long Beach in the Los Angeles-Long Beach-Anaheim urbanized area) qualifies as urban if it meets the weighted-housing-unit-density threshold of 4,000 housing units per square mile.

- Any city or Census-designated place with a population of at least 50,000 and a weighted housing-unit density of at least 5,000 housing units per square mile.

- Any city or Census-designated place with a population of at least 10,000 and a weighted housing-unit density of at least 10,000 housing units per square mile.

The Census Bureau's "urbanized areas" referenced in this definition are similar to OMB's metropolitan areas, but they delineate areas of substantial population rather than utilizing entire counties. The weighted housing-unit density referenced in this definition is discussed in greater detail below.

In addition to developing this definition of urban, BJS has adopted the Census Bureau's definition of rural to replace the historical NCVS definition of rural. The Census Bureau provides specific, carefully drawn boundaries around "urban areas" (both larger "urbanized areas" and smaller "urban clusters") using set criteria, classifying everything outside of those boundaries as rural.

BJS classifies areas that are neither urban nor rural as suburban. In comparison to places that are urban, suburban areas are characterized by lower density, a larger ratio of single-family homes to apartments, and layouts based principally on automobile transportation. Some suburban areas, those that might be thought of as "suburbia proper," do not have their own urban centers but are located near a separate urban city. Other suburban areas are cities or towns that have urban centers, but those centers have smaller populations than their surrounding suburban areas, so the bulk of the city's population lives in suburban areas. (Cities are the smallest geographical designations that can realistically be used in classifying areas as urban.) In short, suburban areas are a mix of "suburbia proper," towns, and some generally smaller cities that are more suburban than urban.

BJS uses weighted housing-unit density in its new NCVS definitions because that measure provides a better indication of the degree of urban density than conventional population density does. Conventional population density is derived by dividing population by land area, and it measures how densely populated a given area of land is. As of the 2010 Census, the U.S. as a whole had a conventional population density of 87 people per square mile; however, most U.S. residents do not live in areas where there are only 87 people per square mile. The experience of most U.S. residents is more fully captured by weighted population density, which is essentially a measure of how densely populated an area is from the perspective of those who live in it.

Weighted housing-unit density is similar to weighted population density, with the difference being that the latter focuses on population and the former on housing units. In comparing weighted housing-unit density to weighted population density, John R. Ottensmann writes, "Housing units better represent the physical pattern of urban development, as they are relatively fixed."

Housing-unit density is the number of housing units per square mile in a given area. Weighted housing-unit density, under BJS's approach, is the weighted average of the housing densities for all census tracts in an area, with the tracts weighted by their number of housing units.

For ease of explanation, imagine an area with only two census tracts. One tract has 2,000 housing units, covers 2 square miles, and thus has a housing-unit density of 1,000 housing units per square mile. The other tract has 6,000 housing units, covers 1 square mile, and thus has a housing-unit density of 6,000 housing units per square mile. The area's weighted housing-unit density is the weighted average of these two tract-level housing-unit densities, or $(1,000 \times 2,000 \times 6,000 \times 6,000) / 8,000 = 4,750$. Otherwise put, the weighted housing-unit density is based one-quarter on the first tract's density (because it contains one-quarter of the housing units) and three-quarters on the second tract's density.

Weighted housing-unit density identifies urban places much more clearly than conventional population density does. Among places with populations of at least 10,000 people in 2010, Chicago rises from number 71 in conventional population density to number 16 in weighted housing-unit density, New Orleans from number 2,212 to number 190, and Urban Honolulu from number 474 to number 13. Meanwhile, Passaic, N.J. falls from number 7 in conventional population density to number 45 in weighted housing-unit density, while Santa Ana, Calif. falls from number 67 to number 237 (moving from 4 places above Chicago to 221 places below).

Comparing the Old and New Definitions

Both the old and new NCVS definitions, as would be expected, classify New York's five boroughs as urban (New York City's weighted housing-unit density is a nation-leading 29,345 housing units per square mile), and they both add Jersey City, N.J. (weighted housing-unit density of 13,837 housing units per square mile), Newark, N.J. (8,788), and White Plains, N.Y. (5,671). The old definition also includes New Brunswick, N.J. (4,908) and Lakewood, N.J. (2,106).

The new definition reclassifies Lakewood and New Brunswick as suburban (although just a 2 percent increase in New Brunswick's weighted housing-unit density would qualify it as urban) and adds the following places as urban: Guttenberg, N.J. (weighted housing-unit density of 29,171 housing units per square mile); Hoboken, N.J. (25,870); West New York (21,763); Union City, N.J. (20,477); Cliffside Park, N.J. (12,001); Mount Vernon, N.Y. (8,811); East Orange, N.J. (8,763); Bayonne, N.J. (8,263); Yonkers, N.Y. (7,930); Elizabeth, N.J. (7,468); Passaic, N.J. (7,424); and Paterson, N.J. (6,739).

As the accompanying map of the Washington, D.C. area shows, both the old and new definitions include Washington, D.C. (weighted housing-unit density of 10,115 housing units per square mile), Arlington, Va. (10,485), Alexandria, Va. (7,714), and Silver Spring, Md. (6,135), as urban places. The new definitions do not classify anywhere else in the D.C. area as urban. The old definitions added as urban Bethesda, Md. (4,325), Gaithersburg, Md. (2,836), Reston, Va. (2,543), Rockville, Md. (2,534), and Frederick, Md. (2,235), all of which the new definitions classify as suburban.

The new definitions more closely fit U.S. residents' own sense of where they live, as reflected in the American Housing Survey (AHS). For each of five metropolitan or micropolitan area designations, the following table and figure show how most AHS respondents in 2017 classified where they lived (and what percentage of respondents gave that classification), what percentage of people would be classified that same way by the new and old NCVS definitions, and the difference between the AHS result and the new and old NCVS results.

As table 11 shows, 58 percent of AHS respondents who lived in the biggest principal city of an MSA said that they lived in an urban place. Forty-three percent of them would be classified as living in an urban place by the new NCVS definitions, a difference of 15 percentage points (58 percent versus 43 percent) from the portion of AHS respondents who gave that answer. In comparison, 100 percent of those respondents would be classified as living in an urban place by the old NCVS definitions, a difference of 42 percentage points (58 percent vs. 100 percent) from the portion of AHS respondents who gave that answer. While AHS respondents' answers about where they live are not necessarily dispositive, the new NCVS definitions fare far better than the old ones versus the AHS in every category, by a margin of at least 21 percentage points per category and an average margin of 33 points per category.

Under the new definitions, 12 percent of the population lives in urban areas, 69 percent in suburban areas, and 19 percent in rural areas, compared to 33 percent in urban areas, 53 percent in suburban areas, and 14 percent in rural areas under the old definitions. Of the main cities in the 15 largest MSAs in the U.S., the new definitions classify 13 as urban. The two classified as suburban—Phoenix, Ariz. and Riverside, Calif.—had 2010 weighted housing-unit densities below that of the U.S. as a whole.

According to the historical NCVS definitions, by far the most urban region in the country is the West, followed by the South (using the Census Bureau's regional classifications). Under the new definitions, the Northeast is by far the most urban region, followed in order by the West, Midwest, and South. The most suburban region according to the old definitions is the Northeast. Under the new definitions, the West is the most suburban region, with the Northeast being the least suburban region.

2016 NCVS SAMPLE REDESIGN

To produce estimates on criminal victimization, the Bureau of Justice Statistics' (BJS) National Crime Victimization Survey (NCVS) collects information from a sample of U.S. households that represents the nation. The sample design is periodically changed to maintain the representativeness of the survey. In 2016, the NCVS sample was redesigned for two reasons:

1. To reflect changes in the U.S. population based on the 2010 Decennial Census

2. To make it possible to produce state- and local-level victimization estimates for the largest 22 states and specific metropolitan areas within those states

Every 10 years, the U.S. Census Bureau conducts the official population count of the United States. In 2016, a redesign of the NCVS sample was necessary to account for shifts in the population identified through the 2010 Decennial Census. From 2000 to 2010, the number of people residing in individual U.S. counties changed. Almost two-thirds of the nation's 3,143 counties gained population. Most counties along coastlines experienced population growth during this period, while others that lost population were clustered by region and were found in areas such as the Great Plains and Mississippi Delta.

The NCVS sampling process involves selecting primary sampling units (PSUs), which are counties, groups of counties, or large metropolitan areas identified through the Decennial Census and the U.S. Census Bureau's American Community Survey. Within the PSUs selected, the sampling process identifies addresses to be included in the sample and interviews are conducted with persons and households at those addresses. Sampled households remain in the NCVS sample for seven waves (each wave is a 6-month period). The decennial sample update ensures that the sample reflects current population distributions. This process requires a phased shift of counties included in the 2000 sample design to those selected for the 2010 sample design, resulting in three types of counties in 2016: (1) continuing counties—those in both the 2000 and 2010 sample designs; (2) outgoing counties—those that were in the 2000 sample design, but not the 2010 sample design; and (3) new counties—those that were selected into the 2010 sample design, but were not in the 2000 sample design.

As part of ongoing efforts to enhance the usefulness and relevance of the NCVS, the sample also was expanded and redistributed to produce state and local estimates of victimization. Because the primary purpose of the NCVS has been to generate national estimates, the sample was initially designed to be representative of the United States as a whole and not individual states and local areas. To produce reliable estimates for the 22 most populous states and specific metropolitan areas within those states, it was necessary to change the NCVS sample design.

IMPLICATIONS OF THE 2016 SAMPLE REDESIGN

When the 2016 NCVS data collection was complete, a comparison of the 2015 and 2016 victimization estimates showed that the violent and property crime rates had increased. Given recent patterns in NCVS data, these increases seemed too large to be a result of actual growth in crime, suggesting that the sample redesign may have affected the victimization rates. To better understand these results, the 2015 and 2016 victimization rates for new and continuing sample counties were examined separately. These comparisons showed that from 2015 to 2016 there were no statistically significant differences for continuing sample counties in the rates of total property crime, total violent crime, and total serious violent crime. In comparison, rates of total violent crime and total serious violent crime were higher in the new sample counties than in the outgoing sample counties.

DIFFERENCES IN RATES OF REPORTING TO POLICE IN THE UCR AND NCVS

For 2016, the Federal Bureau of Investigation's (FBI) Uniform Crime Reporting (UCR) program showed that 3.9 serious violent crimes per 1,000 persons and 24.5 property crimes per 1,000 persons were known to law enforcement. According to the Bureau of Justice Statistics' (BJS) National Crime Victimization Survey (NCVS), 3.6 serious violent crimes per 1,000 persons age 12 or older and 42.6 property crimes per 1,000 households were reported to law enforcement during this same year.

Because the NCVS and UCR measure an overlapping, but not identical, set of offenses and use different methodologies, congruity is not expected between estimates from these two data sources. Restricting the NCVS to serious violence reported to police keeps the measures as similar as possible. However, significant methodological and definitional differences remain between serious violent crimes in the NCVS and the UCR:

- The UCR includes homicide and commercial crimes, while the NCVS excludes these crime types.

- The UCR excludes sexual assault, which the NCVS includes.

- NCVS estimates are based on interviews with a nationally representative sample of persons in U.S. households. UCR estimates are based on counts of crimes reported by an incomplete census of law enforcement agencies and are weighted to compensate for the incomplete reporting.

- The NCVS excludes crimes against children age 11 or younger and persons in institutions (e.g., nursing homes and correctional institutions). It may also exclude highly mobile populations and persons who are homeless. Victimizations against these persons are included in the UCR.

Given these differences, the two measures of crime should not be compared but should be viewed as complementary sources, which together provide a more comprehensive picture of crime in the United States. For additional information about the differences between the two programs, see *The Nation's Two Crime Measures* (NCJ 246832, BJS web, September 2014).

PREVALENCE OF CRIME

Annual estimates of a population's risk for criminal victimization may be examined using victimization or prevalence rates. Historically, Bureau of Justice Statistics (BJS) reports based on National Crime Victimization Survey (NCVS) data rely on victimization rates, which measure the extent to which victimizations occur in a specified population during a specific time. For crimes affecting persons, NCVS victimization rates are estimated by dividing the number of victimizations that occur during a specified time (T) by the population at risk for those victimizations and multiplying the rate by 1,000.

Prevalence rates also describe the level of victimization but are based on the number of unique persons (or households) in the population experiencing at least one victimization during a specified time. The key distinction between a victimization and prevalence rate is whether the numerator consists of the number of victimizations or victims. For example, a person who experienced two robberies on separate occasions within the past year would be counted twice in the victimization rate but once in the prevalence rate. Prevalence rates are estimated by dividing the number of victims in the specified population by the total number of persons in the population and multiplying the rate by 100. This is the percentage of the population victimized at least once in a given period.

Victimization and prevalence rates may also be produced for household crimes, such as burglary. In these instances, numerators and denominators are adjusted to reflect households rather than persons. To better understand the percentage of the population that is victimized at least once in a given period, prevalence rates are presented by type of crime and certain demographic characteristics. (For further information about measuring prevalence in the NCVS, see *Measuring the Prevalence of Crime with the National Crime Victimization Survey*, NCJ 241656, BJS web, September 2013.)

SURVEY METHODOLOGY

The Bureau of Justice Statistics' National Crime Victimization Survey (NCVS) is an annual data collection carried out by the U.S. Census Bureau. The NCVS is a self-reported survey that is administered annually from January 1 to December 31. Annual NCVS estimates are based on the number and characteristics of crimes respondents experienced during the prior 6 months, not including the month in which they were interviewed. Therefore, the 2019 survey covers crimes experienced from July 1, 2018, to November 30, 2019, and March 15, 2019, is the middle of the reference period. Crimes are classified by the year of the survey and not by the year of the crime.

The NCVS is administered to persons age 12 or older from a nationally representative sample of U.S. households. It collects information on nonfatal personal crimes (rape or sexual assault, robbery, aggravated and simple assault, and personal larceny (purse-snatching and pick-pocketing) and household property crimes (burglary/trespassing, motor-vehicle theft, and other types of theft). The survey collects information on threatened, attempted, and completed crimes. It collects data both on crimes reported and not reported to police. Unless specified otherwise, estimates in this report include threatened, attempted, and completed crimes. In addition to providing annual level and change estimates on criminal victimization, the NCVS is the primary source of information on the nature of criminal victimization incidents.

Survey respondents provide information about themselves (including age, sex, race, ethnicity, marital status, educational level, and income) and whether they experienced a victimization. For each victimization incident, respondents report information about the offender (including age, sex, race, ethnicity, and victim-offender relationship), characteristics of the crime (including time and place of occurrence, use of weapons, nature of injury, and economic consequences), whether the crime was reported to police, reasons the crime was or was not reported, and experiences with the criminal justice system.

Household information, including household-level demographics (e.g., income) and property victimizations committed against the household (e.g., burglary/trespassing), is typically collected from the reference person. The reference person is any responsible adult member of the household who is not likely to permanently leave the household. Because an owner or renter of the sampled housing unit is normally the most responsible and knowledgeable household member, this person is generally designated as the reference person and household respondent. However, a household respondent does not have to be one of the household members who owns or rents the unit.

In the NCVS, a household is defined as a group of persons who all reside at a sampled address. Persons are considered household members when the sampled address is their usual place of residence at the time of the interview and when they have no primary place of residence elsewhere. Once selected, households remain in the sample for 3½ years, and eligible persons in these households are interviewed every 6 months, either in person or over the phone, for a total of seven interviews.

First interviews are typically conducted in person, with subsequent interviews conducted either in person or by phone. New households rotate into the sample on an ongoing basis to replace outgoing households that have been in the sample for the full 3½-year period. The sample includes persons living in group quarters, such as dormitories, rooming houses, and religious-group dwellings, and excludes persons living on military bases or in institutional settings such as correctional or hospital facilities.al or hospital facilities, and persons who are homeless.

Measurement of Crime in the National Crime Victimization Survey

BJS presents data from the NCVS on victimization, incident, and prevalence rates. Victimization rates measure the extent to which violent and property victimizations occur in a specified population during a specified time. Victimization numbers show the total number of times that people or households are victimized by crime. For crimes affecting persons, NCVS victimization rates are estimated by dividing the number of victimizations that occur during a specified time by the population at risk for those victimizations and multiplying the rate by 1,000.

For victimization rates, each victimization represents one person (for personal crimes) or one household (for property crimes) affected by a crime. Every victimization experienced by a person or household during the year is counted. For example, if one person experiences two violent crimes during the year, both are counted in the victimization rate. If one household experiences two property crimes, both are counted in the victimization rate. Victimization estimates are presented in figure 3, tables 1 through 10, table 12, and tables 23 through 25 in this report.

Incident rates are another measure of crime. The number of incidents is the number of specific criminal acts involving one or more victims. If every victimization had one victim, the number of incidents would be the same as the number of victimizations. If there was more than one victim, the incident estimate is adjusted to compensate for the possibility that the incident could be reported several times by multiple victims and thus be over-counted. For example, if two people were robbed during the same incident, this crime would be counted as one incident and two victimizations. Incident estimates are presented in tables 13 through 17, and tables 25 through 30 in this report.

A third measure, reflecting a population's risk of experiencing one or more criminal victimizations, is prevalence rates. Like victimization rates, prevalence rates describe the level of victimization, but the latter are based on the number of unique persons or households in the population experiencing at least one victimization during a specified time. The key distinction between a victimization and prevalence rate is whether the numerator consists of the number of victimizations or the number of unique victims. For example, a person who experienced two robberies within the past year would be counted twice in the victimization rate but only once in the prevalence rate. Prevalence rates are estimated by dividing the number of unique victims or victimized households in the specified population by the total number of persons or households in the population and multiplying the rate by 100, yielding the percentage of the population victimized at least once in a period.

Prevalence rates are presented in figures 1 and 2, and tables 18 through 22 in this report. Prevalence rates for property crimes can be produced at the household or person levels by adjusting the numerators and denominators to reflect households or persons. Table 20 presents property-crime prevalence rates at the household level, and table 21 presents serious property-crime prevalence rates at the personal level.

For more information about measuring prevalence in the NCVS, see *Measuring the Prevalence of Crime with the National Crime Victimization Survey* (NCJ 241656, BJS, September 2013).

NONRESPONSE AND WEIGHTING ADJUSTMENTS

The 2019 NCVS data file includes 155,076 household interviews. Overall, 71 percent of eligible households completed interviews. Within participating households, interviews with

249,008 persons were completed in 2019, representing an 83 percent response rate among eligible persons from responding households.

Victimizations that occurred outside of the U.S. were excluded from this report. In 2019, about 1 percent of the unweighted victimizations occurred outside of the U.S.

NCVS data are weighted to produce annual estimates of victimization for persons age 12 or older living in U.S. households. Because the NCVS relies on a sample rather than a census of the entire U.S. population, weights are designed to adjust to known population totals and to compensate for survey non-response and other aspects of the complex sample design.

NCVS data files include person, household, victimization, and incident weights. Person weights provide an estimate of the population represented by each person in the sample. Household weights provide an estimate of the household population represented by each household in the sample. After proper adjustment, both person and household weights are also typically used to form the denominator in calculations of crime rates. For personal crimes, the incident weight is derived by dividing the person weight of a victim by the total number of persons victimized during an incident, as reported by the respondent. For property crimes measured at the household level, the incident weight and the household weight are the same, because the victim of a property crime is considered to be the household as a whole. The incident weight is most frequently used to calculate estimates of offenders' and victims' demographics.

Victimization weights used in this report account for the number of persons victimized during an incident and for high-frequency repeat-victimizations (i.e., series victimizations). Series victimizations are similar in type to one another but occur with such frequency that a victim is unable to recall each individual event or describe each event in detail. Survey procedures allow NCVS interviewers to identify and classify these similar victimizations as series victimizations and to collect detailed information on only the most recent incident in the series.

The weighting counts series victimizations as the actual number of victimizations reported by the victim, up to a maximum of 10. Doing so produces more reliable estimates of crime levels than counting such victimizations only once, while the cap at 10 minimizes the effect of extreme outliers on rates. According to the 2019 data, series victimizations accounted for 1.4 percent of all victimizations and 3.1 percent of all violent victimizations. Additional information on the enumeration of series victimizations is detailed in the report *Methods for Counting High-Frequency Repeat Victimizations in the National Crime Victimization Survey* (NCJ 237308, BJS, April 2012).

Changes to the Household Weighting Adjustment in 2017

The 2017 NCVS weights included a new adjustment that modified household weights to reflect independent housing-unit totals available internally at the U.S. Census Bureau. This new adjustment was applied only to household weights for housing units and does not affect person weights. Historically, the household weights were adjusted to reflect independent totals for the person population. This new weighting adjustment improves on the prior one and better aligns the number of estimated households in the NCVS with other Census household-survey estimates. Due to this new adjustment, the 2017 NCVS estimate for the number of households was about 8 percent lower than the 2016 NCVS estimate. As a result, the estimate of the number of households affected by property crime was also about 8 percent lower. When making comparisons of property crime at the household level between 2017 and prior years, compare victimization or prevalence *rates*. Rates are unaffected by this change in weighting methodology because both the numerator and denominator are equally affected. Comparisons of the number of households that were victimized between 2017 and prior years are inappropriate due to this change in weighting methodology. Property crime measured at the person level is unaffected by the change (as presented in measures of serious crime). For more information on weighting in the NCVS, see the *Non-response and weighting adjustments* section in this methodology and *National Crime Victimization Survey, 2016 Technical Documentation* (NCJ 251442, BJS, December 2017).

Changes to the Classification of Urban, Suburban, and Rural Areas

Beginning in 2019, the NCVS employed a new method for classifying geographical areas (see *Classification of urban, suburban, and rural areas in the National Crime Victimization Survey* on pp. 12–15). All census blocks not in urbanized areas or urbanized clusters, as defined by the Census Bureau, are classified as rural, consistent with the Census Bureau's definition of rural. Census blocks within cities or Census-designated places that meet certain criteria based on population and density are classified as urban (see appendix table 36), while all other census blocks in urbanized areas or urban clusters are classified as suburban.

Classifications of urban places are based on population size, weighted housing-unit density, and the Census Bureau's designations of urbanized areas and urban clusters, using data from the 2010 Census. Housing-unit density is the number of housing units per square mile in a given area. Weighted housing-unit density, under BJS's approach, is the weighted average of the housing-unit densities for all census tracts in an area, with the tracts weighted by their number of housing units. Housing-unit addresses are converted into geographical coordinates through a process called geocoding. Housing units that cannot be geocoded are imputed. For more information on imputation procedures, see *National Crime Victimization Survey, 2016 Technical Documentation* (NCJ 251442, BJS, December 2017).

Table 31 shows the 2019 U.S. resident population for those age 12 or older and the number of households in each category (urban, suburban, rural) under both the new and historical classifications. About one-third of the U.S. resident population age 12 or older were classified as residing in an urban area under the historical definition, compared to about one-eighth under the new definition. The percentage of the resident population classified as residing in a suburban area shifted from 53 percent to 69 percent, while the percentage classified as rural shifted from 14 percent to 19 percent. Similar shifts in the number of households were observed under the new classification.

STANDARD ERROR COMPUTATIONS

When national estimates are derived from a sample, as with the NCVS, caution must be used when comparing one estimate to another or when comparing estimates over time. Although one estimate may be larger than another, estimates based on a sample have some degree of sampling error. The sampling error of an estimate depends on several factors, including the amount of variation in the responses and the size of the sample. When the sampling error around an estimate is taken into account, estimates that appear different may not be statistically significant.

One measure of the sampling error associated with an estimate is the standard error. The standard error may vary from one estimate to the next. Generally, an estimate with a smaller standard error provides a more reliable approximation of the true value than an estimate with a larger standard error. Estimates with relatively large standard errors have less precision and reliability and should be interpreted with caution.

NCVS MEASUREMENT OF RAPE AND SEXUAL ASSAULT

Thee NCVS uses a two-stage measurement approach in the screening and classification of criminal victimization, including rape and sexual assault. In the first stage of screening, survey respondents are administered a series of "short-cue" screening questions designed to help respondents think about different experiences they may have had during the reference period (see NCVS-1 at https://www.bjs.gov/content/pub/pdf/ncvs15_bsq.pdf).

This design improves respondent recall of events, particularly for incidents that may not immediately come to mind as crimes, such as those committed by family members and acquaintances. Respondents who answer affirmatively to any of the short-cue screening items are subsequently administered a crime incident report (CIR) designed to classify incidents into specific crime types (see NCVS-2 at https://www.bjs.gov/content/pub/pdf/ncvs15_cir.pdf).

First Stage of Measurement

Two short-cue screening questions are specifically designed to target sexual violence:

1. Other than any incidents already mentioned, has anyone attacked or threatened you in any of these ways: (a) with any weapon, such as a gun or knife; (b) with anything like a baseball bat, frying pan, scissors, or stick; (c) by something thrown, such as a rock or bottle; (d) by grabbing, punching, or choking; (e) any rape, attempted rape, or other types of sexual attack; (f) any face-to-face threats; *or* (g) any attack or threat or use of force by anyone at all? Please mention it even if you are not certain it was a crime.

2. Incidents involving forced or unwanted sexual acts are often difficult to talk about. Other than any incidents already mentioned, have you been forced or coerced to engage in unwanted sexual activity by (a) someone you did not know; (b) a casual acquaintance; or (c) someone you knew well?

Respondents may screen into a CIR if they respond affirmatively to another short-cue screening question. For instance, a separate screening question cues respondents to think of attacks or threats that took place in specific locations, such as at home, work, or school. A respondent who recalled a sexual victimization that occurred at home, work, or school and answered affirmatively would be administered a CIR even if they did not respond affirmatively to the screening question targeting sexual violence.

Second Stage of Measurement

The CIR is used to collect information on the attributes of each incident. e key attributes of sexual violence that are used to classify a victimization as a rape or sexual assault are the type of attack and physical injury suffered. Victims are asked if "the offender hit you, knock[ed] you down, or actually attack[ed] you in any way;" if "the offender TR[IED] to attack you;" or if "the offender THREATEN[ED] you with harm in any way?" e survey participant is classified as a victim of rape or sexual assault if he or she responds affirmatively to one of these three questions and then responds that the completed, attempted, or threatened attack was (a) rape; (b) attempted rape; (c) sexual assault; (d) verbal threat of rape; (e) verbal threat of sexual assault other than rape; (f) unwanted sexual contact with force (e.g., grabbing, fondling); or (g) unwanted sexual contact without force (e.g., grabbing, fondling).

Whether the victim selects one of these response options to describe the attack, he or she is also classified as a victim of rape or sexual assault if the injuries suffered as a result of the incident are described as: (a) rape; (b) attempted rape; or (c) sexual assault other than rape or attempted rape.

Coercion

Although the CIR does not ask respondents if psychological coercion was used, one screening question targeted to rape and sexual violence asks respondents if force or coercion was used to initiate unwanted sexual activity.

The final classification of incidents by the CIR results in the following definitions of rape and sexual assault used in the NCVS:

Rape: Coerced or forced sexual intercourse. Forced sexual intercourse means vaginal, anal, or oral penetration by the offender(s). is category could include incidents where the penetration was from a foreign object such as a bottle. Includes attempted rapes, male and female victims, and both heterosexual and same-sex rape. Attempted rape includes verbal threats of rape.

Sexual assault: A wide range of victimizations, separate from rape or attempted rape. ese crimes include attacks or attempted attacks generally involving unwanted sexual contact between victim and offender. Sexual assaults may or may not involve force and include such things as grabbing or fondling. Sexual assault also includes verbal threats.

COMPARISON OF NCVS ESTIMATES TO OTHER SURVEY ESTIMATES

During the past several decades, a number of other surveys have also been used to study rape and sexual assault in the general population. BJS estimates of rape and sexual assault from the NCVS have typically been lower than estimates derived from other federal and private surveys. However, the NCVS methodology and definitions of rape and sexual assault differ from many of these surveys in important ways that contribute to the variation in estimates of the prevalence and incidence of these victimizations. Additional information about differences in self-report estimates of rape and sexual assault is available on the BJS website. BJS continues an active research program on the collection of rape and sexual assault data in an effort to improve the quality and accuracy of these estimates.

Despite the current differences in methods and estimates that exist between the NCVS and other surveys measuring rape and sexual assault, a strength of the NCVS is its capacity to be used to make comparisons between population subgroups and over time. Methodological differences that exist between the NCVS and the other surveys should not impact NCVS comparisons between groups or in trends over time.

PART 4

Federal Justice Statistics, 2020

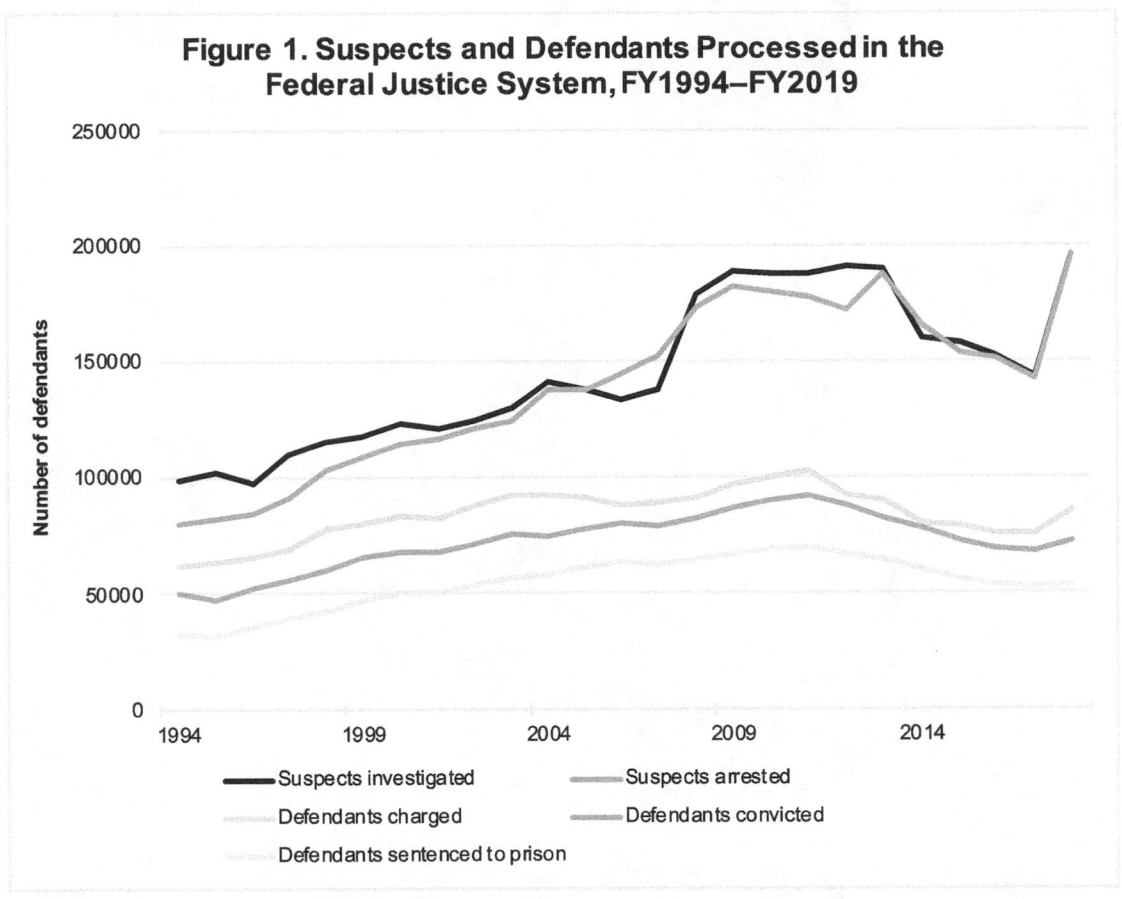

Figure 1. Suspects and Defendants Processed in the Federal Justice System, FY1994–FY2019

Legend:
- Suspects investigated
- Suspects arrested
- Defendants charged
- Defendants convicted
- Defendants sentenced to prison

- Federal law enforcement agencies made a total of 206,630 arrests in fiscal year (FY) 2019, a 6 percent increase from FY2018 (195,771 arrests) and a 14 percent increase from FY2009 (181,726 arrests).

- Nearly two-thirds (66 percent) of all federal arrests in FY2019 took place in the five federal judicial districts along the U.S.-Mexico border. These districts are listed individually in the tables in this section.

- Approximately 57 percent of federal arrests in FY2019 involved an immigration offense as the most serious arrest offense.

- In FY2019, Drug Enforcement Administration (DEA) arrests occurred most frequently for methamphetamine (9,076 arrests) and for heroin and opioids (6,686 arrests) of its 27,543 arrests.

- Approximately 29 percent of defendants charged in U.S. district court in FY2019 were from Mexico, while 10 percent were from Central America and 2 percent were from the Caribbean Islands; non-U.S. citizens made up 44 percent of defendants charged in FY2019.

Table 1. Persons in Federal Confinement or Under Federal Supervision in the Community, FY2009, FY2018, and FY2019 (Yearend)

(Number; percent.)

Characteristic	FY2009		FY2018		FY2019	
	Number	Percent	Number	Percent	Number	Percent
Total	389,031	100.0	372,354	100.0	373,056	100.0
In secure confinement............................	242,846	62.4	222,315	59.7	221,974	59.5
Pre-trial detention.................................	58,202	15.0	60,430	16.2	64,816	17.4
Federal Bureau of Prisons (post-sentencing)[1]	184,644	47.5	161,885	43.5	157,158	42.1
In the community.................................	146,185	37.6	150,039	40.3	151,082	40.5
Pre-trial release supervision...................	26,132	6.7	22,597	6.1	24,595	6.6
Post-sentencing supervision...................	120,053	30.9	127,442	34.2	126,487	33.9
Supervised release	94,703	24.3	111,024	29.8	110,932	29.7
Probation	23,054	5.9	15,465	4.2	14,658	3.9
Parole...	2,296	0.6	953	0.3	897	0.2

Note: Details may not sum to totals due to rounding. Federal populations are shown as of September 30, 2009, 2018, and 2019.
[1]Counts include federally sentenced persons in the custody of the Federal Bureau of Prisons (BOP). Counts exclude persons in federal prison for the District of Columbia code offenses, military code offenses, state boarders, and foreign treaty transfers. Unsentenced federal prisoners in the BOP are counted in pretrial detention counts.

Table 2. Federal Arrests, by Most Serious Offense and Federal District, FY2018 and FY2019

(Number; percent.)

Characteristic	FY2018		FY2019		Percent change, 2018–2019
	Number	Percent	Number	Percent	
Total arrests..............................	195,771	100.0	206,630	100.0	5.5
Most serious offense at arrest					
Violent..	3,811	1.9	3,807	1.8	-0.1
Property..	10,395	5.3	10,363	5.0	-0.3
Fraud...	8,966	4.6	8,954	4.3	-0.1
Other...	1,429	0.7	1,409	0.7	-1.4
Drug...	22,387	11.4	24,432	11.8	9.1
Public order.......................................	7,428	3.8	7,406	3.6	-0.3
Regulatory......................................	234	0.1	222	0.1	-5.1
Other...	7,194	3.7	7,184	3.5	-0.1
Weapons..	10,562	5.4	11,629	5.6	10.1
Immigration	108,667	55.5	117,425	56.8	8.1
Material witness..................................	7,472	3.8	8,302	4.0	11.1
Supervision violation............................	25,049	12.8	23,266	11.3	-7.1
Federal judicial district					
U.S./Mexico border district	126,293	64.5	136,252	65.9	7.9
Arizona...	28,934	14.8	31,475	15.2	8.8
California Southern	13,710	7.0	16,822	8.1	22.7
New Mexico.....................................	9,641	4.9	9,247	4.5	-4.1
Texas Southern	45,740	23.4	48,358	23.4	5.7
Texas Western..................................	28,268	14.4	30,350	14.7	7.4
Other..	69,478	35.5	70,378	34.1	1.3

NOTE: Suspects with more than one arrest are counted separately. The most serious offense at arrest is determined by the deputy U.S. marshal at booking. The federal district is the location of the federal court where booking takes place.

Table 3. Suspects in Matters Opened by U.S. Attorneys, by Referring Authority, FY2009, FY2017, FY2018, and FY2019

(Percent; number.)

Department or authority	FY2009	FY2017	FY2018	FY2019
Defense	2.6	2.2	1.4	1.3
Homeland Security	60.9	47.6	59.1	59.5
Interior	1.6	2.0	1.0	0.7
Justice	22.5	33.2	26.1	26.7
Treasury	1.4	1.2	0.7	0.7
Federal/state task forces	2.1	2.8	2.9	2.6
Other[1]	8.9	11.0	8.8	8.5
Number of suspects	188,341	143,684	195,842	203,030

NOTE: Details may not sum to totals due to rounding. The department or authority is the entity making the referral for criminal action to the U.S. attorneysí offices. Percentages are based on records with nonmissing referring authority data. In 2009, there were 268 records missing referring agency. In 2018, there was one record missing referring agency and in 2019 there were 17 records missing referring agency. The unit of count is a suspect in a matter referred to U.S. attorneys. Suspects in more than one matter are counted separately. A matter is opened when a federal prosecutor spends 1 hour or more investigating.
[1]Includes the Departments of Agriculture, Commerce, Education, Energy, Health and Human Services, Labor, State, and Transportation; and state and local authorities.

Table 4. Outcome and Case Processing Time of Suspects in Matters Concluded, FY2019

(Number; percent; days.)

Characteristic	Outcome[1]				Prosecutor decision/case-processing time (median days)[2]			
	Number of suspects in matters concluded	Prosecuted in U.S. district court	Disposed of by U.S. magistrate	Declined to prosecute	Total	Prosecuted in U.S. district court	Disposed of by U.S. magistrate	Declined to prosecute
Total	205,329	43.8	43.2	13.0	14	22	2	535
Lead charge[3]								
Violent	5,048	51.4	8.8	39.9	97	28	95	333
Property	19,165	51.9	8.0	40.1	319	109	153	695
Fraud	16,785	51.7	6.7	41.6	343	132	95	717
Other	2,380	53.1	17.3	29.6	144	31	526	512
Drug	33,863	74.0	8.8	17.1	43	27	73	573
Public order	18,738	45.3	15.6	39.1	165	35	76	586
Regulatory	3,100	42.4	13.1	44.6	214	32	93	594
Other	15,638	45.9	16.1	38.0	156	35	75	583
Weapon	15,566	75.1	4.1	20.9	42	28	74	265
Immigration	112,922	28.5	71.1	0.5	3	22	1	298
Federal judicial district								
U.S./Mexico border	120,310	29.9	67.8	2.3	3	23	1	548
Arizona	29,372	18.9	77.2	3.9	0	26	0	657
California Southern	15,242	40.4	58.1	1.5	7	26	6	773
New Mexico	9,526	47.1	48.5	4.5	8	12	5	411
Texas Southern	39,143	24.0	75.0	1.0	2	20	1	605
Texas Western	27,027	38.3	59.4	2.3	5	23	1	425
Other	85,019	63.5	8.5	28.0	91	30	97	534

[1]Details may not sum to totals due to rounding. The unit of count is a suspect in a matter referred to U.S. attorneys. Suspects investigated in more than one matter are counted separately. Twenty-seven records were missing the suspect's lead charge.
[2]Case processing time reflects the time from receipt of a matter to the U.S. attorneyís decision to prosecute the matter as a case in U.S. district court, refer the matter for disposal by a U.S. magistrate, or decline the matter, resulting in no further action in U.S. district court. The median is the midpoint of processing time. A median of 1 day means that at least half of suspects received a disposition within a day of the matterís referral.
[3]The lead charge is the substantive statute that is the primary basis for referral. It is most often, but not always, the charge with the greatest potential sentence.

Table 5. Demographic Characteristics of Defendants Charged in U.S. Federal District Court, by Sex of Defendant, FY2019

(Number; percent; years.)

Demographic characteristic	All defendants		Male		Female	
	Number	Percent	Number	Percent	Number	Percent
Total	79,402	100.0	69,060	100.0	10,136	100.0
Race/Ethnicity						
White[1]	14,552	19.0	11,496	17.2	3,053	31.4
Black[1]	14,957	19.5	13,492	20.1	1,458	15.0
Hispanic	44,662	58.2	39,965	59.7	4,679	48.1
Asian/Native Hawaiian/Other Pacific Islander[1]	1081	1.4	856	1.3	224	2.3
American Indian/Alaska Native[1]	1,479	1.9	1,169	1.8	310	3.2
Age						
17 years or younger	22	<0.05	21	<0.05	1	<0.05
18 to 19 years	913	1.2	783	1.1	129	1.3
20 to 24 years	8,977	11.3	7,726	11.2	1,246	12.3
25 to 29 years	13,470	17.0	11,773	17.1	1,694	16.7
30 to 34 years	14,884	18.8	13,084	19.0	1,789	17.7
35 to 39 years	13,413	16.9	11,826	17.1	1,580	15.6
40 to 44 years	10,488	13.2	9,211	13.3	1,277	12.6
45 to 49 years	7,045	8.9	6,137	8.9	906	8.9
50 to 54 years	4,301	5.4	3,694	5.4	602	5.9
55 to 59 years	2,762	3.5	2,342	3.4	417	4.1
60 to 64 years	1,609	2.0	1,347	2.0	262	2.6
65 years or older	1,334	1.7	1100	1.6	232	2.3
Median age (years)	35 yrs.	X	35 yrs.	X	35 yrs.	X
Citizenship						
U.S. citizen	44,507	56.4	36,634	53.2	7,853	78.0
Non-U.S. citizen	34,405	43.6	32,172	46.8	2,214	22.0
Country/Region of Citizenship						
North America	76,829	97.4	66,955	97.3	9,837	97.7
United States	44,507	56.4	36,634	53.2	7,853	78.0
Mexico	23,159	29.4	21,707	31.6	1,444	14.3
Canada	95	0.1	80	0.1	14	0.1
Caribbean Islands[2]	1,306	1.7	1,205	1.8	100	1.0
Central America[2]	7,762	9.8	7,329	10.7	426	4.2
South America[2]	1108	1.4	1004	1.5	104	1.0
Asia and Oceania[2]	419	0.5	350	0.5	68	0.7
Europe[2]	359	0.5	315	0.5	44	0.4
Africa[2]	197	0.3	182	0.3	14	0.1

NOTE: Details may not sum to totals due to rounding. The unit of count is a defendant in a case filed in U.S. district court. Defendants charged in more than one case are counted separately. Includes defendants charged in U.S. district court with a felony or a Class A or B misdemeanor offense as the most serious charge. Percentages are based on nonmissing cases. There were 206 records missing sex of defendant, 2,671 records missing race or ethnicity of defendant, 184 records missing age of defendant, and 490 records missing defendantís citizenship status.
X = Not applicable.
[1]Excludes persons of Hispanic origin (e.g., "White" refers to non-Hispanic Whites and "Black" refers to non-Hispanic Blacks). Represents defendantsí self-reported race and ethnicity during the pretrial interview. Information was collected for one race and one ethnicity category.
[2]Countries aggregated by region.

Table 6. Disposition and Case-Processing Time of Defendants in Cases Terminated in U.S. District Court, FY2019

(Number; percent; days.)

Most serious offense at termination	Total cases terminated	Convicted			Not convicted		
		Total	Guilty plea	Bench/jury trial	Total	Bench/jury trial	Dismissed
All offenses...	84,782	92.3	90.4	2.0	7.7	0.4	7.3
Type of charge							
Felony..	78,543	94.4	92.4	2.0	5.6	0.4	5.2
Violent	2,654	91.9	85.2	6.7	8.1	1.3	6.8
Property	8,581	92.2	88.5	3.8	7.8	0.6	7.2
Fraud..	7,470	92.6	88.6	3.9	7.4	0.5	6.9
Other..	1,111	89.9	87.4	2.5	10.1	0.7	9.4
Drug	22,158	93.0	90.6	2.4	7.0	0.4	6.7
Public order	6,291	93.3	89.7	3.6	6.7	0.7	6.0
Regulatory................................	675	88.3	84.3	4.0	11.7	1.8	9.9
Other..	5,616	93.9	90.4	3.6	6.1	0.6	5.5
Weapon	9,511	93.2	90.6	2.6	6.8	0.6	6.3
Immigration	29,348	97.0	96.7	0.3	3.0	0.1	2.9
Misdemeanor....................................	6,239	65.9	64.8	1.1	34.1	0.3	33.8
Federal judicial district							
U.S./Mexico border	33,357	95.8	95.3	0.6	4.2	0.2	4.0
Arizona..	5,877	96.6	95.9	0.7	3.4	0.1	3.3
California Southern	5,200	89.3	88.3	1.0	10.8	0.3	10.4
New Mexico	4,038	98.8	98.7	0.1	1.2	<0.1	1.2
Texas Southern	8,011	97.2	96.8	0.4	2.8	0.2	2.6
Texas Western.............................	10,231	96.4	95.9	0.6	3.6	0.1	3.5
Other..	51,425	90.0	87.2	2.9	10.0	0.5	9.5
Median time (days) from filing to disposition[1]......	202	202	197	559	219	293	215

NOTE: Includes information on felony defendants; Class A misdemeanants, whether handled by U.S. district judges or U.S. magistrates; and other misdemeanants, provided they were handled by U.S. district judges. Court personnel determine the most serious offense at termination as the offense with the greatest statutory maximum sentence. The unit of count is a defendant in a case terminated in U.S. district court. Defendants in more than one case are counted separately. The median is the midpoint between the slowest and fastest processing times. A median of 202 days means that half of defendants received a disposition in less than 202 days and half received a disposition in more than 202 days. Details may not sum to totals due to rounding.

[1]Includes the interval from the time a case is filed in U.S. district court to sentencing for defendants who were convicted and the interval from case filing to disposition for defendants who were not convicted or whose cases were dismissed.

Table 7. Type and Length of Sentence Imposed for Convicted Defendants, by Offense and District, FY2019

(Number; percent; months.)

Most serious offense at case termination	Number convicted	Type of sentence				Median sentence length (months)	
		Prison[1]	Probation only	Fine only	Suspended sentence	Prison	Probation
All offenses..................................	78,256	72.2	8.1	1.7	18.0	30	36
Type of Offense							
Felony..	74,144	74.8	6.7	0.3	18.2	33	36
Violent................................	2,439	92.7	3.0	0.2	4.1	84	36
Property................................	7,913	64.0	20.3	1.0	14.6	24	36
Fraud................................	6,914	65.8	18.0	1.1	15.1	24	36
Other................................	999	51.7	36.7	0.4	11.2	20	36
Drug................................	20,598	89.8	4.1	0.2	5.9	66	36
Public order............................	5,871	79.8	12.1	0.8	7.3	51	36
Regulatory........................	596	55.7	31.3	2.2	10.8	24	36
Other................................	5,275	82.5	9.9	0.7	6.9	60	36
Weapon................................	8,863	90.9	5.0	0.1	3.9	48	36
Immigration	28,460	59.3	4.6	0.1	35.9	10	36
Misdemeanor..............................	4,112	25.5	32.3	26.5	15.7	4	12
Federal Judicial District							
U.S./Mexico border	31,959	67.2	6.2	0.2	26.5	14	36
Arizona..................................	5,678	67.3	6.9	0.1	25.7	14	36
California Southern	4,641	65.1	5.2	0.1	29.5	18	60
New Mexico	3,988	98.3	1.6	<0.01	0.1	2	24
Texas Southern	7,788	78.2	2.9	0.1	18.9	18	36
Texas Western......................	9,864	46.9	10.6	0.3	42.2	18	36
Other..	46,297	75.7	9.4	0.7	12.2	54	36

NOTE: Details may not sum to totals due to rounding. The unit of count is a defendant in a case terminated with a conviction and sentence in U.S. district court. Defendants convicted and sentenced in more than one case are counted separately. The most serious offense is determined by court personnel as the offense with the greatest statutory maximum sentence. The median prison term is the midpoint of prison terms imposed. A median of 30 months means that half of defendants received a prison term of less than 30 months and half received a prison term of more than 30 months. There were 201 records missing type of sentence.
[1]Includes sentences to incarceration, such as mixed (a prison term followed by a probation term) and life sentences.

Table 8. Admissions and Releases of Federal Prisoners, by Offense, FY2019

(Number.)

Most serious commitment offense[1]	Population at start of the year[2]	Prisoners admitted			Prisoners released			Population at end of year[7]	Net population change
		District court[3]			First release[4]				
		Sentence of 1 year or less	Sentence of more than 1 year	All other[5]	Time served 1 year or less	Time served more than 1 year	All other[6]		
Total	163,853	6,331	39,094	13,461	8,196	42,424	14,961	157,158	-6,695
Violent..................................	9,826	85	1,487	1021	103	1,724	1,182	9,410	-416
Property................................	9,467	703	3,131	1,170	841	3,792	1,349	8,498	-969
Fraud	8,000	527	2,678	833	669	3,242	993	7,136	-864
Other................................	1,467	176	453	337	172	550	356	1,362	-105
Drug.....................................	76,351	456	15,574	5,045	555	18,105	5,623	73,143	-3,208
Public order	25,699	447	5,733	1,427	511	5,258	1,499	26,038	339
Regulatory..........................	3,119	203	1,080	164	183	1063	169	3,151	32
Other................................	22,580	244	4,653	1,263	328	4,195	1,330	22,887	307
Weapon..................................	29,508	202	7,206	2,752	220	7,033	2,856	29,559	51
Immigration..........................	12,338	4,394	5,838	1995	5,891	6,373	2389	9,912	-2,426

NOTE: The unit of count is a person admitted to or released from the Federal Bureau of Prisons. Persons who are admitted and released in the same year are counted separately. Excludes persons sentenced to the Federal Bureau of Prisons by the D.C. Superior Court, military prisoners transferred to Federal Bureau of Prisons' facilities to serve their sentence, U.S. citizen prisoners transferred to the U.S. from another country to serve their sentence closer to home, and persons convicted of a state offense but serving time in a federal prison for their security needs. Percentages are based on nonmissing cases. Offense information was missing at the start of the year for 664 persons and at the end of the year for 598 persons. Persons who entered or left a prison temporarily (such as for transit to another location, for health care, or to serve a weekend sentence) were not counted as admitted or released.
[1]The offense with the longest sentence imposed at conviction.
[2]The population as of October 1, 2018.
[3]Persons committed by a U.S. district court for U.S. Code violations.
[4]Persons released after being committed by a U.S. district court.
[5]Persons who were committed following a return to prison for violating conditions of their supervised release, or were received for examination, treatment, or transfer to another jurisdiction.
[6]Persons released from prison without a new court commitment after they were committed for violating conditions of their supervised release.
[7]The population as of September 30, 2019.

Table 9. Demographic Characteristics of Federally Sentenced Offenders in the Custody of the Federal Bureau of Prisons, Fiscal Yearend 2009 and 2019

(Number; percent.)

Offender characteristic	2009 Number	2009 Percent	2019 Number	2019 Percent	Average annual growth, 2009–2019[1]
All prisoners	184,644	100.0	157,158	100.0	-1.6
Sex					
Male..	172,375	93.4	145,762	92.8	-1.6
Female..	12,269	6.6	11,396	7.3	-0.1
Race/Ethnicity					
White[2]..	50,792	27.5	46,236	29.4	-0.9
Black[2]..	67,654	36.6	54,941	35.0	-2.0
Hispanic..	60,140	32.6	50,196	31.9	-1.7
Asian/Native Hawaiian/Other Pacific Islander[2].....................................	2,818	1.5	2,162	1.4	-2.6
American Indian/Alaska Native[2]...	3,240	1.8	3,623	2.3	1.1
Age					
17 years or younger	31	<0.1	5	<0.1	-5.4
18 to 19 years..	347	0.2	172	0.1	-5.6
20 to 24 years..	10,745	5.8	6,033	3.8	-5.5
25 to 29 years..	28,106	15.2	17,459	11.1	-4.6
30 to 34 years..	37,239	20.2	24,970	15.9	-3.8
35 to 39 years..	34,554	18.7	28,845	18.4	-1.7
40 to 44 years..	25,767	14.0	26,117	16.6	0.2
45 to 49 years..	19,717	10.7	19,880	12.7	0.1
50 to 54 years..	12,898	7.0	13,753	8.8	0.7
55 to 59 years..	7,566	4.1	9,466	6.0	2.3
60 to 64 years..	4,379	2.4	5,446	3.5	2.3
65 years or older..	3,295	1.8	5,012	3.2	4.4
Median age (years)...	37	X	40	X	X
Citizenship					
U.S. citizen...	135,738	73.6	128,634	81.9	-0.5
Non-U.S. citizen..	48,723	26.4	28,523	18.2	-5.0
Country/region of citizenship					
North America	179,128	97.1	152,955	97.3	-1.5
United States..	135,738	73.6	128,634	81.9	-0.5
Mexico...	34,301	18.6	18,570	11.8	-5.7
Canada	404	0.2	192	0.1	-6.8
Caribbean Islands[3]..	5,543	3.0	2,970	1.9	-6.0
Central America[3]...	3,142	1.7	2,589	1.7	-1.5
South America[3]..	2,950	1.6	2,441	1.6	-1.7
Asia and Oceania[3]...	1,386	0.8	819	0.5	-5.1
Europe[3]	526	0.3	491	0.3	-0.6
Africa[3]	471	0.3	451	0.3	-0.3

NOTE: Details may not sum to totals due to rounding. Federal prisoner populations are shown as of September 30, 2009 and 2019. Includes prisoners sentenced in U.S. district court. Excludes persons sentenced to the Federal Bureau of Prisons by the D.C. Superior Court, military prisoners transferred to Federal Bureau of Prisons facilities to serve their sentence, U.S. citizen prisoners transferred to the U.S. from another country to serve their sentence closer to home, and persons convicted of a state offense but serving time in a federal prison for their security needs. Percentages are based on nonmissing cases. There were 183 records missing citizenship in 2009 and one record missing citizenship in 2019.
X = Not applicable.
[1]Average annual percent change measures the change over a period of two or more years. It shows the average rate of increase (or decrease) in persons in federal prison per year from 2009 to 2019.
[2]Excludes persons of Hispanic origin (e.g., White refers to non-Hispanic Whites and Black refers to non-Hispanic Blacks). TDefendants self-reported race and ethnicity during the presentence interview. Information was collected for one race and one ethnicity category.
[3]Countries aggregated by region.

Table 10. Demographic Characteristics of Offenders Under Post-Sentencing Federal Supervision, FY2019

(Number; percent.)

Demographic characteristic	All persons Number	All persons Percent	Probation Number	Probation Percent	Supervised release Number	Supervised release Percent	Parole Number	Parole Percent
All prisoners	126,487	100.0	14,658	11.6	110,932	87.7	897	0.7
Sex								
Male..	105,940	83.9	9,057	62.7	96,008	86.6	875	97.6
Female..	20,326	16.1	5,382	37.3	14,922	13.4	22	2.4
Race/ethnicity								
White[1]...	40,945	33.2	5,767	41.9	34,889	32.1	289	34.6
Black[1]..	44,505	36.1	3,714	27.0	40,366	37.2	425	50.9
Hispanic..	32,194	26.1	3,326	24.1	28,774	26.5	94	11.3
Asian/Native Hawaiian/Other Pacific Islander[1]	2,725	2.2	518	3.8	2,194	2.0	13	1.6
American Indian/Alaska Native[1]..................	2,867	2.3	453	3.3	2,400	2.2	14	1.7
Age								
17 years or younger...................	26	<.01	22	0.2	4	<.01	0	<.01
18 to 19 years............................	208	0.2	126	0.9	82	0.1	0	<.01
20 to 24 years............................	4,320	3.4	1,336	9.3	2,965	2.7	19	2.1
25 to 29 years............................	11,881	9.4	1,913	13.3	9,924	9.0	44	4.9
30 to 34 years............................	17,204	13.6	1,892	13.1	15,256	13.8	56	6.2
35 to 39 years............................	21,036	16.7	1,838	12.7	19,135	17.3	63	7.0
40 to 44 years............................	19,864	15.7	1,561	10.8	18,240	16.4	63	7.0
45 to 49 years............................	16,729	13.3	1,457	10.1	15,172	13.7	100	11.2
50 to 54 years............................	12,219	9.7	1,204	8.3	10,908	9.8	107	11.9
55 to 59 years............................	9,514	7.5	1,112	7.7	8,295	7.5	107	11.9
60 to 64 years............................	6,156	4.9	820	5.7	5,219	4.7	117	13.0
65 years or older........................	7,109	5.6	1,158	8.0	5,730	5.2	221	24.6
Median age (years)......................	X	42.0	X	40.0	X	42.0	X	55.0
Citizenship								
U.S. citizen...................................	122,426	97.1	13,676	94.8	107,899	97.4	851	95.6
Non-U.S. citizen...........................	3,669	2.9	746	5.2	2,884	2.6	39	4.4
Country/region of citizenship								
North America	124,990	99.8	14,153	98.1	109,961	99.3	876	98.4
United States...............................	122,426	97.1	13,676	94.8	107,899	97.4	851	95.6
Mexico...	820	0.7	191	1.3	622	0.6	7	0.8
Canada	29	<0.1	12	<0.1	17	<0.1	0	<.01
Caribbean Islands[2]......................	1,410	1.8	155	1.1	1,239	1.1	16	1.8
Central America[2]	305	0.2	119	0.8	184	0.2	2	0.2
South America[2]............................	168	0.1	44	0.3	115	0.1	9	1.0
Asia and Oceania[2].......................	550	0.4	129	0.9	418	0.4	3	0.3
Europe[2]..	212	0.2	54	0.4	156	0.1	2	0.2
Africa[2]...	175	0.1	42	0.3	133	0.1	0	<.01

NOTE: The unit of count is an individual person under federal supervision on September 30, 2019. Percentages are based on nonmissing cases. There were 221 records missing age of defendant, 221 records missing sex of defendant, 3,251 records missing race or ethnicity of defendant, and 97 records missing defendant's citizenship status.
X = Not applicable
[1]Excludes persons of Hispanic origin (e.g.,"White" refers to non-Hispanic Whites and "Black" refers to non-Hispanic Blacks).
[2]Countries aggregated by region.

Table 11. Characteristics of Sentenced Persons, FY2019

(Number; percent; months.)

Offender characteristic	Number convicted	Type of sentence				Median sentence length (months)	
		Prison[1]	Probation only	Fine only	Suspended	Prison	Probation
Total	78,256	72.2	8.1	1.7	18.0	30	36
Sex							
Male....................	65,357	74.3	6.1	0.9	18.7	30	36
Female..................	8,999	60.4	21.1	2.1	16.4	24	36
Race/Ethnicity							
White[2]	13,980	76.9	14.0	2.0	7.0	57	36
Black[2]	14,563	84.9	8.5	1.1	5.5	60	36
Hispanic.................	42,815	67.4	5.1	0.2	27.2	18	36
Asian/Native Hawaiian/Other Pacific Islander[2]	1,051	68.1	19.3	2.3	10.4	37	36
American Indian/Alaska Native[2].........................	1,302	80.4	13.1	0.9	5.7	37	36
Age							
18 to 19 years..............	1,214	59.8	9.9	2.3	28.0	13	36
20 to 24 years..............	8,557	67.4	9.1	2.1	21.4	24	36
25 to 29 years..............	13,013	72.4	7.1	1.0	19.5	32	36
30 to 34 years..............	13,847	73.3	6.3	0.8	19.7	30	36
35 to 39 years..............	12,583	75.1	6.0	0.7	18.3	33	36
40 to 44 years..............	9,466	75.2	6.4	0.7	17.7	30	36
45 to 49 years..............	6,491	74.3	8.3	0.9	16.6	30	36
50 to 54 years..............	4,070	74.4	9.7	1.1	14.8	31	36
55 to 59 years..............	2,483	71.7	13.2	1.5	13.6	36	36
60 to 64 years..............	1,461	71.1	17.5	1.2	10.3	36	36
65 years or older............	1,196	61.5	25.6	2.4	10.5	36	36
Median age (years)...........	35	35.0	36.0	31.0	33.0	X	X
Citizenship							
U.S. citizen................	40,163	81.2	11.4	1.3	6.1	51	36
Non-U.S. citizen	33,854	63.1	3.5	0.2	33.1	13	36
Country/region of citizenship							
North America	69,262	74.2	7.7	0.6	17.5	37	36
United States................	38,858	81.9	11.2	1.0	5.9	51	36
Mexico....................	21,998	67.7	2.8	0.1	29.4	13	36
Canada	79	70.5	9.0	5.1	15.4	41	60
Caribbean Islands[3]............	1,302	76.7	6.6	0.2	16.5	30	36
Central America[3].............	7,025	51.4	3.8	0.1	44.7	10	36
South America[3]................	929	71.1	4.9	0.2	23.8	57	36
Asia and Oceania[3].............	414	64.0	16.3	3.2	16.6	30	36
Europe[3].................	295	64.8	8.5	2.0	24.8	26	36
Africa[3].................	218	73.4	4.6	0.5	21.6	30	24

NOTE: Details may not sum to totals due to rounding. Federal prisoner populations are shown as of September 30, 2009 and 2019. Includes prisoners sentenced in U.S. district court. Excludes persons sentenced to the Federal Bureau of Prisons by the D.C. Superior Court, military prisoners transferred to Federal Bureau of Prisons facilities to serve their sentence, U.S. citizen prisoners transferred to the U.S. from another country to serve their sentence closer to home, and persons convicted of a state offense but serving time in a federal prison for their security needs. Percentages are based on nonmissing cases. There were 183 records missing citizenship in 2009 and one record missing citizenship in 2019.
X = Not applicable.
[1]Includes sentences to incarceration, such as mixed (a prison term followed by a probation term) and life sentences.
[2]Excludes persons of Hispanic origin (e.g., "White" refers to non-Hispanic Whites and "Black" refers to non-Hispanic Blacks). Defendants self-reported race and ethnicity during the pretrial interview. Information was collected for one race and one ethnicity category.
[3]Countries aggregated by region.

METHODOLOGY

Federal Justice Statistics describes persons processed by the federal criminal justice system. Data are from the Federal Justice Statistics Program (FJSP). The FJSP collects, standardizes, and reports on administrative data received from six federal justice agencies: the U.S. Marshals Service, Drug Enforcement Administration, Executive Office for U.S. Attorneys, Administrative Office of the U.S. Courts, U.S. Sentencing Commission, and Federal Bureau of Prisons.

This report describes the annual activity, workloads, and outcomes of the federal criminal justice system from arrest to imprisonment. Findings are based on data from the U.S. Marshals Service, Drug Enforcement Administration (DEA), Executive Office for U.S. Attorneys, Administrative Office of the U.S. Courts, and Federal Bureau of Prisons. This report presents data on arrests and investigations by law enforcement agency and growth rates by type of offense and federal judicial district. It also examines trends on drug arrests by the DEA, and it includes the most recent available data on sentences imposed and their lengths by type of offense.

Readers should use caution in interpreting data, especially as compared to previous years, due to the conditions imposed by the COVID-19 pandemic.

DEFINITIONS OF MAJOR OFFENSE CATEGORIES

Violent: Includes murder, non-negligent or negligent manslaughter, aggravated or simple assault, sex abuse, robbery, kidnapping, and threats against the president.

Property: Includes fraudulent and other types of property offenses.

Fraudulent property: Includes embezzlement, fraud (including tax fraud), forgery, and counterfeiting.

Other property: Includes burglary, larceny, motor-vehicle theft, arson, transportation of stolen property, and other property offenses, such as destruction of property and trespassing.

Drug: Includes the manufacture, import, export, distribution, or dispensing of a controlled substance (or a counterfeit substance), or the possession of a controlled substance (or a counterfeit substance) with intent to manufacture or distribute.

Public order: Includes regulatory and other types of offenses.

Regulatory public order: Includes violation of agriculture, antitrust, labor, food and drug, motor carrier, and other federal regulations.

Other public order: Includes non-regulatory violations concerning tax law (tax fraud), bribery, perjury, national defense, escape, racketeering and extortion, gambling, liquor, mailing or transporting obscene materials, traffic, migratory birds, conspiracy, aiding and abetting, jurisdiction, and other offenses.

Weapons: Includes violations of any of the provisions of 18 U.S.C. §§ 922–923 concerning the manufacturing, importing, possessing, receiving, and licensing of firearms and ammunition.

Immigration: Includes offenses involving illegal entrance into the United States, illegally reentering after being deported, willfully failing to leave when so ordered, or bringing in or harboring any aliens not admitted by an immigration officer.

Supervision violations: Includes violation of bail, violation of pre-trial or post-sentencing supervision in the community (probation), and failure to appear.

REPORT METHODOLOGY

This report uses data from the Federal Justice Statistics Program (FJSP), a collection from the Bureau of Justice Statistics (BJS). The FJSP receives administrative data files from six federal criminal justice agencies. Data represent the federal criminal case processing stages from arrest to imprisonment. BJS standardizes this information to maximize comparability across and within agencies over time. This includes:

- counting each appearance of an individual in the data during a fiscal year (October 1 through September 30), whether it be for a criminal arrest, matter, case, or imprisonment stay

- delineating fiscal year as the period for reported events

- applying a uniform offense classification across agencies

- classifying disposition and sentences imposed

FJSP DATA SOURCES

U.S. Marshals Service: The Justice Detainee Information System provides information on suspects arrested for federal offenses. Suspects may be counted more than once in a fiscal year if they are arrested multiple times during the period. This report uses most serious arrest offense as classified by the deputy U.S. Marshal at the time of booking. Each of the 94 federal judicial districts in the United States have a U.S. Marshal. Deputy U.S. Marshals take federal suspects who have been charged with a crime into custody, which includes booking, processing, and detaining suspects. They also oversee court security and coordinate prisoner transportation, among other duties.

Drug Enforcement Administration (DEA): The Defendant Statistical System contains data on suspects arrested by DEA agents within the U.S. The data include information on characteristics of arrestees and the type of drug for which they were arrested. Suspects may be counted more than once in a fiscal year if they are arrested multiple times by the DEA during this period.

Executive Office for U.S. Attorneys: The Legal Information Office Network System database contains information on the investigation and prosecution of suspects in criminal matters received and concluded and criminal cases filed and terminated by U.S. attorneys. Suspects may be counted more than once in a fiscal year if they are involved in multiple matters received and concluded during the period. A matter is defined as a referral in which an attorney spends one hour or more investigating. The lead charge is used to classify the most serious offense at referral and is defined as the substantive statute that is the primary basis of referral.

Administrative Office of the U.S. Courts (AOUSC): The Criminal Master File contains information about the criminal proceedings against defendants whose cases were filed and terminated in U.S. district courts. It includes information on felony defendants, Class A misdemeanants—whether handled by U.S. district court judges or U.S. magistrates—and other misdemeanants provided they were handled by U.S. district court judges. A felony is classified as an offense for which the maximum term of imprisonment is more than one year in prison. Offenses classified as misdemeanors include those for which the maximum term of imprisonment is less than one year in prison. Class A misdemeanors include offenses for which the maximum term of imprisonment is one year or less but more than 6 months in prison. Class B misdemeanors include offenses for which the maximum term of imprisonment is 6 months or less but more than 30 days in prison.

Offenses are based on the most serious charged offense, as determined by the probation officer responsible for interviewing the defendant. The probation officer classifies the offense charged into AOUSC four-digit offense codes, which are maintained and updated by the AOUSC. For defendants charged with more than one offense on an indictment, the probation officer chooses as the charged offense the one carrying the most severe penalty or, in the case of two or more charges carrying the same penalty, the one with the highest offense severity. The offense severity level is determined by the AOUSC, which

ranks offenses according to the maximum sentence, type of crime, and maximum fine amount. These four-digit codes are then aggregated into the primary offense charges used for this report.

This report also uses AOUSC data from the Probation and Pretrial Services Automated Case Tracking System (PACTS), which contains information on defendants interviewed and supervised by pre-trial services. These data are used to describe background characteristics of defendants arraigned. Post-sentencing data from PACTS are used to describe persons under post-sentencing supervision in the community.

U.S. Sentencing Commission: The Monitoring Database contains information on criminal defendants sentenced pursuant to the provisions of the Sentencing Reform Act of 1984. Data files are limited to those defendants whose court records have been obtained by the U.S. Sentencing Commission. These data do not appear in this report.

Federal Bureau of Prisons (BOP): The SENTRY database contains information on all federally sentenced offenders admitted into or released from federal prison during a fiscal year and offenders in federal prison at the end of each fiscal year (September 30). The prisoner count reported by the FJSP differs from what is reported by the BOP although data are from the same source (SENTRY). For example, the BOP reports 181,698 prisoners as of September 30, 2018. The FJSP starts with data extracted from SENTRY that differs slightly (down 396) from this total (181,302). Of the 181,302 records, 13,882 records were dropped because the prisoner was not designated at an assigned BOP custodial facility. The excluded records included designations to community confinement, home confinement, hospital, Immigration and Customs Enforcement detention, material witness, and pre-sentence admission. Next, 902 records were excluded due to missing commitment offense, and 4,113 prisoners were dropped as they were sentenced by the District of Columbia Superior Court. Finally, 520 prisoner records were dropped because the prisoner was a state boarder, a treaty transfer, or serving a sentence from a military court commitment. Of the 181,302 prisoners reported by the BOP in custody on September 30, 2018, a total of 161,885 (89 percent of the total population) met the criteria as federally sentenced prisoners.

OTHER RESOURCES

FJSP data are available in the Federal Criminal Case Processing Statistics Tool, an interactive BJS. tool that permits users to query the federal data and download the results as a spreadsheet. This tool is available on the BJS Web site. It provides statistics by the stage of the federal criminal-case process, including law enforcement, prosecution and courts, and incarceration. Users can generate queries for up to three variables using data for the years 1998 to 2016. Users can also generate queries by the title and section of the U.S. criminal code.

PART 5

Hate Crime Statistics, 2020

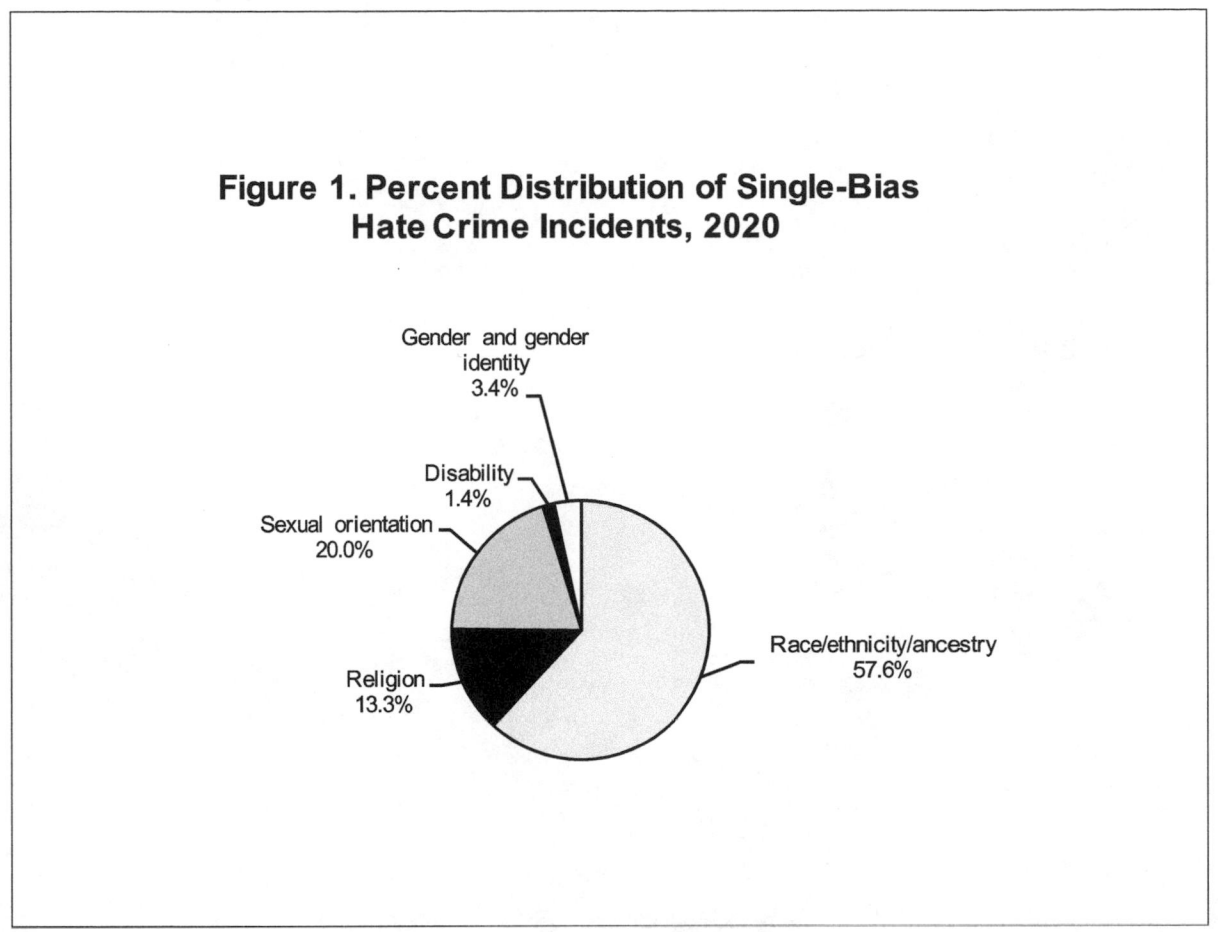

Figure 1. Percent Distribution of Single-Bias Hate Crime Incidents, 2020

Gender and gender identity 3.4%

Disability 1.4%

Sexual orientation 20.0%

Religion 13.3%

Race/ethnicity/ancestry 57.6%

- In 2020, there were 8,052 single-bias incidents that involved 10,790 offenses, 11,472 victims, and 6,780 known offenders; the 211 multiple-bias incidents reported in 2020 involved 339 offenses, 346 victims, and 123 known offenders.

- An analysis of data for victims of single-bias hate crime incidents in 2020 showed that 64.9 percent of the victims were targeted because of the offenders' bias against race/ethnicity/ancestry, 15.4 percent were victimized because of bias against religion, and 13.8 percent were targeted because of bias against sexual orientation.

- In 2020, race was reported for 6,748 known hate crime offenders; of these offenders: 73.5 percent were White, 20.6 percent were Black or African American, 3.3 percent were groups made up of individuals of various races (group of multiple races), 1.1 percent were American Indian or Alaska Native, 1.1 percent were Asian, and 0.4 percent were Native Hawaiian or Other Pacific Islander.

- Of the 7,516 hate crime offenses classified as crimes against persons in 2020, 52.4 percent were for intimidation, 28.4 percent were for simple assault, and 18.2 percent were for aggravated assault. There were 22 murders and 21 rapes reported as hate crimes.

Table 1. Incidents, Offenses, Victims, and Known Offenders, by Bias Motivation, 2020

(Number.)

Bias motivation	Incidents	Offenses	Victims[1]	Known offenders[2]
Total	8,263	11,129	11,472	6,780
Single-Bias Incidents	8,052	10,790	11,126	6,657
Race/Ethnicity/Ancestry	5,227	6,677	6,880	4,339
Anti-White	869	1,048	1,082	825
Anti-Black or African American..............	2,871	3,819	3,915	2,302
Anti-American Indian or Alaska Native....	96	103	108	74
Anti-Asian	279	330	342	239
Anti-Native Hawaiian or Other Pacific Islander	15	15	18	12
Anti-Multiple Races, Group	211	270	281	114
Anti-Arab	71	85	87	52
Anti-Hispanic or Latino	517	664	693	525
Anti-Other Race/Ethnicity/Ancestry	298	343	354	196
Religion	1,244	1,402	1,481	814
Anti-Jewish	683	794	831	401
Anti-Catholic	73	77	80	47
Anti-Protestant.................................	30	31	32	26
Anti-Islamic (Muslim)	110	126	131	126
Anti-Other Religion	76	85	105	44
Anti-Multiple Religions, Group	40	44	49	19
Anti-Mormon.................................	7	8	8	7
Anti-Jehovah's Witness.......................	9	10	10	3
Anti-Eastern Orthodox (Russian, Greek, Other).................................	43	43	43	30
Anti-Other Christian	50	56	62	27
Anti-Buddhist	15	16	16	14
Anti-Hindu	11	11	11	6
Anti-Sikh.................................	89	93	94	59
Anti-Atheism/Agnosticism/etc...............	8	8	9	5
Sexual Orientation	1,110	2,185	2,229	1,043
Anti-Gay (Male)...........................	673	770	791	680
Anti-Lesbian.................................	103	1,021	1,026	89
Anti-Lesbian, Gay, Bisexual, or Transgender (Mixed Group)...................	306	363	380	250
Anti-Heterosexual.............................	11	12	13	10
Anti-Bisexual.................................	17	19	19	14
Disability.................................	130	151	152	117
Anti-Physical.................................	53	60	60	47
Anti-Mental.................................	77	91	92	70
Gender	75	81	82	65
Anti-Male.................................	25	25	25	24
Anti-Female.................................	50	56	57	41
Gender Identity.................................	266	294	302	279
Anti-Transgender.................................	213	237	244	226
Anti-Gender Non-Conforming..............	53	57	58	53
Multiple-Bias Incidents[3]	211	339	346	123

[1] The term *victim* may refer to an individual, business/financial institution, government entity, religious organization, or society/public as a whole.
[2] The term *known offender* does not imply the suspect's identity is known; rather, the term indicates some aspect of the suspect was identified, thus distinguishing the suspect from an unknown offender.
[3] A multiple-bias incident is an incident in which one or more offense types are motivated by two or more biases.

Table 2. Incidents, Offenses, Victims, and Known Offenders, by Offense Type, 2020

(Number.)

Offense type	Incidents[1]	Offenses	Victims[2]	Known offenders[3]
Total	8,263	11,129	11,472	6,780
Crimes Against Persons	5,201	7,750	7,750	5,244
Murder and nonnegligent manslaughter	20	22	22	22
Rape [4]	21	21	21	23
Aggravated assault	1,074	1,390	1,390	1,257
Simple assault	1,867	2,166	2,166	2,061
Intimidation	2,190	4,119	4,119	1,853
Other[5]	29	32	32	28
Crimes Against Property	3,147	3,147	3,490	1,635
Robbery	140	140	155	228
Burglary	132	132	152	94
Larceny-theft	362	362	383	175
Motor vehicle theft	34	34	36	28
Arson	67	67	105	38
Destruction/damage/vandalism	2,333	2,333	2,574	1,031
Other[5]	79	79	85	41
Crimes Against Society[5]	232	232	232	269

[1]The actual number of incidents is 8,263. However, the column figures will not add to the total because incidents may include more than one offense type, and these are counted in each appropriate offense type category.
[2]The term *victim* may refer to an individual, business/financial institution, government entity, religious organization, or society/public as a whole.
[3]The term *known offender* does not imply the suspect's identity is known; rather, the term indicates some aspect of the suspect was identified, thus distinguishing the suspect from an unknown offender. The actual number of known offenders is 6,780. However, the column figures will not add to the total because some offenders are responsible for more than one offense type, and are, therefore, counted more than once in this table.
[4]Only the revised Uniform Crime Reporting definition of rape was used for the figures reported in this row.
[5]The figures shown include additional offenses collected in the National Incident-Based Reporting System.

Table 3. Offenses, Known Offender's Race and Ethnicity, by Offense Type, 2020

(Number.)

Bias motivation	Total offenses	Known offender's race							Known offender's ethnicity[1]				Unknown offender
		White	Black or African American	American Indian or Alaska Native	Asian	Native Hawaiian or Other Pacific Islander	Group of multiple races	Unknown race	Hispanic or Latino	Not Hispanic or Latino	Group of multiple ethnicities	Unknown ethnicity	
Total	11,129	4,958	1,390	73	75	29	223	947	608	2,625	69	2,915	3,434
Crimes Against Persons	7,750	4,194	1,148	64	60	24	187	583	509	2,150	52	2,342	1,490
Murder and nonnegligent manslaughter	22	8	3	0	0	0	1	5	3	6	0	7	5
Rape[2]	21	9	5	0	0	1	1	3	5	6	0	8	2
Aggravated assault	1,390	746	311	12	15	3	48	119	162	530	19	472	136
Simple assault	2,166	1,136	488	37	27	6	92	155	193	742	26	791	225
Intimidation	4,119	2,277	335	14	17	13	45	301	142	856	7	1,051	1,117
Other[3]	32	18	6	1	1	1	0	0	4	10	0	13	5
Crimes Against Property	3,147	628	182	7	12	5	30	360	94	362	15	482	1,923
Robbery	140	38	47	2	0	2	5	25	23	37	4	41	21
Burglary	132	41	9	1	0	0	4	14	0	27	2	32	63
Larceny-theft	362	99	32	0	0	0	2	11	7	60	1	67	218
Motor vehicle theft	34	11	5	0	0	0	0	3	0	8	0	11	15
Arson	67	23	3	0	0	0	1	4	6	7	0	17	36
Destruction/damage/vandalism	2,333	390	78	4	12	3	18	302	54	208	8	298	1,526
Other[3]	79	26	8	0	0	0	0	1	4	15	0	16	44
Crimes Against Society[3]	232	136	60	2	3	0	6	4	5	113	2	91	21

[1]The sum of offenses by the known offender's ethnicity does not equal the sum of offenses by the known offender's race because not all law enforcement agencies that report offender race data also report offender ethnicity data.
[2]Only the revised Uniform Crime Reporting definition of rape was used for the figures reported in this row.
[3]The figures shown include additional offenses collected in the National Incident-Based Reporting System.

Table 4. Offenses, Offense Type, by Bias Motivation, 2020

(Number.)

Bias motivation	Total offenses	Crimes against persons					
		Murder and nonnegligent manslaughter	Rape[1]	Aggravated assault	Simple assault	Intimidation	Other[2]
Total	11,129	22	21	1,390	2,166	4,119	32
Single-Bias Incidents	10,790	22	21	1,370	2,131	3,940	32
Race/Ethnicity/Ancestry	6,677	8	10	976	1,455	2,296	20
Anti-White	1,048	1	7	145	317	231	8
Anti-Black or African American	3,819	5	2	530	660	1,577	5
Anti-American Indian or Alaska Native	103	0	1	5	26	14	3
Anti-Asian	330	0	0	47	99	111	0
Anti-Native Hawaiian or Other Pacific Islander ...	15	0	0	2	2	3	0
Anti-Multiple Races, Group	270	2	0	31	41	77	0
Anti-Arab	85	0	0	9	24	29	0
Anti-Hispanic or Latino	664	0	0	162	215	170	4
Anti-Other Race/Ethnicity/Ancestry	343	0	0	45	71	84	0
Religion	1,402	1	0	73	151	293	0
Anti-Jewish	794	1	0	34	59	209	0
Anti-Catholic	77	0	0	5	5	5	0
Anti-Protestant	31	0	0	2	6	1	0
Anti-Islamic (Muslim)	126	0	0	12	32	43	0
Anti-Other Religion	85	0	0	10	6	10	0
Anti-Multiple Religions, Group	44	0	0	0	6	9	0
Anti-Mormon	8	0	0	1	0	1	0
Anti-Jehovah's Witness	10	0	0	0	1	0	0
Anti-Eastern Orthodox (Russian, Greek, Other) ..	43	0	0	1	5	1	0
Anti-Other Christian	56	0	0	1	8	6	0
Anti-Buddhist	16	0	0	0	2	0	0
Anti-Hindu	11	0	0	0	3	1	0
Anti-Sikh	93	0	0	5	17	7	0
Anti-Atheism/Agnosticism/etc	8	0	0	2	1	0	0
Sexual Orientation	2,185	5	6	223	370	1,254	2
Anti-Gay (Male)	770	5	2	157	252	203	2
Anti-Lesbian	1,021	0	2	17	28	940	0
Anti-Lesbian, Gay, Bisexual, or Transgender (Mixed Group)	363	0	2	45	84	102	0
Anti-Heterosexual	12	0	U	0	1	4	0
Anti-Bisexual	19	0	0	4	5	5	0
Disability	151		2	18	41	21	3
Anti-Physical	60	0	0	6	20	8	3
Anti-Mental	91	0	2	12	21	13	0
Gender	81		2	19	24	16	1
Anti-Male	25	0	0	8	6	2	1
Anti-Female	56	0	2	11	18	14	0
Gender Identity	294	8	1	61	90	60	6
Anti-Transgender	237	8	0	57	76	52	2
Anti-Gender Non-Conforming	57	0	1	4	14	8	4
Multiple-Bias Incidents[3]	339	0	0	20	35	179	0

Table 4. Offenses, Offense Type, by Bias Motivation, 2020—*Continued*

(Number.)

Bias motivation	Crimes against property							Crimes against society[2]
	Robbery	Burglary	Larceny- theft	Motor vehicle theft	Arson	Destruction/ damage/ vandalism	Other[2]	
Total	140	132	362	34	67	2,333	79	232
Single-Bias Incidents	139	130	356	34	63	2,243	78	231
Race/Ethnicity/Ancestry	82	69	166	18	36	1,355	38	148
Anti-White	27	17	56	6	3	150	15	65
Anti-Black or African American	23	32	71	6	25	821	8	54
Anti-American Indian or Alaska Native	1	4	10	2	1	22	5	9
Anti-Asian	7	3	4	2	0	52	0	5
Anti-Native Hawaiian or Other Pacific Islander	0	2	0	0	1	2	3	0
Anti-Multiple Races, Group	1	1	5	0	1	105	3	3
Anti-Arab	0	2	2	0	0	19	0	0
Anti-Hispanic or Latino	18	6	6	0	2	73	2	6
Anti-Other Race/Ethnicity/Ancestry	5	2	12	2	3	111	2	6
Religion	7	34	78	8	18	671	25	43
Anti-Jewish	3	11	9	0	1	460	1	6
Anti-Catholic	0	4	8	2	5	33	5	5
Anti-Protestant	1	2	4	1	0	10	2	2
Anti-Islamic (Muslim)	1	4	7	0	4	23	0	0
Anti-Other Religion	0	2	4	1	3	46	1	2
Anti-Multiple Religions, Group	1	0	5	0	1	19	2	1
Anti-Mormon	0	1	0	0	0	4	0	1
Anti-Jehovah's Witness	0	1	1	0	0	6	0	1
Anti-Eastern Orthodox (Russian, Greek, Other)	0	1	8	2	0	9	3	13
Anti-Other Christian	0	1	3	0	4	33	0	0
Anti-Buddhist	0	0	1	0	0	13	0	0
Anti-Hindu	0	1	0	0	0	5	1	0
Anti-Sikh	1	6	25	2	0	9	9	12
Anti-Atheism/Agnosticism/etc	0	0	3	0	0	1	1	0
Sexual Orientation	34	17	68	2	9	179	4	12
Anti-Gay (Male)	28	7	15	1	2	87	3	6
Anti-Lesbian	0	1	6	0	2	24	0	1
Anti-Lesbian, Gay, Bisexual, or Transgender (Mixed Group)	6	7	45	1	5	63	0	3
Anti-Heterosexual	0	1	1	0	0	3	0	2
Anti-Bisexual	0	1	1	0	0	2	1	0
Disability	5	5	22	4	0	14	6	10
Anti-Physical	3	2	8	1	0	4	0	5
Anti-Mental	2	3	14	3	0	10	6	5
Gender	1	2	4	0	0	4	2	6
Anti-Male	0	1	3	0	0	1	0	3
Anti-Female	1	1	1	0	0	3	2	3
Gender Identity	10	3	18	2	0	20	3	12
Anti-Transgender	8	3	9	2	0	13	2	5
Anti-Gender Non-Conforming	2	0	9	0	0	7	1	7
Multiple-Bias Incidents[3]	1	2	6	0	4	90	1	1

[1] Only the revised Uniform Crime Reporting definition of rape was used for the figures reported in this column.
[2] The figures shown include additional offenses collected in the National Incident-Based Reporting System.
[3] A multiple-bias incident is an incident in which one or more offense types are motivated by two or more biases.

Table 5. Offenses, Known Offender's Race, by Bias Motivation, 2020

(Number.)

Bias motivation	Total offenses	Known offender's race						
		White	Black or African American	American Indian or Alaska Native	Asian	Native Hawaiian or Other Pacific Islander	Group of multiple races	Unknown race
Total	11,129	4,958	1,390	73	75	29	223	947
Single-Bias Incidents	10,790	4,873	1,377	72	74	29	215	859
Race/Ethnicity/Ancestry	6,677	2,843	835	60	59	25	133	465
Anti-White	1,048	175	480	18	7	16	27	46
Anti-Black or African American................	3,819	1,866	87	25	29	6	74	286
Anti-American Indian or Alaska Native............	103	41	12	8	1	0	2	3
Anti-Asian	330	128	44	0	6	1	11	58
Anti-Native Hawaiian or Other Pacific Islander	15	8	1	1	0	0	0	1
Anti-Multiple Races, Group	270	106	12	1	2	1	6	9
Anti-Arab	85	38	10	0	0	1	1	3
Anti-Hispanic or Latino	664	362	144	6	9	0	8	36
Anti-Other Race/Ethnicity/Ancestry	343	119	45	1	5	0	4	23
Religion	1,402	430	90	4	6	1	23	235
Anti-Jewish	794	191	34	2	3	0	14	175
Anti-Catholic	77	26	5	0	0	0	1	14
Anti-Protestant	31	14	3	0	0	0	0	1
Anti-Islamic (Muslim)	126	70	19	0	2	0	3	13
Anti-Other Religion	85	31	7	0	0	0	1	7
Anti-Multiple Religions, Group	44	9	2	1	0	0	1	3
Anti-Mormon	8	0	1	0	0	1	0	2
Anti-Jehovah's Witness	10	2	0	0	0	0	0	1
Anti-Eastern Orthodox (Russian, Greek, Other)	43	19	8	0	0	0	0	0
Anti-Other Christian	56	21	1	0	0	0	0	8
Anti-Buddhist	16	2	0	0	0	0	2	5
Anti-Hindu	11	2	0	1	1	0	0	2
Anti-Sikh	93	39	9	0	0	0	1	4
Anti-Atheism/Agnosticism/etc.	8	4	1	0	0	0	0	0
Sexual Orientation	2,185	1,367	322	4	8	2	48	112
Anti-Gay (Male)	770	284	211	3	4	2	31	82
Anti-Lesbian	1,021	939	32	0	0	0	4	9
Anti-Lesbian, Gay, Bisexual, or Transgender (Mixed Group)	363	131	74	1	4	0	13	19
Anti-Heterosexual	12	7	1	0	0	0	0	0
Anti-Bisexual	19	6	4	0	0	0	0	2
Disability	151	79	27	2	1	0	0	6
Anti-Physical	60	31	8	2	1	0	0	5
Anti-Mental	91	48	19	0	0	0	0	1
Gender	81	44	17	1	0	0	1	4
Anti-Male	25	16	4	0	0	0	0	0
Anti-Female	56	28	13	1	0	0	1	4
Gender Identity	294	110	86	1	0	1	10	37
Anti-Transgender	237	76	78	1	0	0	9	34
Anti-Gender Non-Conforming	57	34	8	0	0	1	1	3
Multiple-Bias Incidents[2]	339	85	13	1	1	0	8	88

Table 5. Offenses, Known Offender's Race, by Bias Motivation, 2020—*Continued*

(Number.)

Bias motivation	Known offender's ethnicity[1]				Unknown offender
	Hispanic or Latino	Not Hispanic or Latino	Group of multiple ethnicities	Unknown ethnicity	
Total	608	2,625	69	2,915	3,434
Single-Bias Incidents	600	2,576	68	2,777	3,291
Race/Ethnicity/Ancestry	387	1,791	43	1,919	2,257
Anti-White	46	323	9	363	279
Anti-Black or African American	218	927	12	1,063	1,446
Anti-American Indian or Alaska Native	9	31	0	27	36
Anti-Asian	40	80	3	80	82
Anti-Native Hawaiian or Other Pacific Islander ...	1	6	0	4	4
Anti-Multiple Races, Group	10	62	3	53	133
Anti-Arab	5	24	0	23	32
Anti-Hispanic or Latino	43	265	15	212	99
Anti-Other Race/Ethnicity/Ancestry	15	73	1	94	146
Religion	42	256	5	274	613
Anti-Jewish	12	121	3	103	375
Anti-Catholic	2	11	0	21	31
Anti-Protestant	1	7	0	8	13
Anti-Islamic (Muslim)	10	34	2	48	19
Anti-Other Religion	3	9	0	32	39
Anti-Multiple Religions, Group	1	7	0	8	28
Anti-Mormon	1	1	0	2	4
Anti-Jehovah's Witness	0	2	0	0	7
Anti-Eastern Orthodox (Russian, Greek, Other) ...	2	18	0	7	16
Anti-Other Christian	4	10	0	16	26
Anti-Buddhist	0	4	0	5	7
Anti-Hindu	1	2	0	1	5
Anti-Sikh	5	25	0	23	40
Anti-Atheism/Agnosticism/etc.	0	5	0	0	3
Sexual Orientation	118	365	16	403	322
Anti-Gay (Male)	92	209	10	262	153
Anti-Lesbian	12	34	1	29	37
Anti-Lesbian, Gay, Bisexual, or Transgender (Mixed Group) ...	13	109	5	107	121
Anti-Heterosexual	0	5	0	3	4
Anti-Bisexual	1	8	0	2	7
Disability	7	51	0	57	36
Anti-Physical	1	19	0	27	13
Anti-Mental	6	32	0	30	23
Gender	7	32	0	21	14
Anti-Male	2	5	0	12	5
Anti-Female	5	27	0	9	9
Gender Identity	39	81	4	103	49
Anti-Transgender	33	65	3	82	39
Anti-Gender Non-Conforming	6	16	1	21	10
Multiple-Bias Incidents[2]	8	49	1	138	143

[1] The aggregate of offenses by the known offender's ethnicity does not equal the aggregate of offenses by the known offender's race because not all law enforcement agencies that report offender race data also report offender ethnicity data.
[2] A multiple-bias incident is an incident in which one or more offense types are motivated by two or more biases.

Table 6. Offenses, Victim Type, by Offense Type, 2020

(Number.)

Offense type	Total offenses	Victim type					
		Individual	Business/ financial institution	Government	Religious organization	Society/ public[1]	Other/ unknown/ multiple
Total	11,129	9,376	577	345	204	232	395
Crimes against persons[2]	7,750	7,750	NA	NA	NA	NA	NA
Crimes against property	3,147	1,626	577	345	204	0	395
Robbery	140	129	2	0	0	0	9
Burglary	132	90	24	2	8	0	8
Larceny-theft	362	266	75	2	4	0	15
Motor vehicle theft	34	30	3	0	0	0	1
Arson	67	40	7	4	9	0	7
Destruction/damage/vandalism	2,333	1,007	456	334	183	0	353
Other[2]	79	64	10	3	0	0	2
Crimes against society[2]	232	NA	NA	NA	NA	193	NA

NA = Not available.
[1]The victim type society/public is collected only in National Incident-Based Reporting System (NIBRS).
[2]Includes additional offenses collected in the NIBRS.

Table 7. Victims, Offense Type, by Bias Motivation, 2020

(Number.)

Bias motivation	Total victims[1]	Total number of adult victims[2]	Total number of juvenile victims[2]	Crimes against persons					
				Murder and nonnegligent manslaughter	Rape[3]	Aggravated assault	Simple assault	Intimidation	Other[4]
Total	11,472	7,729	791	22	21	1,390	2,166	4,119	32
Single-Bias Incidents	11,126	7,469	776	22	21	1,370	2,131	3,940	32
Race/Ethnicity/Ancestry	6,880	5,205	589	8	10	976	1,455	2,296	20
Anti-White	1,082	845	64	1	7	145	317	231	8
Anti-Black or African American	3,915	2,932	408	5	2	530	660	1,577	5
Anti-American Indian or Alaska Native	108	85	6	0	1	5	26	14	3
Anti-Asian	342	262	14	0	0	47	99	111	0
Anti-Native Hawaiian or Other Pacific Islander	18	14	0	0	0	2	2	3	0
Anti-Multiple Races, Group	281	160	24	2	0	31	41	77	0
Anti-Arab	87	74	3	0	0	9	24	29	0
Anti-Hispanic or Latino	693	590	61	0	0	162	215	170	4
Anti-Other Race/Ethnicity/Ancestry	354	243	9	0	0	45	71	84	0
Religion	1,481	740	32	1	0	73	151	293	0
Anti-Jewish	831	361	12	1	0	34	59	209	0
Anti-Catholic	80	39	0	0	0	5	5	5	0
Anti-Protestant	32	20	3	0	0	2	6	1	0
Anti-Islamic (Muslim)	131	97	9	0	0	12	32	43	0
Anti-Other Religion	105	55	6	0	0	10	6	10	0
Anti-Multiple Religions, Group	49	26	0	0	0	0	6	9	0
Anti-Mormon	8	2	0	0	0	1	0	1	0
Anti-Jehovah's Witness	10	4	0	0	0	0	1	0	0
Anti-Eastern Orthodox (Russian, Greek, Other)	43	23	0	0	0	1	5	1	0
Anti-Other Christian	62	24	0	0	0	1	8	6	0
Anti-Buddhist	16	5	0	0	0	0	2	0	0
Anti-Hindu	11	5	0	0	0	0	3	1	0
Anti-Sikh	94	71	2	0	0	5	17	7	0
Anti-Atheism/Agnosticism/etc	9	8	0	0	0	2	1	0	0
Sexual Orientation	2,229	1,090	109	5	6	223	370	1,254	2
Anti-Gay (Male)	791	674	53	5	2	157	252	203	2
Anti-Lesbian	1,026	98	14	0	2	17	28	940	0
Anti-Lesbian, Gay, Bisexual, or Transgender (Mixed Group)	380	294	39	0	2	45	84	102	0
Anti-Heterosexual	13	8	2	0	0	0	1	4	0
Anti-Bisexual	19	16	1	0	0	4	5	5	0
Disability	152	116	19	0	2	18	41	21	3
Anti-Physical	60	48	10	0	0	6	20	8	3
Anti-Mental	92	68	9	0	2	12	21	13	0
Gender	82	64	5	0	2	19	24	16	1
Anti-Male	25	20	1	0	0	8	6	2	1
Anti-Female	57	44	4	0	2	11	18	14	0
Gender Identity	302	254	22	8	1	61	90	60	6
Anti-Transgender	244	209	15	8	0	57	76	52	2
Anti-Gender Non-Conforming	58	45	7	0	1	4	14	8	4
Multiple-Bias Incidents[5]	346	260	15	0	0	20	35	179	0

Table 7. Victims, Offense Type, by Bias Motivation, 2020—*Continued*

(Number.)

Bias motivation	Crimes against property							Crimes against society[4]
	Robbery	Burglary	Larceny- theft	Motor vehicle theft	Arson	Destruction/ damage/ vandalism	Other[4]	
Total	155	152	383	36	105	2,574	85	232
Single-Bias Incidents	154	150	376	36	100	2,479	84	231
Race/Ethnicity/Ancestry	90	79	181	18	41	1,515	43	148
Anti-White	31	18	63	6	4	168	18	65
Anti-Black or African American............	23	38	77	6	27	902	9	54
Anti-American Indian or Alaska Native.........	1	5	11	2	1	25	5	9
Anti-Asian	8	4	4	2	0	62	0	5
Anti-Native Hawaiian or Other Pacific Islander	0	2	0	0	1	4	4	
Anti-Multiple Races, Group	1	1	6	0	1	115	3	3
Anti-Arab	0	2	2	0	0	21	0	0
Anti-Hispanic or Latino	20	7	6	0	4	97	2	6
Anti-Other Race/Ethnicity/Ancestry	6	2	12	2	3	121	2	6
Religion..................................	7	36	79	8	48	716	26	43
Anti-Jewish	3	12	9	0	2	494	2	6
Anti-Catholic		4	8	2	8	33	5	5
Anti-Protestant...........................	1	2	4	1	0	11	2	2
Anti-Islamic (Muslim)....................	1	4	7	0	9	23	0	0
Anti-Other Religion	0	2	4	1	22	47	1	2
Anti-Multiple Religions, Group	1	0	5	0	3	22	2	1
Anti-Mormon	0	1	0	0	0	4	0	1
Anti-Jehovah's Witness....................	0	1	1	0	0	6	0	1
Anti-Eastern Orthodox (Russian, Greek, Other)	0	1	8	2	0	9	3	13
Anti-Other Christian......................	0	1	3	0	4	39	0	0
Anti-Buddhist	0	0	1	0	0	13	0	0
Anti-Hindu	0	1	0	0	0	5	1	0
Anti-Sikh	1	7	25	2	0	9	9	12
Anti-Atheism/Agnosticism/etc.............	0	0	4	0	0	1	1	0
Sexual Orientation.......................	37	25	72	2	11	206	4	12
Anti-Gay (Male)..........................	31	9	16	1	3	101	3	6
Anti-Lesbian..............................	0	1	7	0	2	28	0	1
Anti-Lesbian, Gay, Bisexual, or Transgender (Mixed Group)	6	13	47	1	6	71	0	3
Anti-Heterosexual.........................	0	1	1	0	0	4	0	2
Anti-Bisexual.............................	0	1	1	0	0	2	1	0
Disability................................	5	5	22	4	0	15	6	10
Anti-Physical.............................	3	2	8	1	0	4	0	5
Anti-Mental..............................	2	3	14	3	0	11	6	5
Gender	1	2	4	0	0	5	2	6
Anti-Male................................	0	1	3	0	0	1	0	3
Anti-Female..............................	1	1	1	0	0	4	2	3
Gender Identity	14	3	18	4	0	22	3	12
Anti-Transgender.........................	11	3	9	4	0	15	2	5
Anti-Gender Non-Conforming.............	3		9	0	0	7	1	7
Multiple-Bias Incidents[5]	1	2	7	0	5	95	1	1

NOTE: The aggregate of adult and juvenile individual victims does not equal the total number of victims because total victims include individuals, businesses/financial institutions, government entities, religious organizations, and society/public as a whole. In addition, the aggregate of adult and juvenile individual victims does not equal the aggregate of victims of crimes against persons because not all law enforcement agencies report the ages of individual victims.

[1] The term *victim* may refer to an individual, business/financial institution, government entity, religious organization, or society/public as a whole.

[2] The figures shown are individual victims only.

[3] Only the revised Uniform Crime Reporting definition of rape is used for the figures reported in this column.

[4] The figures shown include additional offenses collected in the National Incident-Based Reporting System.

[5] A multiple-bias incident is an incident in which one or more offense types are motivated by two or more biases.

Table 8. Incidents, Victim Type, by Bias Motivation, 2020

(Number.)

Bias motivation	Total incidents	Victim type					
		Individual	Business/ financial institution	Government	Religious organization	Society/ public[1]	Other/ unknown/ multiple
Total	8,263	6,546	551	343	200	185	438
Single-Bias Incidents	8,052	6,406	535	321	195	185	410
Race/Ethnicity/Ancestry	5,227	4,345	328	212	20	107	215
Religion	1,244	624	162	91	169	41	157
Sexual Orientation	1,110	1,025	25	14	6	9	31
Disability	130	106	11	1	0	10	2
Gender	75	66	1	1	0	6	1
Gender Identity	266	240	8	2	0	12	4
Multiple-Bias Incidents[2]	211	140	16	22	5	0	28

[1]The victim type *society/public* is collected only in the National Incident-Based Reporting System.
[2]A multiple-bias incident is an incident in which one or more offense types are motivated by two or more biases.

Table 9. Known Offenders,[1] by Known Offender's Race, Ethnicity, and Age, 2020

(Number.)

Race/ethnicity/age	Total
Race	6,780
White	3,737
Black or African American	1,438
American Indian or Alaska Native	69
Asian	73
Native Hawaiian or Other Pacific Islander	31
Group of multiple races[2]	366
Unknown race	1,066
Ethnicity[3]	6,169
Hispanic or Latino	629
Not Hispanic or Latino	2,424
Group of multiple ethnicities[4]	146
Unknown ethnicity	2,970
Age[3]	6,264
Total known offenders 18 and over	5,581
Total known offenders under 18	683

[1]The term *known offender* does not imply the suspect's identity is known; rather, the term indicates some aspect of the suspect was identified, thus distinguishing the suspect from an unknown offender.
[2]The term *group of multiple races* is used to describe a group of offenders of varying races.
[3]The total number of known offenders by age and the total number of known offenders by ethnicity do not equal the total number of known offenders by race because not all law enforcement agencies report the age and/or ethnicity of the known offenders.
[4]The term *group of multiple ethnicities* is used to describe a group of offenders of varying ethnicities.

Table 10. Incidents, Bias Motivation, by Location, 2020

(Number.)

Location	Total incidents	Bias motivation						Multiple- bias incidents[1]
		Race/ethnicity/ ancestry	Religion	Sexual orientation	Disability	Gender	Gender identity	
Total	8,263	5,227	1,244	1,110	130	75	266	211
Abandoned/condemned structure................................	10	6	0	0	0	0	2	2
Air/bus/train terminal	118	77	9	20	2	0	6	4
Amusement park................................	4	3	0	1	0	0	0	0
Arena/stadium/fairgrounds/coliseum	9	6	3	0	0	0	0	0
Auto dealership new/used................................	11	6	2	0	0	0	3	0
Bank/savings and loan................................	25	21	1	0	0	1	2	0
Bar/nightclub................................	82	43	4	25	2	1	4	3
Camp/campground................................	12	6	6	0	0	0	0	0
Church/synagogue/temple/mosque................................	285	50	218	10	0	0	0	7
Commercial office building................................	183	114	36	21	2	5	1	4
Community center................................	31	22	5	3	0	0	0	1
Construction site................................	33	24	8	0	0	0	0	1
Convenience store................................	192	146	14	21	2	0	5	4
Cyberspace................................	104	58	19	10	3	2	5	7
Daycare facility................................	6	5	1	0	0	0	0	0
Department/discount store................................	107	76	10	13	3	0	4	1
Dock/wharf/freight/modal terminal	5	5	0	0	0	0	0	0
Drug store/doctor's office/hospital................................	98	70	8	8	2	2	2	6
Farm facility................................	4	4	0	0	0	0	0	0
Field/woods................................	61	35	15	9	0	0	0	2
Gambling facility/casino/race track................................	9	6	2	0	0	0	1	0
Government/public building................................	122	93	16	6	1	1	2	3
Grocery/supermarket................................	122	90	12	11	3	1	3	2
Highway/road/alley/street/sidewalk................................	1,645	1,135	148	240	18	8	66	30
Hotel/motel/etc................................	91	65	11	7	1	0	4	3
Industrial site	15	10	3	0	0	0	0	2
Jail/prison/penitentiary/corrections facility................................	63	45	3	14	0	1	0	0
Lake/waterway/beach................................	24	16	2	4	0	0	0	2
Liquor store................................	26	15	6	4	0	1	0	0
Military installation................................	1	1	0	0	0	0	0	0
Park/playground................................	294	182	50	33	1	2	11	15
Parking/drop lot/garage	540	396	44	70	4	5	12	9
Rental storage facility................................	12	6	4	2	0	0	0	0
Residence/home................................	2,390	1,465	283	397	67	32	92	54
Rest area................................	8	6	1	0	0	1	0	0
Restaurant	207	152	12	34	1	1	2	5
School/college[2]	27	17	6	3	0	0	0	1
School-college/university................................	114	67	23	16	0	1	4	3
School-elementary/secondary................................	209	122	39	24	6	0	3	15
Service/gas station................................	100	65	10	13	2	2	6	2
Shelter-mission/homeless................................	25	15	2	3	2	0	3	0
Shopping mall................................	26	18	2	5	0	0	1	0
Specialty store (TV, fur, etc.)	76	53	9	9	1	0	3	1
Tribal Lands................................	5	4	0	0	0	0	1	0
Other/unknown	713	392	196	73	7	8	18	19
Multiple locations	19	14	1	1	0	0	0	3

[1] A multiple-bias incident is an incident in which one or more offense types are motivated by two or more biases.
[2] The location designation *School/college* has been retained for agencies that have not updated their records management systems to include the new location designations of *School—college/university* and *School—elementary/secondary*, which allow for more specificity in reporting.

Table 11. Offenses, Offense Type, by Participating State/Federal, 2020

(Number.)

State	Total offenses	Crimes against persons					
		Murder and nonnegligent manslaughter	Rape[1]	Aggravated assault	Simple assault	Intimidation	Other[2]
Total	11,129	22	21	1,390	2,166	4,119	32
Alabama	33	0	0	2	3	4	0
Alaska	10	0	1	5	3	0	0
Arizona	332	2	0	54	93	99	3
Arkansas	22	0	0	6	2	7	0
California	1,537	0	2	331	362	358	1
Colorado	343	0	0	52	72	105	0
Connecticut	126	0	0	9	28	53	0
Delaware	18	0	0	0	2	9	0
District of Columbia	151	0	0	35	69	24	0
Florida	112	0	0	28	38	18	U
Georgia	234	0	0	25	56	89	0
Hawaii	39	0	0	5	13	16	1
Idaho	53	0	0	8	18	16	0
Illinois	75	1	0	21	21	22	0
Indiana	229	0	0	33	65	61	0
Iowa	18	0	0	1	7	1	0
Kansas	156	0	0	24	11	38	1
Kentucky	229	0	2	12	52	96	1
Louisiana	53	0	0	17	16	1	0
Maine	93	0	0	6	12	24	0
Maryland	45	0	0	10	8	3	0
Massachusetts	351	0	0	41	65	97	1
Michigan	453	0	1	52	109	189	2
Minnesota	232	0	0	44	39	67	1
Mississippi	16	0	0	1	8	4	0
Missouri	154	0	0	28	55	34	0
Montana	29	0	0	3	7	3	2
Nebraska	985	0	1	16	11	911	0
Nevada	153	1	0	36	48	15	0
New Hampshire	24	0	0	2	5	6	0
New Jersey	389	0	0	12	26	193	0
New Mexico	78	0	1	14	28	8	0
New York	466	1	0	32	149	21	0
North Carolina	243	1	3	34	45	86	1
North Dakota	29	0	0	3	11	8	1
Ohio	633	0	4	51	118	166	5
Oklahoma	9	0	0	1	2	3	0
Oregon	324	0	0	31	72	92	1
Pennsylvania	91	0	0	8	7	38	0
Rhode Island	16	0	0	1	5	1	0
South Carolina	130	0	1	26	25	21	1
South Dakota	19	0	0	2	9	4	0
Tennessee	93	0	0	20	17	38	0
Texas	467	1	4	88	119	94	3
Utah	51	0	0	1	13	6	4
Vermont	64	0	0	4	8	4	1
Virginia	193	0	1	10	60	36	0
Washington	526	0	0	52	101	219	0
West Virginia	58	0	0	4	11	5	1
Wisconsin	88	2	0	17	22	15	1
Wyoming	21	0	0	3	9	5	0
Federal							
Federal Bureau of Investigation, Field Offices.....	832	13	0	69	11	682	0
Pentagon Force Protection Agency	3	0	0	0	0	3	0
United States Marine Corps Law Enforcement...	1	0	0	0	0	1	0

Table 11. Offenses, Offense Type, by Participating State/Federal, 2020—*Continued*

(Number.)

State	Crimes against property							Crimes against society[2]
	Robbery	Burglary	Larceny-theft	Motor vehicle theft	Arson	Destruction/ damage/ vandalism	Other[2]	
Total	140	132	362	34	67	2,333	79	232
Alabama..........................	0	2	3	0	0	4	1	14
Alaska.............................	1	0	0	0	0	0	0	0
Arizona...........................	1	5	5	0	3	62	1	4
Arkansas.........................	0	0	0	0	0	7	0	0
California........................	49	13	8	1	13	399	0	0
Colorado.........................	9	9	13	1	3	74	5	0
Connecticut....................	1	0	3	1	0	29	1	1
Delaware.........................	1	0	0	0	0	5	1	0
District of Columbia........	2	0	0	0	0	21	0	0
Florida............................	1	2	0	0	5	20	0	0
Georgia..........................	0	1	8	2	3	38	6	6
Hawaii............................	2	0	1	0	0	1	0	0
Idaho..............................	1	1	0	0	0	9	0	0
Illinois............................	0	0	0	0	0	10	0	0
Indiana...........................	2	4	19	2	1	24	5	13
Iowa...............................	1	1	0	0	0	6	0	1
Kansas............................	1	2	9	1	2	49	5	13
Kentucky........................	3	2	3	2	3	50	0	3
Louisiana........................	1	2	1	0	0	7	0	8
Maine.............................	0	0	29	0	1	20	0	1
Maryland.........................	3	0	0	0	0	21	0	0
Massachusetts.................	0	1	18	0	0	123	2	3
Michigan.........................	4	6	17	4	1	45	8	15
Minnesota.......................	5	4	12	0	0	57	0	3
Mississippi......................	0	2	0	0	0	1	0	0
Missouri..........................	1	2	2	0	3	25	0	4
Montana.........................	2	1	1	0	0	10	0	0
Nebraska.........................	0	0	3	0	0	27	0	16
Nevada...........................	4	2	5	3	0	25	0	14
New Hampshire...............	0	1	0	0	0	10	0	0
New Jersey......................	2	1	4	0	2	149	0	0
New Mexico.....................	2	2	2	0	0	19	0	2
New York........................	7	9	10	0	0	237	0	0
North Carolina................	3	3	7	0	0	53	1	6
North Dakota..................	0	1	1	0	0	3	1	0
Ohio...............................	11	19	81	9	3	112	14	40
Oklahoma.......................	0	1	0	0	0	1	0	1
Oregon...........................	2	6	8	1	0	104	3	4
Pennsylvania...................	1	0	1	1	1	32	1	1
Rhode Island...................	0	1	1	0	0	7	0	0
South Carolina................	1	3	12	0	0	18	3	19
South Dakota..................	1	0	0	0	0	3	0	0
Tennessee.......................	1	1	1	0	0	14	0	1
Texas..............................	5	11	17	1	3	106	6	9
Utah...............................	0	1	6	0	1	12	4	3
Vermont..........................	0	1	12	1	0	31	2	0
Virginia...........................	0	0	4	0	1	77	1	3
Washington.....................	6	7	20	3	3	106	5	4
West Virginia...................	2	2	10	1	0	6	1	15
Wisconsin........................	0	0	3	0	0	21	2	5
Wyoming........................	0	0	1	0	0	3	0	0
Federal								
Federal Bureau of Investigation, Field Offices.....	1	0	1	0	15	40	0	0
Pentagon Force Protection Agency....................	0	0	0	0	0	0	0	0
United States Marine Corps Law Enforcement...	0	0	0	0	0	0	0	0

[1] Only the revised Uniform Crime Reporting definition of rape was used for the figures shown in this column.
[2] The figures shown include additional offenses collected in the National Incident-Based Reporting System.

Table 12. Agency Hate Crime Reporting, by Participating State/Territory and Federal, 2020

(Number.)

State	Number of participating agencies	Population covered	Agencies submitting incident reports	Total number of incidents reported
Total	15,138	306,085,895	2,389	8,263
Alabama...	409	4,798,528	17	27
Alaska...	32	719,120	4	9
Arizona...	81	5,989,615	25	280
Arkansas...	281	2,818,360	8	19
California..	732	39,361,017	244	1,339
Colorado	227	5,754,151	66	281
Connecticut..	107	3,557,006	38	101
Delaware	62	986,809	7	13
District of Columbia	2	712,816	2	133
Florida	452	19,525,021	54	109
Georgia	401	7,938,166	68	195
Hawaii	1	966,438	1	36
Idaho..	107	1,819,575	15	43
Illinois..	700	11,752,377	26	56
Indiana	174	4,858,228	53	186
Iowa	251	3,083,186	10	15
Kansas..	359	2,586,059	61	124
Kentucky	423	4,472,499	67	166
Louisiana	137	3,491,734	18	39
Maine..	131	1,350,141	23	83
Maryland	152	6,055,802	14	40
Massachusetts..	368	6,835,964	95	310
Michigan	628	9,767,448	168	377
Minnesota	413	5,655,413	61	194
Mississippi..	92	1,306,283	11	16
Missouri..	549	6,089,883	38	115
Montana..	106	1,075,088	12	26
Nebraska...	126	1,807,565	13	72
Nevada..	48	3,128,688	12	113
New Hampshire	193	1,335,848	16	19
New Jersey..	534	8,462,314	182	389
New Mexico..	35	1,114,118	8	55
New York..	559	19,122,405	78	463
North Carolina	378	9,618,194	65	185
North Dakota..	110	765,309	13	21
Ohio..	578	10,035,054	136	538
Oklahoma...	443	3,980,783	4	8
Oregon..	207	4,000,770	67	280
Pennsylvania	734	8,190,948	20	81
Rhode Island	49	1,057,125	9	14
South Carolina..	398	5,139,301	46	110
South Dakota..	128	848,707	14	17
Tennessee...	463	6,886,834	29	78
Texas...	1,073	29,247,610	131	406
Utah	126	3,181,559	23	44
Vermont	88	623,347	28	60
Virginia...	416	8,589,304	65	170
Washington	243	7,663,709	92	451
West Virginia..	251	1,562,004	23	54
Wisconsin	441	5,824,028	48	72
Wyoming...	59	573,644	8	18
Federal[1]				
Board of Governors of the Federal Reserve System and the Consumer Financial Protection Bureau, Office of Inpector General...	1	0	0	0
Central Intelligence Agency Security Protective Service	1	0	0	0
Corporation for National and Community Service, Office of Inspector General..	1	0	0	0
Defense Intelligence Agency	1	0	0	0

Table 12. Agency Hate Crime Reporting, by Participating State/Territory and Federal, 2020—*Continued*

(Number.)

State	Number of participating agencies	Population covered	Agencies submitting incident reports	Total number of incidents reported
Drug Enforcement Administration, Wilmington Resident Office	1	0	0	0
Export-Import Bank of the United States, Office of Inspector General........................	1	0	0	0
Federal Bureau of Investigation, Field Offices	52	0	51	209
Federal Emergency Management Agency........................	1	0	0	0
Federal Housing Finance Agency, Office of Inspector General..	1	0	0	0
National Institute of Health	1	0	0	0
National Security Agency Police........................	1	0	0	0
Peace Corps, Office of Inspector General	1	0	0	0
Pension Benefit Guaranty Corporation, Office of Inspector General........................	1	0	0	0
Pentagon Force Protection Agency........................	1	0	1	3
Tennessee Valley Authority, Office of Inspector General...........	1	0	0	0
United States Agency for International Development, Office of Inspector General	1	0	0	0
United States Air Force, Office of Special Investigations...........	1	0	0	0
United States Army........................	1	0	0	0
United States Department of Agriculture, Office of Inspector General........................	1	0	0	0
United States Department of Defense, Office of Inspector General........................	1	0	0	0
United States Department of Education, Office of Inspector General........................	1	0	0	0
United States Department of Justice, Office of Inspector General........................	1	0	0	0
United States Election Assistance Commission, Office of Inspector General........................	1	0	0	0
United States Environmental Protection Agency, Office of Inspector General........................	1	0	0	0
United States Federal Deposit Insurance Corporation, Office of Inspector General	1	0	0	0
United States Marine Corps Law Enforcement........................	1	0	1	1
United States National Archives and Records Administration, Office of Inspector General	1	0	0	0
United States Navy Law Enforcement........................	1	0	0	0
United States Nuclear Regulatory Commission, Office of Inspector General........................	1	0	0	0
United States Office of Personnel Management, Office of the Inspector General........................	1	0	0	0

[1]Population estimates are not attributed to the federal agencies.

Table 13. Hate Crime Incidents Per Bias Motivation and Quarter, by Selected State and Agency and Federal, 2020

(Number.)

State/agency	Race/ Ethnicity/ Ancestry	Religion	Sexual orientation	Disability	Gender	Gender Identity	1st quarter	2nd quarter	3rd quarter	4th quarter	Population[1]
ALABAMA											
Total	22	5	1	0	0	0					
Cities	8	5	1	0	0	0					
Bayou La Batre	1	0	0	0	0	0	0	1			2,466
Birmingham	1	1	0	0	0	0	1	1			209,081
Carrollton	1	0	0	0	0	0	0	1			935
Dora	0	1	0	0	0	0	1	0			1,890
Evergreen	1	0	0	0	0	0	0	1			3,482
Fayette	1	0	0	0	0	0	0	1			4,239
Hoover	0	1	0	0	0	0	0	1	0	0	86,321
Linden	0	0	1	0	0	0	0	1			1,856
Margaret	1	0	0	0	0	0	1	0			5,222
Mobile[2]	1	2	0	0	0	0	1	1			243,900
Tuskegee	1	0	0	0	0	0	0	1			7,973
Metropolitan Counties	9	0	0	0	0	0					
Etowah	1	0	0	0	0	0	1	0			
Washington	8	0	0	0	0	0	8	0			
Nonmetropolitan Counties	5	0	0	0	0	0					
Crenshaw	1	0	0	0	0	0	1	0			
Dallas	1	0	0	0	0	0	1	0			
DeKalb	2	0	0	0	0	0	1	1			
Walker	1	0	0	0	0	0	0	1			
ALASKA											
Total	5	0	1	0	2	1					
Cities	5	0	1	0	2	1					
Anchorage	3	0	1	0	1	0	0	2	2	1	286,388
Fairbanks	0	0	0	0	0	1	1	0	0	0	30,832
Juneau	2	0	0	0	0	0	0	1	1	0	31,925
North Pole	0	0	0	0	1	0	0	1	0	0	2,090
ARIZONA											
Total	202	37	34	2	1	7					
Cities	178	30	32	1	1	6					
Apache Junction	1	0	0	0	0	0	0	0	0	1	43,385
Casa Grande	2	1	0	0	0	0	0	0	2	1	59,822
Chandler	2	2	0	0	0	0	2	0	1	1	264,071
Fredonia	0	0	1	0	0	0	0	0	0	1	1,275
Gilbert	3	2	1	0	0	0	1	1	2	2	259,629
Glendale	6	0	1	0	0	0	2	2	3	0	255,468
Maricopa	0	0	1	0	0	0	1	0	0	0	53,165
Mesa	7	2	0	0	0	1	2	3	5	0	527,361
Page	1	0	0	0	0	0	0	1	0	0	7,546
Payson	1	0	0	0	0	0	0	1	0	0	15,869
Peoria	2	0	0	0	0	0	0	1	0	1	178,486
Phoenix[2]	140	17	28	0	1	3	24	47	65	51	1,708,960
Prescott	1	0	0	0	0	0	0	0	1	0	44,835
San Luis	0	1	0	0	0	1	1	0	0	1	35,574
Scottsdale	1	1	0	0	0	0	0	0	0	2	263,006
Sierra Vista	0	0	0	0	0	1	0	0	0	1	42,800
Somerton	0	1	0	0	0	0	1	0	0	0	16,811
Surprise	3	0	0	0	0	0	0	1	1	1	144,620
Tempe	3	0	0	0	0	0	0	2	1		199,935
Williams	1	0	0	0	0	0			1	0	3,271
Yuma	4	3	0	1	0	0	1	5	1	1	99,096
Metropolitan Counties	24	7	2	1	0	1					
Coconino	1	0	0	0	0	0	0	0	1	0	
Pima[2]	20	4	2	0	0	1	2	6	6	12	
Yavapai	2	1	0	0	0	0	2	1	0		
Yuma	1	2	0	1	0	0	1	1	1	1	
ARKANSAS											
Total	13	2	4	0	0	0					
Cities	12	1	4	0	0	0					
Conway	1	1	0	0	0	0	0	2	0	0	68,599
Fort Smith	5	0	1	0	0	0	1	4	0	1	88,071
Paragould	1	0	1	0	0	0	1	0	0	1	29,288

(Number.)

State/agency	Race/ Ethnicity/ Ancestry	Religion	Sexual orientation	Disability	Gender	Gender Identity	1st quarter	2nd quarter	3rd quarter	4th quarter	Population[1]
Rogers	4	0	1	0	0	0	0	1	4	0	70,194
Sherwood	1	0	0	0	0	0	0	0	1	0	31,636
Van Buren	0	0	1	0	0	0	0	0	0	1	23,779
Universities and Colleges	1	0	0	0	0	0					
University of Arkansas, Medical Sciences	1	0	0	0	0	0	0	1	0	0	2,996
Metropolitan Counties	0	1	0	0	0	0					
Sebastian	0	1	0	0	0	0	0	1	0	0	
CALIFORNIA											
Total	882	181	210	5	3	59					
Cities	790	160	188	4	2	57					
Alameda	5	0	0	0	0	0	0	0	4	1	78,047
Albany	3	0	0	0	0	0	0	0	1	2	19,830
Alhambra	1	0	0	0	0	0	0	1	0	0	83,817
Aliso Viejo	5	1	0	0	0	0	2	1	2	1	51,244
Antioch	0	0	0	0	0	1	0	0	1	0	112,481
Arcadia	2	0	0	0	0	0	0	0	2	0	58,122
Arcata	0	0	1	0	0	0	0	0	0	1	18,516
Atwater	1	0	0	0	0	0	0	0	1	0	29,704
Auburn	1	0	0	0	0	0	0	0	1	0	14,293
Avalon	0	0	1	0	0	0	0	0	1	0	3,676
Azusa	2	0	0	0	0	0	0	1	1	0	50,373
Bakersfield	1	2	3	0	0	0	0	0	2	4	388,265
Bell	1	0	0	0	0	0	0	1	0	0	35,526
Benicia	2	0	0	0	0	0	0	1	1	0	28,374
Berkeley	3	2	1	0	0	1	1	0	3	3	122,346
Beverly Hills	1	2	2	0	0	0	1	0	2	2	33,776
Big Bear	1	0	1	0	0	0	0	0	2	0	5,305
Brawley	0	0	0	0	0	1	0	1	0	0	26,363
Buena Park	0	0	0	1	0	0	0	0	0	1	81,901
Burbank	6	1	0	0	0	0	0	0	2	5	102,419
Calabasas	1	0	0	0	0	0	0	0	1	0	23,897
Calexico	0	0	1	0	0	0	0	0	0	1	39,957
Camarillo	2	0	0	0	0	0	0	0	1	1	70,424
Campbell	3	0	0	0	0	0	0	1	0	2	41,921
Capitola	0	0	0	0	0	1	1	0	0	0	10,020
Carlsbad	2	1	0	1	0	0	1	3	0	0	116,516
Carson	2	0	0	0	0	0	0	1	0	1	91,372
Cathedral City	1	0	1	0	0	2	0	1	3	0	55,417
Central Marin	5	2	0	0	0	0	0	0	3	4	34,593
Cerritos	1	1	0	0	0	0	1	0	1	0	49,952
Chico	2	0	0	0	0	0	0	1	1	0	105,355
Chino	7	0	0	0	0	0	1	3	1	2	96,309
Chula Vista	4	1	0	0	0	0	0	2	1	2	278,027
Citrus Heights	3	1	0	0	0	0	0	0	3	1	88,314
Clearlake	2	0	0	0	0	0	0	0	1	1	15,268
Clovis	2	0	0	0	0	0	0	1	1	0	116,809
Coalinga	1	0	0	0	0	0	0	0	1	0	17,061
Colusa	1	0	0	0	0	0	0	1	0	0	6,042
Costa Mesa	7	0	1	0	0	0	2	1	3	2	113,317
Covina	3	0	0	0	0	0	2	0	1	0	47,413
Crescent City	1	0	0	0	0	0	0	1	0	0	6,706
Culver City	1	0	0	0	0	0	0	0	1	0	39,218
Cupertino	0	1	0	0	0	0	0	1	0	0	59,343
Cypress	1	0	0	0	0	0	0	0	0	1	49,124
Daly City	1	0	0	0	0	0	0	0	1	0	106,855
Dana Point	1	0	0	0	0	0	0	0	1	0	33,604
Davis	11	2	3	0	0	0	4	2	5	5	69,853
Diamond Bar	1	0	0	0	0	0	0	0	0	1	55,735
El Cajon	1	0	1	0	0	1	1	1	1	0	103,035
El Cerrito	4	0	0	0	0	0	1	1	1	1	25,725
Elk Grove	3	2	0	0	0	0	2	0	2	1	177,331
El Monte	2	0	0	0	0	1	0	2	1	0	115,690
Encinitas	2	1	1	0	0	0	1	0	2	1	63,055
Escondido	1	0	0	0	0	0	0	0	0	1	152,446
Eureka	0	0	0	1	0	0	0	0	1	0	26,656
Fairfax	1	2	0	0	0	1	0	1	0	3	7,530

(Number.)

State/agency	Number of incidents per bias motivation						Number of incidents per quarter				Population[1]
	Race/ Ethnicity/ Ancestry	Religion	Sexual orientation	Disability	Gender	Gender Identity	1st quarter	2nd quarter	3rd quarter	4th quarter	
Fairfield	3	0	1	0	0	0	1	1	0	2	118,491
Fontana	1	1	1	0	0	0	0	0	1	2	216,553
Fort Bragg	1	0	0	0	0	0	0	1	0	0	7,289
Foster City	1	0	0	0	0	0	1	0	0	0	34,291
Fountain Valley	1	0	0	0	0	0	0	1	0	0	55,345
Fremont	4	0	0	0	0	0	0	2	2	0	244,259
Fresno	11	0	1	0	0	0	1	3	3	5	535,472
Fullerton	0	0	1	0	0	0	0	0	1	0	139,011
Galt	1	0	0	0	0	0	0	0	0	1	26,867
Gardena	1	0	0	0	0	0	0	0	1	0	59,385
Garden Grove	4	4	1	0	0	0	1	1	2	5	171,698
Grover Beach	1	0	0	0	0	0	0	0	1	0	13,491
Hawaiian Gardens	1	0	0	0	0	0	0	1	0	0	14,146
Hawthorne	0	0	1	0	0	0	0	0	0	1	86,269
Hayward	3	0	1	0	0	0	0	0	2	2	160,891
Healdsburg	0	0	1	0	0	0	0	0	0	1	11,907
Hermosa Beach	0	1	0	0	0	0	0	0	0	1	19,300
Hesperia	0	1	0	0	0	0	0	0	0	1	96,378
Hillsborough	1	0	0	0	0	0	0	1	0	0	11,447
Hollister	0	0	1	0	0	0	0	1	0	0	41,438
Huntington Beach	2	0	2	0	0	0	2	0	1	1	200,128
Indio	0	2	0	0	0	0	0	0	1	1	93,219
Industry	1	0	0	0	0	0	0	0	0	1	201
Irvine	6	1	0	0	0	0	2	3	0	2	297,069
Jurupa Valley	0	0	1	0	0	0	0	0	1	0	111,198
Laguna Hills	0	0	1	0	0	0	0	1	0	0	31,264
La Habra	0	0	1	0	0	0	0	1	0	0	60,672
Lake Forest	1	0	0	0	0	0	1	0	0	0	86,469
Lakewood	0	0	1	0	0	0	0	1	0	0	79,222
La Mesa	1	0	0	0	0	0	0	1	0	0	59,488
La Mirada	1	0	0	0	0	0	0	0	0	1	48,144
Lancaster	8	0	0	0	0	0	2	3	3	0	157,689
Lodi	1	0	0	0	0	0	0	0	1	0	68,207
Lomita	1	0	0	0	0	0	0	0	1	0	20,327
Long Beach	15	1	2	0	0	0	3	3	3	9	462,654
Los Altos	0	1	0	0	0	0	0	0	0	1	30,203
Los Angeles[2]	187	67	81	1	2	31	69	104	110	85	4,000,587
Los Gatos	1	0	0	0	0	0	0	0	0	1	30,271
Malibu	0	0	1	0	0	0	0	1	0	0	11,736
Manhattan Beach	3	0	0	0	0	0	0	0	2	1	35,190
Martinez	2	0	0	0	0	0	1	0	1	0	38,543
Mendota	1	0	0	0	0	0	0	0	1	0	11,531
Menifee	3	1	0	0	0	0	2	0	1	1	96,837
Merced	2	0	0	0	0	0	0	0	2	0	84,197
Modesto	7	0	4	0	0	0	1	0	3	7	216,560
Montclair	0	1	0	0	0	0	0	0	1	0	40,473
Monterey	4	1	0	0	0	0	1	2	2	0	28,209
Monterey Park	1	0	0	0	0	0	0	0	0	1	59,609
Moorpark	1	0	0	0	0	0	0	0	0	1	36,573
Moreno Valley	1	0	0	0	0	0	0	1	0	0	215,257
Mountain View	1	0	0	0	0	0	0	0	1	0	83,745
National City	2	0	0	0	0	0	0	1	1	0	61,710
Norco	1	0	0	0	0	0	1	0	0	0	26,536
Norwalk	3	0	0	0	0	1	2	0	1	1	103,774
Novato	6	0	0	0	0	0	2	2	2	0	55,926
Oakdale	1	1	0	0	0	0	0	0	0	2	23,926
Oakland	12	1	4	0	0	2	4	6	4	5	437,923
Oceanside	7	0	0	0	0	0	0	2	3	2	176,616
Orange	3	0	1	0	0	0	1	0	1	2	138,846
Oxnard	1	0	0	0	0	0	0	1	0	0	210,064
Pacifica	3	0	0	0	0	0	0	3	0	0	38,677
Pacific Grove	2	0	0	0	0	0	0	0	2	0	15,451
Palmdale	3	0	0	0	0	0	1	0	2	0	155,321
Palm Springs	5	2	3	0	0	0	1	6	1	2	48,952
Palo Alto	4	0	0	0	0	0	1	2	1	0	65,459
Paramount	1	0	0	0	0	0	0	1	0	0	53,939
Pasadena	4	0	0	0	0	1	2	2	1	0	141,473

(Number.)

State/agency	Number of incidents per bias motivation						Number of incidents per quarter				Population[1]
	Race/ Ethnicity/ Ancestry	Religion	Sexual orientation	Disability	Gender	Gender Identity	1st quarter	2nd quarter	3rd quarter	4th quarter	
Perris	1	0	0	0	0	0	0	1	0	0	80,526
Petaluma	5	0	1	0	0	0	1	2	2	1	60,806
Pico Rivera	0	0	0	0	0	1	0	0	1	0	61,925
Pittsburg	1	0	0	0	0	0	0	0	1	0	73,673
Placentia	0	1	0	0	0	0	0	0	1	0	51,260
Pleasanton	1	0	0	0	0	0	0	1	0	0	83,164
Poway	1	1	1	0	0	0	1	1	0	1	49,479
Rancho Cordova	1	0	0	0	0	0	0	0	1	0	76,292
Rancho Cucamonga	4	0	0	0	0	0	2	2	0	0	178,916
Red Bluff	4	0	0	0	0	0	2	0	0	2	14,590
Redding	6	0	0	0	0	0	1	1	4	0	92,895
Redlands	5	1	2	0	0	0	5	1	2	0	71,820
Redondo Beach	1	0	0	0	0	0	0	0	1	0	66,729
Redwood City	2	1	0	0	0	0	0	1	2	0	86,983
Rialto	0	0	2	0	0	0	1	0	1	0	104,004
Richmond	5	0	1	0	0	0	2	1	1	2	111,367
Ridgecrest	1	0	0	0	0	0	0	0	1	0	29,120
Rio Dell	0	1	0	0	0	0	1	0	0	0	3,347
Riverside	9	2	3	0	0	0	7	1	3	3	334,370
Rohnert Park	1	0	0	0	0	0	0	1	0	0	43,572
Rosemead	0	0	2	0	0	0	0	0	1	1	54,087
Roseville	8	1	0	0	0	0	1	4	3	1	144,128
Sacramento	8	0	2	0	0	0	1	6	2	1	519,050
Salinas	1	0	0	0	0	0	0	1	0	0	155,984
San Bernardino	2	1	2	0	0	1	0	0	5	1	216,365
San Bruno	1	0	0	0	0	0	0	1	0	0	42,997
San Clemente	1	0	0	0	0	0	0	1	0	0	64,665
San Diego	17	1	7	0	0	1	6	8	5	7	1,437,608
San Francisco	37	7	8	0	0	2	14	6	18	16	881,514
San Gabriel	0	0	0	0	0	1	0	0	1	0	39,927
San Jose	75	9	9	0	0	1	18	37	23	16	1,029,542
San Leandro	1	0	0	0	0	0	0	1	0	0	89,239
San Luis Obispo	10	0	1	0	0	0	2	3	5	1	47,722
San Marcos	2	1	0	0	0	0	0	0	2	1	98,198
San Mateo	1	0	0	0	0	0	0	1	0	0	105,246
San Pablo	1	0	0	0	0	0	1	0	0	0	31,164
San Rafael	3	1	0	0	0	0	1	2	1	0	58,512
San Ramon	2	0	0	0	0	0	0	0	2	0	76,502
Santa Ana	5	8	2	0	0	1	0	3	4	9	333,107
Santa Barbara	0	0	0	0	0	1	0	0	0	1	91,692
Santa Clarita	4	0	0	0	0	0	0	0	3	1	221,932
Santa Cruz	3	0	2	0	0	1	0	1	4	1	65,073
Santa Maria	0	1	1	0	0	0	1	0	1	0	108,140
Santa Monica	11	0	1	0	0	0	1	6	3	2	90,474
Santa Rosa	6	4	1	0	0	0	0	0	8	3	176,932
Santee	3	0	0	0	0	0	0	1	1	1	58,598
Sausalito	0	1	0	0	0	0	0	1	0	0	7,080
Sierra Madre	2	0	0	0	0	0	0	2	0	0	10,779
Signal Hill	1	0	0	0	0	0	0	1	0	0	11,467
Simi Valley	4	0	1	0	0	0	2	0	1	2	125,742
South Gate	1	0	1	0	0	0	1	0	1	0	93,336
South Lake Tahoe	1	0	2	0	0	0	0	0	3	0	22,286
South San Francisco	0	0	1	0	0	0	0	0	0	1	68,260
Stockton	5	0	1	0	0	0	2	2	1	1	314,981
Sunnyvale	6	1	0	0	0	1	3	0	4	1	154,133
Tehachapi	1	0	0	0	0	0	0	1	0	0	12,873
Temecula	0	0	0	0	0	1	0	0	1	0	116,442
Thousand Oaks	2	0	0	0	0	0	0	0	2	0	126,823
Torrance	10	0	1	0	0	0	1	5	3	2	143,421
Tracy	1	2	0	0	0	0	0	1	1	1	96,067
Tulare	0	1	0	0	0	0	0	0	1	0	66,207
Turlock	1	1	0	0	0	0	0	0	1	1	74,183
Union City	2	0	0	0	0	0	0	1	1	0	74,625
Vacaville	3	0	0	0	0	0	0	2	0	1	101,616
Vallejo	7	0	0	0	0	0	0	3	3	1	122,326
Ventura	3	0	0	0	0	1	1	0	2	1	109,295
Vernon	0	1	0	0	0	0	1	0	0	0	110

Table 13. Hate Crime Incidents Per Bias Motivation and Quarter, by Selected State and Agency and Federal, 2020—Continued

(Number.)

State/agency	Race/Ethnicity/Ancestry	Religion	Sexual orientation	Disability	Gender	Gender Identity	1st quarter	2nd quarter	3rd quarter	4th quarter	Population[1]
Victorville.........	2	0	0	0	0	0	1	1	0	0	123,085
Visalia.........	0	1	0	0	0	0	1	0	0	0	135,733
Vista.........	4	1	0	0	0	0	0	3	1	1	102,600
Walnut Creek.........	7	0	2	0	0	0	2	3	3	1	70,849
West Covina.........	2	0	0	0	0	0	1	0	0	1	104,989
West Hollywood.........	4	1	2	0	0	0	1	1	2	3	36,719
Westminster.........	6	0	0	0	0	0	2	2	1	1	90,741
Woodland.........	1	0	0	0	0	0	0	0	0	1	61,123
Yorba Linda.........	1	1	0	0	0	0	0	1	1	0	68,017
Yuba City.........	4	0	0	0	0	0	0	0	3	1	67,165
Yucaipa.........	0	0	1	0	0	0	0	1	0	0	54,200
Yucca Valley.........	1	0	0	0	0	0	0	0	0	1	21,901
Universities and Colleges.........	11	3	0	0	0	0					
California State University, San Marcos.........	2	0	0	0	0	0	0	1	1	0	17,136
Riverside Community College.........	1	0	0	0	0	0	1	0	0	0	62,345
Sonoma County Junior College.........	1	0	0	0	0	0	0	1	0	0	29,046
University of California											
Irvine.........	3	1	0	0	0	0	2	1	0	1	38,105
Los Angeles.........	3	2	0	0	0	0	2	1	1	1	47,103
San Diego.........	1	0	0	0	0	0	0	0	0	1	39,811
Metropolitan Counties.........	73	15	17	0	1	0					
Alameda.........	1	0	1	0	0	0	1	0	1	0	
Butte.........	0	0	1	0	0	0	0	0	1	0	
Contra Costa.........	1	0	0	0	0	0	0	0	0	1	
El Dorado.........	1	1	0	0	0	0	2	0	0	0	
Fresno.........	0	1	0	0	0	0	0	0	1	0	
Kern.........	1	0	2	0	0	0	0	1	1	1	
Los Angeles.........	21	1	4	0	0	0	5	5	12	4	
Marin.........	1	0	0	0	0	0	0	1	0	0	
Monterey.........	0	1	0	0	0	0	0	1	0	0	
Orange.........	2	5	0	0	0	0	4	1	2	0	
Sacramento.........	2	0	0	0	0	0	0	1	0	1	
San Bernardino.........	6	0	0	0	0	0	0	2	2	2	
San Diego.........	12	3	3	0	1	0	5	5	4	5	
San Luis Obispo.........	1	0	0	0	0	0	0	0	0	1	
San Mateo.........	5	0	2	0	0	0	4	1	1	1	
Santa Barbara.........	1	0	0	0	0	0	0	1	0	0	
Santa Clara.........	3	3	0	0	0	0	4	1	1	0	
Santa Cruz.........	6	0	1	0	0	0	0	0	4	3	
Shasta.........	0	0	1	0	0	0	0	0	1	0	
Sonoma.........	4	0	2	0	0	0	1	4	1	0	
Stanislaus.........	2	0	0	0	0	0	1	1	0	0	
Yolo.........	1	0	0	0	0	0	0	1	0	0	
Yuba.........	2	0	0	0	0	0	0	2	0	0	
Nonmetropolitan Counties.........	2	2	1	0	0	2					
Amador.........	0	0	1	0	0	2	0	3	0	0	
Lake.........	1	0	0	0	0	0	0	1	0	0	
Lassen.........	1	0	0	0	0	0	0	0	0	1	
Nevada.........	0	1	0	0	0	0	0	0	0	1	
Tuolumne.........	0	1	0	0	0	0	0	0	1	0	
Other Agencies.........	6	1	4	1	0	0					
Department of Parks and Recreation, Bay Area....	1	0	0	0	0	0	1	0	0	0	
East Bay Regional Park District.........	1	0	2	0	0	0	0	1	2	0	
Los Angeles Transportation Services Bureau.........	2	0	0	0	0	0	0	0	1	1	
Porterville Developmental Center.........	1	0	0	0	0	0	0	0	1	0	
Port of San Diego Harbor.........	0	0	1	0	0	0	1	0	0	0	
San Francisco Bay Area Rapid Transit:											
Alameda County.........	0	0	1	0	0	0	0	1	0	0	
Contra Costa County.........	0	0	0	1	0	0	0	1	0	0	
Santa Clara Transit District.........	1	1	0	0	0	0	1	1	0	0	
COLORADO											
Total.........	184	35	49	5	0	10					
Cities.........	154	25	39	2	0	6					
Aurora.........	13	0	1	0	0	0	0	7	4	3	385,720
Avon.........	1	0	0	0	0	0	0	1	0	0	6,526
Blue River.........	1	0	0	0	0	0	0	1	0	0	929

Table 13. Hate Crime Incidents Per Bias Motivation and Quarter, by Selected State and Agency and Federal, 2020—*Continued*

(Number.)

State/agency	Number of incidents per bias motivation						Number of incidents per quarter				Population[1]
	Race/ Ethnicity/ Ancestry	Religion	Sexual orientation	Disability	Gender	Gender Identity	1st quarter	2nd quarter	3rd quarter	4th quarter	
Boulder............................	8	1	1	0	0	0	3	4	2	1	106,598
Brighton	0	1	0	0	0	0	0	0	1	0	42,536
Broomfield......................	2	1	0	0	0	0	0	0	1	2	71,795
Canon City......................	3	0	0	0	0	0	1	0	2	0	16,761
Castle Rock.....................	5	0	0	0	0	0	0	3	1	1	71,150
Centennial......................	8	2	0	0	0	0	2	5	2	1	112,104
Colorado Springs.............	15	2	3	0	0	0	4	3	11	2	485,083
Craig..............................	0	0	1	0	0	0	1	0	0	0	8,975
Crested Butte..................	1	0	0	0	0	0	0	0	1	0	1,751
Cripple Creek..................	1	0	0	0	0	0	0	0	1	0	1,261
Denver............................	47	7	21	1	0	4	10	21	24	25	737,709
Durango	2	0	1	0	0	0	0	1	1	1	19,220
Empire............................	1	0	0	0	0	0	1	0	0	0	307
Englewood......................	1	0	0	0	0	0	0	0	1	0	35,464
Erie................................	1	1	0	0	0	0	2	0	0	0	28,198
Estes Park.......................	1	0	0	0	0	0	0	0	1	0	6,480
Fort Collins.....................	2	1	0	0	0	0	0	2	1	0	173,274
Fort Morgan....................	1	0	0	0	0	0	0	1	0	0	11,471
Glendale.........................	0	1	0	0	0	0	0	1	0	0	5,243
Golden...........................	0	0	1	0	0	0	1	0	0	0	20,981
Grand Junction................	2	0	1	0	0	0	0	3	0	0	64,149
Greeley...........................	0	0	1	0	0	0	0	0	0	1	110,505
Hudson...........................	3	0	0	0	0	0	0	1	1	1	2,817
Johnstown......................	1	0	0	0	0	0	0	1	0	0	15,932
Lafayette........................	0	0	1	0	0	0	0	0	0	1	31,457
Lakewood[2].....................	3	1	2	0	0	1	1	2	3	0	159,719
Littleton.........................	1	0	0	0	0	0	0	0	1	0	48,805
Longmont.......................	5	0	0	0	0	1	2	1	1	2	98,545
Louisville........................	1	0	0	0	0	0	0	0	1	0	21,101
Montrose........................	2	0	0	0	0	0	0	1	1	0	19,864
Monument	0	1	0	0	0	0	0	0	1	0	8,361
Northglenn.....................	0	0	1	0	0	0	0	1	0	0	39,161
Parker............................	2	0	0	0	0	0	0	2	0	0	59,245
Pueblo............................	9	0	0	0	0	0	1	0	6	2	113,002
Rifle...............................	1	0	0	0	0	0	1	0	0	0	9,747
Steamboat Springs	0	4	0	0	0	0	2	0	2	0	13,345
Telluride.........................	1	0	0	0	0	0	1	0	0	0	2,508
Thornton	4	1	2	0	0	0	1	2	1	3	144,156
Trinidad..........................	1	0	0	0	0	0	0	1	0	0	8,114
Vail................................	1	0	0	0	0	0	0	0	1	0	5,450
Westminster....................	2	1	1	0	0	0	0	1	2	1	113,941
Wheat Ridge....................	0	0	1	0	0	0	0	0	0	1	31,451
Woodland Park.................	1	0	0	1	0	0	0	1	0	1	7,969
Universities and Colleges	1	3	1	0	0	0					
University of Colorado, Boulder........................	1	3	1	0	0	0	1	2	2	0	40,353
Metropolitan Counties	23	6	6	3	0	3					
Adams............................	4	0	0	0	0	0	1	1	2	0	
Arapahoe........................	8	3	2	0	0	1	1	3	6	4	
Boulder...........................	2	0	0	0	0	0	0	0	1	1	
Douglas..........................	3	0	1	3	0	0	3	2	2	0	
El Paso...........................	0	0	1	0	0	0	1	0	0	0	
Jefferson[2]......................	5	2	0	0	0	1	2	3	2	0	
Larimer...........................	1	0	1	0	0	0	0	0	2	0	
Park...............................	0	1	0	0	0	0	1	0	0	0	
Pueblo............................	0	0	0	0	0	1	0	1	0	0	
Weld..............................	0	0	1	0	0	0	1	0	0	0	
Nonmetropolitan Counties...........	6	1	3	0	0	1					
Crowley..........................	1	0	0	0	0	0	0	0	1	0	
Custer............................	0	0	1	0	0	0	1	0	0	0	
Fremont..........................	0	0	1	0	0	0	0	1	0	0	
Garfield..........................	2	0	0	0	0	0	0	0	1	1	
Gunnison........................	0	0	1	0	0	0	0	1	0	0	
Las Animas	0	0	0	0	0	1	1	0	0	0	
Montrose........................	0	1	0	0	0	0	0	1	0	0	
Routt..............................	1	0	0	0	0	0	0	0	1	0	
Summit...........................	2	0	0	0	0	0	0	0	2	0	

Table 13. Hate Crime Incidents Per Bias Motivation and Quarter, by Selected State and Agency and Federal, 2020—*Continued*

(Number.)

State/agency	Number of incidents per bias motivation						Number of incidents per quarter				Population[1]
	Race/ Ethnicity/ Ancestry	Religion	Sexual orientation	Disability	Gender	Gender Identity	1st quarter	2nd quarter	3rd quarter	4th quarter	
CONNECTICUT											
Total	65	18	15	4	0	0					
Cities	63	15	15	4	0	0					
Bethel	1	0	1	0	0	0	0	2	0	0	19,932
Bridgeport	0	0	3	0	0	0	1	0	2	0	144,350
Coventry	2	0	0	0	0	0	1	1	0	0	12,404
Danbury	4	0	0	0	0	0	2	0	0	2	85,080
Derby	1	1	0	0	0	0	1	0	1	0	12,281
East Haven	1	0	0	0	0	0	0	1	0	0	28,498
East Lyme	0	1	0	0	0	0	0	1	0	0	18,391
Enfield	2	0	0	1	0	0	3	0	0	0	43,551
Fairfield	0	0	2	0	0	0	2	0	0	0	62,311
Glastonbury[2]	7	1	0	1	0	0	0	4	0	4	34,487
Groton	1	0	0	0	0	0	0	0	1	0	8,861
Hartford	2	0	0	0	0	0	1	1	0	0	121,749
Manchester	2	1	0	0	0	0	2	1	0	0	57,510
Middletown	1	0	1	0	0	0	0	0	1	1	46,106
Naugatuck	2	1	0	0	0	0	1	2	0	0	31,024
New Britain	8	2	0	1	0	0	1	2	5	3	72,412
New Haven	7	3	1	0	0	0	2	3	4	2	130,299
North Branford	1	0	0	0	0	0	0	1	0	0	14,115
Norwalk	1	0	0	0	0	0	0	0	1	0	89,140
Norwich	3	0	1	0	0	0	0	1	2	1	38,576
Plymouth	1	0	0	0	0	0	1	0	0	0	11,529
Rocky Hill	1	0	1	0	0	0	0	1	1	0	20,160
Seymour	1	0	1	0	0	0	0	2	0	0	16,426
Shelton	2	0	0	0	0	0	0	1	0	1	41,302
Southington	2	0	0	0	0	0	1	0	1	0	43,906
South Windsor	0	0	1	0	0	0	0	0	1	0	26,213
Stamford	5	1	2	0	0	0	1	3	3	1	130,425
Stonington	1	1	0	0	0	0	1	0	1	0	18,563
Stratford	1	0	0	0	0	0	0	0	0	1	51,895
Torrington	1	0	0	0	0	0	0	1	0	0	33,796
Waterbury	0	2	1	0	0	0	0	1	1	1	107,263
Waterford	1	0	0	0	0	0	0	0	1	0	18,664
West Haven	1	0	0	0	0	0	0	1	0	0	54,516
Westport	0	0	0	1	0	0	0	0	0	1	28,728
Woodbridge	0	1	0	0	0	0	0	0	1	0	8,725
Universities and Colleges	1	1	0	0	0	0					
University of Connecticut, Storrs, Avery Point, and Hartford[3]	1	0	0	0	0	0	0	0	0	1	
Yale University	0	1	0	0	0	0	0	0	0	1	14,389
State Police Agencies	1	2	0	0	0	0					
Connecticut State Police	1	2	0	0	0	0	2	0	1	0	
DELAWARE											
Total	7	2	4	0	0	0					
Cities	2	0	2	0	0	0					
Newark	1	0	0	0	0	0	0	1	0	0	33,752
Rehoboth Beach	1	0	0	0	0	0	0	1	0	0	1,573
Wilmington	0	0	2	0	0	0	0	0	2	0	70,100
Universities and Colleges	1	1	2	0	0	0					
University of Delaware	1	1	2	0	0	0	3	1	0	0	25,885
Metropolitan Counties	1	0	0	0	0	0					
New Castle County Police Department	1	0	0	0	0	0	0	1	0	0	
State Police Agencies	3	1	0	0	0	0					
State Police											
New Castle County	1	0	0	0	0	0	0	0	1	0	
Sussex County	2	1	0	0	0	0	1	2	0	0	
DISTRICT OF COLUMBIA											
Total	63	1	41	0	0	28					
Cities	60	1	38	0	0	27					
Washington	60	1	38	0	0	27	31	21	41	33	712,816
Other Agencies	3	0	3	0	0	1					
Metro Transit Police	3	0	3	0	0	1	4	0	1	2	

(Number.)

State/agency	Number of incidents per bias motivation						Number of incidents per quarter				Population[1]
	Race/ Ethnicity/ Ancestry	Religion	Sexual orientation	Disability	Gender	Gender Identity	1st quarter	2nd quarter	3rd quarter	4th quarter	
FLORIDA											
Total	65	20	22	0	0	2					
Cities	47	13	16	0	0	2					
Boca Raton	2	0	0	0	0	0	1	0	1	0	101,583
Chattahoochee	1	0	1	0	0	0	0	0		2	3,157
Clearwater	0	0	1	0	0	0	0	0	0	1	117,859
Deerfield Beach	2	0	0	0	0	0	2	0	0	0	81,749
Doral	1	0	0	0	0	0	0	0	0	1	68,425
Fort Lauderdale	1	0	0	0	0	0	0	1	0	0	184,347
Fort Myers	1	0	0	0	0	0	1	0	0		90,380
Fort Walton Beach	1	0	0	0	0	0	0	1	0	0	22,871
Gainesville	1	1	1	0	0	0	0	2	1		135,076
Hialeah	1	0	1	0	0	0	1	1	0	0	234,235
Hollywood	0	1	0	0	0	0	1	0	0	0	156,434
Homestead	1	1	0	0	0	0		1		1	70,538
Jacksonville	9	0	1	0	0	1	0	4	4	3	920,508
Jacksonville Beach	1	0	0	0	0	0	0	0	1		23,894
Largo	2	0	0	0	0	0	1	1			85,594
Lauderdale Lakes	1	0	0	0	0	0	0	1	0	0	36,587
Melbourne	1	0	0	0	0	0	0	1	0	0	83,806
Miami Beach	3	4	4	0	0	0	2	1	4	4	89,017
Miami Shores	1	0	0	0	0	0	1	0	0	0	10,358
Milton	1	0	0	0	0	0	0	0		1	10,728
New Port Richey	2	0	0	0	0	0	0	1		1	16,954
New Smyrna Beach	1	0	0	0	0	0	0	0	1		28,380
North Miami Beach	0	2	0	0	0	0	0	1	1		43,273
Ocoee	1	0	0	0	0	0	1	0	0	0	49,877
Orlando	1	0	1	0	0	0	1	0		1	293,363
Palm Bay	0	0	0	0	0	1	1	0	0	0	116,897
Palm Beach Gardens	1	1	0	0	0	0	0	0	1	1	58,629
Pembroke Pines	2	0	0	0	0	0	0	0	1	1	175,757
Pensacola	1	0	0	0	0	0		1	0	0	53,083
Pinellas Park	1	0	1	0	0	0	0	0	0	2	54,114
Port St. Lucie	1	0	0	0	0	0	0	1			206,450
Sarasota	1	2	1	0	0	0	1	2	0	1	59,002
Southwest Ranches	1	1	0	0	0	0	1	1	0		8,025
St. Pete Beach	1	0	1	0	0	0	0	0	2	0	9,616
Tampa	0	0	1	0	0	0	0	0	1	0	407,350
West Palm Beach	2	0	2	0	0	0	0	1	3	0	113,268
Universities and Colleges ...	2	0	1	0	0	0					
Pensacola State College ...	2	0	0	0	0	0	1	1	0	0	13,758
Tallahassee Community College ...	0	0	1	0	0	0	1	0	0	0	16,760
Metropolitan Counties	15	7	5	0	0	0					
Alachua	1	1	0	0	0	0	1	1	0	0	
Collier	3	0	0	0	0	0	0	0	3		
Highlands	0	0	1	0	0	0	0	1	0	0	
Lake	1	0	0	0	0	0	0	1	0	0	
Lee	2	0	0	0	0	0	0	0	2	0	
Marion	1	1	0	0	0	0			1	0	
Martin	1	0	0	0	0	0	0	0	1	0	
Miami-Dade	1	1	1	0	0	0	1	1	1		
Orange	1	1	0	0	0	0	1	0	1	0	
Pasco	1	0	2	0	0	0	1	0	0	2	
Pinellas	1	0	0	0	0	0	0	0	0	1	
Santa Rosa	1	0	0	0	0	0	0	0	0	1	
Sarasota	0	3	0	0	0	0	0	1	2		
St. Johns	1	0	0	0	0	0	0	0	1	0	
Sumter	0	0	1	0	0	0				1	
Nonmetropolitan Counties	1	0	0	0	0	0					
Taylor	1	0	0	0	0	0	1				
GEORGIA											
Total	132	26	24	7	3	4					
Cities	68	11	11	2	1	3					
Athens-Clarke County	4	1	0	0	0	2	0	4	2	1	128,152
Atlanta	3	0	1	0	0	0				4	515,945
Brookhaven	3	1	0	0	0	0	0	2	0	2	56,248

(Number.)

State/agency	Number of incidents per bias motivation						Number of incidents per quarter				Population[1]
	Race/ Ethnicity/ Ancestry	Religion	Sexual orientation	Disability	Gender	Gender Identity	1st quarter	2nd quarter	3rd quarter	4th quarter	
Byron	0	1	0	0	0	0	0	0	1	0	5,304
Cedartown	3	0	0	0	0	0	1	1	1	0	10,020
College Park	0	0	1	0	0	0	1	0	0	0	15,204
Dalton	1	0	0	0	0	0				1	33,723
Decatur	0	0	1	0	0	0	0	0	0	1	26,473
Demorest	1	0	0	0	0	0	1	0			2,157
Douglasville	1	0	0	0	0	0	0	0	0	1	34,409
Dunwoody	3	1	0	0	0	0	1	0	3	0	49,687
Eastman	0	0	1	0	0	0	0	0	0	1	5,018
Forest Park	1	0	1	0	0	0	0	0	0	2	20,202
Gainesville	3	1	0	0	0	0	0	2	1	1	44,398
Hiram	1	0	0	0	0	0	0	1	0	0	4,301
Johns Creek	1	0	0	2	0	0	1	2	0	0	85,408
Marietta	7	1	0	0	1	0	1	3	4	1	61,348
Milton	0	0	1	0	0	0	1	0	0	0	40,368
Newington	1	0	0	0	0	0	0	1	0	0	261
Newnan	4	0	0	0	0	0	0	0	1	3	42,658
Peachtree City	1	1	0	0	0	0	1	0	1	0	36,421
Pine Mountain	1	0	0	0	0	0	1	0	0	0	1,430
Rockmart	1	0	0	0	0	0	0	1	0	0	4,458
Rome	5	0	0	0	0	0		0	2	3	36,747
Sandy Springs	7	0	0	0	0	1	1	2	3	2	111,219
Smyrna	5	2	2	0	0	0	5	1	0	3	57,317
South Fulton	1	0	0	0	0	0	1	0	0	0	100,658
Sparta	2	0	0	0	0	0	0	2	0	0	1,213
Suwanee	0	1	0	0	0	0	0	0	1	0	21,633
Temple	0	0	1	0	0	0	1	0	0	0	4,832
Thomasville	2	0	1	0	0	0	1	0	1	1	18,512
Toccoa	1	0	0	0	0	0	0	0	1	0	8,312
Villa Rica	1	1	0	0	0	0	0	0	1	1	16,296
Warner Robins	4	0	1	0	0	0	0	4	1	0	78,508
Universities and Colleges	1	0	1	0	0	0					
Georgia Institute of Technology	0	0	1	0	0	0	0	0	0	1	38,951
University of West Georgia	1	0	0	0	0	0	1	0	0	0	16,353
Metropolitan Counties	48	14	9	5	0	0					
Brooks	1	0	0	0	0	0	0	0	1	0	
Catoosa	3	0	0	0	0	0	0	1	2	0	
Cherokee	2	0	1	0	0	0	0	2	0	1	
Clayton County Police Department	3	0	2	0	0	0	1	1	1	2	
Cobb County Police Department[2]	15	7	1	1	0	0	3	6	12	2	
Coweta	2	0	0	0	0	0	0	1	1	0	
DeKalb County Police Department	4	1	2	0	0	0	2	1	3	1	
Floyd County Police Department	1	0	0	0	0	0	0	0	1	0	
Forsyth	3	0	2	0	0	0	0	1	1	3	
Glynn County Police Department	1	1	0	0	0	0	2	0	0	0	
Hall	2	0	1	1	0	0	0	3	1	0	
Haralson	1	0	0	0	0	0	0	0	0	1	
Henry County Police Department	0	2	0	0	0	0	0	0	0	2	
Lee	2	0	0	0	0	0	0	0	2	0	
Long	1	0	0	0	0	0	0	0	0	1	
Lowndes	0	1	0	0	0	0	0	0	0	1	
Madison	0	0	0	1	0	0	0	0	0	1	
Oglethorpe	1	0	0	0	0	0	1	0	0	0	
Paulding	4	1	0	0	0	0	0	0	4	1	
Peach	0	0	0	1	0	0	0	1	0	0	
Pickens	0	1	0	0	0	0	0	1	0	0	
Walton	0	0	0	1	0	0	0	0	1	0	
Whitfield	2	0	0	0	0	0	2	0	0	0	
Nonmetropolitan Counties	14	1	2	0	2	1					
Bulloch	5	0	0	0	1	0	4	2	0		
Coffee	0	0	1	0	0	0	0	1	0	0	
Decatur	2	0	0	0	0	0	1	0	0	1	
Grady	2	1	0	0	0	0	1	1	0	1	
Greene	1	0	0	0	0	0	0	0	1	0	
Jackson	1	0	0	0	0	0	0	0	1	0	
Lumpkin	2	0	1	0	1	1	0	2	2	1	
Thomas	1	0	0	0	0	0	0	0	1	0	

(Number.)

State/agency	Number of incidents per bias motivation						Number of incidents per quarter				Population[1]
	Race/ Ethnicity/ Ancestry	Religion	Sexual orientation	Disability	Gender	Gender Identity	1st quarter	2nd quarter	3rd quarter	4th quarter	
Other Agencies..............................	1	0	1	0	0	0					
Fulton County School System...................	1	0	1	0	0	0	0	0	1	1	
HAWAII											
Total	31	0	5	0	0	0					
Cities	31	0	5	0	0	0					
Honolulu..........................	31	0	5	0	0	0	7	8	10	11	966,438
IDAHO											
Total	27	7	6	1	1	1					
Cities	25	6	4	0	1	1					
Boise..........................	10	5	2	0	1	1	2	7	4	6	231,223
Chubbuck..........................	1	0	0	0	0	0	0	1	0	0	15,773
Coeur d'Alene..........................	5	0	0	0	0	0	0	2	2	1	53,405
Fruitland..........................	1	0	0	0	0	0	0	1	0	0	5,505
Jerome..........................	1	0	0	0	0	0	0	1	0	0	12,120
Ketchum..........................	1	0	0	0	0	0	1	0	0	0	2,872
Meridian..........................	2	0	0	0	0	0	1	0	1	0	119,203
Pocatello..........................	0	0	1	0	0	0	0	1	0	0	56,900
Rexburg..........................	1	0	0	0	0	0	0	0	0	1	29,865
Twin Falls..........................	3	1	1	0	0	0	0	2	1	2	50,872
Metropolitan Counties	0	1	0	0	0	0					
Bonneville..........................	0	1	0	0	0	0	0	1	0	0	
Nonmetropolitan Counties..................	2	0	2	1	0	0					
Fremont..........................	0	0	0	1	0	0	0	0	0	1	
Gooding..........................	1	0	1	0	0	0	0	1	1	0	
Lincoln..........................	0	0	1	0	0	0	1	0	0	0	
Teton..........................	1	0	0	0	0	0	0	1	0	0	
ILLINOIS											
Total	38	4	11	0	1	2					
Cities	35	4	10	0	1	2					
Arlington Heights..........................	2	0	0	0	0	0	0		2	0	74,706
Aurora..........................	1	0	0	0	0	0		0	0	1	197,709
Bolingbrook..........................	1	0	0	0	0	0	1	0	0	0	74,665
Carlyle..........................	1	0	0	0	0	0	0	1	0	0	3,174
Centralia..........................	1	0	0	0	0	0	0	0	0	1	12,123
Chicago..........................	9	3	7	0	0	2	5	7	5	4	2,693,598
Crest Hill..........................	1	0	0	0	0	0	0	0	0	1	20,328
Darien..........................	1	0	0	0	0	0	1	0	0	0	21,590
Decatur..........................	1	0	0	0	0	0	0	1	0	0	70,175
Elgin..........................	0	1	0	0	0	0	1	0	0	0	111,127
Fairmont City..........................	1	0	0	0	0	0	0	1	0	0	2,434
Lombard..........................	1	0	0	0	0	0	0	1	0	0	44,392
New Lenox..........................	1	0	0	0	0	0	1	0	0	0	27,230
Palatine..........................	1	0	0	0	1	0	0	0	2		67,358
Peoria..........................	0	0	2	0	0	0	0	0	1	1	109,924
Plainfield..........................	4	0	0	0	0	0	1	1	2	0	44,817
Quincy..........................	1	0	0	0	0	0	0	1	0	0	39,860
Rockford..........................	1	0	1	0	0	0	0	0	1	1	144,795
Skokie..........................	1	0	0	0	0	0	0	1	0	0	62,462
Springfield..........................	2	0	0	0	0	0	1	0	1	0	113,912
Steger..........................	3	0	0	0	0	0	1	1	0	1	9,184
Winnetka..........................	1	0	0	0	0	0	0		1	0	12,328
Metropolitan Counties	2	0	1	0	0	0					
McLean..........................	1	0	0	0	0	0	0	1	0	0	
Peoria..........................	0	0	1	0	0	0	0	0	1		
Sangamon..........................	1	0	0	0	0	0	0	1	0	0	
Other Agencies..........................	1	0	0	0	0	0					
Cook County Forest Preserve...................	1	0	0	0	0	0	0	1	0	0	
INDIANA											
Total	124	34	23	2	2	4					
Cities	109	27	21	1	2	1					
Angola..........................	1	0	0	0	2	0	0	2	1	0	8,748
Avon..........................	1	0	0	0	0	0	0	1	0	0	19,377
Bloomington..........................	4	0	0	0	0	0	2	0	0	2	86,347

(Number.)

State/agency	Number of incidents per bias motivation						Number of incidents per quarter				Population[1]
	Race/Ethnicity/Ancestry	Religion	Sexual orientation	Disability	Gender	Gender Identity	1st quarter	2nd quarter	3rd quarter	4th quarter	
Brownsburg	2	0	0	0	0	0	0	0	2	0	27,621
Columbus	3	0	2	0	0	0	1	3	1	0	48,505
Danville	0	0	1	0	0	0	0	0	0	1	10,247
East Chicago	1	0	0	0	0	0	1	0			27,616
Edinburgh	1	0	0	0	0	0	1	0	0	0	4,603
Evansville	8	0	2	0	0	0		3	3	4	117,747
Fishers	2	0	0	0	0	0	0	0	0	2	97,481
Fort Wayne	5	1	2	0	0	0	0		0	8	272,270
Franklin[2]	3	1	0	0	0	0	0	0	3	0	25,825
Goshen	0	1	0	0	0	0	1	0	0	0	34,409
Greenfield	1	0	0	0	0	0	0	0	1	0	23,273
Greenwood	2	0	0	0	0	0		1	0	1	60,460
Hammond	6	1	0	0	0	0	0	0	7	0	74,966
Hobart	3	0	0	0	0	0	0	0	0	3	27,791
Huntington	3	0	1	0	0	0	0	1	2	1	17,096
Indianapolis[2]	18	0	6	0	0	0	4	7	8	4	890,672
Jeffersonville	5	1	0	0	0	0	0	1	5		48,467
Kokomo	0	3	0	0	0	0	2	0	0	1	58,001
Lafayette	2	0	1	0	0	0	1	1	1		72,040
La Porte	0	0	1	0	0	0	0	0	0	1	21,515
Lawrence[2]	1	2	0	0	0	0	0	2	2	0	49,865
Lebanon	2	0	0	0	0	0	0	1	1	0	16,097
McCordsville	1	0	0	0	0	0	1	0	0	0	7,801
Michigan City	2	1	0	0	0	0	1	0	2	0	30,976
Mishawaka	0	1	0	0	0	0	1	0	0	0	50,610
Muncie	1	0	0	0	0	0	0	1	0	0	67,760
Munster	2	0	0	0	0	0	0	1	1	0	22,357
Noblesville	2	0	0	0	0	0	0	0	1	1	66,127
Plainfield	1	0	0	0	0	0	1	0	0	0	36,239
Schererville	2	0	0	0	0	0	1	1	0		28,454
Seymour	2	0	0	0	0	0	0	2	0	0	20,171
Shelbyville	1	1	0	1	0	0			1	2	19,451
South Bend	11	2	2	0	0	1	4	6	4	2	102,119
Terre Haute	4	12	2	0	0	0	0	10	5	3	60,604
Warsaw	1	0	1	0	0	0	1	1	0	0	15,319
Washington	1	0	0	0	0	0	0	0	0	1	12,612
Westfield	4	0	0	0	0	0	0	0	3	1	45,469
Universities and Colleges	2	0	1	0	0	0					
Indiana University, South Bend	2	0	0	0	0	0	2	0	0	0	6,168
Purdue University	0	0	1	0	0	0			1		47,412
Metropolitan Counties	7	2	1	1	0	1					
Hendricks	1	1	0	0	0	0	0	0	2	0	
Johnson	0	0	0	1	0	0	0	1	0	0	
Lake	1	0	0	0	0	0	1	0	0	0	
Monroe	3	0	1	0	0	0	1	1	2	0	
St. Joseph	0	1	0	0	0	0	1	0	0	0	
Vanderburgh	1	0	0	0	0	0		0	1	0	
Vigo	1	0	0	0	0	1	1	0	1	0	
Nonmetropolitan Counties	1	0	0	0	0	1					
Greene	1	0	0	0	0	0	1	0	0	0	
Steuben	0	0	0	0	0	1	1	0	0	0	
State Police Agencies	5	3	0	0	0	0					
Indiana State Police	5	3	0	0	0	0	2	2	3	1	
Other Agencies	0	2	0	0	0	1					
Indiana Gaming Commission	0	2	0	0	0	1	1	0	2	0	
IOWA											
Total	12	0	3	0	0	0					
Cities	9	0	3	0	0	0					
Adel	1	0	0	0	0	0	0	0	1	0	5,696
Ames	2	0	1	0	0	0	2	1	0	0	67,109
Davenport	1	0	0	0	0	0	0	0	1	0	101,806
Dubuque	0	0	1	0	0	0	1	0	0	0	57,904
Indianola	0	0	1	0	0	0	0	0	0	1	16,154
Iowa City	3	0	0	0	0	0	0	1	2	0	75,964
Marion	1	0	0	0	0	0	0	1	0	0	40,968
Waterloo	1	0	0	0	0	0	0	0	1	0	67,200

Table 13. Hate Crime Incidents Per Bias Motivation and Quarter, by Selected State and Agency and Federal, 2020—*Continued*

(Number.)

State/agency	Number of incidents per bias motivation						Number of incidents per quarter				Population[1]
	Race/ Ethnicity/ Ancestry	Religion	Sexual orientation	Disability	Gender	Gender Identity	1st quarter	2nd quarter	3rd quarter	4th quarter	
Universities and Colleges	2	0	0	0	0	0					
Iowa State University	2	0	0	0	0	0	1	0	1	0	37,944
Nonmetropolitan Counties	1	0	0	0	0	0					
Marshall	1	0	0	0	0	0	1	0	0	0	
KANSAS											
Total	85	28	8	0	3	0					
Cities	62	19	6	0	0	0					
Atchison	1	0	0	0	0	0	0	1	0	0	10,421
Augusta	0	0	1	0	0	0	1	0	0	0	9,339
Bel Aire	2	0	0	0	0	0	0	1	1	0	8,490
Belleville	1	0	0	0	0	0	0	0	0	1	1,869
Beloit	0	0	1	0	0	0	0	0	0	1	3,604
Burlington	0	1	0	0	0	0	0	0	0	1	2,530
Clay Center	16	2	0	0	0	0	3	15	0	0	3,944
Coffeyville	1	1	0	0	0	0	1	0	1	0	9,171
Colby	2	0	0	0	0	0	1	1	0	0	5,365
Concordia	1	1	0	0	0	0	0	1	0	1	4,944
Derby	1	0	0	0	0	0	0	0	1	0	25,229
Dodge City	3	0	0	0	0	0	1	1	0	1	27,066
Edwardsville	1	0	0	0	0	0	0	1	0	0	4,503
El Dorado	1	0	0	0	0	0	1	0	0	0	12,924
Garden City	0	1	0	0	0	0	0	0	1	0	26,360
Goodland	0	1	0	0	0	0	0	1	0	0	4,397
Hays	1	0	0	0	0	0	0	1	0	0	20,769
Hiawatha	0	2	0	0	0	0	0	1	1	0	3,103
Independence	0	0	1	0	0	0	0	0	0	1	8,405
Junction City	2	1	0	0	0	0	0	1	0	2	21,242
Larned	0	1	0	0	0	0	0	0	1	0	3,632
Leavenworth	3	2	1	0	0	0	0	4	1	1	36,023
Leon	1	0	0	0	0	0	0	0	1	0	732
McPherson	1	0	0	0	0	0	1	0	0	0	13,053
Newton	4	1	0	0	0	0	2	2	1	0	18,830
Olathe	1	1	0	0	0	0	0	1	1	0	142,228
Overland Park	5	0	0	0	0	0	0	3	1	1	198,036
Pittsburg	2	0	0	0	0	0	0	0	1	1	20,027
Russell	0	0	1	0	0	0	0	0	1	0	4,412
Salina	2	1	1	0	0	0	0	1	2	1	46,400
Shawnee	3	0	0	0	0	0	0	1	0	2	66,208
Spring Hill	0	1	0	0	0	0	0	0	0	1	7,572
Topeka	1	0	0	0	0	0			1		125,024
Wellington	0	1	0	0	0	0	0	0	1	0	7,608
Wichita	6	1	0	0	0	0	0	3	3	1	390,746
Universities and Colleges	3	0	0	0	0	0					
Fort Hays State University	1	0	0	0	0	0	0	0	0	1	18,343
Kansas State University	1	0	0	0	0	0	0	0	0	1	24,546
University of Kansas, Medical Center[3]	1	0	0	0	0	0	0	0	0	1	
Metropolitan Counties	10	3	1	0	1	0					
Jefferson	0	2	0	0	0	0	1	0	1	0	
Leavenworth	1	0	1	0	0	0	0	2	0	0	
Pottawatomie	1	0	0	0	0	0	0	0	1	0	
Riley County Police Department	5	1	0	0	0	0	0	2	4	0	
Sedgwick	1	0	0	0	1	0	1	1	0	0	
Shawnee	2	0	0	0	0	0	0	2	0	0	
Nonmetropolitan Counties	10	3	0	0	2	0					
Anderson	1	0	0	0	0	0	0	0	1	0	
Barton	0	1	0	0	0	0	0	0	0	1	
Cherokee	1	0	0	0	0	0	1	0	0	0	
Gray	1	0	0	0	0	0	0	0	1	0	
Kingman	1	0	0	0	0	0	0	1	0	0	
Lyon	1	0	0	0	0	0	0	1	0		
Marion	0	1	0	0	0	0	1	0	0	0	
Marshall	1	0	0	0	0	0	0	0	1	0	
McPherson	1	0	0	0	0	0	0	1	0	0	
Montgomery	1	1	0	0	0	0	0	0	1	1	
Rawlins	0	0	0	0	1	0	0	1	0		
Rush	0	0	0	0	1	0	0	0	1	0	

Table 13. Hate Crime Incidents Per Bias Motivation and Quarter, by Selected State and Agency and Federal, 2020—*Continued*

(Number.)

State/agency	Race/ Ethnicity/ Ancestry	Religion	Sexual orientation	Disability	Gender	Gender Identity	1st quarter	2nd quarter	3rd quarter	4th quarter	Population[1]
	Number of incidents per bias motivation						Number of incidents per quarter				
Russell	1	0	0	0	0	0	1	0	0	0	
Saline	1	0	0	0	0	0	0	0	1	0	
State Police Agencies	0	1	0	0	0	0					
Highway Patrol, Troop F	0	1	0	0	0	0	1	0	0	0	
Tribal Agencies	0	0	1	0	0	0					
Potawatomi Tribal	0	0	1	0	0	0	0	0	0	1	
Other Agencies	0	2	0	0	0	0					
Reno County Drug Enforcement Unit	0	2	0	0	0	0	2	0			
KENTUCKY											
Total	134	18	18	1	2	3					
Cities	99	14	14	0	2	3					
Ashland	3	0	0	0	0	0	0	2	1	0	19,979
Bellevue	1	0	0	0	0	0	0	1	0	0	5,695
Berea	2	0	0	0	0	0	0	0	1	1	16,311
Bowling Green[2]	3	2	0	0	0	0	2	0	1	1	71,861
Covington	1	0	1	0	0	1	1	0	1	1	40,324
Cynthiana	3	0	0	0	0	0	1	2	0	0	6,329
Dayton	1	0	0	0	0	0	1	0	0	0	5,639
Eminence	1	0	0	0	0	0	0	0	1	0	2,591
Falmouth	1	0	0	0	0	0	0	0	1	0	2,091
Florence	1	0	0	0	0	0	0	0	0	1	33,397
Frankfort	1	0	0	0	0	0	1	0	0	0	27,803
Glasgow	1	0	0	0	0	0	0	0	1	0	14,537
Grayson	1	0	0	0	0	0	0	0	1	0	3,870
Hopkinsville	2	0	0	0	0	0	1	0	0	1	30,532
Independence	0	0	1	0	0	0	0	0	1	0	28,957
Indian Hills	1	0	0	0	0	0	1	0	0	0	2,978
Jeffersontown	1	0	0	0	0	0	0	0	0	1	27,700
La Grange	1	0	1	0	0	0	0	1	1	0	9,142
Leitchfield	1	0	0	0	0	0	0	0	1	0	6,880
Lexington[2]	18	5	6	0	0	2	5	7	11	5	325,851
Louisville Metro	27	2	3	0	0	0	3	12	9	8	673,730
Marion	1	0	0	0	0	0	0	0	0	1	2,821
Maysville	0	0	1	0	0	0	0	1	0	0	8,695
Middlesboro	1	0	0	0	0	0	0	0	1	0	8,968
Morehead	1	0	0	0	0	0	0	0	1	0	7,644
Murray	4	0	0	0	0	0	0	3	1	0	19,499
Newport	3	0	0	0	0	0	0	2	1	0	14,874
Owensboro	4	1	0	0	0	0	0	2	2	1	60,430
Paducah[2]	3	1	1	0	1	0	1	2	0	1	24,850
Paris	1	0	0	0	0	0	0	0	1	0	9,655
Radcliff	2	0	0	0	0	0	0	2	0	0	22,950
Richmond[2]	1	1	0	0	1	0	1	0	1	0	36,691
Russell Springs	2	0	0	0	0	0	0	1	1	0	2,661
Scottsville	1	1	0	0	0	0	1	0	0	1	4,576
Shively	1	0	0	0	0	0	0	1	0	0	15,735
St. Matthews	1	1	0	0	0	0	0	0	2	0	18,162
Warsaw	1	0	0	0	0	0	0	0	1	0	1,705
Winchester	1	0	0	0	0	0	0	0	0	1	18,570
Universities and Colleges	6	0	1	0	0	0					
University of Kentucky	1	0	0	0	0	0	0	0	1	0	30,981
University of Louisville	4	0	0	0	0	0	1	0	3	0	24,770
Western Kentucky University[2]	1	0	1	0	0	0	0	0	1	0	23,228
Metropolitan Counties	9	1	3	1	0	0					
Boone[2]	4	1	1	0	0	0	0	1	1	3	
Bullitt	1	0	0	0	0	0	0	0	1	0	
Campbell County Police Department	1	0	0	0	0	0	0	0	0	1	
Carter	1	0	0	0	0	0	1	0	0	0	
Jessamine	1	0	0	0	0	0	0	0	0	1	
Kenton County Police Department	0	0	0	1	0	0	0	0	1	0	
Oldham County Police Department[2]	1	0	1	0	0	0	0	1	0	0	
Warren	0	0	1	0	0	0	0	1	0	0	
Nonmetropolitan Counties	14	3	0	0	0	0					
Barren	1	0	0	0	0	0	0	1	0	0	
Bell	0	1	0	0	0	0	0	1	0	0	
Carroll	1	0	0	0	0	0	0	0	1	0	

(Number.)

State/agency	Number of incidents per bias motivation						Number of incidents per quarter				Population[1]
	Race/ Ethnicity/ Ancestry	Religion	Sexual orientation	Disability	Gender	Gender Identity	1st quarter	2nd quarter	3rd quarter	4th quarter	
Graves	2	0	0	0	0	0	0	1	1	0	
Knox	1	0	0	0	0	0	0	1	0	0	
Madison	1	0	0	0	0	0	0	0	0	1	
Mason	1	0	0	0	0	0	0	0	1	0	
McCracken	3	0	0	0	0	0	1	2	0	0	
Montgomery	1	0	0	0	0	0	1	0	0	0	
Pulaski	2	0	0	0	0	0	0	1	1	0	
Rockcastle	0	1	0	0	0	0	0	0	1	0	
Rowan	1	0	0	0	0	0	0	1	0	0	
Whitley	0	1	0	0	0	0	0	0	1	0	
State Police Agencies	5	0	0	0	0	0					
State Police											
Bowling Green	2	0	0	0	0	0	0	1	0	1	
Dry Ridge	1	0	0	0	0	0	0	0	0	1	
Hazard	1	0	0	0	0	0	0	0	1	0	
Madisonville	1	0	0	0	0	0	0	1	0	0	
Other Agencies	1	0	0	0	0	0					
Louisville Regional Airport Authority	1	0	0	0	0	0	0	0	1	0	
LOUISIANA											
Total	27	5	6	1	1	0					
Cities	13	1	4	0	1	0					
Alexandria[2]	1	0	1	0	0	0		1			45,986
Baton Rouge	1	0	0	0	0	0	0	0	0	1	219,245
Bossier City	1	0	0	0	0	0	0	0	1	0	68,869
Gonzales	1	0	0	0	0	0	0	0	1	0	11,092
Jennings	0	0	1	0	0	0	0	0	1	0	9,737
Lake Charles	1	0	0	0	0	0	0	0	1	0	79,077
Mansfield	3	1	0	0	1	0			2	3	4,587
New Orleans	3	0	2	0	0	0	0	2	2	1	393,779
Port Allen	1	0	0	0	0	0	0	0	0	1	4,695
Rayne	1	0	0	0	0	0	0		0	1	7,997
Metropolitan Counties	12	3	2	1	0	0					
Ascension	0	0	1	0	0	0	0	1	0	0	
Calcasieu	1	0	0	0	0	0	0	1	0	0	
Lafourche	4	1	0	1	0	0	0	1	3	2	
Rapides	5	1	1	0	0	0	2	3	1	1	
St. James	0	1	0	0	0	0	0	0	1	0	
St. John the Baptist	2	0	0	0	0	0	0	2	0	0	
Nonmetropolitan Counties	2	1	0	0	0	0					
Lincoln	1	1	0	0	0	0			1	1	
Madison	1	0	0	0	0	0	1	0	0	0	
MAINE											
Total	40	7	36	0	0	1					
Cities	29	6	4	0	0	1					
Augusta	3	0	0	0	0	0	0	3	0	0	18,653
Bangor	0	1	0	0	0	0	0	1	0	0	32,179
Bath	1	0	0	0	0	0	0	0	0	1	8,322
Biddeford	1	0	0	0	0	0	0	1	0	0	21,530
Boothbay Harbor	0	1	0	0	0	0	0	0	0	1	2,219
Brunswick	2	0	0	0	0	0	0	0	2	0	20,566
Cumberland	1	0	0	0	0	0	0	0	0	1	8,327
Fryeburg	1	0	0	0	0	0	0	1	0	0	3,452
Kennebunk	2	0	0	0	0	0	0	2	0	0	11,719
Lewiston	0	0	1	0	0	0	1	0	0	0	36,186
Livermore Falls	2	0	0	0	0	0	0	2	0	0	3,154
Mexico	2	0	0	0	0	0	1	1	0	0	2,624
Norway	1	0	0	0	0	0	0	1	0	0	4,989
Portland	3	1	2	0	0	0	1	1	4	0	66,229
Rockland	0	1	1	0	0	1	0	0	2	1	7,151
Saco	5	1	0	0	0	0	0	3	3	0	20,133
Skowhegan	1	0	0	0	0	0	0	1	0	0	8,202
South Portland	1	1	0	0	0	0	1	1	0	0	25,593
Waterville	1	0	0	0	0	0	0	0	0	1	16,654
Windham	2	0	0	0	0	0	1	0	1	0	18,720
Metropolitan Counties	7	1	29	0	0	0					

(Number.)

State/agency	Number of incidents per bias motivation						Number of incidents per quarter				Population[1]
	Race/Ethnicity/Ancestry	Religion	Sexual orientation	Disability	Gender	Gender Identity	1st quarter	2nd quarter	3rd quarter	4th quarter	
Cumberland	7	1	29	0	0	0	0	2	22	13	
Nonmetropolitan Counties	1	0	0	0	0	0					
Waldo	1	0	0	0	0	0	0	1	0	0	
State Police Agencies	3	0	3	0	0	0					
State Police[2]	3	0	3	0	0	0	1	1	2	1	
MARYLAND											
Total	27	5	7	0	0	1					
Cities	7	0	3	0	0	0					
Annapolis	1	0	0	0	0	0	1	0	0		39,315
Baltimore	3	0	2	0	0	0	1	1	3		588,594
Bowie	3	0	0	0	0	0	0	1	2	0	59,008
Greenbelt	0	0	1	0	0	0	0	1			23,342
Universities and Colleges	2	0	0	0	0	0					
St. Mary's College	1	0	0	0	0	0	0	0	1		1,705
University of Maryland, Baltimore County	1	0	0	0	0	0	0	0	1		15,726
Metropolitan Counties	16	5	4	0	0	1					
Anne Arundel County Police Department	1	0	0	0	0	0	0	0	1		
Baltimore County Police Department	7	2	2	0	0	0	0	4	4	3	
Frederick	0	0	0	0	0	1	1	0	0		
Harford	3	0	0	0	0	0	1	0	2		
Montgomery County Police Department	1	3	1	0	0	0	2	2	1	0	
Prince George's County Police Department	4	0	1	0	0	0	0	2	2	1	
State Police Agencies	1	0	0	0	0	0					
State Police, Harford County	1	0	0	0	0	0	1	0	0		
Other Agencies	1	0	0	0	0	0					
Maryland-National Capital Park Police, Montgomery County	1	0	0	0	0	0	1	0	0		
MASSACHUSETTS											
Total	188	69	51	2	2	11					
Cities	180	65	48	2	2	10					
Acton	3	2	0	0	0	0	2	2	0	1	23,728
Adams[2]	1	1	0	0	0	0	0	0	1	0	7,959
Amherst	0	1	0	0	0	0	0	0	0	1	40,061
Andover	1	0	0	0	0	0	1	0	0	0	36,534
Arlington	6	0	0	0	0	0	1	0	5	0	45,582
Attleboro	0	1	0	0	0	0	0	0	0	1	45,181
Ayer	0	0	1	0	0	0	0	0	1	0	8,237
Barnstable	1	0	0	1	0	0	0	1	1	0	44,169
Bedford	0	1	0	0	0	0	0	1	0	0	14,135
Belmont	1	0	0	0	0	0	0	1	0	0	26,136
Berlin	1	0	0	0	0	0	0	0	1	0	3,266
Beverly	1	0	0	0	0	0	0	0	1	0	42,229
Billerica	0	1	0	0	0	0	1	0	0	0	43,473
Boston[2]	11	9	17	0	0	8	19	6	5	14	697,323
Boxford	1	0	0	0	0	0	0	0	1	0	8,328
Braintree	1	0	0	0	0	1	0	1	1	0	37,278
Brockton	1	0	0	0	0	0	0	0	1	0	99,171
Brookline	1	0	1	0	0	0	0	0	0	2	59,057
Cambridge	10	1	4	0	0	0	2	4	7	2	119,938
Chelmsford	5	1	5	0	0	0	0	3	6	2	35,369
Danvers	1	0	0	0	0	0	0	0	1	0	27,517
Dedham	1	0	0	0	0	0	0	0	0	1	25,217
Douglas	1	0	0	0	0	0	0	1	0	0	9,054
Duxbury	1	0	0	0	0	0	0	0	1	0	16,561
Edgartown	0	0	0	1	0	0	0	0	1	0	4,374
Everett	3	0	0	0	0	0	0	1	2	0	46,765
Fall River	0	1	0	0	0	0	0	0	0	1	89,136
Falmouth	1	0	0	0	0	0	0	0	0	1	30,769
Fitchburg	1	0	0	0	0	0	0	0	0	1	40,443
Great Barrington	0	1	0	0	0	0	0	0	1	0	6,928
Greenfield	1	0	0	0	0	0	0	1	0		17,239
Halifax	1	0	0	0	0	0	0	0	1	0	8,207
Haverhill	6	5	0	0	0	0	1	3	4	3	64,015
Holbrook	0	1	0	0	0	0	1	0	0	0	11,035
Holyoke	1	0	0	0	0	0	1	0	0	0	40,002

(Number.)

State/agency	Race/Ethnicity/Ancestry	Religion	Sexual orientation	Disability	Gender	Gender Identity	1st quarter	2nd quarter	3rd quarter	4th quarter	Population[1]
Ipswich	0	0	0	0	1	0	0	0	0	1	14,097
Leominster	1	0	0	0	0	0	1	0	0	0	41,598
Lowell	1	0	0	0	0	0	1	0	0	0	110,876
Lunenburg	0	0	1	0	0	0	0	0	1	0	11,874
Lynn	13	1	0	0	0	0	2	8	3	1	94,223
Lynnfield	1	0	0	0	0	0	0	0	1	0	13,093
Malden	3	5	0	0	0	1	3	2	4	0	60,231
Manchester-by-the-Sea	1	0	0	0	0	0	0	0	0	1	5,438
Marblehead[2]	1	2	1	0	0	0	0	1	1	1	20,525
Marlborough	1	0	0	0	0	0	0	0	0	1	39,498
Mashpee	1	0	0	0	0	0	0	0	1	0	14,180
Medford	7	3	1	0	0	0	2	0	7	2	57,137
Methuen	2	0	0	0	0	0	0	1	1	0	50,810
Middleton	1	0	0	0	0	0	0	0	1	0	10,189
Monson	1	0	0	0	0	0	0	1	0	0	8,782
Montague[2]	1	1	0	0	0	0	0	1	0	0	8,185
Natick	1	0	0	0	0	0	0	0	0	1	36,200
Newbury	1	0	1	0	0	0	0	0	1	1	7,163
Newburyport	1	0	0	0	0	0	0	1	0	0	18,288
Newton	4	1	0	0	0	0	0	4	0	1	88,281
North Andover	0	0	1	0	0	0	0	0	0	1	31,341
North Attleboro	1	0	0	0	0	0	0	0	1	0	29,280
Norwood	1	0	0	0	0	0	1	0	0	0	29,791
Oakham	1	0	0	0	0	0	0	1	0	0	1,953
Palmer	0	0	1	0	0	0	0	0	1	0	12,200
Plymouth	1	0	0	0	0	0	0	0	1	0	64,199
Provincetown	4	0	1	0	0	0	0	1	2	2	2,947
Quincy[2]	6	3	6	0	0	0	4	6	3	1	94,519
Randolph	1	0	0	0	0	0	0	1	0	0	32,052
Revere	1	0	0	0	1	0	0	1	0	1	52,930
Salem[2]	6	4	0	0	0	0	2	5	1	0	43,154
Somerville	6	1	3	0	0	0	2	1	2	5	81,552
South Hadley	2	0	0	0	0	0	0	2	0	0	17,613
Spencer	0	1	0	0	0	0	0	1	0	0	11,896
Springfield	14	2	1	0	0	0	1	1	10	5	153,084
Sudbury	1	0	0	0	0	0	0	1	0	0	19,778
Sunderland[2]	1	1	0	0	0	0	1	0	0	0	3,622
Swampscott[2]	3	1	0	0	0	0	0	0	2	1	15,391
Taunton	1	0	1	0	0	0	0	2	0	0	57,338
Tisbury	1	0	0	0	0	0	0	1	0	0	4,108
Uxbridge	1	0	0	0	0	0	0	0	1	0	14,202
Waltham[2]	6	1	0	0	0	0	1	2	1	2	62,339
Wareham	0	0	1	0	0	0	0	0	1	0	23,619
Watertown	3	0	0	0	0	0	0	1	2	0	36,201
Wenham	3	0	0	0	0	0	0	0	3	0	5,296
Westford	0	1	0	0	0	0	0	0	1	0	25,011
Westwood	3	7	0	0	0	0	0	0	9	1	16,578
Winchester	1	0	0	0	0	0	1	0	0	0	22,827
Worcester[2]	2	3	1	0	0	0	1	1	2	1	184,850
Yarmouth[2]	5	1	0	0	0	0	0	4	0	1	23,015
Universities and Colleges	7	4	3	0	0	1					
Boston University	2	1	0	0	0	0	0	1	1	1	42,779
Fitchburg State University	1	0	0	0	0	0	0	0	0	1	11,130
Gordon College	1	0	0	0	0	0	0	0	0	1	2,397
Harvard University	0	1	0	0	0	0	0	1	0	0	41,987
Holyoke Community College[2]	0	0	1	0	0	1	1	0	0	0	6,832
Massachusetts Institute of Technology	0	2	1	0	0	0	0	0	3	0	12,321
Salem State University	0	0	1	0	0	0	1	0	0	0	10,069
University of Massachusetts											
Amherst	1	0	0	0	0	0	1	0	0	0	35,116
Medical Center, Worcester	2	0	0	0	0	0	1	1	0	0	1,227
Other Agencies	1	0	0	0	0	0					
Massachusetts General Hospital	1	0	0	0	0	0	1				
MICHIGAN											
Total	273	33	40	9	9	13					
Cities	227	28	34	9	8	11					

Table 13. Hate Crime Incidents Per Bias Motivation and Quarter, by Selected State and Agency and Federal, 2020—*Continued*

(Number.)

State/agency	Number of incidents per bias motivation						Number of incidents per quarter				Population[1]
	Race/ Ethnicity/ Ancestry	Religion	Sexual orientation	Disability	Gender	Gender Identity	1st quarter	2nd quarter	3rd quarter	4th quarter	
Alpena	0	0	1	0	0	0	1	0	0	0	9,900
Ann Arbor	3	0	0	0	0	1	0	1	3	0	120,647
Auburn Hills	1	0	0	0	0	0	0	0	1	0	25,149
Bangor	1	0	0	0	0	0	0	0	1	0	1,827
Bath Township	1	0	0	0	0	0	0	0	1	0	13,167
Battle Creek	4	0	1	1	0	0	1	1	2	2	60,479
Benton Harbor	0	0	1	0	0	0	0	0	1	0	9,710
Benton Township	1	0	0	1	0	0	0	0	0	2	14,251
Birch Run	1	0	0	0	0	0	0	0	1	0	1,468
Bloomfield Township	1	0	0	0	0	0	0	0	1	0	42,059
Boyne City	0	0	0	1	0	0	1	0	0	0	3,729
Bridgeport Township	2	0	0	0	0	0	0	2	0	0	9,736
Buena Vista Township	1	0	0	0	0	0	0	0	1	0	8,047
Burton	2	2	0	0	0	0	1	1	0	2	28,427
Cadillac	1	0	1	0	0	0	1	0	0	1	10,513
Cambridge Township	1	0	0	0	0	0	1	0	0	0	5,679
Canton Township	2	0	1	0	0	0	1	0	1	1	94,128
Cassopolis	1	0	0	0	1	0	1	0	1	0	1,692
Chesaning	0	1	0	0	0	0	0	0	1	0	2,221
Clawson	1	0	0	0	0	0	1	0	0	0	11,846
Clinton Township	1	0	0	0	0	0	0	0	1	0	100,884
Columbia Township	1	0	0	0	0	0	0	0	0	1	7,350
Commerce Township	1	0	0	0	0	0	0	1	0	0	39,689
Covert Township	1	0	0	0	0	0	0	0	1	0	2,891
Dearborn	1	0	0	0	0	0	0	0	0	1	93,507
Dearborn Heights	3	0	0	0	0	0	0	0	2	1	55,105
Decatur	1	0	0	0	0	0	0	1	0	0	1,724
Denton Township	1	0	0	0	0	0	1	0	0	0	5,421
Detroit	17	1	13	2	2	0	4	9	12	10	659,616
DeWitt	1	0	0	0	0	0	0	0	0	1	4,844
DeWitt Township	1	0	0	0	0	0	0	0	0	1	15,756
Durand	0	0	0	0	0	1	0	0	0	1	3,818
East Grand Rapids	1	0	0	0	0	0	0	0	1	0	12,105
East Lansing	2	0	0	0	0	0	0	2	0	0	48,098
Eastpointe	4	0	1	0	0	0	2	0	2	1	32,046
Eaton Rapids	1	0	0	0	0	1	0	2	0	0	5,248
Ecorse	1	1	0	0	0	0	1	0	1	0	9,576
Escanaba	2	0	0	0	1	0	0	1	1	1	12,111
Essexville	1	0	0	0	0	0	0	0	1	0	3,257
Farmington Hills	4	0	0	0	0	0	0	4	0	0	80,708
Ferndale	1	0	0	0	0	0	0	0	0	1	20,048
Flint	1	0	0	0	0	0	0	0	0	1	94,842
Flint Township	1	0	0	0	0	0	0	1	0	0	30,178
Flushing	1	0	0	0	0	0	0	1	0	0	7,827
Flushing Township	0	0	0	0	1	0	0	1	0	0	10,133
Frankenmuth	2	0	0	0	0	0	0	0	2	0	5,595
Fraser	2	0	0	0	0	0	1	0	1	0	14,480
Fremont	0	0	0	0	0	1	0	0	1	0	4,077
Garden City	1	0	0	0	0	0	0	0	0	1	26,282
Gaylord	1	0	0	0	0	0	0	1	0	0	3,692
Gladwin	1	0	0	0	0	0	0	1	0	0	2,887
Grand Blanc Township	1	0	0	0	0	0	0	0	0	1	36,498
Grand Haven	2	0	0	0	0	0	0	1	1	0	11,126
Grand Rapids	1	0	0	0	0	0	1	0	0	0	202,513
Grandville	1	0	0	0	0	0	0	1	0	0	15,913
Greenville	0	0	0	0	0	1	0	0	0	1	8,415
Grosse Pointe	2	0	0	0	0	0	0	0	1	1	5,127
Hamburg Township	0	1	0	0	0	0	0	0	0	1	21,867
Hamtramck	1	2	1	0	0	0	0	3	1	0	21,514
Harper Woods	1	0	0	0	0	0	0	0	1	0	13,679
Highland Park	3	0	1	0	0	0	0	1	0	3	10,680
Houghton	0	0	1	0	0	0	0	0	0	1	7,760
Howell	0	0	1	0	0	0	0	0	0	1	9,620
Huntington Woods	1	1	0	0	0	0	0	0	0	2	6,268
Inkster	4	0	0	0	0	0	0	1	2	1	24,173
Ionia	0	0	1	0	0	0	0	0	1	0	11,153
Jackson	0	1	0	0	0	0	1	0	0	0	32,332

Table 13. Hate Crime Incidents Per Bias Motivation and Quarter, by Selected State and Agency and Federal, 2020—*Continued*

(Number.)

State/agency	Number of incidents per bias motivation						Number of incidents per quarter				Population[1]
	Race/ Ethnicity/ Ancestry	Religion	Sexual orientation	Disability	Gender	Gender Identity	1st quarter	2nd quarter	3rd quarter	4th quarter	
Kalamazoo	1	0	0	0	0	0	0	1	0	0	76,411
Kalamazoo Township	1	0	0	0	0	0	0	0	0	1	24,562
Kentwood	0	1	0	1	0	0	0	0	0	2	52,263
Lansing	7	1	2	0	0	0	2	1	3	4	118,651
Lincoln Park	2	0	0	0	0	0	1	1	0	0	36,140
Livonia	3	0	0	0	0	1	0	0	1	3	93,342
Madison Heights	1	0	0	0	0	0	1	0	0	0	29,906
Manistee	1	0	0	0	0	0	0	1	0	0	6,103
Marshall	0	0	1	0	0	0	0	0	1	0	6,954
Meridian Township	5	0	0	0	0	0	0	2	1	2	43,598
Metro Police Authority of Genesee County	1	0	0	0	0	0	0	0	1	0	19,883
Midland	3	0	0	0	0	0	0	0	3	0	41,682
Montrose Township	1	0	0	0	0	0	0	1	0	0	7,431
Mount Pleasant	2	0	0	0	0	0	1	0	1	0	24,668
Muskegon Township	1	0	0	0	0	0	1	0	0	0	18,022
Negaunee	0	0	0	0	2	0	0	0	0	2	4,520
Niles	1	0	0	0	0	0	0	1	0	0	11,102
Northville Township	1	0	0	0	0	0	1	0	0	0	29,434
Norton Shores	2	0	0	0	0	0	0	0	1	1	24,742
Ontwa Township-Edwardsburg	2	0	0	0	0	0	0	0	1	1	6,602
Ovid	1	0	0	0	0	0	0	0	1	0	1,616
Owosso	5	1	0	0	0	0	1	0	5	0	14,363
Oxford	1	0	0	0	0	0	0	0	1	0	3,570
Paw Paw	0	1	0	0	0	0	0	0	0	1	3,351
Pinckney	2	0	0	0	0	0	1	0	1	0	2,419
Pontiac	3	0	0	0	0	0	0	2	1	0	59,411
Port Huron	1	1	0	0	0	1	0	0	0	3	28,602
Richland Township, Saginaw County	1	0	0	0	0	0	0	0	1	0	3,904
Richmond	0	0	1	0	0	0	0	0	0	1	5,856
River Rouge	0	1	0	0	0	0	0	1	0	0	7,369
Rochester Hills	3	0	0	0	0	0	0	2	1	0	74,913
Rockford	1	0	0	0	0	0	0	1	0	0	6,472
Romeo	1	0	0	0	0	0	0	0	1	0	3,607
Romulus	1	0	1	0	1	1	2	0	1	1	23,533
Roosevelt Park	1	0	0	0	0	0	0	1	0	0	3,793
Roseville	3	0	0	0	0	0	0	1	1	1	46,983
Royal Oak	1	1	0	0	0	1	1	1	0	1	59,506
Saginaw	3	0	0	0	0	0	0	1	1	1	47,767
Saginaw Township	1	0	0	0	0	0	0	1	0	0	38,971
Saline	1	0	0	0	0	0	0	0	1	0	9,400
Shelby	2	0	0	0	0	0	0	1	1	0	2,008
Shelby Township	1	0	0	0	0	0	0	0	1	0	81,416
Southfield	5	0	0	0	0	0	1	0	4	0	72,794
Southgate	1	0	0	0	0	0	0	0	0	1	28,848
South Haven	0	0	0	1	0	0	0	1	0	0	4,341
Spring Arbor Township	1	0	0	0	0	0	1	0	0	0	7,838
Stanton	1	0	0	0	0	0	1	0	0	0	1,423
St. Clair Shores	1	0	0	0	0	0	0	1	0	0	58,898
Sterling Heights	12	3	0	0	0	0	1	4	5	5	132,745
Sumpter Township	2	0	0	0	0	0	0	1	1	0	9,348
Taylor	1	0	0	0	0	0	0	0	1	0	60,698
Tecumseh	2	0	0	0	0	0	0	1	1	0	8,392
Three Oaks	1	0	1	1	0	0	2	0	0	1	1,537
Three Rivers	1	0	0	0	0	0	1	0	0	0	7,604
Traverse City	1	0	0	0	0	0	0	0	1	0	15,855
Troy	7	0	2	0	0	0	1	4	2	2	84,441
Walker	2	0	0	0	0	0	0	0	1	1	25,020
Warren	10	1	0	0	0	0	0	4	6	1	133,928
Waterford Township	1	0	1	0	0	0	1	0	0	1	72,735
Wayne	2	0	0	0	0	0	0	1	0	1	16,734
West Bloomfield Township	4	5	0	1	0	0	2	4	2	2	65,711
Westland	2	1	1	0	0	0	0	1	2	1	81,244
Wyoming	5	1	0	0	0	2	2	0	4	2	76,071
Universities and Colleges	8	1	0	0	0	1					
Grand Valley State University	1	0	0	0	0	0	0	0	1	0	27,752
Michigan Technological University	0	0	0	0	0	1	0	0	1	0	7,657
Oakland Community College	1	0	0	0	0	0	0	0	0	1	25,217

Table 13. Hate Crime Incidents Per Bias Motivation and Quarter, by Selected State and Agency and Federal, 2020—*Continued*

(Number.)

State/agency	Race/ Ethnicity/ Ancestry	Religion	Sexual orientation	Disability	Gender	Gender Identity	1st quarter	2nd quarter	3rd quarter	4th quarter	Population[1]
University of Michigan											
Ann Arbor	5	1	0	0	0	0	1	0	3	2	48,218
Flint	1	0	0	0	0	0	0	1	0	0	8,806
Metropolitan Counties	16	1	5	0	0	1					
Bay	2	0	0	0	0	0	1	1	0	0	
Berrien	0	0	0	0	0	1	0	0	1	0	
Calhoun	1	0	0	0	0	0	0	0	1	0	
Clinton	1	0	0	0	0	0	0	0	0	1	
Genesee	1	1	0	0	0	0	0	0	2	0	
Ingham	2	0	1	0	0	0	0	0	3	0	
Ionia	3	0	0	0	0	0	0	1	1	1	
Kalamazoo	1	0	0	0	0	0	0	1	0	0	
Kent	1	0	1	0	0	0	0	0	0	2	
Oakland	1	0	0	0	0	0	0	1	0	0	
Ottawa	1	0	2	0	0	0	0	0	1	2	
Saginaw	1	0	0	0	0	0	1	0	0	0	
Washtenaw	1	0	1	0	0	0	0	1	1	0	
Nonmetropolitan Counties	12	3	1	0	1	0					
Arenac	2	0	0	0	0	0	0	0	1	1	
Barry	2	0	0	0	0	0	0	1	1	0	
Charlevoix	0	0	1	0	0	0	0	0	0	1	
Dickinson	1	0	0	0	0	0	1	0	0	0	
Grand Traverse	0	1	0	0	0	0	1	0	0	0	
Houghton	1	1	0	0	0	0	0	0	0	2	
Isabella	1	0	0	0	0	0	0	0	1	0	
Lake	1	0	0	0	0	0	0	0	0	1	
Mecosta	2	0	0	0	0	0	0	2	0	0	
Missaukee	0	0	0	0	1	0	0	0	1	0	
Oceana	1	0	0	0	0	0	0	0	0	1	
Ogemaw	1	0	0	0	0	0	0	0	1	0	
Van Buren	0	1	0	0	0	0	0	0	1	0	
State Police Agencies	7	0	0	0	0	0					
State Police											
Lapeer County	1	0	0	0	0	0	0	1	0	0	
Midland County	1	0	0	0	0	0	1	0	0	0	
Saginaw County	1	0	0	0	0	0	0	0	0	1	
Shiawassee County	4	0	0	0	0	0	1	1	0	2	
Tribal Agencies	1	0	0	0	0	0					
Nottawaseppi Huron Band of Potawatomi	1	0	0	0	0	0	0	0	0	1	
Other Agencies	2	0	0	0	0	0					
Department of Natural Resources Law Enforcement Division	1	0	0	0	0	0	0	1	0	0	
Genesee County Parks and Recreation	1	0	0	0	0	0	1	0	0	0	
MINNESOTA											
Total	134	30	27	3	0	2					
Cities	117	23	24	1	0	1					
Alexandria	1	0	0	0	0	0	1	0	0	0	13,978
Blaine	1	0	0	0	0	0	0	0	0	1	66,588
Bloomington	0	0	1	0	0	0	1	0	0	0	85,159
Brainerd	3	0	0	0	0	0	0	1	1	1	13,417
Brooklyn Center	1	0	0	0	0	0	0	0	1	0	30,744
Brooklyn Park	2	0	0	0	0	0	0	1	1	0	80,897
Burnsville	2	0	0	0	0	0	1	1	0	0	61,445
Coon Rapids	1	0	0	0	0	0	0	0	1	0	63,162
Crystal	0	0	1	0	0	0	0	1	0	0	22,987
Dayton	1	0	0	0	0	0	0	0	1	0	6,958
Eden Prairie	2	0	0	0	0	0	0	0	1	1	65,353
Edina	1	0	0	0	0	0	0	0	1	0	53,422
Fairmont	2	0	0	0	0	0	1	1	0	0	9,964
Goodhue	1	0	0	0	0	0	0	1	0	0	1,177
Hastings	1	1	0	0	0	0	0	1	0	1	22,959
Hopkins	4	0	0	0	0	0	0	0	2	2	18,568
Inver Grove Heights	1	0	0	0	0	0	1	0	0	0	35,861
Janesville	0	1	1	0	0	0	0	0	1	1	2,251
Lakes Area	2	0	0	0	0	0	0	0	1	1	10,000

(Number.)

State/agency	Number of incidents per bias motivation						Number of incidents per quarter				Population[1]
	Race/ Ethnicity/ Ancestry	Religion	Sexual orientation	Disability	Gender	Gender Identity	1st quarter	2nd quarter	3rd quarter	4th quarter	
Lakeville	4	1	0	0	0	0	1	2	1	1	68,688
Mankato	4	1	1	1	0	0	0	3	3	1	43,276
Maple Grove	1	0	0	0	0	0	0	0	0	1	73,939
Maplewood	5	1	0	0	0	0	1	2	2	1	41,096
Minneapolis	18	4	5	0	0	0	9	9	5	4	435,116
Minnetonka	1	1	0	0	0	0	0	2	0	0	54,561
Mountain Lake	0	1	0	0	0	0	0	1	0	0	2,029
Plainview	1	0	0	0	0	0	0	0	1	0	3,293
Plymouth	1	1	1	0	0	0	0	0	2	1	80,843
Prior Lake	1	0	0	0	0	0	0	0	1	0	27,748
Red Wing	2	0	5	0	0	0	1	0	3	3	16,304
Rochester	3	0	0	0	0	0	0	0	1	2	120,336
Roseville	13	0	0	0	0	0	0	6	6	1	36,675
Savage	4	1	0	0	0	0	0	1	3	1	33,020
Sleepy Eye	1	0	0	0	0	0	0	1	0	0	3,331
South Lake Minnetonka	1	0	1	0	0	0	0	0	2	0	12,867
South St. Paul	0	0	1	0	0	0	0	0	0	1	20,053
St. Cloud	2	0	1	0	0	0	1	1	1	0	68,751
Stillwater	1	0	0	0	0	0	0	0	0	1	19,736
St. Louis Park	3	2	0	0	0	0	1	2	2	0	49,058
St. Paul	20	5	6	0	0	1	3	14	7	8	309,859
St. Paul Park	0	1	0	0	0	0	0	0	0	1	5,374
Wayzata	0	1	0	0	0	0	0	0	1	0	6,602
Willmar	2	0	0	0	0	0	0	0	1	1	19,901
Winona	0	1	0	0	0	0	0	0	1	0	26,487
Woodbury	3	0	0	0	0	0	2	0	0	1	74,110
Universities and Colleges	1	0	0	0	0	0					
University of Minnesota, Twin **Cities**	1	0	0	0	0	0	1	0	0	0	61,787
Metropolitan Counties	9	6	3	2	0	1					
Anoka	0	1	0	0	0	0	0	0	1	0	
Carver	0	1	0	0	0	0	0	1	0	0	
Olmsted	1	0	0	0	0	0	0	1	0	0	
Ramsey[2]	4	3	1	2	0	1	0	2	7	1	
Sherburne	2	0	0	0	0	0	0	0	0	2	
Washington[2]	2	1	1	0	0	0	0	0	0	3	
Wright	0	0	1	0	0	0	1	0	0	0	
Nonmetropolitan Counties	6	1	0	0	0	0					
Brown	1	0	0	0	0	0	0	0	1	0	
Cook	1	0	0	0	0	0	0	0	1	0	
Crow Wing	1	0	0	0	0	0	1	0	0	0	
Itasca	0	1	0	0	0	0	0	1	0	0	
Jackson	1	0	0	0	0	0	0	0	0	1	
Mahnomen	1	0	0	0	0	0	0	0	0	1	
Pine	1	0	0	0	0	0	0	0	1	0	
Other Agencies	1	0	0	0	0	0					
Metropolitan Transit Commission	1	0	0	0	0	0	0	0	1	0	
MISSISSIPPI											
Total	14	2	0	0	0	0					
Cities	9	2	0	0	0	0					
Cleveland	0	1	0	0	0	0	1	0	0	0	10,944
Corinth	1	0	0	0	0	0	0	0	0	1	14,461
Flowood	0	1	0	0	0	0				1	9,564
Gulfport	3	0	0	0	0	0	0	1	1	1	72,142
Kosciusko	1	0	0	0	0	0	0	0	0	1	6,652
Lucedale	1	0	0	0	0	0	0	0	0	1	3,179
Olive Branch	2	0	0	0	0	0	1	1	0	0	39,566
Southaven	1	0	0	0	0	0	0	0	0	1	56,573
Metropolitan Counties	2	0	0	0	0	0					
DeSoto	1	0	0	0	0	0	0	0	1	0	
Stone	1	0	0	0	0	0	0	0	0	1	
Nonmetropolitan Counties	3	0	0	0	0	0					
Jasper	3	0	0	0	0	0	0	0	1	2	
MISSOURI											
Total	78	15	18	2	3	2					
Cities	69	14	14	2	2	2					

Table 13. Hate Crime Incidents Per Bias Motivation and Quarter, by Selected State and Agency and Federal, 2020—*Continued*

(Number.)

State/agency	Race/ Ethnicity/ Ancestry	Religion	Sexual orientation	Disability	Gender	Gender Identity	1st quarter	2nd quarter	3rd quarter	4th quarter	Population[1]
Belton	1	0	0	0	0	0	0	1	0	0	23,698
Blue Springs[2]	5	3	1	0	0	0	2	1	2	3	56,193
Cameron	1	0	0	0	0	0	0	0	1	0	9,618
Cape Girardeau	2	1	1	0	1	0	0	4	1	0	40,845
Columbia	1	0	0	0	0	0	0	0	0	1	124,829
Creve Coeur	1	0	0	0	0	0	0	1	0	0	18,716
Eldon	0	1	0	0	0	0	1	0	0	0	4,721
Harrisonville	1	0	0	0	0	0	0	0	1	0	10,083
Herculaneum	1	0	0	0	0	0	0	0	1	0	4,216
Independence	4	0	0	0	0	0	1	3	0	0	116,648
Jefferson City	1	0	1	0	0	0	0	0	0	2	42,653
Kansas City[2]	34	5	7	0	1	2	4	18	18	7	499,335
Kirksville	2	0	0	0	0	0	0	0	2	0	17,611
Kirkwood	0	1	0	0	0	0	0	0	1	0	27,834
Lee's Summit	2	0	0	0	0	0	0	1	0	1	100,268
Macon	1	0	0	0	0	0	0	0	1	0	5,326
Marceline	0	1	0	0	0	0	0	0	1	0	2,069
North Kansas City	0	0	1	0	0	0	1	0	0	0	4,615
Odessa	1	0	0	0	0	0	0	0	1	0	5,238
Platte City	1	0	0	0	0	0	0	1	0	0	4,987
Potosi	1	2	0	0	0	0	0	0	2	1	2,568
Rolla	0	0	1	2	0	0	0	0	0	3	20,522
Sikeston	2	0	0	0	0	0	0	0	1	1	15,987
Smithville	0	0	1	0	0	0	0	1	0	0	11,097
St. Louis	1	0	0	0	0	0		0	1		298,422
Strafford	1	0	0	0	0	0	0	0	0	1	2,473
Sullivan	1	0	0	0	0	0	0	0	0	1	7,128
Thayer	1	0	1	0	0	0	0	0	1	1	2,121
Union	2	0	0	0	0	0	1	0	1	0	12,195
University City	1	0	0	0	0	0	0	0	0	1	34,045
Metropolitan Counties	5	0	3	0	0	0					
Franklin	0	0	1	0	0	0	0	0	1	0	
Jackson	1	0	0	0	0	0	0	1	0	0	
St. Louis County Police Department	4	0	2	0	0	0	0	1	5	0	
Nonmetropolitan Counties	4	1	1	0	1	0					
Benton	1	0	0	0	0	0	0	1	0	0	
Butler	1	0	0	0	0	0	0	0	1	0	
Camden	2	0	0	0	1	0	0	0	2	1	
Douglas	0	1	0	0	0	0	0	1	0	0	
Phelps	0	0	1	0	0	0	1	0	0	0	
MONTANA											
Total	16	6	3	1	0	0					
Cities	11	5	2	0	0	0					
Billings	4	3	0	0	0	0	1	4	1	1	110,157
Great Falls	5	0	1	0	0	0	0	2	4	0	58,345
Helena	1	0	0	0	0	0	0	1	0	0	33,629
Kalispell	0	2	0	0	0	0	0	0	2	0	25,125
Livingston	0	0	1	0	0	0	0	0	0	1	7,892
Missoula	1	0	0	0	0	0	0	0	1	0	76,468
Universities and Colleges	1	0	0	0	0	0					
Montana State University	1	0	0	0	0	0	0	0	0	1	18,898
Metropolitan Counties	1	0	0	0	0	0					
Missoula	1	0	0	0	0	0	0	1	0	0	
Nonmetropolitan Counties	3	1	1	1	0	0					
Big Horn	0	1	0	1	0	0	0	0	2	0	
Gallatin	2	0	0	0	0	0	0	2	0	0	
Jefferson	0	0	1	0	0	0	1	0	0	0	
Sheridan	1	0	0	0	0	0	0	1	0	0	
NEBRASKA											
Total	52	11	8	1	0	0					
Cities	35	11	7	1	0	0					
Fremont	1	0	1	0	0	0	1	0	1	0	26,381
Grand Island	2	0	0	0	0	0	1	1	0	0	51,547
Kearney	1	0	0	0	0	0	0	1	0	0	34,201
Lincoln	17	5	3	0	0	0		9	8	8	292,600

(Number.)

State/agency	Number of incidents per bias motivation						Number of incidents per quarter				Population[1]
	Race/ Ethnicity/ Ancestry	Religion	Sexual orientation	Disability	Gender	Gender Identity	1st quarter	2nd quarter	3rd quarter	4th quarter	
McCook............................	10	0	0	0	0	0	5	5	0	0	7,543
Nebraska City....................	1	0	1	0	0	0	1	0	1	0	7,292
North Platte......................	1	0	0	0	0	0	0	0	1	0	23,523
Omaha.............................	1	6	2	0	0	0	1	1	3	4	480,297
Scottsbluff.......................	1	0	0	0	0	0	0	1	0	0	15,665
South Sioux City................	0	0	0	1	0	0	0	1	0	0	12,746
Metropolitan Counties	2	0	1	0	0	0					
Douglas...........................	1	0	1	0	0	0	1	1	0	0	
Sarpy..............................	1	0	0	0	0	0	0	1	0	0	
Nonmetropolitan Counties........	15	0	0	0	0	0					
Keith..............................	15	0	0	0	0	0	1	5	8	1	
NEVADA											
Total	82	14	14	1	2	1					
Cities	72	10	14	1	2	1					
Henderson........................	7	2	0	0	0	0	0	0	2	7	328,056
Las Vegas Metropolitan Police Department[2].........	27	1	9	1	0	1	9	12	6	11	1,693,061
North Las Vegas..................	3	0	3	0	0	0	2	0	2	2	256,217
Reno...............................	30	3	1	0	2	0	6	9	15	6	259,168
Sparks.............................	5	4	1	0	0	0	1	3	1	5	106,664
Universities and Colleges	2	0	0	0	0	0					
University Police Services........	1	0	0	0	0	0	0	0	1	0	92,407
University of Nevada, Reno	1	0	0	0	0	0	0	1	0	0	24,246
Metropolitan Counties	4	3	0	0	0	0					
Washoe............................	4	3	0	0	0	0	1	2	1	3	
Nonmetropolitan Counties........	1	1	0	0	0	0					
Douglas...........................	1	0	0	0	0	0	0	0	1	0	
Mineral...........................	0	1	0	0	0	0	0	0	0	1	
State Police Agencies	1	0	0	0	0	0					
Highway Patrol, Southern Division......................	1	0	0	0	0	0	0	0	1	0	
Other Agencies...................	2	0	0	0	0	0					
Clark County School District............................	2	0	0	0	0	0	2	0	0	0	
NEW HAMPSHIRE											
Total	9	4	4	1	0	1					
Cities	7	4	4	1	0	1					
Charlestown......................	0	0	1	0	0	0	0	0	1	0	5,010
Concord...........................	0	2	0	0	0	0	0	0	0	2	43,737
Dunbarton........................	0	1	0	0	0	0	0	0	1	0	2,894
Hanover...........................	0	1	0	0	0	0	0	0	0	1	11,498
Hudson............................	1	0	0	0	0	0	0	0	0	1	25,748
Laconia............................	1	0	0	0	0	0	0	0	1	0	16,669
Londonderry......................	0	0	1	0	0	0	0	0	1	0	26,812
Manchester.......................	0	0	1	0	0	0	0	0	1	0	113,018
Nashua............................	0	0	1	0	0	0	0	0	1	0	89,671
New Hampton.....................	1	0	0	0	0	0	0	0	1	0	2,231
New Ipswich......................	1	0	0	0	0	0	0	1	0	0	5,425
Salem..............................	2	0	0	0	0	1	0	1	0	2	29,943
Seabrook..........................	1	0	0	0	0	0	0	0	1	0	8,871
Somersworth......................	0	0	0	1	0	0	0	0	0	1	12,005
Universities and Colleges	2	0	0	0	0	0					
Plymouth State University........	1	0	0	0	0	0	0	0	1	0	5,868
University of New Hampshire	1	0	0	0	0	0	1	0	0	0	16,673
NEW JERSEY											
Total	267	136	62	4	8	8					
Cities	250	124	55	4	8	8					
Aberdeen Township	1	1	0	0	0	0	1	0	1	0	19,471
Absecon...........................	1	0	0	0	0	0	0	0	1	0	8,856
Asbury Park.......................	1	0	0	0	0	0	0	1	0	0	15,331
Atlantic City[2]....................	1	0	0	0	1	0	0	1	0	0	37,550
Audubon..........................	1	0	0	0	0	0				1	8,608
Bayonne[2].........................	3	1	1	0	0	0	1	1	1	1	65,013
Belmar............................	1	1	0	0	0	0	1	1	0	0	5,518
Bergenfield[2]......................	1	1	0	0	0	0	0			1	27,347
Berkeley Township[2]..............	3	1	2	0	0	0			3		42,168
Berlin[2]...........................	1	1	1	1	0	0	1	0	0	0	7,517

Table 13. Hate Crime Incidents Per Bias Motivation and Quarter, by Selected State and Agency and Federal, 2020—*Continued*

(Number.)

State/agency	Number of incidents per bias motivation						Number of incidents per quarter				Population[1]
	Race/ Ethnicity/ Ancestry	Religion	Sexual orientation	Disability	Gender	Gender Identity	1st quarter	2nd quarter	3rd quarter	4th quarter	
Bloomingdale	1	0	0	0	0	0	0	1	0		8,098
Branchburg Township[2]	1	1	0	0	0	0	1	0	0	0	14,526
Brick Township[2]	2	4	2	0	0	0	1	1	0	3	76,326
Bridgewater Township[2]	3	1	1	0	0	0	2	0	2	0	44,006
Brigantine	0	1	0	0	0	0	1	0	0	0	8,566
Byram Township[2]	1	1	0	0	0	0	0	0	1	0	7,880
Camden County Police Department	1	0	0	0	0	0	0	1	0	0	73,127
Cape May	0	0	1	0	0	0	0	0	1	0	3,401
Carlstadt[2]	1	1	0	0	0	0	0	1	0	0	6,126
Cedar Grove Township	0	1	0	0	0	0	0	1	0	0	12,483
Cherry Hill Township[2]	2	3	0	1	0	0	0	0	3	0	71,220
Cinnaminson Township	2	0	0	0	0	0	0	0	2	0	16,429
Clark Township	2	1	0	0	0	0	0	1	2		16,026
Clifton	2	0	0	0	0	0	0	0	1	1	85,058
Clinton Township	0	1	0	0	0	0	0	1		0	12,465
Collingswood[2]	1	1	0	0	0	0	0	1	0	0	13,864
Cranford Township[2]	2	1	0	0	0	0	1	0	1	0	24,186
Delran Township	1	0	0	0	0	0	0	0	1	0	16,444
Deptford Township[2]	1	1	0	0	0	0	0	0	0	1	30,275
Dunellen	0	1	0	0	0	0	1	0	0	0	7,192
East Brunswick Township	1	1	0	0	0	0	1	0	0	1	47,573
East Hanover Township	1	1	0	0	0	0	0	0	1	1	10,881
Eatontown[2]	2	2	0	0	0	0	1	0	2	0	12,124
Edison Township	3	1	0	0	0	0	0	3	0	1	99,584
Egg Harbor City	1	0	0	0	0	0	0	0	1	0	4,031
Egg Harbor Township	1	0	2	0	0	0	1	1	1	0	42,110
Elizabeth	0	0	1	0	0	0	0	0	1		129,518
Englewood[2]	4	1	1	0	0	0	2	0	2	1	28,514
Evesham Township	2	1	0	0	0	0	0	2	0	1	45,148
Ewing Township	1	0	0	0	0	0	0	0	1	0	36,325
Fair Lawn	1	0	0	0	0	0	0	1	0	0	32,910
Florence Township	1	0	0	0	0	0	0	1	0	0	12,527
Fort Lee	1	1	0	0	0	0	0	1	1	0	38,921
Franklin	1	0	0	0	0	0	1	0	0	0	4,684
Franklin Township, Gloucester County[2]	2	1	0	0	0	0	1	1	0	0	16,226
Franklin Township, Somerset County	3	0	0	0	0	0	0	3	0	0	66,138
Freehold Borough	0	1	0	0	0	0	1	0	0	0	11,643
Garfield[2]	1	1	0	0	0	0	0	0	0	1	31,908
Garwood[2]	1	1	0	0	0	0	0	0	0	1	4,360
Glen Rock	1	0	0	0	0	0	0	0	0	1	11,705
Gloucester City	0	0	1	0	0	0	0	0	1	0	11,182
Gloucester Township	1	0	0	0	0	0	0	1	0	0	63,755
Hackensack	1	0	0	0	0	0	0	1	0	0	44,264
Hackettstown[2]	1	1	0	0	0	0	1	0	0	0	9,316
Hamburg[2]	1	1	0	0	0	0	0	1	0	0	3,110
Hamilton Township, Mercer County[2]	14	2	1	0	1	0	0	6	7	1	86,805
Hanover Township	1	0	0	0	0	0	0	1	0	0	14,290
Harrison	0	1	1	0	0	0	0	1	1	0	20,937
Hawthorne	0	1	0	0	0	0	0		1	0	18,728
High Bridge	2	0	0	0	0	0	0	0	2		3,385
Highland Park	1	0	0	0	0	0	0	0	0	1	13,666
Hightstown	2	1	0	0	0	0	1	0	2	0	5,273
Hillsborough Township	0	1	0	0	0	0	0	1	0	0	40,210
Hillside Township[2]	1	1	1	0	0	0	1	1	0	0	21,995
Hoboken[2]	2	1	0	0	0	0	1	1	0	0	52,902
Holmdel Township	1	1	0	0	0	0	0	2	0	0	16,726
Hopewell Township[2]	3	0	1	1	0	0	1	1	2	0	17,641
Howell Township[2]	1	1	0	0	0	0	0	0	1	0	52,048
Jackson Township	1	2	0	0	0	0	2	0	1	0	58,120
Jefferson Township	1	0	0	0	0	0	0	1	0	0	20,626
Jersey City	1	1	0	0	0	0	1	0	1	0	263,273
Keansburg	2	0	1	0	0	0	1	1	1	0	9,582
Kearny	1	0	0	0	0	1	0	0	2	0	41,037
Lacey Township	1	0	0	0	0	0	0	1	0	0	29,524
Lakewood Township[2]	3	12	1	0	0	0	6	0	4	4	108,023
Lambertville	1	0	1	0	0	0	0	2	0	0	3,788
Linden	4	0	0	0	0	0	1	1	0	2	42,515

(Number.)

State/agency	Number of incidents per bias motivation						Number of incidents per quarter				Population[1]
	Race/ Ethnicity/ Ancestry	Religion	Sexual orientation	Disability	Gender	Gender Identity	1st quarter	2nd quarter	3rd quarter	4th quarter	
Lodi	0	1	0	0	0	0	0	1	0	0	24,343
Logan Township	1	0	0	0	0	0	0	0	0	1	5,847
Long Branch	0	2	0	0	0	0	0	2	0	0	30,175
Lopatcong Township	1	0	0	0	0	0	1	0	0	0	8,419
Lower Township	3	0	0	0	0	0	1	1	1	0	21,177
Lumberton Township	2	1	1	0	0	0	2	1	1	0	12,153
Madison[2]	1	1	1	0	0	0	0	0	1	0	17,850
Manasquan[2]	1	1	1	0	0	0	0	0		1	5,796
Manchester Township	3	0	0	0	0	0	2	1	0		43,856
Mansfield Township, Burlington County	1	0	0	0	0	0	0	1	0	0	8,527
Mansfield Township, Warren County	1	0	0	0	0	0	0	1	0	0	7,325
Maple Shade Township	3	1	1	0	0	0	2	2	1	0	18,402
Marlboro Township[2]	4	0	2	0	0	0	0	1	1	3	39,593
Medford Township	3	0	3	0	0	0	1	4	0	1	23,433
Middletown Township[2]	4	5	0	0	0	0	0	2	2	3	65,170
Millburn Township	0	1	0	0	0	0	0	1	0	0	20,053
Millville	1	0	0	0	0	0	0	0	0	1	27,272
Monmouth Beach	1	0	0	0	0	0	0	1			3,235
Monroe Township, Gloucester County	1	0	1	0	0	0	0	2	0	0	36,893
Monroe Township, Middlesex County[2]	3	2	1	0	1	0	1	0	2	0	45,653
Montclair[2]	5	3	1	0	0	0	4	3	0	0	38,621
Montgomery Township	2	1	0	0	0	0	2	0	1	0	23,268
Montvale	1	0	0	0	0	0	0	0	0	1	8,643
Montville Township	1	0	0	0	0	0	0	0	1	0	20,982
Mount Laurel Township	4	0	0	0	0	0	0	0	2	2	41,179
Neptune Township	0	0	1	0	0	0	0	1	0	0	27,320
New Brunswick[2]	1	2	3	0	1	1	0	4	1	2	55,701
New Providence	0	1	0	0	0	0	1	0	0	0	13,741
North Bergen Township[2]	1	1	0	0	0	0	0	0	1	0	60,567
Northfield	1	0	0	0	0	0	0	1		0	7,979
North Plainfield	2	0	0	0	0	0	0	1	0	1	21,279
Northvale	1	0	0	0	0	0	0	1	0		4,955
Nutley Township[2]	3	3	0	0	0	0	1	2	0		28,408
Oakland	0	2	0	0	0	0	1	1	0	0	12,929
Ocean City	1	0	0	0	0	0	0	1	0	0	10,893
Ocean Township, Monmouth County[2]	1	2	0	0	0	0	0	1	1	0	26,462
Old Bridge Township[2]	2	1	0	0	0	0	0	0	2	0	65,537
Paramus[2]	4	1	2	0	1	0	1	1	0	5	26,222
Passaic[2]	1	1	1	0	0	1	1	1	1	0	69,610
Paterson	0	1	0	0	0	0	1	0	0	0	144,947
Pemberton Township	1	0	0	0	0	0	0	0	1	0	26,875
Pennington	1	0	0	0	0	0	0	0	1	0	2,575
Pennsauken Township	2	0	0	0	0	0	0	1	1	0	35,698
Pennsville Township	1	0	0	0	0	0	0	0	0	1	12,315
Pequannock Township[2]	0	1	1	0	0	1	0	1		1	14,887
Pine Beach	1	0	0	0	0	0	0	1	0	0	2,192
Piscataway Township[2]	1	1	0	0	0	0	0	0	1	0	56,870
Pitman	1	0	0	0	0	0	0	1		0	8,701
Plainsboro Township	1	0	0	0	0	0	0	1	0	0	22,847
Pohatcong Township	0	0	1	0	0	0	1			0	3,158
Point Pleasant[2]	3	1	0	0	0	0	0	1	1	1	18,842
Princeton	2	0	0	0	0	0	0	2	0	0	31,458
Rahway	2	0	0	0	0	0	1	0	0	1	30,157
Ramsey[2]	0	1	1	0	1	0	0		1	1	14,904
Randolph Township	1	0	0	0	0	0	0	0	0	1	25,311
Raritan	1	0	0	0	0	0	1	0	0	0	7,888
Raritan Township	1	0	0	0	0	1	1	1	0	0	22,402
Red Bank[2]	2	1	0	0	0	0	0	1	0	1	11,929
Ridgewood	0	1	0	0	0	0	0	0	0	1	25,036
River Edge	0	0	0	1	0	0	0	0	1	0	11,431
Riverside Township	0	1	0	0	0	0	1	0	0	0	7,788
Rockaway Township[2]	2	0	2	0	0	0	2	0	0	0	26,046
Roselle[2]	1	1	0	0	0	0	0	0	0	1	21,867
Saddle River	1	0	0	0	0	0	0	0	1		3,170
Scotch Plains Township	1	0	0	0	0	0	0	0	1	0	24,313
Somerville	1	0	0	0	0	0	0	0	0	1	12,084
South Amboy[2]	0	0	1	0	0	1	1	0	0	0	9,235

(Number.)

State/agency	Number of incidents per bias motivation						Number of incidents per quarter				Population[1]
	Race/ Ethnicity/ Ancestry	Religion	Sexual orientation	Disability	Gender	Gender Identity	1st quarter	2nd quarter	3rd quarter	4th quarter	
South Brunswick Township............................	1	0	0	0	0	0	0	0	0	1	45,877
South Plainfield...	2	0	0	0	0	0	0	0	1	1	24,100
Spotswood	1	0	0	0	0	0	0	0	1	0	8,216
Teaneck Township[2].....................................	4	2	0	0	1	0	0	2	2	0	40,290
Toms River Township...................................	1	0	0	0	0	0	0	0	1		94,561
Totowa	0	0	1	0	0	0		1	0		10,777
Trenton	1	0	0	0	0	0	0	1			82,909
Union City[2]	0	0	1	0	0	1	1	0	0	0	68,055
Union Township	0	2	0	0	0	0	0	0	0	2	58,613
Waldwick	0	1	0	0	0	0	0	1	0	0	10,156
Wallington	1	0	0	0	0	0	1	0	0	0	11,499
Warren Township[2].......................................	4	2	0	0	0	0	3	0	1	0	15,689
Washington Township, Bergen County...............	0	1	0	0	0	0	1				9,171
Washington Township, Gloucester County[2]........	2	1	1	0	0	0	1	1	1	0	47,551
Washington Township, Warren County	1	0	0	0	0	0	0	1	0	0	6,323
Wayne Township[2].......................................	12	5	4	0	0	1	1	6	4	4	53,162
Weehawken Township[2]	1	1	0	0	0	0		1	0	0	14,874
Westampton Township	1	0	0	0	0	0	1	0	0	0	8,632
West Amwell Township[2]...............................	2	0	2	0	1	2		1	1		2,728
Westfield	1	1	0	0	0	0	2	0	0	0	29,389
West Milford Township[2]	2	1	0	0	0	0	1	1	0	0	26,310
West New York	1	0	0	0	0	0	0	1	0	0	52,977
Woodbridge Township	2	0	0	0	0	0	0	0	2	0	100,119
Woodbury	4	0	1	0	0	0	0	2	1	2	9,744
Woodcliff Lake[2]..	1	1	0	0	0	0				1	5,845
Wyckoff Township	1	0	0	0	0	0	0	1	0	0	16,950
Universities and Colleges	7	3	5	0	0	0					
Monmouth University	1	0	0	0	0	0		1	0	0	6,704
New Jersey Institute of Technology.....................	1	0	0	0	0	0	0	0	1		13,236
Princeton University	1	2	0	0	0	0	1	1	0	1	8,720
Rutgers University											
Camden[2]..	1	0	1	0	0	0	0	1	0	0	8,154
Newark	1	0	0	0	0	0	1	0	0	0	15,897
New Brunswick	1	1	4	0	0	0	5	1		0	57,162
The College of New Jersey...............................	1	0	0	0	0	0	0	0	0	1	8,825
Metropolitan Counties	2	2	0	0	0	0					
Bergen[2]...	1	1	0	0	0	0	0	0	0	1	
Hudson[2]..	1	1	0	0	0	0	0	0	0	1	
Metropolitan Counties	5	4	0	0	0	0					
State Police[2]...	5	4	0	0	0	0	2	1	2	2	
Other Agencies..	3	3	2	0	0	0					
New Jersey Transit Police[2].............................	3	2	2	0	0	0	3	0	0	3	
Prosecutor, Hudson County...........................	0	1	0	0	0	0	0	0	1	0	
NEW MEXICO											
Total	35	6	9	1	3	2					
Cities	28	5	9	1	3	2					
Albuquerque[2]...	26	3	9	1	2	2	11	9	14	8	562,065
Carlsbad...	1	0	0	0	0	0	0	0	0	1	30,233
Farmington...	1	0	0	0	1	0	1	0	1	0	44,191
Gallup..	0	1	0	0	0	0			1	0	21,460
Sunland Park...	0	1	0	0	0	0	0	0	1	0	18,437
Metropolitan Counties	6	1	0	0	0	0					
Bernalillo..	5	1	0	0	0	0	1	1	2	2	
San Juan...	1	0	0	0	0	0	0	0	1	0	
State Police Agencies	1	0	0	0	0	0					
New Mexico State Police................................	1	0	0	0	0	0			1		
NEW YORK											
Total	200	202	40	0	7	14					
Cities	127	155	30	0	7	12					
Albany..	0	0	1	0	0	0	1	0	0		96,318
Amherst Town	4	0	0	0	0	0	3	1		0	121,304
Binghamton..	0	0	1	0	0	0	0	1	0	0	44,083
Brighton Town	1	1	0	0	0	0	1	0		1	35,853
Buffalo...	5	0	1	0	0	1	0	1	1	5	254,627
Carmel Town	1	0	0	0	0	0	0	0	0	1	34,093

(Number.)

State/agency	Race/ Ethnicity/ Ancestry	Religion	Sexual orientation	Disability	Gender	Gender Identity	1st quarter	2nd quarter	3rd quarter	4th quarter	Population[1]
	Number of incidents per bias motivation						Number of incidents per quarter				
Cheektowaga Town	1	0	0	0	0	0	0	1	0	0	76,536
Clarkstown Town	0	1	0	0	0	0	0	0	0	1	80,462
Cobleskill Village	0	1	0	0	0	0	0	0	1	0	4,323
Colchester Town	1	0	0	0	0	0	1	0		0	1,947
Goshen Village	0	1	0	0	0	0	1	0	0	0	5,361
Greenburgh Town	0	1	0	0	0	0	1	0	0	0	44,727
Hudson	2	0	0	0	0	0	0	2	0	0	6,004
Hyde Park Town	1	0	0	0	0	0	0	0	1		20,766
Ilion Village	1	0	0	0	0	0	0	1	0	0	7,613
Jamestown	1	0	0	0	0	0	0	0	1	0	28,842
Middletown	1	0	0	0	0	0	0	0		1	28,194
Monroe Village	0	1	0	0	0	0	0	0	0	1	8,609
Mount Vernon	4	1	1	0	0	0	0	2	3	1	67,339
New Castle Town	4	0	0	0	0	0	1	0	3	0	17,824
New Rochelle	1	1	0	0	0	0	2	0			78,707
New York	84	144	24	0	7	11	86	50	66	68	8,300,377
Oneida	1	0	0	0	0	0	1	0			10,849
Orangetown Town	0	0	1	0	0	0	0	0	1	0	37,320
Plattsburgh City	1	0	0	0	0	0	0	0	0	1	19,460
Port Washington	0	1	0	0	0	0	0	0	0	1	19,391
Poughkeepsie	1	0	0	0	0	0	0	1	0		30,480
Poughkeepsie Town	2	1	0	0	0	0	1	0	1	1	38,934
Riverhead Town	1	0	0	0	0	0	0	1	0	0	33,461
Rochester	1	0	0	0	0	0	0	0	0	1	205,199
Rome	1	0	0	0	0	0	0	0	1	0	31,978
Southampton Town	1	0	0	0	0	0	0	1		0	51,162
Vestal Town	1	0	0	0	0	0	0	0	1	0	28,639
White Plains	4	0	1	0	0	0	0	1	1	3	58,240
Yorktown Town	1	1	0	0	0	0	1	0	1	0	36,284
Universities and Colleges	3	3	2	0	0	0					
Cornell University	2	0	0	0	0	0	1	0	1	0	24,189
State University of New York Police											
Maritime	0	2	0	0	0	0	2	0	0	0	1,947
Oneonta	0	0	1	0	0	0	1	0			7,131
Plattsburgh	1	1	1	0	0	0	3	0		0	6,475
Metropolitan Counties	23	20	5	0	0	0					
Broome	0	1	0	0	0	0	1	0	0	0	
Monroe	8	0	0	0	0	0	1	2	5	0	
Nassau	7	17	2	0	0	0	4	6	10	6	
Ontario	1	0	0	0	0	0	0	0	0	1	
Saratoga	2	0	2	0	0	0	0	2	1	1	
Suffolk County Police Department	4	1	1	0	0	0	2	3		1	
Westchester Public Safety	1	1	0	0	0	0	1	1		0	
Nonmetropolitan Counties	2	0	0	0	0	0					
Columbia	2	0	0	0	0	0	0	0	0	2	
State Police Agencies	38	17	3	0	0	2					
State Police											
Albany County	1	0	0	0	0	0	1	0	0	0	
Broome County	1	0	3	0	0	0	0	2	1	1	
Cattaraugus County	1	1	0	0	0	0	1	1	0	0	
Cayuga County	1	2	0	0	0	0	2	1	0	0	
Chautauqua County	0	1	0	0	0	0	1	0		0	
Chemung County	1	0	0	0	0	0	0	0	0	1	
Clinton County	5	0	0	0	0	0	1	2	2	0	
Columbia County	2	2	0	0	0	0	2	0	0	2	
Dutchess County	2	1	0	0	0	0	1	0	2	0	
Essex County	3	0	0	0	0	0	0	1	1	1	
Franklin County	1	1	0	0	0	0	1	1	0	0	
Greene County	1	0	0	0	0	0	0	1		0	
Jefferson County	1	1	0	0	0	0	0	1	0	1	
Madison County	1	0	0	0	0	0	0	1	0	0	
New York County	1	0	0	0	0	0	1	0	0	0	
Niagara County	1	0	0	0	0	0	0	1	0		
Ontario County	0	0	0	0	0	1	0	0		1	
Orange County	0	1	0	0	0	1	1	0	1		
Oswego County	2	0	0	0	0	0	0	0	1	1	
Otsego County	0	1	0	0	0	0	1	0	0	0	

Table 13. Hate Crime Incidents Per Bias Motivation and Quarter, by Selected State and Agency and Federal, 2020—*Continued*

(Number.)

State/agency	Number of incidents per bias motivation						Number of incidents per quarter				Population[1]
	Race/Ethnicity/Ancestry	Religion	Sexual orientation	Disability	Gender	Gender Identity	1st quarter	2nd quarter	3rd quarter	4th quarter	
Rockland County	1	1	0	0	0	0	0	1	1	0	
Saratoga County	2	1	0	0	0	0	0	0	1	2	
Schoharie County	1	0	0	0	0	0	0	1	0	0	
Steuben County	1	0	0	0	0	0	0	0	0	1	
Ulster County	1	2	0	0	0	0	0	1	1	1	
Warren County	1	0	0	0	0	0	0	0	1	0	
Wayne County	1	0	0	0	0	0	0	0	1	0	
Westchester County	5	2	0	0	0	0	2	1	2	2	
Other Agencies	7	7	0	0	0	0					
New York City Metropolitan Transportation Authority	7	5	0	0	0	0	6	2	3	1	
State Park											
Finger Lakes Region	0	1	0	0	0	0	0	0	1	0	
Long Island Region	0	1	0	0	0	0	0	0	0	1	
NORTH CAROLINA											
Total	148	12	25	0	1	0					
Cities	120	8	17	0	0	0					
Albemarle	0	0	1	0	0	0	0	1	0	0	16,287
Asheville	5	1	0	0	0	0	0	3	3	0	93,980
Boone	2	0	0	0	0	0	0	0	1	1	19,975
Burgaw	1	0	0	0	0	0	0	0	1	0	4,182
Burlington	3	0	0	0	0	0	0	2	0	1	55,003
Carolina Beach	1	0	0	0	0	0	0	0	1	0	6,479
Chapel Hill	2	0	0	0	0	0	1	0	0	1	64,853
Charlotte-Mecklenburg	13	0	5	0	0	0	4	5	8	1	958,358
Conover	0	0	1	0	0	0	1	0	0	0	8,567
Creedmoor	2	0	0	0	0	0	0	0	2	0	4,669
Durham	12	1	2	0	0	0	4	3	8	0	284,925
Elon	0	1	0	0	0	0	0	1	0	0	12,609
Emerald Isle	1	0	0	0	0	0	0	0	1	0	3,698
Fayetteville	13	0	1	0	0	0	1	6	3	4	212,033
Greensboro	11	1	4	0	0	0	3	5	4	4	299,887
Greenville	2	0	0	0	0	0	1	0	1	0	94,372
High Point	2	0	0	0	0	0	0	1	1	0	113,727
Hope Mills	1	0	0	0	0	0	0	0	1	0	15,924
Kannapolis	1	0	0	0	0	0	1	0	0	0	51,837
Knightdale	1	0	0	0	0	0	0	0	1	0	18,735
Lexington	1	0	0	0	0	0	0	1	0	0	18,933
Lincolnton	2	0	1	0	0	0	1	1	1	0	11,300
Matthews	2	2	0	0	0	0	0	0	1	3	33,860
Mebane	1	0	0	0	0	0	0	0	1	0	16,894
Monroe	1	0	0	0	0	0	0	1	0	0	35,836
Mooresville	1	0	0	0	0	0	0	0	1	0	39,692
Morganton	2	0	0	0	0	0	1	0	0	1	16,550
Morrisville	1	0	0	0	0	0	0	1	0	0	30,264
Newport	1	0	0	0	0	0	0	0	1	0	4,646
Oxford	1	0	0	0	0	0	0	0	1	0	8,934
Pittsboro	1	0	0	0	0	0	0	0	0	1	4,440
Raleigh	16	0	1	0	0	0	0	2	8	7	482,264
Reidsville	6	0	0	0	0	0	0	3	1	2	13,936
Rocky Mount	0	1	0	0	0	0	1	0	0	0	53,520
Salisbury	1	0	0	0	0	0	1	0	0	0	34,045
Scotland Neck	1	0	0	0	0	0	0	0	0	1	1,819
Statesville	5	0	0	0	0	0	1	0	2	2	27,879
Taylortown	0	1	0	0	0	0	0	1	0	0	867
Troy	2	0	0	0	0	0	0	0	0	2	3,194
Warsaw	1	0	0	0	0	0	0	0	1	0	3,086
Weldon	1	0	0	0	0	0	0	0	1	0	1,452
Winston-Salem	0	0	1	0	0	0	1	0		0	250,021
Universities and Colleges	1	0	0	0	0	0					
Western Carolina University	1	0	0	0	0	0	0	0	0	1	13,342
Metropolitan Counties	17	2	6	0	0	0					
Anson	1	0	0	0	0	0	0	0	1	0	
Cabarrus	3	0	1	0	0	0	0	3	1	0	
Currituck	1	0	0	0	0	0	0	0	1	0	
Durham	0	1	0	0	0	0	0	1	0	0	

(Number.)

State/agency	Number of incidents per bias motivation						Number of incidents per quarter				Population[1]
	Race/Ethnicity/Ancestry	Religion	Sexual orientation	Disability	Gender	Gender Identity	1st quarter	2nd quarter	3rd quarter	4th quarter	
Edgecombe	1	0	0	0	0	0	0	0	0	1	
Gaston County Police Department	1	0	0	0	0	0	0	0	1	0	
Guilford	4	0	1	0	0	0	1	2	2	0	
New Hanover	1	0	0	0	0	0	0	0	1	0	
Pamlico	0	0	1	0	0	0	0	0	1	0	
Pitt	1	0	0	0	0	0	0	0	1	0	
Wake	3	1	3	0	0	0	2	0	4	1	
Wayne	1	0	0	0	0	0	0	1	0	0	
Nonmetropolitan Counties	9	2	1	0	1	0					
Carteret[2]	1	0	1	0	0	0	0	1	0	0	
Cleveland	1	0	0	0	0	0	0	0	1	0	
Greene	0	1	0	0	0	0	0	0	1	0	
Hertford	1	0	0	0	0	0	1	0	0	0	
Jackson	2	1	0	0	0	0	0	2	0	1	
McDowell	1	0	0	0	0	0	1	0	0	0	
Montgomery	2	0	0	0	0	0	1	0	0	1	
Swain	1	0	0	0	1	0	0	2	0	0	
Other Agencies	1	0	1	0	0	0					
University of North Carolina Hospitals	1	0	0	0	0	0	0	0	1	0	
WakeMed Campus Police	0	0	1	0	0	0	0	0	0	1	
NORTH DAKOTA											
Total	17	0	3	0	0	1					
Cities	12	0	3	0	0	1					
Bismarck	1	0	0	0	0	0	0	0	0	1	74,997
Dickinson	2	0	0	0	0	0	0	0	1	1	23,801
Fargo	3	0	1	0	0	1	0	1	3	1	126,927
Grand Forks	1	0	1	0	0	0	0	0	2	0	56,163
Napoleon	1	0	0	0	0	0	0	0	1	0	747
Valley City	2	0	0	0	0	0	1	0	0	1	6,288
Watford City	0	0	1	0	0	0	0	0	0	1	9,309
Williston	2	0	0	0	0	0	1	1	0	0	31,046
Universities and Colleges	1	0	0	0	0	0					
University of North Dakota	1	0	0	0	0	0	0	0	1	0	17,050
Metropolitan Counties	2	0	0	0	0	0					
Burleigh	1	0	0	0	0	0	0	1	0	0	
Morton	1	0	0	0	0	0	0	1	0	0	
Nonmetropolitan Counties	2	0	0	0	0	0					
McKenzie	1	0	0	0	0	0	0	1	0	0	
Ward	1	0	0	0	0	0	0	0	1	0	
OHIO											
Total	304	77	69	54	4	34					
Cities	265	57	59	50	3	31					
Akron	3	1	3	2	0	0	1	1	3	4	197,433
Alliance	1	0	1	0	0	0	1	1	0	0	21,356
Arcanum	0	0	2	0	0	0	0	2	0	0	1,997
Ashland	0	0	0	1	0	0	0	0	0	1	20,247
Austintown	1	0	0	0	0	0	0	0	1	0	34,688
Avon Lake	1	0	0	0	0	0	0	0	1	0	24,724
Barberton	2	0	0	0	0	0	0	0	0	2	25,890
Bath Township, Summit County	0	0	0	1	0	0	1	0	0	0	9,635
Bazetta Township	1	0	0	0	0	0	0	0	0	1	5,494
Beavercreek	0	1	0	0	0	0	0	1	0	0	48,029
Beaver Township	1	0	0	0	0	0	0	0	1	0	6,358
Boardman	1	0	0	0	0	0	0	0	0	1	38,625
Butler Township	1	0	1	0	0	0	0	1	0	1	7,816
Canton	2	0	0	0	0	0	0	1	0	1	70,124
Cedarville	0	0	1	0	0	0	0	0	1	0	4,361
Cheviot	1	0	0	0	0	0	1	0	0	0	8,195
Chillicothe	0	4	0	0	0	3	0	3	3	1	21,700
Cincinnati	29	2	3	2	0	0	3	6	18	9	304,724
Circleville	0	2	0	0	0	0	0	2	0	0	14,113
Cleveland[2]	64	13	14	6	3	19	25	26	39	27	379,121
Colerain Township	2	0	0	1	0	0	0	0	2	1	59,307
Columbus[2]	56	7	16	1	0	6	11	25	27	22	911,383
Copley Township	1	0	0	3	0	0	1	1	1	1	17,280

Table 13. Hate Crime Incidents Per Bias Motivation and Quarter, by Selected State and Agency and Federal, 2020—*Continued*

(Number.)

State/agency	Number of incidents per bias motivation						Number of incidents per quarter				
	Race/Ethnicity/Ancestry	Religion	Sexual orientation	Disability	Gender	Gender Identity	1st quarter	2nd quarter	3rd quarter	4th quarter	Population[1]
Dayton	4	0	1	0	0	0	0	3	1	1	140,193
Defiance[2]	1	2	0	0	0	3	0	1	1	3	16,576
Delhi Township	1	0	0	0	0	0	0	0	0	1	29,831
Dublin	1	1	0	0	0	0	0	0	2	0	49,954
Eaton	0	1	0	0	0	0	1	0	0	0	8,118
Elyria	3	0	0	0	0	0	0	0	1	2	53,677
Englewood	3	0	0	0	0	0	0	1	1	1	13,435
Fairfax	0	0	0	1	0	0	0	0	1	0	1,701
Findlay	1	0	0	0	0	0	0	0	1	0	41,237
Gahanna	1	3	0	0	0	0	0	1	0	3	35,738
Garfield Heights	4	0	0	1	0	0		1	4		27,283
Germantown	1	0	0	0	0	0	0	0	1	0	5,517
Green Township	2	0	0	1	0	0	1	0	1	1	59,142
Grove City	1	0	0	0	0	0	0	1	0	0	42,551
Groveport	3	0	0	0	0	0	0	2	0	1	5,649
Hamilton	3	0	0	0	0	0	3				62,053
Hilliard	2	0	0	0	0	0	1	0	0	1	37,585
Huber Heights	0	0	1	6	0	0	1	4	1	1	38,158
Jackson Township, Stark County	2	0	1	0	0	0	0	0	1	2	40,270
Lancaster	3	1	0	0	0	0	1	1	2	0	40,700
Lebanon	2	0	0	0	0	0	1	0	1	0	20,720
Lockland	1	0	0	0	0	0	1	0	0	0	3,440
Lodi	1	0	0	0	0	0	0	0	1	0	2,915
Lyndhurst	1	0	0	0	0	0	0	1	0	0	13,291
Madison Township, Franklin County	0	0	0	1	0	0	0	0	1	0	19,828
Marietta	1	0	0	0	0	0	0	0	1	0	13,281
Mason	4	1	0	0	0	0	1	1	2	1	34,218
Maumee	0	0	1	0	0	0	0	0	1	0	13,605
Medina	0	4	0	0	0	0	0	1	3	0	25,882
Medina Township	1	1	0	0	0	0	0	0	2	0	9,105
Mentor	1	0	0	0	0	0	0	1	0	0	47,275
Miamisburg	1	0	1	0	0	0	1	0	1	0	20,140
Miami Township, Montgomery County	1	0	0	0	0	0	0	1	0	0	29,125
Middletown	6	0	0	2	0	0	3	3	2	0	48,814
Monroe	0	1	0	2	0	0	0	0	1	2	16,663
Mount Healthy	1	0	0	0	0	0	0	1	0	0	6,729
Napoleon	0	1	0	0	0	0	0	1	0	0	8,148
New Albany	3	2	0	0	0	0	2	1	2	0	11,330
Newark	2	0	0	0	0	0	0	2	0	0	50,625
New Franklin	1	0	1	0	0	0	0	1	1	0	14,125
North Canton	0	0	3	0	0	0	2	0	1	0	17,142
North College Hill	1	0	0	0	0	0	0	0	1	0	9,269
North Olmsted	1	0	0	0	0	0	0	0	1	0	31,176
Norton	1	0	0	0	0	0	0	0	0	1	11,951
Norwood	0	0	0	1	0	0	1	0	0		19,843
Perrysburg Township	1	0	0	0	0	0	0	1	0	0	13,011
Pickerington	0	1	0	0	0	0	1	0	0	0	22,631
Pierce Township	1	0	0	0	0	0	0	0	0	1	11,789
Portsmouth	1	1	0	1	0	0	0	1	1	1	20,151
Reynoldsburg	1	0	0	0	0	0	1	0	0	0	38,600
Riverside	1	0	1	0	0	0	0	0	2	0	25,128
Rocky River	1	0	0	0	0	0	0	0	1	0	19,951
Sandusky	0	0	3	0	0	0	0	0	2	1	24,422
Shawnee Township	1	0	0	0	0	0	0	0	1	0	12,044
Shelby	0	0	0	1	0	0	0	1	0	0	9,002
Springfield Township, Hamilton County	3	0	0	1	0	0	1	0	2	1	35,947
Springfield Township, Summit County	1	0	0	2	0	0	0	2	1	0	14,507
St. Clair Township	0	0	0	1	0	0	1	0	0	0	7,436
Streetsboro	1	0	0	0	0	0	0	0	1	0	16,527
Sylvania	1	0	0	0	0	0	0	0	1	0	19,337
Toledo	4	0	1	0	0	0	2	3	0	0	271,237
Trotwood	2	0	0	0	0	0	0	1	1	0	24,399
Troy	1	0	0	0	0	0	0	0	1		26,407
Uniontown	1	0	0	0	0	0	0	0	1	0	3,309
Upper Arlington	0	1	0	0	0	0	0	1	0	0	35,557
Urbana	1	0	1	1	0	0	0	2	1	0	11,351
Vandalia	1	0	0	0	0	0			1		14,968

(Number.)

State/agency	Number of incidents per bias motivation						Number of incidents per quarter				Population[1]
	Race/Ethnicity/Ancestry	Religion	Sexual orientation	Disability	Gender	Gender Identity	1st quarter	2nd quarter	3rd quarter	4th quarter	
Van Wert	0	1	0	0	0	0	0	0	0	1	10,659
Vienna Township	1	0	0	0	0	0	0	0	0	1	3,761
Walbridge	1	0	0	0	0	0		0	0	1	3,169
Wapakoneta	1	0	1	0	0	0	0	0	1	1	9,680
Washington Court House	0	2	0	0	0	0	1	0	1	0	14,076
Waverly	0	2	0	0	0	0	0	2	0	0	4,217
West Chester Township	0	0	0	1	0	0	1	0	0	0	62,685
Willoughby	0	0	0	1	0	0	1	0	0	0	23,058
Wooster	1	0	0	2	0	0	0	2	1	0	26,424
Worthington	0	1	0	1	0	0	0	0	2	0	14,822
Wyoming	0	0	1	0	0	0	0	0	0	1	8,578
Youngstown	1	0	0	0	0	0	1	0			65,316
Zanesville	4	0	1	6	0	0	0	3	5	3	25,136
Universities and Colleges	4	1	0	0	0	0					
Ohio State University, Columbus	3	1	0	0	0	0	0	0	4	0	66,178
Wright State University	1	0	0	0	0	0	0	0	1	0	16,523
Metropolitan Counties	17	2	2	0	0	2					
Clermont	2	0	0	0	0	0	1	0	0	1	
Delaware	1	0	0	0	0	0	0	0	1	0	
Jefferson	1	0	0	0	0	0	0	0	0	1	
Lawrence	1	1	0	0	0	0	0	1	0	1	
Licking	1	0	0	0	0	0	0	0	1	0	
Lorain	1	0	0	0	0	0	1	0	0	0	
Lucas	1	0	0	0	0	0	0	0	1	0	
Medina	1	1	0	0	0	0	0	0	1	1	
Montgomery	4	0	0	0	0	0	1	0	1	2	
Pickaway	1	0	0	0	0	1	1	1	0	0	
Summit	2	0	1	0	0	0	1	1	1	0	
Trumbull	1	0	0	0	0	0	1	0	0	0	
Union	0	0	1	0	0	0	1	0	0	0	
Warren	0	0	0	0	0	1	0	0	0	1	
Nonmetropolitan Counties	13	16	7	4	1	1					
Ashland	1	0	0	0	0	0	0	1	0	0	
Auglaize	1	0	0	0	0	0	0	0	1	0	
Coshocton	0	1	0	0	0	0	0	0	0	1	
Fayette	1	0	0	0	0	0	0	0	1	0	
Logan	1	0	0	1	0	0	0	0	2	0	
Marion	1	0	1	0	0	0	0	0	2	0	
Muskingum	3	0	0	0	0	0	0	0	2	1	
Pike	1	1	1	0	0	0	1	2	0	0	
Preble	0	6	0	0	1	1	1	2	3	2	
Putnam	0	1	0	0	0	0	0	0	0	1	
Ross	2	7	2	0	0	0	0	2	7	2	
Shelby	0	0	0	1	0	0	1	0	0	0	
Vinton	1	0	0	0	0	0	0	0	1	0	
Washington	0	0	3	2	0	0	1	0	2	2	
Wayne	1	0	0	0	0	0	0	0	1		
Other Agencies	5	1	1	0	0	0					
Greater Cleveland Regional Transit Authority	3	0	1	0	0	0	3		1		
Ohio Department of Natural Resources	2	1	0	0	0	0	1	1	1	0	
OKLAHOMA											
Total	4	1	2	1	0	0					
Cities	4	1	1	1	0	0					
Konawa	0	0	1	0	0	0	1	0	0	0	1,186
Oklahoma City	3	1	0	1	0	0	4	1	0	0	663,661
Tulsa	1	0	0	0	0	0	1	0	0	0	402,166
Nonmetropolitan Counties	0	0	1	0	0	0					
McIntosh	0	0	1	0	0	0	1	0	0	0	
OREGON											
Total	203	30	34	6	2	11					
Cities	179	27	29	6	2	9					
Albany	1	0	0	0	0	0	0	0	1	0	55,926
Astoria	2	0	2	0	0	0	3	1	0	0	10,076
Beaverton	1	1	0	0	0	0	0	2	0	0	100,085
Bend	5	7	0	1	0	0	4	1	4	4	103,485

(Number.)

State/agency	Number of incidents per bias motivation						Number of incidents per quarter				Population[1]
	Race/ Ethnicity/ Ancestry	Religion	Sexual orientation	Disability	Gender	Gender Identity	1st quarter	2nd quarter	3rd quarter	4th quarter	
Carlton	1	0	0	0	0	0	0	0	1	0	2,202
Central Point	1	0	0	0	0	0	0	1	0	0	19,032
Coos Bay	1	0	1	0	0	0	0	0	2	0	16,403
Corvallis	1	0	0	0	0	0	0	0	1	0	59,375
Cottage Grove	1	0	0	0	0	0	0	0	0	1	10,556
Dallas	2	1	1	0	0	0	2	1	1	0	17,265
Eugene	29	6	3	3	0	2	11	14	14	4	174,513
Forest Grove	2	0	0	0	0	0	1	0	1	0	26,065
Gladstone	2	0	0	0	0	0	0	1	0	1	12,418
Gresham	1	0	0	0	0	0	1	0	0	0	109,767
Hermiston	1	0	0	0	0	0	0	0	1	0	17,896
Hillsboro[2]	6	0	2	0	0	1	3	1	1	3	111,146
Hood River	2	0	0	0	0	0	0	2	0	0	7,863
Hubbard	0	1	0	0	0	1	0	0	0	2	3,615
Keizer	1	0	0	0	0	0	0	1	0	0	40,087
Klamath Falls	2	0	1	0	0	0	2	0	0	1	22,693
La Grande	4	0	0	1	0	1	0	0	2	4	13,674
Lake Oswego	3	0	0	0	0	0	0	0	1	2	40,171
Lincoln City	6	0	0	0	0	0	1	0	4	1	9,275
McMinnville	2	0	1	0	0	0	0	1	2	0	35,040
Medford	1	0	0	0	0	0	0	1	0	0	84,016
Molalla	0	0	1	0	0	0	0	0	0	1	9,351
Monmouth	1	0	0	0	0	0	0	1	0	0	10,708
Mount Angel	1	0	0	0	0	0	0	0	1	0	3,647
Newberg-Dundee	1	0	0	0	0	0	0	0	1	0	24,081
Newport	2	0	0	0	0	0	2	0	0	0	10,950
North Bend[2]	4	0	1	0	0	0	0	3	0	1	9,778
Ontario	2	0	0	0	0	0	0	0	0	2	10,952
Oregon City	5	0	0	0	0	2	1	3	3	0	37,892
Pendleton	0	0	0	1	0	0	0	1	0	0	16,804
Phoenix	1	0	0	0	0	0	1	0	0	0	4,680
Portland[2]	28	2	9	0	1	0	8	10	10	10	662,941
Rainier[2]	1	0	1	0	0	0	0	0	0	1	2,021
Reedsport	1	1	0	0	0	0	0	2	0	0	4,111
Roseburg	1	0	0	0	0	0	0	1	0	0	23,551
Salem[2]	21	2	5	0	0	2	6	9	8	6	176,632
Sherwood	2	0	0	0	0	0	1	1	0	0	20,052
Silverton	1	0	0	0	0	0	0	1	0	0	10,782
Springfield	7	3	0	0	0	0	0	4	3	3	63,666
Sutherlin	1	0	0	0	0	0	0	0	0	1	8,223
Talent	0	1	0	0	0	0	0	0	0	1	6,671
Tigard	11	1	1	0	0	0	2	5	4	2	56,377
Tualatin	4	0	0	0	1	0	0	1	1	3	28,030
Turner	1	0	0	0	0	0	0	0	1	0	2,153
Umatilla	2	0	0	0	0	0	0	0	1	1	7,366
West Linn	2	1	0	0	0	0	0	0	2	1	26,916
Woodburn	1	0	0	0	0	0	0	0	0	1	26,521
Universities and Colleges	1	1	0	0	0	0					
Portland State University	1	1	0	0	0	0	2	0	0	0	32,445
Metropolitan Counties	15	1	2	0	0	2					
Clackamas	8	0	0	0	0	1	2	0	3	4	
Jackson	1	0	0	0	0	1	1	1	0	0	
Josephine	0	0	2	0	0	0	1	0	1	0	
Linn	1	0	0	0	0	0	0	0	1	0	
Polk	3	0	0	0	0	0	0	3	0	0	
Washington	2	0	0	0	0	0	0	1	0	1	
Yamhill	0	1	0	0	0	0	0	1	0	0	
Nonmetropolitan Counties	5	1	2	0	0	0					
Jefferson	2	0	0	0	0	0	0	0	0	2	
Klamath	2	0	1	0	0	0			1	2	
Lincoln	1	0	0	0	0	0	1	0	0	0	
Tillamook	0	0	1	0	0	0	0	0	0	1	
Union	0	1	0	0	0	0	0	0	1	0	
State Police Agencies	3	0	1	0	0	0					
State Police											
Benton County	1	0	0	0	0	0	0	1	0	0	
Columbia County	1	0	0	0	0	0	0	1	0	0	
Marion County	1	0	1	0	0	0	0	0	2	0	

(Number.)

State/agency	Number of incidents per bias motivation						Number of incidents per quarter				Population[1]
	Race/ Ethnicity/ Ancestry	Religion	Sexual orientation	Disability	Gender	Gender Identity	1st quarter	2nd quarter	3rd quarter	4th quarter	
PENNSYLVANIA											
Total	62	13	5	0	0	2					
Cities	58	13	4	0	0	2					
Altoona.................	2	0	0	0	0	0	0	0	1	1	43,090
East Earl Township	1	0	0	0	0	0	1	0	0	0	6,934
East Pennsboro Township....................	1	1	0	0	0	0	1	1	0	0	21,556
Gettysburg.................	1	0	0	0	0	0				1	7,738
Johnsonburg.................	1	0	0	0	0	0	0	1	0	0	2,271
Meadville.................	2	0	0	0	0	0	0	2	0	0	12,579
New Hope	1	0	0	0	0	0	0	1	0	0	2,530
Philadelphia.................	36	9	3	0	0	2	19	10	15	6	1,586,666
Pittsburgh.................	3	2	0	0	0	0	0	2	2	1	298,608
Pocono Mountain Regional	1	0	0	0	0	0	0	1	0	0	43,250
Pottsville.................	1	0	0	0	0	0			1		13,384
Reading.................	2	0	0	0	0	0	1	1	0	0	88,412
Southern Chester County Regional	0	1	0	0	0	0	0	0	0	1	16,477
South Greensburg.................	1	0	0	0	0	0	0	1	0	0	1,983
State College.................	1	0	0	0	0	0	0	1	0	0	58,471
Upper Darby Township.................	1	0	0	0	0	0	0	0	0	1	82,947
Upper Moreland Township[2]	3	0	1	0	0	0	0	0	2	1	24,031
Universities and Colleges	4	0	1	0	0	0					
Lehigh University.................	1	0	0	0	0	0		0	1	0	7,330
Pennsylvania State University, University Park.......	1	0	1	0	0	0		0	1	1	49,935
Shippensburg University.................	2	0	0	0	0	0	1	0	1	0	7,138
RHODE ISLAND											
Total	4	4	5	0	0	1					
Cities	4	2	3	0	0	0					
Barrington.................	0	1	0	0	0	0	0	0	1	0	15,986
Burrillville.................	0	0	1	0	0	0	1	0	0	0	16,904
Coventry.................	1	0	0	0	0	0	0	1	0	0	34,740
Cranston.................	1	0	0	0	0	0	0	1	0	0	81,313
Lincoln.................	0	1	0	0	0	0	1	0	0	0	22,029
Pawtucket.................	1	0	1	0	0	0	0	1	0	1	72,017
Providence.................	1	0	0	0	0	0	0	1	0	0	179,603
Tiverton.................	0	0	1	0	0	0	0	0	1	0	15,604
Universities and Colleges	0	2	2	0	0	1					
Brown University.................	0	2	2	0	0	1	4	0	1	0	10,760
SOUTH CAROLINA											
Total	58	31	12	1	4	4					
Cities	35	3	8	1	1	3					
Aiken.................	0	1	0	0	1	0	0	1	0	1	31,007
Batesburg-Leesville.................	1	0	0	0	0	0	0	0	1	0	5,419
Calhoun Falls.................	7	0	0	0	0	0	1	0	1	5	1,892
Cayce.................	1	0	0	0	0	0	0	0	0	1	14,117
Charleston.................	5	0	2	0	0	0	1	2	2	2	139,582
Chester.................	1	0	0	0	0	0	0	0	0	1	5,354
Chesterfield.................	1	0	0	0	0	0	0	1	0	0	1,409
Columbia.................	2	0	0	0	0	0	0	1	1	0	131,777
Easley.................	0	0	0	0	0	1	1	0	0	0	21,512
Florence.................	1	0	2	0	0	0	0	1	0	2	38,597
Fort Mill.................	1	0	0	0	0	0	0	1	0	0	23,966
Gaffney.................	2	0	0	0	0	0	0	0	2	0	12,631
Goose Creek.................	1	0	0	0	0	0	0	0	0	1	44,522
Hartsville.................	1	0	1	0	0	0	0	0	1	1	7,519
Lake View.................	3	0	0	0	0	0	0	0	2	1	752
Landrum.................	0	0	0	1	0	0	0	0	1	0	2,713
Lexington.................	1	0	0	0	0	0	0	0	1	0	22,592
Mauldin.................	0	0	0	0	0	1	0	1	0	0	25,662
Moncks Corner.................	1	1	0	0	0	0	0	1	0	1	12,580
Myrtle Beach.................	1	0	1	0	0	0	1	0	0	1	35,658
North Myrtle Beach.................	0	0	1	0	0	1	0	0	1	1	17,183
Orangeburg.................	1	0	0	0	0	0	1	0	0	0	12,529
Pickens.................	1	0	0	0	0	0	0	0	0	1	3,177
Port Royal.................	1	0	0	0	0	0	0	0	0	1	13,553
Rock Hill.................	0	1	0	0	0	0	0	0	1	0	76,016

Table 13. Hate Crime Incidents Per Bias Motivation and Quarter, by Selected State and Agency and Federal, 2020—*Continued*

(Number.)

State/agency	Race/ Ethnicity/ Ancestry	Religion	Sexual orientation	Disability	Gender	Gender Identity	1st quarter	2nd quarter	3rd quarter	4th quarter	Population[1]
Walterboro	0	0	1	0	0	0	1	0	0	0	5,387
Winnsboro	1	0	0	0	0	0	0	0	1	0	3,144
York	1	0	0	0	0	0	1	0	0	0	8,486
Universities and Colleges	1	0	0	0	0	0					
University of South Carolina, Columbia	1	0	0	0	0	0	1	0	0	0	37,510
Metropolitan Counties	12	21	4	0	3	1					
Anderson	1	0	0	0	0	0	0	1	0	0	
Beaufort	2	0	0	0	0	0	0	0	1	1	
Berkeley	0	20	1	0	0	0	5	4	9	3	
Charleston	3	1	0	0	0	0	1	1	2	0	
Laurens	1	0	0	0	0	0	0	0	1	0	
Pickens	2	0	0	0	0	0	0	0	1	1	
Richland	3	0	3	0	3	1	2	4	2	2	
Nonmetropolitan Counties	6	7	0	0	0	0					
Allendale	1	0	0	0	0	0	0	1	0	0	
Bamberg	0	4	0	0	0	0	1	2	0	1	
Chesterfield	1	1	0	0	0	0	2	0	0	0	
Georgetown	2	0	0	0	0	0	1	0	0	1	
Oconee	0	2	0	0	0	0	0	0	1	1	
Orangeburg	2	0	0	0	0	0	0	2	0	0	
State Police Agencies	4	0	0	0	0	0					
Highway Patrol											
Chesterfield County	1	0	0	0	0	0	0	1	0	0	
Lancaster County	1	0	0	0	0	0	0	0	0	1	
Lee County	1	0	0	0	0	0	0	1	0	0	
York County	1	0	0	0	0	0	0	0	1	0	
SOUTH DAKOTA											
Total	15	0	1	0	0	1					
Cities	10	0	1	0	0	1					
Aberdeen	1	0	0	0	0	0	0	0	1	0	28,494
Box Elder	1	0	0	0	0	0	0	0	0	1	10,402
Flandreau	1	0	0	0	0	0	0	0	1	0	2,314
Madison	0	0	1	0	0	0	0	0	1	0	7,357
Mobridge	2	0	0	0	0	0	0	0	1	1	3,442
Rapid City	2	0	0	0	0	1	0	0	2	1	78,492
Sioux Falls	1	0	0	0	0	0	0	0	1	0	187,370
Tea	1	0	0	0	0	0	0	1	0	0	6,340
Watertown	1	0	0	0	0	0	0	0	1	0	22,248
Nonmetropolitan Counties	4	0	0	0	0	0					
Brookings	1	0	0	0	0	0	0	1	0	0	
Brown	1	0	0	0	0	0	1	0	0	0	
Marshall	1	0	0	0	0	0	0	0	1	0	
Roberts	1	0	0	0	0	0	1	0	0	0	
Tribal Agencies	1	0	0	0	0	0					
Sisseton-Wahpeton Tribal	1	0	0	0	0	0	0	0	0	1	
TENNESSEE											
Total	56	4	16	2	0	2					
Cities	43	4	12	2	0	1					
Cleveland	9	0	0	0	0	0	1	3	3	2	45,994
Collierville	1	0	1	0	0	1	1	0	1	1	51,677
Fairview	1	0	0	0	0	0	0	0	1	0	9,300
Franklin	2	1	0	0	0	0	2	1	0	0	85,722
Germantown	2	0	0	0	0	0	0	0	1	1	39,264
Goodlettsville	0	0	1	0	0	0	1	0	0	0	16,896
Hendersonville	0	0	1	0	0	0	0	0	1	0	58,901
Jackson	3	0	1	2	0	0	2	1	1	2	67,234
Knoxville	3	0	2	0	0	0	1	2	2	0	188,672
Lebanon	3	0	0	0	0	0	0	0	2	1	37,832
Manchester	3	0	0	0	0	0	0	1	1	1	11,145
Maryville	1	0	0	0	0	0	0	1	0	0	30,006
Memphis	5	1	4	0	0	0	2	3	2	3	650,937
Metropolitan Nashville Police Department	3	1	2	0	0	0	0	2	2	2	688,013
Murfreesboro	3	0	0	0	0	0	0	1	0	2	151,769
Pigeon Forge	1	0	0	0	0	0	0	1	0	0	6,311
Rogersville	1	0	0	0	0	0	0	0	1	0	4,368

Table 13. Hate Crime Incidents Per Bias Motivation and Quarter, by Selected State and Agency and Federal, 2020—*Continued*

(Number.)

State/agency	Number of incidents per bias motivation						Number of incidents per quarter				Population[1]
	Race/ Ethnicity/ Ancestry	Religion	Sexual orientation	Disability	Gender	Gender Identity	1st quarter	2nd quarter	3rd quarter	4th quarter	
Shelbyville	1	0	0	0	0	0	0	0	0	1	22,306
Spring Hill[2]	1	1	0	0	0	0	1	0	0	0	45,765
Universities and Colleges	1	0	0	0	0	0					
Vanderbilt University	1	0	0	0	0	0	1	0	0	0	13,634
Metropolitan Counties	11	0	2	0	0	1					
Anderson	1	0	1	0	0	0	0	0	0	2	
Blount	4	0	0	0	0	0	1	2	0	1	
Knox[2]	1	0	0	0	0	1	0	0	1	0	
Montgomery	1	0	0	0	0	0	0	1	0	0	
Rutherford	1	0	0	0	0	0	1	0	0	0	
Shelby	2	0	0	0	0	0	1	1	0	0	
Washington	1	0	1	0	0	0	0	2	0	0	
Nonmetropolitan Counties	1	0	2	0	0	0					
Cocke	0	0	1	0	0	0	0	0	0	1	
Warren	1	0	1	0	0	0	1	0	0	1	
TEXAS											
Total	288	31	70	6	9	7					
Cities	248	27	62	3	8	7					
Abilene[2]	3	3	0	0	0	0	0	0	5	0	124,061
Addison	1	0	0	0	0	0	1	0	0	0	16,778
Amarillo	2	0	0	0	0	0	0	0	1	1	200,296
Anna	1	0	0	0	0	0	0	0	0	1	16,036
Aransas Pass	0	0	1	0	0	0	0	1	0	0	8,414
Arlington	13	0	0	0	0	0	4	6	2	1	402,700
Austin[2]	13	2	8	0	0	2	3	9	4	6	1,000,276
Baird	1	0	0	0	0	0	0	0	1	0	1,485
Balch Springs	0	0	1	0	0	0	0	1	0	0	25,189
Beaumont	0	0	1	0	0	0	0	0	0	1	116,766
Bellmead	0	0	1	0	0	0	1	0	0	0	10,835
Benbrook	1	0	0	0	0	0	0	1	0	0	23,766
Brenham	1	1	0	0	0	1	2	0	1	0	18,106
Burkburnett	1	0	0	0	0	0	0	0	1	0	11,321
Burleson	1	0	0	0	0	0	0	0	0	1	49,660
Caldwell	1	0	0	0	0	0	0	0	0	1	4,403
Carrollton	4	0	1	0	0	0	0	1	1	3	141,745
Cedar Park	2	0	1	0	0	0	0	0	2	1	82,653
Cibolo	1	0	0	0	0	0	0	1	0	0	32,777
Cleburne	0	1	0	0	0	0	1	0	0	0	31,486
Clifton	1	0	0	0	0	0	0	1	0	0	3,446
College Station	1	1	0	0	0	0	0	0	1	1	120,831
Comanche	0	1	0	0	0	0	0	1	0	0	4,183
Coppell	4	0	0	0	0	0	1	3	0	0	41,807
Corpus Christi	2	0	0	0	0	0	0	1	1	0	329,050
Corrigan	1	0	0	0	0	0	0	0	1	0	1,613
Crockett	1	0	0	0	0	0	0	0	1	0	6,327
Crowley	1	0	0	0	0	0	0	0	1	0	16,909
Dallas	24	3	11	0	0	0	5	10	17	6	1,363,028
Deer Park	1	0	0	0	0	0	0	0	1	0	33,631
Denton	8	0	0	0	0	0	1	2	2	3	144,569
Elgin	2	1	0	0	0	0	1	1	0	1	10,567
El Paso	2	0	0	0	5	0	0	0	0	7	685,288
Fort Worth	4	1	5	1	0	0	6	2	2	1	929,509
Galena Park	3	0	0	0	0	0	0	0	1	2	10,740
Garland	3	0	0	0	0	0	0	0	2	1	241,845
Gatesville	0	2	0	0	0	0	0	0	2	0	12,394
Greenville	1	0	0	0	0	0	0	1	0	0	29,209
Hamilton	1	0	0	0	0	0	1	0	0	0	3,005
Hempstead	1	0	0	0	0	0	0	0	1	0	8,699
Henderson	2	0	0	0	0	0	0	0	1	1	13,093
Hewitt	1	1	0	0	0	0	1	0	0	1	15,092
Hollywood Park	1	0	0	0	0	0	0	0	1	0	3,370
Houston	31	1	8	0	0	3	7	23	12	1	2,346,155
Huntsville	0	0	1	0	0	0	0	0	1	0	42,648
Hurst	6	0	0	0	0	0	0	2	4	0	38,796
Irving	1	1	1	0	0	0	2	1	0	0	242,976
Jarrell	1	0	0	0	0	0	0	0	0	1	1,953

(Number.)

State/agency	Number of incidents per bias motivation						Number of incidents per quarter				Population[1]
	Race/Ethnicity/Ancestry	Religion	Sexual orientation	Disability	Gender	Gender Identity	1st quarter	2nd quarter	3rd quarter	4th quarter	
Jonestown	1	0	0	0	0	0	0	1	0	0	2,139
Kaufman	0	1	0	0	0	0	0	0	0	1	7,930
Kennedale	1	0	0	0	0	0	0	0	1	0	8,881
Killeen	0	0	1	0	0	0	1	0	0	0	154,417
Kingsville	1	0	0	0	0	0	1	0	0	0	25,195
Kyle	1	0	0	0	0	0	0	0	0	1	51,306
Lacy-Lakeview	1	0	0	0	0	0	0	0	0	1	6,748
Lampasas	1	0	0	0	0	0	0	0	1	0	8,132
Laredo	0	0	1	0	0	0	0	1	0	0	265,515
Leander	2	0	0	0	1	0	0	3	0	0	68,571
Leon Valley	3	1	0	0	0	0	0	0	2	2	12,453
Little Elm	1	0	0	0	0	0	0	0	0	1	57,482
Live Oak	0	0	1	0	0	0	0	0	0	1	16,910
Lockhart	2	0	0	0	0	0	0	0	1	1	14,297
Lubbock	5	0	2	0	0	0	1	0	2	4	262,146
Lytle	1	0	0	0	0	0	1	0	0	0	3,135
Mansfield	1	0	0	0	0	0	0	0	0	1	74,360
McKinney	5	0	2	0	0	0	1	0	3	3	208,335
Mesquite	0	0	1	0	0	0	0	0	1	0	141,325
Midland	1	0	0	0	0	0	1	0	0	0	150,529
Missouri City	0	0	0	1	1	0	0	1	0	1	76,476
Montgomery	0	0	0	0	1	0	1	0	0	0	1,488
Mount Pleasant	1	0	0	0	0	0	0	0	0	1	15,974
Navasota	1	0	0	0	0	0	0	1	0	0	8,104
New Boston	0	1	0	0	0	0	0	0	0	1	4,588
New Braunfels	2	0	0	0	0	0	0	1	0	1	94,751
Odessa	0	0	2	0	0	0	0	0	2	0	126,288
Palestine	2	1	0	0	0	0	0	1	1	1	17,625
Pampa	2	0	0	0	0	0	0	1	1	0	16,975
Pasadena	2	0	0	0	0	0	0	1	1	0	151,421
Pelican Bay	0	0	1	0	0	0	0	0	1	0	2,064
Plainview	1	0	1	0	0	0	0	1	0	1	19,926
Plano	1	1	0	0	0	0	0	2	0	0	290,786
Pleasanton	3	0	0	0	0	0	0	0	2	1	11,006
Rio Grande City	4	0	0	1	0	0	1	2	0	2	14,587
Robinson	1	0	0	0	0	0	1	0	0	0	12,087
Rockport	0	0	1	0	0	0	0	0	0	1	10,672
Round Rock	4	0	0	0	0	0	0	0	3	1	137,593
Rowlett	2	0	0	0	0	0	0	2	0	0	68,810
San Antonio	10	2	3	0	0	1	3	8	4	1	1,573,189
San Saba	3	1	0	0	0	0	2	0	2	0	3,164
Seabrook	6	0	0	0	0	0	0	4	2	0	14,415
Sherman	3	0	0	0	0	0	0	0	2	1	44,611
Silsbee	1	0	0	0	0	0	0	0	0	1	6,613
Spur	4	0	0	0	0	0	2	0	2	0	1,186
Stafford	1	0	0	0	0	0	0	0	1	0	17,423
Sugar Land	1	0	0	0	0	0	1	0	0	0	119,671
Sweeny	1	0	0	0	0	0	0	0	0	1	3,716
Texas City	2	0	1	0	0	0	1	0	2	0	50,660
The Colony	4	0	0	0	0	0	0	1	3	0	45,419
Tyler	1	0	3	0	0	0	1	1	0	2	108,139
University Park	1	0	0	0	0	0	0	0	1	0	25,253
Uvalde	2	0	0	0	0	0	0	0	0	2	16,027
Victoria	1	0	0	0	0	0	0	0	1	0	67,407
Waco	1	0	0	0	0	0	0	0	0	1	140,870
Watauga	2	0	0	0	0	0	0	1	1	0	24,588
West[2]	1	0	1	0	0	0	1	0	0	0	3,008
Willis	0	0	1	0	0	0	0	0	0	1	7,166
Universities and Colleges	7	1	3	0	0	0					
Angelo State University	0	1	0	0	0	0	0	0	1	0	11,737
Trinity Valley Community College	4	0	0	0	0	0	1	0	2	1	9,896
University of Texas											
Arlington	1	0	2	0	0	0	0	0	0	3	60,035
Austin	2	0	0	0	0	0	1	0	0	1	55,128
Permian Basin	0	0	1	0	0	0	0	1	0	0	8,165
Metropolitan Counties	26	2	4	3	0	0					
Ellis	4	0	0	1	0	0	0	1	1	3	

Table 13. Hate Crime Incidents Per Bias Motivation and Quarter, by Selected State and Agency and Federal, 2020—*Continued*

(Number.)

State/agency	Race/Ethnicity/Ancestry	Religion	Sexual orientation	Disability	Gender	Gender Identity	1st quarter	2nd quarter	3rd quarter	4th quarter	Population[1]
Fort Bend	5	0	0	0	0	0	0	4	0	1	
Galveston	1	0	1	0	0	0	0	1	0	1	
Harris	5	1	0	0	0	0	2	2	2	0	
Johnson	1	0	0	0	0	0	0	1	0	0	
Lubbock	1	0	0	2	0	0	0	0	0	3	
Parker	0	0	1	0	0	0	1	0	0		
Potter	1	0	0	0	0	0	1	0	0	0	
Tarrant	1	1	0	0	0	0	0	0	1	1	
Travis	5	0	0	0	0	0	3	0	1	1	
Williamson	2	0	2	0	0	0	0	3	1	0	
Nonmetropolitan Counties	5	1	1	0	1	0					
Cherokee	0	0	1	0	0	0	1	0	0	0	
Hill	1	0	0	0	0	0	0	0	0	1	
Moore	1	0	0	0	0	0	0	1	0	0	
San Augustine	0	0	0	0	1	0	0	1	0	0	
Van Zandt	2	0	0	0	0	0	0	1	0	1	
Willacy	1	0	0	0	0	0	0	0	0	1	
Zavala	0	1	0	0	0	0	0	0	0	1	
Other Agencies	2	0	0	0	0	0					
Independent School District											
Barbers Hill	1	0	0	0	0	0	0	0	0	1	
Houston	1	0	0	0	0	0	0	0	0	1	
UTAH											
Total	20	12	6	1	0	7					
Cities	14	6	4	1	0	5					
Ephraim	3	0	0	0	0	0	0	3	0	0	7,450
Layton	1	1	0	0	0	1	0	1	0	2	79,240
Lindon	0	0	0	0	0	2	0	2	0	0	11,218
North Salt Lake	0	0	1	0	0	0	0	0	0	1	21,540
Ogden	0	0	0	0	0	1	0	0	1	0	88,309
Perry	1	0	0	0	0	0	0	0	1	0	5,335
Price	0	0	0	0	0	1	1	0	0	0	8,291
Roosevelt	2	0	0	0	0	0	0	1	1	0	7,359
Salem	0	1	0	0	0	0	1	0	0	0	8,902
Salt Lake City[2]	1	0	2	0	0	0	0	1	1	0	202,187
Springville	1	0	0	0	0	0	0	0	0	1	33,728
Sunset	0	2	0	0	0	0	0	2	0	0	5,387
Tooele[2]	3	1	0	0	0	0			1	2	36,527
Washington	0	0	1	0	0	0	0	0	0	1	30,622
West Valley	2	1	0	1	0	0	1	1	2	0	135,887
Universities and Colleges	0	0	1	0	0	0					
Dixie State University	0	0	1	0	0	0	0	1	0	0	12,263
Metropolitan Counties	1	4	0	0	0	2					
Davis	1	0	0	0	0	0	0	0	0	1	
Tooele	0	2	0	0	0	2			0	4	
Weber	0	2	0	0	0	0	0	1	0	1	
Nonmetropolitan Counties	0	1	0	0	0	0					
Sanpete	0	1	0	0	0	0	0	1	0	0	
State Police Agencies	1	0	0	0	0	0					
Utah Highway Patrol	1	0	0	0	0	0	0	1	0	0	
Other Agencies	4	1	1	0	0	0					
Parks and Recreation	2	0	0	0	0	0	0	2	0	0	
Utah Transit Authority	2	1	1	0	0	0	1	2	0	1	
VERMONT											
Total	42	9	6	3	0	0					
Cities	24	7	5	3	0	0					
Barre	1	1	0	0	0	0	0	0	1	1	8,471
Bellows Falls	0	0	0	1	0	0	0	0	0	1	2,946
Burlington	1	0	1	0	0	0	0	0	1	1	42,862
Colchester	0	0	1	0	0	0	0	0	1	0	17,129
Dover	0	1	0	0	0	0	0	0	1	0	1,052
Essex	2	0	0	0	0	0	0	0	1	1	22,156
Hartford	0	2	1	0	0	0	1	1	0	1	9,515
Manchester	2	0	0	0	0	0	0	0	1	1	4,206
Middlebury	5	0	0	0	0	0	0	0	3	2	8,813

(Number.)

State/agency	Number of incidents per bias motivation						Number of incidents per quarter				Population[1]
	Race/Ethnicity/Ancestry	Religion	Sexual orientation	Disability	Gender	Gender Identity	1st quarter	2nd quarter	3rd quarter	4th quarter	
Milton	2	0	0	1	0	0	0	1	2	0	10,882
Montpelier	1	1	0	0	0	0	0	1	1	0	7,321
Morristown	2	0	0	0	0	0	0	0	2	0	5,532
Norwich	1	0	0	0	0	0	0	0	1	0	3,409
Rutland	1	0	0	0	0	0	1	0	0	0	14,930
South Burlington	2	1	1	0	0	0	0	1	0	3	19,690
St. Albans	1	1	1	1	0	0	1	1	1	1	6,788
Stowe	1	0	0	0	0	0	0	0	1	0	4,444
Winooski	2	0	0	0	0	0	0	0	0	2	7,341
Universities and Colleges	2	0	0	0	0	0					
University of Vermont	2	0	0	0	0	0	1	0	1	0	15,698
Metropolitan Counties	1	0	0	0	0	0					
Grand Isle	1	0	0	0	0	0	0	1	0	0	
Nonmetropolitan Counties	5	0	0	0	0	0					
Lamoille	2	0	0	0	0	0	0	1	1	0	
Rutland	1	0	0	0	0	0	0	0	1	0	
Windham	2	0	0	0	0	0	0	0	2	0	
State Police Agencies	10	2	1	0	0	0					
State Police											
New Haven	1	2	0	0	0	0	1	0	0	2	
Rutland	1	0	0	0	0	0	0	0	1	0	
St. Albans	1	0	0	0	0	0	0	0	1	0	
Westminster	4	0	0	0	0	0	0	0	4	0	
Williston	3	0	1	0	0	0	0	0	3	1	
VIRGINIA											
Total	123	22	23	1	0	1					
Cities	44	8	9	1	0	0					
Alexandria	0	1	1	0	0	0	0	1	0	1	161,525
Bedford	1	0	0	0	0	0	0	1	0	0	6,601
Bristol	0	1	0	0	0	0	0	0	1	0	16,640
Chesapeake	2	0	0	0	0	0	0	1	0	1	247,118
Christiansburg	1	0	0	0	0	0	0	0	0	1	22,643
Front Royal	1	0	0	0	0	0	0	0	1	0	15,387
Hampton	1	0	0	0	0	0	0	0	0	1	134,082
Harrisonburg	0	0	1	0	0	0	1	0	0	0	53,442
Hopewell	1	0	0	0	0	0	0	0	1	0	22,498
Leesburg	18	4	0	0	0	0	0	16	6	0	55,070
Lynchburg	1	0	1	0	0	0	0	0	1	1	82,871
Manassas Park	1	0	0	0	0	0	0	1	0	0	17,839
Marion	1	0	0	0	0	0	0	1	0	0	5,515
Newport News	2	0	2	0	0	0	3	0	0	1	178,896
Norfolk	1	0	1	0	0	0	0	1	1	0	242,516
Pennington Gap	0	0	1	0	0	0	0	0	1	0	1,705
Portsmouth	1	0	1	0	0	0	1	0	1	0	94,205
Radford	1	0	0	0	0	0	0	0	1	0	18,450
Rich Creek	1	0	0	0	0	0	0	0	0	1	738
Richmond	1	1	0	1	0	0	0	0	1	2	233,350
South Boston	0	0	1	0	0	0	1	0	0	0	7,528
Suffolk	3	0	0	0	0	0	0	2	1	0	92,881
Vienna	1	0	0	0	0	0	1	0	0	0	16,570
Vinton	0	1	0	0	0	0	1	0	0	0	8,117
Virginia Beach	3	0	0	0	0	0	1	2	0	0	450,858
Waynesboro	1	0	0	0	0	0	0	0	0	1	22,801
West Point	1	0	0	0	0	0	0	0	0	1	3,250
Universities and Colleges	8	2	2	0	0	0					
Christopher Newport University	0	0	1	0	0	0	1	0	0	0	5,117
College of William and Mary	1	0	0	0	0	0	1	0	0	0	9,765
George Mason University	0	1	0	0	0	0	1	0	0	0	48,678
James Madison University	1	0	0	0	0	0	0	0	0	1	24,152
Northern Virginia Community College	1	0	0	0	0	0	1	0	0	0	73,642
Old Dominion University	1	0	0	0	0	0	1	0	0	0	28,046
University of Richmond	3	1	0	0	0	0	4	0	0	0	4,602
University of Virginia	0	0	1	0	0	0	0	0	1	0	28,593
Virginia Commonwealth University	1	0	0	0	0	0	0	0	1	0	33,462
Metropolitan Counties	65	10	11	0	0	1					
Albemarle County Police Department	2	0	0	0	0	0	0	0	1	1	

(Number.)

State/agency	Number of incidents per bias motivation						Number of incidents per quarter				Population[1]
	Race/ Ethnicity/ Ancestry	Religion	Sexual orientation	Disability	Gender	Gender Identity	1st quarter	2nd quarter	3rd quarter	4th quarter	
Amherst..	1	0	1	0	0	0	1	0	0	1	
Arlington County Police Department...................	1	1	0	0	0	0	1	0	1	0	
Augusta...	1	0	0	0	0	0	0	1	0	0	
Botetourt...	1	0	0	0	0	0	0	0	1	0	
Chesterfield County Police Department..............	5	1	0	0	0	0	1	4	1	0	
Clarke..	2	0	0	0	0	0	0	0	2	0	
Fairfax County Police Department	30	4	3	0	0	0	10	11	7	9	
Hanover...	3	0	0	0	0	0	0	3	0	0	
Henrico County Police Department	3	0	0	0	0	0	1	0	1	1	
James City County Police Department	1	0	1	0	0	0	1	0	0	1	
Loudoun..	6	3	3	0	0	0	3	1	6	2	
Montgomery...	1	0	0	0	0	0	0	0	1	0	
Nelson...	0	0	1	0	0	0	0	0	1	0	
New Kent..	1	0	0	0	0	0	0	1	0	0	
Powhatan..	0	1	0	0	0	0	1	0	0	0	
Prince William County Police Department...........	1	0	0	0	0	1	0	1	1	0	
Rockingham...	1	0	0	0	0	0	0	1	0	0	
Spotsylvania..	2	0	2	0	0	0	1	0	2	1	
Stafford...	3	0	0	0	0	0	2	1	0	0	
Nonmetropolitan Counties...........................	2	1	1	0	0	0					
King George	0	1	0	0	0	0	0	1	0	0	
Louisa	1	0	0	0	0	0	0	0	1	0	
Orange	1	0	0	0	0	0	0	1	0	0	
Patrick	0	0	1	0	0	0	0	0	0	1	
State Police Agencies	4	1	0	0	0	0					
State Police											
Brunswick County..	1	0	0	0	0	0	0	1	0	0	
Goochland County..	1	0	0	0	0	0	0	0	0	1	
Grayson County..	0	1	0	0	0	0	1	0	0	0	
Roanoke...	1	0	0	0	0	0	0	0	0	1	
Smyth County...	1	0	0	0	0	0	0	1	0	0	
WASHINGTON											
Total	309	52	67	5	6	23					
Cities	258	36	60	4	6	15					
Aberdeen...	0	0	0	0	0	1	1	0	0	0	16,744
Airway Heights	1	0	0	0	0	0	0	1	0		10,010
Arlington	2	0	0	0	0	0	2	0	0	0	20,825
Auburn	1	1	0	0	0	0	1	1	0	0	82,779
Bainbridge Island	0	0	1	0	0	0	0	0	1	0	25,561
Bellevue	11	2	4	0	0	1	4	3	6	5	150,548
Bellingham...	9	2	3	0	0	0	3	7	3	1	93,629
Black Diamond..	2	1	0	0	0	0	0	2	1	0	4,858
Blaine	1	0	0	0	0	0	0	1	0	0	5,717
Bothell	1	0	0	0	0	1	0	0	2	0	48,323
Bremerton	2	0	0	0	0	0	0	1	0	1	41,817
Brier...	1	0	0	0	0	0	0	1	0	0	7,055
Burien...	4	0	3	0	0	0	3	2	2	0	51,879
Carnation	0	1	0	0	0	0	0	0	1	0	2,345
Chehalis..	0	0	2	0	0	0	0	1	0	1	7,700
College Place	1	0	0	0	0	0	0	1	0	0	9,374
Des Moines	1	1	0	0	0	0	1	1	0	0	32,652
East Wenatchee	0	0	1	0	0	0	1	0	0	0	14,336
Edmonds	7	1	0	0	0	0	0	3	2	3	42,934
Ellensburg	2	0	0	0	0	0	0	0	2	0	21,448
Everett...	11	0	3	0	1	0	2	7	3	3	112,439
Federal Way..	2	0	0	0	0	0	0	1	0	1	97,071
Fife..	1	0	0	0	0	0	0	0	1	0	10,301
Fircrest...	1	0	0	0	0	0	0	0	0	1	6,869
Granite Falls...	2	0	0	0	0	0	1	0	1	0	4,341
Hoquiam...	0	1	0	0	0	0	0	0	1	0	8,647
Issaquah	1	1	0	0	0	0	1	0	1	0	40,659
Kent	5	1	1	0	0	0	1	1	3	2	133,883
Kirkland	3	1	0	0	0	0	1	0	2	1	94,470
Lacey	0	0	1	0	0	0	1	0	0	0	53,826
Lake Stevens...	0	1	0	0	0	0	0	0	0	1	34,600
Lakewood..	1	0	0	0	0	0	0	0	0	1	61,432

Table 13. Hate Crime Incidents Per Bias Motivation and Quarter, by Selected State and Agency and Federal, 2020—Continued

(Number.)

State/agency	Number of incidents per bias motivation						Number of incidents per quarter				Population[1]
	Race/ Ethnicity/ Ancestry	Religion	Sexual orientation	Disability	Gender	Gender Identity	1st quarter	2nd quarter	3rd quarter	4th quarter	
Longview	2	0	0	0	0	0	1	1	0	0	38,629
Lynnwood	3	0	1	0	0	0	2	1	0	1	39,517
Maple Valley	1	0	0	0	0	0	0	0	1	0	27,736
Marysville	0	0	0	1	0	0	0	0	0	1	71,522
Mill Creek	0	0	1	0	0	0	0	0	0	1	21,214
Moses Lake	0	1	0	0	0	0	0	1	0	0	24,524
Mount Vernon	1	0	0	0	0	0	0	1	0	0	36,513
Mukilteo	1	1	0	0	0	0	0	1	1	0	21,573
Normandy Park	1	0	0	0	0	0	1	0	0	0	6,633
Olympia	1	0	1	0	0	0	0	0	1	1	53,571
Port Angeles	1	1	0	0	0	0	0	1	1	0	20,364
Port Townsend	1	0	0	0	0	0	0	1	0	0	9,914
Poulsbo	0	1	0	0	0	0	0	0	1	0	11,401
Pullman	2	0	0	0	0	0	1	1	0	0	35,071
Puyallup	1	0	0	0	0	0	0	0	1	0	42,974
Quincy	1	1	0	0	0	0	1	0	1	0	8,183
Redmond	1	0	0	0	0	0	0	0	1	0	74,154
Renton	4	0	0	0	0	0	0	2	0	2	102,856
Richland	4	0	0	0	0	0	0	3	1	0	59,370
Ridgefield	4	1	0	0	0	0	0	4	1	0	9,835
Sammamish[2]	3	1	1	0	0	0	0	2	1	1	66,878
SeaTac	2	1	0	0	0	0	0	2	1	0	29,282
Seattle[2]	100	6	27	3	4	8	28	38	46	28	771,517
Sedro Woolley	2	0	0	0	0	0	0	1	1	0	12,189
Sequim	0	0	0	0	0	1	0	0	0	1	7,768
Shelton	0	0	1	0	0	0	0	1	0	0	10,749
Shoreline	5	3	1	0	0	0	1	2	3	3	57,472
Snohomish	1	0	0	0	0	0	1	0	0	0	10,269
South Bend	1	0	0	0	0	0	0	0	1	0	1,706
Spokane	9	0	1	0	0	2	5	2	4	1	223,524
Spokane Valley	3	0	0	0	0	0	1	1	0	1	102,366
Stanwood	1	0	0	0	0	0	0	0	1	0	7,410
Tacoma	9	0	2	0	0	0	0	3	6	2	220,123
Toppenish	1	0	0	0	0	0	0	0	1	0	8,792
Tukwila	1	1	1	0	0	0	1	1	1	0	20,483
Tumwater	1	0	0	0	0	0	0	1	0	0	24,493
University Place	1	0	0	0	0	0	0	1	0	0	34,339
Vancouver	11	1	3	0	1	0	0	6	2	8	186,440
Walla Walla	2	1	1	0	0	0	1	0	2	1	32,944
Westport	1	0	0	0	0	0	0	1	0	0	2,102
Yakima	2	2	0	0	0	1	1	0	2	2	93,862
Universities and Colleges	1	5	1	0	0	4					
University of Washington	1	5	0	0	0	3	2	1	2	4	56,315
Western Washington University	0	0	1	0	0	1	1	1	0	0	17,966
Metropolitan Counties	37	10	6	1	0	3					
Clark	4	0	1	0	0	0	0	0	2	3	
Cowlitz	0	0	0	1	0	0	0	0	0	1	
King[2]	18	4	5	0	0	1	5	8	9	4	
Pierce	3	0	0	0	0	0	0	1	1	1	
Skagit	2	1	0	0	0	2	0	2	3	0	
Snohomish	4	1	0	0	0	0	3	1	0	1	
Spokane	1	1	0	0	0	0	1	0	0	1	
Stevens	0	1	0	0	0	0	1	0	0	0	
Thurston	1	0	0	0	0	0	0	1	0	0	
Whatcom	2	2	0	0	0	0	2	2	0	0	
Yakima	2	0	0	0	0	0	0	1	1	0	
Nonmetropolitan Counties	9	0	0	0	0	1					
Clallam	4	0	0	0	0	1	1	3	0	1	
Grays Harbor	1	0	0	0	0	0	0	1	0	0	
Island	3	0	0	0	0	0	0	3	0	0	
Okanogan	1	0	0	0	0	0	0	1	0	0	
Tribal Agencies	1	0	0	0	0	0					
Swinomish Tribal	1	0	0	0	0	0	0	0	0	1	
Other Agencies	3	1	0	0	0	0					
Washington State Parks and Recreation Law Enforcement	3	1	0	0	0	0		1	1	2	

Table 13. Hate Crime Incidents Per Bias Motivation and Quarter, by Selected State and Agency and Federal, 2020—*Continued*

(Number.)

State/agency	Number of incidents per bias motivation						Number of incidents per quarter				Population[1]
	Race/ Ethnicity/ Ancestry	Religion	Sexual orientation	Disability	Gender	Gender Identity	1st quarter	2nd quarter	3rd quarter	4th quarter	
WEST VIRGINIA											
Total	30	16	4	1	2	1					
Cities	18	10	3	0	1	1					
Charleston	3	4	0	0	0	0	0	2	1	4	46,038
Clarksburg	0	1	0	0	0	0	0	0	0	1	15,092
Moorefield	3	0	0	0	0	0	0	0	1	2	2,403
Morgantown	2	0	1	0	0	0	1	1	1	0	30,775
Parkersburg	4	4	2	0	1	1	4	2	4	2	29,096
Princeton	1	0	0	0	0	0	0	1	0	0	5,627
Vienna	0	1	0	0	0	0	0	1	0	0	10,049
Weirton	1	0	0	0	0	0	0	1	0	0	18,111
Wheeling	4	0	0	0	0	0	1	1	2	0	26,222
Universities and Colleges	0	1	0	0	0	0					
Marshall University	0	1	0	0	0	0	1	0	0	0	16,452
Metropolitan Counties	3	2	1	0	1	0					
Berkeley	0	0	1	0	0	0	0	1	0	0	
Brooke	1	1	0	0	0	0	0	1	1	0	
Kanawha	1	0	0	0	0	0	0	0	1	0	
Putnam	0	1	0	0	0	0	0	1	0	0	
Raleigh	1	0	0	0	0	0	1	0	0	0	
Wood	0	0	0	0	1	0	0	1	0	0	
Nonmetropolitan Counties	6	1	0	1	0	0					
Hardy	1	0	0	1	0	0	0	1	0	1	
Mason	3	1	0	0	0	0	3	0	1	0	
McDowell	1	0	0	0	0	0	0	0	0	1	
Randolph	1	0	0	0	0	0	0	0	1	0	
State Police Agencies	2	2	0	0	0	0					
State Police											
Beckley	2	1	0	0	0	0	0	0	3	0	
Union	0	1	0	0	0	0	1	0	0	0	
Other Agencies	1	0	0	0	0	0					
Logan County Drug and Violent Crime Task Force	1	0	0	0	0	0	0	1			
WASHINGTON											
Total	43	10	11	3	3	2					
Cities	30	7	6	3	1	2					
Appleton	0	0	0	0	0	1	1	0	0	0	74,255
Beaver Dam	0	0	0	1	0	0	1	0	0	0	16,426
De Pere	1	0	0	0	0	0	0	1	0	0	25,090
Eau Claire	0	0	1	0	0	0	1	0	0	0	69,086
Elkhart Lake	1	0	0	0	0	0	0	0	1	0	1,022
Fond du Lac	1	0	0	0	0	0	0	0	1	0	43,295
Fox Crossing	0	0	2	0	0	0	0	1	1	0	19,099
Green Bay	2	0	0	1	0	0	0	3	0	0	104,649
Janesville	0	1	0	0	1	0	0	0	2	0	64,682
Kenosha	1	0	0	0	0	0	0	1	0	0	100,005
La Crosse	1	0	0	0	0	0	0	0	0	1	51,211
Lodi	1	0	0	0	0	0	0	0	1	0	3,096
Madison	4	0	1	0	0	0	1	3	1	0	262,736
Marinette	1	0	0	0	0	0	0	0	1	0	10,497
Menomonie	2	1	0	0	0	0	0	2	0	1	16,582
Mequon	0	1	0	0	0	0	0	0	1	0	24,527
Milwaukee	1	1	0	0	0	0	1	0	1	0	589,105
Neenah	1	0	0	0	0	0	0	0	1	0	26,390
New Holstein	1	0	0	0	0	0	0	0	1	0	3,088
Oak Creek	1	0	1	0	0	0	1	0	1	0	36,502
Oshkosh	1	0	1	0	0	0	0	1	0	1	67,080
Palmyra	1	0	0	0	0	0	0	1	0	0	1,753
Pewaukee Village	0	1	0	0	0	0	1	0	0	0	8,102
Platteville	3	0	0	0	0	0	0	2	1	0	12,184
Plover	1	0	0	0	0	0	0	0	1	0	13,201
Rhinelander	1	0	0	0	0	1	0	2	0	0	7,629
Stanley	0	1	0	0	0	0	0	0	0	1	3,722
Stevens Point	1	0	0	0	0	0	0	0	1	0	25,790
Stoughton	0	0	0	1	0	0	0	1	0	0	13,164
Waterloo	0	1	0	0	0	0	0	1	0	0	3,332

Table 13. Hate Crime Incidents Per Bias Motivation and Quarter, by Selected State and Agency and Federal, 2020—*Continued*

(Number.)

State/agency	Number of incidents per bias motivation						Number of incidents per quarter				Population[1]
	Race/ Ethnicity/ Ancestry	Religion	Sexual orientation	Disability	Gender	Gender Identity	1st quarter	2nd quarter	3rd quarter	4th quarter	
Wausau	3	0	0	0	0	0	0	1	1	1	38,492
Universities and Colleges	0	0	1	0	0	0					
University of Wisconsin, Eau Claire	0	0	1	0	0	0	0	0	0	1	12,637
Metropolitan Counties	5	3	3	0	1	0					
Calumet	0	0	1	0	0	0	0	0	0	1	
Chippewa	0	0	1	0	0	0	0	0	0	1	
Dane	1	0	1	0	0	0	1	1	0	0	
Fond du Lac	1	0	0	0	0	0	0	0	1	0	
Lincoln	0	2	0	0	1	0	0	2	0	1	
Marathon	1	0	0	0	0	0	0	0	1	0	
Rock	2	0	0	0	0	0	0	0	0	2	
Waukesha	0	1	0	0	0	0	0	0	1	0	
Nonmetropolitan Counties	7	0	1	0	1	0					
Burnett	2	0	0	0	0	0	0	1	1	0	
Dunn	0	0	0	0	1	0	1	0	0	0	
Grant	1	0	1	0	0	0	1	0	1	0	
Menominee	1	0	0	0	0	0	0	0	1	0	
Monroe	1	0	0	0	0	0	0	0	1	0	
Oneida	1	0	0	0	0	0	1	0	0	0	
Taylor	1	0	0	0	0	0	0	0	1	0	
Tribal Agencies	1	0	0	0	0	0					
Oneida Tribal	1	0	0	0	0	0	0	0	1	0	
WYOMING											
Total	11	2	2	0	2	1					
Cities	9	2	2	0	2	1					
Cheyenne	1	0	0	0	0	0	0	1	0	0	64,751
Cody	0	0	0	0	1	0	0	1	0	0	9,816
Evanston	2	0	0	0	1	1	1	0	1	2	11,563
Gillette	0	1	0	0	0	0	0	1	0	0	32,093
Laramie	3	0	0	0	0	0	1	1	1	0	32,913
Sheridan	3	1	2	0	0	0	2	0	2	2	17,991
Nonmetropolitan Counties	2	0	0	0	0	0					
Park	1	0	0	0	0	0	0	0	0	1	
Sheridan	1	0	0	0	0	0	0	0	0	1	
FEDERAL											
Federal Agencies	128	60	24	0	1	10					
Federal Bureau of Investigation Field Offices											
Albany	1	0	0	0	0	0	1				
Albuquerque[2]	3	2	1	0	0	0		2	1	1	
Anchorage	0	1	0	0	0	0	1				
Atlanta	4	2	1	0	0	0	2	2	1	2	
Baltimore	4	3	0	0	0	0	2	3	2		
Birmingham	2	1	0	0	0	0		2		1	
Boston	2	1	0	0	0	0		2		1	
Charlotte	0	0	1	0	0	0	1				
Chicago	1	1	1	0	0	2	2	3			
Cincinnati	0	1	0	0	0	0				1	
Cleveland	2	1	0	0	0	0		1	1	1	
Columbia	1	0	0	0	0	0			1		
Denver	3	0	1	0	0	0	1	2	1		
Detroit	5	0	1	0	0	0		2	3	1	
El Paso[2]	8	2	1	0	0	0	3	5	2		
Honolulu	0	0	1	0	0	0			1		
Indianapolis[2]	3	2	0	0	0	0		2	2		
Jackson	1	2	2	0	0	0	1	2		2	
Jacksonville	1	1	0	0	0	0	1		1		
Kansas City	6	1	0	0	0	0		5	2		
Knoxville	1	0	1	0	0	0	1		1		
Las Vegas	2	2	1	0	0	0	2		2	1	
Little Rock	3	1	0	0	0	1		4		1	
Los Angeles[2]	11	6	1	0	0	1	1	7	3	6	
Louisville	1	1	0	0	0	0			1	1	
Memphis	1	0	1	0	0	0			2		
Miami	1	1	0	0	0	0	1		1		
Milwaukee[2]	2	1	0	0	0	0			1	1	

Table 13. Hate Crime Incidents Per Bias Motivation and Quarter, by Selected State and Agency and Federal, 2020—*Continued*

(Number.)

State/agency	Number of incidents per bias motivation						Number of incidents per quarter				Population[1]
	Race/ Ethnicity/ Ancestry	Religion	Sexual orientation	Disability	Gender	Gender Identity	1st quarter	2nd quarter	3rd quarter	4th quarter	
Minneapolis............................	11	2	1	0	0	0	1	9	4		
Mobile...................................	1	0	0	0	0	0		1			
Newark.................................	2	1	0	0	0	0		2	1		
New Haven............................	2	1	0	0	1	0		3	1		
New Orleans..........................	1	0	2	0	0	0	1	1		1	
New York[2]............................	3	7	0	0	0	0	6		2	1	
Norfolk..................................	0	2	0	0	0	0	1	1			
Omaha...................................	4	2	0	0	0	0		3	2	1	
Philadelphia..........................	1	1	0	0	0	1		1	2		
Phoenix.................................	1	1	0	0	0	0	2				
Pittsburgh.............................	0	0	1	0	0	0			1		
Portland................................	0	0	0	0	0	0		2	3		
Richmond..............................	3	0	0	0	0	0		2	1		
Sacramento[2].........................	3	1	0	0	0	0	1	2	0	0	
Salt Lake City........................	1	0	1	0	0	0	2				
San Antonio...........................	1	0	0	0	0	0		1			
San Diego..............................	0	0	1	0	0	1			2		
San Francisco[2]......................	4	1	1	0	0	0		3	2		
San Juan................................	0	0	0	0	0	3	1	1		1	
Seattle..................................	5	1	2	0	0	0	1	3	3	1	
St. Louis................................	2	2	0	0	0	1	1	2	2		
Tampa....................................	4	4	0	0	0	0		4	4		
Washington...........................	2	0	1	0	0	0		1	1	1	
Pentagon Force Protection Agency.....................	2	1	0	0	0	0	0	1	1	1	
United States Marine Corps Law Enforcement.....	1	0	0	0	0	0	1	0	0	0	

[1]Population figures are published only for the cities. The figures listed for the universities and colleges are student enrollment and were provided by the United States Department of Education for the 2019 school year, the most recent available. The enrollment figures include full-time and part-time students.
[2]The figures shown include one or more incidents reported with more than one bias motivation.
[3]Student enrollment figures were not available.

Table 14. Participation Table, Number of Participating Agencies and Population Covered, by Population Group and Federal, 2020

(Number.)

Population group	Number of participating agencies	Population covered
Total	15,138	306,085,895
Group I (cities 250,000 and over)	89	64,053,353
Group II (cities 100,000-249,999)	226	32,907,848
Group III (cities 50,000-99,999)	487	33,943,172
Group IV (cities 25,000-49,999)	882	30,531,381
Group V (cities 10,000-24,999)	1,787	28,560,177
Group VI1 (cities under 10,000)	7,786	22,084,327
Metropolitan counties[1]	1,654	71,083,178
Nonmetropolitan counties[1]	2,146	22,922,459
Federal[2]	81	0

[1]The figures shown include universities and colleges, state police agencies, and/or other agencies to which no population is attributed.
[2]Population estimates are not attributed to the federal agencies.

METHODOLOGY

The Federal Bureau of Investigation (FBI) began the procedures for implementing, collecting, and managing hate crime data after Congress passed the Hate Crime Statistics Act in 1990. This act required the collection of data "about crimes that manifest evidence of prejudice based on race, religion, sexual orientation, or ethnicity." Beginning in 2013, law enforcement agencies could submit hate crime data in accordance with a number of program modifications. In 1994, the Hate Crime Statistics Act was amended to include bias against persons with disabilities. The Church Arson Prevention Act, which was signed into law in July 1996, removed the sunset clause from the original statute and mandated that the collection of hate crime data become a permanent part of the UCR program. In 2009, Congress further amended the Hate Crime Statistics Act by passing the Matthew Shepard and James Byrd, Jr., Hate Crime Prevention Act. The amendment includes the collection of data for crimes motivated by bias against a particular gender and gender identity, as well as for crimes committed by, and crimes directed against, juveniles. In response to the Shepard/Byrd Act, the FBI modified its data collection so that reporting agencies could indicate whether hate crimes were committed by, or directed against, juveniles.

Readers should use caution in interpreting data, especially as compared to previous years, due to the conditions imposed by the COVID-19 pandemic.

DEFINITIONS

Hate crimes include any crime motivated by bias against race, religion, sexual orientation, ethnicity/national origin, and/or disability. Because motivation is subjective, it is sometimes difficult to know with certainty whether a crime resulted from the offender's bias. Moreover, the presence of bias alone does not necessarily mean that a crime can be considered a hate crime. Only when law enforcement investigation reveals sufficient evidence to lead a reasonable and prudent person to conclude that the offender's actions were motivated, in whole or in part, by his or her bias should an incident be reported as a hate crime.

DATA COLLECTION

The UCR (Uniform Crime Reporting) program collects data about both single-bias and multiple-bias hate crimes. A single-bias incident is defined as an incident in which one or more offense types are motivated by the same bias. A multiple-bias incident is defined as an incident in which more than one offense type occurs and at least two offense types are motivated by different biases.

A table enumerating selected places in the United States that did not report hate crimes in 2019 is available at https://ucr.fbi.gov/hate-crime/2019/topic-pages/tables/participation.xls.

Important Note: Rape Data

In 2013, the UCR Program initiated the collection of rape data under a revised definition and removed the term "forcible" from the offense name. The UCR Program now defines rape as follows:

- **Rape (revised definition)**: Penetration, no matter how slight, of the vagina or anus with any body part or object, or oral penetration by a sex organ of another person, without the consent of the victim. (This includes the offenses of rape, sodomy, and sexual assault with an object as converted from data submitted via the National Incident-Based Reporting System.)

- **Rape (legacy definition)**: The carnal knowledge of a female forcibly and against her will. For tables within this publication that present data for 2018 only or provide a 2-year trend, the rape figures are an aggregate total of the data submitted based on both the legacy and revised UCR definitions. For 5- and 10-year trend tables, the rape figures for the previous year (2014 or 2009) are based on the legacy definition and the 2018 rape figures are an aggregate total based on both the legacy and revised definitions. For this reason, a percent change is not provided.

In 2016, the FBI Director approved the recommendation to discontinue the reporting of rape data using the UCR legacy definition beginning in 2017.

The offenses of fondling, incest, and statutory rape are included in the crimes against persons, *other* category.

Crimes Against Persons, Property, or Society

The UCR program's data collection guidelines stipulate that a hate crime may involve multiple offenses, victims, and offenders within one incident; therefore, the Hate Crime Statistics program is incident-based. According to UCR counting guidelines:

- One offense is counted for each victim in *crimes against persons*

- One offense is counted for each offense type in *crimes against property*

- One offense is counted for each offense type in *crimes against society*

Victims

In the UCR program, the victim of a hate crime may be an individual, a business, an institution, or society as a whole.

Offenders

According to the UCR program, the term *known offender* does not imply that the suspect's identity is known; rather, the term indicates that some aspect of the suspect was identified, thus distinguishing the suspect from an unknown offender. Law enforcement agencies specify the number of offenders, and when possible, the race of the offender or offenders as a group.

Race/Ethnicity

The UCR program uses the following racial designations in its Hate Crime Statistics program: White; Black; American Indian or Alaskan Native; Asian; Native Hawaiian or Other Pacific Islander; and Multiple Races, Group. In addition, the UCR program uses the ethnic designations of Hispanic or Latino and Not Hispanic or Latino.

The law enforcement agencies that voluntarily participate in the Hate Crime Statistics program collect details about an offender's bias motivation associated with 11 offense types already being reported to the UCR program: murder and nonnegligent manslaughter, rape, aggravated assault, simple assault, and intimidation (crimes against persons); and robbery, burglary, larceny-theft, motor vehicle theft, arson, and destruction/damage/vandalism (crimes against property). The law enforcement agencies that participate in the UCR program via the National Incident-Based Reporting System (NIBRS) collect data about additional offenses for *crimes against persons* and *crimes against property*. These data appear in the category of other. These agencies also collect hate crime data for the category called *crimes against society*, which includes drug or narcotic offenses, gambling offenses, prostitution offenses, and weapon law violations.

NATIONAL VOLUME AND PERCENT DISTRIBUTION

In 2019, 2,172 law enforcement agencies (out of 15,588 participating agencies) reported 7,314 hate crime incidents involving 8,559 offenses. Of these, 7,103 were single-bias offenses. An analysis of the single-bias incidents revealed that 55.8 percent were racially/ethnically/ancestrally motivated, 21.4 percent were motivated by religious bias, 16.8 percent resulted from sexual orientation bias, 3.8 percent were motivated by gender and gender-identity bias, and 2.2 percent were prompted by a disability bias.

The majority of the 4,784 hate crime offenses that were racially motivated resulted from an anti-Black or African American bias (48.4 percent) followed by an anti-White bias (15.8 percent). Bias against people of more than one race accounted for 3.6

percent of offenses, while anti-Asian bias accounted for 4.3 percent of racially motivated offenses, anti-Arab bias accounted for 2.6 percent of these offenses, anti–Native Hawaiian and Other Pacific Islander accounted for 0.5 percent of these offenses, and anti–American Indian or Alaska Native bias accounted for 2.6 percent of these offenses. Approximately 14.1 percent of crimes were classified as an anti-Hispanic or Latino bias.

Hate crimes motivated by religious bias accounted for 1,650 offenses reported by law enforcement. A breakdown of these offenses revealed 60.3 percent were motivated by anti-Jewish bias, 13.3 percent by anti-Islamic (Muslim) bias, 2.5 percent were anti–multiple religions or groups, 4.0 percent had an anti-Catholic bias, 1.5 percent were anti-Protestant, 2.8 percent were anti–Eastern Orthodox (Russian, Greek, or other), 3.6 percent were anti–other Christian, 0.4 percent were anti-atheism/agnosticism/etc., 0.8 percent were anti-Mormon, 0.4 percent were anti-Hindu, 0.4 percent were anti–Jehovah's Witness, 0.3 percent were anti-Buddhist, 3.0 percent were anti-Sikh, and the remainder, 6.5 percent, of offenses were based on a bias against other religions—those not specified.

In 2019, 1,395 offenses were committed on the basis of sexual orientation bias. Of the offenses based on sexual orientation, 24.5 percent were classified as having an anti–lesbian, gay, bisexual, or transgender (mixed group) bias; 62.2 percent were classified as having an anti-gay bias; 10.2 percent had an anti-lesbian basis; 1.9 percent had an anti-bisexual bias; and 1.2 percent had an anti-heterosexual bias.

Hate crime offenses committed based on disability totaled 169 offenses. The majority (68.6 percent) were classified as anti-mental disability, with the rest (32.49 percent) classified as anti–physical disability.

Of the 224 gender identity bias offenses reported, 173 (77.2 percent) were anti-transgender and 51 were anti–gender nonconforming. Of the 80 gender bias offenses reported, 62 were anti-female and 18 were anti-male.

CRIMES AGAINST PERSONS

Law enforcement agencies reported 5,512 hate crime offenses against persons in 2019. Approximately 40.0 percent involved intimidation, 36.7 percent involved simple assault, and 21.0 percent involved aggravated assault. There were 51 murders and 30 rapes.

CRIMES AGAINST PROPERTY

In 2019, hate crime offences against property totaled 2,811. Approximately 76.6 percent of offenses involved destruction/damage or vandalism. The remaining 23.4 percent of crimes against property consisted of robbery, burglary, larceny-theft, motor vehicle theft, arson, and other crimes.

PART 6

Indicators of School Crime and Safety, 2020

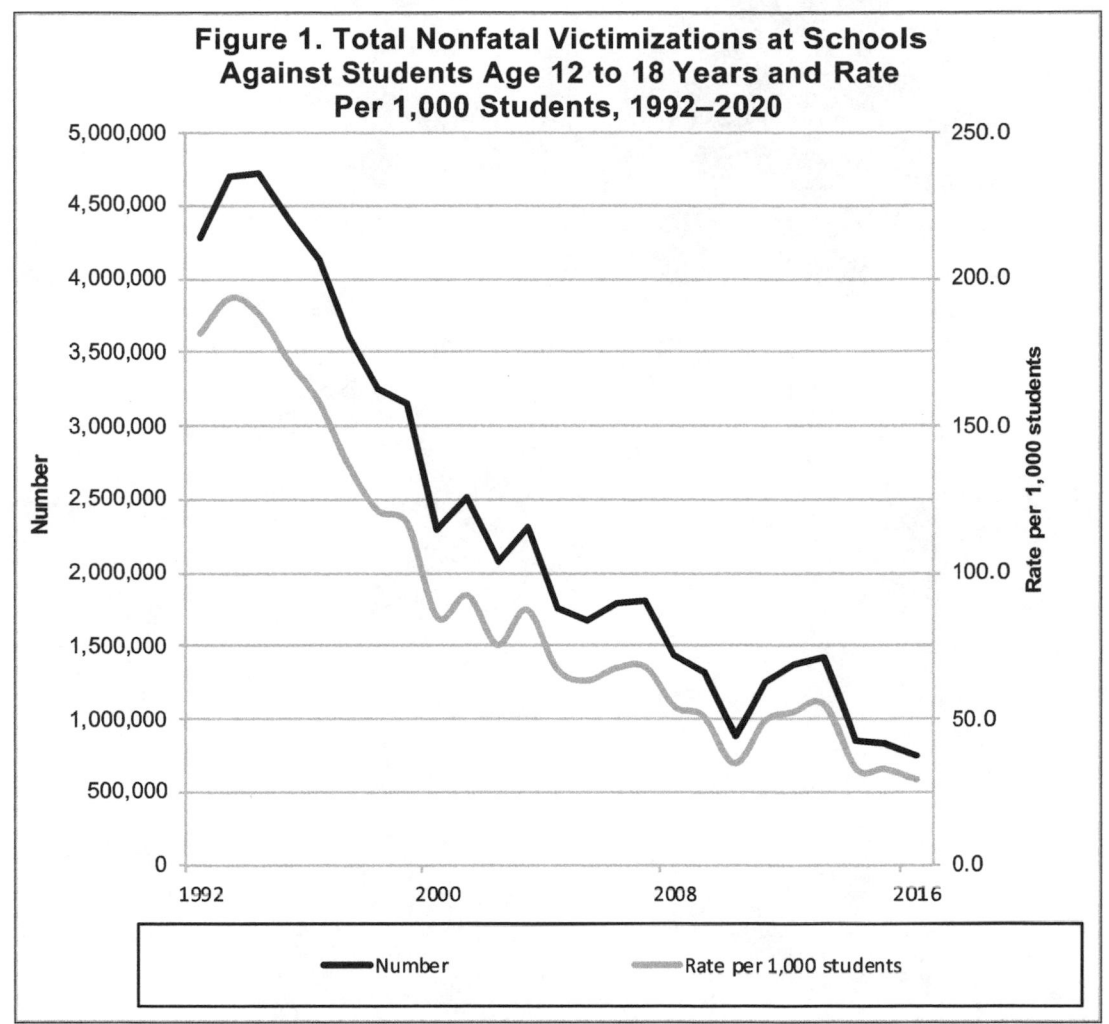

Figure 1. Total Nonfatal Victimizations at Schools Against Students Age 12 to 18 Years and Rate Per 1,000 Students, 1992–2020

- Approximately 285,400 nonfatal victimization incidents occurred at school in 2020 for students between 12 and 18 years of age and approximately 380,900 incidents occurred away from school.

- Between 2001 and 2019, the percentage of students ages 12 to 18 who reported that gangs were present at their school during the school year showed an overall decrease (from approximately 20 percent to approximately 9 percent).

- In 2019, about 6.4 percent of students ages 12 to 18 reported being called hate-related words at school during the school year, representing a decrease from 13.3 percent in 2001. This percentage also decreased between 2001 and 2017 for male and female students and for White, Black, Asian, and Hispanic students. In 2019, about 23 percent of students reported seeing hate-related graffiti at school during the school year, representing a decrease from approximately 36 percent in 2001.

- The percentage of students in grades 9 through 12 who reported that illegal drugs were made available to them on school property in the last 12 months decreased from about 28.5 percent in 2001 to 21.8 percent in 2019.

- Approximately 16 percent of high school students reported being cyberbullied in 2019; while over a quarter (27 percent) of gay, lesbian, and bisexual students reported electronic bullying, only 19 percent of students unsure of their sexual identity and 14 percent of heterosexual students reported this experience.

Table 1. School-Associated Violent Deaths of All Persons, Homicides and Suicides of Youth Ages 5 to 18 Years at School, and Total Homicides and Suicides of Youth Ages 5 to 18 Years, by Type of Violent Death, 1992–1993 to 2018–2019

(Number.)

Year	School-associated violent deaths[1] of all persons (includes students, staff, and other nonstudents)						Homicides of youth age 5 to 18 years		Suicides of youth age 5 to 18 years	
	Total	Homicides	Suicides	Legal interventions	Unintentional firearm-related deaths	Undetermined violent deaths[2]	Homicides at school[3]	Total homicides	Suicides at school[3]	Total suicides[4]
1992–1993	57	47	10	0	0	0	34	3,003	6	1,657
1993–1994	48	38	10	0	0	0	29	3,253	7	1,779
1994–1995	48	39	8	0	1	0	28	3,001	7	1,704
1995–1996	53	46	6	1	0	0	32	2,791	6	1,691
1996–1997	48	45	2	1	0	0	28	2,430	1	1,584
1997–1998	57	47	9	1	0	0	34	2,231	6	1,681
1998–1999	47	38	6	2	1	0	33	1,923	4	1,480
1999–2000	37	26	11	0	0	0	14	1,694	8	1,420
2000–2001	34	26	7	1	0	0	14	1,636	6	1,451
2001–2002	36	27	8	1	0	0	16	1,593	5	1,343
2002–2003	36	25	11	0	0	0	18	1,658	10	1,264
2003–2004	45	37	7	1	0	0	23	1,620	5	1,411
2004–2005	52	40	10	2	0	0	22	1,720	8	1,484
2005–2006	44	37	6	1	0	0	21	1,859	3	1,311
2006–2007	63	48	13	2	0	0	32	1,906	9	1,243
2007–2008	48	39	7	2	0	0	21	1,858	5	1,256
2008–2009	44	29	15	0	0	0	18	1,720	7	1,425
2009–2010	35	27	5	3	0	0	19	1,551	2	1,441
2010–2011	32	26	6	0	0	0	11	1,436	3	1,559
2011–2012	45	26	14	5	0	0	15	1,360	5	1,541
2012–2013	53	41	11	1	0	0	31	1,310	6	1,608
2013–2014	48	26	20	1	0	1	12	1,160	8	1,638
2014–2015	47	28	17	2	0	0	20	1,273	9	1,882
2015–2016	38	30	7	1	0	0	18	1,478	3	1,941
2016–2017	42	28	13	1	0	0	18	1,587	6	2,186
2017–2018	56	46	9	1	0	0	35	1,502	8	2,408
2018–2019	39	29	10	0	0	0	10	1,508	3	2,233

NOTE: All data are reported for the school year, defined as July 1 through June 30. Data from 1999-2000 onward are subject to change until law enforcement reports have been obtained and interviews with school and law enforcement officials have been completed. The details learned during the interviews can occasionally change the classification of a case.

[1]A school-associated violent death is defined as "a homicide, suicide, or legal intervention (involving a law enforcement officer), in which the fatal injury occurred on the campus of a functioning elementary or secondary school in the United States," while the victim was on the way to or from regular sessions at school, or while the victim was attending or traveling to or from an official school-sponsored event.

[2]Violent deaths for which the manner was undetermined; that is, the information pointing to one manner of death was no more compelling than the information pointing to one or more other competing manners of death when all available information was considered.

[3]"At school" includes on the property of a functioning elementary or secondary school, on the way to or from regular sessions at school, and while attending or traveling to or from a school-sponsored event.

[4]Excludes self-inflicted deaths among 5- to 9-year-olds. The number of self-inflicted deaths among 5- to 9-year-olds was generally less than 7 per year during the period covered by this table.

Table 2. Number of Nonfatal Victimizations Against Students Ages 12 to 18 Years and Rate of Victimization Per 1,000 Students, by Type of Victimization and Location, 1992–2020

(Number; rate per 1,000 students.)

Location and year	Number of nonfatal victimizations				Rate of victimization per 1,000 students			
			Violent				Violent	
	Total	Theft	All violent	Violent excluding simple assault[1]	Total	Theft	All violent	Violent excluding simple assault[1]
At School[2]								
1992	4,281,200	2,679,400	1,601,800	197,600	181.5	113.6	67.9	8.4
1993	4,692,800	2,477,100	2,215,700	535,500	193.5	102.1	91.4	22.1
1994	4,721,000	2,474,100	2,246,900	459,100	187.7	98.4	89.3	18.3
1995	4,400,700	2,468,400	1,932,200	294,500	172.2	96.6	75.6	11.5
1996	4,130,400	2,205,200	1,925,300	371,900	158.4	84.5	73.8	14.3
1997	3,610,900	1,975,000	1,635,900	376,200	136.6	74.7	61.9	14.2
1998	3,247,300	1,635,100	1,612,200	314,500	121.3	61.1	60.2	11.7
1999	3,152,400	1,752,200	1,400,200	281,100	117.0	65.1	52.0	10.4
2000	2,301,000	1,331,500	969,500	214,200	84.9	49.1	35.8	7.9
2001	2,521,300	1,348,500	1,172,700	259,400	92.3	49.4	42.9	9.5
2002	2,082,600	1,088,800	993,800	173,500	75.4	39.4	36.0	6.3
2003	2,308,800	1,270,500	1,038,300	188,400	87.4	48.1	39.3	7.1
2004	1,762,200	1,065,400	696,800	107,300	67.2	40.6	26.6	4.1
2005	1,678,600	875,900	802,600	140,300	63.2	33.0	30.2	5.3
2006[3]	1,799,900	859,000	940,900	249,900	67.5	32.2	35.3	9.4
2007	1,801,200	896,700	904,400	116,100	67.8	33.7	34.0	4.4
2008	1,435,500	648,000	787,500	128,700	54.3	24.5	29.8	4.9
2009	1,322,800	594,500	728,300	233,700	51.0	22.9	28.1	9.0
2010	892,000	469,800	422,300	155,000	34.9	18.4	16.5	6.1
2011	1,246,200	647,700	598,600	89,500	49.3	25.6	23.7	3.5
2012	1,364,900	615,600	749,200	89,000	52.4	23.6	28.8	3.4
2013	1,420,900	454,900	966,000	125,500	55.0	17.6	37.4	4.9
2014	850,100	363,700	486,400	93,800	33.0	14.1	18.9	3.6
2015	841,100	309,100	531,900	99,000	32.9	12.1	20.8	3.9
2016[4]	NA	NA	NA	NA	NA	NA	NA	NA
2017	827,000	306,500	520,500	110,600	32.7	12.1	20.6	4.4
2018	836,100	225,600	610,500	152,400	32.9	8.9	24.0	6.0
2019	764,600	239,400	525,300	125,600	30.0	9.4	20.6	4.9
2020[5]	285,400	91,800	193,600	20,400	11.2	3.6	7.6	0.8
Away from School								
1992	4,084,100	1,857,600	2,226,500	1,025,100	173.1	78.7	94.4	43.5
1993	3,835,900	1,731,100	2,104,800	1,004,300	158.2	71.4	86.8	41.4
1994	4,147,100	1,713,900	2,433,200	1,074,900	164.9	68.1	96.7	42.7
1995	3,626,600	1,604,800	2,021,800	829,700	141.9	62.8	79.1	32.5
1996	3,483,200	1,572,700	1,910,600	870,000	133.5	60.3	73.3	33.4
1997	3,717,600	1,710,700	2,006,900	853,300	140.7	64.7	75.9	32.3
1998	3,047,800	1,408,000	1,639,800	684,900	113.8	52.6	61.3	25.6
1999	2,713,800	1,129,200	1,584,500	675,400	100.8	41.9	58.8	25.1
2000	2,303,600	1,228,900	1,074,800	402,100	85.0	45.3	39.6	14.8
2001	1,780,300	961,400	819,000	314,800	65.2	35.2	30.0	11.5
2002	1,619,500	820,100	799,400	341,200	58.6	29.7	28.9	12.4
2003	1,824,100	780,900	1,043,200	412,800	69.1	29.6	39.5	15.6
2004	1,371,800	718,000	653,700	272,500	52.3	27.4	24.9	10.4
2005	1,429,000	637,700	791,300	257,100	53.8	24.0	29.8	9.7
2006[3]	1,413,100	714,200	698,900	263,600	53.0	26.8	26.2	9.9
2007	1,371,700	614,300	757,400	337,700	51.6	23.1	28.5	12.7
2008	1,132,600	498,500	634,100	258,600	42.8	18.9	24.0	9.8
2009	857,200	484,200	372,900	176,800	33.1	18.7	14.4	6.8
2010	689,900	378,800	311,200	167,300	27.0	14.8	12.2	6.5
2011	966,100	541,900	424,300	137,600	38.2	21.4	16.8	5.4
2012	991,200	470,800	520,400	169,900	38.0	18.1	20.0	6.5
2013	778,500	403,000	375,500	151,200	30.1	15.6	14.5	5.8
2014	621,300	288,900	332,400	165,000	24.1	11.2	12.9	6.4
2015	545,100	263,100	281,900	110,900	21.3	10.3	11.0	4.3
2016[4]	NA	NA	NA	NA	NA	NA	NA	NA

Table 2. Number of Nonfatal Victimizations Against Students Ages 12 to 18 Years and Rate of Victimization Per 1,000 Students, by Type of Victimization and Location, 1992–2020—*Continued*

(Number; rate per 1,000 students.)

Location and year	Number of nonfatal victimizations				Rate of victimization per 1,000 students			
			Violent				Violent	
	Total	Theft	All violent	Violent excluding simple assault[1]	Total	Theft	All violent	Violent excluding simple assault[1]
2017.....................................	503,800	188,600	315,200	145,300	19.9	7.4	12.4	5.7
2018.....................................	410,200	158,800	251,400	117,500	16.1	6.3	9.9	4.6
2019.....................................	509,300	160,500	348,800	138,000	20.0	6.3	13.7	5.4
2020[5]	380,900	130,000	250,900	132,300	14.9	5.1	9.8	5.2

NOTE: "All violent" victimization includes the crimes of rape, sexual assault, robbery, aggravated assault, and simple assault. "Theft" includes attempted and completed purse-snatching, completed pickpocketing, and all attempted and completed thefts, with the exception of motor vehicle thefts. Theft does not include robbery, which involves the threat or use of force and is classified as a violent crime. "Total victimization" includes theft and violent crimes. Data in this table are from the National Crime Victimization Survey (NCVS); due to differences in time coverage and administration between the NCVS and the School Crime Supplement (SCS) to the NCVS, data in this table cannot be compared with data in tables that are based on the SCS. Detail may not sum to totals because of rounding.

NA = Not available.

[1] In previous versions of the table, "violent excluding simple assault" was labeled as "serious violent" victimization.

[2] "At school" includes in the school building, on school property, on a school bus, and going to or from school.

[3] Every 10 years, the survey sample is redesigned to reflect changes in the population. Due to the sample redesign and other methodological changes implemented in 2006, use caution when comparing 2006 estimates to other years.

[4] Every 10 years, the survey sample is redesigned to reflect changes in the population. Due to a sample increase and redesign in 2016, victimization estimates among youth in 2016 were not comparable to estimates for other years.

[5] In 2020, schools across the country suspended or modified in-person classes in accordance with federal, state, and local guidance related to the risks associated with the coronavirus pandemic. Students may have spent less time at school than in previous years due to these modified procedures.

Table 3. Number of Nonfatal Victimizations Against Students Ages 12 to 18 Years and Rate of Victimization Per 1,000 Students, by Type of Victimization, Location, and Selected Student Characteristics, 2020

(Number; rate per 1,000 students.)

Location and year	Number of nonfatal victimizations		Violent		Rate of victimization per 1,000 students		Violent	
	Total	Theft	All violent	Violent excluding simple assault[1]	Total	Theft	All violent	Violent excluding simple assault[1]
At School[2]								
Total	285,400	91,800	193,600	20,400	11	4	8	1
Sex								
Male	202,400	58,800	143,600	D	15.4	4.5	10.9	D
Female	83,000	33,000!	50,000	D	6.7	2.7	4.0!	D
Age								
12 to 14 years......................	178,100	61,300	116,700	17,600!	14.3	4.9	9.4	1.4!
15 to 18 years......................	107,400	30,500!	76,900	D	8.2	2.3!	5.9	D
Race/ethnicity[3]								
White....................	159,600	53,100	106,500	17,000!	12.2	4.1	8.1	1.3!
Black	42,100!	15,300!	26,800!	D	12.4!	4.5!	7.9!	D
Hispanic	53,100!	16,300!	36,700!	D	8.1!	2.5!	5.6!	D
Other	30,700!	D	23,600!	D	11.8!	D	9.1!	D
Urbanicity[4]								
Urban.....................	39,600!	D	31,500!	D	14.9!	D	11.8!	D
Suburban	208,300	66,900	141,400	15,000!	11.6	3.7	7.8	0.8
Rural	37,500!	16,800!	20,700!	D	7.7!	3.4!	4.2!	D
Household income[5]								
Less than $25,000.................	25,900!	D	18,300!	D	7.6!	D	5.4!	D
$25,000 to $49,999..............	101,900	19,400!	82,500	D	18.6	3.5!	15.1	D
$50,000 to $99,999..............	89,200	39,400	49,700!	D	11.2	5.0	6.3!	D
$100,000 or more.................	68,400	25,300!	43,100!	D	7.8	2.9!	4.9!	D
Away from School								
Total	380,900	130,000	250,900	132,300	14.9	5.1	9.8	5.2
Sex								
Male	181,100	71,200	109,900	59,200	13.7	5.4	8.3	4.5
Female	199,800	58,800	141,000	73,100	16.1	4.7	11.4	5.9
Age								
12 to 14 years......................	144,200	54,200	90,000	19,500!	11.6	4.4	7.2	1.6!
15 to 18 years......................	236,600	75,800	160,900	112,800	18.0	5.8	12.2	8.6
Race/ethnicity[3]								
White....................	189,700	73,700	115,900	72,000	14.5	5.6	8.9	5.5
Black	31,300!	13,200!	18,100!	D	9.2!	3.9!	5.3!	D
Hispanic	120,300	29,600!	90,700	47,000!	18.5	4.6!	13.9	7.2!
Other	39,600!	13,400!	26,200!	D	15.2!	5.2!	10.1!	D
Urbanicity[4]								
Urban.....................	24,300!	17,700!	D	D	9.1!	6.6!	D	D
Suburban	287,000	100,300	186,700	103,000	15.9	5.6	10.4	5.7
Rural	69,600	D	57,700	29,300!	14.2	D	11.8	6.0!
Household income[5]								
Less than $25,000.................	84,000	D	76,900	40,800!	24.6	D	22.5	11.9!
$25,000 to $49,999..............	66,100	28,700!	37,500!	18,800!	12.1	5.2!	6.9!	3.4!
$50,000 to $99,999..............	126,000	40,400	85,700	42,300!	15.9	5.1	10.8	5.3!
$100,000 or more.................	104,800	53,900	50,900!	30,400!	11.9	6.1	5.8!	3.5

NOTE: "All violent" victimization includes the crimes of rape, sexual assault, robbery, aggravated assault, and simple assault. "Theft" includes attempted and completed purse-snatching, completed pickpocketing, and all attempted and completed thefts, with the exception of motor vehicle thefts. Theft does not include robbery, which involves the threat or use of force and is classified as a violent crime. "Total victimization" includes theft and violent crimes. Data in this table are from the National Crime Victimization Survey (NCVS) and are reported in accordance with Bureau of Justice Statistics standards. In 2020, schools across the country suspended or modified in-person classes in accordance with federal, state, and local guidance related to the risks associated with the coronavirus pandemic. Students may have spent less time at school than in previous years due to these modified procedures. Detail may not sum to totals because of rounding. The population size for students ages 12-18 was 25,587,500 in 2020.
! = Interpret data with caution. The coefficient of variation (CV) for this estimate is between 30 and 50 percent.
D = Reporting standards not met. Either there are too few cases for a reliable estimate or the coefficient of variation (CV) is 50 percent or greater.
[1]In previous versions of the table, "violent excluding simple assault" was labeled as "serious violent" victimization.
[2]"At school" includes in the school building, on school property, on a school bus, and going to or from school.
[3]Race categories exclude persons of Hispanic ethnicity. "Other" includes Asian, Pacific Islander, American Indian/Alaska Native, and two or more races.
[4]Refers to location of the victim's residence and includes urban, suburban, and rural. Areas are categorized based on population size and population density. This differs from previous versions of the table because the Bureau of Justice Statistics revised its definition of urbanicity in 2019.
[5]Income data for 2020 were imputed. For more information, see *Criminal Victimization, 2020*, available at //bjs.ojp.gov/sites/g/files/xyckuh236/files/media/document/cv20.pdf.

Table 4. Percentage of Students Ages 12 to 18 Years Who Reported Criminal Victimization at School During the Previous 6 Months, by Type of Victimization and Selected Student and School Characteristics, Selected Years, 1995–2019

(Percent.)

Characteristic	1995	2001	2003	2005	2007	2009	2011	2013	2015	2017	2019
Total	9.1	5.5	5.1	4.3	4.3	3.9	3.5	3.0	2.7	2.2	2.5
Sex											
Male....................................	9.6	6.1	5.3	4.6	4.5	4.6	3.7	3.2	2.6	2.6	3.1
Female................................	8.5	4.9	4.8	3.9	3.9	3.2	3.4	2.8	2.8	1.8	1.9
Race/ethnicity[1]											
White..................................	9.4	5.7	5.4	4.6	4.2	3.9	3.6	3.0	2.9	2.2	2.5
Black...................................	9.6	6.1	5.1	3.9	4.3	4.4	4.6	3.2	2.2 !	2.6	3.0 !
Hispanic.............................	7.1	4.6	3.9	3.9	3.6	3.9	2.9	3.2	2.3	2.0	1.8
Asian/Pacific Islander	8.3	3.7	3.2	1.4 !	3.4 !	*	2.3 !	2.4 !	*	2.1 !	*
Asian..............................	NA	NA	3.3 !	1.5 !	3.6 !	*	2.5 !	2.6 !	*	2.1 !	*
Pacific Islander..................	NA	NA	*	*	*	*	*	*	*	*	*
American Indian/ Alaska Native	9.6 !	*	*	*	10.1	*	4.9 !	3.0 !	6.5 !	11.1 !	*
Two or more races......................	NA	NA	9.8	*	10.1	*	4.9 !	3.0 !	6.5 !	*	6.5 !
Grade											
6th....................................	8.8	5.9	3.8	4.6	3.9	3.7	3.8	4.1	3.1	3.1	3.1
7th....................................	10.6	5.8	6.3	5.4	4.7	3.4	3.1	2.5	3.4	2.6	2.9
8th....................................	10.1	4.3	5.2	3.6	4.4	3.8	3.8	2.3	2.3	1.8	2.1
9th....................................	11.4	7.9	6.3	4.7	5.3	5.3	5.1	4.1	3.0	2.7	2.6
10th...................................	8.7	6.5	4.7	4.3	4.4	4.2	3.0	3.3	1.6	2.7	3.3
11th...................................	7.0	4.8	5.0	3.6	4.0	4.7	3.1	3.3	4.4	1.4	2.4
12th...................................	5.8	2.9	3.6	3.7	2.7	2.0	2.9	2.0 !	1.3 !	1.4	1.1 !
School locale[2]											
Urban................................	NA	NA	NA	NA	NA	NA	NA	NA	3.1	2.5	3.3
Suburban	NA	NA	NA	NA	NA	NA	NA	NA	3.2	1.9	2.1
Rural	NA	NA	NA	NA	NA	NA	NA	NA	1.3 !	2.3	2.8 !
Town.................................	NA	NA	NA	NA	NA	NA	NA	NA	2.2	2.0	2.4
Control of school[2,3]											
Public................................	9.3	5.7	5.1	4.4	4.5	4.1	3.7	3.1	2.8	2.2	2.7
Private..............................	6.2	3.4	4.9	2.7	1.1 !	1.8 !	1.9 !	2.8 !	*	*	*
Theft	7.0	4.2	4.0	3.1	3.0	2.8	2.6	1.9	1.9	1.5	1.5
Sex											
Male....................................	7.0	4.5	3.9	3.1	3.0	3.4	2.6	2.0	1.7	1.6	1.6
Female................................	7.0	3.8	4.1	3.2	3.0	2.1	2.6	1.8	2.0	1.3	1.4
Race/ethnicity[1]											
White..................................	7.3	4.1	4.3	3.4	3.1	2.9	2.5	1.6	2.0	1.3	1.6
Black...................................	6.9	5.0	3.8	2.7	3.1	2.5	3.7	2.7	1.3 !	1.8	1.7 !
Hispanic.............................	5.7	3.7	3.0	3.1	2.2	3.0	2.0	1.8	1.6	1.4	1.2
Asian/Pacific Islander	6.4	3.5	3.2	*	3.0 !	*	2.3 !	2.4 !	*	2.1 !	*
Asian..............................	NA	NA	3.3 !	*	3.2 !	*	2.5 !	2.6 !	*	2.1 !	*
Pacific Islander..................	NA	NA	*	*	*	*	*	*	*	*	*
American Indian/ Alaska Native	7.2 !	*	*	*	*	*	*	*	*	7.2 !	*
Two or more races......................	NA	NA	8.3 !	*	5.3 !	*	3.7 !	*	4.3 !	*	*
Grade											
6th....................................	5.4	4.0	2.2	2.8	2.6	1.3	2.7	1.4 !	1.6 !	1.0 !	1.4 !
7th....................................	8.1	3.4	4.8	2.9	2.7	2.1	1.9	1.4	1.6 !	1.3 !	1.5 !
8th....................................	7.8	3.3	4.1	2.4	2.5	2.0	2.0	1.0 !	1.8	1.1 !	1.1 !
9th....................................	8.8	6.2	5.2	3.7	4.6	4.9	4.4	2.7	2.1	2.4	1.7
10th...................................	7.6	5.7	3.7	3.8	3.6	3.5	2.1	2.6	1.4 !	2.1	2.1
11th...................................	5.4	3.8	4.1	2.8	2.6	3.3	2.7	2.3	3.4	1.1 !	1.7 !
12th...................................	4.5	2.3	3.1	3.4	1.9	1.5	2.4	1.6 !	1.0 !	1.2 !	0.9!
School locale[2]											
Urban................................	NA	NA	NA	NA	NA	NA	NA	NA	2.3	1.6	2.0
Suburban	NA	NA	NA	NA	NA	NA	NA	NA	1.8	1.4	1.1
Rural	NA	NA	NA	NA	NA	NA	NA	NA	1.1 !	1.0 !	1.9 !
Town.................................	NA	NA	NA	NA	NA	NA	NA	NA	1.6	1.4	1.5
Control of school[2,3]											
Public................................	7.2	4.4	4.0	3.3	3.2	2.9	2.7	1.9	1.9	1.5	1.7
Private..............................	4.9	2.4	4.0	1.3 !	1.1 !	*	1.2 !	2.0 !	*	*	*

Table 4. Percentage of Students Ages 12 to 18 Years Who Reported Criminal Victimization at School During the Previous 6 Months, by Type of Victimization and Selected Student and School Characteristics, Selected Years, 1995–2019—Continued

(Percent.)

Characteristic	1995	2001	2003	2005	2007	2009	2011	2013	2015	2017	2019
All Violent	2.5	1.8	1.3	1.2	1.6	1.4	1.1	1.2	0.9	0.7	1.1
Sex											
Male	3.0	2.1	1.7	1.6	1.7	1.6	1.2	1.3	1.0	1.0	1.6
Female	2.0	1.4	0.9	0.8	1.4	1.1	0.9	1.1	0.9	0.5	0.5
Race/ethnicity[1]											
White	2.5	2.0	1.4	1.3	1.5	1.2	1.2	1.5	1.0	0.9	1.1
Black	3.0	1.3 !	1.5	1.3 !	1.6 !	2.3	1.1 !	*	0.9 !	0.8 !	1.4 !
Hispanic	2.0	1.5	1.1	0.9	1.4	1.3 !	1.0	1.5	0.6 !	0.5 !	0.6 !
Asian/Pacific Islander	2.2 !	*	*	*	*	*	*	*	*	*	*
Asian	NA	NA	*	*	*	*	*	*	*	*	*
Pacific Islander	NA	NA	*	*	*	*	*	*	*	*	*
American Indian/ Alaska Native	*	*	*	*	*	*	*	*	*	*	*
Two or more races	NA	NA	*	*	5.3 !	*	^	*	3.6	*	3.2 !
Grade											
6th	4.3	2.6	1.9	1.9	1.5 !	2.6	1.3 !	2.7	1.6 ~	2.1	1.7 !
7th	3.1	2.6	1.7	2.6	2.4	1.2	1.2 !	1.2 !	1.9	1.4 !	1.7
8th	2.7	1.3	1.4	1.4	2.1	2.0	2.1	1.4	0.6 !	0.7 !	1.0 !
9th	2.9	2.4	1.5	1.0	1.2 !	0.9	1.1 !	1.4 !	0.8 !	*	1.1 !
10th	1.8	1.2	1.3	0.5 !	1.2 !	1.0	0.9 !	1.0 !	*	0.7 !	1.2 !
11th	1.6	1.6	0.9 !	0.7 !	1.5	1.5	*	1.0 !	1.3 !	*	0.8 !
12th	1.6	0.9 !	0.5 !	*	0.8 !	*	*	*	*	*	*
School locale[2]											
Urban	NA	NA	NA	NA	NA	NA	NA	NA	0.8 !	1.0	1.3
Suburban	NA	NA	NA	NA	NA	NA	NA	NA	1.5	0.5 !	1.0
Rural	NA	NA	NA	NA	NA	NA	NA	NA	*	1.3 !	1.2 !
Town	NA	NA	NA	NA	NA	NA	NA	NA	0.6 !	0.5. !	1.2 !
Control of school[2,3]											
Public	2.6	1.8	1.4	1.2	1.7	1.4	1.1	1.2	1.0	0.8	1.2
Private	1.6	1.0 !	0.9 !	1.4 !	*	*	*	*	*	*	*
Violent Excluding Simple Assault[4]	0.5	0.4	0.2	0.3	0.4	0.3	0.1	0.2	0.2	0.2	0.3
Sex											
Male	0.7	0.5	0.3 !	0.3 !	0.5 !	0.6	0.2!	0.2!	0.2!	0.2!	0.4 !
Female	0.3	0.4 !	*	0.3	0.2 !	*	*	0.2	*	0.2!	*
Race/ethnicity[1]											
White	0.5	0.4	0.2	0.3 !	0.2 !	0.3	0.2!	0.2!	0.3 !	0.3 !	0.2!
Black	0.8 !	0.5 !	*	*	*	*	*	*	*	*	*
Hispanic	0.4 !	0.8 !	0.4 !	0.4 !	0.8 !	*	*	0.4 !	*	*	*
Asian/Pacific Islander	*	*	*	*	*	*	*	*	*	*	*
Asian	NA	NA	*	*	*	*	*	*	*	*	*
Pacific Islander	NA	NA	*	*	*	*	*	*	*	*	*
American Indian/ Alaska Native	*	*	*	*	*	*	*	*	*	*	*
Two or more races	NA	NA	*	*	*	*	*	*	*	*	*
Grade											
6th	1.2!	*	*	*	*	*	*	0.8 !	*	*	*
7th	0.5 !	0.6 !	*	*	0.4 !	*	0.5	*	*	*	*
8th	0.6 !	0.3 !	*	*	*	*	#	*	*	*	*
9th	0.5 !	0.8 !	0.6 !	*	*	*	*	*	*	*	*
10th	0.2 !	0.4 !	*	*	*	*	#	*	*	*	*
11th	0.3 !	*	*	*	0.6 !	*	#	*	*	*	*
12th	*	*	*	*	*	*	#	*	*	*	*
School locale[2]											
Urban	NA	NA	NA	NA	NA	NA	NA	NA	*	*	0.3 !
Suburban	NA	NA	NA	NA	NA	NA	NA	NA	0.5 !	*	*
Rural	NA	NA	NA	NA	NA	NA	NA	NA	*	*	*
Town	NA	NA	NA	NA	NA	NA	NA	NA	*	*	*
Control of school[2,3]											
Public	0.5	0.5	0.2	0.3	0.4	0.4	0.1!	0.2!	0.2!	0.2!	0.3 !
Private	*	*	*	*	*	*	*	*	*	*	*

NOTE: "Total victimization" includes theft and violent victimization. A single student could report more than one type of victimization. In the total victimization section, students who reported both theft and violent victimization are counted only once. "Theft" includes attempted and completed purse-snatching, completed pickpocketing, and all attempted and completed thefts, with the exception of motor vehicle thefts. Theft does not include robbery, which involves the threat or use of force and is classified as a violent crime. "All violent" victimization includes the crimes of rape, sexual assault, robbery, aggravated assault, and simple assault. "At school" includes in the school building, on school property, on a school bus, and, from 2001 onward, going to and from school. Some data have been revised from previously published figures.
NA = Not available.
* = Rounds to zero.
! = Interpret data with caution. The coefficient of variation (CV) for this estimate is between 30 and 50 percent.
^ = Reporting standards not met. Either there are too few cases for a reliable estimate or the coefficient of variation (CV) is 50 percent or greater.
[1]Race categories exclude persons of Hispanic ethnicity. Prior to 2003, separate data for Asian students, Pacific Islander students, and students of Two or more races were not collected.
[2]Excludes students with missing information about the school characteristic.
[3]Data for 2013 and prior years were based on school information provided by the respondent. Beginning in 2015, data were based on school information collected in the Common Core of Data and the Private School Universe Survey, which was appended to the School Crime Supplement data file; therefore, these data may not be entirely comparable with figures for earlier years.
[4]In previous versions of this table, "violent excluding simple assault" was labeled as "serious violent" victimization. This category includes all types of violent victimization with the exception of simple assault.

Table 5. Number and Percentage of Public School Teachers Who Reported That They Were Threatened with Injury or Physically Attacked by a Student from School During the Previous 12 Months, by Selected Teacher and School Characteristics, Selected Years, 1993–1994 Through 2015–2016

(Number; percent.)

Incident and year	Total	Sex		Race/ethnicity				Instructional level[1]	
		Male	Female	White	Black	Hispanic	Other[2]	Elementary	Secondary
	Number of teachers								
Threatened with Injury									
1993–1994	326,800	111,200	215,600	281,300	23,400	15,100	6,900	128,000	198,800
1999–2000	287,400	89,600	197,800	237,100	27,200	16,300	6,700	138,000	149,300
2003–2004	242,100	75,300	166,800	189,800	31,900	11,800	8,600	108,800	133,300
2007–2008	276,600	85,200	191,500	223,200	27,600	17,400	8,400	123,800	152,800
2011–2012	338,400	79,800	258,600	266,800	33,400	26,600	11,600	184,000	154,400
2015–2016	327,900	80,700	247,200	262,800	26,200	24,400	14,600	182,100	145,800
Physically Attacked									
1993–1994	112,400	28,700	83,700	96,300	7,600	5,900	2,600	71,600	40,700
1999–2000	125,000	29,100	95,900	103,100	11,000	8,400	2,500	94,400	30,600
2003–2004	121,400	21,700	99,700	95,500	14,800	6,400	4,700	85,100	36,300
2007–2008	146,400	33,400	113,000	124,100	11,600	7,800	2,800!	109,100	37,300
2011–2012	197,400	29,500	167,900	160,700	18,000	11,300	7,400	153,800	43,600
2015–2016	192,500	30,200	162,300	155,600	12,700	14,200	10,000	153,700	38,800
	Percent of teachers								
Threatened with Injury									
1993–1994	12.8	16.0	11.5	12.7	12.4	13.9	14.5	9.6	16.2
1999–2000	9.6	11.9	8.8	9.4	11.9	9.7	9.1	8.6	10.7
2003–2004	7.4	9.3	6.8	7.0	12.4	5.8	9.6	6.3	8.7
2007–2008	8.1	10.4	7.4	7.9	11.5	7.3	8.7	7.2	9.1
2011–2012	10.0	10.0	10.0	9.6	14.5	10.1	9.9	10.7	9.3
2015–2016	9.8	10.4	9.6	9.8	11.7	8.4	10.3	10.8	8.8
Physically Attacked									
1993–1994	4.4	4.1	4.5	4.3	4.0	5.4	5.4	5.4	3.3
1999–2000	4.2	3.9	4.3	4.1	4.8	5.0	3.4	5.9	2.2
2003–2004	3.7	2.7	4.1	3.5	5.8	3.2	5.3	5.0	2.4
2007–2008	4.3	4.1	4.4	4.4	4.9	3.3	3.0!	6.3	2.2
2011–2012	5.8	3.7	6.5	5.8	7.8	4.3	6.3	8.9	2.6
2015–2016	5.7	3.9	6.3	5.8	5.7	4.9	7.1	9.1	2.3

NOTE: Teachers who taught only prekindergarten students are excluded. Includes teachers in both traditional public schools and public charter schools. Race categories exclude persons of Hispanic ethnicity. Detail may not sum to totals because of rounding. Some data have been revised from previously published figures.
! = Interpret data with caution. The coefficient of variation (CV) for this estimate is between 30 and 50 percent.
[1] Instructional level divides teachers into elementary or secondary based on a combination of grades taught, main teaching assignment, and structure of teachers' class(es), rather than the level of school in which teachers taught. Teachers with only ungraded classes were classified based on their main teaching assignment and the structure of their class(es). Among teachers with regularly graded classes, elementary teachers generally include those teaching prekindergarten through grade 6 and those teaching multiple grades, with a preponderance of grades taught being kindergarten through grade 6. In general, secondary teachers include those teaching any of grades 7 through 12 and those teaching multiple grades, with a preponderance of grades taught being grades 7 through 12 and usually with no grade taught being lower than grade 5.
[2] Includes American Indian/Alaska Native, Asian, and Pacific Islander; for 2003-04 and later years, also includes two or more races.

Table 6. Percentage of Public Schools Recording Incidents of Crime at School and Reporting Incidents to Police, Number of Incidents, and Rate Per 1,000 Students, by Type of Crime, Selected Years, 1999–2000 Through 2019–2020

(Percent; number; rate per 1,000 students.)

Type of crime recorded or reported to police	Percent of schools						2015–2016		2017–2018		2019–2020[1]	
	1999–2000	2003–2004	2005–2006	2007–2008	2009–2010	2013–2014[2]	Percent of schools	Number of incidents	Percent of schools	Number of incidents	Percent of schools	Number of incidents
Recorded Incidents												
Total	86.4	88.5	85.7	85.5	85.0	NA	78.9	1,381,200	79.8	1,438,500	77.2	1,425,500
Violent Incidents	71.4	81.4	77.7	75.5	73.8	65.0	68.9	864,900	70.7	962,300	70.2	938,500
Serious violent incidents	19.7	18.3	17.1	17.2	16.4	13.1	15.5	40,800	21.3	54,400	25.4	62,800
Rape or attempted rape	0.7	0.8	0.3	0.8	0.5	0.2!	0.9	1,100	0.9	1,100	1.0	1,000
Sexual assault other than rape[3]	2.5	3.0	2.8	2.5	2.3	1.7	3.4	6,100	5.2	7,100	5.3	7,700
Physical attack or fight with a weapon	5.2	4.0	3.0	3.0	3.9	1.8	2.6	5,300	3.0	10,500	8.9	16,900
Threat of physical attack with a weapon	11.1	8.6	8.8	9.3	7.7	8.7	8.5	18,300	13.2	26,700	10.0	20,500
Robbery with a weapon	0.5!	0.6	0.4	0.4!	0.2	‡	0.5 !	600	0.4	500	0.9!	D
Robbery without a weapon	5.3	6.3	6.4	5.2	4.4	2.5	2.7	9,500	3.5	8,500	5.7	14,000
Physical attack or fight without a weapon	63.7	76.7	74.3	72.7	70.5	57.5	64.9	567,000	65.7	597,300	59.9	583,300
Threat of physical attack without a weapon	52.2	53.0	52.2	47.8	46.4	47.1	39.4	257,000	41.4	310,700	40.1	292,400
Theft/Larceny[4]	45.6	46.0	46.0	47.3	44.1	NA	38.7	166,000	33.4	132,500	31.7	117,300
Other Incidents[5]	72.7	64.0	68.2	67.4	68.1	NA	58.5	350,400	59.8	343,700	56.5	369,700
Possession of a firearm/explosive device	5.5	6.1	7.2	4.7	4.7	NA	4.0	10,500	3.3	3,600	3.7	3,700
Possession of a knife or sharp object	42.6	NA	42.8	40.6	39.7	NA	38.4	70,600	38.2	69,100	32.4	53,200
Distribution of illegal drugs	12.3	12.9	NA	NA	NA	NA	NA	NA	NA	NA	NA	NA
Possession or use of alcohol or illeal drugs[5]	26.6	29.3	NA	NA	NA	NA	NA	NA	NA	NA	NA	NA
Distribution, possession, or use of illegal drugs	NA	NA	25.9	23.2	24.6	NA	24.9	112,100	24.9	120,300	28.5	169,100
Inappropriate distribution, possession, or use of prescription drugs	NA	NA	NA	NA	12.1	NA	9.5	20,100	9.7	21,100	9.0	19,100
Distribution, possession, or use of alcohol	NA	NA	16.2	14.9	14.1	NA	13.3	29,900	13.4	29,000	14.3	29,400
Sexual harassment	36.3	NA	NA	NA	NA	NA	NA	NA	NA	NA	NA	NA
Vandalism	51.4	51.4	50.5	49.3	45.8	NA	33.4	107,200	33.1	100,600	32.4	95,100
Reported Incidents to Police												
Total	62.5	65.2	60.9	62.0	60.0	NA	47.4	448,900	46.9	422,800	46.6	482,400
Violent Incidents	36.0	43.6	37.7	37.8	39.9	NA	32.7	195,600	32.5	192,100	32.4	225,600
Serious violent incidents	14.8	13.3	12.6	12.6	10.4	NA	10.0	20,000	14.9	26,100	13.8	32,500
Rape or attempted rape	0.6	0.8	0.3	0.8	0.5	NA	0.7	900	0.8	1,000	0.9	1,000
Sexual assault other than rape[3]	2.3	2.6	2.6	2.1	1.4	NA	2.7	3,600	4.3	5,600	4.1	6,300
Physical attack or fight with a weapon	3.9	2.8	2.2	2.1	2.2	NA	1.3	2,500 !	1.5	2,400	2.1	5,000!
Threat of physical attack with a weapon	8.5	6.0	5.9	5.7	4.5	NA	5.3	7,500	9.0	12,400	6.5	11,300
Robbery with a weapon	0.3!	0.6	0.4	0.4	0.2	NA	0.3 !	400 !	0.3	400	0.5	500
Robbery without a weapon	3.4	4.2	4.9	4.1	3.5	NA	1.9	5,000	2.4	4,300	3.9	8,300
Physical attack or fight without a weapon	25.8	35.6	29.2	28.2	34.3	NA	25.1	121,500	21.7	107,600	23.0	130,600
Threat of physical attack without a weapon	18.9	21.0	19.7	19.5	15.2	NA	12.9	54,200	14.3	58,400	14.7	62,600
Theft/Larceny[4]	28.5	30.5	27.9	31.0	25.4	NA	18.1	71,600	14.9	53,900	14.6	47,700
Other Incidents[5]	52.0	50.0	50.6	48.7	46.3	NA	33.5	181,700	35.1	176,900	35.9	209,100
Possession of a firearm/explosive device	4.5	4.9	5.5	3.6	3.1	NA	1.9	7,500 !	2.1	2,300	2.4	2,400
Possession of a knife or sharp object	23.0	NA	25.0	23.3	20.0	NA	15.8	27,700	18.0	30,500	16.1	25,900
Distribution of illegal drugs[5]	11.4	12.4	NA	NA	NA	NA	NA	NA	NA	NA	NA	NA
Possession or use of alcohol or illegal drugs[5]	22.2	26.0	NA	NA	NA	NA	NA	NA	NA	NA	NA	NA
Distribution, possession, or use of illegal drugs[6]	NA	NA	22.8	20.7	21.4	NA	19.9	82,200	19.9	84,800	22.5	117,600
Inappropriate distribution, possession, or use of prescription drugs[7]	NA	NA	NA	NA	9.6	NA	7.4	15,100	7.1	15,100	6.5	13,500
Distribution, possession, or use of alcohol[6]	NA	NA	11.6	10.6	10.0	NA	8.6	17,800	8.0	16,900	8.3	18,500
Sexual harassment	14.7	NA	NA	NA	NA	NA	NA	NA	NA	NA	NA	NA
Vandalism	32.7	34.3	31.9	30.8	26.8	NA	12.9	31,600	12.0	27,300	13.6	31,200

NOTE: Responses were provided by the principal or the person most knowledgeable about crime and safety issues at the school. "At school" was defined to include activities that happen in school buildings, on school grounds, on school buses, and at places that hold school-sponsored events or activities. Respondents were instructed to include incidents that occurred before, during, and after normal school hours or when school activities or events were in session. Detail may not sum to totals because of rounding and because schools that recorded or reported more than one type of crime incident were counted only once in the total percentage of schools recording or reporting incidents.
NA = Not available.
! = Interpret data with caution. The coefficient of variation (CV) for this estimate is between 30 and 50 percent.
D = Reporting standards not met. Either there are too few cases for a reliable estimate or the coefficient of variation (CV) is 50 percent or greater.
[1]The coronavirus pandemic affected the 2019-20 data collection activities, while the change to virtual schooling and the adjusted school year may have impacted the data collected by SSOCS. Readers should use caution when comparing 2019-20 estimates with those from earlier years.
[2]Data for 2013-14 were collected using the Fast Response Survey System (FRSS), while data for all other years were collected using the School Survey on Crime and Safety (SSOCS). The 2013-14 FRSS survey was designed to allow comparisons with SSOCS data. However, the mode of the 2013-14 FRSS survey differed from that of SSOCS, which evolved over time. Specifically, all respondents to the 2013-14 survey could choose either to complete the survey on paper (and mail it back) or to complete the survey online. All respondents to SSOCS had only the option of completing a paper survey prior to 2017-18. In 2017-18, SSOCS experimented with offering an online option to some respondents. In 2019-20, SSOCS switched to using primarily an online survey instrument. The 2013-14 FRSS survey also relied on a smaller sample than SSOCS. The FRSS survey's smaller sample size and difference in survey administration may have impacted the 2013-14 results.
[3]Prior to 2015-16, the wording of the survey item was "sexual battery other than rape."
[4]Theft/larceny is taking things worth over $10 without personal confrontation.
[5]Caution should be used when making direct comparisons of "Other incidents" between years because the survey questions about alcohol and drugs changed and because sexual harassment was only included in 1999-2000. In addition, data on "possession of a knife or sharp object" were not included for 2003-04.

Table 7. Percentage of Students Ages 12 to 18 Years Who Reported That Gangs Were Present at School During the School Year, by Sex, Race/Ethnicity, and Urbanicity, Selected Years, 2001–2019

(Percent.)

Student or school characteristic	2001[1]	2003[1]	2005[1]	2007	2009	2011	2013	2015	2017	2019[2]
Total	20.3	21.0	24.2	23.2	20.4	17.5	12.4	10.7	8.6	9.0
Sex										
Male	21.5	22.4	25.3	25.1	20.9	17.5	12.9	10.9	7.9	9.5
Female	18.9	19.6	22.9	21.3	19.9	17.5	12.0	10.4	9.3	8.5
Race/ethnicity[3]										
White	15.5	14.2	16.7	16.0	14.1	11.1	7.4	7.4	5.3	6.3
Black	28.8	29.7	37.5	37.5	31.4	32.7	18.6	17.1	16.6	14.7
Hispanic	32.3	37.3	38.9	36.1	33.0	26.4	20.1	15.3	12.3	12.5
Asian/Pacific Islander	23.3	21.8	21.3	18.1	16.9	10.1	9.8	5.0 !	2.4 !	5.3
Asian	NA	21.2	20.3	17.4	17.2	9.9	9.4	4.1 !	2.0 !	4.5
Pacific Islander	NA	^	^	^	^	^	^	^	^	^
American Indian/ Alaska Native	13.2 !	24.8 !	^	17.2 !	^	^	18.3	^	^	15.8 !
Two or more races	NA	22.3	23.6	28.3	18.0	10.3	13.3	13.5	9.7	9.1
Grade										
6th	11.3	10.9	12.1	15.3	11.0	8.2	5.0	5.7	4.8	5.8
7th	15.8	16.4	17.3	17.4	14.8	10.2	7.7	6.8	5.4	5.5
8th	17.4	17.9	19.1	20.6	15.9	11.3	7.8	7.2	6.6	5.9
9th	24.3	26.2	28.3	28.0	24.9	21.7	13.9	13.3	10.9	11.6
10th	23.8	26.6	32.6	28.1	27.7	23.0	17.7	13.3	11.4	12.1
11th	24.2	23.5	28.0	25.9	22.6	23.2	17.1	13.3	9.7	9.9
12th	21.2	22.4	27.9	24.4	21.9	21.3	14.6	13.1	9.8	11.0
School locale[4]										
Urban	NA	NA	NA	NA	NA	NA	NA	15.4	12.3	13.5
Suburban	NA	NA	NA	NA	NA	NA	NA	11.0	7.4	7.9
Rural	NA	NA	NA	NA	NA	NA	NA	8.3	9.1	8.9
Town	NA	NA	NA	NA	NA	NA	NA	4.9	5.6	6.0
Control of school[4,5]										
Public	21.7	22.6	25.8	24.9	22.0	18.9	13.3	11.4	9.2	9.8
Private	5.0	3.9	4.2	5.2	2.3 !	1.9 !	2.3 !	2.0 !	^	^

NOTE: "At school" includes in the school building, on school property, on a school bus, and going to and from school. Some data have been revised from previously published figures.

NA = Not available.

! = Interpret data with caution. The coefficient of variation (CV) for this estimate is between 30 and 50 percent.

^ = Reporting standards not met. Either there are too few cases for a reliable estimate or the coefficient of variation (CV) is 50 percent or greater.

[1] In 2005 and prior years, the period covered by the survey question was "during the last 6 months," but this was changed to "during this school year" beginning in 2007. Cognitive testing suggested that modifications to the reference period would not have a substantial impact on the survey responses.

[2] The 2019 survey included a split sample design to test alternate introductions for the section assessing the presence of gangs at school. Approximately 60 percent of the sample received the version of the questionnaire that was consistent with prior years, where the section introduction included the definition "All gangs, whether or not they are involved in violent or illegal activity, are included." The remaining 40 percent of the sample received the alternate questionnaire, which excluded the definition. Estimates in this table include all respondents, regardless of which version of the questionnaire they received. For more information about the 2019 survey collection and experiment, see *Methodology Report: Split-Half Administration of the 2019 School Crime Supplement to the National Crime Victimization Survey* (NCES 2021-010).

[3] Race categories exclude persons of Hispanic ethnicity. In 2001, separate data for Asian students, Pacific Islander students, and students of two or more races were not collected.

[4] Excludes students with missing information about the school characteristic.

[5] Data for 2013 and prior years were based on school information provided by the respondent. Beginning in 2015, data were based on school information collected in the Common Core of Data and the Private School Universe Survey, which was appended to the School Crime Supplement data file; therefore, these data may not be entirely comparable with figures for earlier years.

(Percent.)

Student characteristic	1993	1999	2001	2003	2005	2007	2009	2011	2013	2015	2017	2019
Total	24.0	30.2	28.5	28.7	25.4	22.3	22.7	25.6	22.1	21.7	19.8	21.8
Sex												
Male	28.5	34.7	34.6	31.9	28.8	25.7	25.9	29.2	24.5	24.2	20.9	22.8
Female	19.1	25.7	22.7	25.0	21.8	18.7	19.3	21.7	19.7	19.1	18.7	20.8
Race/Ethnicity												
White	24.1	28.8	28.3	27.5	23.6	20.8	19.8	22.7	20.4	19.8	17.7	19.8
Black	17.5	25.3	21.9	23.1	23.9	19.2	22.2	22.8	18.6	20.6	18.9	21.5
Hispanic	34.1	36.9	34.2	36.5	33.5	29.1	31.2	33.2	27.4	27.2	25.4	26.7
Asian[1]	NA	25.7	25.7	22.5	15.9	21.0	18.3	23.3	22.6	15.3	17.7	14.5
Pacific Islander[1]	NA	46.9	50.2	34.7	41.3	38.5	27.6	38.9	27.7	30.1 !	25.7	17.0 !
American Indian/Alaska Native	20.9	30.6	34.5	31.3	24.4	25.1	34.0	40.5	25.5	19.8	17.1	24.2
Two or more races[1]	NA	36.0	34.5	36.6	31.6	24.6	26.9	33.3	26.4	24.7	19.2	27.8
Sexual Identity[2]												
Heterosexual	NA	NA	NA	NA	NA	NA	NA	NA	NA	20.8	18.9	20.8
Gay, lesbian, or bisexual	NA	NA	NA	NA	NA	NA	NA	NA	NA	29.3	28.2	30.3
Not sure	NA	NA	NA	NA	NA	NA	NA	NA	NA	28.4	19.6	23.6
Grade												
9th	21.8	27.6	29.0	29.5	24.0	21.2	22.0	23.7	22.4	21.6	18.9	21.6
10th	23.7	32.1	29.0	29.2	27.5	25.3	23.7	27.8	23.2	21.9	20.3	23.7
11th	27.5	31.1	28.7	29.9	24.9	22.8	24.3	27.0	23.2	22.7	20.0	22.0
12th	23.0	30.5	26.9	24.9	24.9	19.6	20.6	23.8	18.8	20.3	19.6	19.6

NOTE: Students were asked if anyone offered, sold, or gave them an illegal drug on school property during the previous 12 months. "On school property" was not defined for respondents. Race categories exclude persons of Hispanic ethnicity.
NA = Not available.
! = Interpret data with caution. The coefficient of variation (CV) for this estimate is between 30 and 50 percent.
[1]Before 1999, Asian students and Pacific Islander students were not categorized separately, and students could not be classified as two or more races. Because the response categories changed in 1999, caution should be used in comparing data on race from 1993 with data from later years.
[2]Students were asked which of the following ("heterosexual (straight)," "gay or lesbian," "bisexual," or "not sure") best described them.

Table 9. Percentage of Students Age 12 to 18 Years Who Reported Being the Target of Hate-Related Words and Seeing Hate-Related Graffiti at School During the School Year by Selected Student and School Characteristics and Location, Selected Years, 1999–2019

(Percent.)

Student/school characteristic	1999[1]	2001[1]	2003[1]	2005[1]	2007	2009	2011	2013	2015	2017	2019
Hate-Related Words											
Total	13.3	12.3	11.8	11.2	9.7	8.7	9.1	6.6	7.2	6.4	6.7
Sex											
Male.................................	12.4	12.9	12.1	11.7	9.9	8.5	9.0	6.6	7.8	6.0	6.0
Female..............................	14.4	11.8	11.4	10.7	9.6	8.9	9.1	6.7	6.7	6.9	7.5
Race/Ethnicity[2]											
White................................	12.6	12.0	11.0	10.4	8.9	7.2	8.3	5.3	6.3	6.1	5.6
Black.................................	16.6	14.1	14.3	15.0	11.4	11.1	10.7	7.8	9.4	7.4	8.6
Hispanic............................	12.1	11.1	11.4	10.5	10.6	11.2	9.8	7.4	6.5	6.3	6.5
Asian/Pacific Islander...........	13.9	13.0	11.4	10.7	10.5	10.9	9.6	9.8	11.2	4.7	7.7
Asian...........................	NA	NA	11.4	11.0	11.1	10.7	9.0	10.3	10.8	4.8	7.2
Pacific Islander................	NA	NA	^	^	^	^	^	^	^	^	^
American Indian/Alaska Native......	28.5	17.4 !	18.6 !	^	^	^	^	^	^	^	^
Two or more races	NA	NA	19.4	10.6	11.7	9.8	11.1	13.5	8.5	11.4	16.5
Grade											
6th...................................	13.1	12.2	11.9	11.1	12.1	8.3	9.0	6.7	10.1	6.7	7.7
7th...................................	15.8	14.2	12.5	13.1	10.7	9.6	9.9	7.5	7.0	7.3	8.1
8th...................................	16.1	13.0	12.9	11.2	11.0	10.9	8.4	7.4	9.2	7.0	8.6
9th...................................	13.3	12.2	13.5	12.8	10.9	8.0	10.2	6.6	7.4	8.2	6.7
10th..................................	11.9	13.2	11.7	10.9	9.0	9.7	9.6	6.4	6.5	6.3	5.3
11th..................................	10.6	12.7	8.3	9.0	8.6	8.4	8.7	7.5	6.0	4.7	6.8
12th..................................	11.8	8.0	10.9	9.7	6.0	5.8	7.5	4.1	5.4	4.6	4.2
School Locale[3]											
City...................................	NA	NA	NA	NA	NA	NA	NA	NA	7.4	6.7	7.9
Suburban...........................	NA	NA	NA	NA	NA	NA	NA	NA	8.2	5.9	6.5
Town.................................	NA	NA	NA	NA	NA	NA	NA	NA	5.5	7.5	5.8
Rural.................................	NA	NA	NA	NA	NA	NA	NA	NA	6.3	6.7	6.8
Control of School[3,4]											
Public................................	13.9	12.7	11.9	11.6	10.1	8.9	9.3	6.6	7.5	6.7	7.1
Private...............................	8.2	8.2	9.8	6.8	6.1	6.6	6.9	6.7	3.4 !	3.3	2.5 !
Hate-Related Graffiti											
Total	36.6	36.0	36.9	38.4	35.0	29.2	28.4	24.6	27.2	23.2	22.6
Sex											
Male.................................	34.0	35.4	35.6	37.7	34.5	29.0	28.6	24.1	26.3	22.6	22.0
Female..............................	39.3	36.6	38.2	39.1	35.5	29.3	28.1	25.1	28.1	23.8	23.1
Race/Ethnicity[2]											
White................................	36.8	36.5	35.8	38.5	35.6	28.3	28.2	23.7	28.6	24.0	22.9
Black.................................	38.0	34.0	38.7	37.9	33.7	29.0	28.1	26.3	24.9	24.8	21.7
Hispanic............................	35.8	35.6	40.9	38.0	34.9	32.2	29.1	25.6	26.7	21.0	23.2
Asian/Pacific Islander........	30.9	33.5	27.7	34.5	28.5	29.9	29.8	20.8	19.5	15.2	17.0
Asian...........................	NA	NA	26.8	34.7	28.2	31.2	29.9	20.8	17.5	14.6	16.8
Pacific Islander....................	NA	NA	^	^	^	^	^	^	^	^	^
American Indian/Alaska Native......	47.1	31.5	35.9	^	27.3	^	16.8 !	22.0 !	^	27.8 !	30.6 !
Two or more races	NA	NA	40.8	47.7	41.9	30.3	27.4	31.1	29.1	35.0	24.4
Grade											
6th...................................	30.7	35.2	36.1	34.0	35.6	28.1	25.9	21.9	30.0	20.6	20.3
7th...................................	35.1	35.5	37.6	37.0	32.4	27.9	26.0	21.7	24.7	21.2	22.5
8th...................................	35.9	37.2	35.1	35.7	33.5	30.8	25.9	24.0	27.2	22.4	22.3
9th...................................	39.5	36.1	37.6	41.6	34.6	28.1	28.7	27.2	28.2	25.2	25.2
10th..................................	39.3	36.8	41.4	40.7	36.5	31.0	33.3	26.0	28.6	27.0	23.7
11th..................................	37.3	36.5	37.2	40.2	35.4	27.4	32.1	25.8	26.2	22.6	22.0
12th..................................	35.8	33.5	32.6	37.8	37.7	30.4	25.7	24.2	26.1	22.2	20.6
School Locale[3]											
City...................................	NA	NA	NA	NA	NA	NA	NA	NA	27.9	24.3	24.3
Suburban...........................	NA	NA	NA	NA	NA	NA	NA	NA	27.9	23.0	22.4
Town.................................	NA	NA	NA	NA	NA	NA	NA	NA	35.6	28.9	22.3
Rural.................................	NA	NA	NA	NA	NA	NA	NA	NA	22.3	21.4	24.1
Control of School[3,4]											
Public................................	38.3	37.8	38.5	40.0	36.5	30.7	29.7	25.6	28.6	25.1	24.2
Private...............................	20.8	17.3	19.8	18.6	18.5	11.8	13.4	12.6	13.9	4.1	8.6

NOTE: "At school" includes in the school building, on school property, on a school bus, and, from 2001 onward, going to and from school. "Hate-related" refers to derogatory terms used by others in reference to students' personal characteristics. Some data have been revised from previously published figures.
NA = Not available.
! = Interpret data with caution. The coefficient of variation (CV) for this estimate is between 30 and 50 percent.
^ = Reporting standards not met. Either there are too few cases for a reliable estimate or the coefficient of variation (CV) is 50 percent or greater.
[1] In 2005 and prior years, the period covered by the survey question was "during the last 6 months," but this was changed to "during this school year" beginning in 2007. Cognitive testing suggested that modifications to the reference period would not have a substantial impact on the survey responses.
[2] Race categories exclude persons of Hispanic ethnicity. Prior to 2003, separate data for Asian students, Pacific Islander students, and students of two or more races were not collected.
[3] Excludes students with missing information about the school characteristic.
[4] Data for 2013 and prior years were based on school information provided by the respondent. Beginning in 2015, data were based on school information collected in the Common Core of Data and the Private School Universe Survey, which was appended to the School Crime Supplement data file; therefore, these data may not be entirely comparable with figures for earlier years.

Table 10. Percentage of Students Age 12 to 18 Years Who Reported Being Bullied at School During the School Year, by Type of Bullying and Selected Student and School Characteristics, Selected Years, 2005–2019

(Percent.)

Student/school characteristic	2005[1]	2007	2009	2011	2013	2015[2]	2017	2019[3]
Total	28.5	31.7	28.0	27.8	21.5	20.8	20.2	22.2
Sex								
Male....................................	27.5	30.3	26.6	24.5	19.5	18.8	16.7	19.1
Female.................................	29.7	33.2	29.5	31.4	23.7	22.8	23.8	25.5
Race/Ethnicity								
White	30.3	34.1	29.3	31.5	23.7	21.6	22.8	24.6
Black....................................	29.2	30.4	29.1	27.2	20.3	24.7	22.9	22.2
Hispanic................................	22.3	27.3	25.5	21.9	19.2	17.2	15.7	18.0
Asian/Pacific Islander................	20.8	17.2	17.8	13.8	9.3	19.4	7.3	13.7
Asian................................	20.9	18.1	17.3	14.9	9.2	15.6	7.3	13.5
Pacific Islander....................	^	^	^	^	^	^	^	^
American Indian/Alaska Native...........	^	29.8	^	21.1 !	24.3 !	^	27.2	^
Two or more races	34.6	38.2	27.3	26.9	27.6	17.7	23.2	37.1
Grade								
6th.......................................	37.0	42.7	39.4	37.0	27.8	31.0	29.5	28.1
7th.......................................	35.1	35.6	33.1	30.3	26.4	25.1	24.4	28.0
8th.......................................	31.3	36.9	31.7	30.7	21.7	22.2	25.3	26.7
9th.......................................	28.3	30.6	28.0	26.5	23.0	19.0	19.3	18.9
10th.....................................	25.1	27.7	26.6	28.0	19.5	21.2	18.9	18.7
11th.....................................	23.5	28.5	21.1	23.8	20.0	15.8	14.7	21.7
12th.....................................	20.8	23.0	20.4	22.0	14.1	14.9	12.2	15.8
School Locale[4]								
City......................................	NA	NA	NA	NA	NA	21.3	19.9	22.4
Suburban...............................	NA	NA	NA	NA	NA	21.3	18.1	20.5
Town	NA	NA	NA	NA	NA	20.3	26.9	21.7
Rural.....................................	NA	NA	NA	NA	NA	20.0	23.8	27.7
Control of School[4,5]								
Public....................................	29.0	32.0	28.8	28.4	21.5	21.3	21.1	22.7
Private	23.3	29.1	18.9	21.5	22.4	15.3	15.0	21.7

NOTE: "At school" includes in the school building, on school property, on a school bus, and going to and from school. Race categories exclude persons of Hispanic ethnicity. Some data have been revised from previously published figures.
NA = Not available.
! = Interpret data with caution. The coefficient of variation (CV) for this estimate is between 30 and 50 percent.
^ =Reporting standards not met. Either there are too few cases for a reliable estimate or the coefficient of variation (CV) is 50 percent or greater.
[1]In 2005 and prior years, the period covered by the survey question was "during the last 6 months," but this was changed to "during this school year" beginning in 2007. Cognitive testing suggested that modifications to the reference period would not have a substantial impact on the survey responses.
[2]The 2015 survey included a split sample design to compare two versions of an updated questionnaire on bullying that would provide data on repetition and power imbalance aligned with the Centers for Disease Control and Prevention's uniform definition of bullying. Half the sample received version 1, and the other half received version 2. Estimates in this table are based on the 50 percent of the sample who received version 1 of the questionnaire. For more information, see Split-Half Administration of the 2015 School Crime Supplement to the National Crime Victimization Survey Methodology Report (NCES 2017-004).
[3]The 2019 survey included a split sample design to compare two versions of an updated questionnaire on bullying. Approximately 60 percent of the sample received version 1, which was consistent with prior years; the remaining 40 percent received version 2, which included changes such as removing the word "bullying." Estimates in this table are based on the 60 percent of the sample who received version 1 of the questionnaire. For more information, see Methodology Report: Split-Half Administration of the 2019 School Crime Supplement to the National Crime Victimization Survey (NCES 2021-016).
[4]Excludes students with missing information about the school characteristic.
[5]Data for 2013 and prior years were based on school information provided by the respondent. Beginning in 2015, data were based on school information collected in the Common Core of Data and the Private School Universe Survey, which was appended to the School Crime Supplement data file; therefore, these data may not be entirely comparable with figures for earlier years.

Table 11. Percentage of Students in Grades 9–12 Who Reported Having Been Electronically Bullied During the Previous 12 Months, by Selected Student Characteristics, Selected Years, 2011–2019

(Percent.)

Student characteristic	2011	2013	2015	2017	2019
Total	16.2	14.8	15.5	14.9	15.7
Sex					
Male	10.8	8.5	9.7	9.9	10.9
Female	22.1	21.0	21.7	19.7	20.4
Race/ethnicity					
White..........................	18.6	16.9	18.4	17.3	18.6
Black	8.9	8.7	8.6	10.9	8.6
Hispanic	13.6	12.8	12.4	12.3	12.7
Asian	14.4	12.9	13.9	10.0	12.1
Pacific Islander	19.6	15.7	11.8	15.0	19.0!
American Indian/Alaska Native	16.2	18.0	18.7	13.2	21.3!
Two or more races..........................	21.0	18.9	20.4	16.0	19.2
Sexual identity[1]					
Heterosexual	NA	NA	14.2	13.3	14.1
Gay, lesbian, or bisexual	NA	NA	28.0	27.1	26.6
Not sure	NA	NA	22.5	22.0	19.4
Grade					
9th..........................	15.5	16.1	16.5	16.7	16.5
10th..........................	18.1	14.5	16.6	14.8	16.0
11th..........................	16.0	14.9	14.7	14.2	14.4
12th..........................	15.0	13.5	14.3	13.5	15.4

NOTE: Electronic bullying includes "being bullied through e-mail, chat rooms, instant messaging, websites, or texting" for 2011 through 2015, and "being bullied through texting, Instagram, Facebook, or other social media" for 2017 and 2019. Race categories exclude persons of Hispanic ethnicity.
NA = Not available.
! = Interpret data with caution. The coefficient of variation (CV) for this estimate is between 30 and 50 percent.
[1]Students were asked which of the following--"heterosexual (straight)," "gay or lesbian," "bisexual," or "not sure"-- best described them.

Table 12. On-Campus Crimes, Arrests, and Referrals for Disciplinary Action at Degree-Granting Postsecondary Institutions, by Location of Incident, Control and Level of Institution, and Type of Incident, Selected Years, 2001–2019

(Number.)

Control and level of institution and type of incident	Total, in residence halls and at other locations													2019		
	2001	2007	2008	2009	2010	2011	2012	2013	2014	2015	2016	2017	2018	Total	In residence halls	At other locations
All institutions																
Selected crimes against persons and property	41,596	41,829	40,296	34,054	32,097	30,407	29,766	27,236	26,818	27,532	28,239	29,034	28,587	27,334	12,837	14,497
Murder[1]	17	44	12	16	15	16	12	23	11	28	15	22	12	20	6	14
Negligent manslaughter[2]	2	3	3	0	1	1	1	0	2	2	2	3	2	5	1	4
Sex offenses: forcible [3]	2,201	2,694	2,639	2,544	2,927	3,375	4,015	4,977	6,751	8,022	8,908	10,481	12,376	11,767	7,375	4,392
Rape	NA	NA	NA	NA	NA	NA	NA	NA	4,431	5,119	5,840	6,583	6,755	6,212	5,088	1,124
Fondling	NA	NA	NA	NA	NA	NA	NA	2,320	2,903	3,068	3,898	5,621	5,555	2,287	3,268
Sex offenses: non-forcible [4]	461	40	35	65	33	46	46	45	53	63	60	82	63	74	42	32
Robbery [5]	1,663	1,561	1,576	1,409	1,392	1,285	1,368	1,317	1,041	1,044	1,080	1,034	833	806	167	639
Aggravated assault [6]	2,947	2,604	2,495	2,327	2,221	2,239	2,423	2,044	2,048	2,258	2,156	2,257	2,235	2,154	692	1,462
Burglary [7]	26,904	29,488	28,737	23,083	21,335	19,472	18,183	15,232	13,419	12,320	11,918	11,098	9,583	8,991	4,304	4,687
Motor vehicle theft [8]	6,221	4,619	4,104	3,977	3,441	3,334	3,013	2,971	2,890	3,218	3,506	3,448	3,070	3,061	33	3,028
Arson [9]	1,180	776	695	633	732	639	705	627	603	577	594	609	413	456	217	239
Weapons-, drug-, and liquor-related arrests and referrals																
Arrests[10]	40,348	50,558	50,639	50,066	51,519	54,285	52,325	46,975	44,531	40,299	38,992	37,875	32,349	27,731	14,168	13,563
Illegal weapons possession	1,073	1,318	1,190	1,077	1,112	1,023	1,023	1,018	990	1,183	1,198	1,241	1,177	1,145	244	901
Drug law violations	11,854	14,135	15,146	15,871	18,589	20,729	21,212	19,799	19,172	19,431	19,226	19,837	18,190	14,097	6,747	7,350
Liquor law violations	27,421	35,105	34,303	33,118	31,818	32,533	30,090	26,158	24,369	19,685	18,568	16,797	12,982	12,489	7,177	5,312
Referrals for disciplinary action[10]	155,201	216,600	217,526	220,987	230,269	249,694	251,402	244,985	253,315	241,687	228,802	215,288	199,819	187,331	173,015	14,316
Illegal weapons possession	1,277	1,658	1,455	1,275	1,314	1,282	1,404	1,410	1,425	1,425	1,402	1,290	1,231	1,056	718	338
Drug law violations	23,900	28,476	32,469	36,344	42,022	51,562	53,959	53,439	56,575	56,037	55,373	57,602	53,569	46,313	40,170	6,143
Liquor law violations	130,024	186,466	183,602	183,368	186,933	196,850	196,039	190,136	195,315	184,225	172,027	156,396	145,019	139,962	132,127	7,835
Public 4-year																
Selected crimes against persons and property	18,710	19,579	18,695	15,975	15,503	14,675	14,510	13,127	13,346	13,592	14,165	14,950	15,450	15,516	6,851	8,665
Murder[1]	9	42	9	8	9	10	7	10	3	13	8	13	11	12	3	9
Negligent manslaughter[2]	2	2	1	0	0	1	1	0	1	1	2	3	1	4	1	3
Sex offenses: forcible [3]	1,245	1,425	1,317	1,214	1,461	1,638	1,973	2,264	3,211	3,960	4,410	5,315	6,927	6,929	3,937	2,992
Rape	NA	NA	NA	NA	NA	NA	NA	NA	2,118	2,541	2,940	3,426	3,618	3,498	2,814	684
Fondling	NA	NA	NA	NA	NA	NA	NA	NA	1,093	1,419	1,470	1,889	3,309	3,431	1,123	2,308
Sex offenses: non-forcible [4]	207	23	12	40	15	17	17	18	28	37	30	64	38	52	36	16
Robbery [5]	584	722	750	647	662	612	657	635	550	580	589	522	460	468	103	365
Aggravated assault [6]	1,434	1,258	1,182	1,134	1,076	1,076	1,200	1,000	1,016	1,144	1,153	1,150	1,236	1,234	431	803
Burglary [7]	11,520	13,371	12,970	10,708	10,219	9,373	8,821	7,258	6,678	5,782	5,588	5,485	4,794	4,820	2,223	2,597
Motor vehicle theft [8]	3,072	2,266	2,027	1,824	1,604	1,592	1,406	1,537	1,500	1,770	2,048	2,042	1,775	1,757	8	1,749
Arson [9]	637	470	427	400	457	356	428	405	359	305	337	356	208	240	109	131
Weapons-, drug-, and liquor-related arrests and referrals																
Arrests[10]	31,077	39,570	40,607	40,780	41,992	44,891	43,155	38,073	36,249	32,717	31,601	30,393	25,528	21,836	10,878	10,958
Illegal weapons possession	692	825	759	659	669	629	621	637	619	721	759	813	761	781	174	607
Drug law violations	9,125	10,693	11,714	12,186	14,362	16,323	16,792	15,571	15,119	15,509	15,541	15,911	14,641	11,189	5,397	5,792
Liquor law violations	21,260	28,052	28,134	27,935	26,961	27,939	25,742	21,865	20,511	16,487	15,301	13,669	10,126	9,866	5,307	4,559
Referrals for disciplinary action[10]	79,152	106,148	104,585	108,756	116,029	129,667	132,363	127,155	134,310	127,315	118,658	111,724	103,313	97,569	90,418	7,151
Illegal weapons possession	678	867	792	669	664	610	644	604	646	569	602	521	488	449	305	144
Drug law violations	13,179	14,458	16,656	18,260	21,451	27,339	28,880	28,259	30,376	30,599	29,598	31,845	29,051	24,007	20,630	3,377
Liquor law violations	65,295	90,823	87,137	89,827	93,914	101,718	102,839	98,292	103,288	96,147	88,458	79,358	73,774	73,113	69,483	3,630
Private nonprofit 4-year																
Selected crimes against persons and property	14,844	15,452	14,892	11,964	11,202	10,740	10,790	10,290	9,995	10,460	11,013	11,012	10,646	9,358	5,375	3,983
Murder[1]	5	2	1	6	5	3	2	5	5	2	4	6	1	7	2	5
Negligent manslaughter[2]	0	1	0	0	0	0	0	0	0	1	0	0	1	1	0	1
Sex offenses: forcible [3]	820	1,065	1,083	1,102	1,225	1,431	1,741	2,379	3,105	3,510	3,956	4,518	4,854	4,151	3,201	950
Rape	NA	NA	NA	NA	NA	NA	NA	NA	2,152	2,366	2,700	2,894	2,907	2,483	2,121	362
Fondling	NA	NA	NA	NA	NA	NA	NA	NA	953	1,144	1,256	1,624	1,947	1,668	1,080	588
Sex offenses: non-forcible [4]	113	8	16	11	8	13	10	12	7	15	11	9	19	6	3	3
Robbery [5]	649	460	437	366	319	320	386	373	263	280	326	353	237	226	55	171
Aggravated assault [6]	882	768	754	661	641	631	667	681	655	727	657	802	773	694	218	476
Burglary [7]	10,471	11,941	11,551	8,810	8,138	7,421	7,046	5,999	5,020	4,894	5,018	4,282	3,771	3,224	1,788	1,436

(Number.)

Control and level of institution and type of incident	Total, in residence halls and at other locations													2019 Total	2019 In residence halls	2019 At other locations
	2001	2007	2008	2009	2010	2011	2012	2013	2014	2015	2016	2017	2018	Total	In residence halls	At other locations
Motor vehicle theft [8]	1,471	984	859	834	641	704	711	667	754	821	831	842	835	886	7	879
Arson [9]	433	223	191	174	225	217	227	174	186	210	210	200	155	163	101	62
Weapons-, drug-, and liquor-related arrests and referrals																
Arrests [10]	6,329	6,732	6,112	5,777	5,459	5,444	5,477	5,642	4,950	4,583	4,492	4,129	3,653	2,841	1,587	1,254
Illegal weapons possession	167	178	158	148	137	129	127	131	129	168	194	189	199	183	49	134
Drug law violations	1,628	1,804	1,883	2,080	2,248	2,425	2,415	2,503	2,258	2,237	2,195	2,238	2,015	1,567	862	705
Liquor law violations	4,534	4,750	4,071	3,549	3,074	2,890	2,935	3,008	2,563	2,178	2,103	1,702	1,439	1,091	676	415
Referrals for disciplinary action [10]	71,293	103,254	105,289	103,457	104,939	110,607	110,268	109,298	110,150	105,567	102,099	95,198	89,076	82,116	76,116	6,000
Illegal weapons possession	443	545	457	358	393	417	498	535	481	569	571	535	566	463	363	100
Drug law violations	9,688	12,685	14,157	15,845	17,841	21,240	22,168	22,116	23,000	22,180	22,743	22,567	21,599	19,402	17,360	2,042
Liquor law violations	61,162	90,024	90,675	87,254	86,705	88,950	87,602	86,647	86,669	82,818	78,785	72,096	66,911	62,251	58,393	3,858
Private for-profit 4-year																
Selected crimes against persons and property	505	612	574	525	561	446	364	511	442	295	240	284	283	295	127	168
Murder [1]	0	0	0	0	0	1	0	1	0	0	0	0	0	0	0	0
Negligent manslaughter [2]	0	0	0	0	0	0	0	0	0	0	0	0	0	0	0	0
Sex offenses: forcible [3]	4	12	9	9	22	26	18	18	43	34	28	51	60	65	48	17
Rape	NA	NA	NA	NA	NA	NA	NA	NA	26	11	15	29	26	31	28	3
Fondling	NA	NA	NA	NA	NA	NA	NA	NA	17	23	13	22	34	34	20	14
Sex offenses: non-forcible [4]	13	2	0	1	1	0	3	2	2	0	1	0	1	0	0	0
Robbery [5]	64	31	38	86	70	74	51	86	52	24	14	21	13	16	1	15
Aggravated assault [6]	23	31	63	43	51	36	43	58	33	27	32	22	22	25	4	21
Burglary [7]	347	446	385	299	350	249	195	276	251	162	110	139	106	123	54	69
Motor vehicle theft [8]	52	89	79	85	65	58	53	68	59	47	53	48	78	64	18	46
Arson [9]	2	1	0	2	2	2	1	2	2	1	2	3	3	2	2	0
Weapons-, drug-, and liquor-related arrests and referrals																
Arrests [10]	11	28	40	54	165	152	126	74	117	102	109	121	151	377	217	160
Illegal weapons possession	2	3	8	6	13	11	10	12	9	14	11	4	2	6	3	3
Drug law violations	4	16	14	22	66	41	49	48	68	78	78	107	143	240	131	109
Liquor law violations	5	9	18	26	86	100	67	14	40	10	20	10	6	131	83	48
Referrals for disciplinary action [10]	316	519	566	882	760	718	668	1,161	935	804	655	977	763	968	880	88
Illegal weapons possession	11	11	13	23	9	16	23	18	16	11	7	5	8	2	1	1
Drug law violations	92	132	159	231	221	233	254	537	403	330	253	313	231	179	143	36
Liquor law violations	213	376	394	628	530	469	391	606	516	463	395	659	524	787	736	51
Public 2-year																
Selected crimes against persons and property	6,817	5,381	5,464	4,984	4,396	4,141	3,749	3,075	2,845	3,014	2,654	2,648	2,086	2,054	468	1,586
Murder [1]	2	0	2	2	1	2	3	7	3	13	3	2	0	1	1	0
Negligent manslaughter [2]	0	0	0	0	1	0	0	0	1	0	0	0	0	0	0	0
Sex offenses: forcible [3]	118	181	210	205	210	262	263	303	385	495	489	579	519	613	185	428
Rape	NA	NA	NA	NA	NA	NA	NA	NA	132	197	175	223	196	197	124	73
Fondling	NA	NA	NA	NA	NA	NA	NA	NA	253	298	314	356	323	416	61	355
Sex offenses: non-forcible [4]	119	7	7	12	8	16	13	11	16	11	18	9	5	16	3	13
Robbery [5]	245	279	285	251	298	262	244	197	148	149	138	126	118	85	7	78
Aggravated assault [6]	545	462	401	431	409	406	437	278	305	335	281	257	187	171	36	135
Burglary [7]	4,132	3,202	3,430	2,920	2,398	2,235	1,964	1,583	1,383	1,411	1,132	1,149	877	793	231	562
Motor vehicle theft [8]	1,552	1,174	1,059	1,109	1,028	899	776	651	548	541	549	477	335	324	0	324
Arson [9]	104	76	70	54	43	59	49	45	56	59	44	49	45	51	5	46
Weapons-, drug-, and liquor-related arrests and referrals																
Arrests [10]	2,660	4,124	3,764	3,335	3,811	3,723	3,464	3,060	3,121	2,840	2,701	3,161	2,963	2,627	1,474	1,153
Illegal weapons possession	198	304	258	256	282	248	253	230	220	268	215	224	205	167	16	151
Drug law violations	989	1,563	1,490	1,507	1,866	1,892	1,885	1,588	1,671	1,568	1,373	1,524	1,356	1,068	352	716
Liquor law violations	1,473	2,257	2,016	1,572	1,663	1,583	1,326	1,242	1,230	1,004	1,113	1,413	1,402	1,392	1,106	286
Referrals for disciplinary action [10]	3,529	5,987	6,425	7,241	8,017	8,174	7,586	6,845	7,240	7,292	6,870	6,818	6,243	6,339	5,290	1,049
Illegal weapons possession	127	218	183	210	242	228	224	243	269	271	214	218	162	138	45	93
Drug law violations	761	1,006	1,302	1,745	2,336	2,573	2,468	2,304	2,548	2,626	2,575	2,650	2,512	2,571	1,902	669
Liquor law violations	2,641	4,763	4,940	5,286	5,439	5,373	4,894	4,298	4,423	4,395	4,081	3,950	3,569	3,630	3,343	287

Table 12. On-Campus Crimes, Arrests, and Referrals for Disciplinary Action at Degree-Granting Postsecondary Institutions, by Location of Incident, Control and Level of Institution, and Type of Incident, Selected Years, 2001–2019—*Continued*

(Number.)

Control and level of institution and type of incident	2001	2007	2008	2009	2010	2011	2012	2013	2014	2015	2016	2017	2018	2019 Total	2019 In residence halls	2019 At other locations
Private nonprofit 2-year																
Selected crimes against persons and property	248	258	272	147	120	148	107	66	64	53	56	60	35	29	12	17
Murder[1]	1	0	0	0	0	0	0	0	0	0	0	0	0	0	0	0
Negligent manslaughter[2]	0	0	1	0	0	0	0	0	0	0	0	0	0	0	0	0
Sex offenses: forcible[3]	2	9	16	8	7	11	8	4	3	11	16	13	10	5	3	2
Rape	NA	NA	NA	NA	NA	NA	NA	NA	2	1	8	9	8	1	0	1
Fondling	NA	NA	NA	NA	NA	NA	NA	NA	1	10	8	4	2	4	3	1
Sex offenses: non-forcible[4]	2	0	0	0	0	0	0	2	0	0	0	0	0	0	0	0
Robbery[5]	54	2	13	9	5	1	2	3	0	2	5	2	0	2	0	2
Aggravated assault[6]	23	52	66	5	9	53	46	13	27	7	8	12	4	4	1	3
Burglary[7]	142	178	160	120	95	74	47	41	29	27	24	20	12	11	8	3
Motor vehicle theft[8]	23	14	9	4	2	7	4	3	5	4	2	12	8	7	0	7
Arson[9]	1	3	7	1	2	2	0	0	0	2	1	1	1	0	0	0
Weapons-, drug-, and liquor-related arrests and referrals																
Arrests[10]	108	59	93	58	49	52	52	66	39	32	56	47	25	32	8	24
Illegal weapons possession	1	4	3	4	6	5	5	5	5	9	12	9	5	5	1	4
Drug law violations	21	27	33	35	18	34	31	49	28	20	21	37	15	20	2	18
Liquor law violations	86	28	57	19	25	13	16	12	6	3	23	1	5	7	5	2
Referrals for disciplinary action[10]	624	519	413	348	377	360	300	320	448	546	420	488	361	311	296	15
Illegal weapons possession	2	10	6	7	4	1	6	7	11	2	3	7	4	2	2	0
Drug law violations	91	73	85	100	105	109	103	129	155	214	163	185	138	141	130	11
Liquor law violations	531	436	322	241	268	250	191	184	282	330	254	296	219	168	164	4
Private for-profit 2-year																
Selected crimes against persons and property	472	547	399	459	315	257	246	167	126	118	111	80	87	82	4	78
Murder[1]	0	0	0	0	0	0	0	0	0	0	0	1	0	0	0	0
Negligent manslaughter[2]	0	0	1	0	0	0	0	0	0	0	0	0	0	0	0	0
Sex offenses: forcible[3]	12	2	4	6	2	7	12	9	4	12	9	5	6	4	1	3
Rape	NA	NA	NA	NA	NA	NA	NA	NA	1	3	2	2	0	2	1	1
Fondling	NA	NA	NA	NA	NA	NA	NA	NA	3	9	7	3	6	2	0	2
Sex offenses: non-forcible[4]	7	0	0	1	1	0	3	0	0	0	0	0	0	0	0	0
Robbery[5]	67	67	53	50	38	16	28	23	28	9	8	10	5	9	1	8
Aggravated assault[6]	40	33	29	53	35	37	30	14	12	18	25	14	13	26	2	24
Burglary[7]	292	350	241	226	135	120	110	75	58	44	46	23	23	20	0	20
Motor vehicle theft[8]	51	92	71	121	101	74	63	45	24	35	23	27	39	23	0	23
Arson[9]	3	3	0	2	3	3	0	1	0	0	0	0	1	0	0	0
Weapons-, drug-, and liquor-related arrests and referrals																
Arrests[10]	163	45	23	62	43	23	51	60	55	25	33	24	29	18	4	14
Illegal weapons possession	13	4	4	4	5	1	7	3	8	3	7	2	5	3	1	2
Drug law violations	87	32	12	41	29	14	40	40	28	19	18	20	20	13	3	10
Liquor law violations	63	9	7	17	9	8	4	17	19	3	8	2	4	2	0	2
Referrals for disciplinary action[10]	287	173	248	303	147	168	217	206	232	163	100	83	63	28	15	13
Illegal weapons possession	16	7	4	8	2	10	9	3	2	3	5	4	3	2	2	0
Drug law violations	89	122	110	163	68	68	86	94	93	88	41	42	38	13	5	8
Liquor law violations	182	44	134	132	77	90	122	109	137	72	54	37	22	13	8	5

NOTE: Data are for degree-granting institutions, which are institutions that grant associate's or higher degrees and participate in Title IV federal financial aid programs. Some institutions that report Clery data--specifically, non-degree-granting institutions and institutions outside of the 50 states and the District of Columbia--are excluded from this table. Crimes, arrests, and referrals include incidents involving students, staff, and on-campus guests. Excludes off-campus crimes and arrests even if they involve college students or staff. Duplicate reporting of a small number of incidents may occur among institutions sharing all or part of a building, institutions in close proximity to each other that rely on the same crime statistics from local law enforcement agencies, or institutions operating more than one campus in close proximity to each other. Some data have been revised from previously published figures.
NA = Not available.
[1]Excludes suicides, fetal deaths, traffic fatalities, accidental deaths, and justifiable homicide (such as the killing of a felon by a law enforcement officer in the line of duty).
[2]Killing of another person through gross negligence (excludes traffic fatalities).
[3]Any sexual act directed against another person forcibly and/or against that person's will.
[4]Includes only statutory rape or incest.
[5]Taking or attempting to take anything of value using actual or threatened force or violence.
[6]Attack upon a person for the purpose of inflicting severe or aggravated bodily injury.
[7]Unlawful entry of a structure to commit a felony or theft.
[8]Theft or attempted theft of a motor vehicle.
[9]Willful or malicious burning or attempt to burn a dwelling house, public building, motor vehicle, or personal property of another.
[10]If an individual is both arrested and referred to college officials for disciplinary action for a single offense, only the arrest is counted.

Table 13. On-Campus Hate Crimes at Degree-Granting Postsecondary Institutions, by Level and Control of Institution, Type of Crime, and Category of Bias Motivating the Crime, Selected Years, 2010–2019

(Number.)

Type of crime and category of bias motivating the crime	Total, 2010	Total, 2014	Total, 2015	Total, 2016	Total, 2017	2018 Total	2018 4-year Public	2018 4-year For profit	2018 4-year Non-profit	2018 2-year Public	2018 2-year For profit	2018 2-year Non-profit	2019 Total	2019 4-year Public	2019 4-year For profit	2019 4-year Non-profit	2019 2-year Public	2019 2-year For profit	2019 2-year Non-profit
All On-Campus Hate Crimes	928	782	846	1,057	954	814	365	319	7	119	0	4	757	343	297	8	108	0	1
Murder[1]	0	0	0	0	1	0	0	0	0	0	0	0	0	0	0	0	0	0	0
Sex offenses: forcible[2]	7	4	7	8	5	7	3	2	0	2	0	0	5	2	3	0	0	0	0
Race	0	1	0	1	0	1	1	0	0	0	0	0	0	0	0	0	0	0	0
Ethnicity	0	0	0	0	0	0	0	0	0	0	0	0	0	0	0	0	0	0	0
Religion	0	0	1	0	0	0	0	0	0	0	0	0	0	0	0	0	0	0	0
Sexual orientation	4	1	3	1	0	2	1	1	0	0	0	0	2	1	1	0	0	0	0
Gender	3	2	1	5	3	3	0	1	0	2	0	0	1	0	1	0	0	0	0
Gender identity	NA	0	2	1	2	1	1	0	0	0	0	0	2	1	1	0	0	0	0
Disability	0	0	0	0	0	0	0	0	0	0	0	0	0	0	0	0	0	0	0
Sex offenses: non-forcible[3]	0	0	0	0	0	0	0	0	0	0	0	0	0	0	0	0	0	0	0
Robbery[4]	2	1	0	2	2	3	1	2	0	0	0	0	3	2	1	0	0	0	0
Aggravated assault[5]	17	17	16	32	10	27	14	10	0	2	0	1	16	9	3	0	4	0	0
Race	6	5	5	6	5	17	7	9	0	1	0	0	8	3	2	0	3	0	0
Ethnicity	1	4	2	14	1	3	3	0	0	0	0	0	5	4	1	0	0	0	0
Religion	1	1	0	1	1	0	0	0	0	0	0	0	0	0	0	0	0	0	0
Sexual orientation	9	7	7	8	2	5	4	1	0	0	0	0	3	2	0	0	1	0	0
Gender	0	0	1	1	0	1	0	0	0	0	0	1	0	0	0	0	0	0	0
Gender identity	NA	0	1	2	0	1	0	0	0	1	0	0	0	0	0	0	0	0	0
Disability	0	0	0	0	1	0	0	0	0	0	0	0	0	0	0	0	0	0	0
Burglary[6]	11	28	0	5	1	7	0	7	0	0	0	0	1	0	1	0	0	0	0
Race	7	24	0	1	0	4	0	4	0	0	0	0	1	0	1	0	0	0	0
Ethnicity	0	0	0	0	0	0	0	0	0	0	0	0	0	0	0	0	0	0	0
Religion	0	3	0	0	0	2	0	2	0	0	0	0	0	0	0	0	0	0	0
Sexual orientation	2	1	0	2	0	0	0	0	0	0	0	0	0	0	0	0	0	0	0
Gender	1	0	0	2	1	0	0	0	0	0	0	0	0	0	0	0	0	0	0
Gender identity	NA	0	0	0	0	1	0	1	0	0	0	0	0	0	0	0	0	0	0
Disability	1	0	0	0	0	0	0	0	0	0	0	0	0	0	0	0	0	0	0
Motor vehicle theft[7]	0	0	1	0	0	0	0	0	0	0	0	0	0	0	0	0	0	0	0
Arson[8]	0	1	2	2	1	0	0	0	0	0	0	0	1	1	0	0	0	0	0
Simple assault[9]	67	61	80	97	82	75	37	26	0	11	0	1	85	43	32	0	9	0	1
Race	25	14	36	42	40	28	16	8	0	4	0	0	49	23	22	0	3	0	1
Ethnicity	5	11	9	13	8	8	2	5	0	0	0	1	10	4	6	0	0	0	0
Religion	4	2	9	12	9	10	5	3	0	2	0	0	7	5	1	0	1	0	0
Sexual orientation	23	23	18	16	18	22	12	7	0	3	0	0	13	7	2	0	4	0	0
Gender	9	7	2	11	2	4	1	1	0	2	0	0	4	3	0	0	1	0	0
Gender identity	NA	3	5	2	5	3	1	2	0	0	0	0	2	1	1	0	0	0	0
Disability	1	1	1	1	0	0	0	0	0	0	0	0	0	0	0	0	0	0	0
Larceny[10]	9	14	25	29	22	12	4	6	1	1	0	0	11	1	10	0	0	0	0
Race	1	5	1	12	4	2	1	0	0	1	0	0	2	0	2	0	0	0	0
Ethnicity	3	1	0	1	3	0	0	0	0	0	0	0	1	0	1	0	0	0	0
Religion	1	3	19	5	1	4	0	4	0	0	0	0	3	0	3	0	0	0	0
Sexual orientation	1	1	1	5	6	5	3	2	0	0	0	0	4	0	4	0	0	0	0
Gender	3	4	3	2	7	1	0	0	1	0	0	0	1	1	0	0	0	0	0
Gender identity	NA	0	1	3	1	0	0	0	0	0	0	0	0	0	0	0	0	0	0
Disability	0	0	0	1	0	0	0	0	0	0	0	0	0	0	0	0	0	0	0
Intimidation[11]	260	336	353	425	393	335	145	141	3	45	0	1	340	159	126	5	50	0	0
Race	79	111	141	170	178	158	62	75	3	18	0	0	147	70	55	1	21	0	0
Ethnicity	17	32	37	48	46	36	16	17	0	3	0	0	47	23	14	1	9	0	0
Religion	38	35	48	67	49	41	19	13	0	8	0	1	36	18	15	0	3	0	0
Sexual orientation	87	77	77	83	67	70	40	21	0	9	0	0	79	40	31	0	8	0	0
Gender	37	61	32	28	24	16	4	7	0	5	0	0	23	4	11	3	5	0	0
Gender identity	NA	13	11	20	20	12	3	7	0	2	0	0	4	2	0	0	2	0	0
Disability	2	7	7	9	9	2	1	1	0	0	0	0	4	2	0	0	2	0	0

Table 13. On-Campus Hate Crimes at Degree-Granting Postsecondary Institutions, by Level and Control of Institution, Type of Crime, and Category of Bias Motivating the Crime, Selected Years, 2010–2019—*Continued*

(Number.)

Type of crime and category of bias motivating the crime	Total, 2010	Total, 2014	Total, 2015	Total, 2016	Total, 2017	2018 Total	2018 4-year Public	2018 4-year For profit	2018 4-year Non-profit	2018 2-year Public	2018 2-year For profit	2018 2-year Non-profit	2019 Total	2019 4-year Public	2019 4-year For profit	2019 4-year Non-profit	2019 2-year Public	2019 2-year For profit	2019 2-year Non-profit
Destruction, damage, and vandalism[12]	555	320	362	457	437	348	161	125	3	58	0	1	295	126	121	3	45	0	0
Race	257	116	149	174	184	140	67	50	1	21	0	1	133	60	51	3	19	0	0
Ethnicity	43	29	25	30	34	34	13	13	0	8	0	0	31	12	12	0	7	0	0
Religion	103	67	108	133	111	73	31	30	1	11	0	0	60	19	30	0	11	0	0
Sexual orientation	135	88	61	67	62	76	38	23	1	14	0	0	63	29	26	0	8	0	0
Gender	17	12	10	31	20	9	4	2	0	3	0	0	1	1	0	0	0	0	0
Gender identity	NA	6	8	22	26	15	8	6	0	1	0	0	6	5	1	0	0	0	0
Disability	0	2	1	0	0	1	0	1	0	0	0	0	1	0	1	0	0	0	0

NOTE: Data are for degree-granting institutions, which are institutions that grant associate's or higher degrees and participate in Title IV federal financial aid programs. Bias categories correspond to characteristics against which the bias is directed (i.e., race, ethnicity, religion, sexual orientation, gender, gender identity, or disability). Some institutions that report Clery data--specifically, non-degree-granting institutions and institutions outside of the 50 states and the District of Columbia--are excluded from this table. A hate crime is a criminal offense that is motivated, in whole or in part, by the perpetrator's bias against a group of people based on their race, ethnicity, religion, sexual orientation, gender, gender identity, or disability. Includes on-campus incidents involving students, staff, and on-campus guests. Excludes off-campus crimes and arrests even if they involve college students or staff. Duplicate reporting of a small number of incidents may occur among institutions sharing all or part of a building, institutions in close proximity to each other that rely on the same crime statistics from local law enforcement agencies, or institutions operating more than one campus in close proximity to each other. Some data have been revised from previously published figures.

NA = Not available.

[1] Excludes suicides, fetal deaths, traffic fatalities, accidental deaths, and justifiable homicide (such as the killing of a felon by a law enforcement officer in the line of duty).

[2] Any sexual act directed against another person forcibly and/or against that person's will.

[3] Includes only statutory rape or incest.

[4] Taking or attempting to take anything of value using actual or threatened force or violence.

[5] Attack upon a person for the purpose of inflicting severe or aggravated bodily injury.

[6] Unlawful entry of a structure to commit a felony or theft.

[7] Theft or attempted theft of a motor vehicle.

[8] Willful or malicious burning or attempt to burn a dwelling house, public building, motor vehicle, or personal property of another.

[9] A physical attack by one person upon another where neither the offender displays a weapon, nor the victim suffers obvious severe or aggravated bodily injury involving apparent broken bones, loss of teeth, possible internal injury, severe laceration, or loss of consciousness.

[10] The unlawful taking, carrying, leading, or riding away of property from the possession of another.

[11] Placing another person in reasonable fear of bodily harm through the use of threatening words and/or other conduct, but without displaying a weapon or subjecting the victim to actual physical attack.

[12] Willfully or maliciously destroying, damaging, defacing, or otherwise injuring real or personal property without the consent of the owner or the person having custody or control of it.

METHODOLOGY

This annual report, a joint effort by the Bureau of Justice Statistics and the National Center for Education Statistics (NCES), provides the most current statistical information on the nature of crime in schools. It presents data on crime and safety at school from the perspectives of students, teachers, and principals. This report contains 23 indicators of crime and safety at school from a number of sources, including the National Crime Victimization Survey (NCVS), the School Crime Supplement to the NCVS, the Youth Risk Behavior Survey, the School Survey on Crime and Safety, and the School and Staffing Survey. Topics covered include victimization at school, teacher injury, bullying and cyberbullying, school conditions, fights, weapons, availability and student use of drugs and alcohol, student perceptions of personal safety at school, and crime at postsecondary institutions. For more information or to access the full report, please see https://nces.ed.gov/programs/coe.

The indicators in this report are based on information drawn from a variety of independent data sources, including national and international surveys of students, teachers, principals, and postsecondary institutions and universe data collections from federal departments and agencies and international organizations. These sources include the Bureau of Justice Statistics, the National Center for Education Statistics, the Centers for Disease Control and Prevention, the Office of Postsecondary Education, the Center for Homeland Defense and Security of the U.S. Department of Defense, and the Organization for Economic Cooperation and Development. Each data source has an independent sample design, data collection method, and questionnaire design or is the result of a universe data collection. Universe data collections include a census of all known entities in a specific universe (e.g., all deaths occurring on school property). Readers should be cautious when comparing data from different sources. Differences in sampling procedures, populations, time periods, and question phrasing can all affect the comparability of results. For example, some questions from different surveys may appear the same, but were asked of different populations of students (e.g., students ages 12–18 or students in grades 9–12); in different years; about experiences that occurred within different periods of time (e.g., in the past 30 days or during the past 12 months); or at different locations (e.g., in school or anywhere).

In 2020—and to a lesser extent in 2021—schools across the country suspended or modified in-person classes in accordance with federal, state, and local guidance related to the risks associated with the coronavirus pandemic. Students might have spent less time at school than in previous years due to these modified procedures. Thus, readers are encouraged to interpret the 2020 and 2021 data in the context of these pandemic-related modifications.

DATA

The Bureau of Justice Statistics' (BJS) **National Crime Victimization Survey (NCVS)** is the nation's primary source of information on criminal victimization. The survey has undergone several recent revisions and redesigns.

The accuracy of any statistic is determined by the joint effects of nonsampling and sampling errors. Both types of error affect the estimates presented in this report. Several sources can contribute to nonsampling errors. For example, members of the population of interest are inadvertently excluded from the sampling frame; sampled members refuse to answer some of the survey questions (item nonresponse) or all of the survey questions (questionnaire nonresponse); mistakes are made during data editing, coding, or entry; the responses that respondents provide differ from the "true" responses; or measurement instruments such as tests or questionnaires fail to measure the characteristics they are intended to measure. Although nonsampling errors due to questionnaire and item nonresponse can be reduced somewhat by the adjustment of sample weights and imputation procedures, correcting nonsampling errors or gauging the effects of these errors is usually difficult.

Sampling errors occur because observations are made on samples rather than on entire populations. Surveys of population universes are not subject to sampling errors. Estimates based on a sample will differ somewhat from those that would have been obtained by a complete census of the relevant population using the same survey instruments, instructions, and procedures. The standard error of a statistic is a measure of the variation due to sampling; it indicates the precision of the statistic obtained in a particular sample. In addition, the standard errors for two sample statistics can be used to estimate the precision of the difference between the two statistics and to help determine whether the difference based on the sample is large enough so that it represents the population difference.

Most of the data used in this report were obtained from complex sampling designs rather than a simple random design. The features of complex sampling require different techniques to calculate standard errors than are used for data collected using a simple random sampling. Therefore, calculation of standard errors requires procedures that are markedly different from the ones used when the data are from a simple random sample.

The Taylor series approximation technique or the balanced repeated replication (BRR) method was used to estimate most of the statistics and their standard errors in this report.

Standard error calculation for data from the School Crime Supplement was based on the Taylor series approximation method using PSU and strata variables available from each dataset. For statistics based on all years of NCVS data, standard errors were derived from a formula developed by the U.S. Census Bureau, which consists of three generalized variance function (gvf) constant parameters that represent the curve fitted to the individual standard errors calculated using the Balanced Repeated Replication (BRR) technique.

The coefficient of variation (CV) represents the ratio of the standard error to the mean. As an attribute of a distribution, the CV is an important measure of the reliability and accuracy of an estimate. With the exception of *Indicator 2*, the CV was calculated for all estimates in this report, and in cases where the CV was between 30 and 50 percent the estimates were noted with an "!" symbol (interpret data with caution). In *Indicator 2*, the "!" symbol cautions the reader that estimates marked indicate that the reported statistic was based on fewer than 10 cases or the CV was greater than 50 percent. With the exception of *Indicator 2*, in cases where the CV was 50 percent or greater, the estimate was determined not to meet reporting standards and was suppressed.

The **School-Associated Violent Deaths Study (SAVD)** is an epidemiological study developed by the Centers for Disease Control and Prevention in conjunction with the U.S. Department of Education and the U.S. Department of Justice. SAVD seeks to describe the epidemiology of school-associated violent deaths, identify common features of these deaths, estimate the rate of school-associated violent deaths in the United States, and identify potential risk factors for these deaths. The study includes descriptive data on all school-associated violent deaths in the United States, including all homicides, suicides, or legal intervention deaths in which the fatal injury occurred on the campus of a functioning elementary or secondary school; while the victim was on the way to or from regular sessions at such a school; or while attending or on the way to or from an official school-sponsored event. Victims of such incidents include nonstudents, as well as students and staff members. SAVD includes descriptive information about the school, event, victim(s), and offender(s). The SAVD study has collected data from July 1, 1992, through the present.

SAVD uses a four-step process to identify and collect data on school-associated violent deaths. Cases are initially identified through a search of the LexisNexis newspaper and media database. Then law enforcement officials from the office that investigated the deaths are contacted to confirm the details of the case and to determine if the event meets the case definition. Once a case is confirmed, a law enforcement official and a school official are interviewed regarding details about the school, event, victim(s), and offender(s). A copy of the full law enforcement report is also sought for each case. The information obtained on schools includes school demographics, attendance/absentee rates, suspensions/expulsions and mobility, school history of weapon-carrying incidents, security measures, violence prevention activities, school response to the event, and school policies about weapon carrying. Event information includes the location of injury, the context of injury (while classes were being held, during break, etc.), motives for injury, method of injury, and school and community events happening around the time period. Information obtained on victim(s) and offender(s) includes demographics, circumstances of the event (date/time, alcohol or drug use, number of persons involved), types and origins of weapons, criminal history, psychological risk factors, school-related problems, extracurricular activities, and family history, including structure and stressors.

For some recent data, the interviews with school and law enforcement officials to verify case details have not been completed. The details learned during the interviews can occasionally change the classification of a case. Also, new cases may be identified because of the expansion of the scope of the media files used for case identification. Sometimes other cases not identified during earlier data years using the independent case finding efforts (which focus on nonmedia sources of information) will be discovered. Also, other cases may occasionally be identified while the law enforcement and school interviews are being conducted to verify known cases.

Created as a supplement to the NCVS and co-designed by the National Center for Education Statistics and Bureau of Justice Statistics, the School Crime Supplement (SCS) survey has been conducted in 1989, 1995, and biennially since 1999 to collect additional information about school-related victimizations on a national level. This report includes data from the 1995, 1999, 2001, 2003, 2005, 2007, 2009, 2011, 2013, 2015, and 2017 collections. The 1989 data are not included in this report as a result of methodological changes to the NCVS and SCS. The SCS was designed to assist policymakers, as well as academic researchers and practitioners at federal, state, and local levels, to make informed decisions concerning crime in schools. The survey asks students a number of key questions about their experiences with and perceptions of crime and violence that occurred inside their school, on school grounds, on the school bus, or on the way to or from school. Students are asked additional questions about security measures used by their school, students' participation in after-school activities, students' perceptions of school rules, the presence of weapons and gangs in school, the presence of hate-related words and graffiti in school, student reports of bullying and reports of rejection at school, and the availability of drugs and alcohol in school. Students are also asked attitudinal questions relating to fear of victimization and avoidance behavior at school.

The SCS survey was conducted for a 6-month period from January through June in all households selected for the NCVS (see discussion above for information about the NCVS sampling design and changes to the race/ethnicity variable beginning in 2003). Within these households, the eligible respondents for the SCS were those household members who had attended school at any time during the 6 months preceding the interview, were enrolled in grades 6–12, and were not homeschooled. In 2007, the questionnaire was changed and household members who attended school sometime during the school year of the interview were included. The age range of students covered in this report is 12–18 years of age. Eligible respondents were asked the supplemental questions in the SCS only after completing their entire NCVS interview. It should be noted that the first or unbounded NCVS interview has always been included in analysis of the SCS data and may result in the reporting of events outside of the requested reference period.

The **Youth Risk Behavior Surveillance System (YRBSS)** is an epidemiological surveillance system developed by the Centers for Disease Control and Prevention (CDC) to monitor the prevalence of youth behaviors that most influence health. The YRBSS focuses on priority health-risk behaviors established during youth that result in the most significant mortality, morbidity, disability, and social problems during both youth and adulthood. The YRBSS includes a national school-based Youth Risk Behavior Survey (YRBS) as well as surveys conducted in states and large urban school districts. This report uses 1993, 1995, 1997, 1999, 2001, 2003, 2005, 2007, 2009, 2011, 2013, 2015, and 2017 YRBSS data.

The national YRBS uses a three-stage cluster sampling design to produce a nationally representative sample of students in grades 9–12 in the United States. The target population consisted of all public and private school students in grades 9–12 in the 50 states and the District of Columbia. The first-stage sampling frame included selecting primary sampling units (PSUs) from strata formed on the basis of urbanization and the relative percentage of Black and Hispanic students in the PSU. These PSUs are either counties; subareas of large counties; or groups of smaller, adjacent counties. At the second stage, schools were selected with probability proportional to school enrollment size.

The final stage of sampling consisted of randomly selecting, in each chosen school and in each of grades 9–12, one or two classrooms from either a required subject, such as English or social studies, or a required period, such as homeroom or second period. All students in selected classes were eligible to participate. In surveys conducted before 2013, three strategies were used to oversample Black and Hispanic students: (1) larger sampling rates were used to select PSUs that are in high-Black and high-Hispanic strata; (2) a modified measure of size was used that increased the probability of selecting schools with a disproportionately high minority enrollment; and (3) two classes per grade, rather than one, were selected in schools with a high percentage of combined Black, Hispanic, Asian/Pacific Islander, or American Indian/Alaska Native enrollment. In 2013, only selection of two classes per grade was needed to achieve an adequate precision with minimum variance.

The **School Survey on Crime and Safety (SSOCS)** is managed by the National Center for Education Statistics (NCES) on behalf of the U.S. Department of Education. SSOCS collects extensive crime and safety data from principals and school administrators of U.S. public schools. Data from this collection can be used to examine the relationship between school characteristics and violent and serious violent crimes in primary schools, middle schools, high schools, and combined schools. In addition, data from SSOCS can be used to assess what crime prevention programs, practices, and policies are used by schools.

DEFINITIONS

General Terms

Crime: Any violation of a statute or regulation or any act that the government has determined is injurious to the public, including felonies and misdemeanors. Such violation may or may not involve violence, and it may affect individuals or property.

Incident: A specific criminal act or offense involving one or more victims and one or more offenders.

Multistage sampling: A survey sampling technique in which there is more than one wave of sampling. That is, one sample of units is drawn, and then another sample is drawn within that sample. For example, at the first stage, a number of Census blocks may be sampled out of all the Census blocks in the United States. At the second stage, households are sampled within the previously sampled Census blocks.

Prevalence: The percentage of the population directly affected by crime in a given period. This rate is based upon specific information elicited directly from the respondent regarding crimes committed against his or her person, against his or her property, or against an individual bearing a unique relationship to him or her. It is not based upon perceptions and beliefs about, or reactions to, criminal acts.

School: An education institution consisting of one or more of grades K–12.

School crime: Any criminal activity that is committed on school property.

School year: The 12-month period of time denoting the beginning and ending dates for school accounting purposes, usually from July 1 through June 30.

Stratification: A survey sampling technique in which the target population is divided into mutually exclusive groups or strata based on some variable or variables (e.g., metropolitan area) and sampling of units occurs separately within each stratum.

Unequal probabilities: A survey sampling technique in which sampled units do not have the same probability of selection into the sample. For example, the investigator may oversample rural students in order to increase the sample sizes of rural students. Rural students would then be more likely than other students to be sampled.

Specific Terms Used in Various Surveys

School-Associated Violent Deaths Study (SAVD)

Homicide: An act involving a killing of one person by another resulting from interpersonal violence.

Legal intervention death: An act involving the killing of one person by a law enforcement agent in the course of arresting or attempting to arrest a lawbreaker, suppressing a disturbance, maintaining order, or engaging in another legal action.

School-associated violent death: A homicide or suicide in which the fatal injury occurred on the campus of a functioning elementary or secondary school in the United States, while the victim was on the way to or from regular sessions at such a school, or while the victim was attending or traveling to or from an official school-sponsored event. Victims included non-students as well as students and staff members.

Suicide: An act of taking one's own life voluntarily and intentionally.

National Crime Victimization Survey (NCVS)

Aggravated assault: Attack or attempted attack with a weapon, regardless of whether or not an injury occurs, and attack without a weapon when serious injury results.

At school (students): Inside the school building, on school property (school parking area, play area, school bus, etc.), or on the way to or from school.

Metropolitan Statistical Areas (MSAs): Geographic entities defined by the U.S. Office of Management and Budget (OMB) for use by federal statistical agencies in collecting, tabulating, and publishing federal statistics.

Rape: Forced sexual intercourse including both psychological coercion as well as physical force. Forced sexual intercourse means vaginal, anal, or oral penetration by the offender(s). Includes attempts and verbal threats of rape. This category also includes incidents where the penetration is from a foreign object, such as a bottle.

Robbery: Completed or attempted theft, directly from a person, of property or cash by force or threat of force, with or without a weapon, and with or without injury.

Serious violent victimization: Rape, sexual assault, robbery, or aggravated assault.

Sexual assault: A wide range of victimizations, separate from rape or attempted rape. These crimes include attacks or attempted attacks generally involving unwanted sexual contact between the victim and offender. Sexual assault may or may not involve force and includes such things as grabbing or fondling. Sexual assault also includes verbal threats.

Simple assault: Attack without a weapon resulting either in no injury, minor injury, or an undetermined injury requiring less than 2 days of hospitalization. Also includes attempted assault without a weapon.

Theft: Completed or attempted theft of property or cash without personal contact.

Victimization: A crime as it affects one individual person or household. For personal crimes, the number of victimizations is equal to the number of victims involved. The number of victimizations may be greater than the number of incidents because more than one person may be victimized during an incident.

Victimization rate: A measure of the occurrence of victimizations among a specific population group. For personal crimes, the number of victimizations is equal to the number of victims involved. Each victimization that is reported by the respondents is counted, so there may be one incident with two victims, which would be counted as two victimizations. The number of victimizations may be greater than the number of incidents because more than one person may be victimized during an incident.

Violent victimization: Includes serious violent victimization, rape, sexual assault, robbery, aggravated assault, or simple assault.

School Crime Supplement (SCS)

At school: In the school building, on school property, on a school bus, or going to or from school.

Bullied: Students were asked if any student had bullied them at school in one or more ways during the school year. Specifically, students were asked if another student had made fun of them, called them names, or insulted them; spread rumors about them; threatened them with harm; pushed, shoved, tripped, or spit on them; tried to make them to do something they did not want to do; excluded them from activities on purpose; or destroyed their property on purpose.

Gang: Street gangs, fighting gangs, crews, or something else. Gangs may use common names, signs, symbols, or colors. All gangs, whether or not they are involved in violent or illegal activity, are included.

Hate-related graffiti: Hate-related words or symbols written in school classrooms, school bathrooms, school hallways, or on the outside of the school building.

Hate-related words: Students were asked if anyone called them an insulting or bad name at school having to do with their race, religion, ethnic background or national origin, disability, gender, or sexual orientation.

Serious violent victimization: Rape, sexual assault, robbery, or aggravated assault.

Total victimization: Combination of violent victimization and theft. If a student reported an incident of either type, he or she is counted as having experienced any victimization. If the student reported having experienced both, he or she is counted once under "total victimization."

Violent victimization: Includes serious violent victimization, rape, sexual assault, robbery, aggravated assault, or simple assault.

Youth Risk Behavior Survey (YRBS)

On school property: On school property is included in the question wording, but was not defined for respondents.

Rural school: A school located outside a Metropolitan Statistical Area (MSA).

Suburban school: A school located inside an MSA, but outside the "central city."

Urban school: A school located inside an MSA and inside the "central city."

Weapon: Examples of weapons appearing in the questionnaire include guns, knives, and clubs.

School Survey on Crime and Safety (SSOCS)

Gang: An ongoing loosely organized association of three or more persons, whether formal or informal, that has a common name, signs, symbols, or colors, whose members engage, either individually or collectively, in violent or other forms of illegal behavior.

Hate crime: A criminal offense or threat against a person, property, or society that is motivated, in whole or in part, by the offender's bias against a race, color, national origin, ethnicity, gender, religion, disability, or sexual orientation.

Intimidation: To frighten, compel, or deter by actual or implied threats. It includes bullying and sexual harassment. (Intimidation was not defined in the front of the questionnaire in 2005–06.)

Physical attack or fight: An actual and intentional touching or striking of another person against his or her will, or the intentional causing of bodily harm to an individual.

Rape: Forced sexual intercourse (vaginal, anal, or oral penetration). Includes penetration from a foreign object.

Robbery The taking or attempting to take anything of value that is owned by another person or organization, under confrontational circumstances by force or threat of force or violence and/or by putting the victim in fear. A key difference between robbery and theft/larceny is that a threat or battery is involved in robbery.

Serious violent incidents: Include rape, sexual battery other than rape, physical attacks or fights with a weapon, threats of physical attack with a weapon, and robbery with or without a weapon.

Sexual battery: An incident that includes threatened rape, fondling, indecent liberties, child molestation, or sodomy. Principals were instructed that classification of these incidents should take into consideration the age and developmentally appropriate behavior of the offenders.

Sexual harassment: Unsolicited, offensive behavior that inappropriately asserts sexuality over another person. The behavior may be verbal or nonverbal.

Theft/larceny: Taking things valued at over $10 without personal confrontation. Specifically, the unlawful taking of another person's property without personal confrontation, threat, violence, or bodily harm. Included are pocket picking, stealing purse or backpack (if left unattended or no force was used to take it from owner), theft from a building, theft from a motor vehicle or motor vehicle parts or accessories, theft of bicycles, theft from vending machines, and all other types of thefts.

Vandalism: The willful damage or destruction of school property, including bombing, arson, graffiti, and other acts that cause property damage. Includes damage caused by computer hacking.

Violent incidents: Include rape, sexual battery other than rape, physical attacks or fights with or without a weapon, threats of physical attack with or without a weapon, and robbery with or without a weapon.

Weapon: Any instrument or object used with the intent to threaten, injure, or kill. Includes look-alikes if they are used to threaten others.

PART 7

Jail Inmates in 2020

HIGHLIGHTS

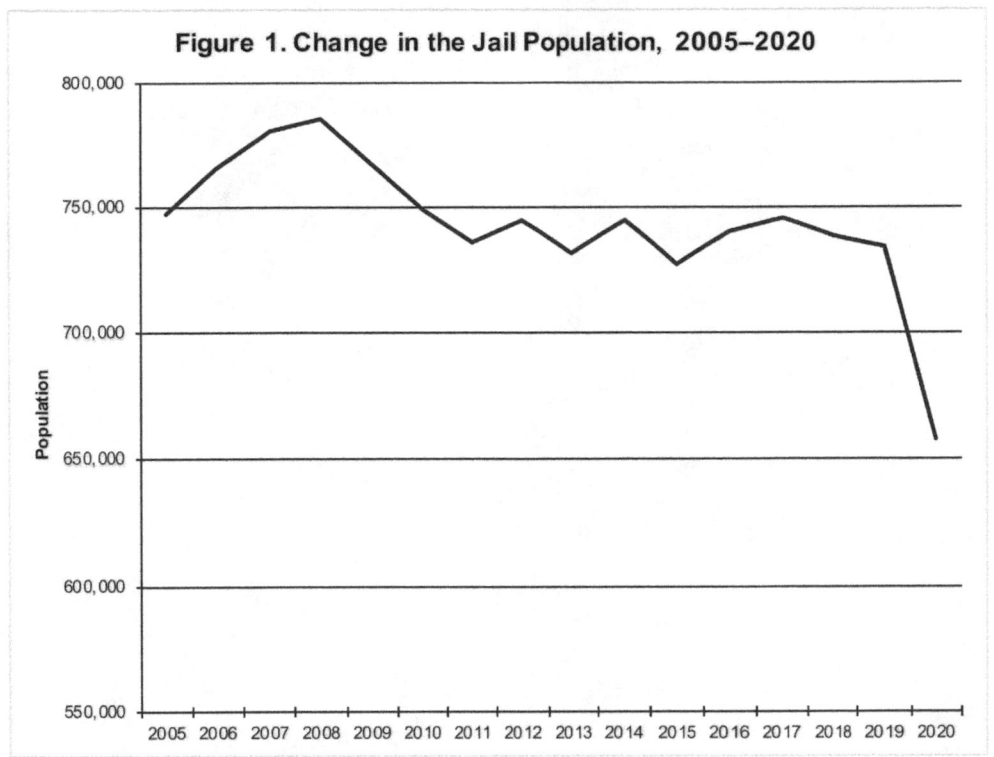

Figure 1. Change in the Jail Population, 2005–2020

- After a decade of relative stability, the number of inmates confined in county and city jails was an estimated 549,100 at midyear 2020, 25 percent lower than the 734,500 inmates on an average day at midyear 2019.

- At midyear 2020, the jail incarceration rate had decreased from a peak of 258 per 100,000 U.S. residents at midyear 2008 and a rate of 224 per 100,000 U.S. residents at midyear 2019 to about 167 per 100,000 population.

- Approximately 8.7 million admissions to jail occurred in 2020, continuing the trend of steady decline that has been experienced since 2008.

- Fewer than 3,000 (2,300) juveniles age 17 years or younger were held in local jails at midyear 2020; this was significantly below the peak of about 7,600 at midyear 2000 and 2010 and 21 percent less than the 2,900 held at midyear 2019.

- Approximately 81 percent of jail beds were occupied in 2019, down from 95 percent in 2007, while 15 percent of jails were operating at or above 100 percent of their operating capacity.

- At yearend 2020, Blacks (465 per 100,000 Black residents) were incarcerated in jail at a rate 3.5 times that of Whites (133 per 100,000 White residents).

Table 1. Inmates Confined at Midyear, Average Daily Population and Incarceration Rates, 2010–2020

(Number; percent.)

Year	Confined inmates[1]	Average daily population[2]	Annual admissions[3]	Jail incarceration rate[4]
2010[A]	748,700	748,600	12,900,000	242
2011[A]	735,600	735,600	11,800,000	236
2012[A]	744,500	737,400	11,600,000	237
2013[A]	731,200	731,400	11,700,000	231
2014[A]	744,600	739,000	11,400,000	234
2015[A]	727,400	719,500	10,700,000	227
2016[A]	740,700	731,300	10,600,000	229
2017[A]	745,200	745,600	10,600,000	229
2018[A]	738,400	737,900	10,700,000	226
2019[A]	734,500	741,900	10,300,000	224
2020*	549,100	658,100	8,700,000	167
Average Annual Percent Change				
2010–2019	-0.2	-0.1	-2.5	-0.9
2019–2020	-25.2	-11.3	-16.2	-25.5

NOTE: Data are rounded to the nearest 100 for confined inmates and for average daily population (ADP), and to the nearest 100,000 for annual admissions. Results may differ from previous reports in the series due to data updates from jail authorities.
* = Comparison year.
A = Difference with comparison year is significant at the 95% confidence level at all values.
[1]Number of inmates held on the last weekday in June.
[2]The ADP is the sum of all inmates in jail each day for 1 year, divided by the number of days in the year. The ADP for 2015 and 2016 was calculated for the calendar year ending on December 31. The ADP for all other years was calculated for the 12-month period ending on June 30.
[3]Annual admissions from 2010 to 2014 were estimated based on admissions during a 1-week period in June. The 2015 and 2016 annual admissions were for the calendar year ending on December 31. The 2017 to 2020 annual admissions were for the 12-month period ending on June 30.
[4]Number of confined inmates in local jails at midyear per 100,000 U.S. residents.

Table 2. Jail Incarceration Rates, by Sex, Race, and Ethnicity, Midyear 2010 and 2015–2020

(Rate; percent.)

Characteristic	2010	2015[1]	2016[1]	2017	2018	2019	2020*	Average annual percent change, 2010–2019	Percent change, 2019–2020
Total	242[A]	227[A]	229[A]	229[A]	226[A]	224[A]	167	-0.9	-25.5
Sex									
Male	431[A]	395[A]	398[A]	394[A]	387[A]	386[A]	295	-1.2	-23.4
Female	59[A]	64[A]	66[A]	69[A]	69[A]	66[A]	42	1.4	-37.2
Adults[2]	315[A]	293[A]	295[A]	295[A]	290[A]	287[A]	213	-1.1	-25.7
18 to 24 years	NC	NC	NC	NC	NC	NC	329	NC	NC
25 to 34 years	NC	NC	NC	NC	NC	NC	421	NC	NC
35 to 44 years	NC	NC	NC	NC	NC	NC	337	NC	NC
45 to 54 years	NC	NC	NC	NC	NC	NC	177	NC	NC
55 to 64 years	NC	NC	NC	NC	NC	NC	78	NC	NC
65 years and over	NC	NC	NC	NC	NC	NC	13	NC	NC
Race/Ethnicity									
White[3]	167[A]	178[A]	180[A]	187[A]	186[A]	184[A]	133	1.1	-27.6
Black[3]	745[A]	640[A]	633[A]	616[A]	592[A]	600[A]	465	-2.4	-22.5
Hispanic	235[A]	185[A]	197[A]	186[A]	184[A]	177[A]	134	-3.1	-24.5
American Indian/Alaska Native[3]	426[A]	379[A]	380[A]	367[A]	403[A]	422[A]	274	-0.1	-35.1
Asian[3]	31[A]	30[A]	29[A]	26[A]	26[A]	25[A]	19	-2.5	-22.2
Native Hawaiian/Other Pacific Islander[3]	136[A]	153[A]	116	164[A]	174[A]	127[A]	104	-0.8	-17.6
Two or more races[3]	16	25[A]	33[A]	28[A]	40	25[A]	19	5	-22.6

NOTE: Rates are based on the number of confined inmates at midyear in local jails per 100,000 U.S. residents (for total) or per 100,000 U.S. residents of a given demographic group. Data are based on the inmate population confined on the last weekday in June and include both adults and juveniles, unless specified. Results may differ from previous reports in the series due to data updates.
* = Comparison year.
A = Difference with comparison year is significant at the 95% confidence level.
NC = Not collected. The Annual Survey of Jails (ASJ) began collecting inmate counts by adult age category in 2020.
[1]In 2015 and 2016, the ASJ collected jail population data at midyear and yearend but only collected demographic data on the yearend population. Because jails typically hold fewer inmates at yearend than at midyear, the 2015 and 2016 demographic data reported here were adjusted for seasonal variation and represent estimated midyear counts.
[2]Excludes persons under age 18.
[3]Excludes persons of Hispanic/Latino origin (e.g., White refers to non-Hispanic Whites and Black refers to non-Hispanic Blacks).

Table 3. Number of Confined Inmates in Local Jails, by Demographic Characteristics, 2010 and 2015–2019

(Number; percent.)

Characteristic	2010	2015[1]	2016[1]	2017	2018	2019	2020*	Average annual percent change, 2010–2019	Percent change, 2019–2020
Total	748,700[A]	727,400[A]	740,700[A]	745,200[A]	738,400[A]	734,500[A]	549,100	-0.2	-25.2
Sex									
Male..	656,400[A]	623,600[A]	633,100[A]	631,500[A]	623,400[A]	623,700[A]	479,300	-0.6	-23.2
Female..	92,400[A]	103,800[A]	107,600[A]	113,700[A]	115,100[A]	110,700[A]	69,800	2.0	-37.0
Age Group									
Juveniles[2]..................................	7,600[A]	3,600[A]	3,900[A]	3,600[A]	3,400[A]	2,900[A]	2,300	-10.7	-21.1
Held as adult[3]............................	5,600[A]	3,200[A]	3,200[A]	3,200[A]	2,700[A]	2,200[A]	2,000	-10.4	-10.7
Held as juvenile...........................	1,900[A]	400	700[A]	300	700[A]	700[A]	300	-11.6	-55.4
Adults....................................	741,200[A]	723,800[A]	736,800[A]	741,600[A]	735,000[A]	731,600[A]	546,800	-0.1	-25.3
18 to 24 years..............................	NC	NC	NC	NC	NC	NC	98,800	NC	NC
25 to 34 years..............................	NC	NC	NC	NC	NC	NC	193,900	NC	NC
35 to 44 years..............................	NC	NC	NC	NC	NC	NC	142,200	NC	NC
45 to 54 years..............................	NC	NC	NC	NC	NC	NC	71,400	NC	NC
55 to 64 years..............................	NC	NC	NC	NC	NC	NC	33,100	NC	NC
65 years and over	NC	NC	NC	NC	NC	NC	7,400	NC	NC
Race/ethnicity									
White[4]......................................	331,600[A]	351,600[A]	356,100[A]	370,100[A]	368,500[A]	362,900[A]	262,100	1.0	-27.8
Black[4].......................................	283,200[A]	255,200[A]	254,600[A]	250,100[A]	242,300[A]	247,100[A]	192,600	-1.5	-22.0
Hispanic.....................................	118,100[A]	103,900[A]	112,700[A]	108,400[A]	109,300[A]	106,900[A]	81,900	-1.1	-23.4
American Indian/Alaska Native[4].............	9,900[A]	9,000[A]	9,000[A]	8,800[A]	9,700[A]	10,200[A]	6,700	0.3	-34.9
Asian[4].......................................	4,400[A]	5,200[A]	5,200[A]	4,800[A]	4,800[A]	4,700[A]	3,700	0.7	-21.1
Native Hawaiian/Other Pacific Islander[4]	700[A]	900	700	1,000[A]	1,000[A]	800[A]	600	1.8	-16.4
Two or more races[4]........................	800[A]	1,700	2,300[A]	2,000	2,800	1,900	1,500	8.9	-20.7

NOTE: Data are based on the inmate population confined on the last weekday in June, unless specified. Data are adjusted for nonresponse and rounded to the nearest 100. Details may not sum to totals due to rounding. See table 3 in Jail Inmates in 2017 (NCJ 251774, BJS, April 2019) for data from 2011 to 2014. Results may differ from previous reports in the series due to data updates from jail authorities.
* = Comparison year.
A = Difference with comparison year is significant at the 95% confidence level.
NC = Not collected. The Annual Survey of Jails (ASJ) began collecting inmate counts by adult age category in 2020.
[1]In 2015 and 2016, the ASJ collected jail population data at midyear and yearend but only collected demographic data on the yearend population. Because jails typically hold fewer inmates at yearend than at midyear, the 2015 and 2016 demographic data reported here were adjusted for seasonal variation and represent estimated midyear counts.
[2]Persons younger than age 18.
[3]Includes juveniles who were tried or awaiting trial as adults.
[4]Excludes persons of Hispanic/Latino origin (e.g., White refers to non-Hispanic Whites and Black refers to non-Hispanic Blacks).

Table 3A. Percent of Confined Inmates in Local Jails, of Confined Inmates in Local Jails, by Characteristics, 2010 and 2015–2019

(Percent.)

Characteristic	2010	2015[1]	2016[1]	2017	2018	2019	2020
Sex							
Male..	87.7[A]	85.7[A]	85.5[A]	84.7[A]	84.4[A]	84.9[A]	87.3
Female...	12.3[A]	14.3[A]	14.5[A]	15.3[A]	15.6[A]	15.1[A]	12.7
Age group							
Juveniles[2]..	1.0[A]	0.5[A]	0.5[A]	0.5[A]	0.5	0.4	0.4
Held as adult[3].....................................	0.8[A]	0.4[A]	0.4[A]	0.4[A]	0.4	0.3[A]	0.4
Held as juvenile...................................	0.3[A]	0.1	0.1[A]	<0.05	0.1	0.1[A]	0.1
Adults...	99.0[A]	99.5[A]	99.5[A]	99.5[A]	99.5	99.6	99.6
18 to 24 years.....................................	NC	NC	NC	NC	NC	NC	18.0
25 to 34 years.....................................	NC	NC	NC	NC	NC	NC	35.3
35 to 44 years.....................................	NC	NC	NC	NC	NC	NC	25.9
45 to 54 years.....................................	NC	NC	NC	NC	NC	NC	13.0
55 to 64 years.....................................	NC	NC	NC	NC	NC	NC	6.0
65 years and over	NC	NC	NC	NC	NC	NC	1.3
Race/ethnicity							
White[4]...	44.3[A]	48.3	48.1	49.7[A]	49.9[A]	49.4[A]	47.7
Black[4]...	37.8[A]	35.1	34.4	33.6[A]	32.8[A]	33.6[A]	35.1
Hispanic..	15.8	14.3	15.2	14.5	14.8	14.6	14.9
American Indian/Alaska Native[4]..............	1.3	1.2	1.2	1.2	1.3	1.4	1.2
Asian[4]...	0.6[A]	0.7	0.7	0.6	0.7	0.6	0.7
Native Hawaiian/Other Pacific Islander[4]	0.1[A]	0.1	0.1[A]	0.1	0.1	0.1	0.1
Two or more races[4]	0.1[A]	0.2	0.3	0.3	0.4	0.3	0.3

NOTE: Data are based on the inmate population confined on the last weekday in June, unless specified. Data are adjusted for nonresponse and rounded to the nearest 100. Details may not sum to totals due to rounding. See table 3 in *Jail Inmates in 2017* (NCJ 251774, BJS, April 2019) for data from 2011 to 2014. Results may differ from previous reports in the series due to data updates from jail authorities.
* = Comparison year.
A = Difference with comparison year is significant at the 95% confidence level.
NC = Not collected. The Annual Survey of Jails (ASJ) began collecting inmate counts by adult age category in 2020.
[1]In 2015 and 2016, the ASJ collected jail population data at midyear and yearend but only collected demographic data on the yearend population. Because jails typically hold fewer inmates at yearend than at midyear, the 2015 and 2016 demographic data reported here were adjusted for seasonal variation and represent estimated midyear counts.
[2]Persons younger than age 18.
[3]Includes juveniles who were tried or awaiting trial as adults.
[4]Excludes persons of Hispanic/Latino origin (e.g., White refers to non-Hispanic Whites and Black refers to non-Hispanic Blacks).

Table 4. Average Daily Jail Population, by Size of Jurisdiction, 2020

(Number; percent.)

Jail jurisdiction size	Jail jurisdictions		Total average daily population		Mean average daily population	Median average daily population
	Number	Percent	Number	Percent		
Total	2,843	100.0	658,100	100.0	231	75
49 or fewer..............................	1120	39.4	23,400	3.6	21	19
50 to 99	482	16.9	34,700	5.3	72	70
100 to 249	619	21.8	98,500	15.0	159	159
250 to 499	308	10.8	109,000	16.6	354	349
500 to 999	199	7.0	140,900	21.4	707	696
1,000 to 2,499	90	3.2	132,800	20.2	1,472	1,351
2,500 and over	25	0.9	118,800	18.0	4,704	3,939

NOTE: The average daily population (ADP) is the sum of all inmates in jail each day for the 12-month period from July 1, 2019 to June 30, 2020, divided by the number of days in the period. Details may not sum to totals due to rounding.

Table 5. Jail Capacity, Midyear Population, and Percent of Capacity Occupied in Local Jails, 2010–2020

(Number; percent.)

Year	Midyear population[1]	Rated capacity[2]	Percent of capacity occupied[3]	Percent of jail jurisdictions operating at more than 100% of rated capacity
2010...	748,700[A]	866,800[A]	86.4[A]	18.5[A]
2011...	735,600[A]	879,700[A]	83.6[A]	17.2[A]
2012...	744,500[A]	870,400[A]	84.9[A]	18.5[A]
2013...	731,200[A]	872,900[A]	83.9[A]	15.4[A]
2014...	744,600[A]	890,500	83.6[A]	15.5[A]
2015...	727,400[A]	901,400	80.7[A]	14.5[A]
2016...	740,700[A]	915,400	80.9[A]	16.5[A]
2017...	745,200[A]	915,100	81.4[A]	20.0[A]
2018...	738,400[A]	907,000	81.4[A]	20.1[A]
2019...	734,500[A]	907,700	80.9[A]	15.0[A]
2020*...	549,100	913,700	60.1	7.0
Average annual percent change, 2010–2019.......	-0.2	0.5	NC	NC
Percent change, 2019–2020	-25.2	0.7	NC	NC

NOTE: Data are rounded to the nearest 100 for midyear population and rated capacity. Results may differ from previous reports in the series due to data updates from jail authorities.
* = Comparison year.
A = Difference with comparison group is significant at the 95% confidence level.
NC = Not calculated.
[1]The number of inmates held on the last weekday in June.
[2]The maximum number of beds or inmates assigned by a rating official to a facility, excluding separate temporary holding areas.
[3]The midyear inmate population divided by the rated capacity.

Table 6. Percent of Jail Capacity Occupied at Midyear, by Size of Jurisdiction, 2020

(Number; percent.)

Jail jurisdiction size (ADP)	Midyear population[1]	Rated capacity[2]	Percent of capacity occupied at midyear[3]	Percent of jail jurisdictions operating at more than 100% of rated capacity at midyear
Total	549,100	913,700	60.1	7.0
49 or fewer..	19,100	48,500	39.5[A]	3.1
50 to 99	29,700	49,500	60.0	11.8[A]
100 to 249	83,800	139,500	60.1	9.2[A]
250 to 499	90,900	146,400	62.1	8.9[A]
500 to 999	115,100	190,800	60.4	10.5[A]
1,000 to 2,499	112,400	180,300	62.3	3.4[A]
2,500 or more*	98,000	158,700	61.8	0.0

NOTE: The average daily population (ADP) is the sum of all inmates in jail each day for the 12-month period from July 1, 2019 to June 30, 2020, divided by the number of days in the period. Jail jurisdiction size is based on the ADP. Data are rounded to the nearest 100 for midyear population and rated capacity. Details may not sum to totals due to rounding.
* = Comparison group.
A = Difference with comparison group is significant at the 95% confidence level.
[1]The number of inmates held on the last weekday in June.
[2]Maximum number of beds or inmates assigned by a rating official to a facility, excluding separate temporary holding areas.
[3]The midyear population divided by the rated capacity.

Table 7. Inmate Turnover Rate and Expected Average Length of Stay, by Size of Jurisdiction, 2020

(Number; percent.)

Jail jurisdiction size (ADP)	Average daily population[1]	Annual admissions	Weekly inmate turnover rate[2]	Expected average time in jail (days)
Total	658,100	8,652,200	50.3	27.8
49 or fewer....................................	23,400	704,600	113.8 A	12.2 A
50 to 99	34,700	672,400	71.7 A	18.9 A
100 to 249	98,500	1,577,300	61.3 A	22.9 A
250 to 499	109,000	1,444,300	50.2 A	27.6 A
500 to 999	140,900	1,637,400	44.8 A	31.5 A
1,000 to 2,499	132,800	1,512,200	43.7 A	32.1 A
2,500 or more*	118,800	1,104,100	36.3	39.4

NOTE: The average daily population (ADP) is the sum of all inmates in jail each day for the 12-month period from July 1, 2019 to June 30, 2020, divided by the number of days in the period. Jail jurisdiction size is based on the ADP. Data are rounded to the nearest 100 for ADP. Details may not sum to totals due to rounding.
* = Comparison group.
A = Difference with comparison group is significant at the 95% confidence level.
[1]The sum of all inmates in jail each day for the 12-month period from July 1, 2019 to June 30, 2020, divided by the number of days in the period.
[2]The sum of weekly admissions and releases, divided by the ADP. Weekly admissions and releases are calculated using the annual admissions and releases, divided by the number of weeks in the 12-month period.

Table 8. Persons Under Jail Supervision, by Confinement Status, 2010–2020

(Number; percent.)

Year	Total[1]	Held in jail[1]		Supervised outside of a jail facility[2]	
		Number	Percent	Number	Percent
2010................................	799,500 A	748,700 A	93.7 A	50,800	6.3 A
2011................................	787,000 A	735,600 A	93.5 A	51,400	6.5 A
2012................................	798,300 A	744,500 A	93.3 A	53,700	6.7 A
2013................................	779,700 A	731,200 A	93.8 A	48,500	6.2 A
2014................................	798,400 A	744,600 A	93.3 A	53,800	6.7 A
2015................................	774,500 A	727,400 A	93.9 A	47,100	6.1 A
2016................................	789,300 A	740,700 A	93.8 A	48,700	6.2 A
2017................................	794,200 A	745,200 A	93.8 A	49,100	6.2 A
2018................................	790,400 A	738,400 A	93.4 A	52,000	6.6 A
2019................................	773,100 A	734,500 A	95.0 A	38,700 A	5.0 A
2020*..............................	599,100	549,100	91.6	50,100	8.4

NOTE: Based on the number of inmates supervised on the last weekday in June, unless specified. Data are rounded to the nearest 100. Details may not sum to totals due to rounding.
* = Comparison year.
A = Difference with comparison year is significant at the 95% confidence level.
[1]The total population under jail supervision differs from past reports because persons serving weekend-only sentences are listed separately in this report instead of being added to the population supervised outside of jail.
[2]Includes unconfined persons under jail supervision in various programs such as electronic monitoring, home detention, day reporting, community service, alcohol or drug treatment programs, and other pretrial supervision and work programs. Excludes persons supervised by a probation or parole agency and persons in weekend programs. In 2015 and 2016, data on the population supervised outside jail were collected at December 31. For all other years, the data were collected on the last weekday in June.

Table 9. Staff Employed in Local Jails, by Sex, 2013 and 2015–2020

(Number; percent, ratio.)

Job function	Number							Percent of all staff						
	2013[1]	2015[1]	2016[1]	2017[2]	2018[2]	2019[2]	2020[2,*]	2013[1]	2015[1]	2016[1]	2017[2]	2018[2]	2019[2]	2020[2,*]
Job Function														
Total	220,000[A]	213,000[A]	226,300	225,700	221,600[A]	237,500	233,200	100.0	100.0	100.0	100.0	100.0	100.0	100.0
Correctional Officers[3].....................	173,900[A]	169,300[A]	178,800	179,500	174,500[A]	184,100	184,900	79.1	79.5	79.0	79.5	78.7	77.5[A]	79.3
Male	123,400	117,300[A]	124,300	123,200	119,900	127,300	125,700	56.1[A]	55.1[A]	54.9[A]	54.6	54.1	53.6	53.9
Female	50,500[A]	51,900[A]	54,500[A]	56,300	54,600[A]	56,800	59,100	22.9[A]	24.4[A]	24.1[A]	25.0	24.6	23.9[A]	25.3
Inmate-to-correctional-officer ratio[4]	4.2[A]	4.1[A]	3.9[A]	4.2[A]	4.2[A]	4.0[A]	3.0							
All Other Staff[5]..............................	46,100[A]	43,700[A]	47,500	46,200	47,100	53,400[A]	48,400	20.9	20.5	21.0	20.5	21.3	22.5[A]	20.7
Male	20,800	19,700	21,000	20,300	20,600	25,400[A]	20,100	9.5[A]	9.3[A]	9.3[A]	9.0	9.3[A]	10.7[A]	8.6
Female	25,200[A]	24,000[A]	26,500[A]	25,900[A]	26,500[A]	28,000	28,300	11.5[A]	11.3[A]	11.7	11.5[A]	12.0	11.8	12.1

NOTE: Data are rounded to the nearest 100 for the number of staff employed in local jails. Details may not sum to totals due to rounding. Results may differ from previous reports in the series due to data updates from jail authorities. BJS did not collect national data on the number of jail staff by job function and sex in 2010–2012 and 2014.
* = Comparison year.
A = Difference with comparison year is significant at the 95% confidence level.
[1]Data are based on staff employed at yearend.
[2]Data are based on staff employed on the last weekday in June.
[3]Includes deputies, monitors, and other custody staff who spend more than 50% of their time with the incarcerated population.
[4]The number of inmates in custody per correctional officer.
[5]Includes administrators, clerical and maintenance staff, educational staff, professional and technical staff, and other unspecified staff who spend more than 50% of their time in the facility.

Table 10. Number of Persons Serving Weekend-Only Sentences on the Weekend Before the Last Weekday in June, 2010–2020

(Number.)

Year	Number
2010..	9,900[A]
2011..	11,400[A]
2012..	10,400[A]
2013..	11,000[A]
2014..	9,700[A]
2015..	7,800[A]
2016..	5,500[A]
2017..	6,800[A]
2018..	5,900[A]
2019..	6,500[A]
2020*..	2,200

NOTE: Includes persons who served their sentences of confinement on weekends only (i.e., Friday to Sunday) on the weekend before the last weekday in June. In 2015 and 2016, the number of weekenders was collected for the weekend before December 31. Data are rounded to the nearest 100. Details may not sum to totals due to rounding.
* = Comparison year.
A = Difference with comparison year is significant at the 95% confidence level.

Table 11. Confined Inmates Held in Local Jails for Federal Correctional Authorities, State Prison Authorities, and American Indian and Alaska Native Tribal Governments, Midyears 2015 and 2019–2020

(Number; percent.)

Authority for which inmates were held	Number			Percent			Average annual percent change, 2015–2019	Percent change, 2019–2020
	2015	2019	2020*	2015	2019	2020*		
Total inmates in custody..	727,400 A	734,500 A	549,100	100.0	100.0	100.0	0.2	-25.2
All federal/state/tribal authorities	117,900 A	117,100 A	107,100	16.2 A	15.9 A	19.5	-0.2	-8.5
Federal authorities[1]	42,100	53,500 A	43,900	5.8 A	7.3 A	8.0	6.0	-17.9
U.S. Marshals Service....................................	25,200 A	32,900 A	31,500	3.5 A	4.5 A	5.7	6.6	-4.4
Federal Bureau of Prisons	1,700 A	1,800 A	2,600	0.2 A	0.2 A	0.5	2.1	41.0
U.S. Immigration and Customs Enforcement	14,400 A	17,300 A	9,300	2.0	2.4 A	1.7	4.6	-46.4
Bureau of Indian Affairs................................	140	230	150	<0.05	<0.05	<0.05	11.8	-34.9
State prison authorities...	75,600 A	63,300	63,000	10.4 A	8.6 A	11.5	-4.4	-0.6
American Indian/Alaska Native tribal governments	240	270	190	<0.05	<0.05	<0.05	3.6	-30.5

NOTE: Data are based on the inmate population confined on the last weekday in June. Data are rounded to the nearest 100, except for the Bureau of Indian Affairs and American Indian and Alaska Native tribal governments, which are rounded to the nearest 10. Details may not sum to totals due to rounding. Results may differ from previous reports in the series due to data updates from jail authorities.
* = Comparison year.
A = Difference with comparison year is significant at the 95% confidence level.
[1]Includes a small number inmates held for unspecified federal authorities and other federal authorities in addition to the listed categories.

Table 12. Confined Inmates in Local Jails, by Conviction Status and Offense Severity, 2010 and 2015–2020

(Number; percent.)

Job function	Number							Percent							Average annual percent change		Percent change, 2019–2020
	2010	2015[1]	2016[1]	2017	2018	2019	2020*	2010	2015[1]	2016[1]	2017	2018	2019	2020*	2010–2019	2015–2019	
Total	748,700ᴬ	727,400ᴬ	740,700ᴬ	745,200ᴬ	738,400ᴬ	734,500ᴬ	549,100	100.0	100.0	100.0	100.0	100.0	100.0	100.0	-0.2	-0.2	-25.2
Conviction status																	
Convicted[2]......................	291,300ᴬ	273,000ᴬ	258,500ᴬ	263,200ᴬ	248,500ᴬ	253,700ᴬ	168,400	38.9ᴬ	37.5ᴬ	34.9ᴬ	35.3ᴬ	33.6ᴬ	34.5ᴬ	30.7	-1.5	-1.8	-33.6
Unconvicted[3]	457,500ᴬ	454,400ᴬ	482,100ᴬ	482,000ᴬ	490,000ᴬ	480,700ᴬ	380,700	61.1ᴬ	62.5ᴬ	65.1ᴬ	64.7ᴬ	66.4ᴬ	65.5ᴬ	69.3	0.6	1.4	-20.8
Most serious type of offense																	
Felony..............................	NC	494,100ᴬ	516,400ᴬ	516,800ᴬ	504,900ᴬ	513,900ᴬ	421,200	NC	67.9ᴬ	69.7ᴬ	69.4ᴬ	68.4ᴬ	70.0ᴬ	76.7	NC	1.0	-18.0
Misdemeanor....................	NC	193,100ᴬ	188,000ᴬ	194,700ᴬ	192,000ᴬ	170,300ᴬ	94,000	NC	26.5ᴬ	25.4ᴬ	26.1ᴬ	26.0ᴬ	23.2ᴬ	17.1	NC	-3.1	-44.8
Other[4].............................	NC	40,200ᴬ	36,300	33,600	41,600ᴬ	50,300ᴬ	33,800	NC	5.5	4.9ᴬ	4.5ᴬ	5.6	6.8ᴬ	6.2	NC	5.6	-32.7

NOTE: Data are based on the inmate population confined on the last weekday in June, unless specified. Details may not sum to totals due to rounding. See table 3 in *Jail Inmates in 2017* (NCJ 251774, BJS, April 2019) for conviction status data from 2011 to 2014. Collection of the most serious type of offenses started in 2015. Results may differ from previous reports in the series due to data updates from jail authorities.
* = Comparison year.
A = Difference with comparison year is significant at the 95% confidence level.
NC = Not collected. The Annual Survey of Jails (ASJ) began collecting inmate counts by offense severity in 2015.
[1]In 2015 and 2016, the ASJ jail population data at midyear and yearend but only collected demographic data on the yearend population. Because jails typically hold fewer inmates at yearend than at midyear, the 2015 and 2016 demographic data reported here were adjusted for seasonal variation and represent estimated midyear counts.
[2]Sentenced or awaiting sentencing on a conviction.
[3]Awaiting court action on a current charge or held in jail for other reasons.
[4]Includes civil infractions and unknown offenses.

METHODOLOGY

Findings in this report are based on the 2005, 2013, and 2020 Census of Jails (COJ) and the 2006 to 2019 Annual Survey of Jails (ASJ). The large decreases in jail admissions and midyear populations can be attributed to the COVID-19 pandemic. The Bureau of Justice Statistics (BJS) periodically conducts the COJ, collecting a complete enumeration of local jail facilities and Federal Bureau of Prisons (BOP) detention facilities. The 2020 COJ was the twelfth collection in the series since 1970. In the years between complete enumerations of jails, BJS conducts the ASJ, a national survey administered to a sample of approximately 900 jails (BOP detention facilities are excluded from the ASJ), to provide nationwide statistics on the number and characteristics of local jail inmates.

In 2013, BJS conducted both the COJ and ASJ. The 2013 ASJ collected jail population data at midyear, and the 2013 COJ collected jail population and facility data at yearend. Statistics for 2013 in the *Jail Inmates* series are based on the 2013 ASJ midyear data, except for statistics on staff employed in local jails, which are based on the 2013 COJ yearend data. COJ and ASJ collections are currently conducted through Web-based surveys. RTI International is the data collection agent for the COJ and ASJ.

Data from 2020 should be interpreted with caution due to the conditions imposed by the global COVID-19 pandemic. For more information, see *Impact of COVID-19 on the Local Jail Population, January–June 2020* (NCJ 255888, BJS, March 2021) at https://bjs.ojp.gov/content/pub/pdf/icljpjj20.pdf.

THE UNIVERSE OF THE CENSUS OF JAILS AND THE ANNUAL SURVEY OF JAILS

The COJ and ASJ gather data from jails that hold inmates beyond arraignment, usually for a period exceeding 72 hours. Jail facilities are intended to hold adults, but some also hold juveniles (persons age 17 or younger). The universe of the COJ consists of all local jail jurisdictions (including county, city, regional, and privately operated jail facilities) and BOP detention facilities that function as jails. The universe of the ASJ includes all local jail jurisdictions but excludes BOP detention facilities. For consistency of historical comparisons, data from BOP detention facilities are excluded from BJS's *Jail Inmates* series, including this report.

The universe of the COJ and ASJ excludes separate temporary holding facilities (such as drunk tanks and police lockups) that do not hold persons after they have been formally charged in court. However, temporary holding facilities that are operated as part of a local jail are included. Also excluded are combined jail and prison systems in Alaska, Connecticut, Delaware, Hawaii, Rhode Island, and Vermont. These combined systems are operated by state departments of corrections and included in BJS's National Prisoner Statistics program. However, there are 15 independently operated jails in Alaska that are included in the universe of the COJ and ASJ.

JAIL JURISDICTIONS AND FACILITIES

A jail jurisdiction is a legal entity that has responsibility for managing jail facilities. Jail jurisdictions typically operate at the county level, with a sheriff's office or jail administrator managing the local facilities. Most jail jurisdictions have one facility each, but some jail jurisdictions have multiple facilities under a central authority. The 2020 ASJ sample consisted of 897 active jail jurisdictions, represented by 943 reporting units.

ADJUSTING FOR SEASONAL VARIATION IN THE JAIL POPULATION

Prior to 2015, the ASJ asked jails to report total and detailed inmate counts on the last weekday in June (the midyear reference date). In 2015 and 2016, the ASJ collected the total confined population at midyear, but detailed inmate counts by characteristic (i.e., sex, race or ethnicity, age category, conviction status, and most serious type of offense) on December 31 (the yearend reference date). Starting with the 2017 collection, the ASJ reverted back to the midyear reference. Comparisons of yearend data with midyear data need to consider seasonal variations, as jails typically hold fewer inmates at yearend than at midyear.

To adjust for seasonal variation, the numbers of inmates by characteristics for 2015 and 2016 in table 3 were multiplied by the ratio of the midyear confined population to the yearend confined population of the corresponding year.

TERMS AND DEFINITIONS

Admissions: Persons who are officially booked and housed in jails by formal legal document and the authority of the courts or some other official agency. Jail admissions include persons sentenced to weekend programs and those who are booked into the facility for the first time. Excluded from jail admissions are inmates re-entering the facility after an escape, work release, medical appointment or treatment facility appointment, and bail and court appearances. BJS collects jail admissions for the last 7 days in June.

Average daily population (ADP): The average is derived by the sum of inmates in jail each day for a year, divided by the number of days in the year.

Average annual change: The mean average change across a 12-month time period.

Calculating annual admissions: Annual jail admissions are calculated by multiplying weekly admissions by the sum of 365 days divided by 7 days.

Calculating weekly jail turnover rate: This rate is calculated by adding admissions and releases and dividing by the average daily population.

Inmates confined: The number of inmates held in custody.

Jail incarceration rate: The number of inmates held in the custody of local jails, per 100,000 U.S. residents.

Percent of capacity occupied: This percentage is calculated by taking the number of inmates, dividing by the rated capacity, and multiplying by 100.

Rated capacity: The number of beds or inmates assigned by a rating official to a facility, excluding separate temporary holding areas.

Releases: Persons released after a period of confinement (e.g., sentence completion, bail or bond releases, other pretrial releases, transfers to other jurisdictions, and deaths). Releases include those persons who have completed their weekend program and who are leaving the facility for the last time. Excluded from jail releases are temporary discharges including work release, medical appointment or treatment center, court appearance, furlough, day reporting, and transfers to other facilities within the jail's jurisdiction.

Standard errors and tests of significance: As with any survey, the ASJ estimates are subject to error arising from sampling rather than using a complete enumeration of the jail population. A common way to express this sampling variability is to construct a 95% confidence interval around each survey estimate. Typically, multiplying the standard error by 1.96 and then adding or subtracting the result from the estimate produces the confidence interval. This interval expresses the range of values that could result among 95% of the different samples that could be drawn.

Under jail supervision but not confined: This classification includes all persons in community-based programs operated by a jail facility. These programs include electronic monitoring, house arrest, community service, day reporting, and work programs. The classification excludes persons on pretrial release and who are not in a community-based program run by the jail, as well as persons under supervision of probation, parole, or other agencies; inmates on weekend programs; and inmates who participate in work release programs and return to the jail at night.

Weekend programs: Offenders in these programs are allowed to serve their sentences of confinement only on weekends (i.e., Friday to Sunday).

PART 8

Law Enforcement Officers Killed and Assaulted, 2020

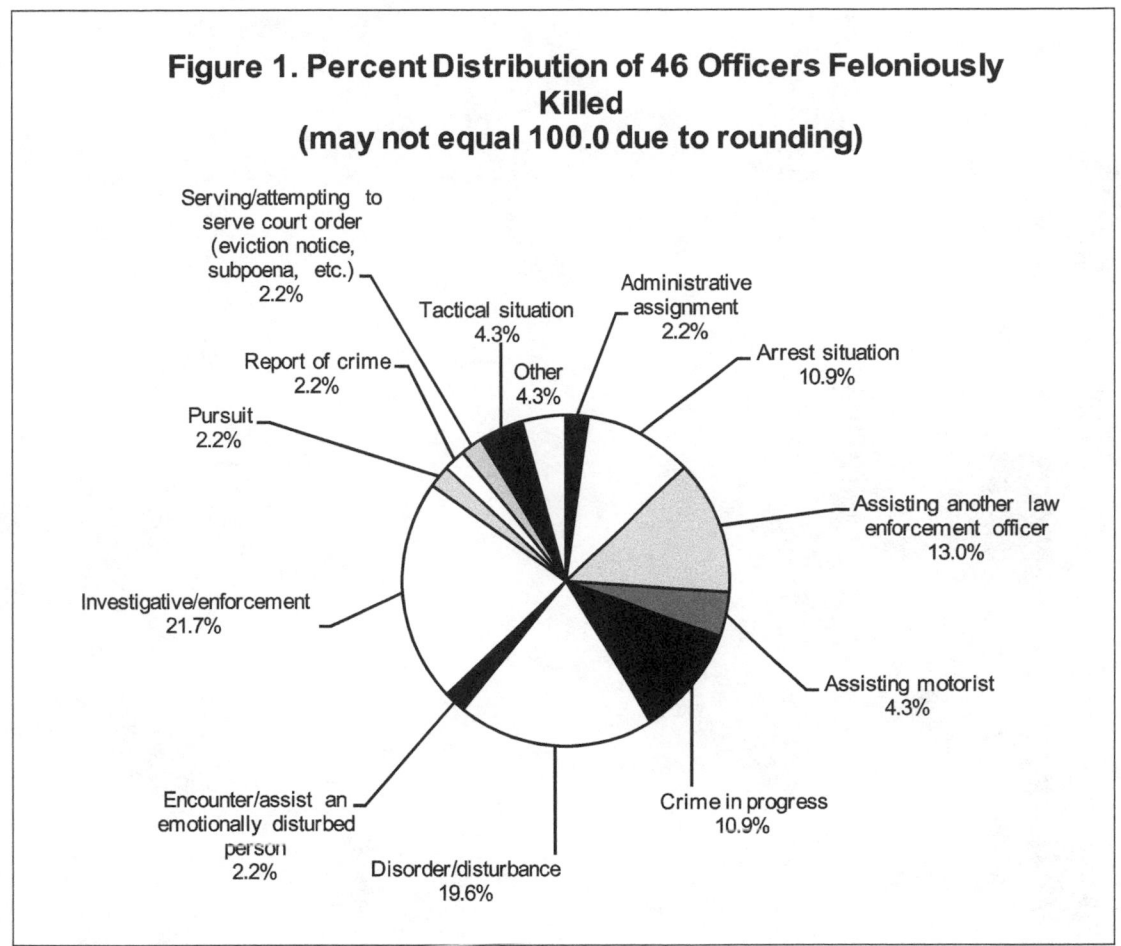

Figure 1. Percent Distribution of 46 Officers Feloniously Killed
(may not equal 100.0 due to rounding)

Serving/attempting to serve court order (eviction notice, subpoena, etc.) 2.2%

Tactical situation 4.3%

Administrative assignment 2.2%

Report of crime 2.2%

Other 4.3%

Arrest situation 10.9%

Pursuit 2.2%

Assisting another law enforcement officer 13.0%

Investigative/enforcement 21.7%

Assisting motorist 4.3%

Encounter/assist an emotionally disturbed person 2.2%

Crime in progress 10.9%

Disorder/disturbance 19.6%

- In 2020, 46 law enforcement officers died from injuries incurred in the line of duty during felonious incidents. Of the officers feloniously killed, 35 were employed by city police departments, including 13 who were members of law enforcement agencies in cities with 250,000 or more inhabitants.

- Line-of-duty deaths in 2020 occurred in 25 states. By region, 24 officers were feloniously killed in the South, 11 officers in the Midwest, 10 officers in the West, and 1 officer in the Northeast.

- The average age of the officers who died in 2020 was 39 years old. The slain officers' average length of law enforcement service was 12 years. Of these officers, 41 were male and 5 were female.

- In 2020, 46 law enforcement officers died as the result of accidents that occurred in the line of duty. Accidental line-of-duty deaths of law enforcement officers occurred in 25 states.

- Participating federal law enforcement agencies reported that 18,568 officers were injured but nonfatally assaulted while performing their duties in 2020.

- One federal law enforcement officers was feloniously killed in 2020. Of the 1,692 reported assaulted, 586 were reported as injured.

Table 1. Law Enforcement Officers Feloniously Killed, by Region, Geographic Division, and State/Territory, 2011–2020

(Number.)

Area	Total	2011	2012	2013	2014	2015	2016	2017	2018	2019	2020
Number of Victim Officers	503	72	49	27	51	41	66	46	57	48	46
Northeast	44	10	6	2	8	4	4	3	5	1	1
New England	9	0	2	1	1	0	1	0	4	0	0
Connecticut	1	0	0	0	0	0	0	0	1	0	0
Maine	1	0	0	0	0	0	0	0	1	0	0
Massachusetts	5	0	1	1	0	0	1	0	2	0	0
New Hampshire	2	0	1	0	1	0	0	0	0	0	0
Rhode Island	0	0	0	0	0	0	0	0	0	0	0
Vermont	0	0	0	0	0	0	0	0	0	0	0
Middle Atlantic	35	10	4	1	7	4	3	3	1	1	1
New Jersey	4	2	0	0	1	0	0	0	0	1	0
New York	18	4	2	1	5	2	1	2	1	0	0
Pennsylvania	13	4	2	0	1	2	2	1	0	0	1
Midwest	100	21	6	4	8	5	13	11	12	9	11
East North Central	61	12	2	3	5	3	6	8	8	8	6
Illinois	10	1	0	1	0	1	0	2	2	3	0
Indiana	11	2	0	1	3	0	1	1	2	0	1
Michigan	14	4	1	1	0	0	2	2	1	1	2
Ohio	18	4	1	0	1	1	2	2	2	2	3
Wisconsin	8	1	0	0	1	1	1	1	1	2	0
West North Central	39	9	4	1	3	2	7	3	4	1	5
Iowa	5	1	0	1	0	0	2	1	0	0	0
Kansas	10	1	2	0	1	0	2	0	3	0	1
Minnesota	4	1	1	0	1	1	0	0	0	0	0
Missouri	12	3	1	0	1	0	2	1	1	1	2
Nebraska	2	0	0	0	0	1	0	0	0	0	1
North Dakota	4	1	0	0	0	0	1	1	0	0	1
South Dakota	2	2	0	0	0	0	0	0	0	0	0
South	233	29	22	15	17	19	30	24	26	27	24
South Atlantic	99	18	10	5	10	3	13	8	15	7	10
Delaware	3	1	0	0	0	0	0	2	0	0	0
District of Columbia	0	0	0	0	0	0	0	0	0	0	0
Florida	24	6	2	2	4	1	0	3	4	0	2
Georgia	23	3	1	0	2	1	7	1	5	3	0
Maryland	7	0	0	1	0	0	2	1	2	1	0
North Carolina	13	2	3	0	2	0	1	0	1	1	3
South Carolina	12	2	1	0	1	1	1	0	3	0	3
Virginia	11	3	0	1	1	0	2	1	0	2	1
West Virginia	6	1	3	1	0	0	0	0	0	0	1
East South Central	42	6	5	3	0	5	4	1	6	9	3
Alabama	12	1	2	0	0	0	0	0	1	6	2
Kentucky	6	0	1	1	0	2	0	0	2	0	0
Mississippi	13	1	1	2	0	2	1	1	2	2	1
Tennessee	11	4	1	0	0	1	3	0	1	1	0
West South Central	92	5	7	7	7	11	13	15	5	11	11
Arkansas	11	1	0	0	1	1	1	2	0	2	3
Louisiana	22	0	2	1	1	6	4	4	1	1	2
Oklahoma	4	0	0	0	0	0	0	2	1	0	1
Texas	55	4	5	6	5	4	8	7	3	8	5
West	103	10	9	6	14	9	17	6	13	9	10
Mountain	49	5	5	1	7	7	8	4	6	1	5
Arizona	17	3	2	0	3	0	2	1	3	0	3
Colorado	10	2	1	0	0	2	2	1	2	0	0
Idaho	1	0	0	0	0	1	0	0	0	0	0
Montana	2	0	0	0	1	0	0	1	0	0	0
Nevada	6	0	1	0	2	1	0	1	0	0	1
New Mexico	5	0	0	0	0	3	2	0	0	0	0
Utah	8	0	1	1	1	0	2	0	1	1	1
Wyoming	0	0	0	0	0	0	0	0	0	0	0
Pacific	54	5	4	5	7	2	9	2	7	8	5
Alaska	3	0	0	0	2	0	1	0	0	0	0
California	38	3	2	5	5	2	6	2	5	6	2
Hawaii	3	0	0	0	0	0	0	0	1	0	2
Oregon	3	2	0	0	0	0	1	0	0	0	0
Washington	7	0	2	0	0	0	1	0	1	2	1
Puerto Rico and other outlying areas	23	2	6	0	4	4	2	2	1	2	0
American Samoa	0	0	0	0	0	0	0	0	0	0	0
Guam	0	0	0	0	0	0	0	0	0	0	0
Mariana Islands	0	0	0	0	0	0	0	0	0	0	0
Puerto Rico	22	2	5	0	4	4	2	2	1	2	0
U.S. Virgin Islands	1	0	1	0	0	0	0	0	0	0	0

Table 2. Law Enforcement Officers Feloniously Killed, by Population Group/Agency Type, 2011–2020

(Number.)

Population group/agency type	Total	2011	2012	2013	2014	2015	2016	2017	2018	2019	2020
Number of Victim Officers..........................	503	72	49	27	51	41	66	46	57	48	46
Group I (cities 250,000 and over)....................	87	13	6	4	8	10	12	8	7	6	13
Group II (cities 100,000–249,999)....................	48	9	4	2	6	2	8	2	2	7	6
Group III (cities 50,000–99,999).....................	35	9	2	2	2	1	2	4	4	5	4
Group IV (25,000–49,999).............................	35	4	2	3	2	4	6	2	5	3	4
Group V (cities 10,000–24,999)......................	36	5	3	2	4	2	5	2	7	2	4
Group VI (cities under 10,000).......................	53	10	4	3	5	5	8	8	4	2	4
Metropolitan counties.................................	108	14	11	6	11	5	15	7	21	12	6
Nonmetropolitan counties.............................	32	4	5	3	4	2	3	5	2	4	0
State agencies...	34	0	5	2	4	4	4	4	3	4	4
Federal agencies	12	2	1	0	1	2	1	2	1	1	1
Puerto Rico and other outlying areas..............	23	2	6	0	4	4	2	2	1	2	0

Table 3. Law Enforcement Officers Feloniously Killed, by Time of Incident, 2011–2020

(Number.)

Time of day	Total	2011	2012	2013	2014	2015	2016	2017	2018	2019	2020
Number of Victim Officers	503	72	49	27	51	41	66	46	57	48	46
Total A.M. hours	208	36	24	13	20	22	28	17	20	13	15
12:01 a.m.–2 a.m.	47	7	5	3	4	4	7	4	5	6	2
2:01 a.m.–4 a.m.	38	9	3	3	6	6	3	2	1	1	4
4:01 a.m.–6 a.m.	20	2	3	3	3	1	1	1	3	1	2
6:01 a.m.–8 a.m.	21	5	3	0	1	1	1	5	3	1	1
8:01 a.m.–10 a.m.	37	3	4	1	0	8	10	2	2	3	4
10:01 a.m.–noon	45	10	6	3	6	2	6	3	6	1	2
Total P.M. hours	284	36	23	14	31	18	37	29	37	34	25
12:01 p.m.–2 p.m.	40	5	2	3	7	1	10	2	5	3	2
2:01 p.m.–4 p.m.	52	6	3	3	9	2	8	5	8	2	6
4:01 p.m.–6 p.m.	44	8	3	1	6	2	3	5	8	4	4
6:01 p.m.–8 p.m.	42	5	6	2	1	5	2	3	7	7	4
8:01 p.m.–10 p.m.	55	3	6	2	4	7	9	5	2	13	4
10:01 p.m.–midnight	51	9	3	3	4	1	5	9	7	5	5
Not reported	11	0	2	0	0	1	1	0	0	1	6

Table 3A. Law Enforcement Officers Feloniously Killed, by Lighting and Weather/Environmental Conditions by Location of Incident, 2020

(Number.)

Characteristic	Total	Commercial			Government		
		Inside of structure	Outside	Location not reported	Inside of structure	Outside	Location not reported
Number of Victim Officers............................	46	0	7	0	1	1	0
Lighting							
Artificial	12	0	3	0	0	0	0
Dark...	2	0	0	0	0	1	0
Dawn...	2	0	0	0	0	0	0
Daylight	12	0	0	0	0	0	0
Dusk	2	0	1	0	0	0	0
Not reported	16	0	3	0	1	0	0
Weather/environmental							
Blizzard	0	0	0	0	0	0	0
Blowing dirt/sand/soil.....................	0	0	0	0	0	0	0
Clear...	22	0	5	0	0	1	0
Cloudy/partly cloudy........................	0	0	0	0	0	0	0
Earthquake.......................................	0	0	0	0	0	0	0
Fire/fog/smog/smoke.........................	0	0	0	0	0	0	0
Flooding...	0	0	0	0	0	0	0
Freezing rain/hail/sleet......................	0	0	0	0	0	0	0
Hurricane	0	0	0	0	0	0	0
Indoors (no adverse conditions)................	6	0	0	0	1	0	0
Rain	1	0	0	0	0	0	0
Severe crosswinds/high winds..............	0	0	0	0	0	0	0
Snow...	0	0	0	0	0	0	0
Tornado...	0	0	0	0	0	0	0
Other	0	0	0	0	0	0	0
Unknown..	1	0	0	0	0	0	0
Not reported	16	0	2	0	0	0	0

Table 3A. Law Enforcement Officers Feloniously Killed, by Lighting and Weather/Environmental Conditions by Location of Incident, 2020—*Continued*

(Number.)

Characteristic	Public space[1]			Residential			Other		
	Inside of structure	Outside	Location not reported	Inside of structure	Outside	Location not reported	Inside of structure	Outside	Location not reported
Number of Victim Officers..........................	0	17	0	5	13	0	0	0	2
Lighting									
Artificial	0	5	0	3	1	0	0	0	0
Dark...	0	0	0	0	1	0	0	0	0
Dawn...	0	1	0	1	0	0	0	0	0
Daylight	0	4	0	1	7	0	0	0	0
Dusk...	0	0	0	0	1	0	0	0	0
Not reported	0	7	0	0	3	0	0	0	2
Weather/environmental									
Blizzard	0	0	0	0	0	0	0	0	0
Blowing dirt/sand/soil	0	0	0	0	0	0	0	0	0
Clear...	0	7	0	0	9	0	0	0	0
Cloudy/partly cloudy........................	0	0	0	0	0	0	0	0	0
Earthquake.....................................	0	0	0	0	0	0	0	0	0
Fire/fog/smog/smoke	0	0	0	0	0	0	0	0	0
Flooding...	0	0	0	0	0	0	0	0	0
Freezing rain/hail/sleet	0	0	0	0	0	0	0	0	0
Hurricane	0	0	0	0	0	0	0	0	0
Indoors (no adverse conditions)	0	0	0	5	0	0	0	0	0
Rain	0	1	0	0	0	0	0	0	0
Severe crosswinds/high winds............	0	0	0	0	0	0	0	0	0
Snow	0	0	0	0	0	0	0	0	0
Tornado..	0	0	0	0	0	0	0	0	0
Other	0	0	0	0	0	0	0	0	0
Unknown..	0	1	0	0	0	0	0	0	0
Not reported	0	8	0	0	4	0	0	0	2

[1]Examples of public space include, but are not limited to, alleys, highways, lakes, parks, rivers, roads, and sidewalks.

Table 4. Law Enforcement Officers Feloniously Killed, by Day of Incident, 2011–2020

(Number.)

Day of the week	Total	2011	2012	2013	2014	2015	2016	2017	2018	2019	2020
Number of Victim Officers	503	72	49	27	51	41	66	46	57	48	46
Sunday	77	13	7	2	9	5	13	8	5	6	9
Monday	60	12	5	3	7	6	4	8	7	5	3
Tuesday	66	11	10	5	5	6	6	3	7	6	7
Wednesday	76	8	5	3	4	9	15	7	14	5	6
Thursday	71	9	9	6	7	3	12	6	7	5	7
Friday	68	11	5	5	8	4	7	9	8	6	5
Saturday	85	8	8	3	11	8	9	5	9	15	9

Table 5. Law Enforcement Officers Feloniously Killed, by Month of Incident, 2011–2020

(Number.)

Month	Total	2011	2012	2013	2014	2015	2016	2017	2018	2019	2020
Number of Victim Officers	503	72	49	27	51	41	66	46	57	48	46
January	37	9	6	2	2	0	2	4	4	4	4
February	41	3	4	5	1	0	9	2	8	5	4
March	51	9	1	1	8	6	5	4	7	3	7
April	34	9	4	3	1	0	1	4	6	2	4
May	48	3	3	1	9	10	3	7	4	5	3
June	37	6	4	2	4	3	3	2	3	5	5
July	42	8	2	1	4	1	10	4	6	3	3
August	42	7	8	2	3	6	5	5	0	3	3
September	38	1	5	4	6	4	3	2	7	3	3
October	39	5	1	1	4	4	9	5	4	1	5
November	45	2	4	0	5	4	13	5	4	6	2
December	49	10	7	5	4	3	3	2	4	8	3

Table 6. Law Enforcement Officers Feloniously Killed, by Age Group of Victim Officer, 2011–2020

(Number; years.)

Age group	Total	2011	2012	2013	2014	2015	2016	2017	2018	2019	2020
Number of Victim Officers	503	72	49	27	51	41	66	46	57	48	46
Under 25 years	20	2	2	0	5	2	2	1	1	3	2
25–30 years	82	17	8	2	3	5	10	11	16	7	3
31–35 years	108	11	12	9	11	9	15	8	14	9	10
36–40 years	72	12	8	7	7	2	8	7	7	7	7
41–45 years	86	10	8	4	12	9	12	9	9	6	7
46–50 years	68	13	6	1	9	10	9	6	2	6	6
51–55 years	41	4	5	2	3	2	8	2	6	3	6
56–60 years	12	3	0	1	0	1	0	2	0	4	1
Over 60 years	11	0	0	1	1	1	2	0	2	2	2
Not reported	3	0	0	0	0	0	0	0	0	1	2
Average age (years)	388	38	38	39	39	40	40	38	37	40	39

Table 7. Law Enforcement Officers Feloniously Killed, by Years of Service of Victim Officer, 2011–2020

(Number.)

Years of service	Total	2011	2012	2013	2014	2015	2016	2017	2018	2019	2020
Number of Victim Officers......................	503	72	49	27	51	41	66	46	57	48	46
Less than 1	19	0	2	0	2	4	2	1	3	3	2
1–5..	120	17	12	4	11	8	13	14	14	12	15
6–10..	123	24	13	10	8	11	13	10	18	7	9
11–15..	78	8	5	8	11	4	13	7	10	8	4
16–20..	76	8	10	1	13	5	13	9	5	8	4
21–25..	42	12	1	1	5	6	4	2	2	4	5
26–30..	28	1	4	2	0	2	8	2	3	5	1
More than 30	9	2	1	1	1	0	0	0	1	1	2
Not reported..................................	8	0	1	0	0	1	0	1	1	0	4
Average years of service...........................	121	12	12	13	13	12	13	11	10	13	12

Table 8. Law Enforcement Officers Feloniously Killed, by Profile of Victim Officer, Average Demographics, 2001–2020

(Number.)

Average	2020	5-year averages		10-year averages	
		2011–2015	2016–2020	2001–2010	2011–2020
Age	39	39	39	38	39
Years of service	12	12	12	11	12
Height	5'9"	5'11"	5'10"	5'11"	5'10"
Weight	185	201	202	200	202

Note: The deaths of the 72 law enforcement officers that resulted from the events of September 11, 2001, are not included in this table.

Table 9. Law Enforcement Officers Feloniously Killed, by Race, Ethnicity, and Sex of Victim Officer, 2011–2020

(Number.)

Characteristic	Total	2011	2012	2013	2014	2015	2016	2017	2018	2019	2020
Number of Victim Officers...........................	503	72	49	27	51	41	66	46	57	48	46
Race											
White..	428	68	43	25	47	29	61	35	48	40	32
Black/African American	58	3	6	2	2	8	4	9	7	7	10
American Indian/Alaska Native	6	1	0	0	0	2	0	2	0	0	1
Asian/Native Hawaiian/Other Pacific Islander...........	6	0	0	0	2	2	1	0	0	1	0
Asian..	4	0	0	0	0	0	0	0	2	0	2
Native Hawaiian/Other Pacific Islander	1	0	0	0	0	0	0	0	0	0	1
Ethnicity											
Hispanic or Latino...........................	65	7	9	2	11	4	7	6	5	11	3
Not Hispanic or Latino......................	406	65	35	24	39	36	57	37	52	33	28
Not reported	32	0	5	1	1	1	2	3	0	4	15
Sex											
Male..	474	69	44	25	51	38	64	43	54	45	41
Female	29	3	5	2	0	3	2	3	3	3	5

Table 10. Law Enforcement Officers Feloniously Killed, by Use of Firearm by Victim Officer, Assisting Officer, and Offender During Incident, 2011–2020

(Number; percent.)

Characteristic	Total	2011	2012	2013	2014	2015	2016	2017	2018	2019	2020
Number of victim officers.............................	503	72	49	27	51	41	66	46	57	48	46
Average number of rounds fired by victim officers................		2.1	0.7	0.9	1.0	1.7	1.2	1.0	1.4	1.8	1.5
Average number of rounds fired by assisting officers[1]............		10.4	7.8	2.8	12.8	8.2	13.8	9.4	20.2	16.8	9.4
Average number of rounds fired by offenders[2] .		4.9	6.6	5.0	4.7	5.8	8.0	5.7	5.7	14.3	11.0
Number of victim officers who fired own weapon.....................	102	18	6	5	5	6	15	10	16	10	11
Average number of rounds fired by victim officers who fired own weapon..............		9.7	6.0	5.8	9.6	11.2	6.1	4.4	4.8	9.4	7.3
Average number of victim officer's rounds that struck offenders		0.8	1.5	0.7	4.0	0.7	0.3	1.5	1.7	1.9	1.7
Percentage hit rate of victim officers' rounds striking offenders		6.3	40.0	13.3	41.7	6.0	1.5	32.4	35.3	19.7	35.7
Average number of rounds fired by assisting officers............		8.0	14.7	2.7	2.5	2.0	6.0	6.0	7.4	11.4	28.3
Average number of rounds fired by offenders...		9.5	7.8	6.7	4.3	10.0	3.4	8.4	6.3	8.1	6.8
Number of victim officers who attempted to (but did not) use own firearm(s)	68	11	2	3	8	7	11	10	5	6	5
Average number of rounds fired by assisting officers............		5.8	0.0	1.0	15.2	23.0	40.0	15.7	33.5	2.5	19.0
Average number of rounds fired by offenders...		3.2	2.0	2.3	8.2	3.4	11.2	3.1	15.0	3.3	22.4
Number of victim officers who did not use and did not attempt to use own firearm(s)	302	40	38	18	34	26	39	24	30	32	21
Average number of rounds fired by assisting officers[1]............		12.4	6.0	3.0	12.5	3.4	18.2	8.1	24.7	21.0	2.8
Average number of rounds fired by offenders...		4.2	5.0	5.3	4.3	5.9	9.8	5.6	5.3	18.9	10.6
Number of victim officers who did not use own firearm(s), but attempt to use own firearm(s) information was not reported........	7	1	0	0	2	0	1	0	2	0	1
Average number of rounds fired by assisting officers[3]............			0.0	0.0	41.0	0.0		0.0		0.0	0.0
Average number of rounds fired by offenders[4] .		4.0	0.0	0.0	2.0	0.0	9.0	0.0	5.7	0.0	6.8
Number of victim officers in which victim officer's use of firearm(s) was unknown or not reported........	24	2	3	1	2	2	0	2	4	0	8

NOTE: When calculating the averages presented in this table, the FBI's Law Enforcement Officers Killed and Assaulted Program used all available data for each incident. For example, in a specific incident, if the number of rounds fired by the victim officer is known, but the number of rounds fired by the offender is not known, the known number was included in the calculation for the average number of rounds fired by victim officers.
[1]The number of rounds fired (1,100) during an incident in 2013 was excluded when calculating the average number of rounds fired by assisting officers to provide more accurate statistics.
[2]The number of rounds fired (1,046) during an incident in 2017 was excluded when calculating the average number of rounds fired by offenders to provide more accurate statistics.
[3]For 2011, 2016, and 2018, the victim officers were alone at the time of the incident; therefore, the number of rounds fired by assisting officers is not relevant.
[4]For 2011, number of rounds data were not available for inclusion in these averages.

Table 11. Law Enforcement Officers Feloniously Killed, by Victim Officer Killed with Own Weapon, Disarmed[1] of Weapon, and Weapon Stolen[2] by Offender, 2011–2020

(Number.)

Characteristic	Total	2011	2012	2013	2014	2015	2016	2017	2018	2019	2020
Number of victim officers	503	72	49	27	51	41	66	46	57	48	46
Killed with own weapon	16	3	1	1	1	4	0	1	4	0	1
Disarmed of weapon/weapon taken from victim officer	16	3	1	1	1	4	0	1	4	0	1
Weapon stolen[3]	8	1	0	0	0	3	0	1	2	0	1
Weapon not stolen	8	2	1	1	1	1	0	0	2	0	0
Weapon stolen information not reported	0	0	0	0	0	0	0	0	0	0	0
Not disarmed of weapon/weapon not taken from victim officer	0	0	0	0	0	0	0	0	0	0	0
Weapon stolen	0	0	0	0	0	0	0	0	0	0	0
Weapon not stolen	0	0	0	0	0	0	0	0	0	0	0
Weapon stolen information not reported	0	0	0	0	0	0	0	0	0	0	0
Disarmed of weapon/weapon taken information not reported	0	0	0	0	0	0	0	0	0	0	0
Weapon stolen	0	0	0	0	0	0	0	0	0	0	0
Weapon not stolen	0	0	0	0	0	0	0	0	0	0	0
Weapon stolen information not reported	0	0	0	0	0	0	0	0	0	0	0
Killed with weapon other than own	487	69	48	26	50	37	66	45	53	48	45
Disarmed of weapon/weapon taken from victim officer	35	10	5	3	7	5	3	0	2	0	0
Weapon stolen	21	4	3	2	6	2	2	0	2	0	0
Weapon not stolen	14	6	2	1	1	3	1	0	0	0	0
Weapon stolen information not reported	0	0	0	0	0	0	0	0	0	0	0
Not disarmed of weapon/weapon not taken from victim officer	452	59	43	23	43	32	63	45	51	48	45
Weapon stolen	1	0	0	0	0	0	0	1	0	0	0
Weapon not stolen	451	59	43	23	43	32	63	44	51	48	45
Weapon stolen information not reported	0	0	0	0	0	0	0	0	0	0	0
Disarmed of weapon/weapon taken information not reported	1	1	0	0	0	0	0	0	0	0	0
Weapon stolen	0	0	0	0	0	0	0	0	0	0	0
Weapon not stolen	1	1	0	0	0	0	0	0	0	0	0
Weapon stolen information not reported	0	0	0	0	0	0	0	0	0	0	0

NOTE: The term "weapon" includes all weapon types that may be issued to a law enforcement officer.
[1] The term "disarmed" indicates the victim officer was physically disarmed of one or more of his or her weapons by the offender(s) during the incident.
[2] The term "stolen" indicates a weapon issued to the victim officer was taken from the scene of the incident by the offender(s).

Table 12. Law Enforcement Officers Feloniously Killed with Own Weapons, by Victim Officer's Type of Weapon, 2011–2020

(Number.)

Type of weapon	Total	2011	2012	2013	2014	2015	2016	2017	2018	2019	2020
Number of Victim Officers Killed with Own Weapon.	17	3	1	1	1	4	0	1	4	0	2
Total, handgun...............	14	3	1	1	1	3	0	1	4	0	0
.38 caliber..................	1	1	0	0	0	0	0	0	0	0	0
.40 caliber..................	7	2	0	0	1	1	0	1	2	0	0
.45 caliber..................	0	0	0	0	0	0	0	0	0	0	0
9 millimeter................	4	0	0	1	0	1	0	0	2	0	0
Not reported................	2	0	1	0	0	1	0	0	0	0	0
Rifle, total..................	0	0	0	0	0	0	0	0	0	0	0
Shotgun, total...............	0	0	0	0	0	0	0	0	0	0	0
Other.......................	3	0	0	0	0	1	0	0	0	0	2

Table 13. Law Enforcement Officers Feloniously Killed, Time of Incident, by Type of Assignment, 2020

(Number.)

Characteristic and time	Total	2-officer patrol	1-officer patrol		Court/prisoner security		Investigative/detective		Plainclothes assignment	
			Alone	Assisted	Alone	Assisted	Alone	Assisted	Alone	Assisted
Number of Victim Officers............	46	3	5	26	0	0	0	0	0	0
Total A.M. hours	15	0	3	7	0	0	0	0	0	0
12:01 a.m.–2 a.m.	2	0	1	1	0	0	0	0	0	0
2:01 a.m.–4 a.m.	4	0	0	2	0	0	0	0	0	0
4:01 a.m.–6 a.m.	2	0	1	0	0	0	0	0	0	0
6:01 a.m.–8 a.m.	1	0	0	0	0	0	0	0	0	0
8:01 a.m.–10 a.m.	4	0	0	4	0	0	0	0	0	0
10:01 a.m.–noon	2	0	1	0	0	0	0	0	0	0
Total P.M. hours	25	3	0	17	0	0	0	0	0	0
12:01 p.m.–2 p.m.	2	0	0	2	0	0	0	0	0	0
2:01 p.m.–4 p.m.	6	0	0	5	0	0	0	0	0	0
4:01 p.m.–6 p.m.	4	1	0	2	0	0	0	0	0	0
6:01 p.m.–8 p.m.	4	0	0	4	0	0	0	0	0	0
8:01 p.m.–10 p.m.	4	0	0	2	0	0	0	0	0	0
10:01 p.m.–midnight	5	2	0	2	0	0	0	0	0	0
Not reported................	6	0	2	2	0	0	0	0	0	0

Table 13. Law Enforcement Officers Feloniously Killed, Time of Incident, by Type of Assignment, 2020—*Continued*

(Number.)

Characteristic and time	Special assignment		Tactical assignment (uniformed)		Undercover		Other[1]		Off duty
	Alone	Assisted	Alone	Assisted	Alone	Assisted	Alone	Assisted	
Number of Victim Officers............	1	1	0	2	1	1	2	2	2
Total A.M. hours	0	1	0	1	1	0	1	0	1
12:01 a.m.–2 a.m.	0	0	0	0	0	0	0	0	0
2:01 a.m.–4 a.m.	0	0	0	0	1	0	0	0	1
4:01 a.m.–6 a.m.	0	0	0	1	0	0	0	0	0
6:01 a.m.–8 a.m.	0	0	0	0	0	0	1	0	0
8:01 a.m.–10 a.m.	0	0	0	0	0	0	0	0	0
10:01 a.m.–noon	0	1	0	0	0	0	0	0	0
Total P.M. hours	1	0	0	0	0	1	1	1	1
12:01 p.m.–2 p.m.	0	0	0	0	0	0	0	0	0
2:01 p.m.–4 p.m.	1	0	0	0	0	0	0	0	0
4:01 p.m.–6 p.m.	0	0	0	0	0	0	0	0	1
6:01 p.m.–8 p.m.	0	0	0	0	0	0	0	0	0
8:01 p.m.–10 p.m.	0	0	0	0	0	1	0	1	0
10:01 p.m.–midnight	0	0	0	0	0	0	1	0	0
Not reported................	0	0	0	1	0	0	0	1	0

[1]Includes officers on overtime/extra duty activities and other types of assignments not listed.

Table 14. Law Enforcement Officers Feloniously Killed, by Circumstance Encountered by Victim Officer Upon Arrival at Scene of Incident, 2011–2020

(Number.)

Circumstance	Total	2011	2012	2013	2014	2015	2016	2017	2018	2019	2020
Total	503	72	49	27	51	41	66	46	57	48	46
Administrative assignment	7	1	2	0	0	1	0	1	2	0	0
Prisoner transport	6	1	1	0	0	1	0	1	2	0	0
Other administrative assignment	1	0	1	0	0	0	0	0	0	0	0
Ambush (entrapment/premeditation)	75	3	5	3	11	7	19	5	11	2	9
Arrest situation	21	2	0	1	0	2	4	4	2	3	3
Attempting to restrain/control/handcuff offender(s)	10	0	0	0	0	2	0	1	2	3	2
Attempting to restrain/control/handcuff other individual[1]	0	NA	NA	NA	NA	NA	NA	NA	NA	0	0
Maintaining custody of prisoner (in vehicle, precinct, etc.)[1]	0	NA	NA	NA	NA	NA	NA	NA	NA	0	0
Verbal advisement only	11	2	0	1	0	0	4	3	0	0	1
Assisting another law enforcement officer	33	7	2	0	4	2	4	2	2	3	7
Foot pursuit	5	1	0	0	0	1	0	0	2	1	0
High-risk traffic stop[1]	1	NA	NA	NA	NA	NA	NA	NA	NA	0	1
Officer down (requiring emergency assistance)	1	0	0	0	0	0	0	0	0	0	1
Officer requiring emergency assistance (not pursuit)	3	1	0	0	0	0	1	0	0	0	1
Providing/deploying flares, traffic cones, etc.	9	4	1	0	1	1	1	1	0	0	0
Providing/deploying spike strips/stop sticks[1]	2	NA	NA	NA	NA	NA	NA	NA	NA	0	2
Traffic control (crash scene, directing traffic, etc.)[1]	0	NA	NA	NA	NA	NA	NA	NA	NA	0	0
Vehicular pursuit	7	1	1	0	0	0	1	1	0	2	1
Other emergency circumstance	3	0	0	0	2	0	1	0	0	0	0
Other nonemergency circumstance	2	0	0	0	1	0	0	0	0	0	1
Assisting motorist	3	0	0	0	1	1	0	0	0	0	1
Citizen complaint	2	0	0	0	0	0	0	0	0	0	2
Animal bite	0	0	0	0	0	0	0	0	0	0	0
Animal disturbance (barking dog, unleashed dog, etc.)	0	0	0	0	0	0	0	0	0	0	0
Business check	0	0	0	0	0	0	0	0	0	0	0
Check on welfare of citizen	0	0	0	0	0	0	0	0	0	0	0
Drug complaint	0	0	0	0	0	0	0	0	0	0	0
Traffic complaint	1	0	0	0	0	0	0	0	0	0	1
Trespassing[1]	0	NA	NA	NA	NA	NA	NA	NA	NA	0	0
Verbal complaint of noncriminal violation	1	0	0	0	0	0	0	0	0	0	1
Other citizen complaint[1]	0	NA	NA	NA	NA	NA	NA	NA	NA	0	0
Crime in progress	27	3	1	2	3	1	2	2	4	4	5
Active shooter[1]	0	NA	NA	NA	NA	NA	NA	NA	NA	0	0
Assault	1	0	0	0	1	0	0	0	0	0	0
Burglary	5	0	1	0	0	0	1	0	2	0	1
Larceny-theft	1	0	0	0	0	0	0	0	0	1	0
Mass casualty[1]	0	NA	NA	NA	NA	NA	NA	NA	NA	0	0
Motor vehicle theft	0	0	0	0	0	0	0	0	0	0	0
Person with firearm (no shots fired)	3	0	0	0	2	0	0	0	1	0	0
Robbery	7	2	0	1	0	0	1	1	0	2	0
Shooting/shots being fired (not "active shooter" situation)	6	1	0	1	0	1	0	1	0	0	2
Tampering with vehicle	0	0	0	0	0	0	0	0	0	0	0
Other crime against person	0	0	0	0	0	0	0	0	0	0	0
Other crime against property	4	0	0	0	0	0	0	0	1	1	2
Disorder/disturbance	29	6	2	1	5	1	2	1	4	3	4
Civil disorder (mass disobedience, riot, etc.)	0	0	0	0	0	0	0	0	0	0	0
Disturbance (disorderly subject, fight, etc.)	15	4	1	0	4	0	1	0	3	2	0
Domestic disturbance (family quarrel, no assault)	7	1	1	0	0	0	1	1	0	0	3
Domestic violence	7	1	0	1	1	1	0	0	1	1	1
Encounter/assist an emotionally disturbed person	7	1	2	0	1	0	0	1	0	0	2
Investigative/enforcement	208	34	28	13	20	17	28	21	24	16	7
Active shooter[1]	0	NA	NA	NA	NA	NA	NA	NA	NA	0	0
Animal cruelty[1]	0	NA	NA	NA	NA	NA	NA	NA	NA	0	0
Drug-related matter (drug bust, buy, etc.)	8	0	2	0	0	0	1	1	0	2	2
Handling person with mental illness	7	0	2	0	0	2	0	0	1	0	2
High-risk traffic stop[2]	7	2	2	0	1	0	0	1	0	0	1
Investigative activity	25	1	3	2	2	1	6	2	8	0	0
Mass casualty[1]	0	NA	NA	NA	NA	NA	NA	NA	NA	0	0
Motor vehicle crash	5	1	2	0	0	0	0	1	0	0	1
Official contact (not an arrest situation)[1]	0	NA	NA	NA	NA	NA	NA	NA	NA	0	0

(Number.)

Circumstance	Total	2011	2012	2013	2014	2015	2016	2017	2018	2019	2020
Possible DUI/DWI suspect (operating a vehicle)	1	0	0	0	1	0	0	0	0	0	0
Serving/attempting to serve search warrant (non-tactical)[1]	0	NA	NA	NA	NA	NA	NA	NA	NA	0	0
Surveillance activity[1]	5	NA	NA	NA	NA	NA	NA	NA	NA	5	0
Suspicious package[1]	0	NA	NA	NA	NA	NA	NA	NA	NA	0	0
Suspicious person/circumstance	54	8	8	6	6	5	11	6	3	1	0
Tactical situation[3]	49	13	4	4	4	4	7	6	7	NA	NA
Traffic violation stop	28	3	5	1	2	4	1	3	2	6	1
Undercover situation	2	0	0	0	2	0	0	0	0	0	0
Wanted person	17	6	0	0	2	1	2	1	3	2	0
Out of service (court, dining, etc.)[3]	0	NA	NA	NA	NA	NA	NA	NA	NA	0	0
Providing/deploying equipment (flares, traffic cones, etc.)[3]	0	NA	NA	NA	NA	NA	NA	NA	NA	0	0
Pursuit	42	9	5	1	4	4	4	6	6	3	0
Foot	22	5	3	0	1	2	4	3	4	0	0
Vehicular (anything other than foot)	20	4	2	1	3	2	0	3	2	3	0
Report of crime	1	0	0	0	1	0	0	0	0	0	0
Active shooter[1]	0	NA	NA	NA	NA	NA	NA	NA	NA	0	0
Assault	0	0	0	0	0	0	0	0	0	0	0
Burglary	0	0	0	0	0	0	0	0	0	0	0
Homicide	0	0	0	0	0	0	0	0	0	0	0
Larceny-theft	0	0	0	0	0	0	0	0	0	0	0
Mass casualty[1]	0	NA	NA	NA	NA	NA	NA	NA	NA	0	0
Motor vehicle theft	0	0	0	0	0	0	0	0	0	0	0
Person with firearm (no shots fired)	1	0	0	0	1	0	0	0	0	0	0
Robbery	0	0	0	0	0	0	0	0	0	0	0
Shooting/shots fired (not "active shooter" situation)	0	0	0	0	0	0	0	0	0	0	0
Tampering with vehicle	0	0	0	0	0	0	0	0	0	0	0
Other crime against person	0	0	0	0	0	0	0	0	0	0	0
Other crime against property	0	0	0	0	0	0	0	0	0	0	0
Respond to alarm (audible/silent)	0	0	0	0	0	0	0	0	0	0	0
Burglary	0	0	0	0	0	0	0	0	0	0	0
Fire[1]	0	NA	NA	NA	NA	NA	NA	NA	NA	0	0
Medical emergency[1]	0	NA	NA	NA	NA	NA	NA	NA	NA	0	0
Robbery	0	0	0	0	0	0	0	0	0	0	0
Serving/attempting to serve court order (eviction notice, subpoena, etc.)[2]	2	NA	NA	NA	NA	NA	NA	NA	NA	1	1
Tactical situation[3]	10	NA	NA	NA	NA	NA	NA	NA	NA	8	2
Active shooter[1]	0	NA	NA	NA	NA	NA	NA	NA	NA	0	0
Barricaded/hostage situation[1]	2	NA	NA	NA	NA	NA	NA	NA	NA	2	0
Mass casualty[1]	0	NA	NA	NA	NA	NA	NA	NA	NA	0	0
Serving/attempting to serve arrest warrant[1]	4	NA	NA	NA	NA	NA	NA	NA	NA	2	2
Serving/attempting to serve search warrant[1]	3	NA	NA	NA	NA	NA	NA	NA	NA	3	0
Other tactical situation[1]	1	NA	NA	NA	NA	NA	NA	NA	NA	1	0
Traffic control (crash scene, directing traffic, etc.)	2	0	0	0	0	1	0	0	1	0	0
Unprovoked attack	31	6	1	6	1	3	3	3	1	5	2
Other	3	0	1	0	0	1	0	0	0	0	1
Not applicable[2]	0	NA	NA	NA	NA	NA	NA	NA	NA	0	0

NA = Not available.

[1] Beginning in 2019, this category/subcategory was added as an option to the list of circumstances.
[2] Prior to 2019, the circumstance "High-risk traffic stop" was collected as "Traffic stop (felony traffic stop)."
[3] Prior to 2019, the circumstance "Tactical situation" was collected under the category of "Investigative/enforcement" and did not include subcategories.

Table 15. Law Enforcement Officers Feloniously Killed, by Specific Activity Being Performed by Victim Officer at Time of Attack, 2011–2020

(Number.)

Circumstance	Total	2011	2012	2013	2014	2015	2016	2017	2018	2019	2020
Total	503	72	49	27	51	41	66	46	57	48	46
Administrative assignment	14	1	5	0	0	4	0	1	2	0	1
Prisoner transport	8	1	3	0	0	1	0	1	2	0	0
Other administrative assignment	6	0	2	0	0	3	0	0	0	0	1
Arrest situation	74	12	5	8	4	5	7	9	12	7	5
Attempting to restrain/control/handcuff offender(s)	43	10	4	4	2	5	4	5	9	0	0
Attempting to restrain/control/handcuff other individual[1]	9	NA	NA	NA	NA	NA	NA	NA	NA	6	3
Maintaining custody of prisoner (in vehicle, precinct, etc.)[1]	0	NA	NA	NA	NA	NA	NA	NA	NA	0	0
Verbal advisement only	22	2	1	4	2	0	3	4	3	1	2
Assisting another law enforcement officer	33	10	4	1	3	1	2	2	1	3	6
Foot pursuit	3	1	0	0	0	0	0	0	1	1	0
High-risk traffic stop[1]	1	NA	NA	NA	NA	NA	NA	NA	NA	0	1
Officer down (requiring emergency assistance)	5	2	2	0	0	0	0	0	0	0	1
Officer requiring emergency assistance (not pursuit)	2	1	0	1	0	0	0	0	0	0	0
Providing/deploying flares, traffic cones, etc.	10	5	1	0	1	1	1	1	0	0	0
Providing/deploying spike strips/stop sticks[1]	2	NA	NA	NA	NA	NA	NA	NA	NA	0	2
Traffic control (crash scene, directing traffic, etc.)[1]	0	NA	NA	NA	NA	NA	NA	NA	NA	0	0
Vehicular pursuit	4	0	1	0	0	0	0	0	0	2	1
Other emergency circumstance	4	1	0	0	2	0	1	0	0	0	0
Other nonemergency circumstance	2	0	0	0	0	0	0	1	0	0	1
Assisting motorist	5	0	0	1	0	1	0	1	0	0	2
Citizen complaint	4	0	0	0	0	1	0	0	2	1	0
Animal bite	0	0	0	0	0	0	0	0	0	0	0
Animal disturbance (barking dog, unleashed dog, etc.)	0	0	0	0	0	0	0	0	0	0	0
Business check	0	0	0	0	0	0	0	0	0	0	0
Check on welfare of citizen	3	0	0	0	0	1	0	0	2	0	0
Drug complaint	0	0	0	0	0	0	0	0	0	0	0
Traffic complaint	1	0	0	0	0	0	0	0	0	1	0
Trespassing[1]	0	NA	NA	NA	NA	NA	NA	NA	NA	0	0
Verbal complaint of noncriminal violation	0	0	0	0	0	0	0	0	0	0	0
Other citizen complaint[1]	0	NA	NA	NA	NA	NA	NA	NA	NA	0	0
Crime in progress	26	4	0	1	2	2	3	3	4	2	5
Active shooter[1]	0	NA	NA	NA	NA	NA	NA	NA	NA	0	0
Assault	2	0	0	0	0	0	0	0	0	0	2
Burglary	4	0	0	0	0	0	1	0	2	0	1
Larceny-theft	1	0	0	0	0	0	0	0	0	1	0
Mass casualty[1]	0	NA	NA	NA	NA	NA	NA	NA	NA	0	0
Motor vehicle theft	0	0	0	0	0	0	0	0	0	0	0
Person with firearm (no shots fired)	4	0	0	0	2	1	0	0	1	0	0
Robbery	7	3	0	1	0	1	1	1	0	0	0
Shooting/shots being fired (not "active shooter" situation)	6	1	0	0	0	0	1	2	1	0	1
Tampering with vehicle	0	0	0	0	0	0	0	0	0	0	0
Other crime against person	0	0	0	0	0	0	0	0	0	0	0
Other crime against property	2	0	0	0	0	0	0	0	0	1	1
Disorder/disturbance	31	3	2	0	4	1	4	0	3	5	9
Civil disorder (mass disobedience, riot, etc.)	0	0	0	0	0	0	0	0	0	0	0
Disturbance (disorderly subject, fight, etc.)	13	2	1	0	3	0	1	0	2	2	2
Domestic disturbance (family quarrel, no assault)	7	0	0	0	1	0	1	0	0	2	3
Domestic violence	11	1	1	0	0	1	2	0	1	1	4
Encounter/assist an emotionally disturbed person	4	2	0	0	1	0	0	0	0	0	1
Investigative/enforcement	213	31	28	10	22	18	33	22	25	14	10
Active shooter[1]	0	NA	NA	NA	NA	NA	NA	NA	NA	0	0
Animal cruelty[1]	0	NA	NA	NA	NA	NA	NA	NA	NA	0	0
Drug-related matter (drug bust, buy, etc.)	5	0	2	0	0	0	1	0	0	0	2
Handling person with mental illness	5	0	2	0	1	1	0	0	1	0	0
High-risk traffic stop[2]	7	1	2	0	1	0	1	0	1	0	1
Investigative activity	24	1	3	0	2	1	6	5	6	0	0
Mass casualty[1]	0	NA	NA	NA	NA	NA	NA	NA	NA	0	0
Motor vehicle crash	5	1	1	0	0	0	0	1	0	1	1
Official contact (not an arrest situation)[1]	2	NA	NA	NA	NA	NA	NA	NA	NA	2	0
Possible DUI/DWI suspect (operating a vehicle)	1	0	0	0	0	0	1	0	0	0	0
Serving/attempting to serve search warrant (non-tactical)[1]	0	NA	NA	NA	NA	NA	NA	NA	NA	0	0

Table 15. Law Enforcement Officers Feloniously Killed, by Specific Activity Being Performed by Victim Officer at Time of Attack, 2011–2020—*Continued*

(Number.)

Circumstance	Total	2011	2012	2013	2014	2015	2016	2017	2018	2019	2020
Surveillance activity[1]	5	NA	NA	NA	NA	NA	NA	NA	NA	3	2
Suspicious package[1]	0	NA	NA	NA	NA	NA	NA	NA	NA	0	0
Suspicious person/circumstance	57	8	8	6	6	6	12	5	4	1	1
Tactical situation[3]	57	11	6	3	4	6	9	7	11	NA	NA
Traffic violation stop	33	5	4	1	4	3	3	4	2	5	2
Undercover situation	3	0	0	0	2	0	0	0	0	0	1
Wanted person	9	4	0	0	2	1	0	0	0	2	0
Out of service (court, dining, etc.)[3]	0	NA	NA	NA	NA	NA	NA	NA	NA	0	0
Providing/deploying equipment (flares, traffic cones, etc.)[3]	0	NA	NA	NA	NA	NA	NA	NA	NA	0	0
Pursuit	40	6	2	2	7	2	8	5	5	2	1
Foot	29	5	2	0	5	1	7	4	4	1	0
Vehicular (anything other than foot)	11	1	0	2	2	1	1	1	1	1	1
Report of crime	3	0	0	0	1	0	0	0	0	1	1
Active shooter[1]	0	NA	NA	NA	NA	NA	NA	NA	NA	0	0
Assault	0	0	0	0	0	0	0	0	0	0	0
Burglary	0	0	0	0	0	0	0	0	0	0	0
Homicide	0	0	0	0	0	0	0	0	0	0	0
Larceny-theft	1	0	0	0	0	0	0	0	0	1	0
Mass casualty[1]	0	NA	NA	NA	NA	NA	NA	NA	NA	0	0
Motor vehicle theft	0	0	0	0	0	0	0	0	0	0	0
Person with firearm (no shots fired)	1	0	0	0	1	0	0	0	0	0	0
Robbery	0	0	0	0	0	0	0	0	0	0	0
Shooting/shots fired (not "active shooter" situation)	0	0	0	0	0	0	0	0	0	0	0
Tampering with vehicle	0	0	0	0	0	0	0	0	0	0	0
Other crime against person	1	0	0	0	0	0	0	0	0	0	1
Other crime against property	0	0	0	0	0	0	0	0	0	0	0
Respond to alarm (audible/silent)	0	0	0	0	0	0	0	0	0	0	0
Burglary	0	0	0	0	0	0	0	0	0	0	0
Fire[1]	0	NA	NA	NA	NA	NA	NA	NA	NA	0	0
Medical emergency[1]	0	NA	NA	NA	NA	NA	NA	NA	NA	0	0
Robbery	0	0	0	0	0	0	0	0	0	0	0
Serving/attempting to serve court order (eviction notice, subpoena, etc.)[2]	2	NA	NA	NA	NA	NA	NA	NA	NA	1	1
Tactical situation[3]	11	NA	NA	NA	NA	NA	NA	NA	NA	9	2
Active shooter[1]	0	NA	NA	NA	NA	NA	NA	NA	NA	0	0
Barricaded/hostage situation[1]	2	NA	NA	NA	NA	NA	NA	NA	NA	2	0
Mass casualty[1]	0	NA	NA	NA	NA	NA	NA	NA	NA	0	0
Serving/attempting to serve arrest warrant[1]	4	NA	NA	NA	NA	NA	NA	NA	NA	2	2
Serving/attempting to serve search warrant[1]	4	NA	NA	NA	NA	NA	NA	NA	NA	4	0
Other tactical situation[1]	1	NA	NA	NA	NA	NA	NA	NA	NA	1	0
Traffic control (crash scene, directing traffic, etc.)	6	0	0	0	0	1	4	0	1	0	0
Other	37	3	3	4	7	5	5	3	2	3	2

[1]Beginning in 2019, this category/subcategory was added as an option to the list of circumstances.
[2]Prior to 2019, the circumstance "High-risk traffic stop" was collected as "Traffic stop (felony traffic stop)."
[3]Prior to 2019, the circumstance "Tactical situation" was collected under the category of "Investigative/enforcement" and did not include subcategories.

Table 16. Law Enforcement Officers Feloniously Killed During Traffic-Related Incidents,[1] Location of Offender by Location of Victim Officer, 2020

(Number.)

Location of offender	Total	Approaching offender(s)	Approaching suspect vehicle		Returning to victim officer's vehicle	Seated in victim officer's vehicle	
			On driver's side	On passenger's side		Prior to approaching suspect vehicle	After obtaining contact with offenders
Number of Victim Officers Killed During Traffic-Related Incidents	4	1	1	0	0	0	0
Prone	0	0	0	0	0	0	0
On ground	0	0	0	0	0	0	0
On vehicle/object	0	0	0	0	0	0	0
Seated	1	1	0	0	0	0	0
In suspect's vehicle	1	1	0	0	0	0	0
In victim officer's vehicle	0	0	0	0	0	0	0
Outside in vicinity of suspect's vehicle	0	0	0	0	0	0	0
Outside in vicinity of victim officer's vehicle	0	0	0	0	0	0	0
Standing	2	0	1	0	0	0	0
In vicinity of suspect's vehicle	1	0	0	0	0	0	0
In vicinity of victim officer's vehicle	1	0	1	0	0	0	0
Unrestricted Movement	0	0	0	0	0	0	0
Outside of suspect's vehicle	0	0	0	0	0	0	0
Outside of victim officer's vehicle	0	0	0	0	0	0	0
Other	0	0	0	0	0	0	0
Multiple locations due to multiple offenders	0	0	0	0	0	0	0
Unknown	0	0	0	0	0	0	0
Not reported	1	0	0	0	0	0	0

NOTE: For 2020, 2 of the 4 victim officers who were feloniously killed during traffic-related incidents contacted radio dispatchers prior to or during the attack.
[1] Traffic-related incidents include traffic stops (high-risk traffic stops and traffic violation stops), investigating possible DUI/DWI suspects, and assisting motorists.

Table 16. Law Enforcement Officers Feloniously Killed During Traffic-Related Incidents,[1] Location of Offender by Location of Victim Officer, 2020—*Continued*

(Number.)

Location of offender	Standing in vicinity of suspect's vehicle		Standing in vicinity of victim officer's vehicle		Other	Unknown	Not reported
	On driver's side	On passenger's side	On driver's side	On passenger's side			
Number of Victim Officers Killed During Traffic-Related Incidents	1	0	0	0	0	0	1
Prone................................	0	0	0	0	0	0	0
On ground		0	0	0	0	0	0
On vehicle/object.................		0	0	0	0	0	0
Seated...............................	0	0	0	0	0	0	0
In suspect's vehicle..............	0	0	0	0	0	0	0
In victim officer's vehicle.........	0	0	0	0	0	0	0
Outside in vicinity of suspect's vehicle	0	0	0	0	0	0	0
Outside in vicinity of victim officer's vehicle..........	0	0	0	0	0	0	0
Standing	1	0	0	0	0	0	0
In vicinity of suspect's vehicle...........	1	0	0	0	0	0	
In vicinity of victim officer's vehicle	0	0	0	0	0		0
Unrestricted Movement	0	0	0	0	0	0	0
Outside of suspect's vehicle................	0	0	0	0	0	0	0
Outside of victim officer's vehicle...........	0	0	0	0	0	0	0
Other.................................	0	0	0	0	0	0	0
Multiple locations due to multiple offenders............	0	0	0	0	0	0	0
Unknown..............................	0	0	0	0	0	0	0
Not reported...........................	0	0	0	0	0	0	1

NOTE: For 2020, 2 of the 4 victim officers who were feloniously killed during traffic-related incidents contacted radio dispatchers prior to or during the attack.
[1] Traffic-related incidents include traffic stops (high-risk traffic stops and traffic violation stops), investigating possible DUI/DWI suspects, and assisting motorists.

Table 17. Law Enforcement Officers Feloniously Killed, by Type of Weapon, 2011–2020

(Number.)

Type of weapon	Total	2011	2012	2013	2014	2015	2016	2017	2018	2019	2020
Number of victim officers...........................	503	72	49	27	51	41	66	46	57	48	46
Total firearms	458	63	44	26	46	38	62	42	52	44	41
Handgun.................................	326	49	34	18	33	29	37	32	39	34	21
Rifle......................................	95	7	7	5	10	7	23	9	10	7	10
Shotgun.................................	21	6	3	3	3	1	1	1	2	1	0
Multiple firearms used by offender(s), unable to determine which caused fatal injury..................................	2	1	0	0	0	0	1	0	0	0	0
Type of firearm unknown	3	0	0	0	0	1	0	0	0	1	1
Type of firearm not reported......................	11	0	0	0	0	0	0	0	1	1	9
Knife...	3	1	1	0	0	0	0	1	0	0	0
Other cutting instrument	0	0	0	0	0	0	0	0	0	0	0
Blunt instrument....................................	0	0	0	0	0	0	0	0	0	0	0
Bomb...	0	0	0	0	0	0	0	0	0	0	0
Personal weapons (hands, feet, fists, etc.)......	7	2	2	0	1	0	0	0	1	0	1
Vehicle..	35	6	2	1	4	3	4	3	4	4	4
Other...	0	0	0	0	0	0	0	0	0	0	0
Number of victim officers who had prior knowledge that a weapon might be involved in the incident...........................	160	25	6	8	15	17	26	11	24	15	13

Table 18. Law Enforcement Officers Feloniously Killed, by Number of Victim Officers Wearing Uniform, Body Armor, or Holster, 2011–2020

(Number.)

Characteristic	Total	2011	2012	2013	2014	2015	2016	2017	2018	2019	2020
Number of Victim Officers......................	503	72	49	27	51	41	66	46	57	48	46
Wearing body armor.................................	355	52	25	19	40	30	51	35	46	31	26
In uniform.............................	337	47	25	18	40	28	50	33	40	30	26
Not in uniform	18	5	0	1	0	2	1	2	6	1	0
Wearing holster	461	69	43	27	48	37	65	44	52	43	33
In uniform.............................	409	61	38	20	43	35	59	39	45	38	31
Not in uniform	44	8	2	7	5	2	4	5	6	4	1
Wearing uniform not reported................	8	0	3	0	0	0	2	0	1	1	1

Table 19. Law Enforcement Officers Feloniously Killed, Age Group of Known Offender, 2011–2020

(Number.)

Age group	Total	2011	2012	2013	2014	2015	2016	2017	2018	2019	2020
Number of Known Offenders	502	76	51	28	60	37	56	44	57	49	44
Under 18	16	5	1	0	3	0	3	1	1	2	0
18–24	111	20	14	9	13	4	12	3	15	12	9
25–30	122	19	15	7	18	14	6	10	14	11	8
31–35	79	9	6	6	10	10	10	12	10	5	1
36–40	50	7	4	2	9	1	6	5	5	4	7
41–45	34	3	5	0	1	1	5	6	4	6	3
46–50	33	5	2	3	3	2	6	3	1	5	3
51–55	18	4	1	1	1	3	2	1	3	0	2
56–60	14	4	0	0	2	2	3	0	1	0	2
Over 60	10	0	1	0	0	0	1	3	3	0	2
Not reported	15	0	2	0	0	0	2	0	0	4	7
Average age	33	32	31	31	31	34	35	36	33	31	37

Table 20. Law Enforcement Officers Feloniously Killed, by Profile of Known Offender, Average Demographics, 2001–2020

(Number.)

Characteristic	2020	5-year averages		10-year averages	
		2011–2015	2016–2020	2001–2010	2011–2020
Age	36	32	34	30	33
Height	5'10"	5'10"	5'10"	5'10"	5'10"
Weight	183	182	184	178	183

NOTE: The 14 known offenders involved in the events of September 11, 2001, are not included in this table.

Table 21. Law Enforcement Officers Feloniously Killed, by Race, Ethnicity, and Sex of Known Offender, 2011–2020

(Number.)

Characteristic	Total	2011	2012	2013	2014	2015	2016	2017	2018	2019	2020
Number of known offenders	502	76	51	28	60	37	56	44	57	49	44
Race											
White	289	44	32	15	43	18	33	26	33	28	17
Black/African American	173	28	17	12	14	18	17	16	23	15	13
American Indian/Alaska Native	9	2	1	0	2	1	1	1	0	0	1
Asian	3	1	0	0	1	0	0	1	0	0	0
Native Hawaiian/Other Pacific Islander .	3	0	1	0	0	0	0	0	1	1	0
Not reported	25	1	0	1	0	0	5	0	0	5	13
Ethnicity											
Hispanic or Latino	84	7	7	3	19	3	9	5	10	14	7
Not Hispanic or Latino	374	68	41	23	39	33	41	38	46	25	20
Not reported	44	1	3	2	2	1	6	1	1	10	17
Sex											
Male	487	74	50	27	55	37	56	44	55	48	41
Female	12	2	1	1	5	0	0	0	2	1	0
Not reported	3	0	0	0	0	0	0	0	0	0	3

Table 22. Law Enforcement Officers Feloniously Killed, by Status of Known Offender at Time of Incident, 2011–2020

(Number.)

Characteristic	Total	2011	2012	2013	2014	2015	2016	2017	2018	2019	2020
Number of known offenders	502	76	51	28	60	37	56	44	57	49	44
Under judicial supervision	130	19	12	6	12	11	15	18	20	12	5
Conditional release, pending criminal prosecution	28	5	2	2	1	3	1	3	6	3	2
Escapee from mental institution[1]	0	NA	NA	NA	NA	NA	NA	NA	NA	0	0
Escapee from penal institution	1	0	0	0	0	0	0	0	1	0	0
Halfway house	2	1	0	0	0	0	0	1	0	0	0
Home confinement/house arrest[1]	0	NA	NA	NA	NA	NA	NA	NA	NA	0	0
Parole	35	4	4	2	5	3	3	5	3	6	0
Patient in mental institution[1]	0	NA	NA	NA	NA	NA	NA	NA	NA	0	0
Probation	51	7	5	2	5	4	10	5	8	3	2
Serving time in penal institution	1	0	0	0	0	0	0	1	0	0	0
Other judicial supervision	11	2	1	0	1	1	1	3	1	0	1
Multiple forms of judicial supervision	1	0	0	0	0	0	0	0	1	0	0
Known to agency as:											
Anti-government/political[2]	0	NA	NA	NA	NA	NA	NA	NA	NA	0	0
Anti-law enforcement[2]	1	NA	NA	NA	NA	NA	NA	NA	NA	1	0
Controlled substance dealer	59	9	6	4	12	2	4	2	10	8	2
Controlled substance possessor	57	9	5	2	10	2	9	1	10	4	5
Controlled substance user	69	13	6	3	8	2	12	4	10	4	7
Domestic terrorist[3]	0	NA	NA	NA	NA	NA	NA	NA	NA	0	0
Gang member/affiliated with gang member(s)	37	8	4	2	7	4	7	0	2	2	1
Having history of assaulting/threatening law enforcement officer(s)[2]	3	NA	NA	NA	NA	NA	NA	NA	NA	2	1
International terrorist[4]	0	NA	NA	NA	NA	NA	NA	NA	NA	0	0
Known or suspected terrorist (domestic or international)[3]	2	1	0	0	0	0	0	1	0	NA	0
Militia member[2]	0	NA	NA	NA	NA	NA	NA	NA	NA	0	0
Sovereign citizen[2]	0	NA	NA	NA	NA	NA	NA	NA	NA	0	0
Survivalist[2]	0	NA	NA	NA	NA	NA	NA	NA	NA	0	0
Violent offender[2]	10	NA	NA	NA	NA	NA	NA	NA	NA	4	6
Other	84	11	2	7	6	7	12	15	24	0	0
Use of alcohol and/or controlled substance											
Under influence	110	12	13	4	13	13	16	6	16	9	8
Alcohol	26	4	3	3	2	3	1	1	2	3	4
Controlled substance	0	NA	NA	NA	NA	NA	NA	NA	NA	NA	0
Amphetamines/methamphetamines	15	0	0	1	3	0	4	1	2	3	1
Barbiturates	1	0	0	0	1	0	0	0	0	0	0
Cocaine (all forms except Crack)	1	0	1	0	0	0	0	0	0	0	0
Crack/cocaine	1	0	0	0	1	0	0	0	0	0	0
Hashish/hash oil	0	0	0	0	0	0	0	0	0	0	0
Heroin	2	0	0	0	0	2	0	0	0	0	0
Lysergic Acid Diethylamide (a.k.a. LSD)	0	0	0	0	0	0	0	0	0	0	0
Marijuana	22	2	2	0	3	2	4	2	7	0	0
Morphine	0	0	0	0	0	0	0	0	0	0	0
Opium/opiate	0	0	0	0	0	0	0	0	0	0	0
Phencyclidine (a.k.a. PCP)	1	0	0	0	1	0	0	0	0	0	0
Synthetic cathinones (a.k.a. Bath salts)[4]	0	NA	NA	NA	NA	NA	NA	NA	NA	0	0
Other drug/substance	3	1	0	0	0	0	1	0	1	0	0
Multiple forms of substances	37	5	7	0	2	6	6	2	4	2	3
Type of drug/substance not reported	1	0	0	0	0	0	0	0	0	1	0
Not under influence	42	11	3	3	4	2	3	3	4	4	5
Use of alcohol/controlled substance unknown	303	48	28	20	42	19	31	35	33	27	20
Use of alcohol/controlled substance not reported	47	5	7	1	1	3	6	0	3	10	11
Known to agency as having prior mental disorders	28	7	2	2	1	3	2	2	5	1	3
Relationship between victim officer and offender											
Prior relationship through law enforcement (arrest, investigation, etc.)	49	11	4	3	3	4	10	3	5	0	6
Prior relationship through non-law enforcement (acquaintance, neighbor, relative, etc.)	5	0	0	2	0	0	0	0	1	1	1
No known relationship	435	65	47	23	57	33	45	40	51	47	27
Not reported	13	0	0	0	0	0	1	1	0	1	10

[1] Beginning in 2019, new options were added, including: "Escapee from mental institution," "Home confinement/house arrest," and "Patient in mental institution."
[2] Beginning in 2019, new options were added, including: "Anti-government/political," "Anti-law enforcement," "Having history of assaulting/threatening law enforcement officer(s)," "Militia member," "Sovereign citizen," "Survivalist," and "Violent offender."
[3] From 2011 through 2018, "Domestic terrorist" and "International terrorist" were combined.
[4] Beginning in 2019, a new option was added to the list of controlled substances: "Synthetic cathinones (a.k.a. Bath salts)."

Table 23. Law Enforcement Officers Feloniously Killed, by Judicial History of Known Offender Prior to Incident, 2011–2020

(Number.)

Judicial history prior to incident	Total	2011	2012	2013	2014	2015	2016	2017	2018	2019	2020
Number of known offenders	502	76	51	28	60	37	56	44	57	49	44
Previously arrested	404	64	42	20	51	32	47	40	51	37	20
Conviction as adult	311	48	29	13	35	29	39	34	39	31	14
Conviction as juvenile	100	18	6	2	10	9	14	12	15	12	2
Halfway house	9	1	1	0	2	0	1	2	2	0	0
House arrest	0	0	0	0	0	0	0	0	0	0	0
Incarceration in penal institution[1]	92	19	4	4	9	10	11	13	22	NA	NA
House arrest	0	NA	0	0	0	0	0	0	0	0	0
Incarceration in penal institution	92	NA	19	4	4	9	10	11	13	22	NA
Parole	95	14	7	3	12	12	13	11	9	11	3
Probation	217	37	17	8	26	18	31	22	32	21	5
Prior arrest for:											
Aggravated assault (excluding officers)[2]	17	NA	NA	NA	NA	NA	NA	NA	NA	12	5
Assault on law enforcement officer (aggravated or simple)	59	10	1	1	7	5	7	7	5	10	6
Crime of violence (includes arrests for aggravated assault, murder, rape, and robbery)[3]	0	NA	NA	NA	NA	NA	NA	NA	NA	NA	NA
Domestic violence[2]	13	NA	NA	NA	NA	NA	NA	NA	NA	8	5
Drug law violation	221	27	20	8	34	15	27	22	33	23	12
Murder	17	1	2	0	1	3	4	2	2	2	0
Other crime of violence (includes arrests for aggravated assault, rape, and robbery)[3]	210	38	19	12	22	24	35	30	30	NA	NA
Resisting arrest	109	19	9	3	15	11	14	13	13	10	2
Robbery[2]	14	NA	NA	NA	NA	NA	NA	NA	NA	9	5
Sex offense[2]	1	NA	NA	NA	NA	NA	NA	NA	NA	0	1
Threats against law enforcement[2]	1	NA	NA	NA	NA	NA	NA	NA	NA	1	0
Weapons violation	178	32	15	7	26	19	21	16	20	18	4
None of the above[2]	7	NA	NA	NA	NA	NA	NA	NA	NA	5	2

NA = Not available.

[1] In 2019, counts for "Incarceration in penal institution" stopped being collected.

[2] In 2019, "Aggravated assault (excluding officers)," "Domestic violence," "Robbery," "Sex offense," "Threats against law enforcement," and "None of the above" were added as options for prior arrests.

[3] In 2019, "Other crime of violence" was eliminated from the list of options for prior arrests because the specific violent crimes were added as options.

Table 24. Law Enforcement Officers Feloniously Killed, by Disposition of Known Offender, 2009–2018

(Number.)

Disposition	2009–2013	2014–2018	2009–2018
Number of known offenders	280	254	534
Fugitive	1	0	1
Arrested and charged	175	122	297
Guilty of murder	117	76	193
Received death sentence	16	9	25
Received life imprisonment	68	47	115
Received prison term (ranging from 8.75 years to 205 years)	32	19	51
Sentence unknown	1	1	2
Guilty of lesser offense related to murder	18	2	20
Guilty of crime other than murder	9	6	15
Acquitted/dismissed/nolle prosequi	16	5	21
Indeterminate charge and sentence	0	0	0
Committed to psychiatric institution	7	6	13
Case pending/disposition unknown	7	26	33
Died in custody prior to sentencing	1	1	2
Not arrested	166	162	328
Justifiably killed	62	65	127
by victim officer	18	13	31
by person(s) other than victim officer[1]	17	0	17
by assisting officer(s)[1]	18	31	49
by officer(s) responding to scene of incident[1]	0	5	5
by officer(s) at other scene of incident[1]	9	16	25
Committed suicide	36	27	63
Killed by civilian(s)	2	0	2
Died under other circumstance	3	3	6
Died by unknown cause	0	1	1
Other	1	1	2
Not reported	0	35	35

NOTE: Due to delays in court proceedings, this table runs two years behind the publication year.
[1] Beginning in 2011, new options were added to identify the other persons who justifiably killed the offender(s).

Table 25. Law Enforcement Officers Accidentally Killed, by Region, Geographic Division, and State/Territory, 2011–2020

(Number.)

Area	Total	2011	2012	2013	2014	2015	2016	2017	2018	2019	2020
Number of victim officers..................	477	53	48	49	45	45	52	48	50	41	46
Northeast..	56	8	9	5	8	5	5	6	5	3	2
New England..............................	12	2	4	0	1	0	1	1	1	1	1
Connecticut............................	1	0	0	0	0	0	0	0	1	0	0
Maine....................................	3	1	0	0	0	0	0	1	0	1	0
Massachusetts........................	7	1	3	0	1	0	1	0	0	0	1
New Hampshire......................	0	0	0	0	0	0	0	0	0	0	0
Rhode Island..........................	1	0	1	0	0	0	0	0	0	0	0
Vermont................................	0	0	0	0	0	0	0	0	0	0	0
Middle Atlantic...........................	44	6	5	5	7	5	4	5	4	2	1
New Jersey.............................	12	1	1	0	2	3	2	1	2	0	0
New York...............................	21	5	2	3	3	0	2	3	1	2	0
Pennsylvania..........................	11	0	2	2	2	2	0	1	1	0	1
Midwest..	71	7	3	4	4	6	12	9	11	8	7
East North Central......................	48	3	3	4	3	4	8	6	8	5	4
Illinois..................................	16	0	1	2	1	1	2	2	3	3	1
Indiana..................................	4	0	0	0	1	0	0	0	1	1	1
Michigan................................	12	1	0	1	1	2	2	2	2	0	1
Ohio......................................	11	2	1	1	0	0	3	1	1	1	1
Wisconsin..............................	5	0	1	0	0	1	1	1	1	0	0
West North Central	23	4	0	0	1	2	4	3	3	3	3
Iowa......................................	5	1	0	0	0	0	3	0	0	1	0
Kansas...................................	2	0	0	0	0	0	1	0	0	0	1
Minnesota..............................	2	0	0	0	0	0	0	1	0	1	0
Missouri.................................	11	3	0	0	1	2	0	1	2	0	2
Nebraska................................	2	0	0	0	0	0	0	1	0	1	0
North Dakota..........................	1	0	0	0	0	0	0	0	1	0	0
South Dakota	0	0	0	0	0	0	0	0	0	0	0
South..	262	27	28	31	19	29	24	27	27	22	28
South Atlantic............................	109	16	14	9	4	12	8	14	13	6	13
Delaware................................	0	0	0	0	0	0	0	0	0	0	0
District of Columbia.................	0	0	0	0	0	0	0	0	0	0	0
Florida...................................	22	1	2	1	1	1	4	4	4	3	1
Georgia..................................	31	6	4	2	1	5	2	2	1	1	7
Maryland................................	9	2	3	0	0	3	1	0	0	0	0
North Carolina........................	18	4	2	1	1	0	1	0	6	1	2
South Carolina........................	14	1	0	2	0	2	0	4	1	1	3
Virginia..................................	14	2	3	3	1	1	0	3	1	0	0
West Virginia..........................	1	0	0	0	0	0	0	1	0	0	0
East South Central.....................	51	3	3	7	7	9	1	5	5	8	3
Alabama.................................	14	2	1	3	2	2	0	1	1	1	1
Kentucky................................	6	0	1	0	0	2	0	1	2	0	0
Mississippi.............................	14	0	0	4	2	2	0	1	2	2	1
Tennessee...............................	17	1	1	0	3	3	1	2	0	5	1
West South Central	102	8	11	15	8	8	15	8	9	8	12
Arkansas................................	7	0	0	4	0	0	1	1	0	0	1
Louisiana...............................	23	3	2	3	1	2	5	1	3	1	2
Oklahoma..............................	13	0	2	2	2	1	0	2	1	1	2
Texas	59	5	7	6	5	5	9	4	5	6	7
West...	83	10	8	9	13	5	9	6	6	8	9
Mountain....................................	37	4	6	4	4	2	5	2	1	5	4
Arizona..................................	12	2	1	2	2	0	2	0	0	2	1
Colorado................................	13	0	4	0	1	2	1	0	1	2	2
Idaho.....................................	1	0	0	0	0	0	0	0	0	0	1
Montana................................	2	1	0	0	0	0	0	0	0	1	0
Nevada..................................	2	0	0	1	0	0	0	1	0	0	0
New Mexico	4	0	0	1	1	0	1	1	0	0	0
Utah......................................	2	0	1	0	0	0	1	0	0	0	0
Wyoming................................	1	1	0	0	0	0	0	0	0	0	0
Pacific	46	6	2	5	9	3	4	4	5	3	5
Alaska	1	0	0	1	0	0	0	0	0	0	0
California................................	34	5	0	3	9	2	4	4	4	1	2
Hawaii....................................	4	1	2	0	0	0	0	0	0	0	1
Oregon...................................	1	0	0	0	0	1	0	0	0	0	0
Washington............................	6	0	0	1	0	0	0	0	1	2	2
Puerto Rico and other outlying areas.....	5	1	0	0	1	0	2	0	1	0	0
American Samoa........................	0	0	0	0	0	0	0	0	0	0	0
Guam.......................................	0	0	0	0	0	0	0	0	0	0	0
Mariana Islands	0	0	0	0	0	0	0	0	0	0	0
Puerto Rico................................	5	1	0	0	1	0	2	0	1	0	0
U.S. Virgin Islands......................	0	0	0	0	0	0	0	0	0	0	0

(Number.)

Area	Total	2011	2012	2013	2014	2015	2016	2017	2018	2019	2020
Number of Victim Officers	477	53	48	49	45	45	52	48	50	41	46
Group I (cities 250,000 and over)	55	5	9	5	6	4	4	4	10	4	4
Group II (cities 100,000–249,999)	32	3	3	4	1	3	3	2	5	4	4
Group III (cities 50,000–99,999)	25	5	1	5	2	3	2	0	3	2	2
Group IV (25,000–49,999)	25	3	6	1	2	1	1	1	5	0	5
Group V (cities 10,000–24,999)	16	0	1	3	2	1	1	4	1	2	1
Group VI (cities under 10,000)	60	7	2	6	7	7	10	7	7	2	5
Metropolitan counties	105	11	12	10	10	10	12	9	9	6	16
Nonmetropolitan counties	49	3	4	5	7	4	4	8	3	8	3
State agencies	85	12	6	8	5	12	9	13	3	12	5
Federal agencies	20	3	4	2	2	0	4	0	3	1	1
Puerto Rico and other outlying areas	5	1	0	0	1	0	2	0	1	0	0

Table 27. Law Enforcement Officers Accidentally Killed, by Time of Incident, 2011–2020

(Number.)

Time of day	Total	2011	2012	2013	2014	2015	2016	2017	2018	2019	2020
Number of victim officers	477	53	48	49	45	45	52	48	50	41	46
Total A.M. hours	215	22	25	16	26	17	25	25	22	17	20
12:01 a.m.–2 a.m.	45	5	6	3	6	2	6	4	4	3	6
2:01 a.m.–4 a.m.	44	9	5	5	4	4	5	3	3	4	2
4:01 a.m.–6 a.m.	24	3	4	1	1	2	3	4	3	1	2
6:01 a.m.–8 a.m.	50	3	5	3	7	4	5	7	7	5	4
8:01 a.m.–10 a.m.	24	1	4	2	3	2	1	3	3	2	3
10:01 a.m.–noon	28	1	1	2	5	3	5	4	2	2	3
Total P.M. hours	238	31	23	30	19	27	24	22	25	24	13
12:01 p.m.–2 p.m.	34	6	3	3	4	4	6	2	3	3	0
2:01 p.m.–4 p.m.	34	6	5	4	4	4	3	3	1	3	1
4:01 p.m.–6 p.m.	37	7	2	4	3	5	5	4	4	2	1
6:01 p.m.–8 p.m.	44	4	2	3	2	2	3	5	9	8	6
8:01 p.m.–10 p.m.	45	3	5	10	2	5	4	5	4	2	5
10:01 p.m.–midnight	44	5	6	6	4	7	3	3	4	6	0
Not reported	24	0	0	3	0	1	3	1	3	0	13

Table 28. Law Enforcement Officers Accidentally Killed, by Day and Time of Incident, 2020

(Number.)

Time of day	Total	Sunday	Monday	Tuesday	Wednesday	Thursday	Friday	Saturday
Number of victim officers	46	5	4	7	8	8	9	5
Total A.M. hours	20	3	2	2	5	2	3	3
12:01 a.m.–2 a.m.	6	1	1	0	1	0	1	2
2:01 a.m.–4 a.m.	2	1	0	0	0	1	0	0
4:01 a.m.–6 a.m.	2	0	1	0	0	1	0	0
6:01 a.m.–8 a.m.	4	0	0	2	1	0	1	0
8:01 a.m.–10 a.m.	3	0	0	0	1	0	1	1
10:01 a.m.–noon	3	1	0	0	2	0	0	0
Total P.M. hours	13	2	1	0	1	3	5	1
12:01 p.m.–2 p.m.	0	0	0	0	0	0	0	0
2:01 p.m.–4 p.m.	1	0	0	0	0	0	1	0
4:01 p.m.–6 p.m.	1	0	0	0	0	0	1	0
6:01 p.m.–8 p.m.	6	1	0	0	1	1	2	1
8:01 p.m.–10 p.m.	5	1	1	0	0	2	1	0
10:01 p.m.–midnight	0	0	0	0	0	0	0	0
Not reported	13	0	1	5	2	3	1	1

Table 29. Law Enforcement Officers Accidentally Killed, by Day of Incident, 2011–2020

(Number.)

Day of the week	Total	2011	2012	2013	2014	2015	2016	2017	2018	2019	2020
Number of victim officers	477	53	48	49	45	45	52	48	50	41	46
Sunday	66	7	6	6	9	6	10	7	8	2	5
Monday	61	7	7	6	5	12	7	3	6	4	4
Tuesday	70	10	5	7	9	3	6	11	4	8	7
Wednesday	49	2	2	6	4	5	7	5	6	4	8
Thursday	65	10	8	4	5	6	7	5	7	5	8
Friday	85	7	8	12	8	4	8	9	10	10	9
Saturday	81	10	12	8	5	9	7	8	9	8	5

Table 30. Law Enforcement Officers Accidentally Killed, by Month of Incident, 2011–2020

(Number.)

Month	Total	2011	2012	2013	2014	2015	2016	2017	2018	2019	2020
Number of Victim Officers	477	53	48	49	45	45	52	48	50	41	46
January	40	4	4	1	6	6	2	6	2	4	5
February	27	4	1	0	2	1	1	6	4	5	3
March	50	8	3	5	2	5	9	3	6	5	4
April	36	1	3	5	5	5	1	5	4	3	4
May	51	8	4	9	6	2	3	6	6	3	4
June	38	5	4	2	1	5	5	4	4	4	4
July	42	5	8	6	1	3	4	3	2	3	7
August	32	3	2	3	1	5	5	6	3	2	2
September	44	4	6	3	5	3	9	4	3	2	5
October	39	2	4	5	6	2	7	2	4	3	4
November	34	3	5	3	4	5	4	1	5	3	1
December	44	6	4	7	6	3	2	2	7	4	3

Table 31. Law Enforcement Officers Accidentally Killed, by Age Group of Victim Officer, 2011–2020

(Number.)

Age group	Total	2011	2012	2013	2014	2015	2016	2017	2018	2019	2020
Number of Victim Officers	477	53	48	49	45	45	52	48	50	41	46
Under 25	35	3	2	1	4	7	2	1	11	2	2
25–30	87	9	6	6	7	10	12	11	6	9	11
31–35	81	3	9	5	9	4	12	11	10	10	8
36–40	66	11	6	11	8	7	6	6	4	5	2
41–45	68	8	13	11	5	7	5	5	8	2	4
46–50	51	9	8	5	3	2	7	4	7	3	3
51–55	39	5	3	8	5	3	4	1	2	4	4
56–60	22	2	1	2	2	3	1	5	0	1	5
Over 60	20	3	0	0	2	1	2	4	2	4	2
Unknown	3	0	0	0	0	0	0	0	0	0	3
Not reported	5	0	0	0	0	1	1	0	0	1	2
Average age (years)	39	41	40	41	39	37	38	40	36	40	40

Table 32. Law Enforcement Officers Accidentally Killed, by Years of Service of Victim Officer, 2011–2020

(Number; years.)

Years of service	Total	2011	2012	2013	2014	2015	2016	2017	2018	2019	2020
Number of Victim Officers	477	53	48	49	45	45	52	48	50	41	46
Less than 1	34	2	2	2	5	4	6	3	5	3	2
1–5	145	13	9	9	14	18	14	16	17	17	18
6–10	92	13	14	12	13	3	9	10	8	4	6
11–15	67	7	9	8	3	7	8	7	7	6	5
16–20	52	6	8	7	3	9	5	3	6	2	3
21–25	28	5	3	5	0	2	2	3	3	3	2
26–30	28	3	3	3	5	2	5	1	0	3	3
More than 30	20	4	0	2	2	0	2	5	1	2	2
Not reported	11	0	0	1	0	0	1	0	3	1	5
Average years of service	11	13	12	13	10	9	11	12	9	11	10

Table 33. Law Enforcement Officers Accidentally Killed, by Profile of Victim Officer, Average Demographics, 2001–2020

(Number.)

Characteristic	2020	5-year averages		10-year averages	
		2011–2015	2016–2020	2001–2010	2011–2020
Age	40	40	39	38	39
Years of service	10	12	11	10	11
Height	5'11"	5'11"	5'11"	5'11"	5'11"
Weight	208	2,011	209	199	210

Table 34. Law Enforcement Officers Accidentally Killed, by Race, Ethnicity, and Sex of Victim Officer, 2011–2020

(Number.)

Characteristic	Total	2011	2012	2013	2014	2015	2016	2017	2018	2019	2020
Number of Victim Officers.....................	477	53	48	49	45	45	52	48	50	41	46
Race											
White..	396	45	36	43	43	33	40	42	38	39	37
Black/African American	62	7	10	6	0	9	9	3	7	2	9
American Indian/Alaska Native	8	0	0	0	0	0	2	2	4	0	0
Asian.......................................	6	0	2	0	2	0	0	1	1	0	0
Native Hawaiian/Other Pacific Islander .	2	1	0	0	0	1	0	0	0	0	0
Not reported	3	0	0	0	0	2	1	0	0	0	0
Ethnicity											
Hispanic or Latino............................	41	4	6	2	7	3	7	3	5	2	2
Not Hispanic or Latino........................	411	46	40	47	38	40	43	44	45	38	30
Not reported	25	3	2	0	0	2	2	1	0	1	14
Sex											
Male	450	50	46	49	42	41	50	46	46	38	42
Female......................................	27	3	2	0	3	4	2	2	4	3	4

Table 35. Law Enforcement Officers Accidentally Killed, Time of Incident, by Type of Assignment, 2020

(Number.)

Characteristic and time	Total	2-officer patrol	1-officer patrol Alone	1-officer patrol Assisted	Investigative/detective Alone	Investigative/detective Assisted	Tactical assignment (uniformed) Alone	Tactical assignment (uniformed) Assisted	Plainclothes assignment Alone	Plainclothes assignment Assisted
Number of Victim Officers.....................	46	6	21	4	3	1	0	0	0	0
Total A.M. hours	20	2	10	2	3	0	0	0	0	0
12:01 a.m.–2 a.m.	6	1	3	1	0	0	0	0	0	0
2:01 a.m.–4 a.m.	2	1	1	0	0	0	0	0	0	0
4:01 a.m.–6 a.m.	2	0	1	1	0	0	0	0	0	0
6:01 a.m.–8 a.m.	4	0	2	0	2	0	0	0	0	0
8:01 a.m.–10 a.m.	3	0	2	0	1	0	0	0	0	0
10:01 a.m.–noon	3	0	1	0	0	0	0	0	0	0
Total P.M. hours	13	2	6	2	0	0	0	0	0	0
12:01 p.m.–2 p.m.	0	0	0	0	0	0	0	0	0	0
2:01 p.m.–4 p.m.	1	0	1	0	0	0	0	0	0	0
4:01 p.m.–6 p.m.	1	0	0	0	0	0	0	0	0	0
6:01 p.m.–8 p.m.	6	0	4	1	0	0	0	0	0	0
8:01 p.m.–10 p.m.	5	2	1	1	0	0	0	0	0	0
10:01 p.m.–midnight	0	0	0	0	0	0	0	0	0	0
Not reported..	13	2	5	0	0	1	0	0	0	0

Table 35. Law Enforcement Officers Accidentally Killed, Time of Incident, by Type of Assignment, 2020—Continued

(Number.)

Characteristic and time	Special assignment		Undercover		Court/prisoner security		Overtime/extra duty activity		Other		Unknown
	Alone	Assisted	Alone	Assisted	Alone	Assisted	Alone	Assisted	Alone	Assisted	
Number of Victim Officers	1	2	0	0	0	0	1	0	3	3	1
Total A.M. hours	1	0	0	0	0	0	0	0	2	0	0
12:01 a.m.–2 a.m.	0	0	0	0	0	0	0	0	1	0	0
2:01 a.m.–4 a.m.	0	0	0	0	0	0	0	0	0	0	0
4:01 a.m.–6 a.m.	0	0	0	0	0	0	0	0	0	0	0
6:01 a.m.–8 a.m.	0	0	0	0	0	0	0	0	0	0	0
8:01 a.m.–10 a.m.	0	0	0	0	0	0	0	0	0	0	0
10:01 a.m.–noon	1	0	0	0	0	0	0	0	1	0	0
Total P.M. hours	0	0	0	0	0	0	1	0	1	1	0
12:01 p.m.–2 p.m.	0	0	0	0	0	0	0	0	0	0	0
2:01 p.m.–4 p.m.	0	0	0	0	0	0	0	0	0	0	0
4:01 p.m.–6 p.m.	0	0	0	0	0	0	1	0	0	0	0
6:01 p.m.–8 p.m.	0	0	0	0	0	0	0	0	1	0	0
8:01 p.m.–10 p.m.	0	0	0	0	0	0	0	0	0	1	0
10:01 p.m.–midnight	0	0	0	0	0	0	0	0	0	0	0
Not reported	0	2	0	0	0	0	0	0	0	2	1

Table 36. Law Enforcement Officers Accidentally Killed, by Lighting and Weather/Environmental Conditions by Location of Incident, 2020

(Number.)

Characteristic	Total	Aircraft accident	Drowning	Fall	Firearm-related incident	Motor vehicle crash	Pedestrian officer struck by vehicle
Number of victim officers	46	1	2	1	5	25	12
Lighting							
Artificial	2	0	0	0	0	1	1
Dark	8	0	0	0	0	5	3
Dawn	1	0	0	0	0	1	0
Daylight	11	0	0	0	1	6	4
Dusk	4	0	1	0	0	3	0
Not reported	20	1	1	1	4	9	4
Weather/environmental							
Blizzard	0	0	0	0	0	0	0
Blowing dirt/sand/soil	0	0	0	0	0	0	0
Clear	12	0	0	0	1	6	4
Cloudy/partly cloudy	4	0	0	0	0	3	1
Earthquake	0	0	0	0	0	0	0
Fire/fog/smog/smoke	1	0	0	0	0	1	0
Flooding	0	0	0	0	0	0	0
Freezing rain/hail/sleet	1	0	0	0	0	0	1
Hurricane	0	0	0	0	0	0	0
Indoors (no adverse conditions)	0	0	0	0	0	0	0
Rain	2	0	0	0	0	1	1
Severe crosswinds/high winds	1	0	1	0	0	0	0
Snow	0	0	0	0	0	0	0
Tornado	0	0	0	0	0	0	0
Other	1	0	0	0	0	1	0
Not reported	24	1	1	1	4	12	5

Table 37. Federal Law Enforcement Officers Killed and Assaulted, Department and Agency, by Number of Victim Officers and Known Offenders, 2019–2020

(Number.)

Department and agency	Victim officers		Known offenders	
	2019	2020	2019	2020
Number of victim officers/known offenders	2,136	1,692	1,469	1,181
Amtrak (National Railroad Passenger Corporation)[1,2]	0	0	0	0
Architect of the Capitol[1,2,3]	NA	0	NA	0
Corporation for National and Community Service[1,2]	0	0	0	0
Federal Deposit Insurance Corporation[1,2]	0	0	0	0
Federal Housing Finance Agency[1,2]	0	0	0	0
Library of Congress[1,2]	0	0	0	0
National Aeronautics and Space Administration[1,2]	0	0	0	0
National Science Foundation[1,2,3]	0	NA	0	NA
Pension Benefit Guaranty Corporation[1,2]	0	0	0	0
Smithsonian Institution[1,2]	0	0	0	0
Tennessee Valley Authority[1,2]	0	0	0	0
U.S. Agency for International Development[1,2,3]	NA	0	NA	0
U.S. Department of Agriculture[2,3]	4	NA	4	NA
U.S. Department of Commerce[1,2]	0	0	0	0
U.S. Department of Defense	47	186	37	185
Defense Intelligence Agency Police[1,2]	0	0	0	0
Defense Logistics Agency[1,2,3]	0	NA	0	NA
Office of Inspector General (Defense Criminal Investigation Service)	0	0	0	0
U.S. Department of the Air Force[1,2]	0	0	0	0
U.S. Department of the Army[1,2]	0	158	0	170
U.S. Department of the Navy[1,2]	0	28	0	15
U.S. Marine Corps[2,3]	47	NA	37	NA
U.S. Department of Education[1,2]	0	0	0	0
U.S. Department of Health and Human Services[1,2]	0	0	0	0
U.S. Department of Homeland Security	733	430	420	96
Federal Emergency Management Agency, Mount Weather Police[1,2]	0	0	0	0
Federal Protective Service	3	258	3	20
U.S. Coast Guard[1,2,3]	0	NA	0	NA
U.S. Customs and Border Protection (CBP)	609	29	335	5
CBP, Air and Marine Operations	13	29	2	5
CBP, Office of Field Operations[2,3]	135	NA	88	NA
CBP, U.S. Border Patrol[2,3]	461	NA	245	NA
U.S. Immigration and Customs Enforcement	94	129	54	57
U.S. Secret Service	27	14	28	14
Not reported	0		0	
U.S. Department of the Interior[2]	978	826	777	811
Bureau of Indian Affairs	765	810	764	797
Bureau of Land Management	4	3	4	3
National Park Service (NPS)	206	13	6	11
U.S. Fish and Wildlife Service (FWS)	3	0	3	0
FWS, Division of Refuge Law Enforcement[3]	3	NA	3	NA
FWS, Office of Law Enforcement[1,2,3]	0	NA	0	NA
U.S. Department of Justice[2]	369	243	227	85
Bureau of Alcohol, Tobacco, Firearms and Explosives	16	13	4	4
Federal Bureau of Investigation	17	54	18	19
U.S. Drug Enforcement Administration	8	10	11	10
U.S. Marshals Service	328	166	194	52
Not Reported	0	0	0	0

Table 37. Federal Law Enforcement Officers Killed and Assaulted, Department and Agency, by Number of Victim Officers and Known Offenders, 2019–2020—*Continued*

(Number.)

Department and agency	Victim officers		Known offenders	
	2019	2020	2019	2020
U.S. Department of Labor[1,2,3]	NA	0	NA	0
U.S. Department of State[1,2]	0	0	0	0
U.S. Department of Transportation[1,2]	0	0	0	0
U.S. Department of the Treasury[1,2]	0	1	0	1
Bureau of Engraving and Printing Police	0	0	0	0
Not Reported	0	0	0	0
Treasury Inspector General for Tax Administration	0	1	0	1
U.S. Environmental Protection Agency[1,2]	0	0	0	0
U.S. General Services Administration[1,2]	0	0	0	0
Government Publishing Office[3]	0	NA	0	NA
U.S. National Archives and Records Administration[1,2]	0	0	0	0
U.S. Nuclear Regulatory Commission[1,2]	0	0	0	0
U.S. Office of Personnel Management[1,2]	0	0	0	0
U.S. Peace Corps[1,2,3]	0	NA	0	NA
U.S. Postal Service[2]	5	6	4	3
U.S. Securities and Exchange Commission[1,2]	0	0	0	0

NA = Not available.
[1] This table includes federal agencies that indicated one or more of their law enforcement officers were killed or assaulted.
[2] For 2020, data were not reported by these departments, agencies, or offices.
[3] NA indicates the agency did not submit data.

Table 38. Federal Law Enforcement Officers Killed and Assaulted, Department and Agency, by Number of Victim Officers Killed and Injured, 2020[1]

(Number.)

Department and agency	Killed		Injured	
	Firearms	Other weapons	Firearms	Other weapons
Number of victim officers..	1	0	10	576
U.S Department of Defense	0	0	1	124
U.S Department of the Army	0	0	0	116
U.S Department of the Navy	0	0	1	8
U.S. Department of Homeland Security	NA	0	NA	330
Federal Protective Service	NA	0	NA	258
U.S. Customs and Border Protection (CBP):................................	NA	NA	NA	4
CBP, Air and Marine Operations	NA	NA	NA	4
CBP, Office of Field Operations...	NA	0	NA	0
CBP, U.S. Border Patrol	NA	0	NA	0
U.S. Immigration and Customs Enforcement	NA	0	NA	65
U.S. Coast Guard	NA	0	NA	0
Enforcement and Removal Operations	NA	0	NA	0
Transportation Security Administration	NA	0	NA	0
Homeland Security Investigations	NA	0	NA	0
Federal Emergency Management Agency (Mout Weather Police)........	NA	0	NA	0
U.S. Secret Service..	0	0	NA	3
U.S. Department of Interior	NA	0	NA	74
Bureau of Indian Affairs	NA	0	NA	64
Bureau of Land Management	NA	0	NA	1
National Park Service	NA	0	NA	9
U.S. Department of Justice	1	0	9	47
Bureau of Alcohol, Tobacco, Firearms and Explosives	1	0	1	0
Federal Bureau of Investigations	0	0	4	2
U.S. Drug Enforcement Administration	0	0	0	1
U.S. Marshals Service	0	0	4	44
U.S. Postal Service	0	0	0	1
Not reported	0	0	0	1

[1]This table includes federal agencies that indicated one or more of their law enforcement officers were killed or assaulted.
NA indicates agency did not submit data.

Table 39. Federal Law Enforcement Officers Killed and Assaulted, Department and Agency, by Extent of Injury of Victim Officer, 2016–2020[1]

(Number.)

Department and agency	2016			2017			2018			2019			2020		
	Killed	Injured	Not injured	Killed	Injured	Not injured	Killed	Injured	Not injured	Killed	Injured	Not injured	Killed	Injured	Not injured
Number of victim officers[2]	1	324	1,122	0	426	1,358	2	374	1,392	0	372	1,764	1	586	1,105
U.S. Capitol Police[2]	0	4	21	0	9	7	0	3	15	NA	NA	NA	0	0	0
U.S. Department of Agriculture[2]	NA	NA	NA	NA	NA	NA	0	0	8	0	1	3	0	0	0
U.S. Department of Defense[2,3,4]	NA	NA	NA	0	2	21	0	5	11	0	1	46	0	125	61
Defense Intelligence Agency Police	NA	NA	NA	NA	NA	NA	0	0	0	0	0	0	0	0	0
Defense Logistics Agency	NA	NA	NA	NA	NA	NA	0	0	0	0	0	0	0	0	0
Department of the Air Force	NA	NA	NA	0	0	0	NA	NA	NA	NA	NA	NA	NA	NA	NA
National Security Agency	NA	NA	NA	0	0	0	0	1	0	NA	NA	NA	0	0	0
Pentagon Force Protection Agency	NA	NA	NA	0	0	0	0	0	1	NA	NA	NA	0	0	0
Department of the Army	NA	NA	NA	0	0	0	0	3	9	0	0	0	0	116	42
Department of the Navy[4]	NA	NA	NA	0	2	21	0	1	1	0	0	0	0	9	19
U.S. Marine Corps[5]	NA	NA	NA	NA	NA	NA	NA	NA	NA	0	1	46	0	0	0
U.S. Department of Health and Human Services[2]	NA	NA	NA	NA	NA	NA	0	3	0	0	0	0	0	0	0
U.S. Department of Homeland Security[2]	0	146	357	0	225	462	0	219	532	0	240	493	0	330	100
Federal Protective Service	NA	NA	NA	NA	NA	NA	0	20	2	0	3	0	0	258	0
Homeland Security Investigations	NA	NA	NA	NA	NA	NA	NA	NA	NA	NA	NA	NA	0	0	0
U.S. Customs and Border Protection															
Air and Marine Operations	NA	NA	NA	NA	NA	NA	0	3	27	0	1	12	0	4	25
CBP, Office of Air and Marine	NA	NA	NA	0	5	7	NA	NA	NA	NA	NA	NA	NA	NA	NA
CBP, Office of Border Patrol	0	132	265	0	103	329	NA	NA	NA	NA	NA	NA	NA	NA	NA
CBP, Office of Field Operations	NA	NA	NA	0	29	33	NA	NA	NA	NA	NA	NA	NA	NA	NA
Not reported	0	7	80	NA	NA	NA	NA	NA	NA	NA	NA	NA	NA	NA	NA
Office of Field Operations	NA	NA	NA	NA	NA	NA	0	24	51	0	61	74	0	0	0
U.S. Border Patrol	NA	NA	NA	NA	NA	NA	0	135	394	0	115	346	0	0	0
U.S. Immigration and Customs Enforcement[6]	0	0	0	0	76	83	0	30	45	0	57	37	0	65	64
U.S. Secret Service	0	7	12	0	12	10	0	7	13	0	3	24	0	3	11
U.S. Department of Justice	1	57	240	0	66	267	2	52	217	0	19	350	1	56	186
Bureau of Alcohol, Tobacco, Firearms and Explosives	0	0	11	0	0	18	0	2	11	0	1	15	1	1	11
Federal Bureau of Investigation	0	5	11	0	4	12	0	7	8	0	4	13	0	6	48
U.S. Drug Enforcement Administration	0	2	3	0	1	9	0	4	12	0	1	7	0	1	9
U.S. Marshals Service	1	50	215	0	61	228	2	39	186	0	13	315	0	48	118
U.S. Department of the Interior[2]	0	117	504	0	124	600	0	83	606	0	107	871	0	74	752
Bureau of Indian Affairs	0	86	418	0	105	504	0	72	439	0	75	690	0	64	746
Bureau of Land Management	0	0	4	0	0	4	0	3	3	0	0	4	0	1	2
Bureau of Reclamation	NA	NA	NA	NA	NA	NA	NA	NA	NA	NA	NA	NA	0	0	0
National Park Service	0	31	76	0	15	83	0	8	159	0	31	175	0	9	4
U.S. Fish and Wildlife Service															
Division of Refuge Law Enforcement	NA	NA	NA	NA	NA	NA	0	0	5	0	1	2	0	0	0
FWS, National Wildlife Refuge System	NA	NA	NA	0	4	9	NA	NA	NA	NA	NA	NA	NA	NA	NA
FWS, Office of Law Enforcement	NA	NA	NA	0	0	0	NA	NA	NA	NA	NA	NA	NA	NA	NA
Not reported	0	0	6	NA	NA	NA	NA	NA	NA	NA	NA	NA	NA	NA	NA
U.S. Department of the Treasury[2]	0	0	0	0	0	1	0	0	1	0	0	0	0	0	1
Internal Revenue Service	0	0	0	0	0	1	NA	NA	NA	NA	NA	NA	0	0	0
Treasury Inspector General for Tax Administration	0	0	0	0	0	0	0	0	0	0	0	0	0	0	1
U.S. Mint Police	NA	NA	NA	NA	NA	NA	0	0	1	NA	NA	NA	0	0	0
U.S. Postal Service[2]	NA	NA	NA	NA	NA	NA	0	9	2	0	4	1	0	1	5

[1]This table includes federal agencies that indicated one or more of their law enforcement officers were killed or assaulted.
[2]For 2016 and 2017, data were not reported by these departments, agencies, or offices.
[3]For 2016, data were not reported by the U.S. Department of Defense.
[4]For 2017, data reported by the U.S. Department of the Navy were aggregated and not submitted separately.
[5]For 2016, 2017, 2018 data were not reported by the U.S. Marine Corps.
[6]For 2016, data requests to the U.S. Immigration and Customs Enforcement (ICE) were inadvertent received and addressed by entities within ICE that did not possess the appropriate resources to provide comprehensive and complete data; therefore, caution must be taken when comparing 2016 data to 2017, 2018, 2019, and 2020 data.
NA indicates the agency did not submit data.

Table 40. Federal Law Enforcement Officers Killed and Assaulted, by Region, Geographic Division, and State/Territory, 2020

(Number.)

Area	Total	Firearm	Knife or other cutting instrument	Bomb	Blunt instrument	Personal weapons	Vehicle	Other
Number of Victim Officers.....................................	1,692	143	24	23	219	659	156	468
Northeast...	41	10	0	0	1	19	2	9
New England...	1	0	0	0	0	0	1	0
Connecticut.................................	0	0	0	0	0	0	0	0
Maine..	0	0	0	0	0	0	0	0
Massachusetts...........................	1	0	0	0	0	0	1	0
New Hampshire.........................	0	0	0	0	0	0	0	0
Rhode Island..............................	0	0	0	0	0	0	0	0
Vermont......................................	0	0	0	0	0	0	0	0
Middle Atlantic...................................	40	10	0	0	1	19	1	9
New Jersey.................................	4	4	0	0	0	0	0	0
New York....................................	24	2	0	0	1	15	0	6
Pennsylvania..............................	12	4	0	0	0	4	1	3
Midwest	324	51	7	0	5	46	7	208
East North Central.............................	49	13	0	0	3	23	0	10
Illinois..	12	1	0	0	2	3	0	6
Indiana..	2	2	0	0	0	0	0	0
Michigan......................................	11	5	0	0	1	2	0	3
Ohio...	5	5	0	0	0	0	0	0
Wisconsin....................................	19	0	0	0	0	18	0	1
West North Central...........................	275	38	7	0	2	23	7	198
Iowa...	0	0	0	0	0	0	0	0
Kansas...	10	0	0	0	0	7	2	1
Minnesota...................................	21	2	5	0	1	4	2	7
Missouri......................................	39	35	0	0	1	1	0	2
Nebraska.....................................	0	0	0	0	0	0	0	0
North Dakota.............................	70	0	1	0	0	3	0	66
South Dakota	135	1	1	0	0	8	3	122
South...	184	32	3	0	2	89	16	42
South Atlantic	89	7	1	0	1	47	5	28
Delaware.....................................	0	0	0	0	0	0	0	0
District of Columbia.................	22	1	0	0	1	1	0	19
Florida...	28	2	0	0	0	22	0	4
Georgia.......................................	12	3	0	0	0	9	0	0
Maryland.....................................	4	1	1	0	0	0	1	1
North Carolina..........................	15	0	0	0	0	12	1	2
South Carolina..........................	1	0	0	0	0	1	0	0
Virginia.......................................	7	0	0	0	0	2	3	2
West Virginia.............................	0	0	0	0	0	0	0	0
East South Central.............................	26	5	0	0	0	12	6	3
Alabama......................................	5	0	0	0	0	1	2	2
Kentucky.....................................	12	0	0	0	0	9	2	1
Mississippi..................................	3	3	0	0	0	0	0	0
Tennessee...................................	6	2	0	0	0	2	2	0
West South Central...........................	69	20	2	0	1	30	5	11
Arkansas.....................................	4	2	0	0	0	0	2	0
Louisiana....................................	4	1	0	0	0	3	0	0
Oklahoma...................................	2	0	0	0	0	2	0	0
Texas	59	17	2	0	1	25	3	11
West...	1,071	50	11	23	210	448	128	201
Mountain...	523	47	4	0	4	337	99	32
Arizona.......................................	97	7	1	0	1	64	5	19
Colorado.....................................	24	0	0	0	0	17	7	0
Idaho..	287	21	0	0	1	183	82	0
Montana.....................................	23	5	0	0	2	13	3	0
Nevada..	28	2	0	0	0	23	2	1
New Mexico...............................	58	12	2	0	0	33	0	11
Utah..	0	0	0	0	0	0	0	0
Wyoming.....................................	6	0	1	0	0	4	0	1
Pacific..	548	3	7	23	206	111	29	169
Alaska...	5	2	0	0	0	1	0	2
California....................................	37	0	0	0	3	22	6	6
Hawaii...	15	1	3	0	0	11	0	0
Oregon..	401	0	4	23	203	13	2	156
Washington................................	90	0	0	0	0	64	21	5

Table 40. Federal Law Enforcement Officers Killed and Assaulted, by Region, Geographic Division, and State/Territory, 2020—*Continued*

(Number.)

Area	Total	Firearm	Knife or other cutting instrument	Bomb	Blunt instrument	Personal weapons	Vehicle	Other
Puerto Rico and other outlying areas........................	8	0	1	0	0	1	2	4
American Samoa........................	0	0	0	0	0	0	0	0
Guam........................	0	0	0	0	0	0	0	0
Mariana Islands........................	0	0	0	0	0	0	0	0
Puerto Rico........................	8	0	1	0	0	1	2	4
U.S. Virgin Islands........................	0	0	0	0	0	0	0	0
Foreign (selected)........................	36	0	0	0	0	31	1	4
Santo Domingo........................	0	0	0	0	0	0	0	0
South Korea........................	28	0	0	0	0	28	0	0
Jamaica........................	0	0	0	0	0	0	0	0
Japan........................	3	0	0	0	0	0	1	2
Italy........................	3	0	0	0	0	3	0	0
Costa Rica........................	0	0	0	0	0	0	0	0
Douala, Cameroon........................	0	0	0	0	0	0	0	0
Ecuador........................	0	0	0	0	0	0	0	0
Okinawa, Japan........................	0	0	0	0	0	0	0	0
Iwakuni, Japan........................	0	0	0	0	0	0	0	0
Mexico........................	2	0	0	0	0	0	0	2
Location not reported[1]........................	28	0	2	0	1	25	0	0

[1]Location data for 170 victim officers were not provided by the National Park Service Rangers.

METHODOLOGY

For all sections, data for 2020 should be interpreted with caution, especially in regard to comparison with previous years, due to the circumstances imposed by the COVID-19 pandemic.

OFFICERS KILLED

When an officer is killed in the line of duty, the FBI gathers data about circumstances pertaining to the death. The data come from various sources:

- City, university and college, county, state, tribal, and federal law enforcement agencies participating in the Uniform Crime Reporting Program may report line-of-duty deaths that occur in their jurisdictions

- FBI field offices report line-of-duty deaths of law enforcement officers that occur in the United States and its outlying areas

- Several nonprofit organizations, such as the Concerns of Police Survivors and the National Law Enforcement Officers Memorial Fund, which provide various services to the families of fallen officers, also furnish information about line-of-duty deaths

When the FBI receives notification of a line-of-duty death, the Law Enforcement Officers Killed and Assaulted (LEOKA) Program's staff works with FBI field offices to contact the fallen officer's employing agency and request additional details about the fatal incident. The LEOKA staff also obtains criminal history data from the FBI's Interstate Identification Index about individuals who are identified in connection with line-of-duty felonious deaths.

OFFICERS ASSAULTED

The Uniform Crime Reporting (UCR) Program collects information monthly about assaults on duly sworn city, university and college, county, state, and tribal law enforcement officers. The agencies that employ these officers collect and submit data either through their state UCR Programs or, for non-Program states, directly to the FBI. For assault data to be included in this publication, law enforcement agencies must have submitted information for all 12 months of 2019 regarding their sworn officers who were assaulted as well as the number of officers and civilians their agencies employed full time for the reporting year.

Law enforcement agencies report to the UCR Program the number of assaults resulting in injuries to their officers or instances in which an offender used a weapon that could have caused injury or death. Law enforcement agencies report other assaults (i.e., those not causing injury) if they involved more than verbal abuse or minor resistance to an arrest.

The data in this report pertain to felonious deaths, accidental deaths, and assaults of duly sworn law enforcement officers who, at the time of the incident, met the following criteria. These law enforcement officers:

- Wore/carried a badge (ordinarily).

- Carried a firearm (ordinarily).

- Were duly sworn and had full arrest powers.

- Were members of a law enforcement agency.

- Were acting in an official capacity, whether on or off duty, at the time of incident.

- If killed, the deaths were directly related to the injuries received during the incident.

An exception to the above criteria includes individuals who were killed or assaulted while acting in a law enforcement capacity at the request of a law enforcement agency whose officers meet the LEOKA criteria. (See below for further explanation in reference to this exception.)

EXCLUSIONS FROM THE LEOKA PROGRAM'S DATA COLLECTION

Deaths resulting from the following are not included in the LEOKA Program's statistics:

- Natural causes, such as, heart attack, stroke, aneurism, etc.

- On duty, but death is attributed to their own personal situation, such as, domestic violence, neighbor conflict, etc.

- Suicide

Examples of job positions not typically included in the LEOKA Program's statistics (unless they meet the above exception):

- Corrections/correctional officers

- Bailiffs

- Probation/parole officers

- Federal judges

- U.S. and Assistant U.S. Attorneys

- Bureau of Prison Officers

- Private Security Officers

In September 2014, the LEOKA Program expanded its collection criteria to include the data of individuals who are killed or assaulted while temporarily serving as a law enforcement officer at the request of a law enforcement agency whose officers meet the general current collection criteria. These individuals must be under the supervision of a certified law enforcement officer from the requesting agency at the time of the incident, but they are not required to be in the physical presence of the supervisory officer while they are working an assigned duty. Examples of permitted exceptions:

- An unpaid reserve officer responded to a structure fire along with a law enforcement officer. As the reserve officer exited the patrol unit, he was immediately confronted in an ambush-style attack and was fatally shot by the offender.

- A correctional officer was fatally shot while assisting local law enforcement agencies who were tracking a man wanted for murdering his parents. The officer was a canine handler at a local correctional facility and was asked to assist during the incident based on the need for the canine. (If the correctional officer was working in his/her normal capacity as a correctional officer when killed, that correctional officer would not be counted in the LEOKA Program's statistics.)

FEDERAL LAW ENFORCEMENT OFFICERS KILLED AND ASSAULTED

Data published by the FBI concerning federal officers who were killed or assaulted in the line of duty are provided by the following six federal departments:

- U.S. Capitol Police

- U.S. Department of Defense

- U.S. Department of Homeland Security

- U.S. Department of the Interior

- U.S. Department of Justice

- U.S. Department of the Treasury

- U.S. Postal Inspection Service

Within these departments are the agencies, bureaus, and services that employ most of the personnel who are responsible for protecting government officials and enforcing and investigating violations of federal law. Every year, the FBI contacts these agencies and requests information about the officers who were killed or assaulted in the line of duty.

The information concerning federal officers differs slightly from the data regarding assaults on city, university and college,

county, state, and tribal law enforcement officers. First, the data regarding federal officers include all reports of assaults regardless of the extent (or the absence) of personal injury. Second, the circumstance categories are tailored to represent the unique duties of federal law enforcement personnel.

DATA CONSIDERATIONS

When reviewing the tables, charts, and summaries presented in this publication, readers should be aware of certain features of the LEOKA data collection process that could affect their interpretation of the information.

- The data in the tables and charts reflect the number of victim officers, not the number of incidents or weapons used.

- The UCR Program considers any parts of the body that can be used as weapons (such as hands, fists, or feet) to be personal weapons and designates them as such in its data.

- Law enforcement agencies use a different methodology for collecting and reporting data about officers who were killed than the methodology used for those who were assaulted. As a result, information about officers killed and information about officers assaulted reside in two separate databases, and the data are not comparable.

- Because the information in the tables of this publication is updated each year, the FBI cautions readers against making comparisons between the data in this publication and those in prior editions.

CAUTION AGAINST COMPARISONS WITH DATA FROM OTHER ORGANIZATIONS

The FBI's LEOKA Program is one of a number of entities that report information concerning line-of-duty deaths and/or assaults of law enforcement officers in the United States. Each organization has its own purpose and may use different methods to collect and report information or focus on somewhat different aspects of these important topics. Therefore, care should be taken not to compare LEOKA data to data provided by other entities, such as the Officer Down Memorial Page, National Law Enforcement Officers Memorial Fund, and others.

HISTORY

Beginning in 1937, the FBI's UCR Program collected and published statistics on law enforcement officers killed in the line of duty in its annual publication, *Crime in the United States*. Statistics regarding assaults on officers were added in 1960. In June 1971, executives from the law enforcement conference, "Prevention of Police Killings," called for an increase in the FBI's involvement in preventing and investigating officers' deaths. In response to this directive, the UCR Program expanded its collection of data to include more details about the incidents in which law enforcement officers were killed and assaulted.

Using this comprehensive set of data, the FBI began in 1972 to produce two reports annually, the *Law Enforcement Officers Killed Summary* and the *Analysis of Assaults on Federal Officers*. These two reports were combined in 1982 to create the annual publication, *Law Enforcement Officers Killed and Assaulted*.

DEFINITIONS

Type of Incident

Feloniously Killed: Incident type in which an officer, while engaged in or on account of the performance of their official duties, was fatally injured as a direct result of a willful and intentional act by an offender.

Accidentally Killed: Incident type in which an officer was fatally injured as a result of an accident or negligence that occurred while the officer was acting in an official capacity. Due to the hazardous nature of the law enforcement profession, deaths of law enforcement officers are considered accidental if the act causing the death is found not to be willful and intentional.

Assaulted: An unlawful attack by one person upon another for the purpose of inflicting severe or aggravated bodily injury. This type of assault is accompanied by the use of a weapon or by a means likely to produce death or great bodily injury.

Detailed Assault Data: The detailed data collection is limited to officers who are assaulted and injured with firearms or knives/other cutting instruments. Incident type in which an officer, while engaged in or on account of the performance of their official duties, received nonfatal injuries as a direct result of a willful and intentional act by an offender.

Race

White: A person having origins in any of the original peoples of Europe, the Middle East, or North Africa.

Black/African American: A person having origins in any of the black racial groups of Africa. Terms such as "Haitian" or "Negro" can be used in addition to "Black or African American."

Asian: Included within "Asian/Pacific Islander" in LEOKA publication tables referring to Race: A person having origins in any of the original peoples of the Far East, Southeast Asia, or the Indian subcontinent, including, for example, Cambodia, China, India, Japan, Korea, Malaysia, Pakistan, the Philippine Islands, Thailand, and Vietnam.

Native Hawaiian/Other Pacific Islands: Included within "Asian/Pacific Islander" in LEOKA publication tables referring to Race: A person having origins in any of the original peoples of Hawaii, Guam, Samoa, or other Pacific Islands, e.g., individuals who are Carolinian, Fijian, Kosraean, Melanesian, Micronesian, Northern Mariana Islander, Palauan, Papua New Guinean, Ponapean (Pohnpelan), Polynesian, Solomon Islander, Tahitian, Tarawa Islander, Tokelauan, Tongan, Trukese (Chuukese), and Yapese. (*NOTE:* The term "Native Hawaiian" does not include individuals who are native to the state of Hawaii simply by virtue of being born there.)

American Indian/Alaska Native: A person having origins in any of the original peoples of North and South America (including Central America), and who maintains tribal affiliation or community attachment.

Type of Assignment

2-Officer vehicle: An assignment where the officer is on patrol and is accompanied by another law enforcement officer(s) in the agency's marked patrol vehicle.

1-Officer vehicle: An assignment where the officer is on patrol and is not accompanied by another officer in the agency's marked patrol vehicle.

Foot patrol: An assignment where the officer is patrolling a designated route on foot.

Administrative: Included within "Other" in LEOKA publication tables referring to Type of Assignment: An assignment in which an officer is working management, performance, or executive duties of the local, state, or federal jurisdiction. Examples include, but are not limited to:

- handling, transporting, or maintaining custody of persons who are in the custodial care of a law enforcement agency subsequent to an arrest and/or while dealing with persons who are being detained in accordance with the law;

- attending community meetings, crime preventive programs, or other organized functions as an official representative of a law enforcement agency;

- performing duties and recreational activities associated with agency sanctioned programs such as D.A.R.E., Boys and Girls Clubs, or other youth programs; or

- serving of writs, notices, summonses, subpoenas, hearing notices, notifications, and other civil processes; and transporting of papers, equipment, or persons associated with official agency sanctioned activities, functions, and programs.

Investigative/detective: Included within "Other" in LEOKA publication tables referring to Type of Assignment: An officer whose occupation is mainly to investigate and solve crimes.

Plainclothes assignment: Included within "Other" in LEOKA publication tables referring to Type of Assignment: A non-uniformed assignment where the officer's role and identity as a sworn law enforcement officer is not intended to be confidential or clandestine.

Tactical assignment (uniformed): Included within "Other" in LEOKA publication tables referring to Type of Assignment: A uniformed assignment where an officer is strategically deployed in order to achieve a specific goal or objective. These are typically high-risk assignments.

Undercover: Included within "Other" in LEOKA publication tables referring to Type of Assignment: A non-uniformed assignment where the officer requires anonymity or blending into a group or environment to gather evidence or intelligence. The disclosure of the officer's identity would pose a significant safety risk.

Off duty: An officer who is off duty at the time of incident, but is acting in such a way which is sanctioned by, recognized by, or derived from authority.

Circumstances at Scene of Incident

Disturbance (bar fight, person with firearm, etc.): A breach of the peace type of circumstance resulting in a call for law enforcement to respond. Examples include, but are not limited to: curfew violations, disorderly persons, drinking in public, fights, fireworks violations, gambling in public space, persons under the influence, landlord/tenant disputes, loitering, loud noise of any type (excluding animal disturbance complaints by a citizen), littering, nuisance complaints, prostitution offenses, trespassing or unwanted guests, vagrancy violations, and verbal altercations.

Domestic disturbance (family quarrel, etc.): A breach of the peace or crime against a person occurring within a family, families, or other relatives or members of the household. Examples include, but are not limited to: family disputes, family intimidations, family arguments, and assisting citizens with the removal of legally owned possessions at locations where prior domestic disturbances or other related offenses have occurred. (Family includes a current or former spouse, parent, or guardian of the victim; a person with whom the victim shares a child in common; a person who is or has been in a social relationship of a romantic or intimate nature with the victim; a person who is cohabiting with or has cohabited with the victim as a spouse, parent, or guardian; or by a person who is or has been similarly situated to a spouse, parent, or guardian of the victim.)

Domestic violence: Included within "Domestic disturbance (family quarrels, etc.)" in LEOKA publication tables referring to Circumstance at Scene of Incident: The use, attempted use, or threatened use of physical force, or a weapon; or the use of coercion or intimidation; or committing a crime against property by a current or former spouse, parent, or guardian of the victim; a person with whom the victim shares a child in common; a person who is or has been in a social relationship of a romantic or intimate nature with the victim; a person who is cohabiting with or has cohabited with the victim as a spouse, parent, or guardian; or by a person who is or has been similarly situated to a spouse, parent, or guardian of the victim.

Burglary: The unlawful entry of a structure with the intent to commit a felony or a theft.

Burglary in progress/pursuing burglary suspect: Situation where an officer is pursuing, arresting, or attempting to arrest an offender involved in a burglary.

Robbery: The taking, or attempting to take, anything of value under confrontational circumstances from the care, custody, or control of a person by force, threat of force, or violence and/or by putting the victim in fear of immediate harm.

Robbery in progress/pursuing robbery suspect: Situation where an officer is pursuing, arresting, or attempting to arrest an offender involved in a robbery.

Drug-related matter: Situation where an officer is pursuing, arresting, or attempting to arrest an offender involved in a drug-related matter, such as, drug busts, buys, etc.

Drug complaint: Included within "Drug-related matter" in LEOKA publication tables referring to Circumstance at Scene of Incident: Incident where a citizen reports the use or presence of illegal drugs or drug paraphernalia. Examples include, but are not limited to, the possession, buying, or selling of illegal drugs or drug paraphernalia.

Attempting other arrest: Situation where an officer is arresting or attempting to arrest an offender either through verbal advisement or through physical contact, such as, attempting to restrain, control, or handcuff the offender.

Civil disorder (mass disobedience, riot, etc.): An activity where an officer is to control, disperse, or terminate a riot or mass disobedience.

Handling, transporting, custody of prisoner: Situation where an officer is handling, transporting, or maintaining custody of persons who are in the custodial care of a law enforcement agency subsequent to an arrest and/or while dealing with persons who are being detained in accordance with the law.

Investigating suspicious person/circumstance: An activity where an officer's intent is to investigate an unusual occurrence, an out-of-the-ordinary condition, or a suspicious person or circumstance.

Ambush: Situation where an officer is assaulted, unexpectedly, as the result of premeditated design by the perpetrator.

Ambush (entrapment/premeditation): Situation where an unsuspecting officer was targeted or lured into danger as the result of conscious consideration and planning by the offender.

Unprovoked attack: An attack on an officer not prompted by official contact at the time of the incident between the officer and the offender.

Investigative activity (surveillance, search, interview, etc.): An activity where an officer is making official inquiries relating to prior criminal offenses and/or perpetrators. Examples include, but are not limited to, obtaining follow-up information or additional information relating to any crime (excluding drug offense complaints) or interviewing a citizen relating to any criminal matter (excluding drug offenses).

Handling person with mental illness: Situation where an officer is handling a person who is known or suspected to be suffering from a mental illness that impairs judgment, behavior, perceptions of reality, or their ability to cope with the ordinary demands of life. Examples include, but are not limited to: mental patients, suicidal persons, service of commitment orders, and calls to investigate persons or activities where it is suspected that a person is suffering from a mental illness.

Felony vehicle stop: A vehicle stop made by an officer that is considered to be high-risk in nature.

Traffic violation stop: A vehicle stop made by an officer due to a motorist's violation of traffic rules and regulations.

Tactical situation (barricaded offender, hostage taking, high-risk entry, etc.): Situation where an officer is strategically deployed in order to achieve a specific goal or objective. Examples include, but are not limited to: serving search warrants, hostage situations, barricaded offenders, search warrants for drug violations, and any other situations that could be deemed "high-risk," such as, serving an arrest warrant on a known armed felon.

PART 9

Probation and Parole in the United States, 2020

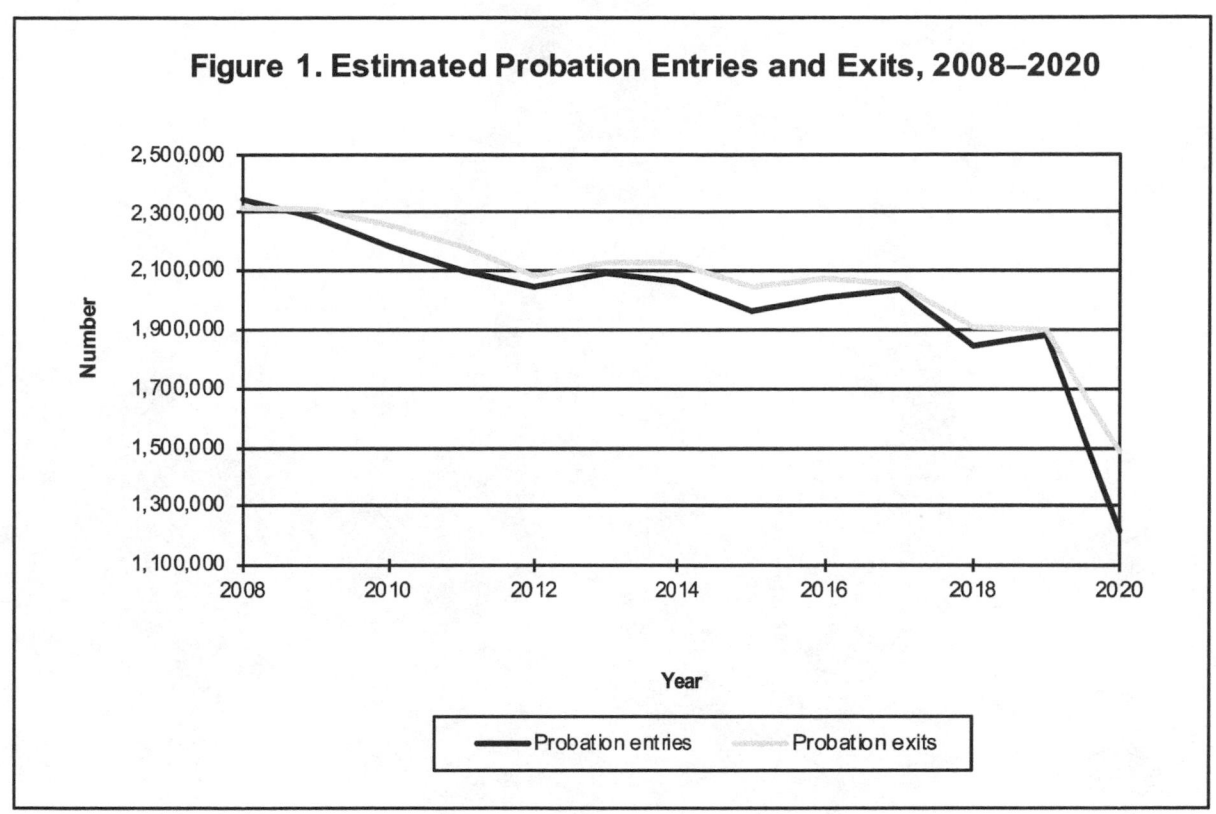

Figure 1. Estimated Probation Entries and Exits, 2008–2020

- At yearend 2020, an estimated 3,890,400 adults were under community supervision, down by about 276,500 offenders from January 1, 2020; the total community supervision population in 2020 was at its lowest level since 1998.

- Approximately 1 in 66 adults in the United States was under community supervision at yearend 2020, down from 1 in 58 in 2018.

- The adult probation population declined by approximately 8.3 percent (about 52,500 offenders) in 2020, the largest annual decrease since this series was initiated by the Bureau of Justice Statistics in 1981.

- The adult parole population increased by 1.3 percent between January 1, 2020, and yearend 2020; the parole population increased in 30 states and decreased in 9 states, the District of Columbia, and the U.S. federal system's term of supervised release.

- Probation exits in 2020 outpaced entries, the 12th consecutive year of this trend.

Table 1. Adults Under Community Supervision on Probation or Parole, 2005–2020

(Number; percent.)

Year	Total[1]	Probation	Parole
2005	4,946,600	4,162,300	784,400
2006	5,035,000	4,236,800	798,200
2007	5,115,500	4,293,000	826,100
2008	5,093,400	4,271,200	826,100
2009	5,019,900	4,199,800	824,600
2010	4,888,500	4,055,900	840,800
2011	4,818,300	3,973,800	855,500
2012	4,790,700	3,944,900	858,400
2013	4,749,800	3,912,900	849,500
2014	4,713,200	3,868,400	857,700
2015	4,650,900	3,789,800	870,500
2016	4,537,100	3,673,100	874,800
2017	4,508,900	3,647,200	875,000
2018	4,399,000	3,540,000	878,000
2019	4,357,700	3,492,900	878,900
2020			
January 1	4,167,100	3,330,200	851,000
December 31	3,890,400	3,053,700	862,100
Percent change, December 31			
2005–2020	-21.4	-26.6	9.9
January 1, 2020–December 31, 2020	-6.6	-8.3	1.3

NOTE: Counts are rounded to the nearest 100. Detail may not sum to total due to rounding. Estimates are based on most recent data and may differ from previously published statistics. Reporting methods for some probation agencies changed over time.
[1]Details may not sum to totals because community-supervision counts were adjusted to exclude parolees who were also on probation.

Table 2. Rates of U.S. Adult Residents on Community Supervision, Probation, and Parole, 2005–2020

(Number; rate.)

Year	Number per 100,000 U.S. adult residents			U.S. adult residents on:		
	Community supervision[1]	Probation	Parole	Community supervision[1]	Probation	Parole
2005	2215	1864	351	1 in 45	1 in 54	1 in 285
2006	2228	1875	353	1 in 45	1 in 53	1 in 283
2007	2237	1878	361	1 in 45	1 in 53	1 in 277
2008	2,202	1,847	357	1 in 45	1 in 54	1 in 280
2009	2,148	1,797	353	1 in 47	1 in 56	1 in 283
2010	2,067	1,715	356	1 in 48	1 in 58	1 in 281
2011	2,017	1,663	358	1 in 50	1 in 60	1 in 279
2012	1,984	1,634	356	1 in 50	1 in 61	1 in 281
2013	1,949	1,606	349	1 in 51	1 in 62	1 in 287
2014	1,916	1,572	349	1 in 52	1 in 64	1 in 287
2015	1,873	1,527	351	1 in 53	1 in 66	1 in 285
2016	1,811	1,466	349	1 in 55	1 in 68	1 in 287
2017	1,786	1,444	347	1 in 56	1 in 69	1 in 289
2018	1,729	1,391	345	1 in 58	1 in 72	1 in 290
2019	1,701	1,363	343	1 in 59	1 in 73	1 in 291
2020	1,511	1,186	335	1 in 66	1 in 84	1 in 299

NOTE: Counts for 2019 and earlier may differ from previously published statistics. Rates are based on the total community supervision, probation, and parole population counts as of December 31 of the reporting year and were calculated using U.S. Census Bureau estimates of the U.S. resident population of persons age 18 or older for January 1 of the following year.
[1]Includes adults on probation or parole. Details may not sum to totals because community supervision counts were adjusted to exclude adults on parole who were also on probation.

Table 3. Parolees on Probation Excluded from the January 1 and December 31 Community Supervision Populations, 2017–2020

(Number.)

Year	January 1[1]	December 31
2007	NA	3,562
2008	3,562	3,905
2009	3,905	4,959
2010	8,259	8,259
2011	8,259	10,958
2012	10,958	12,672
2013	12,672	12,511
2014	12,511	12,919
2015	12,919	9,375
2016	9,375	10,822
2017	10,822	13,302
2018	13,302	18,878
2019	18,878	14,057
2020	14,057	25,414

NOTE: Counts for 2019 and earlier may differ from previously published statistics. The community supervision counts were adjusted to exclude adults on parole who were also on probation.
NA = Not available.
[1]Data are based on the December 31 count of the prior reporting year for all years except 2010. For 2010, the December 31, 2010 count was used as a proxy because additional states reported these data in 2010.

Table 4. One-Day Difference Based on Reporting Changes for Probation and Parole, 2007–2019

(Number.)

Year	Probation population difference from December 31 to January 1 of the following year	Parole population difference from December 31 to January 1 of the following year
2007	-59280	-4920
2008	-33670	1390
2009	-73120	13700
2010	-2400	-80
2011	9,770	-2,830
2012	2,960	-23640
2013	20,980	540
2014	9,750	170
2015	-64,150	130
2016	5,030	2200
2017	-45,010	-1240
2018	-18,950	-1,040
2019	-162,650	-27,890

NOTE: Counts are calculated as the difference between December 31 of the year displayed and January 1 of the following year. Counts are rounded to the nearest 10.

Table 5. Estimated Total Probation Movements, Entries, and Exits, 2005–2020

(Number.)

Year	Total movements	Probation entries	Probation exits
2005	4,453,100	2,235,600	2,217,500
2006	4,489,200	2,279,800	2,209,400
2007	4,666,400	2,371,400	2,295,000
2008	4,663,500	2,346,600	2,316,900
2009	4,597,000	2,283,300	2,313,700
2010	4,442,300	2,185,500	2,256,800
2011	4,287,600	2,104,800	2,182,800
2012	4,122,900	2,042,900	2,080,000
2013	4,220,200	2,093,600	2,126,600
2014	4,194,900	2,065,800	2,129,100
2015	4,009,300	1,966,100	2,043,200
2016	4,083,600	2,012,200	2,071,400
2017	4,100,300	2,039,500	2,060,800
2018	3,755,700	1,845,200	1,910,500
2019	3,780,800	1,880,300	1,900,500
2020	2,703,400	1,216,100	1,487,300

Table 6. Estimated Total Parole Movements, Entries, and Exits, 2005–2020

(Number.)

Year	Total movements	Parole entries	Parole exits
2005	1,036,300	524,400	511,900
2006	1,069,300	543,100	526,200
2007	1,100,600	562,900	537,700
2008	1,141,900	575,500	566,400
2009	1,144,000	570,700	573,300
2010	1,128,300	565,500	562,800
2011	1,080,900	546,300	534,600
2012	997,700	500,900	496,800
2013	921,100	467,200	453,900
2014	913,900	461,100	452,800
2015	938,900	475,200	463,700
2016	913,100	457,100	456,000
2017	887,700	442,000	445,700
2018	901,100	447,200	453,900
2019	885,000	442,800	442,200
2020	780,800	392,400	388,400

Table 7. Adults Under Community Supervision, 2020

(Number; percent; rate.)

Jurisdiction	Community supervision population, January 1, 2020[1]	Entries Reported	Entries Estimated[2]	Exits Reported	Exits Estimated[2]	Community supervision population, December 31, 2020[1]	Change, 1/1/19–12/31/19 Number	Change, 1/1/19–12/31/19 Percent	Number under community supervision per 100,000 adult residents, 12/31/20[3]
U.S. Total	4,167,100	1,471,600	1,608,500	1,767,800	1,875,700	3,890,400	-276,700	-6.6	1,511
Federal	122,500	50,300	50,300	53,800	53,800	120,300	-2,200	-1.8	47
State	4,044,700	1,421,300	1,558,300	1,714,000	1,821,900	3,770,100	-274,500	-6.8	1,465
Alabama	64,200	12,200	12,200	21,100	21,100	55,400	-8800	-13.8	1,440
Alaska[4]	3,300	3800	4,200	3,500	4,000	3,400	200	5.5	623
Arizona	85,200	25,300	25,300	30,800	30,800	79,800	-5400	-6.4	1,366
Arkansas	63,800	20,700	20,700	20,100	20,100	64,900	1,100	1.7	2,775
California[3,4]	306,500	97,100	118,200	113,100	131,000	293,700	-12,800	-4.2	960
Colorado[4]	93,900	53,600	53,900	56,700	56,900	90,800	-3000	-3.2	1,980
Connecticut[4]	41,400	12,000	12,000	17,900	17,900	35,600	-5900	-14.2	1,253
Delaware	13,400	5,600	5,600	8,400	8,400	10,500	-2800	-21.3	1,336
District of Columbia	7,300	2,300	2,300	3,700	3,700	5,900	-1400	-18.9	1,015
Florida[4]	207,900	87,700	95,800	109,900	121,100	183,900	-24,100	-11.6	1,046
Georgia[4]	370,400	34,800	70,900	84,000	84,000	357,500	-13,000	-3.5	4,331
Hawaii	21,100	2,600	2,600	4,400	4,400	18,800	-2300	-10.9	1,698
Idaho	32,600	13,300	14,100	12,800	13,600	33,400	800	2.3	2,394
Illinois	117,400	74,300	74,300	78,100	78,100	113,600	-3800	-3.2	1,161
Indiana	115,900	77,400	77,400	87,400	87,400	105,900	-10000	-8.6	2,036
Iowa[4]	31,500	15,600	15,600	15,300	15,300	31,800	200	0.8	1,302
Kansas	21,200	22,400	22,400	22,300	22,300	21,300	100	0.4	959
Kentucky[4]	71,100	23,300	28,200	25,400	30,300	69,900	-1,200	-1.7	2,008
Louisiana	53,400	21,800	21,800	27,700	27,700	48,000	-5,300	-10.0	1,348
Maine	6,600	2,100	2,100	3,000	3,000	6,000	-600	-9.5	541
Maryland	79,900	22,100	22,100	36,000	36,000	66,000	-13,900	-17.3	1,398
Massachusetts[4]	52,700	31,600	31,600	48,300	48,300	35,900	-16,800	-31.8	647
Michigan[4]	151,300	55,900	70,400	70,500	84,300	132,200	-19,000	-12.6	1,686
Minnesota	105,600	37,500	37,500	50,500	50,500	92,600	-13,000	-12.3	2,121
Mississippi	38,900	12,900	12,900	12,300	12,300	39,500	600	1.7	1,738
Missouri	64,700	30,400	30,400	35,600	35,700	59,500	-5,200	-8.1	1,241
Montana[4]	11,100	4,700	5,000	4,600	4,900	11,200	100	0.7	1,309
Nebraska	14,000	10,200	10,200	11,300	11,300	12,600	-1400	-9.8	860
Nevada	17,300	U	U	9,100	9,100	18,400	1,100	6.3	749
New Hampshire	5,000	4,300	4,300	1,400	1,400	4,600	-400	-7.5	412
New Jersey	150,200	15,900	15,900	38,100	38,100	128,000	-22,200	-14.8	1,843
New Mexico[4]	12,200	6,600	6,600	6,900	6,900	11,700	-500	-4.1	712
New York	135,300	25,900	25,900	40,900	40,900	120,300	-15,000	-11.1	786
North Carolina	89,800	41,900	41,900	52,700	52,700	79,000	-10,800	-12.0	946
North Dakota	7,000	4,300	4,300	4,700	4,700	6,600	-400	-5.7	1,124
Ohio[4]	242,500	105,100	113,600	122,000	130,200	224,200	-18200	-7.5	2,455
Oklahoma	25,300	10,200	10,200	10,200	10,200	25,300	-100	-0.3	831
Oregon	59,900	34,600	34,600	34,900	34,900	59,600	-400	-0.6	1,753
Pennsylvania[4]	184,400	68,900	68,900	52,600	52,600	200,700	16,300	8.8	1,974
Rhode Island[4]	20,500	300	4,100	200	6,200	18,400	-2,000	-9.9	2,152
South Carolina	35,300	11,500	11,500	16,000	16,000	30,800	-4400	-12.6	746
South Dakota	9,800	5,400	5,400	3,900	3,900	11,200	1500	15.1	1,659
Tennessee	72,700	19,600	22,900	19,300	22,600	73,000	200	0.3	1,350
Texas	473,700	173,000	173,000	204,700	204,700	442,100	-31,600	-6.7	2,000
Utah	15,900	7,600	7,600	8,800	8,800	14,700	-1200	-7.6	625
Vermont	4,700	U	2,600	U	3,400	4,000	-700	-14.6	790
Virginia	67,400	28,000	28,000	29,000	29,000	66,300	-1100	-1.6	984
Washington[4]	87,600	27,000	37,900	25,700	37,500	73,700	-13900	-15.9	1,215
West Virginia	10,500	7,300	7,300	7,900	7,900	9,900	-600	-5.9	696
Wisconsin[4]	65,000	8000	29,200	7100	32,600	61,600	-3400	-5.3	1,343
Wyoming	6,500	3,000	3,000	3,200	3,200	6,400	-100	-2.1	1,415

NOTE: Counts are rounded to the nearest 100. Details may not sum to totals due to rounding. Data quality may vary across jurisdictions for counts of entries and exits. Therefore, the population on December 31, 2019 does not equal the population on January 1, 2019 plus entries, minus exits. Rates are based on the total community supervision, probation, and parole population counts as of December 31 of the reporting year and were calculated using U.S. Census Bureau estimates of the U.S. resident population of persons age 18 or older for January 1 of the following year.
U = Not known.
[1]The January 1 population excludes 14,057 adults under community supervision who were on both probation and parole and the December 31 population excludes 13,669.
[2]Reported data will equal estimated data in cases where no imputation was required.
[3]Rates were calculated using the estimated U.S. adult resident population in each jurisdiction on January 1, 2021.
[4]See Methodology for more detail.

Table 8. Adults on Probation, 2020

(Number; percent; rate.)

Jurisdiction	Probation population, January 1, 2020	Entries		Exits		Probation population, December 31, 2020	Change, January 1, 2020– December 31, 2020		Number on probation per 100,000 adult residents, 12/31/20[2]
		Reported	Estimated[1]	Reported	Estimated[1]		Number	Percent	
U.S. Total..........................	3,330,232	1,101,091	1,216,100	1,398,289	1,487,300	3,053,742	-276,490	-8.3	1,186
Federal..............................	14,137	5,153	5,153	6,964	6,964	12,394	-1,743	-12.3	5
State.................................	3,316,095	1,095,938	1,211,000	1,391,325	1,480,300	3,041,348	-274,747	-8.3	1,181
Alabama............................	55,349	9,051	9,051	16,993	16,993	47,407	-7942	-14.3	1,233
Alaska[3].............................	2,100	3791	3791	3,453	3,453	2,438	338	16.1	442
Arizona..............................	78,214	16,253	16,253	21,521	21,521	72,946	-5268	-6.7	1,249
Arkansas............................	39,759	9,944	9,944	9,937	9,937	39,871	112	0.3	1,705
California...........................	199,313	73,111	73,111	89,115	89,115	183,334	-15,979	-8.0	599
Colorado	82,739	45,179	45,400	49,319	49,600	78,562	-4177	-5.0	1,712
Connecticut	37,816	9,334	9,334	15,785	15,785	31,473	-6,343	-16.8	1,110
Delaware...........................	13,010	5,465	5,465	8,325	8,325	10,150	-2860	-22.0	1,289
District of Columbia............	4,859	1,385	1,385	2,749	2,749	3,495	-1364	-28.1	598
Florida[3]	203,597	81,871	89,900	103,981	115,200	179,594	-24,003	-11.8	1,021
Georgia[3]	354,650	25,090	61,200	74,378	74,378	341,434	-13,216	-3.7	4,136
Hawaii	19,619	1,529	1,529	3,857	3,857	17,291	-2328	-11.9	1,559
Idaho................................	27,499	10,310	11,100	10,633	11,500	27,418	-81	-0.3	1,966
Illinois	91,148	56,583	56,583	58,837	58,837	88,894	-2,254	-2.5	908
Indiana	109,850	73,015	73,015	83,102	83,102	99,763	-10087	-9.2	1,918
Iowa[3]...............................	24802	11656	11656	11619	11619	24839	37	0.1	1018
Kansas	15,683	18,409	18,409	18,218	18,218	15,874	191	1.2	715
Kentucky[3]	57,008	14,238	19,100	15,786	20,700	55,460	-1,548	-2.7	1,593
Louisiana	31,822	8,881	8,881	12,805	12,805	27,898	-3,924	-12.3	783
Maine................................	6,595	2,114	2,114	3,023	3,023	5,966	-629	-9.5	540
Maryland	70,227	18,463	18,463	32,139	32,139	56,551	-13,676	-19.5	1,197
Massachusetts	51,338	29,454	29,454	46,168	46,168	34,624	-16,714	-32.6	624
Michigan[3]	137,798	47,123	61,800	61,798	75,700	118,778	-19,020	-13.8	1,514
Minnesota	98,344	32,421	32,421	45,511	45,511	85,254	-13,090	-13.3	1,952
Mississippi.........................	28,458	7,535	7,535	6,969	6,969	29,024	566	2.0	1,276
Missouri............................	43,216	16,715	16,700	21,182	21,200	38,749	-4,467	-10.3	809
Montana[3]	9,617	3,844	4,100	3,934	4,200	9,524	-93	-1.0	1,113
Nebraska...........................	13,023	8,940	8,940	10,301	10,301	11,454	-1569	-12.0	781
Nevada..............................	10,260	U	U	4,759	4,759	9,222	-1038	-10.1	374
New Hampshire	2,728	3,655	3,655	614	614	2,723	-5	-0.2	244
New Jersey.........................	135,020	10,456	10,456	32,969	32,969	112,507	-22,513	-16.7	1,619
New Mexico[3]	12,257	4,482	4,500	5,279	5,300	11,682	-575	-4.7	712
New York...........................	90,352	10,774	10,774	24,803	24,803	76,323	-14,029	-15.5	499
North Carolina	76,169	28,709	28,709	39,070	39,070	65,808	-10,361	-13.6	788
North Dakota......................	6,199	3,363	3,363	3,717	3,717	5,845	-354	-5.7	1,000
Ohio[3]...............................	220,625	93,232	101,700	111,051	119,200	201,455	-19170	-8.7	2,206
Oklahoma..........................	23,378	9,391	9,391	9,742	9,742	23,027	-351	-1.5	758
Oregon..............................	35,732	25,847	25,847	25,847	25,847	35,732	0	0.0	1,052
Pennsylvania	99,798	40,510	40,510	27,868	27,868	112,440	12,642	12.7	1,106
Rhode Island[3].....................	19,897	U	3,900	U	6,000	17,805	-2,092	-10.5	2,080
South Carolina....................	30,845	8,899	8,899	13,364	13,364	26,389	-4456	-14.4	639
South Dakota......................	6,300	2,852	2,852	1,602	1,602	7,550	1250	19.8	1116
Tennessee[3]........................	61,723	14,988	18,300	16,161	19,500	60,550	-1173	-1.9	1,120
Texas................................	367,326	137,798	137,798	170,771	170,771	334,353	-32,973	-9.0	1,513
Utah	11,806	4,083	4,083	5,658	5,658	10,231	-1575	-13.3	436
Vermont	3,861	U	2,200	U	2,900	3,125	-736	-19.1	612
Virginia.............................	65,520	27,305	27,305	28,545	28,545	64,280	-1240	-1.9	954
Washington[3]......................	74,128	21,291	32,100	21,100	32,900	72,181	-1947	-2.6	1,191
West Virginia	6,454	4,315	4315	4,526	4,526	6,243	-211	-3.3	438
Wisconsin[3]........................	42,680	U	21,200	U	25,500	38,385	-4295	-10.1	837
Wyoming	5,584	2,284	2,284	2,441	2,441	5,427	-157	-2.8	1,204

NOTE: Data quality may vary across jurisdictions for counts of entries and exits. Therefore, the population on December 31, 2020 does not equal the population on January 1, 2020 plus entries, minus exits. Counts may not be actual as reporting agencies may provide estimates on some or all detailed data. Rates are based on the probation population counts as of December 31 of the reporting year and were calculated using U.S. Census Bureau estimates of the U.S. resident population of persons age 18 or older for January 1 of the following year.
U = Not known.
[1]Reported data will equal estimated data in cases where no imputation was required.
[2]Rates were calculated using the estimated U.S. adult resident population in each jurisdiction on January 1, 2020.
[3]See "Probation: Explanatory Notes" in Methodology for more detail.

Table 9. Adults Exiting Probation, by Type of Exit, 2020

(Number.)

Jurisdiction	Total reported	Completion	Incarcerated				Unsatisfactory reason other than incarceration			Death	Other[2]	Unknown or not reported
			With new sentence	Under current sentence	To receive treatment	Other/ unknown	Absconder	Discharged to warrant or detainer	Other unsatisfactory[1]			
U.S. Total	1,398,289	644,798	40,138	67,894	2,626	28,867	38,308	6,566	30,315	14,611	106,176	417,990
Federal	6,964	6,038	0	427	0	0	0	0	47	101	0	351
State	1,391,325	638,760	40,138	67,467	2,626	28,867	38,308	6,566	30,268	14,510	106,176	417,639
Alabama*	16,993	10,082	1,522	468	0	U	101	5	35	451	4329	0
Alaska*	3,453	695	1607	1095	NA	NA	594	NA	NA	19	NA	-557
Arizona*	21,521	16,795	U	3,535	NA	726	U	U	NA	447	18	0
Arkansas*	9,937	6,683	1766	765	361	0	0	12	0	335	15	0
California*	89,115	U	U	U	U	U	U	U	U	U	U	89115
Colorado*	49,319	30,153	79	527	0	6,494	5,596	0	253	445	4,704	1,068
Connecticut*	15,785	13,913	U	U	0	0	152	1,337	0	0	383	0
Delaware*	8,325	6,497	185	513	U	U	U	U	602	153	375	0
District of Columbia	2,749	2,440	0	0	0	202	0	0	28	49	30	0
Florida*	103,981	60,551	9,323	11,432	10	15	298	1,259	3,007	1,250	1,674	15,162
Georgia*	74,378	32,337	2,538	1,011	0	0	1,531	0	0	889	0	36072
Hawaii*	3,857	2,566	155	461	0	619	0	0	0	50	6	0
Idaho*	10,633	2,204	680	22	951	0	1041	0	0	99	0	5,636
Illinois*	58,837	33,568	U	U	U	325	4,030	U	4,406	U	8,866	7642
Indiana*	83,102	50,542	7,569	7,371	U	U	8,409	U	U	U	9,211	0
Iowa	11,619	8,411	953	236	0	0	0	0	1,845	154	20	0
Kansas*	18,218	14,959	81	1629	U	U	1,549	U	U	U	NA	0
Kentucky	15,786	9,792	872	4,213	0	2	213	0	19	564	111	0
Louisiana*	12,805	8,857	897	1,408	NA	0	NA	NA	1,313	288	42	0
Maine*	3,023	2,346	U	320	U	U	U	U	U	U	282	75
Maryland	32,139	19,032	1,447	991	U	NA	U	U	4,352	693	2,046	3578
Massachusetts*	46,168	U	U	U	U	U	U	U	U	U	U	46,168
Michigan*	61,798	32,793	547	1,168	61	1	85	412	654	419	10	25,648
Minnesota	45,511	U	U	U	U	U	U	U	U	U	U	45,511
Mississippi	6,969	4,500	506	1,176	NA	305	NA	NA	NA	86	379	17
Missouri*	21,182	9,725	643	2,070	475	21	6,169	U	U	482	U	1597
Montana*	3,934	1,855	257	444	U	149	U	U	U	102	U	1,127
Nebraska*	10,301	7,461	U	1657	U	U	U	U	822	81	280	0
Nevada	4,759	4,694	U	U	U	NA	U	U	U	65	NA	0
New Hampshire*	614	220	50	65	45	0	155	35	0	33	11	0
New Jersey*	32,969	U	U	U	U	U	1	U	U	32	U	32,936
New Mexico*	5,279	5,156	U	U	U	U	28	9	U	86	U	0
New York	24,803	16,604	U	U	U	U	U	U	U	479	U	7,720
North Carolina	39,070	22,958	2,211	977	NA	NA	3,905	NA	8,136	883	NA	0
North Dakota*	3,717	U	U	U	U	NA	U	U	NA	60	3657	0
Ohio*	111,051	48,984	2,995	5,139	723	1,231	4,228	2,642	2,702	1,080	1,165	40,162
Oklahoma*	9,742	7,979	368	509	U	U	U	U	70	125	U	691
Oregon	25,847	U	U	U	U	U	U	U	U	U	U	25,847
Pennsylvania*	27,868	1,889	207	239	0	0	0	26	479	84	0	24944
Rhode Island	U	U	U	U	U	U	U	U	U	U	U	U
South Carolina	13,364	11,454	218	1,350	0	0	0	0	0	308	34	0
South Dakota*	1,602	984	U	U	U	618	U	U	U	U	U	0
Tennessee*	16,161	11,238	1,368	2,857	0	0	0	0	0	698	0	0
Texas*	170,771	79,374	U	12020	U	10,977	U	U	65	2,088	66,247	0
Utah	5,658	2,669	301	229	0	0	112	0	990	86	1,271	0
Vermont	U	U	U	U	U	U	U	U	U	U	U	U
Virginia	28,545	21,933	U	U	U	5,194	U	U	U	896	338	184
Washington*	21,100	10,460	487	826	0	268	25	829	409	302	209	7,285
West Virginia*	4,526	1,609	156	385	U	1720	33	NA	38	111	463	11
Wisconsin	U	U	U	U	U	U	U	U	U	U	U	U
Wyoming	2,441	1,798	150	359	0	0	53	0	43	38	0	0

NOTE: Based on reported data only. Counts may not be actual as reporting agencies may provide estimates on some or all detailed data.
* = Some or all data were estimates.
U = Not known.
X = Not applicable.
[1]Includes adults on probation who were discharged from supervision when they did not complete the conditions of probation or fulfill obligations.
[2]Includes 12,160 adults on probation who transferred to another jurisdiction and 94,016 who exited supervision for other reasons.

Table 10. Characteristics of Adults on Probation, 2005 and 2020

(Percent.)

Characteristic	Percent of total adults on probation		Percent with known characteristics[1]	
	2005	2020	2005	2020
Total	100.0	100.0	100.0	100.0
Sex	56.0	55.0	77.0	75.0
Male	17.0	19.0	23.0	25.0
Female	27.0	26.0	NA	NA
Race/ethnicity	100.0	100.0	100.0	100.0
White[2]	35.0	38.0	54.0	54.0
Black[2]	19.0	21.0	29.0	30.0
Hispanic	8.0	9.0	13.0	13.0
American Indian/Alaska Native[2]	1.0	1.0	1.0	1.0
Asian[2]	<1	1.0	1.0	1.0
Native Hawaiian or Other Pacific Islander[2]......	<1	0.0	<1	1.0
Two or more races[2]	<1	0.0	<1	1.0
Unknown	36.0	30.0	NA	NA
Status of supervision	100.0	100.0	100.0	100.0
Active	51.0	55.0	72.0	70.0
Residential/other treatment program	1.0	0.0	1.0	1.0
Financial conditions remaining	NA	2.0	NA	2.0
Inactive	6.0	4.0	9.0	4.0
Absconder	7.0	6.0	10.0	9.0
Supervised out of jurisdiction	4.0	2.0	6.0	3.0
Warrant status	1.0	4.0	2.0	5.0
Other	<1	4.0	<1	6.0
Unknown	29.0	22.0	NA	NA
Type of offense	100.0	100.0	100.0	100.0
Felony	39.0	52.0	50.0	69.0
Misdemeanor	39.0	28.0	49.0	30.0
Other infractions	0.0	1.0	1.0	1.0
Unknown	22.0	19.0	NA	NA
Most serious offense	100.0	100.0	100.0	100.0
Violent	10.0	15.0	18.0	25.0
Domestic violence	2.0	3.0	6.0	5.0
Sex offense	2.0	2.0	3.0	4.0
Other violent offense	6.0	10.0	10.0	16.0
Property	13.0	14.0	23.0	24.0
Drug	15.0	13.0	25.0	26.0
Public order	9.0	8.0	19.0	13.0
DWI/DUI	7.0	7.0	14.0	11.0
Other traffic offense	2.0	1.0	5.0	2.0
Other[3]	5.0	7.0	14.0	11.0
Unknown[4]	47.0	43.0	NA	NA

NOTE: Details may not sum to totals due to rounding. Estimates for 2005 may have been revised based on updated reporting and may differ from numbers in past reports.
NA = Not applicable.
[1]Excludes unknown and unreported characteristics.
[2]Excludes persons of Hispanic origin (e.g., White refers to non-Hispanic Whites and Blakc refers to non-Hispanic Blacks).
[3]Includes other offenses, such as public intoxication, disorderly conduct, false statement, insufficient funds, and other miscellaneous charges.
[4]Many agencies face challenges in reporting detailed characteristics on adults on probation who are supervised for misdemeanor offenses.

Table 11. Adults on Parole, 2020

(Number; percent; rate.)

Jurisdiction	Parole population, January 1, 2020	Entries Reported	Entries Estimated[1]	Exits Reported	Exits Estimated[1]	Parole population, December 31, 2020	Change, January 1, 2020– December 31, 2020[2] Number	Change, January 1, 2020– December 31, 2020[2] Percent	Number on parole per 100,000 adult residents, 12/31/20[2]
U.S. Total	850,964	370,501	392,400	369,528	388,400	862,113	11,149	1.3	335
Federal	108,343	45,105	45,105	46,820	46,820	107,922	-421	-0.4	42
State	742,621	325,396	347,300	322,708	341,600	754,191	11,570	1.6	293
Alabama	9,223	3,149	3,149	4,127	4,127	8,245	-978	-10.6	214
Alaska[3]	1,163	U	400	U	600	1,003	-160	-13.8	182
Arizona	7,043	9,081	9,081	9,237	9,237	6,887	-156	-2.2	118
Arkansas	24,976	10,761	10,761	10,147	10,147	25,852	876	3.5	1,106
California[4]	107,139	23,959	45,000	23,959	41,800	110,349	3,210	3	361
Colorado	11,155	8,465	8,465	7,336	7,336	12,284	1129	10.1	268
Connecticut[3]	3,601	2,636	2,636	2,157	2,157	4,080	479	13.3	144
Delaware	362	132	132	121	121	373	11	3	47
District of Columbia	2,595	920	920	968	968	2,547	-48	-1.8	436
Florida	4,349	5,845	5,845	5,914	5,914	4,280	-69	-1.6	24
Georgia	19,241	9,705	9,705	9,583	9,583	19,447	206	1.1	236
Hawaii	1,513	1,088	1,088	578	578	1,544	31	2	139
Idaho	5,121	2,963	2,963	2,117	2,117	5,967	846	16.5	428
Illinois	26,251	17,713	17,713	19,220	19,220	24,744	-1,507	-5.7	253
Indiana	6,050	4,362	4,362	4,276	4,276	6,136	86	1.4	118
Iowa	6,999	3,959	3,959	3,697	3,697	7,261	262	3.7	297
Kansas	5,530	3,954	3,954	4,056	4,056	5,428	-102	-1.8	244
Kentucky	14,977	9,097	9,097	9,645	9,645	14,429	-548	-3.7	414
Louisiana	23,582	12,920	12,920	14,936	14,936	21,566	-2,016	-8.5	605
Maine	19	0	0	1	1	18	-1	-5.3	2
Maryland	9,669	3,664	3,664	3,843	3,843	9,490	-179	-1.9	201
Massachusetts[3]	1,382	2,099	2,099	2,165	2,165	1,316	-66	-4.8	24
Michigan	13,488	8,630	8,630	8,657	8,657	13,461	-27	-0.2	172
Minnesota	7,243	5,085	5,085	4,969	4,969	7,359	116	1.6	169
Mississippi	10,432	5,408	5,408	5,330	5,330	10,510	78	0.7	462
Missouri	21,507	13,688	13,688	14,466	14,466	20,729	-778	-3.6	433
Montana	1,512	855	855	684	684	1,683	171	11.3	197
Nebraska	956	1,221	1,221	1,023	1,023	1156	200	20.9	79
Nevada	7,086	U	U	4,329	4,329	9,222	2,136	30.1	374
New Hampshire	2,250	625	625	795	795	1,882	-368	-16.4	168
New Jersey	15,194	5,488	5,488	5,166	5,166	15,516	322	2.1	223
New Mexico	2,608	2,075	2,075	1,588	1,588	2,725	117	4.5	166
New York	44,917	15,157	15,157	16,095	16,095	43,979	-938	-2.1	287
North Carolina	13,820	13,216	13,216	13,617	13,617	13,419	-401	-2.9	161
North Dakota	767	960	960	1,003	1,003	724	-43	-5.6	124
Ohio	21,832	11,877	11,877	10,940	10,940	22,769	937	4.3	249
Oklahoma	1,959	761	761	483	483	2,237	278	14.2	74
Oregon	24,183	8,723	8,723	9,074	9,074	23,832	-351	-1.5	702
Pennsylvania[3]	84,592	28,372	28,372	24,701	24,701	88,263	3,671	4.3	868
Rhode Island	557	250	250	188	188	619	62	11.1	72
South Carolina	4,638	2,619	2,619	2,651	2,651	4,638	0	0	112
South Dakota	3,452	2,516	2,516	2,295	2,295	3,673	221	6.4	543
Tennessee	10,993	4,562	4,562	3,148	3,148	12,407	1414	12.9	230
Texas	109,159	35,197	35,197	33,919	33,919	110,437	1278	1.2	500
Utah	4,061	3,507	3,507	3,135	3,135	4,433	372	9.2	189
Vermont	875	U	400	U	400	909	34	3.9	178
Virginia	1,860	660	660	503	503	2,017	157	8.4	30
Washington	13,427	5,742	5,742	4,633	4,633	14,536	1109	8.3	240
West Virginia	4,090	3,001	3,001	3,409	3,409	3,682	-408	-10	258
Wisconsin	22,292	7988	7,988	7106	7,106	23,174	882	4	505
Wyoming	931	741	741	718	718	954	23	2.5	212

NOTE: Data quality may vary across jurisdictions for counts of entries and exits. Therefore, the population on December 31, 2020 does not equal the population on January 1, 2020 plus entries, minus exits. Counts may not be actual as reporting agencies may provide estimates on some or all detailed data. Rates are based on the parole population counts as of December 31 of the reporting year and were calculated using U.S. Census Bureau estimates of the U.S. resident population of persons age 18 or older for January 1 of the following year.
U = Not known.
[1]Reported data will equal estimated data in cases where no imputation was required.
[2]Rates were calculated using the estimated U.S. adult resident population in each jurisdiction on January 1, 2021.
[3]See Methodology for more details.
[4]Includes adults on Post-Release Community Supervision and Mandatory Supervision: 45,899 on January 1, 2020 and 55,216 on December 31, 2020, with 28,324 entries and 31,699 exits.

Table 12. Adults Exiting Parole, by Type of Exit, 2020

(Number.)

Jurisdiction	Total reported	Completion	Returned to incarceration — With new sentence	Returned to incarceration — With revocation	Returned to incarceration — To receive treatment	Returned to incarceration — Other/ unknown	Unsatisfactory reason other than incarceration — Absconder	Unsatisfactory reason other than incarceration — Other unsatisfactory[1]	Death	Other[2]	Unknown or not reported
U.S. Total	369,528	211,276	18,654	45,878	1,281	5,574	6,188	2,995	7,962	6,635	63,085
Federal	46,820	29,295	0	8,406	0	0	2	291	1129	0	7,697
State	322,708	181,981	18,654	37,472	1,281	5,574	6,186	2,704	6,833	6,635	55,388
Alabama*	4,127	2,314	1123	370	NA	NA	NA	NA	177	143	0
Alaska	U	U	U	U	U	U	U	U	U	U	U
Arizona	9,237	8,022	91	944	0	0	39	29	112	0	0
Arkansas*	10,147	4,438	558	4,860	0	0	0	0	281	10	0
California	23,959	U	U	U	U	U	U	U	U	U	23,959
Colorado	7,336	5,541	794	832	0	0	0	0	122	47	0
Connecticut*	2,157	1,183	65	39	51	660	159	NA	U	NA	0
Delaware*	121	25	0	0	U	U	U	2	6	88	0
District of Columbia	968	553	0	0	0	279	0	0	33	103	0
Florida	5,914	3,863	296	539	0	0	0	0	2	1,015	199
Georgia*	9,583	7,318	145	19	0	1,953	0	0	148	0	0
Hawaii	578	0	NA	364	NA	NA	80	0	13	121	0
Idaho*	2,117	720	4	U	2	U	486	U	62	U	843
Illinois	19,220	13,686	351	4,060	NA	NA	48	NA	413	662	0
Indiana	4,276	2,798	185	708	NA	NA	491	NA	62	32	0
Iowa	3,697	1,995	806	586	0	0	0	249	61	0	0
Kansas	4,056	2,982	81	352	0	96	308	0	48	189	0
Kentucky	9,645	6,780	202	994	0	0	1492	0	177	0	0
Louisiana*	14,936	9,335	1,160	539	NA	937	NA	792	264	1,909	0
Maine	1	0	0	0	0	0	0	0	1	0	0
Maryland	3,843	2,427	222	111	U	NA	U	576	161	78	268
Massachusetts	2,165	1,526	86	368	0	0	0	146	34	5	0
Michigan	8,657	6,907	508	1,109	0	0	0	0	133	0	0
Minnesota	4,969	3,374	252	1,262	0	0	0	0	81	0	0
Mississippi	5,330	3,333	286	1,239	NA	U	NA	NA	81	166	225
Missouri	14,466	6,065	760	2,582	480	1,506	1,564	NA	438	NA	1071
Montana*	684	361	16	281	NA	NA	NA	NA	24	2	0
Nebraska	1,023	677	NA	338	NA	NA	NA	NA	6	2	0
Nevada*	4,329	4,264	U	U	U	NA	U	U	65	NA	0
New Hampshire	795	25	170	110	150	0	320	0	20	0	0
New Jersey	5,166	3,965	78	918	0	0	NA	0	186	0	19
New Mexico	1,588	666	33	808	U	22	U	U	59	U	0
New York	16,095	12,210	508	2,311	598	0	NA	NA	468	NA	0
North Carolina	13,617	10,693	1,006	191	NA	NA	1050	489	188	NA	0
North Dakota*	1,003	711	132	106	NA	NA	24	NA	18	12	0
Ohio	10,940	6,676	1,594	2,670	0	0	0	0	0	0	0
Oklahoma*	483	459	NA	NA	NA	NA	NA	NA	20	4	0
Oregon	9,074	U	U	U	U	U	U	U	U	U	9074
Pennsylvania*	24,701	5,358	2,063	2,642	0	0	0	279	508	1,580	12271
Rhode Island	188	U	U	U	U	U	U	U	U	U	188
South Carolina	2,651	2,391	29	132	0	0	0	40	59	0	0
South Dakota*	2,295	1328	136	566	NA	28	0	NA	40	197	0
Tennessee	3,148	1,970	420	580	0	0	0	0	178	0	0
Texas	33,919	27,613	3,547	659	NA	92	NA	8	1,836	NA	164
Utah	3,135	770	349	1,596	0	0	1	88	62	269	0
Vermont	U	U	U	U	U	U	U	U	U	U	U
Virginia	503	391	70	28	0	1	0	U	11	1	1
Washington	4,633	3,447	497	566	NA	NA	NA	NA	123	NA	0
West Virginia	3,409	2,235	17	1001	0	0	115	0	41	0	0
Wisconsin	7106	U	U	U	U	U	NA	U	U	U	7106
Wyoming	718	586	14	92	0	0	9	6	11	0	0

NOTE: Based on reported data only. See appendix table 9 for imputed exits from parole. Counts may not be actual as reporting agencies may provide estimates on some or all detailed data.
* = Some or all data were estimates.
U = Not known.
NA = Not applicable.
[1]Includes persons discharged because they were released to special sentence. Also includes closure due to deportation, pending parole institutional hearing, other revocations, other unsuccessful discharges, and early terminations.
[2]Includes 1,089 adults on parole who were transferred to another state and 5,546 who exited for other reasons.

METHODOLOGY

ABOUT THE DATA

The Bureau of Justice Statistics' (BJS) Annual Probation Survey and Annual Parole Survey began in 1980 and collect data from probation and parole agencies in the United States that supervise adults. In these data, adults are persons subject to the jurisdiction of an adult court or correctional agency. Juveniles prosecuted as adults in a criminal court are considered adults. Juveniles under the jurisdiction of a juvenile court or correctional agency are excluded from these data.

The National Criminal Justice Information and Statistics Service of the Law Enforcement Assistance Administration, BJS's predecessor agency, began a statistical series on parole in 1976 and on probation in 1979. The two surveys collect data on the total number of adults supervised in the community on January 1 and December 31 each year, the number of entries and exits to supervision during the reporting year, and characteristics of the population at yearend.

Both surveys cover all 50 states, the District of Columbia, and the federal system. BJS depends on the voluntary participation of state central reporters and separate state, county, and court agencies for these data.

In response to the COVID-19 pandemic, BJS added a special addendum to the 2020 Annual Survey of Probation and Annual Survey of Parole to measure the impact of this public health emergency on community corrections. The nine-question addendum collected information on the effects of the COVID-19 pandemic on probation and parole agencies' populations, policies, and procedures. BJS collected quarterly population numbers, a midyear count of entries and exits, and information on closures and changes in supervision techniques during 2020. Data should be interpreted with caution in comparison to previous years due to the impact of the pandemic.

PROBATION

The 2020 Annual Probation Survey was sent to 498 eligible agencies, which included 40 central state agencies; the federal system; the District of Columbia; and 458 separate state, county, or court agencies. Jurisdictions with multiple agencies included Alabama (3), Colorado (8), the District of Columbia (2), Florida (41), Georgia (2), Idaho (46), Kansas (4), Kentucky (3), Michigan (129), Missouri (2), Montana (4), New Mexico (2), Ohio (182), Oklahoma (3), Pennsylvania (3), Tennessee

(3), Texas (3), and Washington (32). Georgia and Pennsylvania are included as central state agencies, but each provides data from two departments within the state government. Idaho has historically reported probation data through two agencies: the Idaho Department of Correction and the Idaho Supreme Court. However, beginning in 2020, the Idaho Supreme Court announced that it will no longer be reporting represents 63 percent of Idaho's total probation population), 35 reporting local agencies representing 34 percent of Idaho's total probation population, and 9 nonreporting local agencies.

Of the 498 eligible agencies in the Annual Probation Survey population frame, 427 (86 percent) provided at least a population estimate for one of these four key items: January 1, 2020; December 31, 2020; number of entries in 2020; or number of exits in 2020. The remaining 71 (14 percent) did not provide any data for the 2020 collection. This included 2 agencies in Colorado, 7 in Florida, 8 in Idaho, 1 in Kentucky, 27 in Michigan, 1 in Missouri, 1 in New Mexico, 17 in Ohio, 1 in Tennessee, and 6 in Washington.

In 2020, about 79 percent of the 498 eligible agencies responded to all four key items asking about the population at the beginning or end of the year and the number of probation entries and exits. The remaining 21 percent did not respond to at least one of the four key items, including the 71 agencies that provided no data and 33 agencies that provided incomplete data: 4 in Florida, 1 in Georgia, 2 in Idaho, 7 in Michigan, 1 in Montana, 10 in Ohio, 1 in Rhode Island, 1 in Vermont, 5 in Washington, and 1 in Wisconsin.

The 2020 Annual Parole Survey was sent to 56 eligible agencies: 52 state reporters; 2 separate state, county, or court agencies; the District of Columbia; and the federal system. In this report, federal parole includes a term of supervised release from prison, mandatory release, parole, military parole, or special parole. A federal judge orders a term of supervised release at the time of sentencing, which is served after release from a federal prison sentence. In the case of Alaska, people on probation and parole are supervised under a common program, and the data provider is unable to report probation and parole counts separately. Combined counts of people on probation and parole were reported to BJS through the probation questionnaire. January 1 and December 31 counts of people on parole were imputed for Alaska, and these figures were deducted from the combined reported totals for the calculation of the state's January 1 and December 31 probation counts.

Of the 56 total agencies surveyed for 2020, 98 percent provided the population count for the beginning or end of the year or the number of parole exits or entries, and 95 percent responded to all of these key items. Vermont and one of the reporting agencies for California did not provide complete data on the four key survey items, and Alaska's data were estimated using the combined community supervision data provided.

PROBATION: EXPLANATORY NOTES, 2020

Probation agencies vary in their ability to provide counts each year consistent with Bureau of Justice Statistics (BJS) definitions. Some agencies report the number of cases, while others report the number of persons they supervise. Because a person can have multiple probation sentences, counting cases can artificially inflate probation totals. BJS requests that agencies report the number of persons under supervision, and each year some agencies make the conversion, resulting in what appears to be a large decrease from previous years' data. BJS documents these and other reporting anomalies below.

Alaska: The state supervises probation and parole in a combined program. The state agency was unable to report probation and parole data separately, so both populations were reported in the probation survey. The January 1, 2020, and December 31, 2020, probation population counts were derived based on the difference between the reported probation and imputed parole count (imputed using the December 31, 2019, parole population count).

Colorado: Nonreporting agencies in 2020—two local agencies did not report data. The December 31, 2019, population counts were used to estimate January 1, 2020, and December 31, 2020, populations. Fiscal year 2020 (ending June 30, 2020) quarter 3 and quarter 4 data were significantly impacted due to the COVID-19 pandemic as courts and probation operations were limited.

Florida: Nonreporting agencies in 2020—seven local agencies did not report data. The December 31, 2019, population count was used to estimate January 1, 2020, and December 31, 2020, counts for these agencies. Four other agencies did not report the number of entries and exits.

Georgia: Nonreporting agencies in 2020—one state agency did not report the number of entries or exits to probation. The January 1, 2020, reported population varied from the December 31, 2019, reported population. This caused a 1-day difference of 57,118. The respondent reported that the January 1, 2020, population was the better estimate of the population at that time.

Idaho: Nonreporting agencies in 2020 and change in reporting—nine local agencies did not report. Idaho has historically reported probation data through two agencies: the Idaho

Department of Correction and the Idaho Supreme Court. However, beginning in 2020 the Idaho Supreme Court announced that it will no longer be reporting data and instead requested that all local probation agencies report directly. This means that Idaho now has 1 state agency, the Idaho Department of Correction (which provides information on felons and represents 63 percent of Idaho's total probation population), 35 reporting local agencies, and 9 nonreporting local agencies. This change resulted in a decrease of 8,017 people on probation from December 31, 2019, to January 1, 2020.

Kentucky: Nonreporting agencies in 2020—one local agency did not report data. The December 31, 2019, population counts were used to estimate January 1, 2020, and December 31, 2020, populations.

Michigan: Nonreporting agencies in 2020—Michigan has 129 agencies: 1 state agency, representing 44 percent of Michigan's total probation population; 100 reporting local agencies; and 28 nonreporting local agencies. For the 28 nonreporting agencies, December 31, 2019, population counts were used to estimate January 1, 2020, populations, where available. Other agencies did not report the number of entries to or exits from probation.

Missouri: Nonreporting agencies in 2020—one local agency did not report data. The December 31, 2019, population counts were used to estimate January 1, 2020, and December 31, 2020, populations.

New Mexico: Nonreporting agencies in 2020—one local agency did not report data. The December 31, 2019, population counts were used to estimate January 1, 2020, and December 31, 2020, populations.

Ohio: Nonreporting agencies in 2020—22 local agencies did not report data. The December 31, 2019, population counts were used to estimate January 1, 2020, and December 31, 2020, populations. Many agencies reporting switching their case management systems in 2020, resulting in changes to reporting.

Oklahoma: Starting in 2020, reporting in Oklahoma changed parameters to exclude those on warrant status. This change in reporting resulted in a decrease of 16,211 people on probation from December 31, 2019, to January 1, 2020.

Pennsylvania—Pennsylvania has two reporting units that provide counts for portions of the probation population. The Pennsylvania Board of Probation and Parole provides state data that represented 6 percent of Pennsylvania's total probation population. Previously, the Pennsylvania Department of Corrections provided county-level probation data, but beginning in 2020 the Pennsylvania Commission on Crime and Delinquency assumed authority to collect that information. Their reporting for 2020 represented 94 percent of Pennsylvania's total probation population. In 2019, many county populations were estimated. This change in reporting resulted in a decrease of 72,254 people on probation from December 31, 2019, to January 1, 2020.

Rhode Island: Nonreporting agencies in 2020—the state agency did not report data on entries to or exits from probation.

Tennessee: Nonreporting agencies in 2020—one local agency did not report data. December 31 probation population counts from the last reported year going back to 2015 were used to estimate January 1, 2020, and December 31, 2020, populations.

Washington: Nonreporting agencies in 2020—five local agencies did not report data. The December 31, 2019, population counts were used to estimate January 1, 2020, and December 31, 2020, populations. Other agencies did not report the number of entries to or exits from probation. After a change in leadership at one agency, the December 31, 2019, population was a rough estimate due to lack of knowledge of how the numbers were presented in the past. Another agency reported a change in their case management system. These reporting changes resulted in a decrease of 6,967 people on probation from December 31, 2019, to January 1, 2020.

Wisconsin: The state probation agency, overseeing the entire state probation population, was unable to report either the total number of exits or the total number of entries to probation during 2020.

PAROLE: EXPLANATORY NOTES, 2020

Each year, changes in legislation or offender management systems require states to alter previously submitted data or the data they can currently submit. The Bureau of Justice Statistics documents these changes as reported by the respondents.

Alaska: Alaska supervises probation and parole in a combined program. The state agency was unable to report probation and parole data separately, so both populations were reported in the probation survey. The January 1, 2020, and December 31, 2020, parole population counts were imputed based on the December 31, 2019, parole population count.

Arizona: Reporting changes from 2019 to 2020—Data totals were estimates due to a transition to a new computerized database. This transition resulted in no data collected in January or February.

California: One of the reporting agencies did not provide complete data on entries and exits. Parole data for January 1, 2020, included 45,899 individuals on Post-Release Community Supervision or Mandatory Supervision. The parole population on December 31, 2020, included 55,216 individuals on Post-Release Community Supervision or Mandatory Supervision.

Louisiana: Reporting changes from 2019 to 2020—A revised program code was used to obtain information for the 2020 survey. This change in reporting resulted in a decrease of 4,701 people on parole from December 31, 2019, to January 1, 2020.

Oklahoma: Parole eligibility has accelerated in Oklahoma. On November 1, 2018, the general parole eligibility decreased from 33 percent of a sentence to 25 percent of a sentence, meaning inmates were serving one-sixth less time before becoming eligible for parole. This should have caused some compression in the numbers. Furthermore, the Oklahoma Pardon and Parole Board (PPB) is a separate agency with complete discretion over granting and denying parole in nonviolent cases. The governor has full discretion on violent cases after approval by a majority of the PPB.

Pennsylvania: Pennsylvania has two reporting units that provide counts for portions of the parole population. The Pennsylvania Board of Probation and Parole provides data on the state parole population; their report represented 39 percent of Pennsylvania's total parole population. Previously the Pennsylvania Department of Corrections provided data on the county parole population, but beginning in 2020 the Pennsylvania Commission on Crime and Delinquency assumed authority to collect that information; their report represented 61 percent of Pennsylvania's total parole population. This change in reporting resulted in a decrease of 21,346 people on parole from December 31, 2019, to January 1, 2020.

Vermont: Vermont did not report entries or exits for 2020.

West Virginia: Reporting changes from 2019 to 2020—West Virginia reported that the December 31, 2019, population count was incorrect. This change resulted in a decrease of 628 people on parole from December 31, 2019, to January 1, 2020.

IMPUTING FOR NON-REPORTING AGENCIES

BJS used the following methods to impute missing probation and parole data for key items, including the January 1 population, entries, and exits and the December 31 population.

Imputing the January 1 Probation Population

When the January 1 probation population was missing, the December 31 probation population from the last reported year going back to 2010 was carried forward. This method was used to estimate the January 1, 2018, probation population in 38 non-reporting counties and district agencies in Florida, Michigan, Montana, New Mexico, Ohio, and Washington. The January 1, 2018, population was imputed for 0.8percent of the total probation population. This method was used to estimate the January 1, 2017, probation population in 45 non-reporting counties and district agencies in Alabama, Florida, Kentucky,

Michigan, New Mexico, Ohio, and Washington. The January 1, 2017, population was imputed for 1.4 percent of the total probation population.

Imputing the December 31 Probation Population

When counts were missing for the December 31 probation population, the missing values were imputed by assuming no intra-year growth and setting the missing value to the January 1 population size.

This method was used to estimate the December 31, 2018, probation population in 37 non-reporting counties and district agencies in Florida, Kentucky, Michigan, Montana, New Mexico, Ohio, and Washington. The December 31, 2018, population was imputed for 0.9 percent of the total probation population. This method was used to estimate the December 31, 2017, probation population in 48 non-reporting counties and district agencies in Alabama, Alaska, Florida, Kentucky, Michigan, New Mexico, Ohio, and Washington. The December 31, 2017, population was imputed for 1.7 percent of the total probation population.

Imputing the January 1 Parole Population

When the January 1 parole population was missing, the December 31 probation population from the prior year was carried forward. This method was used to estimate the January 1 parole population in both 2018 and 2017 for Alaska, which represented 0.2 percent of the total parole population.

Imputing the December 31 Parole Population

When counts were missing for the December 31 parole population, the missing values were imputed by adding to (or subtracting from) the January 1 parole population to estimate population change based on what was observed in the prior year. The intra-year change in population from January 1 to December 31 of the prior year was multiplied by the January 1 reporting-year count to estimate the reporting-year population change. This method was used to estimate the December 31 parole population for Alaska, which represented 0.2 percent of the total parole population in 2018 and 2017.

Imputing Parole Entries

To estimate parole entries for agencies that did not report these data in the reporting year but did report in the prior year, BJS calculated the ratio of entries in the prior year to the agency's parole population on January 1 of the prior year and applied that ratio to the agency's January 1 population of the reporting year. This method was used to estimate parole entries in Alaska, Vermont, and Wisconsin. Total entries were imputed for 1.7 percent of the entering parole population in 2018 and 1.9 percent in 2017.

Imputing Probation and Parole Exits

A single method was used to estimate exits from probation that were not imputed with the first method noted above and for all parole agencies. For both probation and parole, BJS added each agency's estimated entries to that agency's population on January 1 and subtracted that estimate from the population on December 31.

For probation, this method was used for 46 non-reporting agencies in Colorado, Florida, Michigan, Ohio, Rhode Island, Vermont, Washington, and Wisconsin in 2018 and totaled 2.1 percent of the exiting probation population. In 2017, this method was used for 24 non-reporting agencies in Alaska, Colorado, Florida, Michigan, Ohio, Rhode Island, Vermont, Washington, and Wisconsin, totaling 2.3 percent of the exiting probation population.

For parole, this method was used in Alaska, Vermont, and Wisconsin. Total exits were imputed for 1.8 percent of the exiting parole population in 2018 and 2.0 percent in 2017.

ESTIMATING CHANGE IN POPULATION COUNTS

Technically, the change in the probation and parole populations from the beginning of the year to the end of the year should equal the difference between entries and exits during the year. However, those numbers may not be equal. Some probation and parole information systems track the number of cases that enter and exit community supervision, not the number of offenders. This means that entries and exits may include case counts as opposed to counts of individuals, while the beginning and yearend population counts represent individuals. Some individuals are being supervised for more than one charge or case simultaneously. Additionally, all of the data on entries and exits may not have been logged into the information systems, or the information systems may not have fully processed all of the data before the data were submitted to BJS.

Jurisdiction counts reported for January 1 may differ from December 31 counts reported in the previous year. As a result, the direction of change based on yearend data could be in the opposite direction of the within-year change.

TYPES OF FEDERAL OFFENDERS UNDER COMMUNITY SUPERVISION

Since the Sentencing Reform Act of 1984 was enacted on November 1, 1987, offenders sentenced to federal prison are no longer eligible for parole but are required to serve a term of supervised release following release from prison. Those sentenced to prison prior to November 1, 1987, continue to be eligible for parole, as do persons violating laws of the District of Columbia, military offenders, and foreign treaty transfer offenders. (See http://www.uscourts.gov/news/TheThirdBranch/11-05-01/Parole_in_the_Federal_Probation_System.aspx.)

In 2008, the Annual Parole Survey included a new type of entry-to-parole category—term of supervised release—to better classify the large majority of entries to parole reported by the federal system. It is a fixed period of release to the community that follows a fixed period of incarceration based on a determinate sentencing statute. Both are determined by a judge at the time of sentencing. For details about estimating methods used to analyze national trends for all types of entry to parole, see *Probation and Parole in the United States, 2010* (NCJ 236019, BJS web, November 2011).

The Sentencing Reform Act also required the adoption and use of sentencing guidelines, which took effect on the same day. Many offenses for which probation had been the typical sentence prior to this date, particularly property and regulatory offenses, subsequently resulted in sentences to prison. Changes in how federal o enders are supervised in the community were first described in the BJS report *Federal Offenders Under Community Supervision, 1987-96* (NCJ 168636, BJS web, August 1998) and updated in *Federal Criminal Case Processing, 2002: With Trends 1982-2002, Reconciled Data* (NCJ 207447, BJS web, January 2005).

EFFECTS OF COVID-19 ON COMMUNITY SUPERVISION POPULATION

In response to the COVID-19 pandemic, BJS added a special addendum to the 2020 Annual Survey of Probation and Annual Survey of Parole to measure the impact of this public health emergency on community corrections. The nine-question addendum collected information on the effects of the COVID-19 pandemic on probation and parole agencies' populations, policies, and procedures. BJS collected quarterly population numbers, a midyear count of entries and exits, and information on closures and changes in supervision techniques during 2020.

Quarterly probation data were reported by 69 percent of agencies in 46 states and the District of Columbia for 2020. The reporting jurisdictions account for 83 percent of the total December 31, 2020, probation population of 3,053,700 persons. Quarterly probation population was not reported from the U.S. federal system, Minnesota, North Carolina, Oregon, or Virginia. Some agencies in Colorado, Florida, Idaho, Michigan, Missouri, Montana, New Mexico, Ohio, Tennessee, and Washington were unable to report quarterly data.

The probation population in reporting agencies fell in each of the first three quarters of 2020, while slightly increasing in the fourth. The largest drop occurred in the second quarter, from April 1 to June 30, 2020, with a 5 percent decrease among reporting agencies. Agencies reported smaller changes during the second half of 2020: a decrease of 1 percent between July 1 and September 30 and an increase of less than 1 percent between October 1 and December 31. About half of responding agencies reported that they suspended all supervision and closed their agencies for a period of time during 2020.

Quarterly data were reported by 90 percent of parole agencies in 47 states for 2020. The reported population represents 70 percent of the total December 31, 2020, parole population of 862,100 persons. Quarterly populations were not reported by the U.S. federal system, Alaska, North Carolina, Oregon, or Virginia. Quarterly populations were unavailable for a portion of the population in California and Pennsylvania. Quarterly changes to the parole population also saw the largest change in the second quarter, with a less than 2 percent increase from April 1 to June 30, 2020. Responding agencies reported changes of less than 1 percent for other quarters. About a fourth of responding parole agencies reported a suspension of reporting requirements during at least one quarter of 2020.

Recidivism of Prisoners Released in 24 States in 2008: A 10-Year Follow-Up Period (2008–2018)

HIGHLIGHTS

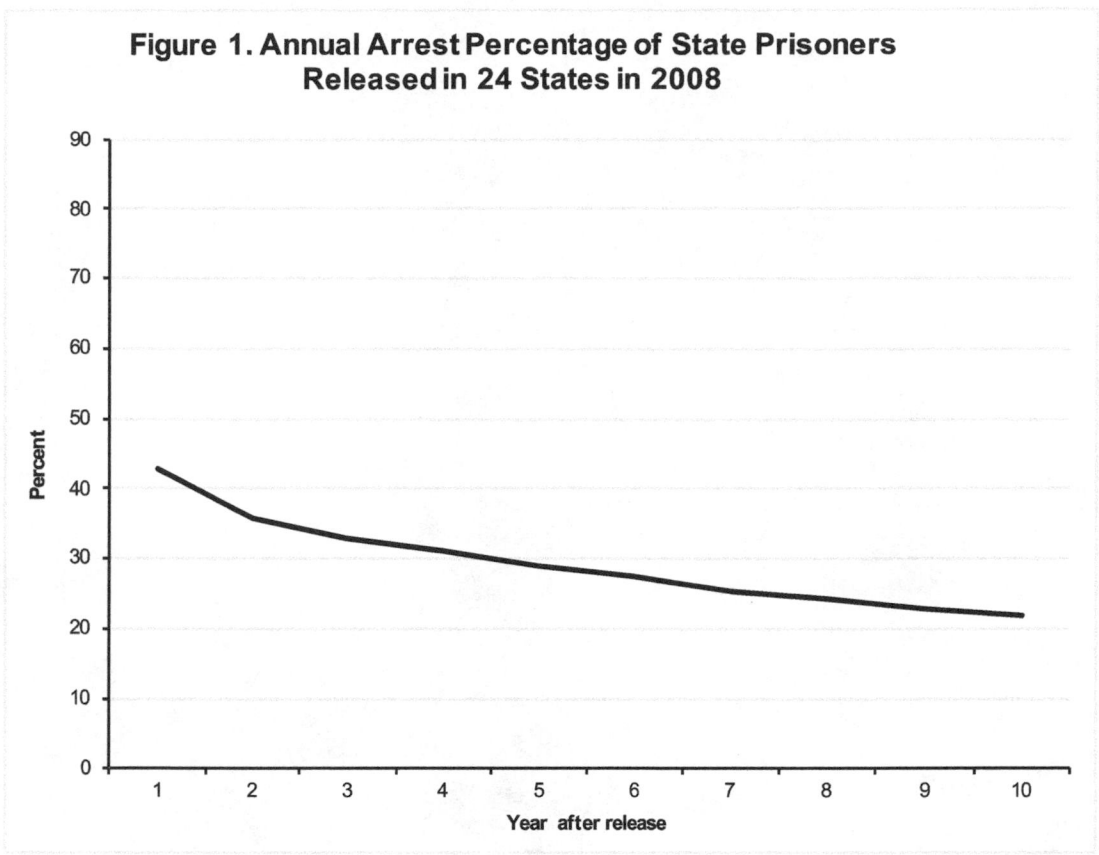

Figure 1. Annual Arrest Percentage of State Prisoners Released in 24 States in 2008

- The 24 states studied accounted for 69 percent of all state prisoners released nationwide in 2008; the study randomly sampled about 73,600 released prisoners to represent the approximately 409,300 state prisoners released across 24 states in 2008.

- Approximately 409,300 state prisoners released in 2008 had 2.2 million arrests during the 10-year period; approximately 75 percent of drug offenders released from prison in 2008 were arrested for a nondrug crime within 10 years.

- About 61 percent of prisoners released in 2008 returned to prison within 10 years for a parole or probation violation or a new sentence.

- An estimated 82 percent of released prisoners were arrested at least once in the 10 years following release, with approximately 43 percent arrested the first year, 29 percent in the fifth year, and 22 percent in the tenth year.

- Ninety percent of prisoners who were age 24 or younger at the time of release in 2008 were arrested within 10 years of release. A smaller percentage of those who were ages 25 to 39 (85 percent) and age 40 or older (75 percent) at the time of release were arrested within 10 years of release.

Table 1. Characteristics of Prisoners Released in 24 States in 2008

(Percent; number.)

Characteristic	Percent
Total	100.0
Sex	
Male	89.0
Female	11.0
Race/Hispanic origin	
White[1]	39.5
Black/African American[1]	37.1
Hispanic	21.0
American Indian/Alaska Native[1]	1.2
Asian/Native Hawaiian/Other Pacific Islander[1]	0.6
Other[1,2]	0.6
Age at release	
24 years or younger	15.3
25 to 39 years	50.3
25 to 29 years	20.5
30 to 34 years	15.9
35 to 39 years	14.0
40 years and over	34.3
40 to 54 years	30.5
55 to 64 years	3.3
65 years and over	0.6
Median (years)	34
Mean	35.4
Type of prison admission	
New court commitment[3]	66.4
Conditional release violation[4]	31.7
Other admission	1.9
Type of release	
Conditional[5]	77.5
Unconditional[6]	22.5
Number of released prisoners	409,300

NOTE: Data on prisoners' sex were reported for 100% of cases; age at release, for over 99%; race or ethnicity, for over 99%; type of prison admission, for 98%; and type of prison release, for 98%. Percentages exclude missing data. The number of released prisoners is rounded to the nearest 100. Details may not sum to totals due to rounding.
[1]Excludes persons of Hispanic/Latino origin (e.g., White refers to non-Hispanic Whites and Black refers to non-Hispanic Blacks).
[2]Includes persons of two or more races or other unspecified races.
[3]Includes admissions of persons convicted and sentenced by a court.
[4]Includes admissions of persons who returned to prison after being released to community supervision.
[5]Includes releases of persons to community supervision.
[6]Includes expirations of sentences, commutations, and other releases not followed by community supervision.

Table 2. Prisoners Released in 24 States in 2008 Who Were Arrested Within 9 Years Following Release, by Most Serious Commitment Offense and Types of Post-Release Arrest Charges

(Percent.)

Most serious commitment offense	Any offense	Violent post-release arrest offense					Property post-release arrest offense				Other post-release arrest offense	
		Total violent[1]	Homicide	Rape/ sexual assault	Robbery	Assault	Total property[2]	Burglary	Larceny/ motor vehicle theft	Fraud/ forgery	Drug	Public order
All released..........................	81.9	39.6	1.2	2.5	7.4	31.3	47.4	14.5	28.9	16.0	47.1	68.3
Violent[1]................................	76.7	44.2	1.7	3.6	8.5	35.4	40.1	11.2	22.1	11.8	36.3	65.1
Homicide..........................	57.4	28.1	2.3	1.8	4.0	21.9	22.9	5.2	11.5	5.8	25.1	45.9
Rape/sexual assault..........	62.8	25.8	0.5	6.3	2.7	17.5	21.2	4.9	10.4	6.6	17.4	55.8
Robbery	82.5	47.5	1.9	3.0	15.6	36.0	48.9	14.3	31.5	15.2	45.9	67
Assault..............................	82.0	52.8	2.2	3.0	7.4	45.0	45.7	13.4	22.9	13.1	39.5	70.9
Property..............................	86.7	39.7	0.9	2.3	8.4	30.8	63.6	24.1	44.0	23.3	48.3	72.1
Burglary	87.4	41.4	0.9	2.7	8.5	32.4	62.9	30.9	42.0	19.3	46.8	72.3
Larceny/motor vehicle theft	87.6	40.2	1.2	2.5	10.0	30.3	66.7	22.4	49.7	24.0	51.9	73.8
Fraud/forgery	82.2	31.7	0.7	1.4	5.4	25.3	59.8	12.9	38.9	33.5	42.4	65.5
Drug	81.4	34.8	1.1	1.9	6.2	27.7	40.3	10.0	22.5	13.9	57.6	65.8
Public order	82.1	41.4	1.3	2.5	6.2	33.0	42.2	10.5	23.2	12.9	41.4	70.9

NOTE: Detail may not sum to total due to rounding. The numerator for each percentage is the number of persons arrested for that offense during the 9-year follow-up period, and the denominator is the number released after serving time for each type of commitment offense. Persons could have been in prison for more than one offense, the most serious of which is reported. Details may not sum to totals because a person may be arrested more than once for different types of offenses and each arrest may involve more than one offense.
[1]Includes other violent offenses that are not shown separately.
[2]Includes other property offenses that are not shown separately.

Table 3. Most Serious Commitment Offense of Prisoners Released in 24 States in 2008

(Number; percent.)

Most serious commitment offense	Percent
Number of released prisoners..	409,300
Violent..	24.5
Homicide...	1.8
Rape/sexual assault..	4.3
Robbery	7.0
Assault..	8.9
Other violent...	2.5
Property...	29.6
Burglary..	11.1
Larceny/motor vehicle theft	9.7
Fraud/forgery..	4.9
Other property	3.7
Drug...	30.3
Possession..	11.3
Trafficking...	12.5
Other drug..	6.4
Public order	15.7
Weapons..	4.3
Other public order...	11.4

NOTE: For prisoners serving time for more than one offense, the most serious offense is the one with the longest sentence length. The number of released prisoners is rounded to the nearest 100. Details may not sum to totals due to rounding.

Table 4. Prior Criminal History of State Prisoners Released in 24 States in 2008

(Number; percent.)

Characteristic	Percent
Number of released prisoners..	100.0
Prior arrests[1]	
4 or fewer	21.5
2 or fewer	9.3
3 to 4..	12.3
5 to 9..	29.6
10 or more..	48.9
Median arrests	9
Mean arrests	12.1
Prior convictions[2]	
Median arrests	5
Mean arrests	5.8
Age at first arrest	
17 years or younger	29.4
18 to 19 years	32.9
20 to 24 years	23.0
25 to 29 years..	7.6
30 to 34 years..	3.6
35 to 39 years..	1.9
40 years or over..	1.7

NOTE: Data on prisonersi age at first arrest were reported for over 99% of cases. Some juvenile offenses may not be accounted for in the analysis for persons not prosecuted as an adult or due to state laws and practices regarding record sealing or expungement. Percentages exclude missing data. Details may not sum to totals due to rounding.
[1]Includes arrests in the prisoners' criminal history and the arrest that resulted in the imprisonment.
[2]Includes convictions prior to the prisonersi date of release in 2008 and the conviction that resulted in the imprisonment.

Table 5. Cumulative Percent of State Prisoners Released in 24 States in 2008 Who Were Arrested Following Release, by Sex, Race, Ethnicity, Age at Release, and Year Following Release

(Number; percent.)

Characteristic	Number of released prisoners	Year 1	Year 2	Year 3	Year 4	Year 5	Year 6	Year 7	Year 8	Year 9	Year 10
All released prisoners	409,300	42.9	58.0	66.2	71.2	74.8	77.3	79.0	80.2	81.1	81.9
Sex											
Male*	364,200	43.9	59.2	67.3	72.3	75.9	78.3	79.9	81.0	82.0	82.7
Female[A]..	45,100	34.4	48.8	57.0	62.3	66.3	69.6	71.6	73.2	74.4	75.5
Race/ethnicity											
White[1]*	161,400	39.6	54.8	63.2	68.4	72.3	75.0	76.9	78.3	79.4	80.2
Black/African American[1,A]	151,700	45.2	61.4	69.7	75.1	78.6	81.1	82.7	83.7	84.7	85.6
Hispanic[A]	86,100	44.2	57.8	65.4	69.6	72.8	75.3	76.7	77.5	78.3	78.9
American Indian/Alaska Native[1,A]	4,800	50.7	65.7	72.8	76.3	78.8	80.8	82.1	83.1	84.3	84.7
Asian/Native Hawaiian/Other Pacific Islander[1]	2,300	41.3	57.2	63.5	67.2	68.9	70.2	70.8	73.2	73.8	74.4
Other[1,2]	2,600	44.6	57.4	63.0	67.1	72.4	74.3	74.4	77.0	77.2	77.3
Age at release											
24 years or younger*	62,700	49.8	66.8	75.0	79.5	82.7	85.2	86.8	87.8	88.6	89.5
25 to 39 years[A]..	206,000	44.1	60.3	68.7	73.8	77.6	80.0	81.6	82.9	83.9	84.7
40 years or older[A]..	140,600	37.9	50.8	58.6	63.7	67.2	69.9	71.6	72.8	73.7	74.5
40 to 54 years	124,600	39.2	52.6	60.7	66.0	69.6	72.3	74.1	75.4	76.3	77.2
55 to 64 years	13,600	28.5	37.3	43.6	47.2	49.9	52.6	54.1	54.9	55.6	56.1
65 years and over	2,300	22.9	33.6	36.0	37.3	38.4	38.5	39.5	39.7	39.9	40.1

NOTE: Data on prisonersi sex were reported for 100% of cases; age at release, for over 99%; and race or ethnicity, for over 99%. The number of released prisoners is rounded to the nearest 100. Details may not sum to totals due to rounding.
* = Comparison group.
A = Difference with comparison group for percentages is significant at the 95% confidence level. The significance tests were not conducted on age subcategories.
[1]Excludes persons of Hispanic/Latino origin (e.g., White refers to non-Hispanic Whites and Black refers to non-Hispanic Blacks).
[2]Includes persons of two or more races or unspecified race.

Table 6. Cumulative Percent of State Prisoners Released in 24 States in 2008 Who Were Arrested Following Release, by Most Serious Commitment Offense Type of Prison Admission, and Year Following Release

(Number; percent.)

Characteristic	Number of released prisoners	Year 1	Year 2	Year 3	Year 4	Year 5	Year 6	Year 7	Year 8	Year 9	Year 10
All released prisoners	409,300	42.9	58.0	66.2	71.2	74.8	77.3	79.0	80.2	81.1	81.9
Most serious commitment offense											
Violent	100,100	38.4	52.6	60.7	65.6	69.4	71.8	73.5	74.8	75.7	76.7
Homicide[1]	7,300	22.1	33.5	40.4	45.1	48.8	51.3	53.4	54.9	56.3	57.4
Murder/nonnegligent manslaughter	4,700	21.1	32.5	39.6	44.1	47.6	50.1	52.1	53.8	55.1	56.1
Negligent manslaughter	2,400	24.3	35.9	42.3	47.2	51.1	53.9	56.1	57.3	58.7	60.0
Rape/sexual assault	17,600	27.6	39.2	45.9	50.5	54.1	56.5	58.7	60.4	61.7	62.8
Robbery	28,700	40.2	56.6	64.6	70.4	75.2	77.8	79.6	80.6	81.4	82.5
Assault	36,400	44.8	59.6	68.0	72.7	75.7	77.7	79.1	80.4	81.2	82.0
Other violent	10,100	41.3	52.7	63.2	66.9	72.2	74.7	76.3	77.3	78.1	79.6
Property	121,000	49.3	64.6	72.5	77.3	80.8	83.0	84.2	85.2	86.1	86.7
Burglary	45,600	47.7	63.8	72.0	77.6	81.6	83.7	85.1	86.1	87.0	87.4
Larceny/motor vehicle†theft	39,900	54.7	68.7	76.1	79.6	82.7	84.6	85.4	86.1	86.9	87.6
Fraud/forgery	20,200	41.7	56.8	65.3	70.7	73.9	76.7	78.5	79.9	81.1	82.2
Other property	15,200	49.9	67.2	74.0	79.4	82.9	84.8	86.0	86.7	87.7	88.0
Drug	123,900	40.7	56.2	64.8	70.0	73.6	76.4	78.2	79.5	80.5	81.4
Possession	46,500	44.6	59.8	67.8	72.7	76.1	78.9	80.6	81.7	82.4	83.0
Trafficking	51,300	40.7	56.0	64.5	69.7	73.3	76.0	77.6	78.8	79.9	80.9
Other drug	26,100	33.8	50.6	59.9	65.8	69.9	72.8	75.1	76.9	78.2	79.4
Public order	64,300	41.8	57.6	65.8	70.7	74.1	77.2	79.3	80.4	81.5	82.1
Weapons	17,500	46.6	64.7	72.5	76.8	79.7	82.5	84.7	85.7	86.9	87.4
Other public order	46,900	40.0	54.9	63.3	68.5	72.1	75.2	77.3	78.5	79.4	80.1
Type of prison admission[2]											
New court commitment	266,600	36.8	52.1	61.0	66.3	70.2	73.0	74.9	76.2	77.3	78.3
Conditional release violation....................	127,400	56.3	71.3	78.0	82.1	85.2	87.0	88.0	89.0	89.6	90.0

NOTE: For prisoners serving time for more than one offense, the most serious offense is the one with the longest sentence length. Data on prisoners' type of prison admission were reported for 98 percent of cases. The number of released prisoners is rounded to the nearest 100.
[1]Includes unspecified homicide offenses that are not shown separately.
[2]Excludes missing data.

Table 7. Cumulative Percent of State Prisoners Released in 24 States in 2008 Who Were Arrested Following Release, by Number of Prior Arrests, Age at First Arrest, and Year Following Release

(Number; percent.)

Characteristic	Number of released prisoners	Year 1	Year 2	Year 3	Year 4	Year 5	Year 6	Year 7	Year 8	Year 9	Year 10
All released prisoners	409,300	42.9	58.0	66.2	71.2	74.8	77.3	79.0	80.2	81.1	81.9
Number of prior arrests[1]											
4 or fewer*	88,100	24.3	38.0	46.5	52.3	56.9	60.3	62.6	64.3	65.9	67.2
2 or fewer	37,900	19.9	31.6	38.8	44.3	48.4	51.7	54.5	56.4	58.3	59.8
3 to 4	50,200	27.6	42.8	52.2	58.4	63.3	66.7	68.7	70.3	71.6	72.8
5 to 9^A	121,100	35.9	52.8	62.1	68.0	72.3	75.3	77.4	78.8	80.0	80.9
10 or more^A	200,100	55.2	70.0	77.4	81.4	84.2	86.1	87.2	88.0	88.5	89
Age at first arrest[2]											
17 years or younger*	119,900	51.8	67.8	76.0	80.6	83.8	86.1	87.3	88.2	89.0	89.7
18 to 19 years^A	134100	46.0	62.2	70.3	75.3	79.3	81.6	83.3	84.3	85.3	86
20 to 24 years^A	93,900	37.2	52.3	61.0	66.5	70.2	73.1	75.1	76.6	77.6	78.6
25 to 29 years^A	30,900	30.8	44.6	53.1	57.6	61.7	64.6	66.7	68.3	69.4	70.2
30 to 34 years^A	14,700	25.7	36.1	43.8	48.5	52.9	56.4	58.5	60.1	61.6	62.8
35 to 39 years^A	7,600	20.3	28.7	35.4	41.5	44.9	47.2	48.9	50.7	52.6	54
40 years and over^A	7,000	16.3	24.2	30.1	33.1	35.1	36.6	38.3	38.8	40.6	41.3

NOTE: Data on prisoners' age at first arrest were reported for over 99% of cases. Some juvenile offenses may not be accounted for in the analysis for persons not prosecuted as an adult or due to state laws and practices regarding record sealing or expungement. The number of released prisoners is rounded to the nearest 100.
*= Comparison group.
A = Difference with comparison group for percentages is significant at the 95% confidence level. The significance tests were not conducted on age subcategories.
[1]Includes arrests in the prisoners' criminal history and the arrest that resulted in the imprisonment.
[2]Excludes missing data.

Table 8. Cumulative Percent of State Prisoners Released in 18 States in 2008 Who Returned to Prison for a Probation or Parole Violation or an Arrest That Led to a New Sentence, by Sex, Race, Ethnicity, Age at Release, and Year Following Release

(Percent.)

Characteristic	Year 1	Year 2	Year 3	Year 4	Year 5	Year 6	Year 7	Year 8	Year 9	Year 10
All released prisoners	30.7	42.8	48.6	52.3	55.0	56.9	58.4	59.3	60.1	60.7
Sex										
Male*	31.7	44.2	50.1	53.9	56.6	58.5	60.0	61.0	61.8	62.4
Female[A]	22.9	31.6	36.3	39.3	41.5	43.6	44.8	45.8	46.5	47.2
Race/ethnicity										
White[1]*	28.6	40.0	46.1	50.0	52.8	54.7	56.1	57.2	58.1	58.7
Black/African American[1,A]	31.3	44.2	50.7	54.8	57.4	59.5	61.1	62.0	62.9	63.4
Hispanic[A]	33.1	45.0	49.6	52.6	55.0	56.8	58.1	58.9	59.5	60.0
American Indian/Alaska Native[1]	33.1	43.6	48.0	51.5	53.9	56.2	57.6	59.1	61.2	61.9
Asian/Native Hawaiian/Other Pacific Islander[1]	37.8	48.5	52.3	53.1	55.1	55.5	55.5	55.7	56.9	58.8
Other[1,2]	30.9	43.1	49.5	50.5	55.7	56.6	59.1	59.8	59.9	62.2
Age at release										
24 years or younger*	34.3	48.6	55.3	59.4	62.7	64.7	66.5	67.6	68.5	69.0
25 to 39 years[A]	31.6	44.3	50.2	54.3	57.1	59.3	60.9	61.9	62.9	63.5
40 years or older[A]	27.9	38.0	43.4	46.4	48.5	50.1	51.2	51.9	52.6	53.0
40 to 54 years	28.8	39.3	44.9	48.0	50.2	51.9	53.1	53.9	54.6	55.1
55 to 64 years	20.4	28.4	32.3	34.5	35.8	36.6	37.2	37.4	37.5	37.7
65 years and over	25.5	28.0	31.3	31.8	32.1	32.5	32.6	32.7	32.7	32.7

NOTE: Estimates are based on prisoners released across the 18 states that could provide the necessary data on persons returned to prison for a probation or parole violation or an arrest that led to a new sentence.
* = Comparison group.
A = Difference with comparison group for percentages is significant at the 95% confidence level. The significance tests were not conducted on age subcategories.
[1]Excludes persons of Hispanic/Latino origin (e.g., White refers to non-Hispanic Whites and Black refers to non-Hispanic Blacks).
[2]Includes persons of two or more races or unspecified race.

Table 9. Post-Release Arrests of State Prisoners Released in 24 States in 2008, by Year of Arrest

(Number; percent.)

Year	Number of arrests	Percent of arrests
Total	2,197,000	100.0
Year 1	301,000	13.7
Year 2	254,000	11.6
Year 3	235,000	10.7
Year 4	229,000	10.4
Year 5	224,000	10.2
Year 6	215,000	9.8
Year 7	199,000	9.0
Year 8	188,000	8.5
Year 9	184,000	8.4
Year 10	169,000	7.7

NOTE: Persons could have been arrested more than once for different types of offenses, and each arrest may involve more than one offense. The number of post-release arrests is rounded to the nearest 1,000. Details may not sum to totals due to rounding.

Table 10. Percent of State Prisoners released in 24 States in 2008 Who Were Arrested Within 10 Years Following Release, by Type of Post-Release Arrest Offense

(Number; percent.)

Post-release arrest offense	Percent
All released prisoners	409,300
Violent	39.6
Homicide	1.2
Rape/sexual assault	2.5
Robbery	7.4
Assault	31.3
Other violent	13.5
Property	47.4
Burglary	14.5
Larceny/motor vehicle theft	28.9
Fraud/forgery	16.0
Other property	28.2
Drug	47.1
Possession	31.7
Trafficking	17.5
Other drug	28.3
Public order	68.3
Weapons	14.4
DUI/DWI	14.2
Other public order	63.4

NOTE: Details may not sum to totals because a person may be arrested for more than one offense. The number of released prisoners is rounded to the nearest 100.

Table 11. Cumulative Percent of State Prisoners Released in 18 States in 2008 Who Were Arrested Following Release for a Type of Offense That Was the Same as or Different from the Most Serious Commitment Offense

(Percent.)

Characteristic	Year 1	Year 2	Year 3	Year 4	Year 5	Year 6	Year 7	Year 8	Year 9	Year 10
Any arrest after release										
All released prisoners	42.9	58.0	66.2	71.2	74.8	77.3	79.0	80.2	81.1	81.9
Violent*	38.4	52.6	60.7	65.6	69.4	71.8	73.5	74.8	75.7	76.7
Property^A	49.3	64.6	72.5	77.3	80.8	83.0	84.2	85.2	86.1	86.7
Drug^A	40.7	56.2	64.8	70.0	73.6	76.4	78.2	79.5	80.5	81.4
Public order^A	41.8	57.6	65.8	70.7	74.1	77.2	79.3	80.4	81.5	82.1
Arrest after release for violent offense										
All released prisoners	8.8	15.2	20.6	24.9	28.3	31.4	33.9	36.1	38.0	39.6
Violent*	10.4	17.8	24.4	29.3	33.2	36.1	38.5	40.7	42.6	44.2
Property^A	8.6	15.1	20.0	24.5	28.0	31.2	33.7	36.3	38.2	39.7
Drug^A	7.3	12.4	17.0	21.1	24.2	27.1	29.5	31.4	33.1	34.8
Public order^A	9.7	16.8	22.4	26.2	29.5	32.9	35.7	38.0	39.8	41.4
Arrest after release for same type of offense as most serious commitment offense[1]										
All released prisoners	20.0	30.5	37.8	43.3	47.6	50.5	53.0	55.0	56.7	58.2
Violent*	10.4	17.8	24.4	29.3	33.2	36.1	38.5	40.7	42.6	44.2
Property^A	24.1	35.0	42.5	48.6	53.4	56.4	58.8	60.6	62.2	63.6
Drug^A	18.2	29.4	36.7	42.2	46.4	49.6	52.1	54.3	56.0	57.6
Public order^A	30.5	43.9	51.8	57.5	61.1	64.0	66.5	68.3	70.0	70.9
Arrest after release for different type of offense as most serious commitment offense[1]										
All released prisoners	35.3	49.3	57.3	62.7	66.8	69.7	71.8	73.4	74.7	75.8
Violent*	35.6	49.0	56.4	61.5	65.4	67.9	69.6	71.1	72.2	73.3
Property^A	41.0	55.9	64.2	69.7	73.7	76.4	78.4	79.7	81.0	82.0
Drug^A	34.1	48.0	56.3	61.8	65.7	68.8	71.0	72.6	74.1	75.2
Public order^A	26.5	40.2	47.8	53.2	58.0	62.1	64.6	66.6	68.0	69.2

NOTE: For prisoners serving time for more than one offense, the most serious offense is the one with the longest sentence length. Each arrest may include more than one type of offense. "Type of offense" refers to the categories of violent, property, drug, and public order.
* = Comparison group.
A = Difference with comparison group for percentages is significant at the 95% confidence level. The significance tests were not conducted on age subcategories.
[1]Percentages for "arrest after release for same type of offense" and "arrest after release for different type of offense" do not sum to the "any arrest after release" category because categories overlap.

Table 12. Time Served Before First Release Among State Prisoners Released in 24 States in 2008, by Most Serious Commitment Offense

(Percent; months.)

Time served in prison	All first releases	Most serious commitment offense			
		Violent	Property	Drug	Public order
Total	100.0	100.0	100.0	100.0	100.0
6 months or less	19.8	11.4	24.1	21.9	21.4
7 to 12 months	23.7	13.2	26.9	27.6	26.7
13 to 18 months	14.5	10.8	15.3	16.3	15.2
19 to 24 months	10.8	10.3	9.9	10.9	12.6
25 to 36 months	11.3	12.6	10.8	11.1	10.7
37 to 60 months	10.2	16.5	7.9	8.1	8.7
61 to 80 months	3.4	6.9	2.5	2.2	2.2
81 months or more	6.3	18.3	2.6	2.0	2.4
Median (months)	15 mos.	29 mos.	13 mos.	13 mos.	14 mos.

NOTE: First releases include prisoners released in 2008 for the first time since beginning their sentence and exclude those released under the same sentence who returned to prison for a conditional release violation. For prisoners serving time for more than one offense, the most serious offense is the one with the longest sentence length. Estimates exclude prisoners missing data on type of prison admission. Data on prisoners' time served were reported for 100% of new court commitments. Details may not sum to totals due to rounding.

Table 13. Percent of State Prisoners Released in 24 States in 2008 Who Were Arrested Within 10 Years, by Most Serious Commitment Offense and Median Time Served in Prison Before First Release

(Months; percent.)

Most serious commitment offense	Median time served in prison (months)	Percent of released prisoners who were arrested within 10 years after serving:	
		Less than the median time served before first release*	More than the median time served before first release
All first releases	15	81.1	75.5 A
Violent[1]	29	78.3	66.4 A
Murder/nonnegligent manslaughter	129	57.0	42.5 A
Rape/sexual assault	49	63.3	51.9 A
Robbery	38	84.7	75.4 A
Assault	19	83.2	75.1 A
Property[2]	13	84.9	83.0
Burglary	15	84.5	86.3
Larceny/motor vehicle theft	11	85.6	82.1
Fraud/forgery	12	82.1	77.9 A
Drug	13	79.4	75.3 A
Public order	14	79.4	78.2

NOTE: First releases include prisoners released in 2008 for the first time since beginning their sentence and exclude those released under the same sentence who returned to prison for a conditional release violation. For prisoners serving time for more than one offense, the most serious offense is the one with the longest sentence length. Estimates exclude prisoners missing data on type of prison admission. Data on prisoners' time served were reported for 100% of new court commitments. Time served was rounded to the nearest month.
* = Comparison group.
A = Difference with comparison group is significant at the 95% confidence level.
[1]Includes other violent offenses that are not shown separately.
[2]Includes other property offenses that are not shown separately.

METHODOLOGY

SAMPLING

This study estimates the recidivism patterns of persons released in 2008 from state prisons across 24 states. States were included if the state departments of corrections (DOCs) provided the prisoner records and the FBI or state identification numbers of the released prisoners for the study. The prisoner records and identification numbers were collected through the National Corrections Reporting Program (NCRP), which is administered by the Bureau of Justice Statistics (BJS). The identification numbers were needed to obtain criminal history data from the FBI and state repositories on the released prisoners. The prisoner records included information on each prisoner's sex, race, ethnicity, date of birth, commitment offenses, sentence length, type of prison admission and release, and date of release.

The 24 states in the study were Alabama, Arizona, Arkansas, California, Colorado, Florida, Georgia, Hawaii, Iowa, Louisiana, Michigan, Missouri, Nebraska, New Jersey, New York, North Dakota, Oklahoma, Oregon, Pennsylvania, South Carolina, Texas, Washington, Wisconsin, and Wyoming. These states were responsible for 69 percent of all persons released from state prisons in 2008 nationwide.

The study excludes prisoners who were sentenced to less than 1 year, were transferred to the custody of another authority, died in prison, were released on bond, were released to participate in an appeal of a case, escaped from prison, or were absent without official leave. When a prisoner was released multiple times in the same state during 2008, the first release during the year was used for the study.

A stratified random sample of all prisoners eligible for the study was selected. All prisoners released after serving time for homicide, rape, or sexual assault were included in the sample. Within each state, prisoners released after serving time for other offenses were sorted by the county in which the sentence was imposed, race or ethnicity, age, and most serious commitment offense. Male and female prisoners were sampled separately from each state at sizes that yielded estimates with equal variance to increase the sample of female prisoners and improve the precision of their recidivism estimates. Each prisoner in the sample was assigned a weight based on the probability of selection within the state.

COLLECTING AND PROCESSING CRIMINAL HISTORY DATA FOR RECIDIVISM RESEARCH

BJS used the state and FBI identification numbers to collect criminal history data on released prisoners through the FBI's Interstate Identification Index (III) via the International Justice and Public Safety Network (Nlets), which is a computer-based network responsible for interstate transmissions of federal and state criminal history records. After BJS received approval from the FBI's Institutional Review Board to conduct this recidivism study, Nlets transmitted the identification numbers of sampled prisoners to the FBI's III system to collect criminal history data on behalf of BJS. To conduct this recidivism study with a 10-year follow-up period, criminal history data on the prisoners released in 2008 were collected in 2019.

The criminal history data collected on prisoners released in 24 states included arrests and dispositions, from state and federal criminal justice agencies across the 50 states and the District of Columbia, prior to and following release from prison in 2008. Nlets parsed fields from individual criminal history records into a relational database with a uniform record layout consisting of state- and federal-specific numeric codes and text descriptions (e.g., criminal statutes and case outcome information). BJS assessed the accuracy and completeness of the criminal history data, which included an examination of the identification numbers that failed to match a record in the FBI's III. BJS also compared individual identifiers in the NCRP data to those reported in the criminal history data to ensure the demographic information was accurate and complete.

BJS standardized the content of the relational database into a uniform coding structure to support analysis. During data processing and analysis, the impact of varying criminal history reporting practices on overall recidivism estimates were minimized. For example, administrative records (e.g., criminal registrations or issuances of a warrant) and procedural records (e.g., transfers of a suspect to another jurisdiction) that did not refer to an actual arrest were identified and removed from the criminal history data. Among traffic offenses, only vehicular manslaughter, driving under the influence or driving while intoxicated (DUI/DWI), and hit-and-run offenses were included in this report because state criminal history data vary widely in their coverage of other traffic offenses.

This study used death information from the FBI's III to identify individuals who died during the 10-year follow-up period. BJS removed from its recidivism analysis about 600 prisoners who died during the 10-year follow-up period from among the approximately 77,300 released prisoners who were originally sampled for this study.

Among the approximately 76,700 prisoners in the final sample, excluding those who were deceased, BJS obtained criminal history data on approximately 73,600 (95.9 percent) prisoners during the follow-up period. BJS did not receive criminal history data on about 3,100 prisoners because either the state DOCs were unable to provide their FBI or state identification number or the prisoner had an identification number that did not link to a criminal history record. To ensure the recidivism statistics were representative of the approximately 76,700 prisoners in the analysis, BJS developed weighting-class adjustments to account for prisoners without criminal history information and for nonresponse error.

To create the statistical adjustments, the approximately 76,700 sampled prisoners were stratified into groups with the same categories of sex, age at release, race or ethnicity, and most serious commitment offense. Within each subgroup, statistical weights were applied to data for the approximately 73,600 prisoners with criminal history information, so their data could represent the approximately 3,100 prisoners without criminal history information. The adjusted weights for the final sample of about 73,600 prisoners were used to produce recidivism estimates representative of the approximately 409,300 persons released from prison across the 24 states in 2008.

This study was based on a sample, not a complete enumeration, so the estimates are subject to sampling error. One measure of the sampling error associated with an estimate is the standard error. The standard error can vary from one estimate to the next. In general, an estimate with a smaller standard error provides a more accurate approximation of the true value than an estimate with a larger standard error. Estimates with relatively large standard errors should be interpreted with caution.

BJS conducted tests to determine whether differences in the estimates were statistically significant when the sampling error is taken into account. All differences discussed in this report are statistically significant at the 95 percent confidence level, unless noted otherwise.

RECIDIVISM DEFINITIONS

Cumulative arrest percentage is the percentage of released prisoners who were arrested at least once during the follow-up period. For example, the cumulative arrest percentage for Year 3 is the percentage of prisoners who had at least one arrest during the first, second, or third years following their release.

Annual arrest percentage is the percentage of released prisoners who were arrested at least once during a particular year within the follow-up period. The denominator for each percentage from Years 1 through 10 is the total number of prisoners released in the 24 states during 2008. The numerator is the number of former prisoners arrested during the particular year, regardless of whether they had been arrested during a prior year.

Volume of arrest offenses is the total number of arrest offenses among the released prisoners during the follow-up period. A former prisoner may have had multiple arrests for different types of offenses during the follow-up period, and a single arrest may have involved charges for more than one crime.

Cumulative percent with an arrest that led to conviction is based on the time from release to the first date of arrest that led to a conviction, not the date of the conviction. The arrests that occurred within the follow-up period were tracked for 4 more months after Year 10 to determine whether the case outcomes led to a subsequent conviction. This measure included prisoners released in 22 of the study's 24 states. Prisoners released in Alabama and Louisiana were excluded because the disposition information from these states were generally not linked to the associated arrest.

Cumulative percent who returned to prison is the percentage who had an arrest or a technical violation of a condition of release within 10 years of release from prison in 2008 that resulted in a return to prison. This measure incorporates the criminal history data from the FBI and state repositories and the prisoner records obtained from the state DOCs through the NCRP. The criminal history data provided information on arrests that resulted in a prison sentence during the 10-year follow-up period either within or outside of the state that released the prisoner. BJS used 2008 to 2018 NCRP prison admission data to supplement the criminal history data with information on released prisoners who returned to prison within the state that released them on probation or parole violations or for sentences for new crimes. The return-to-prison analysis included prisoners released in 18 states for which the necessary data were available for the 10-year follow-up period. The 18 states were Arizona, California, Colorado, Florida, Georgia, Iowa, Michigan, Missouri, New Jersey, New York, North Dakota, Oklahoma, Oregon, Pennsylvania, Texas, Washington, Wisconsin, and Wyoming.

OFFENSE DEFINITIONS

Violent offenses include homicide, rape or sexual assault, robbery, assault, and other unspecified violent offenses.

Homicide includes murder, nonnegligent and negligent manslaughter, and unspecified homicide offenses.

Murder is (1) intentionally causing the death of another person without extreme provocation or legal justification, or (2) causing the death of another while committing or attempting to commit another crime.

Nonnegligent (or voluntary) manslaughter is intentionally and without legal justification causing the death of another when acting under extreme provocation.

Negligent (or involuntary) manslaughter is causing the death of another person through recklessness or gross negligence, without intending to cause death. Negligent manslaughter also includes vehicular manslaughter but excludes vehicular murder (intentionally killing someone with a motor vehicle), which is classified as murder.

Rape or sexual assault includes (1) forcible intercourse (vaginal, anal, or oral) with a female or male; (2) forcible sodomy or penetration with a foreign object (sometimes called "deviate sexual assault"); (3) forcible or violent sexual acts not involving intercourse; (4) nonforcible sexual acts with a minor (such as statutory rape or incest with a minor); and (5) nonforcible sexual acts with someone unable to give legal or factual consent due to intellectual or physical disability or intoxication.

Robbery is the unlawful taking of property that is in the immediate possession of another, by force or the threat of force. It includes forcible purse snatching but excludes nonforcible purse snatching.

Assault includes aggravated, simple, and unspecified assault.

Aggravated assault includes (1) intentionally and without legal justification causing serious bodily injury, with or without a deadly weapon; and (2) using a deadly or dangerous weapon to threaten, attempt, or cause bodily injury, regardless of the degree of injury, if any. It also includes attempted murder, aggravated battery, felonious assault, and assault with a deadly weapon.

Simple assault includes intentionally and without legal justification causing less-than-serious bodily injury without a deadly or dangerous weapon, and attempting or threatening bodily injury without a dangerous or deadly weapon.

Property offenses include burglary, fraud or forgery, larceny, motor vehicle theft, and other unspecified property offenses.

Burglary is the unlawful entry of a fixed structure used for regular residence, industry, or business, with or without the use of force, to commit a felony or theft.

Larceny is the unlawful taking of property other than a motor vehicle from the possession of another, by stealth and without force or deceit. It includes pocket picking, nonforcible purse snatching, shoplifting, and thefts from motor vehicles. It excludes receiving or reselling stolen property (or both) and thefts through fraud or deceit.

Motor vehicle theft is the unlawful taking of a self-propelled road vehicle owned by another. It includes the theft of automobiles, trucks, and motorcycles but not the theft of boats, aircraft, or farm equipment (classified as larceny). It also includes receiving, possessing, stripping, transporting, and reselling stolen vehicles and unauthorized use of a vehicle (joyriding).

Fraud/forgery is the use of deceit or intentional misrepresentation to unlawfully deprive persons of their property or legal rights. It also includes offenses such as embezzlement, check fraud, confidence games, counterfeiting, and credit card fraud.

Other property offenses include arson, stolen property offenses, possession of burglary tools, damage to property, trespassing, and other unspecified property crimes.

Drug offenses include possession, trafficking, and other unspecified drug offenses.

Drug possession includes possession of an illegal drug but excludes possession with intent to sell.

Drug trafficking includes manufacturing, distributing, selling, smuggling, and possessing a drug with intent to sell.

Other drug offenses include offenses involving drug paraphernalia, forged or unauthorized prescriptions, and other unspecified drug offenses.

Public order offenses include violations of the peace or order of the community or threats to public health or safety through unacceptable conduct, interference with a governmental authority, and the violation of civil rights or liberties. It includes weapons, DUI/DWI, nonviolent sex offenses, liquor law violation, and other unspecified public order offenses.

Weapons offenses include the unlawful sale, distribution, manufacture, alteration, transportation, possession, and use of a deadly or dangerous weapon or accessory.

DUI/DWI is driving under the influence or driving while intoxicated.

Other public order offenses include probation and parole violations, obstruction of justice, contempt of court, failure to appear, commercialized vice, nonviolent sex offenses, liquor law violations, bribery, invasion of privacy, disorderly conduct, contributing to the delinquency of a minor, and other unspecified offenses. In this report, arrests for probation and parole violations were included as public order offenses. Excluding such arrests from the analysis would have a small impact on the recidivism rates. The percentage of state prisoners released across 24 states in 2008 who were arrested at least once within 10 years would be 80.5 percent if arrests for probation and parole violations were excluded and 81.9 percent if they were included. In other words, 98 percent of released prisoners who were arrested during the 10-year follow-up period were arrested for an offense other than a probation or parole violation.

PART 11

Impact of COVID-19 on the Local Jail Population, January–June 2020

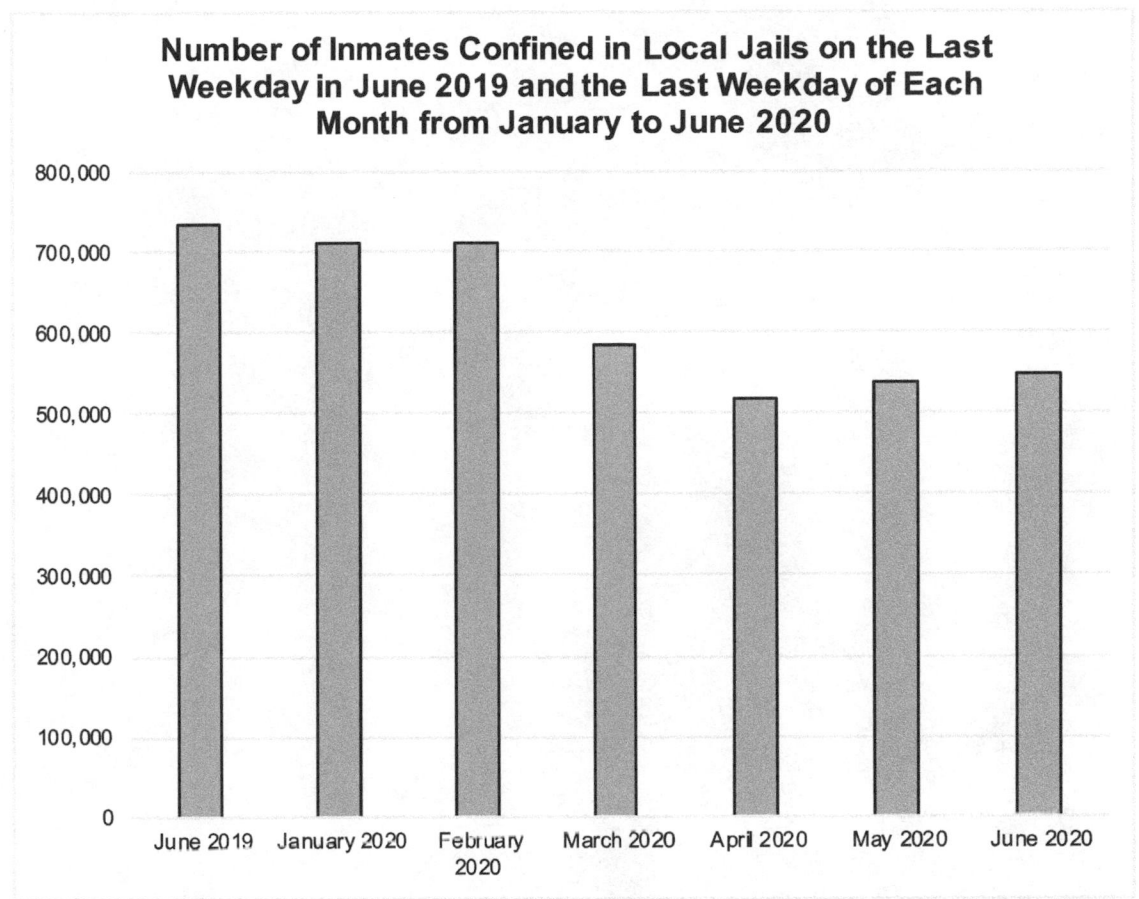

Number of Inmates Confined in Local Jails on the Last Weekday in June 2019 and the Last Weekday of Each Month from January to June 2020

- Local jails in the United States experienced a large decline (down 185,400 inmates) in their inmate populations from June 30, 2019 to June 30, 2020, which can be attributed mainly to the COVID-19 pandemic; from March to June 2020, about 208,500 inmates received expedited release.

- The impact of COVID-19 on local jails began in March 2020, with a drop of 18 percent in the inmate population between the end of February and the end of March, followed by an 11 percent drop by the end of April; occupied bedspace dropped from 81 percent at midyear 2019 to 60 percent at midyear 2020.

- From March to June 2020, jails conducted 215,360 inmate COVID-19 tests, and more than 11 percent of these tests were positive; nearly 5 percent (10,850) of all local jail staff (233,220) tested positive for COVID-19.

- The number of inmates held for a misdemeanor declined about 45 percent since midyear 2019, outpacing the decline in the number of inmates held for a felony (down 18 percent).

Table 1. Number of Inmates Confined in Local Jails on the Last Weekday in June 2019 and the Last Weekday of Each Month, January–June 2020

(Number.)

Last weekday in:	Number
June 2019*	734,500
January 2020	711,900 B
February 2020	710,300 B
March 2020	585,900 B
April 2020	519,500 B
May 2020	536,600 B
June 2020	549,100 B

*Comparison month.
B = Difference with comparison month is significant at the 95% confidence level.

Table 2. Local Jail Population as a Percentage of the June 2019 Jail Population, by Region, January–June 2020

(Number.)

Region	June 2019*	January 2020	February 2020	March 2020	April 2020	May 2020	June 2020
U.S. Total	100.0	96.9[B]	96.7[B]	79.8[B]	70.7[B]	73.1[B]	74.8[B]
Northeast	100.0	103.4	102.7	75.8[B]	66.2[B]	70.2[B]	75.5[B]
Midwest	100.0	96.2[B]	95.8[B]	81.9[B]	74.6[B]	77.4[B]	78.6[B]
South	100.0	95.7	96.6	78.4[B]	66.7[B]	67.6[B]	67.9[B]
West	100.0	92.0	91.5	78.3[B]	66.3[B]	65.9[B]	67.0[B]

NOTE: Data are based on the inmate population confined on the last weekday of each month.
*Comparison month.
B = Difference with comparison month is significant at the 95% confidence level.

Table 3. Inmate Population Change and Inmate and Staff COVID-19 Testing and Cases in the 50 Largest Local Jail Jurisdictions, March–June 2020

(Number; percent.)

Location	Inmates in custody[1]			Inmate tests[2]				Staff tests[3]	
	Number in 2019	Number in 2020	Percent change	Total tests conducted	Percent of admissions that were tested	Number of positive tests	Percent of tests that were positive	Number who tested positive	Percent who tested positive
U.S. total[4]..	734,500	549,100	-25.2	215,360	9.0	24,550	11.4	10,850	4.7
50 largest local jail jurisdictions									
Estimated[4]........................	180,700	134,200	-25.7	88,900	18.7	12,670	14.3	4,570	6.7
Reported........................	173,966	125,949	NC	77,087	NC	11,471	NC	4,277	NC
Los Angeles County, CA........................	17,385	12,045	-30.7	13,197	57.8	2,640	20.0	292	6.3
Harris County, TX........................	8,883	8,517	-4.1	4,401	22.4	1,120	25.4	366	6.9
Maricopa County, AZ........................	7,873	4,501	-42.8	2,837	13.3	804	28.3	131	5.5
New York City, NY........................	7,341	3,927	-46.5	NR	NR	NR	NR	1,432	14.7
San Diego County, CA........................	5,959	3,650	-38.7	1,681	9.3	18	1.1	12	0.6
Cook County, IL........................	5,666	4,617	-18.5	7,477	56.6	776	10.4	387	10.4
San Bernardino County, CA........................	5,623	4,553	-19.0	409	2.0	159	38.9	33	2.5
Orange County, CA........................	5,480	3,070	-44.0	2,113	18.4	403	19.1	30	2.0
Dallas County, TX........................	4,817	5,125	6.4	1,058	6.1	563	53.2	6	0.3
Shelby County, TN........................	4,776	3,429	-28.2	1,504	17.5	280	18.6	153	12.3
Philadelphia City, PA........................	4,670	3,872	-17.1	4,540	76.6	229	5.0	199	10.1
Miami-Dade County, FL........................	4,302	3,271	-24.0	746	5.8	262	35.1	210	7.4
Tarrant County, TX........................	4,144	4,008	-3.3	565	3.8	215	38.1	67	7.0
Bexar County, TX........................	3,963	3,620	-8.7	4,164	25.5	518	12.4	86	8.7
Riverside County, CA........................	3,796	3,140	-17.3	3,418	24.0	271	7.9	NR	NR
Broward County, FL........................	3,758	2,878	-23.4	294	3.5	56	19.0	13	0.9
Las Vegas, NV........................	3,749	2,464	-34.3	5,227	26.1	93	1.8	36	2.9
Sacramento County, CA........................	3,546	2,515	-29.1	1,182	9.8	9	0.8	14	2.0
Hillsborough County, FL[5]........................	3,302	NR	NR	NR	NR	NR	NR	NR	NR
Santa Clara County, CA........................	3,200	2,102	-34.3	2,036	33.5	40	2.0	16	1.6
Jacksonville City, FL........................	3,199	2,791	-12.8	NR	NR	NR	NR	NR	NR
Fresno County, CA........................	3,090	2,191	-29.1	1,948	26.6	598	30.7	42	7.1
Pinellas County, FL........................	3,019	2,144	-29.0	63	0.7	15	23.8	28	2.6
Fulton County, GA[5]........................	2,945	NR	NR	NR	NR	NR	NR	NR	NR
Allegheny County, PA........................	2,720	1,996	-26.6	205	6.0	46	22.4	17	2.1
Polk County, FL[5,6]........................	NR	NR	NR	NR	NR	NR	NR	NR	NR
Gwinnett County, GA........................	2,603	1,872	-28.1	312	4.1	18	5.8	12	1.3
Orange County, FL........................	2,530	2,149	-15.1	881	8.9	8	0.9	47	2.9
Alameda County, CA........................	2,458	1,733	-29.5	1,409	15.6	65	4.6	37	8.5
El Paso County, TX........................	2,279	2,030	-10.9	215	2.6	79	36.7	13	2.0
Marion County, IN........................	2,204	1,756	-20.3	755	10.8	177	23.4	11	1.4
Southwest Virginia Regional Jail Authority, VA........................	2,181	1,703	-21.9	0	0.0	0	NR	0	0.0
Cuyahoga County, OH........................	2,179	1,161	-46.7	1,464	23.1	162	11.1	40	5.4
Davidson County, TN........................	2,168	1,743	-19.6	981	12.8	218	22.2	40	5.1
Salt Lake County, UT........................	2,153	1,179	-45.2	147	2.1	23	15.6	34	4.6
Franklin County, OH........................	2,124	1,673	-21.2	130	2.0	29	22.3	33	5.4
Travis County, TX........................	2,057	1,778	-13.6	340	3.9	9	2.6	29	2.8
Clayton County, GA........................	2,055	1,998	-2.8	200	3.0	40	20.0	21	11.5
King County, WA[6]........................	NR	1,312	NR	235	3.3	8	3.4	16	2.3
Palm Beach County, FL........................	2,045	1,580	-22.7	207	2.6	58	28.0	36	4.1
Denver County, CO........................	2,044	974	-52.3	4,692	65.9	648	13.8	58	8.2
Milwaukee County, WI........................	2,027	1,362	-32.8	1,761	22.0	139	7.9	15	2.6
Cobb County, GA[5]........................	2,022	NR	NR	NR	NR	NR	NR	NR	NR
Essex County, NJ........................	2,021	1,778	-12.0	2,422	48.2	499	20.6	102	15.0
El Paso County, CO........................	2,020	1,316	-34.9	16	0.3	0	0.0	7	1.5
York County, PA........................	2,013	1,214	-39.7	151	7.1	0	0.0	0	0.0
Dekalb County, GA[6]........................	NR	1,217	NR	117	1.6	25	21.4	44	8.4
Kern County, CA........................	1,892	1,769	-6.5	145	1.9	23	15.9	24	5.6
Chatham County, GA........................	1,857	1,207	-35.0	370	11.0	4	1.1	4	1.0
Delaware County, PA........................	1,828	1,019	-44.3	1,072	57.8	124	11.6	89	18.6

NOTE: Jail jurisdictions are listed in order of their confined inmate population at midyear 2019. Data were estimated for jail jurisdictions that did not respond in 2019. Most jail jurisdictions consist of a single facility, but some have multiple facilities, or multiple facility operators, called reporting units (RU). If at least one RU responded, the jail jurisdiction is counted as a responding jail jurisdiction and data were estimated for the non-responding RU in that jail jurisdiction. For 2020, data were estimated for one RU in Marion County, IN, Davidson County, TN, and Franklin County, OH, that did not report on the number of confined inmates at midyear 2020, the number of inmates tested for COVID-19 and positive tests, or the number of staff that tested positive for COVID-19. Data were estimated for one RU in Sacramento County, CA, that did not report on the number of staff that tested positive for COVID-19. For 2019, data were estimated for one RU in El Paso County, TX, Gwinnett County, GA, and Milwaukee County, WI, that did not report on the number of confined inmates at midyear 2019.
NC = Not calculated because the numerator and denominator are not based on the same jail jurisdictions.
NR = Not reported.
[1]Number of inmates confined on the last weekday in June.
[2]Inmates may be tested more than once and may account for multiple positive tests.
[3]Includes deputies, monitors, and other custody staff who spend more than 50% of their time with the incarcerated population, and administrators, clerical and maintenance staff, educational staff, professional and technical staff, and other unspecified staff who spend more than 50% of their time in the facility. Multiple positive results for the same employee were counted only once. The 2020 Annual Survey of Jails (ASJ) did not capture the number of staff who were tested for COVID-19, due to potential employee testing practices (i.e., tests conducted in jail versus employees who tested during their personal time).
[4]Data were adjusted for survey and item non-response. Imputed values were used to calculate aggregate statistics but are not displayed for individual jail jurisdictions in this table.
[5]Did not respond or provide complete data to the 2020 ASJ.
[6]Did not respond to the 2019 Census of Jails.

Table 4. COVID-19 Deaths Among Local Jail Inmates and Staff, March 1–June 30, 2020

(Number; percent.)

COVID-19 deaths in responding jails[1]	Inmates	Staff[2]
Total Deaths	43	40
Confirmed[3]	33	32
Suspected[4]	10	8
Deaths based on medical examiner's or coroner's evaluation	30	27
Inmate and staff population at midyear 2020 in jails that reported on COVID-19 deaths		
Number of inmates and staff	376,500	160,500
As percentage of inmate population and staff employed in all jails	68.6	67.8

[1]Includes deputies, monitors, and other custody staff who spend more than 50 percent of their time with the incarcerated population, and administrators, clerical and maintenance staff, educational staff, professional and technical staff, and other unspecified staff who spend more than 50 percent of their time in the facility.
[2]Unweighted and unadjusted for item non-response. The number of deaths are based on 841 jail reporting units that reported data on inmate and staff deaths from March 1 to June 30, 2020, out of a total of 943 jail reporting units that were selected for the 2020 Annual Survey of Jails.
[3]COVID-19 was a significant contributor as determined by a positive test for COVID-19 before or after death.
[4]COVID-19 was a significant contributor based on the person having symptoms of COVID-19 before death but no positive test to confirm COVID-19.

Table 5. Number and Percent of Confined Inmates in Local Jails, by Characteristics, Midyear 2019 and Midyear 2020

(Number; percent.)

Characteristic	2019* Number	2019* Percent	2020 Number	2020 Percent	Change Number	Change Percent
Total	734,500	100.0	549,100 B	100.0	-185,400	-25.2
Sex						
Male	623,700	84.9	479,300 B	87.3 B	-144,400	-23.2
Female	110,700	15.1	69,800 B	12.7 B	-41,000	-37.0
Race/Ethnicity						
White[1]	362,900	49.4	262,100 B	47.7 B	-100,800	-27.8
Black[1]	247,100	33.6	192,600 B	35.1 B	-54,400	-22.0
Hispanic	106,900	14.6	81,900 B	14.9	-25,000	-23.4
American Indian/Alaska Native[1]	10,200	1.4	6,700 R	1.2	-3,600	-34.9
Asian[1]	4,700	0.6	3,700 B	0.7 B	-1,000	-21.1
Native Hawaiian/Pacific Islander[1]	800	0.1	600 B	0.1	-100	-16.4
Two or more races[1]	1,900	0.3	1,500 B	0.3	-400	-20.7
Conviction Status						
Convicted	253,700	34.5	168,400 B	30.7 B	-85,300	-33.6
Unconvicted	480,700	65.5	380,700 B	69.3 B	-100,000	-20.8
Most Serious Type of Offense						
Felony	513,900	70.0	421,200 B	76.7 B	-92,600	-18.0
Misdemeanor	170,300	23.2	94,000 B	17.1 B	-76,300	-44.8
Other[2]	50,300	6.8	33,800 B	6.2 B	-16,400	-32.7

NOTE: Data are based on the inmate population confined on the last weekday in June, unless specified. Data are adjusted for non-response and rounded to the nearest 100. Details may not sum to totals due to rounding. Results may differ from previous reports in the series due to data updates from jail authorities.
* = Comparison year.
B = Difference with comparison year is significant at the 95% confidence level.
[1]Excludes persons of Hispanic/Latino origin (e.g., White refers to non-Hispanic Whites and Black refers to non-Hispanic Blacks).
[2]Includes civil infractions and unknown offenses.

Table 6. Local Jail Incarceration Rates, by Sex and Race or Ethnicity, Midyear 2019 and Midyear 2020

(Number; rate.)

Characteristic	Number per 100,000 U.S. residents		Change	
	2019[1]*	2020[2]	Per 1,000 U.S. Residents	Percent
Total	224	167 B	-57	-25.5
Sex				
Male	386	295 B	-90	-23.4
Female	66	42 B	-25	-37.2
Race/Ethnicity				
White[3]	184	133 B	-51	-27.6
Black[3]	600	465 B	-135	-22.6
Hispanic	176	134 B	-43	-24.3
American Indian/Alaska Native[3]	420	274 B	-146	-34.8
Asian[3]	25	19 B	-6	-22.9
Native Hawaiian/Pacific Islander[3]	129	104 B	-24	-18.7
Two or more races[3]	25	19 B	-6	-23.7

NOTE: Rates are based on the number of confined inmates at midyear in local jails per 100,000 U.S. residents (for total) or per 100,000 U.S. residents of a given demographic group. Data are based on the inmate population confined on the last weekday in June and include both adults and juveniles, unless otherwise specified.
* = Comparison year.
B = Difference with comparison year is significant at the 95% confidence level.
[1]The population of U.S. residents in 2019 is based on the U.S. Census Bureau's population estimation for July 1, 2019.
[2]The population of U.S. residents in 2020 is based on the U.S. Census Bureau's population estimation for July 1, 2020.
[3]Excludes persons of Hispanic/Latino origin (e.g., White refers to non-Hispanic Whites and Black refers to non-Hispanic Blacks).

METHODOLOGY

Findings in this report are based on the 2019 Census of Jails (COJ) and the 2020 Annual Survey of Jails (ASJ). The Bureau of Justice Statistics (BJS) uses the COJ to periodically conduct a complete enumeration of local jail facilities and Federal Bureau of Prisons (BOP) detention facilities to collect data on inmate population and jail programs. The 2019 COJ was the eleventh collection in this series since 1970. In the years between complete enumerations of jails, BJS conducts the ASJ, a survey administered to a sample of approximately one-third of the nation's jails, to provide national estimates of the size and characteristics of the jail inmate population. The COJ and ASJ collections are currently conducted through web-based surveys. Numerous jurisdictions nationwide released inmates from jails in an effort to lessen the spread of COVID-19. BJS added a special addendum to the 2020 and 2021 ASJ to gather data on these pandemic-related releases.

The COJ and ASJ gather data from jails that hold inmates beyond arraignment, usually for a period exceeding 72 hours. Jail facilities are intended to hold adults, but some also hold juveniles (persons age 17 or younger). The universe of the COJ consists of all local jail jurisdictions (including county, city, regional, and privately operated jail facilities) and BOP detention facilities that function as jails. (Regional jail jurisdictions are created by two or more local governing bodies through cooperative agreements.)

The universe of the COJ and ASJ excludes separate temporary holding facilities (such as drunk tanks and police lockups) that do not hold persons after they have been formally charged in court, unless the temporary holding facilities are operated as part of a local jail. Also excluded are combined jail and prison systems in Alaska, Connecticut, Delaware, Hawaii, Rhode Island, and Vermont. These combined systems are operated by state departments of corrections and included in BJS's National Prisoner Statistics program. However, there are 15 independently operated jails in Alaska that are included in the universe of the COJ and ASJ.

A jail jurisdiction is a legal entity that has responsibility for managing jail facilities. Jail jurisdictions typically operate at the county level, with a sheriff's office or jail administrator managing the local facilities. Most jail jurisdictions consist of a single facility, but some have multiple facilities, or multiple facility operators, called reporting units. For example, three reporting units in Allegheny County, Pennsylvania, represent a single jail jurisdiction.

ITEM NON-RESPONSE IMPUTATION

Item response rates ranged from 90 percent to 100 percent in the 2019 COJ. Key population items (including one-day counts of the confined population, population by sex and juvenile status, population by race or ethnicity, admissions by sex, average daily population (ADP) by sex, and rated capacity) had item response rates of more than 95 percent. For responding jail jurisdictions that were unable to provide some requested items, a LOCF procedure was used to replace missing values with prior-year (2016, 2017, or 2018) ASJ or MCI data from the same jails, adjusted for year-to-year difference in the jail's confined population.

For cases with no prior-year data, a WSHD procedure was implemented to impute missing data, where the donor for each missing item was randomly selected from a set of similar jails, sorted by related auxiliary population values. Donor pools, also referred to as imputation classes, are formed by state, ADP category, and regional jail indicator. Within each imputation class, jails are sorted by confined jail population at midyear 2019.

Item response rates ranged from 95 percent to 100 percent for the 2020 ASJ. For responding jail jurisdictions that were unable to provide some requested items, missing data were imputed using LOCF or WSHD. In LOCF, missing values were substituted by last-observed values (i.e., data that the same jail jurisdictions submitted to the 2019 COJ). Specifically, missing values in rated capacity and inmate population supervised outside of jail were replaced with 2019 values without any adjustment, while missing values in inmate population counts, admissions, and ADP were replaced with 2019 values after adjustment for average year-to-year change. The average year-to-year adjustment factor was calculated, for each sampling stratum, as the ratio of the weighted sum of data reported in 2020 to that in 2019. Only data from jails that provided data in both years were included in the calculation. By applying the average year-to-year adjustment factor, BJS assumed that jails with missing items experienced the average year-to-year percentage change as other jails in the same sampling stratum.

In the scenario where no prior-year data were available, a WSHD procedure was used to impute missing values. This applies to missing values in variables that were not collected in 2019 (for example, the COVID-19 variables) and missing values for jails that did not respond, or provide valid data, to the 2019 COJ. In the WSHD procedure, the donor for each missing item was randomly selected from a group of similar jails (called the imputation class), sorted by related auxiliary population values. The imputation class and sorting variables differed by the variable being imputed. For variables in the COVID-19 module, including expedited releases, COVID-19 tests, and positive tests, and the number of staff tested positive, the imputation class was formed by the sampling stratum and the number of confirmed COVID-19 cases in the county (0–99, 100–1,399, 1400–1,499, and 1,500 or more). Within each imputation class, jails were sorted by confined inmate population at midyear 2020 (for imputing expedited releases and COVID-19 tests), total number of staff (for imputing the number of staff tested positive), or the number of positive tests (for imputing the number of inmates tested positive). Missing values in COVID-19-related death counts were not imputed.

Missing COVID-19 variables for New York City Department of Corrections (including expedited release count, number of COVID tests conducted, number of positive tests, and number of inmates tested positive) were imputed using a series of regression models instead of the WSHD procedure described above. This is because no suitable single donor could be found for New York City due to its unique experience during the first wave of the COVID-19 pandemic, coupled with a rapidly declining inmate population. The models used Poisson regressions to predict counts (e.g., releases or tests) based on annual admissions and releases, inmate population at the end of February 2020, and at midyear 2020, occupancy rate at the end of February, 2020, staff positive rate and county COVID-19 positive rate category as of midyear 2020, jail size category

(measured by ADP), and region. Missing values for New York City were then imputed using the regression results.

ESTIMATION OF ADMISSIONS

Admissions from March 1, 2020, to June, 30, 2020, were estimated in two steps. In step 1, monthly ADP was estimated for the 12 months from July 2019 to June 2020 as the average number of inmates held on the last weekday of the month and prior month. For example, the March ADP was estimated as the average number of inmates held on the last weekdays of February and March. The COVID-19 addendum to the 2020 ASJ collected inmate counts held on the last weekday of each month from January 2020 to June 2020. For the months when inmate counts were unavailable (i.e., July through December 2019), end-of-month inmate counts were interpolated from inmate counts on the last weekday of June 2019 and January 2020. In step 2, admissions from March 2020 to June 2020 were estimated as the reported annual admissions from July 2019 to June 2020, divided by the sum of estimated monthly ADP for the year, and then multiplied by the sum of estimated monthly ADP from March 2020 to June 2020.

CONFIRMED INFECTION RATE

The infection rate was calculated as the cumulative number of confirmed COVID-19 cases in the county, through June 30, 2020, as a percentage of the county population.

APPENDIX: SOURCES FOR TABLES

PART 1: CAPITAL PUNISHMENT, 2020

1	Bureau of Justice Statistics, National Prisoner Statistics program (NPS-8), 2020
2	Bureau of Justice Statistics, National Prisoner Statistics program (NPS-8), 2020
3	Bureau of Justice Statistics, National Prisoner Statistics program (NPS-8), 2020
4	Bureau of Justice Statistics, National Prisoner Statistics program (NPS-8), 2020
5	Bureau of Justice Statistics, National Prisoner Statistics program (NPS-8), 2020
6	Bureau of Justice Statistics, National Prisoner Statistics program (NPS-8), 2020
7	Bureau of Justice Statistics, National Prisoner Statistics program (NPS-8), 1930–2020
8	Bureau of Justice Statistics, National Prisoner Statistics program (NPS-8), 1953–2020
9	Bureau of Justice Statistics, National Prisoner Statistics program (NPS-8), 1973–2020
10	Bureau of Justice Statistics, National Prisoner Statistics program (NPS-8), 1968–2020
11	Bureau of Justice Statistics, National Prisoner Statistics program (NPS-8), 2020
12	Bureau of Justice Statistics, National Prisoner Statistics program (NPS-8), 2020
13	Bureau of Justice Statistics, National Prisoner Statistics program (NPS-8), 2020
14	Bureau of Justice Statistics, National Prisoner Statistics program (NPS-8), 2020
15	Bureau of Justice Statistics, National Prisoner Statistics program (NPS-8), 2020

PART 2: CRIME IN THE UNITED STATES, 2020

1	Bureau of Justice Statistics, Census of Jails, 2020; and Annual Survey of Jails, 2020
2	United States Department of Justice, Federal Bureau of Investigation, Uniform Crime Reports, 2020
3	United States Department of Justice, Federal Bureau of Investigation, Uniform Crime Reports, 2020
4	United States Department of Justice, Federal Bureau of Investigation, Uniform Crime Reports, 2020
5	United States Department of Justice, Federal Bureau of Investigation, Uniform Crime Reports, 2020
6	United States Department of Justice, Federal Bureau of Investigation, Uniform Crime Reports, 2020
7	United States Department of Justice, Federal Bureau of Investigation, Uniform Crime Reports, 2020
8	United States Department of Justice, Federal Bureau of Investigation, Uniform Crime Reports, 2020
9	United States Department of Justice, Federal Bureau of Investigation, Uniform Crime Reports, 2020
10	United States Department of Justice, Federal Bureau of Investigation, Uniform Crime Reports, 2020
11	United States Department of Justice, Federal Bureau of Investigation, Uniform Crime Reports, 2020
12	United States Department of Justice, Federal Bureau of Investigation, Uniform Crime Reports, 2020
13	United States Department of Justice, Federal Bureau of Investigation, Uniform Crime Reports, 2020
14	United States Department of Justice, Federal Bureau of Investigation, Uniform Crime Reports, 2020
15	United States Department of Justice, Federal Bureau of Investigation, Uniform Crime Reports, 2020
16	United States Department of Justice, Federal Bureau of Investigation, Uniform Crime Reports, 2020
17	United States Department of Justice, Federal Bureau of Investigation, Uniform Crime Reports, 2020

18 United States Department of Justice, Federal Bureau of Investigation, Uniform Crime Reports, 2020

19 United States Department of Justice, Federal Bureau of Investigation, Uniform Crime Reports, 2020

20 United States Department of Justice, Federal Bureau of Investigation, Uniform Crime Reports, 2020

21 United States Department of Justice, Federal Bureau of Investigation, Uniform Crime Reports, 2020

22 United States Department of Justice, Federal Bureau of Investigation, Uniform Crime Reports, 2020

23 United States Department of Justice, Federal Bureau of Investigation, Uniform Crime Reports, 2020

24 United States Department of Justice, Federal Bureau of Investigation, Uniform Crime Reports, 2020

25 United States Department of Justice, Federal Bureau of Investigation, Uniform Crime Reports, 2020

26 United States Department of Justice, Federal Bureau of Investigation, Uniform Crime Reports, 2020

27 United States Department of Justice, Federal Bureau of Investigation, Uniform Crime Reports, 2020

28 United States Department of Justice, Federal Bureau of Investigation, Uniform Crime Reports, 2020

29 United States Department of Justice, Federal Bureau of Investigation, Uniform Crime Reports, 2020

30 United States Department of Justice, Federal Bureau of Investigation, Uniform Crime Reports, 2020

31 United States Department of Justice, Federal Bureau of Investigation, Uniform Crime Reports, 2020

32 United States Department of Justice, Federal Bureau of Investigation, Uniform Crime Reports, 2020

33 United States Department of Justice, Federal Bureau of Investigation, Uniform Crime Reports, 2020

34 United States Department of Justice, Federal Bureau of Investigation, Uniform Crime Reports, 2020

35 United States Department of Justice, Federal Bureau of Investigation, Uniform Crime Reports, 2020

36 United States Department of Justice, Federal Bureau of Investigation, Uniform Crime Reports, 20209

37 United States Department of Justice, Federal Bureau of Investigation, Uniform Crime Reports, 2020

38 United States Department of Justice, Federal Bureau of Investigation, Uniform Crime Reports, 2020

39 United States Department of Justice, Federal Bureau of Investigation, Uniform Crime Reports, 2020

40 United States Department of Justice, Federal Bureau of Investigation, Uniform Crime Reports, 2020

41 United States Department of Justice, Federal Bureau of Investigation, Uniform Crime Reports, 2020

42 United States Department of Justice, Federal Bureau of Investigation, Uniform Crime Reports, 2020

43 United States Department of Justice, Federal Bureau of Investigation, Uniform Crime Reports, 2020

44 United States Department of Justice, Federal Bureau of Investigation, Uniform Crime Reports, 2020

45 United States Department of Justice, Federal Bureau of Investigation, Uniform Crime Reports, 2020

PART 3: CRIMINAL VICTIMIZATION, 2020

1 Bureau of Justice Statistics, National Crime Victimization Survey, 2016–2020

2 Bureau of Justice Statistics, National Crime Victimization Survey, 2016–2020

3 Bureau of Justice Statistics, National Crime Victimization Survey, 2020 and 2020

4 Bureau of Justice Statistics, National Crime Victimization Survey, 2020–2020; and Federal Bureau of Investigation, Crime in the United States, 2020

5 Bureau of Justice Statistics, National Crime Victimization Survey, 2020 and 2020

6 Bureau of Justice Statistics, National Crime Victimization Survey, 2020 and 2020

7 Bureau of Justice Statistics, National Crime Victimization Survey, 2020 and 2020

8 Bureau of Justice Statistics, National Crime Victimization Survey, 2020 and 2020

PART 4: FEDERAL JUSTICE STATISTICS, 2018–2020

1   Bureau of Justice Statistics, based on data from the Administrative Office of the U.S. Courts, Probation and Pretrial Services Automated Case Tracking System; U.S. Marshals Service, Justice Detainee Information System; and Federal Bureau of Prisons, SENTRY database, fiscal yearend 2009, 2018, and 2020.

2   Bureau of Justice Statistics, based on data from the U.S. Marshals Service, Justice Detainee Information System, fiscal years 2018 and 2020.

3   Bureau of Justice Statistics, based on data from the Executive Office for U.S. Attorneys, National Legal Information Office Network System database, fiscal years 2009 and 2017–2020.

4   Bureau of Justice Statistics, based on data from the Executive Office for U.S. Attorneys, National Legal Information Office Network System database, fiscal year 2020.

5   Bureau of Justice Statistics, based on data from the Administrative Office of the U.S. Courts, Probation and Pretrial Services Automated Case Tracking System, fiscal year 2020.

6   Bureau of Justice Statistics, based on data from the Administrative Office of the U.S. Courts, Criminal Master File, fiscal year 2020.

7   Bureau of Justice Statistics, based on data from the Administrative Office of the U.S. Courts, Criminal Master File, fiscal year 2020.

8   Bureau of Justice Statistics, based on data from the Federal Bureau of Prisons, SENTRY database, fiscal year 2020.

9   Bureau of Justice Statistics, based on data from the Federal Bureau of Prisons, SENTRY database, fiscal yearend 2009 and 2020.

10   Bureau of Justice Statistics, based on data from the Administrative Office of the U.S. Courts, Office of Probation and Pretrial Services, Pretrial Services Act Information System, fiscal year 2020.

11   Bureau of Justice Statistics, based on data from the Administrative Office of the U.S. Courts, Criminal Master File; U.S. Sentencing Commission, Monitoring data file; and Probation and Pretrial Services Automated Case Tracking System, fiscal year 2020.

PART 5: HATE CRIME STATISTICS, 2020

1   Federal Bureau of Investigation, Hate Crime Statistics, 2020

2   Federal Bureau of Investigation, Hate Crime Statistics, 2020

3   Federal Bureau of Investigation, Hate Crime Statistics, 2020

4   Federal Bureau of Investigation, Hate Crime Statistics, 2020

5   Federal Bureau of Investigation, Hate Crime Statistics, 2020

6   Federal Bureau of Investigation, Hate Crime Statistics, 2020

7   Federal Bureau of Investigation, Hate Crime Statistics, 2020

8   Federal Bureau of Investigation, Hate Crime Statistics, 2020

9   Federal Bureau of Investigation, Hate Crime Statistics, 2020

10   Federal Bureau of Investigation, Hate Crime Statistics, 2020

11   Federal Bureau of Investigation, Hate Crime Statistics, 2020

12   Federal Bureau of Investigation, Hate Crime Statistics, 2020

13   Federal Bureau of Investigation, Hate Crime Statistics, 2020

14   Federal Bureau of Investigation, Hate Crime Statistics, 2020

PART 6: INDICATORS OF SCHOOL CRIME AND SAFETY, 2021

1   Centers for Disease Control and Prevention (CDC), 1992–2019 School-Associated Violent Death Surveillance System (SAVD-SS) (partially funded by the U.S. Department of Education, Office of Safe and Healthy Students), previously unpublished tabulation; and CDC, National Center for Health Statistics, 1992–2019 National Vital Statistics System (NVSS), previously unpublished tabulation prepared by CDC's National Center for Injury Prevention and Control.

2   U.S. Department of Justice, Bureau of Justice Statistics, National Crime Victimization Survey (NCVS), 1992 through 2020

3   U.S. Department of Justice, Bureau of Justice Statistics, National Crime Victimization Survey (NCVS), 2020

4   U.S. Department of Justice, Bureau of Justice Statistics, School Crime Supplement (SCS) to the National Crime Victimization Survey, 1995 through 2020

5   U.S. Department of Education, National Center for Education Statistics, Schools and Staffing Survey (SASS), "Public School Teacher Data File," 1993–94, 1999–2000, 2003–04, 2007–08, and 2011–12; "Charter School Teacher Data File," 1999–2000; and National Teacher and Principal Survey (NTPS), "Public School Teacher Data File," 2015–16

6   U.S. Department of Education, National Center for Education Statistics, 1999–2000, 2003–04, 2005–06, 2007–08, 2009–10, 2015–16, 2017–18, and 2019–20 School Survey on Crime and Safety (SSOCS), 2000, 2004, 2006, 2008, 2010, 2016, 2018, and 2020; and Fast Response Survey System (FRSS), "School Safety and Discipline: 2013–14," FRSS 106, 2014

7   U.S. Department of Justice, Bureau of Justice Statistics, School Crime Supplement (SCS) to the National Crime Victimization Survey, 1995 through 2020

8   Centers for Disease Control and Prevention, Division of Adolescent and School Health, Youth Risk Behavior Surveillance System (YRBSS), 1993 through 2020

9   U.S. Department of Justice, Bureau of Justice Statistics, School Crime Supplement (SCS) to the National Crime Victimization Survey, 1999 through 2020 U.S. Department of Justice, Bureau of Justice Statistics, School Crime Supplement (SCS) to the National Crime Victimization Survey, 1999 through 2020

10   U.S. Department of Justice, Bureau of Justice Statistics, School Crime Supplement (SCS) to the National Crime Victimization Survey, selected years, 2005 through 2020

11   Centers for Disease Control and Prevention, Division of Adolescent and School Health, Youth Risk Behavior Surveillance System (YRBSS), 2011 through 2019

12   U.S. Department of Education, Office of Postsecondary Education, Campus Safety and Security Reporting System, 2001 through 2019; and National Center for Education Statistics, Integrated Postsecondary Education Data System (IPEDS), Fall 2002 through Fall 2019, Institutional Characteristics component

13   U.S. Department of Education, Office of Postsecondary Education, Campus Safety and Security Reporting System, 2010 through 2019

PART 7: JAIL INMATES, 2020

1   Bureau of Justice Statistics, Annual Survey of Jails, 2010–2018 and 2020, and Census of Jails, 2019; and U.S. Census Bureau, Population Estimates by Age, Sex, Race, and Hispanic Origin for the United States: January 1, 2010 to January 1, 2021

2   Bureau of Justice Statistics, Annual Survey of Jails, 2010, 2015–2018, and 2020; and Census of Jails, 2019

3, 3A   Bureau of Justice Statistics, Annual Survey of Jails, 2010, 2015–2018, and 2020; and Census of Jails, 2019

4   Bureau of Justice Statistics, Census of Jails, 2020

5   Bureau of Justice Statistics, Annual Survey of Jails, 2010–2018 and 2020; and Census of Jails, 2019

6   Bureau of Justice Statistics, Census of Jails, 2020

7   Bureau of Justice Statistics, Census of Jails, 2020

8   Bureau of Justice Statistics, Annual Survey of Jails, 2010–2018 and 2020; and Census of Jails, 2019

9	Bureau of Justice Statistics, Annual Survey of Jails, 2015–2018 and 2020; and Census of Jails, 2013 and 2019
10	Bureau of Justice Statistics, Annual Survey of Jails, 2006–2018; and Census of Jails, 2005 and 2020
11	Bureau of Justice Statistics, Annual Survey of Jails, 2015 and 2020; and Census of Jails, 2019
12	Bureau of Justice Statistics, Annual Survey of Jails, 2010, 2015–2018, and 2020; and Census of Jails, 2019

PART 8: LAW ENFORCEMENT OFFICERS KILLED AND ASSAULTED, 2020

1	United States Department of Justice, Federal Bureau of Investigation, Uniform Crime Reports, 2020
2	United States Department of Justice, Federal Bureau of Investigation, Uniform Crime Reports, 2020
3, 3A	United States Department of Justice, Federal Bureau of Investigation, Uniform Crime Reports, 2020
4	United States Department of Justice, Federal Bureau of Investigation, Uniform Crime Reports, 2020
5	United States Department of Justice, Federal Bureau of Investigation, Uniform Crime Reports, 2020
6	United States Department of Justice, Federal Bureau of Investigation, Uniform Crime Reports, 2020
7	United States Department of Justice, Federal Bureau of Investigation, Uniform Crime Reports, 2020
8	United States Department of Justice, Federal Bureau of Investigation, Uniform Crime Reports, 2020
9	United States Department of Justice, Federal Bureau of Investigation, Uniform Crime Reports, 2020
10	United States Department of Justice, Federal Bureau of Investigation, Uniform Crime Reports, 2020
11	United States Department of Justice, Federal Bureau of Investigation, Uniform Crime Reports, 2020
12	United States Department of Justice, Federal Bureau of Investigation, Uniform Crime Reports, 2020
13	United States Department of Justice, Federal Bureau of Investigation, Uniform Crime Reports, 2020
14	United States Department of Justice, Federal Bureau of Investigation, Uniform Crime Reports, 2020
15	United States Department of Justice, Federal Bureau of Investigation, Uniform Crime Reports, 2020
16	United States Department of Justice, Federal Bureau of Investigation, Uniform Crime Reports, 2020
17	United States Department of Justice, Federal Bureau of Investigation, Uniform Crime Reports, 2020
18	United States Department of Justice, Federal Bureau of Investigation, Uniform Crime Reports, 2020
19	United States Department of Justice, Federal Bureau of Investigation, Uniform Crime Reports, 2020
20	United States Department of Justice, Federal Bureau of Investigation, Uniform Crime Reports, 2020
21	United States Department of Justice, Federal Bureau of Investigation, Uniform Crime Reports, 2020
22	United States Department of Justice, Federal Bureau of Investigation, Uniform Crime Reports, 2020
23	United States Department of Justice, Federal Bureau of Investigation, Uniform Crime Reports, 2020
24	United States Department of Justice, Federal Bureau of Investigation, Uniform Crime Reports, 2020
25	United States Department of Justice, Federal Bureau of Investigation, Uniform Crime Reports, 2020
26	United States Department of Justice, Federal Bureau of Investigation, Uniform Crime Reports, 2020
27	United States Department of Justice, Federal Bureau of Investigation, Uniform Crime Reports, 2020
28	United States Department of Justice, Federal Bureau of Investigation, Uniform Crime Reports, 2020
29	United States Department of Justice, Federal Bureau of Investigation, Uniform Crime Reports, 2020
30	United States Department of Justice, Federal Bureau of Investigation, Uniform Crime Reports, 2020
31	United States Department of Justice, Federal Bureau of Investigation, Uniform Crime Reports, 2020
32	United States Department of Justice, Federal Bureau of Investigation, Uniform Crime Reports, 2020
33	United States Department of Justice, Federal Bureau of Investigation, Uniform Crime Reports, 2020
34	United States Department of Justice, Federal Bureau of Investigation, Uniform Crime Reports, 2020

35   United States Department of Justice, Federal Bureau of Investigation, Uniform Crime Reports, 2020

36   United States Department of Justice, Federal Bureau of Investigation, Uniform Crime Reports, 2020

37   United States Department of Justice, Federal Bureau of Investigation, Uniform Crime Reports, 2020

38   United States Department of Justice, Federal Bureau of Investigation, Uniform Crime Reports, 2020

39   United States Department of Justice, Federal Bureau of Investigation, Uniform Crime Reports, 2020

40   United States Department of Justice, Federal Bureau of Investigation, Uniform Crime Reports, 2020

PART 9: PROBATION AND PAROLE, 2020

1   Bureau of Justice Statistics, Annual Probation Survey and Annual Parole Survey, 2005–2020

2   Bureau of Justice Statistics, Annual Probation Survey and Annual Parole Survey, 2005–2020; and U.S. Census Bureau, National Intercensal Estimates, 2006–2021

3   Bureau of Justice Statistics, Annual Probation Survey and Annual Parole Survey, 2007–2020

4   Bureau of Justice Statistics, Annual Probation Survey and Annual Parole Survey, 2007–2019

5   Bureau of Justice Statistics, Annual Probation Survey, 2007–2020

6   Bureau of Justice Statistics, Annual Parole Survey, 2005–2020

7   Bureau of Justice Statistics, Annual Probation Survey and Annual Parole Survey, 2020; and U.S. Census Bureau, National Intercensal Estimates, 2021

8   Bureau of Justice Statistics, Annual Probation Survey, 2020; and U.S. Census Bureau, National Intercensal Estimates, 2021

9   Bureau of Justice Statistics, Annual Probation Survey, 2020

10   Bureau of Justice Statistics, Annual Probation Survey, 2005 and 2020

11   Bureau of Justice Statistics, Annual Parole Survey, 2020; and U.S. Census Bureau, National Intercensal Estimates, 2020

12   Bureau of Justice Statistics, Annual Parole Survey, 2020

13   Bureau of Justice Statistics, Annual Parole Survey, 2020

14   Bureau of Justice Statistics, Annual Parole Survey, 2005 and 2020

PART 10: RECIDIVISM OF PRISONERS RELEASED IN 24 STATES IN 2008: A 10-YEAR FOLLOW-UP PERIOD (2008–2018)

1   Bureau of Justice Statistics, Recidivism of State Prisoners Released in 2008 data collection, 2008–2018

2   Bureau of Justice Statistics, Recidivism of State Prisoners Released in 2008 data collection, 2008–2018

3   Bureau of Justice Statistics, Recidivism of State Prisoners Released in 2008 data collection, 2008–2018

4   Bureau of Justice Statistics, Recidivism of State Prisoners Released in 2008 data collection, 2008–2018

5   Bureau of Justice Statistics, Recidivism of State Prisoners Released in 2008 data collection, 2008–2018

6   Bureau of Justice Statistics, Recidivism of State Prisoners Released in 2008 data collection, 2008–2018

7   Bureau of Justice Statistics, Recidivism of State Prisoners Released in 2008 data collection, 2008–2018

8   Bureau of Justice Statistics, Recidivism of State Prisoners Released in 2008 data collection, 2008–2018

9   Bureau of Justice Statistics, Recidivism of State Prisoners Released in 2008 data collection, 2008–2018

10   Bureau of Justice Statistics, Recidivism of State Prisoners Released in 2008 data collection, 2008–2018

11   Bureau of Justice Statistics, Recidivism of State Prisoners Released in 2008 data collection, 2008–2018

12   Bureau of Justice Statistics, Recidivism of State Prisoners Released in 2008 data collection, 2008–2018

13   Bureau of Justice Statistics, Recidivism of State Prisoners Released in 2008 data collection, 2008–2018

PART 11: IMPACT OF COVID-19 ON THE LOCAL JAIL POPULATION, JANUARY-JUNE 2020

1   Bureau of Justice Statistics, Census of Jails, 2020, and Annual Survey of Jails, 2020

2   Bureau of Justice Statistics, Census of Jails, 2020, and Annual Survey of Jails, 2020

3   Bureau of Justice Statistics, Census of Jails, 2020; and Annual Survey of Jails, 2020

4   Bureau of Justice Statistics, Annual Survey of Jails, 2020

5   Bureau of Justice Statistics, Census of Jails, 2020; and Annual Survey of Jails, 2020

6   Bureau of Justice Statistics, Census of Jails, 2020; and Annual Survey of Jails, 2020

INDEX

CPSIA information can be obtained
at www.ICGtesting.com
Printed in the USA
BVHW022104080523
663793BV00010B/125